A People and a Nation

Brief Edition

A PEOPLE AND A NATION

A History of the United States

Volume 2 • Since 1865

BRIEF SIXTH EDITION

Mary Beth Norton
Cornell University

David M. Katzman
University of Kansas

David W. Blight
Amherst College

Howard P. Chudacoff
Brown University

Thomas G. Paterson
University of Connecticut

William M. Tuttle, Jr.
University of Kansas

Paul D. Escott
Wake Forest University

and

William J. Brophy
Stephen F. Austin State University

Houghton Mifflin Company   Boston   New York

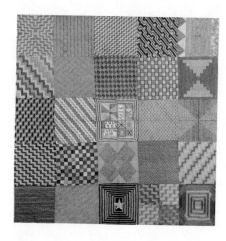

The icons used throughout Chapter 16 are details from "Sampler Block Quilt" by Evelyn Derr. National Museum of American Art, Smithsonian Institution, Washington, D.C./Art Resource, N.Y.

Sponsoring Editor: Mary Dougherty
Development Editor: Leah Strauss
Senior Project Editor: Christina M. Horn
Editorial Assistant: Talia M. Kingsbury
Senior Production/Design Coordinator: Carol Merrigan
Senior Manufacturing Coordinator: Marie Barnes
Senior Marketing Manager: Sandra McGuire

Cover image: *Mother and Child,* © by Margard Walter/Superstock.

Text credits:

Pages 489–490: Adapted from *The Greatest Generation,* by Tom Brokaw. Copyright © 1998 by Tom Brokaw. Used by permission of Random House, Inc.

Printed in the U.S.A.

Library of Congress Control Number: 2001097962

ISBN: 0-618-21470-4

1 2 3 4 5 6 7 8 9-DOC-06 05 04 03 02

Brief Contents

CONTENTS

MAPS

CHARTS

PREFACE TO THE BRIEF SIXTH EDITION

Almost two decades have passed since the publication of the first brief edition of *A People and a Nation*. In that initial brief edition, as well as each subsequent one, the intent was to preserve the uniqueness and integrity of the complete work while condensing it. This Brief Sixth Edition once again reflects the scholarship, readability, and comprehensiveness of the full-length version. It also maintains the integration of social, cultural, political, economic, and foreign relations history that has been a hallmark of *A People and a Nation*.

Creation of the Brief Edition

William J. Brophy has again prepared the brief text. As in the past, he worked closely with the authors. This collaboration ensured that the changes in content and organization incorporated in the full-length Sixth Edition were retained in the condensation. By reviewing each line, the authors attained reductions by paring down details rather than deleting entire sections. The Brief Sixth Edition thus contains fewer statistics, fewer quotations, and fewer examples than the unabridged version. A sufficient number of quotations and examples were retained, however, to maintain the richness in style created by the authors.

The Brief Sixth Edition is available in both one-volume and two-volume formats. The two-volume format is divided as follows: Volume 1 contains Chapters 1 through 16, beginning with a discussion of three cultures—American, African, and European—that intersected during the exploration and colonization of the New World and ending with a discussion of the Reconstruction era. Volume 2 contains Chapters 16 through 33, beginning its coverage at Reconstruction and extending the history of the American people to the present. The chapter on Reconstruction appears in both volumes to provide greater flexibility in matching a volume to the historical span covered by a specific course.

While the following Preface to the full-length Sixth Edition elaborates on specific content changes,

Changes in This Edition

we note briefly that the authors paid increased attention to the following: the interaction of the private sphere of everyday life with the public sphere of politics and government; grassroots movements; religion; the emerging cultural globalism of American foreign relations; the development of the American West; and the relationship of the people to the land, including conflict over access to natural resources. These new emphases, as well as the up-to-date scholarship on which they are based, are retained in the Brief Sixth Edition.

Although each author feels answerable for the whole of *A People and a Nation*, we take primary responsibility for particular chapters: Mary Beth Norton, Chapters 1–8; David M. Katzman, Chapters 9–12; David Blight, Chapters 13–16; Howard P. Chudacoff, Chapters 17–21 and 24; Thomas G. Paterson, Chapters 22–23, 26, 29, 31, and shared responsibility for 33; William M. Tuttle, Jr., Chapters 25, 27, 28, 30, 32, and shared responsibility for 33.

A number of useful learning and teaching aids accompany the Brief Sixth Edition of *A People and a Nation*. They are designed to help instructors and students achieve their teaching and learning goals. *@history: an interactive American history source* is a multimedia teaching/learning package that combines a variety of material on a cross-platformed CD-ROM—primary sources (text and graphic), video, and audio—with activities that can be used to analyze, interpret, and discuss primary sources; to enhance collaborative learning; and to create multimedia lecture presentations.

Study and Teaching Aids

American History GeoQuest is a CD-ROM designed to improve students' geographical literacy. The program consists of thirty interactive historical maps, each of which provides background information and a series of self-correcting quizzes so that students can master the information on their own.

The *Online Study Guide*, prepared by George Warren and Cynthia Ricketson of Central Piedmont Community College, includes an introductory chapter on studying history that focuses on interpreting historical facts, test-taking hints, and critical analysis. The guide also includes learning objectives, a thematic guide, lists of terms, multiple-choice and essay questions for each chapter, as well as map exercises and sections on organizing information of some chapters. An answer key alerts students to the correct response and also explains why the other choices are wrong. This *Online Study Guide* is free to students and may be found at **college.hmco.com/students.**

An *Online Instructor's Resource Manual*, also created by George Warren, will now be downloadable from Houghton Mifflin's web site. For each chapter, the manual includes a content overview, a brief list of learning objectives, a comprehensive chapter outline, ideas for classroom activities, discussion questions, and ideas for paper topics.

A *Test Bank*, also prepared by George Warren, provides multiple-choice questions, identification questions, and essay questions. This content is also available in a *Computerized Test Bank* for both Windows and Macintosh platforms.

An *Instructor's Web Site* includes the *Online Instructor's Resource Manual*, interactive Legacy activities, online primary sources with teaching instructions, and annotated links to other sites. The *Student's Web Site* includes ACE self-quizzes; online primary sources, including text, photo, and audio resources; an annotated guide of the top historical research web sites; and interactive Legacy activities.

The *HM ClassPrep CD-ROM with HM Testing* is a complete electronic resource for instructors that features the text's maps and charts in PowerPoint for presentations, and other documents in Word, such as lecture outlines. Also included is *HM Testing* for Macintosh and Windows. This computerized version of the printed *Test Bank* allows instructors to create customized tests by editing and adding questions. Most electronic resources can be customized to complement the way you teach your course.

There is also a set of full-color *American History Map Transparencies*, available in two-volume sets upon adoption.

Please visit us on the Web at **college.hmco.com** or contact your local Houghton Mifflin representative for more information about the ancillary items or to obtain desk copies.

Acknowledgments

Author teams rely on review panels to help create and execute successful revision plans. Many historians advised us on the revision of this Brief Sixth Edition, and the book is better because of their thoughtful insights and recommendations. We heartily thank

S. Carol Berg, *College of St. Benedict*
Trace' Etienne-Gray, *Southwest Texas State University*
Irene Guenther, *Houston Community College*
Martin Haas, *Adelphi University*
Andrew C. Holman, *Bridgewater State College*
Eric Juhnke, *Southwest Missouri State University*
Eric Mogren, *Northern Illinois University*
Seth Wigderson, *University of Maine–Augusta*

Finally, we want to thank the many people who have contributed their thoughts and labors to this work, including the talented staff at Houghton Mifflin.

For the authors, WILLIAM J. BROPHY

PREFACE TO THE FULL-LENGTH SIXTH EDITION

"What? Another edition?" asked one of our friends. "History hasn't changed that much in the last few years!" Wrong. "History" *has* changed, in several ways. More of "history's" story has been told in new books and articles and revealed in newly released documents. Our interpretation of "history" has changed because new perspectives on familiar topics have continued to emerge from the prolific writings of historians, anthropologists, and other scholars. And, last, our understanding of "history" has changed as our engagement with current events reshapes how we remember the past.

Like other teachers and students, we are always recreating our past, restructuring our memory, rediscovering the personalities and events that have influenced us, inspired us, and bedeviled us. This book represents our rediscovery of America's history—its diverse people and the nation they created and have nurtured. As this book demonstrates, there are many different Americans and many different memories. We have sought to present all of them, in both triumph and tragedy, in both division and unity.

Although much is new in this Sixth Edition in coverage, interpretation, and organization, we have sustained the qualities that have marked *A People and a Nation* from the beginning: our approach of telling the story of all the people; our study of the interaction of the private sphere of everyday life with the public sphere of politics and government; our integration of political and social history; our spirited narrative based on diaries, letters, oral histories, and other sources; and our effort to challenge readers to think about the meaning of American history, not just to memorize facts. Students and instructors have commented on how enjoyable the book is to read. Scholars have commended the book for its up-to-date scholarship.

About *A People and a Nation*

Readers have also told us that we have demonstrated, in section after section and in the "How Do Historians Know?" feature, how the historian's mind works asking questions and teasing conclusions out of vast and often conflicting evidence. Each chapter's highlighted "How Do Historians Know?" explains how historians go about using sources—such as artifacts, cartoons, census data, medical records, and popular art—to arrive at conclusions. This feature also helps students understand how scholars can claim knowledge about historical events and trends. Chapter-opening vignettes, dramatically recounting stories of people contending with their times, continue to define the key questions of each chapter. Succinct introductions and summaries still frame each chapter. As before, myriad illustrations, maps, tables, and graphs tied closely to the text encourage visual and statistical explorations. Readability, scholarship, critical thinking, clear structure, instructive illustrative material—these strengths have been sustained in this edition.

Guided by Houghton Mifflin's excellent editorial and design staffs, by instructors' thorough reviews, by the authors' ongoing research, and by our frank and friendly planning sessions and critical reading of one another's chapters, we worked to improve every aspect of the book. We added a distinguished new author, David W. Blight, whose expertise on the antebellum period, slavery, the Civil War, and historical memory has strengthened these topics in the book. To reflect new scholarship and to satisfy instructors' needs for improved chronological flow, we substantially reorganized the chapters that cover the antebellum and post-1945 periods. We have expanded our treatment of slavery, women, religion in America's social and political life, race theory and the social construction of racial identity, the West, the South's relationship to the nation, cultural expansion as a dimension of foreign relations, and the globalization of the U.S. economy. Throughout the book, we reexamined every sentence, interpretation, map,

What's New in This Edition

chart, illustration, and caption, refining the narrative, presenting new examples, and rethinking and labeling the Summary section for each chapter. More than half of the chapter-opening vignettes are new to this edition, as are more than one-third of the "How Do Historians Know?" entries. The "Important Events" tables have been trimmed for easier reference. The "Suggestions for Further Reading" have been revised to include new literature and conveniently consolidated at the end of the book.

Eager to help students link the past to the present, to identify the origins of issues of current interest, we have introduced in each chapter a new feature: "Legacy for a People and a Nation." Appearing after each chapter's Summary, the Legacy feature spotlights a specific contemporary topic; examples include Columbus Day, women's education, Bible Belt, revolutionary violence, Fourteenth Amendment, ethnic food, intercollegiate athletics, Peace Corps, atomic waste, and the Internet. After exploring the subject's beginnings, a few tightly focused paragraphs trace its important history to the present, inviting students to think about the historical roots of their world today and to understand the complexity of issues that on the surface seem so simple. For students who ask what history has to do with the immediate events and trends that swirl around them—or who wonder why we study history at all—these timely legacies provide telling answers.

New "Legacy for a People and a Nation"

As in previous editions, several themes and questions stand out in our concerted effort to incorporate the most recent scholarship that integrates political, social, and cultural history. We study the many ways Americans have defined themselves—gender, race, class, region, ethnicity, religion, sexual orientation—and the many subjects that have reflected their multidimensional experiences: social, political, economic, diplomatic, military, environmental, intellectual, cultural, technological, and more. We highlight the remarkably diverse everyday life of the American people—in cities and on farms and ranches, in factories and in corporate headquarters, in neighborhood meetings and in powerful political chambers, in love relationships and in hate groups, in recreation and in work, in the classroom and in military uniform, in secret national security conferences and in public foreign relations debates, in church and in prison, in polluted environments and in conservation areas. We pay particular attention to lifestyles, diet and dress, family life and structure, labor conditions, gender roles, and childbearing and child rearing. We explore how Americans have entertained and informed themselves by discussing their music, sports, theater, print media, film, radio, television, graphic arts, and literature, in both "high" culture and "low" culture. We study how technology has influenced Americans' lives, such as through the internal combustion engine and the computer.

Themes in This Book

The private sphere of everyday life always interacts with the public sphere of politics and government. To understand how Americans have sought to protect their different ways of life and to work out solutions to thorny problems, we emphasize their expectations of governments at the local, state, and federal levels; governments' role in providing answers; the lobbying of interest groups; the campaigns and outcomes of elections; and the hierarchy of power in any period. Because the United States has long been a major participant in world affairs, we explore America's descent into wars, interventions in other nations, empire-building, immigration patterns, images of foreign peoples, cross-national cultural ties, and international economic trends.

Mary Beth Norton, who had primary responsibility for Chapters 1–8, expanded and revised her coverage of the peopling of the Americas and early settlements, the Salem witchcraft crisis, and masculinity and public rituals in the colonial period. She reorganized Chapter 3 to highlight new scholarship identifying the 1670s as a crucial turning point in the relationships of Europeans and Indians in several regions of North America, and to emphasize the key role of the slave trade in the economy of all the colonies. In Chapter 4, she added a discussion of regional differences in African American family life. Chapters 3, 4, and 8, moreover, all incorporate recent scholarship on the complex relationship between the development of the slave system and the creation of racial categories.

Section-by-Section Changes in This Edition

David M. Katzman, who had primary responsibility for Chapters 9–12, substantially reorganized the early-nineteenth-century chapters. Chapters 9–11 now have a more focused chronological narrative, integrating political events with related social, economic, and cultural developments. The antebellum chapters give added emphasis to regional interconnections in the emerging market economy, Indian–white relations and Native American adaptations to the market economy, demographic changes, internal migration, popular culture, and the formation of racial ideas. Katzman also gives new attention to the Barbary captives, the Lewis and Clark expedition, early Texas settlement, and population movements. He also explores anew immigration, ethnicity and race, frontier communities in the West, and the links between reform politics and religion.

David W. Blight, who had primary responsibility for Chapters 13–16, brought fresh perspectives to the antebellum South and its relation to the nation's cultural life and market revolution. He added new material on slave culture and resistance, slavery's intersection with westward expansion, the War with Mexico, and the Underground Railroad. In his discussion of the South, he increased coverage of free blacks and social reform movements. In the Civil War and Reconstruction chapters, Blight has revised the history of military battles, women and nursing, emancipation, wartime reconstruction, the meanings of freedom for former slaves, and the Fourteenth Amendment. He has introduced the problem of memory—especially Americans' difficulty in confronting the Reconstruction period of their history. Replacing Paul D. Escott, who brought distinction to *A People and a Nation* for five editions and whose fine writing and scholarship remain evident throughout, Blight has worked with co-author Katzman to reorganize all the antebellum period chapters.

Howard P. Chudacoff, who had primary responsibility for Chapters 17–21 and 24, reconfigured material throughout these chapters. Chapter 17 now focuses solely on the West, with additions on Indian economic and cultural life, women in frontier communities, mining, irrigation, and transportation. In his other chapters, he has increased the coverage of southern industrialization, immigrants and migrants in southern cities, and southern Progressivism. He also presents new discussion of the characteristics of the industrial revolution, race and ethnicity in urban bor-

derlands, Mexican American farmers, religion and science, technology, the clash between modernism and fundamentalism, women's political activities, and the causes of the Great Depression.

Thomas G. Paterson, who had primary responsibility for Chapters 22–23, 26, 29, and 31, and shared responsibility for 33, and who served as the book's co-ordinating author, offers new material throughout on cultural expansion and on the influence of ideology and images of foreign peoples on foreign policy decisions. He has augmented coverage of religious missionaries, Anglo-American cooperation, and navalism. Labor issues, Indian soldiers, weapons technology, and gas warfare receive new treatment for World War I. As part of the restructuring of the post-1945 chapters, Chapters 29 and 31 are newly designed to parallel chapters on domestic history. Paterson reexamines the Korean War, U.S. Information Agency activities, and popular fears of nuclear war. For the Vietnam War, he has revisited presidential leadership, the war's impact on domestic reform, and military experiences. The last chapter newly explores environmental diplomacy, the globalization of U.S. culture, intrastate wars, and humanitarian intervention.

William M. Tuttle, Jr., had primary responsibility for Chapters 25, 27, 28, 30, and 32, and shared responsibility for 33. In Chapter 25, he expanded treatment of New Deal cultural programs, unionism, and the question of "whiteness." For World War II, he added new material on the cultural history of the home front, the wartime economy, technological research, and homosexuals in the armed forces. In his post-1945 chapters, Tuttle has revised his coverage of McCarthyism, race relations, the New Left and counterculture, Indian protest, immigration legislation, the Reagan presidency, AIDS, and the anti-abortion movement. In the last chapter, Tuttle has expanded his discussion of political violence and public dissatisfaction with government, and he has included new material on school shootings and the presidential impeachment crisis.

The multidimensional Appendix, prepared by Thomas G. Paterson, has been brought up to date. Once again, the Appendix includes a guide to reference works on key subjects in American history. Students may wish to use this updated and enlarged list of encyclopedias, atlases, chronologies, and other books, for example, when they start to explore topics for research papers, when they seek precise definitions or dates, when they need biographical profiles, or when they chart territorial or demographic changes. The tables of statistics on key features of the American people and nation also have been updated, as have the tables on the states (and the District of Columbia and Puerto Rico), presidential elections, presidents and vice presidents, party strength in Congress, and the justices of the Supreme Court. Other information, including the Articles of Confederation and a complete table of the cabinets by administration, is available on the *A People and a Nation* web site.

A People and a Nation continues to be supported by an extensive supplements package. For this edition, many more resources will be available to students and instructors online and on CD-ROM. We have also revised and updated all elements of our existing package.

Study and Teaching Aids

A new version of *@history*, Houghton Mifflin's CD-ROM featuring nearly one thousand primary source materials, including video, audio, visual, and textual resources, has been keyed to the organization of the Sixth Edition of *A People and a Nation*. Available in both instructor's and student's versions, *@history* is an interactive multimedia tool that can improve the analytical skills of students and introduce them to historical sources.

American History GeoQuest is a CD-ROM designed to improve students' geographical literacy. The program consists of thirty interactive historical maps, each of which provides background information and a series of self-correcting quizzes so that students can master the information on their own.

The *A People and a Nation* web site has been redesigned, updated, and augmented for users of the Sixth Edition. An *Instructor's Web Site* includes the *Online Instructor's Resource Manual* (see below), downloadable PowerPoint lecture outline slides, interactive Legacy activities, online primary sources with teaching instructions, and annotated links to other sites. The *Student's Web Site* includes ACE reading self-quizzes; online primary sources, including text, photo, and audio resources; an annotated guide of the top historical research Web sites; and interactive Legacy activities.

The *Study Guide*, prepared by George Warren of Central Piedmont Community College, includes an introductory chapter on studying history that focuses on interpreting historical facts, test-taking hints, and critical analysis. The guide also includes learning objectives, a thematic guide, lists of terms, multiple choice and essay questions with answer keys, and map exercises.

A new *Online Instructor's Resource Manual*, also created by George Warren, will now be downloadable from Houghton Mifflin's web site. For each chapter, the manual includes a content overview, a brief list of learning objectives, a comprehensive chapter outline, ideas for classroom activities, discussion questions, and ideas for paper topics.

A *Test Bank*, also prepared by George Warren, provides approximately 1,700 new multiple choice questions, more than 1,000 identification questions, and approximately 500 essay questions. This content is also available in a *Computerized Test Bank* for both Windows and Macintosh platforms.

A set of *American History Map Transparencies* is also available to instructors upon adoption.

At each stage of this revision, a sizable panel of historian reviewers read drafts of our chapters. Their suggestions, corrections, and pleas helped guide us through this momentous revision. We could not include all of their recommendations, but the book is better for our having heeded most of their advice. We heartily thank

Acknowledgments

Patrick Allitt, *Emory University*

Cara Anzilotti, *Loyola Marymount University*

Felix Armfield, *Western Illinois University*

Robert Becker, *Louisiana State University*

Jules Benjamin, *Ithaca College*

Roger Bromert, *Southwestern Oklahoma State University*

Jonathan Chu, *University of Massachusetts at Boston*

Nathaniel Comfort, *George Washington University*

Mary DeCredico, *U.S. Naval Academy*

Judy DeMark, *Northern Michigan University*

Jonathan Earle, *University of Kansas*

Alice Fahs, *University of California, Irvine*

Neil Foley, *University of Texas*

Colin Gordon, *University of Iowa*

Robert Gough, *University of Wisconsin at Eau Claire*

Brian Greenberg, *Monmouth University*

Harland Hagler, *University of North Texas*

Elizabeth Haiken, *University of British Columbia*

Benjamin Harrison, *University of Louisville*

Elizabeth Cobbs Hoffman, *San Diego State University*

Marianne Holdzkom, *Ohio State University*

John Inscoe, *University of Georgia*

Frank Lambert, *Purdue University*

David Rich Lewis, *Utah State University*

Nancy Mitchell, *North Carolina State University*

Patricia Moore, *University of Utah*

John Neff, *University of Mississippi*

James Reed, *Rutgers University*

Joseph Rowe, *Sam Houston State University*

Sharon Salinger, *University of California, Riverside*

Richard Stott, *George Washington University*

Daniel B. Thorp, *Virginia Polytechnic Institute and State University*

Marilyn Westerkamp, *University of California, Santa Cruz*

John Wigger, *University of Missouri, Columbia*

John Scott Wilson, *University of South Carolina*

The authors once again thank the extraordinary Houghton Mifflin people who designed, edited, produced, and nourished this book. Their high standards and acute attention to both general structure and fine detail are cherished in the publishing industry. Many thanks, then, to Colleen Shanley Kyle, sponsoring editor; Ann Hofstra Grogg, freelance development editor; Christina Horn, senior project editor; Jean Woy, editor-in-chief; Sandra McGuire, senior marketing manager; Pembroke Herbert, photo researcher; Charlotte Miller, art editor; and Michael Kerns, editorial assistant.

The authors also extend their thanks to the following for helping us: Sandra Greene, Karin Beckett, Nancy Board, Frank Couvares, Jan D. Emerson, Alice Fahs, Jeffrey Ferguson, Irwin Hyatt, Steven Jacobson, Andrea Katzman, Eric Katzman, Henry W. Katzman, Julie Stephens Katzman, Sharyn Katzman, Ariela Katzman-Jacobson, Elizabeth Mahan, Terri Rockhold, Martha Sandweiss, Martha Saxton, Barry Shank, John David Smith, Kathryn Nemeth Tuttle, and Samuel Watkins Tuttle.

We welcome comments from instructors and students about this new edition of *A People and a Nation*, which can be communicated through its accompanying web site, found at **http://college.hmco.com**.

For the authors, THOMAS G. PATERSON

A People and a Nation

Brief Edition

16

RECONSTRUCTION: AN UNFINISHED REVOLUTION

1865–1877

Wartime Reconstruction
The Meanings of Freedom
Johnson's Reconstruction Plan
The Congressional Reconstruction Plan
Reconstruction Politics in the South
Reconstruction Reversed

LEGACY FOR A PEOPLE AND A NATION
The Fourteenth Amendment

In 1861 Robert Smalls was a slave in South Carolina, while Wade Hampton was a South Carolina legislator and one of the richest planters in the South. The events of the next fifteen years turned each man's world upside down more than once.

Robert Smalls became a Union hero in 1862 when he stole a Confederate ship from Charleston harbor and piloted it to the blockading federal fleet. After the war, Smalls began a career in politics and served in both the South Carolina legislature and Congress. There he worked for educational and economic opportunity for his people. But Smalls was helpless to prevent the return of white control in South Carolina in 1877.

Wade Hampton joined the Confederate Army in 1861 and soon became a general. The South's defeat

profoundly shocked him. The postwar years brought further painful changes, including forced bankruptcy. By 1876, though, Hampton's fortunes were again on the rise: the Democrats nominated him for governor, promising that he would "redeem" South Carolina from Republican misrule. Among Hampton's white supporters were the paramilitary Red Shirts, who pledged to "control the vote of at least one Negro, by intimidation, purchase," or other means. Hampton won the governor's chair, then a seat in the U.S. Senate.

As the careers of Smalls and Hampton suggest, Reconstruction was revolutionary. Robert Smalls rose from bondage to experience glory, emancipation, political power, and, ultimately, disappointment. Wade Hampton fell from privilege to endure defeat, failure, bankruptcy, and, eventually, a return to leadership in his state. Unprecedented changes took place in American society, but the underlying realities of economic power, racial prejudice, and judicial conservatism limited Reconstruction's revolutionary potential.

Nowhere was the turmoil of Reconstruction more evident than in national politics. Lincoln's successor, Andrew Johnson, fought bitterly with Congress over the shaping of a plan for Reconstruction. Though a southerner, Johnson had always been a foe of the South's wealthy planters, and his first acts as president suggested that he would be tough on "traitors." Before the end of 1865, however, Johnson's policies changed direction. Jefferson Davis stayed in prison for two years, but Johnson quickly pardoned other rebel leaders and allowed them to occupy high offices. He also ordered the return of plantations to their original owners, including abandoned Georgia and South Carolina coastal lands on which forty thousand freed men and women had settled as a result of General William Tecumseh Sherman's Field Order Number 15 of February 1865.

Johnson imagined a lenient and rapid "restoration" of the South to the Union rather than the fundamental "reconstruction" that Republican congressmen favored. Between 1866 and 1868, the president and the Republican leadership in Congress engaged in a bitterly antagonistic power struggle over how to put the United States back together again.

Before these struggles were over, Congress had impeached the president, enfranchised the freedmen, and given them a role in reconstructing the South. The nation also adopted the Fourteenth and Fifteenth Amendments. Yet little was done to open the doors of economic opportunity to black southerners. Moreover, by 1869 the Ku Klux Klan was employing extensive violence and terror to thwart Reconstruction and undermine black freedom.

As the 1870s advanced, industrial growth accelerated, creating new opportunities and raising new priorities. A new economic depression after 1873 refocused northerners' attention. Political corruption became a nationwide scandal, bribery a way of doing business. "Money has become the God of this country," wrote one disgusted observer, "and men, otherwise good men, are almost compelled to worship at her shrine."

Thus Reconstruction became a revolution eclipsed. White southerners' desire to take back control of their states and of race relations overwhelmed the national interest in stopping them. But Reconstruction left enduring legacies the nation has struggled with ever since. ■

Wartime Reconstruction

 Civil wars leave immense challenges of healing, justice, and physical rebuilding. Anticipating that process, Reconstruction of the Union was an issue as early as 1863. The very idea of Reconstruction raised many questions: How would the nation be restored? How would southern states and leaders be treated? What was the constitutional basis for readmission of states to the Union? More specifically, four vexing problems compelled early thinking and would haunt the country throughout the Reconstruction era. One, *who* would rule in the South once it was defeated? Two, *who* would rule in the federal government, Congress or the president? Three, what were the dimensions of *black freedom*, and what rights under law would the freedmen enjoy? And four, would Reconstruction be a preservation of the *old* republic or a second revolution, a re-invention of a *new* republic?

Abraham Lincoln had never been antisouthern. He planned early for a swift and moderate Reconstruction process. In his Second Inaugural Address, Lincoln promised "malice toward none; with charity for all" as Americans strove to "bind up the nation's wounds."

Lincoln's 10 Percent Plan

In his "Proclamation of Amnesty and Reconstruction," issued in December 1863, Lincoln proposed to replace majority rule with "loyal rule" as a means of reconstructing southern state governments. He proposed pardoning all ex-Confederates except the highest-ranking military and civilian officers. Then, as soon as 10 percent of the voting population in the 1860 election had taken an oath and established a government, that government would be recognized. Lincoln did not consult Congress in these plans, and "loyal" assemblies (known as "Lincoln governments") were created in Louisiana, Tennessee, and Arkansas in 1864, states largely occupied by Union troops.

Congress responded with great hostility to Lincoln's moves to readmit southern states in what seemed such a premature manner. Many Radical Republicans considered the 10 percent plan a "mere

IMPORTANT EVENTS

1865 Johnson begins rapid and lenient
Reconstruction
Confederate leaders regain power
White southern governments pass
restrictive black codes
Congress refuses to seat southern
representatives
Thirteenth Amendment ratified

1866 Congress passes Civil Rights Act and
renewal of Freedmen's Bureau over
Johnson's veto
Congress approves Fourteenth Amendment
Most southern states reject Fourteenth
Amendment
In *Ex parte Milligan* the Supreme Court
reasserts its influence
In congressional elections, Republicans
win more than two-thirds majority, a
renunciation of Johnson's plan of
Reconstruction

1867 Congress passes Reconstruction Acts and
Tenure of Office Act
Secretary of State William Seward arranges
purchase of Alaska
Constitutional conventions called in
southern states

1868 House impeaches Johnson; Senate
acquits him
Most southern states gain readmission to
the Union under Radical plan
Fourteenth Amendment ratified
Grant elected president

1869 Congress approves Fifteenth Amendment
(ratified in 1870)

1870 Congress passes first Enforcement Act

1871 Congress passes Ku Klux Klan Act

1872 Amnesty Act frees almost all remaining
Confederates from restrictions on holding
office
Liberal Republicans organize and oppose
Grant
Debtors urge government to keep greenbacks
in circulation
Grant reelected

1873 *Slaughter-House* cases limit power of
Fourteenth Amendment
Panic of 1873 sends economy into extended
depression, leading to widespread
unemployment and labor strife

1874 Grant vetoes increase in supply of paper
money
Democrats win majority in House of
Representatives

1875 Several Grant appointees indicted for
corruption
Congress passes weak Civil Rights Act
Congress requires that after 1878 greenbacks
be convertible into gold
Democratic Party continues to "redeem"
control of southern states with white
supremacy campaigns

1876 *U.S. v. Cruikshank* and *U.S. v. Reese* further
weaken Fourteenth Amendment
Presidential election disputed

1877 Congress elects Hayes president
Exodusters migrate to Kansas
"Home rule" returns to three remaining
southern states not yet controlled by
Democrats; Reconstruction over

Congress and the Wade-Davis Bill

mockery" of democracy. Thaddeus Stevens of Pennsylvania advocated a "conquered provinces" theory, and Charles Sumner of Massachusetts employed an argument of "state suicide." Both contended that by seceding, southern states had destroyed their status as states. They there-fore must be treated as "conquered foreign lands" and revert to the status of "unorganized territories" before Congress could entertain any process of readmission.

In July 1864, the Wade-Davis bill, named for its sponsors, Senator Benjamin Wade of Ohio and Congressman Henry W. Davis of Maryland, emerged from Congress with three specific conditions for southern readmission: one, it demanded a "majority" of white male citizens participating in the creation of a new government; two, to vote or be a delegate to constitutional conventions, men had to take an "iron-clad" oath (declaring they had never aided the Confederate war effort); and three, all officers above the rank of lieutenant, and all civil officials in the Confederacy, would be disfranchised and deemed "not a citizen of the United States." Lincoln pocket-vetoed the bill and issued a conciliatory proclamation of his own, announcing that he would not be inflexibly committed to any "one plan" of Reconstruction.

The timing of this exchange came during Grant's bloody campaign in Virginia against Lee. The outcome of the war and Lincoln's reelection were still in doubt. Radical members of his own party, indeed, were organizing a dump-Lincoln campaign for the 1864 election. What emerged in 1864–1865 was a clear-cut debate and a potential constitutional crisis. Lincoln saw Reconstruction as a means of weakening the Confederacy and winning the war; the Radicals saw it as a longer-term transformation of the political and racial order of the country.

In early 1865, Congress and Lincoln joined in passing two important measures that recognized slavery's centrality to the war. On January 31, with strong administration backing, Congress passed the Thirteenth Amendment, which had two provisions: it abolished involuntary servitude everywhere in the United States, and it declared that Congress shall have power to enforce this outcome by "appropriate legislation."

Thirteenth Amendment and the Freedmen's Bureau

Potentially as significant, on March 3, 1865, Congress created the Bureau of Refugees, Freedmen, and Abandoned Lands—the Freedmen's Bureau, an unprecedented agency of social uplift, necessitated by the ravages of the war. In the mere four years of its existence, the Freedmen's Bureau supplied food and medical services, built several thousand schools and some colleges, negotiated several hundred thousand employment contracts between freedmen and their former masters, and tried to manage confiscated land.

The Bureau would be a controversial aspect of Reconstruction, both within the South, where whites generally hated it, and within the federal government, where politicians divided over its constitutionality.

The war had forced into the open an eternal question of republics: What are the social welfare obligations of the state toward its people, and what do people owe their governments in return?

The Meanings of Freedom

 Black southerners entered into life after slavery with hope and circumspection. Expecting hostility from southern whites, freed men and women tried to gain as much as they could from their new circumstances. Often the changes they valued the most were personal—alterations in location, employer, or living arrangements.

For America's former slaves, Reconstruction had one paramount meaning: a chance to explore freedom.

The Feel of Freedom

Former slaves remembered singing far into the night after federal troops, who confirmed rumors of their emancipation, reached their plantations. The slaves on a Texas plantation shouted for joy, their leader proclaiming, "We is free—no more whippings and beatings." One man recalled that he and others "started on the move," either to search for family members or just to exercise the human right of mobility.

Many freed men and women reacted more cautiously and shrewdly, taking care to test the boundaries of their new condition. As slaves they had learned to expect hostility from white people, and they did not presume it would instantly disappear. Life in freedom might still be a matter of what was allowed, not what was right. One sign of their caution was the way freedpeople evaluated potential employers. "Most all the Negroes that had good owners stayed with 'em, but the others left. Some of 'em come back and some didn't," explained one man. After considerable wandering in search of better circumstances, a majority of blacks eventually settled as agricultural workers back on their former farms or plantations. But they relocated their houses and did their utmost to control the conditions of their labor.

The search for family members who had been sold away during slavery was awe-inspiring. With only shreds of information to guide them, thousands of freedpeople embarked on odysseys in search of a husband, wife, child, or parent. Some succeeded in their quest, sometimes almost miraculously. Others trudged through several states and never found loved ones.

Parents in African American Families

Husbands and wives who had belonged to different masters established homes together for the first time, and parents asserted the right to raise their own children. A mother bristled when her old master claimed a right to whip her children. She informed him that "he warn't goin' to brush none of her chilluns no more." The freed men and women were too much at risk to act recklessly, but, as one man put it, they were tired of punishment and "sure didn't take no more foolishment off of white folks."

Many black people wanted to minimize contact with whites. To avoid contact with overbearing whites who were used to supervising them,

Blacks' Search for Independence

blacks abandoned the slave quarters and fanned out to distant corners of the land they worked. Some described moving "across the creek to [themselves]" or building a "saplin house . . . back in the woods." Others established small all-black settlements that still exist today along the back roads of the South.

In addition to a fair employer, what freed men and women most wanted was the ownership of land. Land

African Americans' Desire for Land

represented their chance to enjoy the independence that self-sufficient farmers value. It represented compensation for generations of travail in bondage. A northern observer noted that slaves freed in the Sea Islands of South Carolina and Georgia made "plain, straightforward" inquiries as they settled the land set aside for them by General Sherman. They wanted to be sure the land "would be theirs after they had improved it."

But how much of a chance would whites give to blacks? Most members of both political parties opposed genuine land redistribution to the freedmen. Even northern reformers showed little sympathy for black aspirations. The former Sea Island slaves wanted to establish small, self-sufficient farms. Northern soldiers, officials, and missionaries insisted that they grow cotton.

"The Yankees preach nothing but cotton, cotton!" complained one Sea Island black. "We wants land," wrote another, but tax officials "make the lots too big, and cut we out." Indeed, the U.S. government sold thousands of acres in the Sea Islands for nonpayment

African Americans of all ages eagerly pursued the opportunity in freedom to gain an education. This young woman in Mt. Meigs, Alabama, is helping her mother learn to read. (Smithsonian Institute, photo by Rudolf Eickemeyer)

of taxes, but 90 percent of the land went to wealthy investors from the North.

Ex-slaves reached out for valuable things in life that had been denied them. One of these was education. Blacks of all ages hungered for

The Black Embrace of Education

the knowledge in books that had been permitted only to whites. With freedom, they started schools and filled classrooms both day and night. On log seats and dirt floors, freed men and women studied their letters in old almanacs and discarded dictionaries. Young children brought infants to school with them, and adults attended at night or after "the crops were laid by."

The federal government and northern reformers of both races assisted this pursuit of education. In its brief life, the Freedmen's Bureau founded over four thousand schools, and idealistic men and women from the North established and staffed others founded by private northern philanthropy. Thus did African Americans seek a break from their pasts through learning. The results included the beginnings of a public school system in each southern state and the enrollment of over six hundred thousand African Americans in elementary school by 1877.

Blacks and their white allies also saw the need for colleges and universities to train teachers, ministers, and professionals for leadership. The American Missionary Association founded seven colleges, including Fisk and Atlanta Universities, between 1866 and 1869. The Freedmen's Bureau helped to establish Howard University in Washington, D.C., and northern religious groups supported dozens of seminaries and teachers' colleges. By the late 1870s black churches had joined in the effort, founding numerous colleges despite limited resources.

During Reconstruction, African American leaders often were highly educated individuals; many of them came from the prewar elite of free people of color. This group had benefited from its association with wealthy whites, many of whom were blood relatives; some planters had given their mulatto children an outstanding education. Francis Cardozo, who held various offices in South Carolina, had attended universities in Scotland and England. The two black senators from Mississippi, Blanche K. Bruce and Hiram Revels, possessed privileged educations. These men and many self-educated former slaves brought to political office their experience as artisans, businessmen, lawyers, teachers, and preachers.

Freed from the restrictions and regulations of slavery, blacks could build their own institutions as they saw fit. The secret churches of slavery came into the open; throughout the South, ex-slaves "started a brush arbor." A brush arbor was merely "a sort of . . . shelter with leaves for a roof," but the freed men and women worshiped in it enthusiastically. Within a few years, however, independent branches of the Methodist and Baptist denominations had attracted the great majority of black Christians in the South.

Growth of Black Churches

The desire to gain as much independence as possible also shaped the former slaves' economic arrangements. Since most of them lacked the money to buy land, they preferred the next best thing: renting the land they worked. But the South had a cash-poor economy with few sources of credit. Therefore, black farmers and white landowners turned to sharecropping, a system in which farmers kept part of their crop and gave the rest to the landowner while living on his property. The landlord or a merchant "furnished" food and supplies needed before the harvest, and he received payment from the crop. Although landowners tried to set the laborers' share at a low level, black farmers had some bargaining power, at least at first. Sharecroppers would hold out, or move and try to switch employers from one year to another.

Rise of the Sharecropping System

The sharecropping system originated as a desirable compromise. It eased landowners' problems with cash and credit, and provided them a permanent, dependent labor force; blacks accepted it because it gave them more freedom from daily supervision. Instead of working under a white overseer, as in slavery, they farmed a plot of land on their own in family groups. But sharecropping later proved to be a disaster. Owners and merchants developed a monopoly of control over the agricultural economy, and sharecroppers found themselves riveted into ever-increasing debt. Coinciding with the emergence of a southern economy based on sharecropping was the nation's struggle to put its political house back in order.

Johnson's Reconstruction Plan

When Reconstruction began under President Andrew Johnson, many expected his policies to be harsh. Throughout his career in Tennessee he had criticized the wealthy planters and championed the small farmers. When an assassin's bullet thrust Johnson into the presidency, many former slaveowners, as well as northern Radicals, had reason to believe that Johnson would deal sternly with the South. When one Radical suggested the exile or execution of ten or twelve leading rebels to set an example, Johnson replied, "How are you going to pick out so small a number?"

Like his martyred predecessor, Johnson followed a path in antebellum politics from obscurity to power.

Who Was Andrew Johnson?

With no formal education, he became a tailor's apprentice. But from 1829, while in his early twenties, he held nearly every office in Tennessee politics: alderman, state representative, congressman, two terms as governor, and U.S. senator by 1857. Although elected as a southern Democrat, Johnson was the only senator from a seceded state who refused to follow his state out of the Union. Lincoln appointed him war governor of Tennessee in 1862, and hence, his symbolic place on the ticket in the president's bid for reelection in 1864.

Although a staunch Unionist, Johnson was also an ardent states' rightist. And while he vehemently opposed secession, Johnson advocated limited government. Above all, when it came to race, Johnson was a thoroughgoing white supremacist. He accepted emancipation as a result of the war, but he did not favor black civil and political rights. His philosophy toward Reconstruction may be summed up in the slogan he adopted: "The Constitution as it is, and the Union as it was."

Through 1865 Johnson alone controlled Reconstruction policy, for Congress recessed shortly before he became president and did not reconvene until December. In the following eight months, Johnson put into operation his own plan, forming new state governments in the South by using his power to grant pardons. But what role, if any, would blacks have in these governments?

Johnson's Leniency and Racial Views

Johnson held that black suffrage could never be imposed on a southern state by the federal government. His racism put him on a collision course with the Radicals. In perhaps the most blatantly racist official statement ever delivered by an American president, Johnson declared in his annual message of 1867 that blacks possessed less "capacity for government than any other race of people. No independent government of any form has ever been successful in their hands."

This racial conservatism had an enduring effect on Johnson's policies. Where whites were concerned, however, Johnson seemed to be pursuing changes in class relations. He proposed rules that would keep the wealthy planter class at least temporarily out of power. White southerners were required to swear an oath of loyalty as a condition of gaining amnesty or pardon, but Johnson barred several categories of people from taking the oath: former federal officials, high-ranking Confederate officers, and political leaders or graduates of West Point or Annapolis who had violated their oaths to support the United States by aiding the Confederacy. To this list Johnson added another important group: all southerners who aided the rebellion and whose taxable property was worth more than $20,000. These individuals had to apply personally to the president for pardon and restoration of their political rights. It thus appeared that the leadership class of the Old South would be removed from power and replaced by deserving yeomen.

Johnson appointed provisional governors who began the Reconstruction process by calling constitutional conventions. The delegates chosen for these conventions had to draft new constitutions that eliminated slavery and invalidated secession.

Johnson's Pardon Policy

After ratification of these constitutions, new governments could be elected, and the states would be restored to the Union with full congressional representation. But only those southerners who had taken the oath of amnesty and been eligible to vote on the day the state seceded could participate in this process. Thus unpardoned whites and former slaves were not eligible.

If Johnson intended to strip the old elite of its power, he did not hold to his plan. Surprisingly, he helped to subvert his own plan by pardoning aristocrats and leading rebels. These pardons, plus the rapid return of planters' abandoned lands, restored the old elite to power.

Why did Johnson allow the planters to regain power? Part of the answer is tied to his determination to implement a rapid Reconstruction in order to deny the Radicals the opportunity for the more thorough racial and political changes they desired in the South. Another reason was Johnson's need for southern support in the 1866 elections. Such factors led him to endorse the new governments and declare Reconstruction complete only eight months after Appomattox. Thus in December 1865 many Confederate leaders, including the vice president of the Confederacy, traveled to Washington to claim seats in the U.S. Congress.

The election of such prominent rebels troubled many northerners. So did other results of Johnson's program. Some of the state conven-

Black Codes tions were slow to repudiate secession; others admitted only grudgingly that slavery was dead. Furthermore, to define the status of freed men and women and control their labor, some legislatures merely revised large sections of the slave codes by substituting the word *freedmen* for *slaves*. The new black codes compelled the former slaves to carry passes, observe a curfew, live in housing provided by a landowner, and give up hope of entering many desirable occupations. Stiff vagrancy laws and restrictive labor contracts bound supposedly free laborers to plantations.

It seemed to northerners that the South was intent on returning African Americans to servility. Thus the Republican majority in Congress decided to call a halt to the results of Johnson's plan. On reconvening, the House and Senate considered the credentials of the newly elected southern representatives and decided not to admit them. Instead, they bluntly challenged the president's authority and established a joint committee to study and investigate a new direction for Reconstruction.

The Congressional Reconstruction Plan

 Northern congressmen were hardly unified, but they did not doubt their right to shape Reconstruction policy. The Constitution mentioned neither secession nor reunion, but it gave Congress the primary role in the admission of states. Moreover, the Constitution declared that the United States shall guarantee to each state a republican form of government. This provision, legislators believed, gave them the authority to devise policies for Reconstruction.

They soon found that other constitutional questions affected their policies. What, for example, had rebellion done to the relationship between southern states and the Union? Lincoln had always insisted that states could not secede—they had engaged in an "in-

surrection"—and that the Union remained intact. Johnson also argued that the Union had endured, though individuals had erred. In contrast, congressmen who favored vigorous Reconstruction measures argued that the war had broken the Union, and that the South was subject to the victor's will. Moderate congressmen held that the states had forfeited their rights through rebellion and thus had come under congressional supervision.

These theories mirrored the diversity of Congress itself. Northern Democrats denounced any idea of racial equality and supported John-

The Radicals son's policies. Conservative Republicans favored a limited federal role in Reconstruction. The Radical Republicans wanted to transform the South. Although they were a minority within their party, they had the advantage of a clearly defined goal. They believed it was essential to democratize the South, establish public education, and ensure the rights of freedpeople. They favored black suffrage, often supported land confiscation and redistribution, and were willing to exclude the South from the Union for several years if necessary to achieve their goals. A large group of moderate Republicans did not want to go as far as the Radicals but believed some reworking of Johnson's policies was necessary.

Ironically, Johnson and the Democrats sabotaged the possibility of a conservative coalition. They refused to cooperate with conservative or moderate Republicans and insisted that Reconstruction was over, that the new state governments were legitimate, and that southern representatives should be admitted to Congress. To devise a Republican program, conservative and moderate elements in the party had to work with the Radicals, whose influence grew in proportion to Johnson's intransigence.

Trying to work with Johnson, Republicans believed a compromise had been reached in the spring of

Congress Wrests Control from Johnson 1866. Under its terms Johnson would agree to two modifications of his program: extension of the life of the Freedmen's Bureau for another year and passage of a civil rights bill to counteract the black codes. This bill would force southern courts to practice equality before the law by allowing federal judges to remove from state courts cases in which blacks were treated unfairly.

Its provisions applied to public, not private, acts of discrimination. The civil rights bill of 1866 was the first statutory definition of the rights of American citizens.

Johnson destroyed the compromise, however, by vetoing both bills (they later became law when Congress overrode the president's veto). All hope of presidential-congressional cooperation was now dead. In 1866 newspapers reported daily violations of blacks' rights in the South and carried alarming accounts of antiblack violence. In Memphis, for instance, forty blacks were killed and twelve schools burned by white mobs. Such violence convinced Republicans, and the northern public, that more needed to be done. A new Republican plan took the form of a proposed amendment to the Constitution, forged out of a compromise between radical and conservative elements of the party. The Fourteenth Amendment, passed and sent to the states in June 1866, was Congress's alternative to Johnson's program of Reconstruction.

Of the four parts of the Fourteenth Amendment, the first was to have the greatest legal significance in later years. It conferred citizenship

The Fourteenth Amendment

on the freedmen and prohibited states from abridging their constitutional "privileges and immunities." It also barred any state from taking a person's life, liberty, or property "without due process of law" and from denying "equal protection of the laws." These resounding phrases became powerful guarantees of African Americans' civil rights—indeed, of the rights of all citizens—in the twentieth century.

Nearly universal agreement emerged among Republicans on the amendment's second and third provisions. The second declared the Confederate debt null and void and guaranteed the war debt of the United States. The third provision barred Confederate leaders from holding state and federal office. Only Congress, by a two-thirds vote of each house, could remove the penalty.

The fourth part of the amendment dealt with representation and embodied the compromises that produced the document. Emancipation made every former slave a full person rather than three-fifths of a person, which would increase southern representation. Thus the postwar South stood to gain power in Congress, and if white southerners did not allow blacks to vote, former secessionists would derive the political benefit from emancipation. So Republicans determined that if a southern state did not grant black men the vote, its representation would be reduced proportionally. If a state did enfranchise black men, its representation would be increased proportionally. This compromise avoided a direct enactment of black suffrage, but would deliver future black voters to the Republican Party.

The Fourteenth Amendment paved the way for black male suffrage but ignored female citizens, black and white. For this reason it provoked a strong reaction from the women's rights movement. When legislators defined women as nonvoting citizens, prominent leaders such as Elizabeth Cady Stanton and Susan B. Anthony decided that it was time to end their alliance with abolitionists and fight more determinedly for themselves. Thus the amendment infused new life into the women's rights movement and caused considerable strife among old allies.

In 1866, however, the major question in Reconstruction politics was how the public would respond to the congressional initiative. Johnson

The South's and Johnson's Defiance, 1866

did his best to block the Fourteenth Amendment in both North and South. Condemning Congress for its refusal to seat southern representatives, the president urged state legislatures in the South to vote against ratification. Every southern legislature except Tennessee's rejected the amendment by a wide margin.

To present his case to northerners, Johnson organized a National Union Convention and took to the stump himself. In an age when active personal campaigning was rare for a president, Johnson boarded a special train for a "swing around the circle" that carried his message deep into the Northeast, the Midwest, and then back to Washington. In city after city, he criticized the Republicans in a ranting, undignified style. Increasingly, audiences rejected his views and hooted and jeered at him.

The elections of 1866 were a resounding victory for Republicans in Congress. Radicals and moderates whom Johnson had denounced won reelection by large margins, and the Republican majority grew to two-thirds of both houses of Congress. The North had spoken clearly: Johnson's policies were prematurely giving the advantage to rebels and traitors. Thus Republican congressional leaders won a mandate to pursue their Reconstruction plan.

After some embittered debate, Congress, in March 1867, passed the First Reconstruction Act. This

The Reconstruction Acts of 1867–1868

plan, under which the southern states were actually readmitted to the Union, incorporated only a part of the Radical program. Union generals, commanding small garrisons of troops and charged with supervising all elections, assumed control in five military districts in the South (see Map 16.1). Confederate leaders designated in the Fourteenth Amendment were barred from voting until new state constitutions were ratified. The act guaranteed freedmen the right to vote in elections for state constitutional conventions and in subsequent elections. In addition, each southern state was required to ratify the Fourteenth Amendment, to ratify its new constitution by majority vote, and to submit that constitution to Congress for approval. The Second, Third, and Fourth Reconstruction Acts, passed between March 1867 and March 1868, provided for the details of operation of voter registration boards, the adoption of constitutions, and the administration of "good faith" oaths on the part of white southerners.

In the words of one historian, the Radicals succeeded in "clipping Johnson's wings." But they had

The Failure of Land Redistribution

hoped Congress could do much more. Thaddeus Stevens, for example, argued that economic opportunity was essential to the freedmen. Stevens therefore drew up a plan for extensive confiscation and redistribu-

Map 16.1   The Reconstruction   This map shows the five military districts established when Congress passed the Reconstruction Act of 1867. As the dates within each state indicate, conservative Democratic forces quickly regained control of government in four southern states. So-called Radical Reconstruction was curtailed in most of the others as factions within the weakened Republican Party began to cooperate with conservative Democrats.

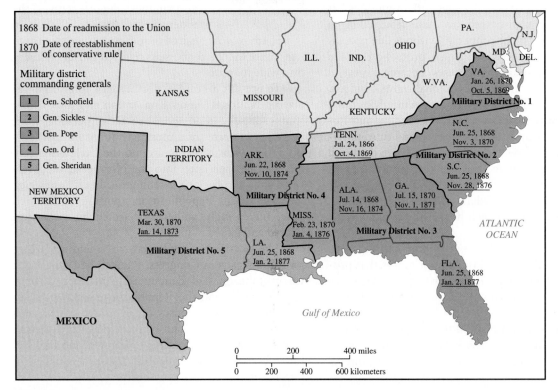

tion of land. Only one-tenth of the land affected by his plan was earmarked for freedmen, in 40-acre plots. The rest was to be sold to generate money for Union veterans' pensions, compensation to loyal southerners for damaged property, and payment of the federal debt.

By these means Stevens hoped to win support for a basically unpopular measure. But he failed. Northerners were accustomed to a limited role for government, and the business community staunchly opposed any interference with private property rights, even for former Confederates.

Congress's role as the architect of Reconstruction was not quite over. To restrict Johnson's influence and safeguard its plan, Congress passed a number of controversial laws. First, it set the date for its own reconvening—an unprecedented act, for the president traditionally summoned legislators to Washington. Then it limited Johnson's power over the army by requiring the president to issue military orders through the General of the Army, Ulysses S. Grant, who could not be dismissed without the Senate's consent. Finally, Congress passed the Tenure of Office Act, which gave the Senate power to approve changes in the president's cabinet. Designed to protect Secretary of War Edwin M. Stanton, who sympathized with the Radicals, this law violated the tradition that a president controlled appointments to his own cabinet. All of these measures, as well as each of the Reconstruction Acts, were passed by a two-thirds override of presidential vetoes.

Constitutional Crisis

Johnson took several belligerent steps of his own. He issued orders to military commanders in the South limiting their powers and increasing the powers of the civil governments he had created in 1865. Then he removed military officers who were conscientiously enforcing Congress's new law, preferring commanders who allowed disqualified Confederates to vote. Finally, he tried to remove Secretary of War Stanton. With that attempt the confrontation reached its climax.

Twice in 1867, the House Judiciary Committee had considered impeachment of Johnson, rejecting the idea once and then recommending it by only a 5-to-4 vote. That recommendation was decisively defeated by the House. After Johnson tried to remove Stanton, however, a third attempt to impeach the president car-

Impeachment of President Johnson

ried easily. The indictment concentrated on his violation of the Tenure of Office Act, though modern scholars regard his efforts to impede enforcement of the Reconstruction Act of 1867 as a far more serious offense.

Johnson's trial in the Senate began promptly and lasted more than three months. The prosecution attempted to prove that Johnson was guilty of "high crimes and misdemeanors." But they also argued that the trial was a means to judge Johnson's performance, not a judicial determination of guilt or innocence. The Senate ultimately rejected such reasoning, which could have made removal from office a political weapon against any chief executive who disagreed with Congress. Although a majority of senators voted to convict Johnson, the prosecution fell one vote short of the necessary two-thirds majority. Johnson remained in office, politically weakened and with only a few months left in his term.

In the 1868 presidential election Ulysses S. Grant, running as a Republican, defeated Horatio Seymour, a New York Democrat. Grant was not a Radical, but his platform supported congressional Reconstruction and endorsed black suffrage in the South. (Significantly, Republicans stopped short of endorsing it in the North.) The Democrats vigorously denounced Reconstruction. For the first time African Americans participated in a presidential election on a wide scale; they voted en masse for General Grant.

Election of 1868

In office Grant acted as an administrator of Reconstruction but not as its enthusiastic advocate. He vacillated in his dealings with the southern states, sometimes defending Republican regimes and sometimes currying favor with Democrats. On occasion Grant called out federal troops to stop violence or enforce acts of Congress. But he never imposed a true military occupation on the South. The later legend of "military rule," so important to southern claims of victimization during Reconstruction, was steeped in myth.

In 1869, in an effort to write democratic principles into the Constitution, the Radicals passed the Fifteenth Amendment. This measure forbade states to deny the right to vote "on account of race, color, or previous condition of servitude." Such wording did not guarantee the right to vote. It deliberately left states free to restrict

Fifteenth Amendment

suffrage on other grounds so that northern states could continue to deny suffrage to women and certain groups of men—Chinese immigrants, illiterates, and those too poor to pay poll taxes. Ironically, the votes of four uncooperative southern states—compelled by Congress to approve the amendment as an added condition to rejoining the Union—proved necessary to impose even this language on parts of the North. Although several states outside the South refused to ratify, three-fourths of the states approved the measure, and the Fifteenth Amendment became law in 1870.

With passage of the Fifteenth Amendment, many Americans, especially supportive northerners, considered Reconstruction essentially completed. "Let us have done with Reconstruction," pleaded the *New York Tribune* in April 1870. "The country is tired and sick of it. . . . Let us have Peace!"

Reconstruction Politics in the South

From the start, Reconstruction encountered the resistance of white southerners. In the black codes and in private attitudes, many whites stubbornly opposed emancipation, and the former planter class proved especially unbending. In 1866 a Georgia newspaper frankly observed that "most of the white citizens believe that the institution of slavery was right, and . . . they will believe that the condition, which comes nearest to slavery, that can now be established will be the best."

Fearing loss of control over their slaves, some planters attempted to postpone freedom by denying or misrepresenting events. Former slaves reported that their owners "didn't tell them it was freedom" or "wouldn't let [them] go." To hold onto their workers, some landowners claimed control over black children and used guardianship and apprentice laws to bind black families to the plantation. Whites also blocked blacks from acquiring land.

White Resistance

After President Johnson encouraged the South to resist congressional Reconstruction, white conservatives worked hard to capture the new state governments. Many whites also boycotted the polls in an attempt to defeat Congress's plans; by sitting out the

Thomas Nast, in this 1868 cartoon, pictured the combination of forces that threatened the success of Reconstruction: southern opposition and the greed, partisanship, and racism of northern interests.   (Library of Congress)

elections, whites might block the new constitutions, which had to be approved by a majority of registered voters. This tactic was tried in North Carolina and succeeded in Alabama, forcing Congress to base ratification of the Fourteenth Amendment and of new state constitutions on a majority of "votes cast."

Very few black men stayed away from the polls. Enthusiastically and hopefully, they voted Republican. Most agreed with one man who felt he should "stick to the end with the party that freed me." Illiteracy did not prohibit blacks (or uneducated whites) from making intelligent choices. A Mississippi black testified that he and his friends had no difficulty selecting the Republi-

Black Voters and Emergence of a Southern Republican Party

can ballot. "We stood around and watched," he explained. "We saw D. Sledge vote; he owned half the county. We knowed he voted Democratic so we voted the other ticket so it would be Republican."

Thanks to a large black turnout and the restrictions on prominent Confederates, a new southern Republican Party came to power in the constitutional conventions of 1868–1870. Republican delegates consisted of a sizable contingent of blacks (265 out of the total of just over 1,000 delegates throughout the South), some northerners who had moved to the South, and native southern whites who favored change. Together these Republicans brought the South into line with progressive reforms adopted earlier in the rest of the nation. The new constitutions were more democratic. They eliminated property qualifications for voting and holding office, and they turned many appointed offices into elective posts. They provided for public schools and institutions to care for the mentally ill, the blind, the deaf, the destitute, and the orphaned.

The conventions broadened women's rights in property holding and divorce. Usually, the goal was not to make women equal with men but to provide relief to thousands of suffering debtors. In families left poverty-stricken by the war and weighed down by debt, it was usually the husband who had contracted the debts. Thus giving women legal control over their own property provided some protection to their families. The goal of some delegates, however, was to elevate women. Blacks in particular called for laws to provide for woman suffrage, but they were ignored by their white colleagues.

Under these new constitutions the southern states elected Republican-controlled governments. For the first time, the ranks of state legislators in 1868 included some black southerners. These new biracial regimes appreciated the realities of power and the depth of racial enmity. In most states, whites were in the majority and former slaveowners controlled the best land and other sources of economic power. James Lynch, a leading black politician from Mississippi, explained why African Americans shunned the "folly" of disfran-

Triumph of Republican Governments

chisement of ex-Confederates. Unlike northerners who "can leave when it becomes too uncomfortable," landless former slaves "must be in friendly relations with the great body of the whites in the state."

Blacks also believed in the principle of universal suffrage and the Christian goal of reconciliation. Far from being vindictive toward the race that had enslaved them, they treated leading rebels with generosity and appealed to white southerners to adopt a spirit of fairness and cooperation. In this way the South's Republican Party condemned itself to defeat if white voters would not cooperate. Within a few years Republicans were reduced to the embarrassment of making futile appeals to whites while ignoring the claims of their strongest supporters, blacks. But for a time both Republicans and their opponents, who called themselves Conservatives or Democrats, moved to the center and appealed for support from a broad range of groups. Some propertied whites accepted congressional Reconstruction as a reality and declared themselves willing to compete under the new rules. All sides found an area of agreement in economic policies.

Reflecting northern ideals and southern necessity, the Reconstruction governments enthusiastically promoted industry. Confederates had seen how industry aided the North during the war. Accordingly, Reconstruction legislatures encouraged investment with loans, subsidies, and exemptions from taxation for periods up to ten years. The southern railroad system was rebuilt and expanded, and coal and iron mining made possible Birmingham's steel plants. Between 1860 and 1880, the number of manufacturing establishments in the South nearly doubled. This emphasis on big business, however, produced higher state debts and taxes, drew money away from schools and other programs, and multiplied possibilities for corruption.

Industrialization

Policies appealing to African American voters never went beyond equality before the law. In fact, the whites who controlled the southern Republican Party were reluctant to allow blacks a share of offices proportionate to their electoral strength. Aware of their weakness, black leaders did not push very far for revolutionary economic or social change. In every southern

Republican Policies on Racial Equality

state, they led efforts to establish public schools, although they did not press for integrated facilities.

Economic progress was uppermost in the minds of most freedpeople. Black southerners needed land, but only a few promoted confiscation. In fact, much land did fall into state hands for nonpayment of taxes and was offered for sale in small lots. But most freedmen had too little cash to bid against investors or speculators, and few acquired land in this way. Any widespread redistribution of land had to arise from Congress, which never supported such action. The lack of genuine land redistribution remained the significant lost opportunity of Reconstruction.

Within a few years, as centrists in both parties met with failure, white hostility to congressional Reconstruction began to dominate. Some conservatives had always desired to fight Reconstruction through pressure and racist propaganda. Charging that the South had been turned over to ignorant blacks, conservatives deplored "black domination," which became a rallying cry for a return to white supremacy.

The Myth of "Negro Rule"

Such attacks were inflammatory propaganda, and part of the growing myth of "Negro rule." African Americans participated in politics but hardly dominated or controlled events. They were a majority in only two out of ten state constitution–writing conventions (transplanted northerners were a majority in one). In the state legislatures, only in the lower house in South Carolina did blacks ever constitute a majority; among officeholders, their numbers generally were far fewer than their proportion in the population. Sixteen blacks won seats in Congress before Reconstruction was over, but none was ever elected governor. Only eighteen served in a high state office such as lieutenant governor, treasurer, superintendent of education, or secretary of state. However, elected officials, such as Robert Smalls in South Carolina, labored tirelessly for cheaper land prices, better healthcare, access to schools, and the enforcement of civil rights for their people.

Conservatives also assailed the allies of black Republicans. Their propaganda denounced whites from the North as "carpetbaggers," greedy crooks planning to pour stolen tax revenues into their sturdy luggage made of carpet material. In fact, most northerners who settled in the South had come seeking business opportunities or a warmer climate and never entered politics. Those who did enter politics generally wanted to democratize the South and to introduce northern ways, such as industry, public education, and the spirit of enterprise.

Carpetbaggers and Scalawags

In addition to tagging northern interlopers as carpetbaggers, Conservatives invented the term *scalawag* to discredit any native white southerner who cooperated with the Republicans. A substantial number of southerners did so. Most scalawags were yeoman farmers, men from mountain areas and nonslaveholding districts who saw that they could benefit from the education and opportunities promoted by Republicans. Banding together with freedmen, they pursued common class interests and hoped to make headway against the power of long-dominant planters. A majority of scalawags, however, did not support racial equality. The black-white coalition was thus vulnerable on the race issue. Republican tax policies also cut into upcountry yeoman support because reliance on the property tax hit many small landholders hard.

Taxation was a major problem for the Reconstruction governments. Republicans wanted to maintain prewar services, repair the war's destruction, stimulate industry, and support important new ventures such as public schools. But the Civil War had destroyed much of the South's tax base. Thus an increase in taxes was necessary even to maintain traditional services, and new ventures required still higher taxes.

Tax Policy and Corruption as Political Wedges

Corruption was another serious charge levied against the Republicans. Unfortunately, it often was true. Many carpetbaggers and black politicians engaged in fraudulent schemes, sold their votes, or padded expenses, taking part in what scholars recognize was a nationwide surge of corruption. Corruption carried no party label, but the Democrats successfully pinned the blame on unqualified blacks and greedy carpetbaggers among southern Republicans.

All these problems hurt the Republicans, but in many southern states the deathblow came through violence. The Ku Klux Klan began in Tennessee in 1866; it spread through the South and rapidly evolved into a terrorist organization. Violence against African Americans occurred from the first days of Re-

Ku Klux Klan

construction but became far more organized and purposeful after 1867. Klansmen rode to frustrate Reconstruction and keep the freedmen in subjection. Nighttime harassment, whippings, beatings, and murder became common, and terrorism dominated some counties and regions.

The Klan's main purpose was political. Lawless nightriders made active Republicans the target of their attacks. Leading white and black Republicans were killed in several states. After freedmen who worked for a South Carolina scalawag started voting, terrorists visited the plantation and, in the words of one victim, "whipped every nigger man they could lay their hands on." Klansmen also attacked Union League clubs—Republican organizations that mobilized the black vote—and schoolteachers who were aiding the freedmen.

Klan violence was not a spontaneous outburst of racism; very specific social forces shaped and directed it. In North Carolina, for example, Alamance and Caswell Counties were the sites of the worst Klan violence. Slim Republican majorities there rested on cooperation between black voters and white yeomen. Together, these black and white Republicans had ousted officials long entrenched in power. The wealthy and powerful men in Alamance and Caswell who had lost their accustomed political control then organized a deliberate campaign of terror. The campaign weakened the Republican coalition and restored a Democratic majority.

Klan violence injured Republicans across the South. No fewer than one-tenth of the black leaders who had been delegates to the 1867–1868 state constitutional conventions were attacked, seven fatally. A single attack on Alabama Republicans in the town of Eutaw left four blacks dead and fifty-four wounded. In South Carolina five hundred masked Klansmen lynched eight black prisoners at the Union County jail. According to historian Eric Foner, the Klan "made it virtually impossible for Republicans to campaign or vote in large parts of Georgia."

Thus a combination of difficult fiscal problems, Republican mistakes, racial hostility, and terror brought down the Republican regimes. In most southern states, "Radical Reconstruction" lasted only a few years (see Map 16.1). The most enduring failure of Reconstruction, however, was not political; it was social and economic. Recon-

Failure of Reconstruction

struction failed to alter the South's social structure or its distribution of wealth and power. Without land of their own, freed men and women were dependent on white landowners, who could and did use their economic power to compromise blacks' political freedom. Armed only with the ballot, freedmen in the South had little chance to effect major changes.

Reconstruction Reversed

Northerners had always been more interested in suppressing rebellion than in aiding southern blacks, and by the early 1870s the North's commitment to bringing about change in the South was weakening. Criticism of the southern governments grew, new issues captured public attention, and sentiment for national reconciliation gained popularity in politics. In one southern state after another, Democrats regained control. And for one of only a few times in American history, violence and terror emerged as a tactic in normal politics.

In 1870 and 1871 the violent campaigns of the Ku Klux Klan forced Congress to pass two Enforcement Acts and an anti-Klan law. These laws made actions by individuals against the civil and political rights of others a federal criminal offense for the first time. They also provided for election supervisors and permitted martial law and suspension of the writ of habeas corpus to combat murders, beatings, and threats by the Klan. Federal prosecutors used the laws rather selectively. In 1872 and 1873 Mississippi and the Carolinas saw many prosecutions; but in other states where violence flourished, the laws were virtually ignored. Southern juries sometimes refused to convict Klansmen.

Political Implications of Klan Terrorism

Some conservative but influential Republicans opposed the anti-Klan laws. Rejecting other Republicans' arguments that the Thirteenth, Fourteenth, and Fifteenth Amendments had made the federal government the protector of the rights of citizens, these dissenters echoed an old Democratic charge that Congress was infringing on states' rights. This opposition foreshadowed a more general revolt within Republican ranks in 1872.

Disenchanted with Reconstruction, a group calling itself the Liberal Republicans bolted the party in 1872 and nominated Horace Greeley, the well-known

The Liberal Republican Revolt

editor of the *New York Tribune*, for president. The Liberal Republicans were a varied group, including civil service reformers, foes of corruption, and advocates of a lower tariff. Normally such disparate elements would not cooperate with one another, but two popular and widespread attitudes united them: distaste for federal intervention in the South and an elitist desire to let market forces and the "best men" determine events, both in the South and in Washington. The Democrats also gave their nomination to Greeley in 1872. The combination was not enough to defeat Grant, who won reelection, but it reinforced Grant's desire to avoid confrontation with white southerners.

Dissatisfaction with Grant's administration grew during his second term. Strong-willed but politically naive, Grant made a series of poor appointments. His secretary of war, his private secretary, and officials in the Treasury and Navy Departments were involved in bribery or tax-cheating scandals. Instead of exposing the corruption, Grant defended some of the culprits. In 1874, as Grant's popularity and his party's prestige declined, the Democrats recaptured the House of Representatives.

The effect of Democratic gains in Congress was to weaken legislative resolve on southern issues. Congress had already lifted the political disabilities of the Fourteenth Amendment from many former Confederates. In 1872 it had adopted a sweeping Amnesty Act, which pardoned most of the remaining rebels and left only five hundred barred from political officeholding. In 1875 Congress passed a Civil Rights Act purporting to guarantee black people equal accommodations in public places, such as inns and theaters, but the bill was watered down and contained no effective provisions for enforcement. And by 1876 the Democrats had regained control in all but three southern states. Meanwhile, new concerns were capturing the public's attention.

A General Amnesty

Both industrialization and immigration were surging, hastening the pace of change in national life. Within only eight years, postwar industrial production increased by an impressive 75 percent. For the first time, nonagricultural workers outnumbered farmers, and only Britain's industrial output was greater than

Reconciliation and Industrial Expansion

that of the United States. Many of those finding employment in the expanding economy were among the 3 million immigrants who entered the country between 1865 and 1873.

Then the Panic of 1873 ushered in over five years of economic contraction. Three million people lost their jobs, and the clash between labor and capital became the major issue of the day. Class attitudes diverged, especially in the large cities. Debtors and the unemployed sought easy money policies to spur economic expansion. Businessmen, disturbed by the widespread strikes and industrial violence that accompanied the panic, became increasingly concerned about the defense of property.

Class conflict fueled a monetary issue: whether paper money—the Civil War greenbacks—should be kept in circulation. In 1872 Democratic farmers and debtors urged this policy to expand the money supply and raise prices, but businessmen, bankers, and creditors overruled them. Now hard times swelled the ranks of the "greenbackers"—voters who favored easy money.

Greenbacks Versus Sound Money

Congress voted in 1874 to increase the number of greenbacks in circulation, but Grant vetoed the bill in deference to the opinions of financial leaders. The next year, "sound money" interests prevailed in Congress, winning passage of a law requiring that greenbacks be convertible into gold after 1878. The chasm between farmers and workers and wealthy industrialists grew even wider.

Meanwhile, the Supreme Court played its part in the northern retreat from Reconstruction. During the Civil War the Court had been cautious and inactive. Reaction to the *Dred Scott* decision (1857) had been so violent, and the Union's wartime emergency so great, that the Court avoided interference with government actions. In 1866, however, *Ex parte Milligan* reached the Court.

Judicial Retreat from Reconstruction

Lambdin P. Milligan of Indiana had plotted to free Confederate prisoners of war and overthrow state governments. For these acts a military court sentenced Milligan, a civilian, to death. Milligan challenged the authority of the military tribunal, claiming that he had a right to a civil trial. The Supreme Court declared that military trials were illegal when civil courts were open and functioning, and its language indicated that the Court intended to reassert its authority.

In the 1870s the Court successfully renewed its challenge to Congress's actions when it narrowed the meaning and effectiveness of the Fourteenth Amendment. The *Slaughter-House* cases (1873) began in 1869, when the Louisiana legislature granted one company a monopoly on the slaughtering of livestock in New Orleans. Rival butchers in the city promptly sued. Their attorney, former Supreme Court justice John A. Campbell, argued that the Fourteenth Amendment had revolutionized the constitutional system by bringing individual rights under federal protection. Campbell thus articulated an original goal of the Republican Party: to nationalize civil rights and guard them from state interference.

The Court rejected Campbell's argument and thus dealt a stunning blow to the scope and vitality of the Fourteenth Amendment. Indeed, it interpreted the "privileges and immunities" of citizens so narrowly that it reduced them almost to trivialities. State citizenship and national citizenship were separate, the Court declared. National citizenship involved only matters such as the right to travel freely from state to state and to use the navigable waters of the nation, and only these narrow rights were protected by the Fourteenth Amendment.

The Supreme Court also concluded that the butchers who sued had not been deprived of their rights or property in violation of the due-process clause of the amendment. The Court's majority declared that the framers of the recent amendments had not intended to "destroy" the federal system, in which the states exercised "powers for domestic and local government, including the regulation of civil rights." Thus the justices severely limited the amendment's potential for securing and protecting the rights of black citizens—its original intent.

The next day the Court decided *Bradwell v. Illinois*, a case in which Myra Bradwell, a female attorney, had been denied the right to practice law in Illinois on account of her gender. Pointing to the Fourteenth Amendment, Bradwell's attorneys contended that the state had unconstitutionally abridged her "privileges and immunities" as a citizen. The Supreme Court rejected her claim, alluding to women's traditional role in the home.

In 1876 the Court weakened the Reconstruction era amendments even further by emasculating the enforcement clause of the Fourteenth Amendment and revealing deficiencies inherent in the Fifteenth Amendment. In *U.S. v. Cruikshank* the Court overruled the conviction under the 1870 Enforcement Act of Louisiana whites who had attacked a meeting of blacks and conspired to deprive them of their rights. The justices ruled that the Fourteenth Amendment did not give the federal government power to act against these whites. The duty of protecting citizens' equal rights, the Court said, "rests alone with the States." In *U.S. v. Reese* the Court noted that the Fifteenth Amendment did not guarantee the right to vote but merely listed certain impermissible grounds for denying suffrage. The decision opened the door for southern states to deny blacks the vote on grounds other than "race, color, or previous condition of servitude." Such judicial conservatism had profound impact down through the next century, as the revolutionary potential in the Civil War amendments was blunted, if not destroyed.

As the 1876 elections approached, most political observers saw that the North was no longer willing to pursue the goals of Reconstruction. The results of a disputed presidential election confirmed this fact. Samuel J. Tilden, the Democratic governor of New York, ran strongly in the South and needed only one more electoral vote to triumph over Rutherford B. Hayes, the Republican nominee. Nineteen electoral votes from Louisiana, South Carolina, and Florida (the only southern states yet "unredeemed" by Democratic rule) were disputed; both Democrats and Republicans claimed to have won in those states despite fraud committed by their opponents. One vote from Oregon was undecided because of a technicality (see Map 16.2).

Disputed Election of 1876 and the Compromise of 1877

To resolve this unprecedented situation Congress established a fifteen-member electoral commission. In the interest of impartiality, membership on the commission was to be balanced between Democrats and Republicans. But one independent Republican, Supreme Court Justice David Davis, refused appointment in

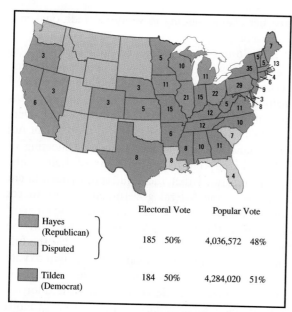

	Electoral Vote	Popular Vote
Hayes (Republican)		
Disputed	185 50%	4,036,572 48%
Tilden (Democrat)	184 50%	4,284,020 51%

Map 16.2 Presidential Election of 1876 and the Compromise of 1877 In 1876 a combination of solid southern support and Democratic gains in the North gave Samuel Tilden the majority of popular votes, but Rutherford B. Hayes won the disputed election in the electoral college, after a deal satisfied Democratic wishes for an end to Reconstruction.

who was not going to continue Reconstruction. Thus Hayes became president.

Southern Democrats rejoiced, but African Americans grieved over the betrayal of their hopes for equality. In the minds of many of these people, the only hope lay outside the South. Thus from South Carolina, Louisiana, Mississippi, and other southern states, thousands gathered up their possessions and migrated to Kansas. They were known as Exodusters, disappointed people still searching for their share in the American dream. Even in Kansas they met disillusionment, as the welcome extended by the state's governor soon gave way to hostile public reactions.

Betrayal of Black Rights and the Exodusters

Summary

Reconstruction left a contradictory record. It was an era of tragic aspirations and failures, but also of unprecedented legal, political, and social change. The Union victory brought about an increase in federal power, stronger nationalism, sweeping federal intervention in the southern states, and landmark amendments to the Constitution. But northern commitment to make these changes endure had eroded, and the revolution remained unfinished.

The North embraced emancipation, black suffrage, and constitutional alterations strengthening the central government. But it did so to defeat the rebellion and secure the peace. As the pressure of these crises declined, strong underlying continuities emerged and placed their mark on Reconstruction. The American people and the courts maintained a preference for state authority and a distrust of federal power. The ideology of free labor dictated that property should be respected and that individuals should be self-reliant. Racism endured and was transformed into the even more virulent forms of Klan terror. Concern for the human rights of African Americans was strongest when their plight threatened to undermine the interests of whites, and reform frequently had less appeal than moneymaking in an individualistic, enterprising society.

In the wake of the Civil War Americans faced two profound tasks—the achievement of healing and the dispensing of justice. Both had to occur, but they never

order to accept his election as a senator. A regular Republican took his place, and the Republican Party prevailed 8 to 7 on every attempt to count the returns, along strict party lines. Hayes would become president if Congress accepted the commission's findings.

Congressional acceptance was not certain, and many citizens worried that the nation had entered a major constitutional crisis and would slip once again into civil war. The crisis was resolved when Democrats acquiesced in the election of Hayes based on a "deal" cut in a Washington hotel. Negotiations took place between Hayes's supporters and southerners who wanted federal aid to railroads, internal improvements, federal patronage, and removal of troops from southern states. Neither party was well enough organized to implement and enforce the various parts of this bargain between the sections. Northern and southern Democrats simply decided they could not win and did not contest the election of a Republican

developed in historical balance. Making sectional re-union compatible with black freedom and equality overwhelmed the imagination in American political culture, and the nation still faced much of this dilemma more than a century later.

LEGACY FOR A PEOPLE AND A NATION
The Fourteenth Amendment

Before the Civil War, no definition of civil rights existed in America. Reconstruction legislation, especially the Fourteenth Amendment, changed that forever. Approved by Congress in 1866, the Fourteenth Amendment enshrined in the Constitution the ideas of birthright citizenship and equal rights. The Fourteenth Amendment was designed to secure and protect the rights of the freedpeople. But over time, the "equal protection of the law" clause has been used at times to support the rights of states, cities, corporations, immigrants, women, religious organizations, gays and lesbians, students, and labor unions. It has advanced both tolerance and intolerance, affirmative action and anti–affirmative action programs. It provides the legal well-spring for the generations-old civil rights movement in the United States.

The amendment as originally written required individuals to pursue grievances through private litigation, alleging state denial of a claimed federal right. At first the Supreme Court interpreted it conservatively, especially on racial matters, and by 1900 the idea of color-blind liberty in America was devastated by Jim Crow laws, disfranchisement, and unpunished mob violence.

But Progressive reformers used the equal protection clause to advocate government support of health, union organizing, municipal housing, and the protection of woman and child laborers. In the 1920s and 1930s, a judicial defense of civil liberties and free speech took hold. The Supreme Court expanded the amendment's guarantee of equality by a series of decisions upholding the rights of immigrant groups to resist "forced Americanization," especially Catholics in their creation of parochial schools. And, from its inception in 1910, the NAACP waged a long campaign to reveal the inequality of racial segregation in schooling and every other kind of public facility. Led by Charles Houston and Thurgood Marshall, this epic legal battle culminated in the *Brown v. Board of Education* desegregation decision of 1954. In the Civil Rights Act of 1964, the equal protection tradition was reenshrined into American law. Since 1964 Americans have lived in a society where the Fourteenth Amendment's legacy is the engine of expanded liberty for women and all minorities, as well as a political battleground for defining the nature and limits of human equality, and for redistributing justice long denied.

For Further Reading, see the Appendix. For Web resources, go to history.college.hmco.com/students.

THE DEVELOPMENT OF THE WEST

1877–1900

In 1893 a young historian named Frederick Jackson Turner delivered a stunning scholarly paper at the Columbian Exposition in Chicago. Titled "The Significance of the Frontier in American History," the paper argued the "frontier thesis" that the existence of "free land, its continuous recession, and the advancement of American settlement westward" had created a distinctively American spirit of democracy and egalitarianism. The conquest of a succession of frontier Wests, in other words, explained American progress and character.

At a covered arena just across the street from this same world's fair, the folk character Buffalo Bill Cody staged two performances daily of an extravaganza he called the "Wild West." Though Cody also dramatized the conquest of frontiers, his perspective differed markedly from Turner's. While Turner described the relatively peaceful settlement of largely empty western land, Cody portrayed the violent conquest of territory formerly occupied by savage Indians. Turner's heroes were persevering farmers who tamed the wilderness with axes and plows and in the process fashioned a new progressive race. Buffalo Bill's heroes were rugged scouts who braved danger and defeated Indians with rifles and bullets.

Both Turner and Cody believed that by the 1890s the era of the frontier had come to an end. In fact, Turner's essay had been sparked by an announcement from the superintendent of the 1890 census that "at present the unsettled area [of the West] has been so broken into by isolated bodies of settlement that there can be hardly said to be a frontier line." Over time,

IMPORTANT EVENTS

1862 Homestead Act grants free land to citizens who live on and improve the land

Morrill Land Grant Act gives states public lands to finance agricultural and industrial colleges

1864 Chivington's militia massacres Black Kettle's Cheyennes at Sand Creek

1872 Yellowstone becomes first national park

1873 Barbed wire invented, enabling western farmers to enclose and protect fields cheaply

1876 Sioux annihilate Custer's federal troops at Little Big Horn

1878 Timber and Stone Act allows citizens to buy timberland cheaply but also enables large companies to acquire huge tracts of forestland

1879 Utes surrender after resisting territorial concessions in western Colorado

Carlisle School for Indians established in Pennsylvania

Colorado creates water divisions to regulate water rights

1880–81 Manypenny's *Our Indian Wards* and Jackson's *A Century of Dishonor* influence public conscience about poor government treatment of Indians

1881–82 Chinese Exclusion Acts prohibit Chinese immigration to the U.S.

1883 National time zones standardized

1884 U.S. Supreme Court first defines Indians as wards under government protection

1887 Dawes Severalty Act ends communal ownership of Indian lands and grants land allotments to individual Native American families

Hatch Act provides for agricultural experiment stations in every state

California passes law permitting farmers to organize into districts that would sponsor the construction and operation of irrigation projects

1889 Statehood granted to North Dakota, South Dakota, Washington, and Montana

1890 Final suppression of Plains Indians by U.S. Army at Wounded Knee

Census Bureau announces closing of the frontier

Statehood granted to Wyoming and Idaho

Yosemite National Park established

Wyoming makes its rivers public property subject to state supervision

1893 Turner presents "frontier thesis" at Columbian Exposition

1896 Rural Free Delivery made available

Statehood granted to Utah

1902 Newlands Reclamation Act passed

Turner's theory was abandoned (even by Turner himself) as too simplistic, and Buffalo Bill was relegated to the gallery of rogues and showmen. Even so, both of the Wests that they depicted persist in the romance of American history, while the real story of western development in the late nineteenth century is much more complex than either myth.

One fact is certain: much of the West was never empty, and those who inhabited it utilized its resources in quite different ways. Indians had managed the environment and sustained their needs for centuries before white settlers arrived on the scene. The Pawnees of the Plains, for example, planted crops in the spring, left their fields to hunt buffalo, then returned for harvesting. Though Pawnees sometimes splurged when feasting on buffalo, they survived by developing and using natural resources in limited ways. Concepts of private property and profit had little meaning for them.

For white Americans, land and water were assets to be utilized for economic gain. As whites settled the West in the late nineteenth century, they exploited the environment for profit. They excavated deep into the earth for minerals, cut down forests for lumber, built railroads to carry goods and link markets, and dammed the rivers and plowed the soil. Their goal was not survival; rather, it was buying and selling and opening markets nationally and internationally.

The West, which by 1870 referred to the vast area between the Mississippi River and the Pacific Ocean, actually consisted of several regions and a variety of economic potential. Abundant rainfall along the northern Pacific Coast fed huge forests. Farther south into California, woodlands and grasslands existed, with fertile valleys capable of supporting vegetable fields and orange groves. Eastward, between the Cascade and Sierra Mountains and the Rocky Mountains where gold, silver, and other minerals lay buried, was an arid, desolate plateau that descended into the hot desert of southeastern California and western Arizona. On the eastern side of the Rockies were the Great Plains, divided into a semiarid western side of few trees and tough buffalo grass and an eastern area of ample rainfall and tall grasses. The Plains could support grain crops and livestock.

Between 1870 and 1890, the abundance of exploitable land, food, and raw materials in the West led to a migration that swelled the region's population from 7 million to nearly 17 million. This abundance also filled white Americans with faith that anyone eager and persistent enough could succeed. But this self-confidence rested on a belief that white people were somehow special, and individual advantage often asserted itself at the expense of people of color, the poor, and the environment. Americans rarely thought about conserving resources because there always seemed to be more territory to exploit and bring into the market economy.

By 1890 farms, ranches, mines, towns, and cities could be found in almost every corner of the present-day continental United States. Though of great symbolic importance, the fading of the frontier had little direct impact on people's behavior, for vast stretches of land remained unsettled. The expanses of seemingly uninhabited land gave Americans the feeling that they would always have a second chance. It was this belief in an infinity of second chances that left a deep imprint on the American character. ■

The Economic Activities of Native Peoples

Historians once defined the American frontier as "the edge of the unused," implying that the frontier disappeared once white men and women arrived to occupy supposedly open land for farming or the building of cities. Scholars now acknowledge that Native Americans had settled and developed the West long before other Americans migrated there. Nevertheless, almost all native economic systems weakened in the late nineteenth century.

Western Indian cultures varied, but all Indians based their economies to differing degrees on four activities: crop raising; livestock raising; hunting, fishing, and gathering; and trading and raiding. Corn was the most common crop; sheep and horses, acquired from Spanish colonizers, were the livestock; and buffalo were the primary prey of hunts. Indians raided one another for food, tools, hides, and horses, which in turn they used in trading with other Indians and with whites. To achieve their standards of living, Indians tried to balance their economic systems. When a buffalo hunt failed, they could subsist on crops. When their crops failed, they could still hunt buffalo and steal food and horses in a raid or trade livestock and furs for necessities.

Subsistence Cultures

For Indians on the Great Plains, everyday life focused on the buffalo. They cooked and preserved buffalo meat; fashioned hides into clothing, shoes, and blankets; used sinew for thread and bowstrings; and carved tools from bones and horns. They also depended on horses, which they used for transportation and hunting, and as symbols of wealth. To provide food for their herds, Plains Indians altered the environment by periodically setting fire to tall-grass prairies. The fires burned away dead plants, facilitating the growth of new grass in the spring so horses could feed all summer.

In the Southwest, Indians were herders and placed great value on sheep, goats, and horses. To the Navajos, the herds provided status and security. Like many Indians, the Navajos emphasized generosity and distrusted private property and wealth. Within the family, sharing was expected; outside the family, gifts and reciprocity governed personal relations. Southwestern Indians, too, altered the environment, building elaborate irrigation systems to maximize use of scarce water supplies.

What buffalo were to the Plains Indians and sheep were to Southwestern Indians, salmon were to Indians of the Northwest. Along the Columbia River and its tributaries, the Clatsops, Klamathets, and S'Klallam applied their own technology of stream diversion, platform construction over the water, and special baskets to better harvest fish. Like natives of other regions, many of these Indians also traded for horses, buffalo robes, beads, cloth, and knives.

On the Plains and in parts of the Southwest, this native world began to dissolve after 1850 when whites,

Slaughter of Buffalo

perceiving the buffalo and the Indians as hindrances to their ambitions, endeavored to eliminate both. Railroads sponsored hunts in which eastern sportsmen shot at the bulky targets from slow-moving trains. The army refused to enforce treaties that reserved hunting grounds for exclusive Indian use. Some hunters collected from $1 to $3 from tanneries for hides; others did not even stop to pick up their kill.

Indians themselves contributed to the depletion of the herds by increasing their kills, especially to obtain hides for trade. Also, a period of generally dry years in the 1840s and 1850s had forced Indians to set up camps in more fertile river basins, where they competed with buffalo for space and water. As a result, the bison were pushed out of important grazing territory and faced the threat of starvation. And the livestock that whites brought to the Plains exposed buffalo to lethal animal diseases such as anthrax and brucellosis. The increased numbers of horses, oxen, and sheep owned by white newcomers, as well as by some Indians, also upset the grazing patterns of the bison by devouring grasses that buffalo depended on at certain times of the year. In sum, a convergence of human and environmental shocks decimated the buffalo herds. By the 1880s only a few hundred remained of the estimated 25 million bison that had existed in 1820.

In the Northwest, the basic wild source of Indian food supply, salmon, suffered a similar fate. As white

Decline of Salmon

commercial fishermen and canneries moved into the region, they greatly diminished the salmon runs on the Columbia by the 1880s. Increasing numbers of salmon running up the river to spawn were being caught before they laid their eggs so that the fish supply was not being replenished. By the twentieth century, the construction of dams on the river and its tributaries further impeded the salmon's ability to reproduce. The government protected Indian fishing rights on the river and hatcheries helped restore some of the fish supply, but the need for electrical power from dams, combined with depletion of the salmon from overfishing and pollution, ended the abundance of this resource in the Northwest.

The Transformation of Native Cultures

Buffalo slaughter and salmon reduction undermined Indian subsistence, but a unique mix of human circumstances contributed as well. For most of the nineteenth century, the white population that migrated into western lands inhabited by Indians was overwhelmingly male. Most

Violence

of these males were in their twenties and thirties, unmarried, and at the stage of life when they were most prone to violent behavior. In other words, the first whites that Indians were most likely to come into contact with possessed guns and had few qualms about using their weapons against animals and humans who got in their way. Moreover, these men subscribed to prevailing attitudes that Indians were primitive, lazy, devious, and cruel. Such contempt made exploiting and killing natives all the easier, and violence was often "justified" by claims of preempting threats to life and property.

Indian warriors also were young, armed, and prone to violence. But Indian communities contrasted with those of whites in that they contained excesses of women and children, making native bands less mobile and therefore vulnerable to attack. Also, the syphilis and gonorrhea Indian males contracted from Indian women infected by whites killed many and reduced the ability of natives to reproduce, a consequence that their already declining population could not afford. Thus the age and gender structure of the white frontier population combined with attitudes of racial contempt created a serious threat to Indian existence in the West.

Government policy reinforced individual efforts to remove Indians from the path of white ambitions.

Lack of Native Unity

North American natives were organized not so much into tribes, as whites believed, as into hundreds of bands and confederacies in the Plains and in towns and villages in the Southwest and Northwest. Some two hundred distinct languages and dialects separated these groups. Although a language group could be defined as a tribe, separate bands and clans within each language group had their own leaders, and seldom did a tribal chief hold significant power.

Nevertheless, to help it fashion a policy toward Indians, the U.S. government gave more meaning to tribal organization than was warranted. After the Treaty of Greenville in 1795, American officials considered Indian tribes to be separate nations with which they could make treaties. But a chief or chiefs who agreed to a treaty could not guarantee that all bands within the group would abide by it. Moreover, whites seldom accepted treaties as guarantees of the Indians' future land rights. They assumed that they could settle wherever they wished on the Plains or take the best fishing sites in the Northwest.

Territorial Treaties

From the 1860s to the 1880s, the federal government tried to force Indians onto reservations, where, it was thought, they could be "civilized." Reservations usually consisted of those areas of a group's previous territory that were least desirable to whites. When assigning Indians to such parcels, the government promised protection from white encroachment and agreed to provide food, clothing, and other necessities.

Reservation Policy

Reservation policy had degrading consequences. First, Indians had no say over their own affairs on reservations. Supreme Court decisions in 1884 and 1886 defined natives as wards (falling, like helpless

children, under government protection) and denied them the right to become U.S. citizens. Thus they were unprotected by the Fourteenth and Fifteenth Amendments. Second, pressure from whites seeking Indian lands for their own purposes made it difficult for the government to preserve reservations intact. Third, the government ignored native history, even combining on the same reservation Indian bands that habitually had waged war against each other. Rather than serving as civilizing communities, reservations weakened Indian life.

Not all Indians succumbed to market forces and reservation restrictions. Some natives tried to preserve their cultures even as they became dependent on whites. Pawnees, for example, agreed to leave their Nebraska homelands for a reservation in the hope that they could hunt buffalo and grow corn as they once had done.

Native Resistance

As they had done earlier in the East, whites responded to western Indian recalcitrance and revolt with organized military aggression. In 1864, for example, in order to eliminate Indians who blocked white ambitions in the Sand Creek region of Colorado, a militia force led by Methodist minister John Chivington attacked a Cheyenne band under Black Kettle, killing almost everyone. And in 1879 four thousand U.S. soldiers mobilized and forced a surrender from Utes, who already had given up most of their ancestral territory in western Colorado but were resisting further concessions.

Indian Wars

The most infamous of Indian battles occurred in June 1876 when 2,500 Lakotas led by Chiefs Rain-in-the-Face, Sitting Bull, and Crazy Horse surrounded and annihilated 256 government troops led by the rash Colonel George A. Custer near the Little Big Horn River in southern Montana. Though Indians consistently demonstrated military skill in such battles, shortages of supplies and relentless pursuit by U.S. soldiers eventually overwhelmed armed Indian resistance.

By the 1870s and 1880s, government officials and reformers sought more peaceful means of dealing with western natives. With government encouragement, white missionaries and teachers would attempt to persuade Native Americans to adopt the values of the new American work ethic: ambition, thrift, and material-

**Reform of
Indian Policy**

ism. To achieve this transformation, however, Indians would have to abandon their traditional cultures. Also, reform treatises—George Manypenny's *Our Indian Wards* (1880) and Helen Hunt Jackson's *A Century of Dishonor* (1881), for example—and unfavorable comparison with Canada's management of Indian affairs aroused the American conscience. Canada had granted native peoples the rights of British subjects, and the Royal Mounted Police defended them against whites. A high rate of intermarriage between Indians and Canadian whites also promoted smoother relations.

In the United States, most reformers believed Indians were culturally inferior to whites and assumed Indians could succeed economically only if they adopted the middle-class values of diligence, monogamy, and education. Reformers particularly deplored Indians' sexual division of labor. Women seemed to do all the work—tending crops, raising children, cooking, curing hides, making tools and clothes—and to be servile to men, who hunted but were otherwise idle. White-dominated reform groups wanted Indian men to bear more responsibilities, to treat Indian women more respectfully, and to resemble male heads of white middle-class households.

In 1887 Congress reversed its reservation policy and passed the Dawes Severalty Act. The act authorized dissolution of community-owned Indian property and granted land allotments to individual Native American

Reformers established boarding schools to take Indian children off the reservations and teach them a new and allegedly better culture. As one white leader remarked, "They should be educated, not as Indians, but as Americans." At the Carlisle School in Pennsylvania, one of twenty-four such schools, Sioux youths (*left*) received new attire to make them look (*right*) as their teachers wanted them to look.   (Smithsonian Institute, Washington, D.C.)

Dawes Severalty Act

families. The land was held in trust by the government for twenty-five years so the families could not sell their allotments. The act also awarded citizenship to all who accepted allotments and entitled the government to sell unallocated land to whites.

In an attempt to foster assimilation, Indian policy now took on two main features. First and foremost, as required by the Dawes Act, the federal government distributed reservation land to individual families in the belief that the American institution of private property would fashion good citizens and integrate Indians into the larger society. Second, officials believed that Indians would abandon their "barbaric" habits more quickly if their children were educated in boarding schools away from the reservations.

Attempts at Assimilation

The Dawes Act reflected the Euro-American and Christian world-view, an earnest but narrow belief that a society of families headed by men was the most desired model. The reformers were joined by professional educators who viewed schools as tools to create a well-integrated, patriotic, industrial nation. Educators helped establish the Carlisle School in Pennsylvania in 1879, which served as the flagship of the government's Indian school system. In keeping with Euro-American custom, the boarding schools sought to impose white-defined sex roles: boys were taught farming and carpentry, while girls learned sewing, cleaning, and cooking.

The Losing of the West

The Dawes Act effectively reduced native control over land. Eager speculators induced Indians to sell their newly acquired property, in spite of federal safeguards against such practices. Between 1887 and the 1930s, Indian landholdings dwindled from 138 million acres to 52 million. Land-grabbing whites were particularly cruel to the Ojibwas of the northern plains. In 1906 an Indian appropriations bill contained a rider declaring that mixed-blood adults on the White Earth reservation were "competent" enough to sell their land without having to observe the twenty-five-year waiting period stipulated in the Dawes Act. Speculators then duped many Ojibwas, whom white experts had declared mixed-bloods, into signing away their land in return for counterfeit money and worthless merchandise.

The Ojibwas lost more than half of their original holdings, and economic ruin overtook them.

The government's policy had other harmful effects on Indians' ways of life. The boarding-school program enrolled thousands of children and tried to teach them that their inherited customs were inferior, but most returned to their families demoralized and confused rather than ready to assimilate into white society. Polingaysi Qoyawayma, a Hopi woman forced to take the Christian name Elizabeth Q. White, recalled after four years spent at the Sherman Institute in Riverside, California, "As a Hopi, I was misunderstood by the white man; as a convert of the missionaries, I was looked upon with suspicion by the Hopi people."

Ultimately, political and ecological crises overwhelmed most western Indian groups. Buffalo extinction, enemy raids, and disease, in addition to white violence and military superiority, combined to hobble subsistence culture to the point that Native Americans had no alternative but to yield their lands to market-oriented whites. Although Indians tried to retain their culture by both adapting and yielding to the various demands they faced, by the end of the century they had lost control of the land and were under increasing pressure to shed their group identity. To this day they remain casualties of an aggressive age.

The Extraction of Natural Resources

In sharp contrast to the Indians, who used land and water mostly to meet subsistence needs, most whites who migrated to the West and the Great Plains were driven by the desire to get rich quick. To their eyes, the vast stretches of territory lay as untapped reservoirs of resources and wealth (see Map 17.1). Extraction of these resources advanced settlement and created new markets at home and abroad; it also fueled the revolutions in transportation, agriculture, and industry that swept the United States in the late nineteenth century. At the same time, extraction of nature's wealth gave rise to wasteful interaction with the environment and fed habits of racial and sexual oppression.

In the mid-1800s, eager prospectors began to comb western forests and mountains for gold, silver, timber, and copper. The mining frontier advanced

Mining and Lumbering

rapidly, drawing thousands of people to California, Nevada, Idaho, Montana, Utah, and Colorado. Prospectors tended to be restless optimists, willing to climb mountains and trek across deserts in search of a telltale glint of precious metal.

Digging for and transporting minerals was extremely expensive, so prospectors who did discover veins of metal seldom mined them. Instead, they sold their claims to large mining syndicates. Financed by eastern capital, these companies could bring in engineers, heavy machinery, railroad lines, and work crews. Although discoveries of gold and silver first drew attention to the West and its resources, mining companies usually exploited less romantic but equally lucrative metals, such as copper and lead.

Map 17.1 The Development and Natural Resources of the West By 1890 mining, lumbering, and cattle ranching had penetrated many areas west of the Mississippi River, and railroads had linked together the western economy. These characteristics, along with the spread of agriculture, contributed to the Census Bureau's observation that the frontier had disappeared; yet, as the map shows, large areas remained undeveloped.

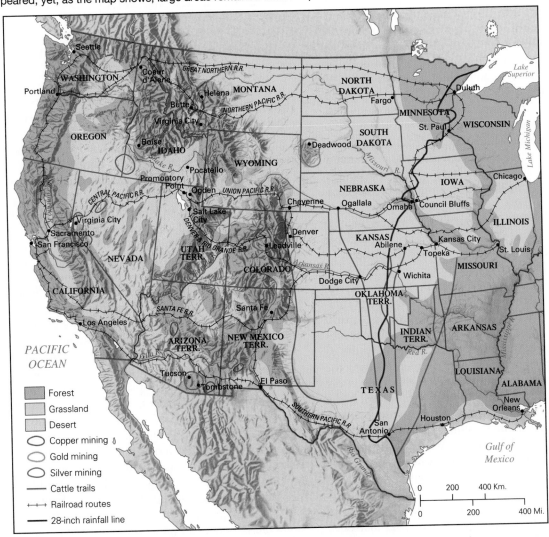

Timber harvesting, another large-scale extractive industry, needed vast tracks of forestland to be profitable. Lumber companies moving into the Northwest grabbed millions of acres under the Timber and Stone Act, passed by Congress in 1878 to stimulate settlement in California, Nevada, Oregon, and Washington. It allowed private citizens to buy, at a low price, 160-acre plots "unfit for cultivation" and "valuable chiefly for timber." Lumber companies hired seamen from waterfront boarding houses to register private claims to timberland and then transfer those claims to the companies. By 1900 private citizens had bought over 3.5 million acres, but most of that land belonged to corporations.

While lumber companies were acquiring timberlands in the Northwest, oil companies were beginning to drill for wells in the Southwest. In 1900 most of the nation's petroleum still came from the Appalachians and the Midwest, but rich oil reserves had been discovered in southern California and eastern Texas. Although oil and kerosene were still used mostly for lubrication and lighting, oil discovered in the Southwest later became a vital new source of fuel.

Though single white men numerically dominated the western natural-resource frontier, many communities did have substantial populations of white women who had come for the same reason as men: to find a fortune. But on the mining frontier as elsewhere, women's independence was limited; they usually accompanied a husband or father and seldom prospected themselves. Even so, many women used their labor as a resource and realized opportunities to earn money by cooking and laundering. And while some women provided sexual services for the miners in houses of prostitution, others helped to bolster family and community life as members of the home mission movement. During the mid-nineteenth century, many women broke away from male-dominated missionary organizations. In the West, they exercised moral authority by building homes to rescue women—unmarried mothers, Mormons, Indians, and Chinese immigrants—who they believed had fallen prey to men or who had not yet accepted the conventions of Christian virtue.

Women in Mining Regions

The West became a rich multiracial society, including not only Native Americans and native-born white migrants but also Hispanics, African Americans,

A Complex Population

and Asians. A crescent of territory, a borderland stretching from western Texas through New Mexico and Arizona to northern California, supported Hispanic ranchers and sheepherders, descendants of the Spanish who originally had claimed the land. In New Mexico, Hispanics had mixed with Indians to form a *mestizo* population of small farmers and ranchers. Some returned to Mexico seasonally; others stayed. And, before federal law excluded them in 1881 and 1882, some two hundred thousand Chinese immigrants—most of them young, male, and single—came to the United States and constituted a sizable proportion of the work force in California, Oregon, and Washington. Japanese and eastern European immigrants also inhabited mining and agricultural communities.

To control labor and social relations within this complex population, white settlers made race an important distinguishing social characteristic in the West. They usually identified four nonwhite races: Indians, Mexicans, "Mongolians" (a term applied to Chinese), and African Americans. Whites using these categories ascribed demeaning characteristics to all nonwhites, judging them to be not only inferior but permanently so.

Significance of Race

Racial minorities in western communities occupied the bottom half of a two-tiered labor system. Whites dominated the top tier of managerial and skilled labor positions. Unskilled laborers, often Irish, Chinese, and Mexicans, worked in the mines, on railroad construction, and as agricultural laborers. Blacks also worked in railroad and mining camps, doing cooking and cleaning, while Indians barely participated in the white-controlled labor system at all. All nonwhite groups plus the Irish encountered prejudice.

The multiracial quality of western society, however, also included a cross-racial quality. Because so many male migrants to these states, as well as to Texas and New Mexico, were single, intermarriage with Mexican and Indian women was common. Such intermarriage was acceptable for white men, but not for white women, especially where Asian immigrants were involved.

As whites were wresting control of the land from the Indians and Spanish inhabitants of the Southwest and California, questions arose over control of the nation's oil, mineral, and timber resources. Much of the

Dressed formally for the opening ceremony of the Mullan Tunnel in Montana in 1884, these Chinese railroad workers, who helped build the tunnel, have temporarily cast aside their traditional work clothes and are showing their embrace of a new culture. (Montana Historical Society)

Conservation Movement

remaining undeveloped land west of the Mississippi was in the public domain, and some people believed that the federal government, as its owner, should limit its exploitation. Others, however, believed in unlimited use of the land.

Questions about natural resources caught Americans between a desire for progress and a fear of spoiling the land. By the late 1870s, people eager to protect the natural landscape began to organize a conservation movement. They made Yellowstone Park in Wyoming the first national park in 1872. A prominent conservationist, naturalist John Muir, helped to establish Yosemite National Park in 1890. The next year, Congress authorized President Benjamin Harrison to create forest reserves—public lands protected from private-interest cutting. Such policies met with strong objections. Opposition came from those wanting to freely exploit the West's natural resources. Public

opinion also split along sectional lines. As a rule, easterners favored conservation; westerners opposed it.

Development of the mining and forest regions, and of the farms and cities that followed, brought western territories to the threshold of statehood. In 1889 Republicans seeking to solidify their control of Congress passed an omnibus bill granting statehood to North Dakota, South Dakota, Washington, and Montana. Wyoming and Idaho were admitted the following year. Congress denied statehood to Utah until 1896, wanting assurances from the Mormons, who constituted a majority of the territory's population and controlled its government, that they would give up polygamy.

Admission of New States

Those states' mining towns and lumber camps spiced American folk culture and fostered a go-getter optimism that distinguished the American spirit. The lawlessness and hedonism of places such as Deadwood,

Legends of the West

in Dakota Territory, and Tombstone, in Arizona Territory, gave the West notoriety and romance. Mark Twain, Bret Harte, and other writers captured for posterity the flavor of mining life, and characters like Buffalo Bill, Annie Oakley, Wild Bill Hickok, Poker Alice, and Bedrock Tom became western folk heroes. But violence and eccentricity were far from common. Most miners and lumbermen worked long hours and had little time, energy, or money for gambling, carousing, or gunfights. Women worked as long or longer as teachers, cooks, laundresses, storekeepers, and housewives. Only a few were sharpshooters or dance-hall queens. For most, western life was a matter of adapting and surviving.

Irrigation and Transportation

Glittering gold, tall trees, and gushing oil shaped the popular image of the West, but water gave it life. If western territories and states promised wealth from mining, cutting, and drilling, their agricultural potential promised more—but only if settlers could find a way to bring water to the arid land. The economic development of the West is the story of how public and private interests used technology and organization to develop the region's river basins and make the land agriculturally productive.

For centuries, Indians had irrigated southwestern lands to sustain their subsistence farming. When the Spanish arrived, they began tapping the Rio Grande to irrigate farms in southwest Texas and New Mexico. Later they channeled water to the California mission communities of San Diego and Los Angeles. The first Americans of northern European ancestry to practice extensive irrigation were the Mormons. Arriving in Utah in 1847, they quickly diverted streams and rivers into networks of canals, whose water enabled them to farm the hard-baked soil.

Efforts at land reclamation through irrigation in Colorado and California raised controversies over rights to the precious streams that flowed through the West. Americans had inherited the English common-law principle of riparian rights, which held that only those who owned land along the banks of a river could appropriate from the water's flow. The stream itself,

Rights to Water

according to riparianism, belonged to God; those who lived on its banks could take water for normal needs but were not to diminish the river by damming or diverting water at the expense of others who lived along its banks.

The Americans who settled the West rejected riparianism in favor of the doctrine of prior appropriation, which awarded a river's water to the first person who claimed it. Westerners asserted that water, like timber, minerals, and other natural resources, existed to serve human needs and advance profits. They argued that anyone intending a beneficial or "reasonable" (economically productive) use of river water should have the right to appropriation, and the courts ultimately agreed.

Under appropriation, those who dammed and diverted water often reduced the flow of water downstream. People disadvantaged by such action could protect their interests either by suing those who deprived them of water or by establishing a public authority to regulate water usage. Thus in 1879 Colorado created a number of water divisions, each with a commissioner to determine and regulate water rights. In 1890 Wyoming enlarged the concept of control with a constitutional provision declaring that the state's rivers were public property subject to state supervision of their use.

California developed a dramatic solution to the problem of water rights, sometimes called the "California Solution." Unlike western states

California's Solution

that had opted for appropriation rights over riparian rights, California maintained a mixed legal system that upheld riparianism while allowing for some appropriation. This system put irrigators at a disadvantage and prompted them to seek a change in state law. In 1887 the state legislature passed a bill permitting farmers to organize into districts that would sponsor the construction and operation of irrigation projects. An irrigation district could use its public authority to purchase water rights, seize private property to build irrigation canals, and finance its projects through taxation or by issuing bonds. As a result of this legislation, California became the nation's leader in irrigated acreage and boasted the most profitable agricultural economy in the country.

Though state irrigation provisions stimulated development, the federal government still owned most of western lands in the 1890s. Prodded by land-hungry developers, the states wanted the federal government to transfer to them at least part of the public domain lands. States claimed that they could make these lands profitable through reclamation—providing them with irrigation water. For the most part, Congress refused such transfers. If federal lands were transferred to state control for the purpose of water development, who would regulate waterways that flowed through more than one state or that potentially could provide water to a nearby state? If, for example, California received control of the Truckee River, which flowed westward out of Lake Tahoe on the California-Nevada border, how would Nevadans be assured that California would give them any water? Only the federal government, it seemed, had the power to regulate regional water development.

In 1902, Congress passed the Newlands Reclamation Act, which allowed the federal government to sell

Newlands Reclamation Act

western public lands to individuals in parcels not to exceed 160 acres, and to use the proceeds from such sales to finance irrigation projects. The Newlands Act provided for control but not conservation of water, because three-fourths of the water used in open-ditch irrigation, the most common form, was lost to evaporation. Thus the legislation fell squarely within the tradition of exploitation of nature for human profit. It also represented a decision by the federal government to aid the agricultural and general economic development of the West.

Railroad construction boomed after the Civil War. Between 1865 and 1890, total track in the United

Post–Civil War Railroad Construction

States grew from 35,000 to 200,000 miles (see Map 17.1). By the turn of the century, the United States contained one-third of all the railroad track in the world. After 1880, when steel rails began to replace iron rails, railroads helped to boost the nation's steel industry to international leadership. Railroad expansion also spawned a number of related industries, including coal production, passenger- and freight-car manufacture, and depot construction.

Influential and essential, railroads performed a uniquely American function. Europeans usually built railroads to link established market centers. In the United States, railroads often created many of the very communities they were meant to serve.

Rails and Markets

With their ability to transport large loads of people and freight, lines such as the Union Pacific and Southern Pacific accelerated the growth of western regional centers such as Omaha, Kansas City, Cheyenne, Los Angeles, Portland, and Seattle.

Railroads accomplished these feats with the help of some of the largest government subsidies in American history. Executives argued that because railroads benefited the public, the government should aid them by giving them land from the public domain. Sympathetic officials at the federal, state, and local levels responded with massive subsidies. The federal government granted railroad companies over 180 million acres; states granted some 50 million acres. Local governments assisted by offering loans or by purchasing railroad bonds or stocks.

Government subsidies had mixed effects. Though capitalists often argued against government interference in the economic affairs of private companies, privately owned railroads nevertheless accepted government aid and pressured governments into meeting their needs. The Southern Pacific, for example, threatened to bypass Los Angeles unless the city came up with a bonus and built a depot. Without public help, few railroads could have prospered sufficiently to attract private investment, yet public aid was not always salutary. During the 1880s, the policy of assistance haunted communities whose zeal had prompted them to commit too much to railroads that were never built or that defaulted on loans. Some laborers and farmers fought subsidies, arguing that companies like the Southern Pacific would become too powerful. Many communities boomed, however, because they had linked their fortunes to the iron horse. Moreover, railroads drew farmers into the market economy.

Railroads also altered conceptions of time and space. First, by surmounting physical barriers to travel, railroads transformed space into time. Instead of expressing the distance between places in miles, people began to refer to the amount of time it took to travel from one place to another. Second, railroad scheduling

Train schedules not only changed the American economy but also altered how Americans timed their daily lives. As people and businesses ordered their day according to the arrival and departure of trains, distances became less important than hours and minutes.   (Library of Congress)

Standard Time

required nationwide standardization of time. Before railroads, local church bells and clocks struck noon when the sun was directly overhead, and people set their clocks and watches accordingly. But because the sun was not overhead at exactly the same moment everywhere, time varied from place to place. To impose regularity, railroads created their own time zones. By 1880 there were nearly fifty different standards, but in 1883 the railroads finally agreed—without consulting anyone in government—to establish four standard time zones for the whole country. Railroad time became national time.

Farming the Plains

During the 1870s and 1880s, hundreds of thousands of hopeful farmers streamed into the Great Plains region. More acres were put under cultivation in states such as Kansas, Nebraska, and Texas during these two decades

Settlement of the Plains

than in the entire country during the previous 250 years. The number of farms tripled from 2 million to over 6 million between 1860 and 1910. Several states opened offices in the East and in European ports to lure migrants westward. Land-rich railroads were especially aggressive, advertising cheap land, arranging credit terms, offering reduced fares, and promising instant success. Railroad agents—often former immigrants—traveled to Denmark, Sweden, Germany, and other European nations to recruit settlers and greeted newcomers at eastern ports. In California after the turn of the century, fruit and vegetable growers imported laborers from Japan and Mexico to work in the fields and canneries.

Most migrants went west because opportunities there seemed to promise a better life. Farm life on the Plains, however, was much harder than the advertisements and railroad agents suggested. Migrants often encountered scarcities of essentials they had once taken for granted. The open prairies contained little lumber for housing and fuel. Pioneer families were forced to build houses of sod and to burn manure for heat. Water for cooking and cleaning was sometimes as scarce as timber. Machinery for drilling wells was expensive, as were windmills for drawing the water to the surface.

Hardship of Life on the Plains

Even more formidable than the terrain was the climate. The climate between the Missouri River and the Rocky Mountains divides along a line running from Minnesota southwest through Oklahoma, then south, bisecting Texas. West of this line, annual rainfall averages less than 28 inches, not enough for most crops or trees.

Weather seldom followed predictable cycles. In summer, weeks of torrid heat and parching winds suddenly gave way to violent storms that washed away crops and property. The wind and cold of winter blizzards piled up mountainous snowdrifts that halted all outdoor movement. In springtime, melting snow swelled streams, and floods threatened millions of acres. In the fall, a week without rain could turn dry grasslands into tinder, and the slightest spark could ignite a raging prairie fire.

Nature could be cruel even under good conditions. Weather that was favorable for crops was also good for breeding insects. Worms and flying pests ravaged corn and wheat. In the 1870s and 1880s swarms of grasshoppers virtually ate up entire farms. As one farmer lamented, the "hoppers left behind nothing but the mortgage."

Settlers also had to contend with social isolation. Farmers in New England and in Europe lived in villages and traveled each day to nearby fields. This pattern was rare in the vast expanses of the Plains—and in the Far West and South as well—where peculiarities of land division compelled American rural dwellers to live apart from each other. The Homestead Act of 1862 and other measures to encourage western settlement offered cheap or free plots to people who would live on and improve their property. Because most plots acquired by small farmers were rectangular—usually encompassing 160 acres—at most four families could live near each other, and then only if they congregated around the shared four-corner intersection. In practice, farm families usually lived back from their boundary lines, and at least a half-mile separated farmhouses.

Social Isolation

Farm families survived by sheer resolve and by organizing churches and clubs where they could socialize a few times a month. By 1900 two developments had brought rural settlers into closer contact with modern consumer society. First, mail-order companies—Montgomery Ward and Sears, Roebuck—made new products available to almost everyone by the 1870s and 1880s. Emphasizing personal attention to customers, Ward's and Sears were outlets for sociability as well as material goods. Letters from customers to Mr. Ward often reported family news and sought advice on everything from gifts to childcare.

Mail-Order Companies and Rural Free Delivery

Second, in 1896 the government made Rural Free Delivery (RFD) widely available. Farmers previously had to go to town to pick up their mail. Now, they could receive letters, newspapers, and catalogues in a mailbox on a road near their home nearly every day. In 1913 the postal service inaugurated parcel post, which enabled people to receive packages, such as orders from Ward's and Sears, more cheaply.

The agricultural revolution that followed the Civil War would not have been possible without the expanded use of machinery. When the Civil War drew men away from farms in the upper Mississippi River valley, the women and older men who remained behind began using reapers and other mechanical implements to satisfy the demand for food and take advantage of high grain prices. After the war, continued demand and high prices encouraged farmers to depend more on machines, and inventors developed new implements for farm use.

Mechanization of Agriculture

For centuries, the acreage of grain a farmer could plant had been limited by the amount that could be harvested by hand. Before mechanization, for example, a farmer working alone could harvest about 7.5 acres of wheat. Using an automatic binder that cut and bundled the grain, the same farmer could harvest 135 acres. Machines dramatically reduced the time and cost of farming other crops as well.

Meanwhile, Congress and scientists worked to improve existing crops and develop new ones. The 1862 Morrill Land Grant Act gave each state federal lands to sell in order to finance educational institutions that aided agricultural development. A second Morrill Act in 1890 aided more schools, including a number of black colleges. The Hatch Act of 1887 provided for agricultural experiment stations in every state, further encouraging the advancement of farming science and technology.

Legislative and Scientific Aids to Farming

Scientific advances enabled farmers to use the soil more efficiently. Researchers developed dry farming, a technique of plowing and harrowing that minimized the evaporation of precious moisture. Botanists perfected varieties of "hard" wheat whose seeds could withstand northern winters. Californian Luther Burbank developed a multitude of new plants by crossbreeding, and chemist George Washington Carver of Alabama's Tuskegee Institute created hundreds of new products from peanuts, soybeans, sweet potatoes, and cotton wastes. These and other scientific and technological developments helped feed a burgeoning population and make America what one journalist called "the garden of the world."

The Ranching Frontier

While commercial farming was overspreading the West, it ran headlong into one of the region's most romantic industries—cattle ranching. Early in the nineteenth century

Longhorns and the Long Drive

herds of cattle, introduced by the Spanish and expanded by Mexican ranchers, roamed southern Texas and bred with cattle brought by Anglo settlers. The resulting longhorn breed multiplied and became valuable by the 1860s, when population growth boosted the demand for beef and railroads simplified the transportation of food. By 1870 drovers (as many as 25 percent of whom were African American) were herding thousands of Texas cattle northward to Kansas, Missouri, and Wyoming (see Map 17.1).

The long drive gave rise to romantic lore but was not very efficient. Trekking 1,000 miles or more for two to three months made cattle sinewy and tough. Herds traveling through Indian lands and farmers' fields were sometimes shot at and later prohibited from such trespass by state laws. Ranchers adjusted by raising herds nearer to railroad routes. When ranchers discovered that crossing Texas longhorns with heavier Hereford and Angus breeds produced animals better able to survive northern winters, cattle raising spread across the Great Plains.

The Open Range

Cattle raisers needed vast pastures to graze their herds, and they wanted to incur as little expense as possible in using such land. Thus they often bought a few acres bordering a stream and turned their herds loose on adjacent public domain that no one wanted because it lacked water access. By this method, called open-range ranching, a cattle raiser could control thousands of acres by owning only a hundred or so. Neighboring ranchers often formed associations and allowed their herds to graze together. Owners identified their cattle by burning a brand into each animal's hide. Cowboy crews rounded up the cattle twice each year, in the spring to brand new calves and in the fall to drive mature animals to market. Roundups delighted easterners with colorful images of western life: bellowing cattle, rope-swinging cowboys, and smoky campfires.

Grazing Wars

Meanwhile, sheepherders from California and New Mexico also were using the public domain, sparking conflict over land. Ranchers complained that sheep ruined grassland by eating down to the roots and that cattle refused to graze where sheep had been because the "woolly critters" left a re-

pulsive odor. Armed conflict occasionally erupted between cowboys and sheepherders.

More important, however, the farming frontier was advancing and generating new demands for land. Devising a way to organize the land resulted in an unheralded but highly significant invention. The problem was fencing. Lacking sufficient timber and stone for traditional fencing, western settlers faced a critical problem in defining and protecting their property.

Barbed Wire

The solution was barbed wire. Invented in 1873 by Joseph F. Glidden, a farmer in DeKalb, Illinois, these fences consist of two wires held in place by sharp spurs twisted around them. Barbed wire provided a cheap and durable means of enclosure. It opened the Plains to homesteaders by enabling them to protect their farms from grazing cattle. It also ended open-range ranching, not only because it removed grazing land that often had been used illegally, but also because it enabled large-scale ranchers to isolate their herds within massive stretches of private property.

Open-range ranching made beef a staple of the American diet and created a few fortunes, but its features could not survive the spurs of barbed wire and the rush of history. Moreover, a devastating winter in 1887–1888 destroyed countless herds and drove small ranchers out of business. By 1890 big businesses were taking over the cattle industry and applying scientific methods of breeding and feeding. Most ranchers now owned or leased the land they used, though some illegal fencing persisted.

Summary

Americans of all races developed the West with courage and creativity. Indians, the region's original inhabitants, had used, and sometimes abused, the land to support subsistence cultures. Living mostly in small groups, they depended heavily on fragile resources such as buffalo herds and salmon runs. When they came into contact with aggressive, migratory Euro-Americans, their resistance to the market economy, the diseases, and the violence that the whites brought into the West failed.

White miners, timber cutters, farmers, and builders accomplished extraordinary feats. The extraction of raw minerals, the use of irrigation and mechanization to bring forth agricultural abundance, and the construction of railroads to tie the nation together transformed half of the continent within a few decades. The new settlers, however, employed power, violence, and greed that sustained discrimination within a multiracial society, left many farmers feeling cheated and betrayed, kindled contests over use of water, and sacrificed environmental balance for market profits.

LEGACY FOR A PEOPLE AND A NATION
The West and Rugged Individualism

Though born in New York State, Theodore Roosevelt, twenty-sixth president of the United States, thought of himself as a westerner. In 1884, at the age of twenty-five, he moved to Dakota Territory to live on ranches he had bought there. He loved the uncharted world of what he called "vast silent spaces, a place of grim beauty." In such a place, Roosevelt believed, he developed a character of "rugged individualism," an ability to conquer challenges through independent strength and fortitude.

Americans have long shared Roosevelt's fascination with the West and its reputation for rugged individualism. They have popularized western settings and characters in movies and on television. The film *Cimarron* (1930) was one of the first to win an Academy Award, and *Gunsmoke* held the record as one of the longest-running television series (1955–1975). From *The Virginian*, first published in 1902, to the recent novels of Larry McMurtry, Americans have made stories about the West bestsellers. In each instance, a lone individual, usually male, overcomes danger and hardship through solitary effort. In their appreciation of this quality, Americans have not only infused political and moral rhetoric with references to rugged individualism; they also have tried to exhibit the quality in their attire. Over the years they have bought millions of dollars worth of Stetson cowboy hats, denim jeans, and buckskin jackets.

At the same time, however, the myth of rugged individualism that Roosevelt thought he could cultivate in the West had a different, ironic reality. In the late nineteenth century, migrants to the West traveled on railroads built with government subsidies, acquired land cheaply from the federal government under the Homestead and Timber and Stone Acts, depended on the army to remove Indians, and destroyed forests and diverted rivers with federal support. More recently, western politicians who oppose big government have received votes from constituents who depend on federal farm subsidies and price supports, free or subsidized water, and government-financed disaster relief from droughts, floods, and tornadoes.

Perhaps more important, the West could not have been settled and developed without both individualism *and* government assistance. Here was the West's true legacy to a people and a nation. The federal government, with state assistance, created opportunities that tenacious miners, ranchers, and farmers took advantage of. Those who populated the West had to be rugged. Like Roosevelt they had to have the vision and determination to endure "toil and hardship and hunger and thirst." They survived, but they had—and continue to need—help.

For Further Reading, see the Appendix. For Web resources, go to history.college.hmco.com/students.

THE MACHINE AGE

1877–1920

The shoemaker known only as "S" appeared a beaten and bitter man. Interviewed by the Massachusetts Bureau of the Statistics of Labor in 1871, "S" reported that he and his three children each worked in a shoe factory ten hours a day, five days a week, and nine hours on Saturdays. His wife toiled in another factory from 5:30 A.M. to 10 A.M. every day.

"S" told the interviewer that ever since his factory had introduced machinery, he had lost control of his craft. He could no longer teach his sons the skill of shoemaking because they had been moved to another room to carry out just one task instead of assembling the whole shoe or boot. "S" hoped his sons would not be factory workers all their lives, but he also realized they had little other choice. The cost of living had risen, making it impossible for his family to sustain itself in any other way.

"S" felt embittered by the homage being paid to supply and demand: "We have it constantly dinned in our ears that supply and demand govern prices, but we have found out to a certainty that this is not so. . . . [W]ithout the aid of machinery, six men will make a case of 60 pairs [of shoes] in a day, . . . which would give each man about $1.70 a day; on the other hand, with the machinery, three men will do the same amount of work in the same time, and get about the same pay [$1.70] each, as the men on hand work. . . . Who gets the difference in money saved by machinery? and how far does supply and demand govern in these things?"

The new order of which "S" spoke was both exciting and daunting. Factories and machines divided pro-

IMPORTANT EVENTS

1860 Knights of Labor founded

1873–78 Economic decline results from overly rapid expansion

1876 Bonsack invents machine for rolling cigarettes

1877 Widespread railroad strikes protest wage cuts

1878 Edison Electric Light Company founded

1879 George's *Progress and Poverty* argues against economic inequality

1880s Chain-pull toilets spread across the United States

Doctors begin to accept germ theory of disease

Mass production of tin cans begins

1881 First federal trademark law begins spread of brand names

1882 Standard Oil Trust formed

1884–85 Economic decline results from numerous causes

1886 Haymarket riot in Chicago protests police brutality against labor demonstrators

American Federation of Labor (AFL) founded

1888 Bellamy's *Looking Backward* depicts utopian world free of monopoly, politicians, and class divisions

1890 Sherman Anti-Trust Act outlaws "combinations in restraint of trade"

1892 Homestead (Pennsylvania) steelworkers strike against Carnegie Steel Company

1893–97 Economic depression causes high unemployment and business failures

1894 Workers at Pullman Palace Car Company strike against exploitative policies

1895 *U.S. v. E. C. Knight Co.* limits Congress's power to regulate manufacturing

1896 *Holden v. Hardy* upholds law regulating miners' work hours

1898 Taylor promotes scientific management as efficiency measure in industry

1901–03 U.S. Steel Corporation founded

Ford Motor Company founded

1903 Women's Trade Union League founded

1905 *Lochner v. New York* overturns law limiting bakery workers' work hours and limits labor protection laws

Industrial Workers of the World (IWW) founded

1908 *Muller v. Oregon* upholds law limiting women to ten-hour workday

First Ford Model T built

1913 First moving assembly line begins operation at Ford Motor Company

1914 Ford offers Five-Dollar-Day plan to workers

1919 Telephone operator unions strike in New England

duction into minute, repetitive tasks and organized work according to the dictates of the clock. Workers like "S" who had long thought of themselves as valued producers found themselves struggling to avoid becoming slaves to machines. Meanwhile, in their quest for productivity, profits, and growth, corporations merged and amassed great power.

Industrialization is a complex process whose chief feature is production of goods by machine rather than by hand. In the latter part of the nineteenth century,

technological developments, including the rise of electric-powered machines and the expansion of engines powered by internal combustion, propelled industrialization. Earlier industrialization influenced the new technologies. Steam engines had reached their peak of utility, generating a need for a new power source—electricity. And the potential of railroad transportation spurred progress in automobile manufacture.

In 1860 only about one-fourth of the American labor force worked in manufacturing and transportation;

by 1900 over half did so. As the twentieth century dawned, the United States was not only the world's largest producer of raw materials and food but also the most productive industrial nation (see Map 18.1). Between 1880 and 1920 migrants from farms and from abroad swelled the industrial work force; but machines, more than people, boosted American productivity. Innovations in business organization and marketing also fueled the drive for profits.

These developments had momentous effects on standards of living and everyday life. Between the end of Reconstruction and the end of the First World War, a new consumer society took shape. Farms and factories produced so much that growing numbers of Americans could afford to satisfy their material wants. What had once been accessible to only a few was becoming available to many. Yet the accomplishments of industrialism involved waste and greed. ■

Technology and the Triumph of Industrialism

In 1876 Thomas A. Edison and his associates set up a laboratory in Menlo Park, New Jersey. There they intended to turn out "a minor invention every ten days and a big thing every six months or so." Edison envisioned his laboratory as an invention factory, where creative people would pool ideas and skills to fashion marketable products. Here he would blend brash enthusiasm with a systematic work ethic. If Americans wanted new products, Edison believed, they had to organize and work purposefully to bring about progress.

In the closing years of the nineteenth century, mechanization fired American optimism and the machine symbolized opportunity. Between 1790 and 1860 the U.S. Patent Office granted a total of 36,000 patents; between 1860 and 1930, 1.5 million were registered. These inventions often sprang from a marriage between technology and business organization. The harnessing of electricity and internal combustion illustrates how this marriage worked.

Most of Edison's more than one thousand inventions used electricity to transmit light, sound, and images. Perhaps his biggest "big thing" project began in 1878 when he formed the Edison Electric Light Com-

Birth of the Electrical Industry

pany and embarked on a search for a cheap, efficient means of indoor lighting. After tedious trial-and-error experiments, Edison perfected an incandescent bulb. At the same time, he devised a system of power generation and distribution—an improved dynamo and a parallel circuit of wires—to provide convenient power to a large number of customers. To market his ideas, Edison acted as his own publicist. During the 1880 Christmas season he illuminated Menlo Park with forty incandescent bulbs, and in 1882 he built a power plant that could light eighty-five buildings in New York's Wall Street financial district.

Edison's system of direct current could transmit electric power only a mile or two. George Westinghouse,

George Westinghouse

a young inventor from Schenectady, New York, solved the problem. Westinghouse purchased patent rights to generators that used alternating current and transformers that reduced high-voltage power to lower voltage levels, thus making transmission over long distances cheaper.

Other entrepreneurs utilized new business practices to market Edison's and Westinghouse's technological breakthroughs. Samuel Insull, Edison's private secretary, attracted investors and organized Edison power plants across the country, amassing an electric-utility empire. In the late 1880s and early 1890s financiers Henry Villard and J. P. Morgan bought up patents in electric lighting and merged small equipment-manufacturing companies into the General Electric Company. Equally important, General Electric and Westinghouse Electric established research laboratories to create electrical products for everyday use.

Some inventors worked for corporations; others worked alone. One independent inventor, Granville T. Woods, an engineer called by some the "black Edison," patented thirty-five devices vital to electronics and communications. Among his inventions were an automatic circuit breaker, an electromagnetic brake, and various instruments to aid communications between railroad trains.

Like Edison, Henry Ford had a scheme as well as a product. In 1909 Ford, who first began experimenting with an internal combustion engine in the 1890s,

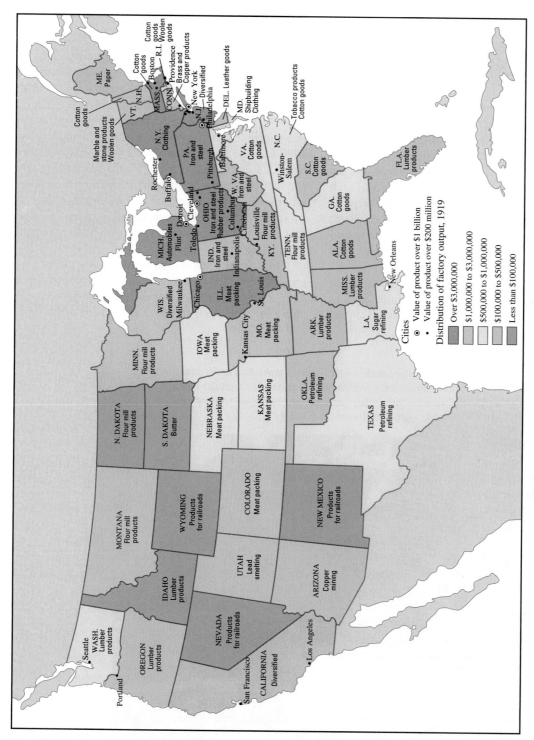

Map 18.1   Industrial Production, 1919 By the early twentieth century, each state could boast of at least one kind of industrial production. Although the value of goods produced was still highest in the Northeast, states like Minnesota and California had impressive dollar values of outputs.   (Source: Data from U.S. Bureau of the Census, *Fourteenth Census of the United States, 1920,* Vol. IX, *Manufacturing* [Washington, D.C.: U.S. Government Printing Office, 1921].)

Henry Ford and the Automobile Industry

declared, "I am going to democratize the automobile. When I'm through, everybody will be able to afford one, and about everyone will have one." Ford proposed to reach this goal by mass-producing thousands of identical cars in exactly the same way. His engineers set up assembly lines that drastically reduced the time and cost of producing cars. Instead of performing numerous tasks, each worker was assigned only one task, performed repeatedly, using the same specialized machine. A conveyor belt moved past stationary workers who fashioned each component part, and progressively the entire car was assembled.

The Ford Motor Company began operation in 1903. In 1908, the first year it built the Model T, Ford sold 10,000 cars. In 1913 the company's first full assembly line began producing cars; the next year, 248,000 Fords were sold. Rising automobile production created more jobs, higher earnings, and greater profits in related industries such as oil, paint, rubber, and glass.

By 1914 many Ford cars cost $490, only about one-fourth of their price a decade earlier. Yet even $490 was too much for many workers, who earned at best $2 a day. That year, however, Ford tried to spur productivity, prevent high labor turnover, head off unionization, and better enable his workers to buy the cars they produced by offering them the Five-Dollar-Day plan—combined wages and profit sharing equal to $5 a day.

The South's two major staple crops, tobacco and cotton, propelled that region into the machine age. In 1876 a Virginian named James Bonsack invented a machine for rolling cigarettes. Sales soared when James

The assembly line broke the production process down into simple tasks that individual workers could efficiently repeat hour after hour. Here, assembly-line workers at the Ford plant in Highland Park, Michigan, outside Detroit, are installing pistons in engines of the Model T around 1914.   (Henry Ford Museum and Greenfield Village)

Technology and Southern Industry

B. Duke of North Carolina began marketing cigarettes in the North by enticing consumers with free samples, trading cards, and billboards. By 1900 his American Tobacco Company was a huge nationwide business.

New technology also aided southern textile mills, which by 1900 numbered over four hundred and contained 4 million spindles. As the machinery of northern mills became obsolete, the South had space for factory construction as well as a cheap labor force to tend new machines.

Southern Textile Mills

Aided by electric motors rather than waterpower, southern mills utilized automatic looms, which required fewer and less skilled workers. The textile mills, financed mostly by local investors, paid women and children 50 cents a day for twelve or more hours of work—about half the wages northern workers received. Many companies built villages around their mills, where they controlled housing, stores, schools, and churches; banned criticism of the company; and squelched attempts at union organization.

Northern and European capitalists financed other southern industries. Between 1890 and 1900, northern lumber syndicates moved into the pine forests of the Gulf states. During the 1880s, northern investors developed southern iron and steel manufacturing, much of it in the boom city of Birmingham. Except for some modernized plants, however, the South lacked the technological innovations that had enabled northern industries to compete with those of other industrializing nations. Nevertheless, southern boosters heralded the emergence of a New South.

In all regions of the country, the timing of technological innovation varied from one industry to another, but machines broadly altered the economy and everyday life.

Influence of New Machines

Telephones and typewriters revolutionized communications. Sewing machines made mass-produced clothing available to almost everyone. Refrigeration changed dietary habits by enabling the preservation and shipment of food products. Cash registers and adding machines revamped accounting and created new clerical jobs.

Profits resulted from higher production at lower costs, and technological innovations made large-scale production more economical. Only large companies could afford to buy complex machines and operate them at full capacity. And large companies could best take advantage of discounts for shipping products in bulk and for buying raw materials in quantity. Economists call such advantages economies of scale.

Profitability depended as much on how production was arranged as on the machines in use. By the 1890s engineers and managers with specialized knowledge acquired in specialized schools had assumed control over how a product was made and planned every task to increase output. Their efforts standardized production, which then required less skill and virtually no independent judgment from workers.

The most influential advocate of efficient production was Frederick W. Taylor. In 1898 Taylor took his stopwatch to the Bethlehem Steel Company to illustrate how his principles of scientific management worked.

Frederick W. Taylor and Efficiency

His experiments, he explained, required studying workers and devising "a series of motions which can be made quickest and best." Applying this technique to the shoveling of ore, Taylor designed fifteen kinds of shovels and prescribed the proper motions for using each one. He succeeded in reducing a crew of 600 men to 140.

As a result of Taylor's writings and experiments, time, as much as quality, became the measure of acceptable work, and science rather than experience determined the ways of doing things. As integral features of the assembly line, where work was divided into specific time-determined tasks, employees like "S" became another kind of interchangeable part.

Mechanization and the Changing Status of Labor

By 1880 the status of labor had undergone a dramatic shift. Technological innovation and assembly-line production created new jobs, but because most machines were labor-saving, fewer workers could produce more in less time. Moreover, workers could no longer accurately be termed producers, as farmers and craftsmen had traditionally thought of themselves. The working class now consisted mainly of employees—people who worked only when someone hired them. Producers had been paid by consumers in accordance with the quality of what they produced; employees received wages for time spent on the job.

As mass production subdivided manufacturing into small tasks, workers continually repeated the same specialized operation. By coordinating production with the running of machinery, the process deprived employees of their independence. Workers could no longer decide when to begin and end the workday, when to rest, and what tools and techniques to use.

Workers affected by these changes did not accept them passively. Employees struggled to retain independence and self-respect in the face of employers' ever-increasing power. As new groups encountered the industrial system, they resisted in various ways. Artisans such as cigar makers, glass workers, and coopers (barrel makers) fought to preserve their work pace and to retain shop customs such as appointing a fellow worker to read a newspaper aloud while they worked. Conversely, employers endeavored to establish standards of behavior and work incentives that they thought would enhance efficiency and productivity.

As machines and assembly lines reduced the need for skilled workers, employers cut labor costs by hiring women and children. Between 1880 and 1900, the numbers of employed women soared from 2.6 million to 8.6 million. At the same time their occupational patterns underwent striking changes. The proportion of women in domestic-service jobs (maids, cooks, laundresses)—the most common and lowest-paid form of female employment— dropped dramatically as jobs opened in other sectors. In manufacturing, women usually held menial positions in textile mills and food-processing plants that paid as little as $1.56 a week for seventy hours of labor. (Unskilled men received $7 to $10 for a similar workweek.)

Employment of Women

General expansion of the industrial and retail sectors, however, caused the numbers and percentages of women in clerical jobs—typists, bookkeepers, sales clerks—to skyrocket. By 1920 nearly half of all clerical workers were women; in 1880 only 4 percent had been women. Previously, when sales and office positions had required accounting and letter-writing skills, men had dominated such jobs. Then new inventions such as the typewriter, cash register, and adding machine simplified these tasks. Companies eagerly hired women who had taken trade-school courses in typing and shorthand and were looking for the better pay and conditions that clerical jobs offered compared to factory and domestic work. Nevertheless, sex discrimination pervaded the clerical sector. The new jobs offered women some opportunities for advancement to supervisory positions, but males dominated the managerial ranks.

Although most children who worked toiled on their parents' farms, the number in nonagricultural occupations tripled between 1870 and 1900. In 1890 over 18 percent of all children between ages ten and fifteen were gainfully employed. Textile and shoe factories in particular employed many workers below age sixteen. Conditions were especially hard for child laborers in the South, where burgeoning textile mills needed unskilled hands.

Child Labor

Several states, especially in the Northeast, passed laws specifying minimum ages and maximum workday hours for child labor. But most large companies could evade these regulations because state statutes could regulate only firms operating within state borders, not those engaged in interstate commerce. Enforcing age requirements proved difficult because many parents, needing income from child labor, lied about their children's ages. By 1900 state laws and automation had reduced the number of children employed in manufacturing, but many more worked at street trades— shining shoes and peddling newspapers and other merchandise—and as helpers in stores.

Although working conditions were often dangerous and unhealthy, low wages most often acted as the catalyst of worker unrest. Many employers believed in the "iron law of wages," which dictated that employees be paid according to conditions of supply and demand. As practiced, the "iron law" meant that employers could pay as little as possible, as long as there were workers willing to accept whatever wages were offered. Employers justified the system by invoking individual freedom: a worker who did not like the wages being paid was free to quit and find a job elsewhere. Courts reinforced the system by regularly denying workers the right to organize and bargain collectively on the grounds that wages should be individually negotiated between employee and employer.

Wage Work

Factories employed children from the early nineteenth century well into the twentieth. In textile mills like the one pictured here, girls operated machines, and boys ran messages and carried materials back and forth. Mill girls had to tie up their hair to keep it from getting caught in the machines. The girl posing here with a shawl over her head would not have worn that garment while she was working.   (National Archives)

Even steady employment proved insecure. Repetitive tasks using high-speed machinery dulled concentration, and the slightest mistake could cause serious injury. Industrial accidents rose steadily before 1920, killing or maiming hundreds of thousands of people each year. As late as 1913, after factory owners had installed safety devices, some 25,000 people died in industrial mishaps, and close to 1 million were injured. Each year sensational disasters, such as explosions and mine cave-ins, aroused public clamor for better safety regulations.

Industrial Accidents

Prevailing free-market views hampered the passage of legislation that would regulate hours and working conditions, and employers denied responsibility for employees' well-being. The only recourse for a stricken family was to sue and prove in court that the killed or injured worker had not realized the risks involved and had not caused the accident, an expensive route that very few took.

Reformers and union leaders lobbied Congress for laws to improve working conditions, but the Supreme Court limited the scope of such legislation by narrowly defining what jobs were dangerous and which workers needed protection. In *Holden v. Hardy* (1896), the Court upheld a law regulating working hours of miners because overly long hours would increase the threat of injury. In *Lochner v. New York* (1905), however, the Court struck down a law limiting bakery workers to a sixty-hour week and a ten-hour day. Responding to the argument that states had the authority to protect workers' health and safety, the Court ruled that baking was not a dangerous enough occupation to justify restricting the right of workers to sell their labor freely.

Courts Restrict Labor Reform

In *Muller v. Oregon* (1908), the Court used a different rationale to uphold a law limiting women to a ten-hour workday in laundries. In this case, the Court asserted that women's health and reproductive functions required protection. According to the Court, a woman's well-being "becomes an object of public interest and care in order to preserve the strength and vigor of the race." As a result of *Muller's* success, later laws barred women from occupations such as printing and transportation, which required long hours or night work, and thus further confined women to menial, dead-end jobs.

Throughout the nineteenth century, tensions rose and fell as workers confronted mechanization. Some people submitted to the demands of the factory, machine, and time clock. Some tried to blend old ways of working into the new system. Others, however, turned to organized resistance.

The year 1877 marked a crisis for labor. In July a series of strikes broke out among unionized railroad workers who were protesting wage

Railroad Strikes of 1877

cuts. Violence spread from Pennsylvania and West Virginia to the Midwest, Texas, and California. Venting pent-up anger, rioters attacked railroad property, derailing trains and burning railroad yards. State militia companies, organized and commanded by employers, broke up picket lines and fired into threatening crowds.

The worst violence occurred in Pittsburgh, where on July 21 militiamen bayoneted and fired on rock-throwing demonstrators, killing ten and wounding many more. Infuriated, the mob drove the soldiers into a railroad roundhouse and set fires that destroyed 39 buildings, 104 engines, and 1,245 freight and passenger cars. The next day, the troops shot their way out of the roundhouse and killed twenty more citizens before fleeing the city. After more than a month of unprecedented carnage, President Rutherford B. Hayes sent federal troops to end the strikes—the first significant use of soldiers to quell labor unrest.

The Union Movement

After 1877 anxiety over the loss of independence and a desire for better wages, hours, and working conditions pushed more workers into unions. Trade unions, which excluded everyone except skilled workers in particular crafts such as printing and iron molding, dated from the early nineteenth century, but the narrowness

of their membership left them without broad power. The National Labor Union, founded in 1866, claimed 640,000 in 1868 but collapsed during the hard times of the 1870s. The only broad-based labor organization to survive that depression was the Knights of Labor.

Founded in 1869 by Philadelphia garment cutters, the Knights began recruiting other workers in the 1870s. In 1879 Terence V. Powderly,

Knights of Labor

a machinist and mayor of Scranton, Pennsylvania, was elected grand master. Under his forceful guidance and, in contrast to most craft unions, willingness to welcome women, African Americans, immigrants, and all unskilled and semiskilled workers, Knights membership mushroomed, peaking at 730,000 in 1886.

The Knights tried to avert the bleak future that they believed industrialism portended by building a workers' alliance that would offer an alternative to profit-oriented industrial capitalism. They believed they could eliminate conflict by establishing a cooperative society in which laborers worked for themselves, not for those who possessed capital. The cooperative idea, attractive in the abstract, gave laborers little bargaining power because employers held all the economic leverage. Strikes offered one means of achieving immediate goals, but Powderly and other Knights leaders opposed strikes, arguing that they tended to divert attention from the long-term goal of a cooperative society and that workers tended to lose more strikes than they won.

Some Knights, however, did support militant action. In 1886 the Knights, demanding higher wages and union recognition from railroads in the Southwest, launched a strike in Texas on March 1. The strike then spread to Kansas, Missouri, and Arkansas. When Powderly, concerned about violence, tried to end the strike by making concessions to the owners, the more militant craft unions broke away from the Knights. Membership dwindled, the special interests of craft unions replaced the Knights' broad-based but often vague appeal, and dreams of labor unity faded.

Nevertheless, workers continued to strive to regain control of their work, and several groups rallied around the issue of an eight-hour

Haymarket Riot

workday. Among those agitating were radical anarchists who believed in using violence to replace all government with voluntary cooperation. On May 3, 1886, Chicago police stormed an area near the McCormick reaper factory and broke up a battle between striking unionists and nonunion strikebreakers. Police shot and killed two unionists and wounded several others.

The next evening, labor groups rallied at Haymarket Square, near downtown Chicago, to protest police brutality. As a police company approached, a bomb exploded, killing seven and injuring sixty-seven. Mass arrests of anarchists and unionists followed. Eventually a court convicted eight anarchists of the bombing, though the evidence of their guilt was questionable. Four were executed and one committed suicide in prison. The remaining three were pardoned in 1893 by Illinois governor John P. Altgeld, who believed they had been victims of the "malicious ferocity" of the courts.

The Haymarket bombing drew attention to the growing discontent of labor and revived fear of radicalism. Some local governments strengthened police forces and armories. And employer associations, coalitions of manufacturers in the same industry, countered labor militancy by drawing up blacklists of union activists whom they would not employ, and by agreeing to resist strikes.

The American Federation of Labor (AFL) emerged from the 1886 upheavals as the major workers' organization. An alliance of national craft unions, the AFL at that time had about 140,000 members, most of them skilled workers. Led by Samuel Gompers, a pragmatic and opportunistic immigrant who headed the Cigar Makers' Union, the AFL avoided the Knights' and anarchists' idealistic rhetoric of worker solidarity and pressed for concrete goals: higher wages, shorter hours, and the right to bargain collectively. The AFL accepted capitalism and worked to improve conditions within the wage-and-hour system. Its national organization required constituent unions to hire organizers to expand membership, and it collected dues for a fund to aid members on strike. The AFL avoided party politics, adhering instead to Gompers's dictum to support labor's friends and oppose its enemies, regardless of party. By 1917 the 111 national unions in the AFL had a combined membership of 2.5 million.

American Federation of Labor

The AFL and the labor movement suffered a series of setbacks in the early 1890s, when once again labor violence stirred public fears. In July 1892 the AFL-affiliated Amalgamated Association of Iron and Steelworkers refused to accept pay cuts and went on strike in Homestead, Pennsylvania. Henry C. Frick, president of Carnegie Steel Company, then closed the plant. Shortly thereafter angry workers attacked and routed three hundred Pinkerton guards hired to protect the plant. State militiamen intervened, and after five months the strikers gave in.

In 1894 workers at the Pullman Palace Car Company walked out in protest over exploitative policies at the company town near Chicago. The paternalistic George Pullman owned everything in his so-called model town named after him. As one laborer grumbled, "We are born in a Pullman house, fed from the Pullman shop, taught in the Pullman school, catechized in the Pullman church, and when we die we shall be buried in the Pullman cemetery and go to the Pullman hell."

Pullman Strike

When the hard times that began in 1893 threatened his prosperity, Pullman protected profits and stock dividends by cutting wages 25 to 40 percent while holding firm on rents and prices in the town. Hard-pressed workers sent a committee to Pullman to protest his policies. He reacted by firing three members of the committee. Enraged workers, most of them from the American Railway Union, called a strike; Pullman retaliated by closing the factory. The union, led by the charismatic Eugene V. Debs, voted to aid the strikers by refusing to handle any Pullman cars attached to any trains. The railroad owners' association then enlisted aid from U.S. Attorney General Richard Olney, who obtained a court injunction to prevent the union from "obstructing the railways and holding up the mails." President Grover Cleveland ordered federal troops to Chicago, ostensibly to protect the rail-carried mails but in reality to crush the strike. Within a month the strikers gave in, and Debs went to prison for defying the court injunction.

In the West, radical labor activity arose among Colorado miners. In 1905 these workers helped form a new labor organization, the Industrial Workers of the World (IWW). Unlike the AFL, the IWW strove to unify all laborers and to organize them into "One

IWW

Big Union." But the "Wobblies," as IWW members were known, also espoused socialism and tactics of violence and sabotage.

Embracing the rhetoric of class conflict—"The final aim is revolution," according to IWW creed—Wobblies believed workers should seize and run the nation's industries. Though the Wobblies' anticapitalist goals and aggressive tactics attracted considerable publicity, IWW membership probably never exceeded 150,000. The organization collapsed during the First World War when federal prosecution sent many of its leaders to jail.

Many unions, notably those of the AFL, openly rejected female members. Of 6.3 million employed

Women and the Labor Movement

women in 1910, fewer than 2 percent belonged to unions. Mostly, male unionists feared competition. Because women were paid less than men, males worried that their own wages would be lowered or that they would lose their jobs if women invaded the workplace. Moreover, male workers, accustomed to sex segregation in employment, could not imagine working side by side with women.

Yet female employees could organize and fight employers as strenuously as men could. Since the early years of industrialization, women had formed their own unions. Some, such as the Collar Laundry Union of Troy, New York, organized in the 1860s, had successfully struck for higher wages. The "Uprising of the 20,000" in New York City, a 1909 strike by immigrant members—most of them women—of the International Ladies Garment Workers Union (ILGWU), was one of the country's largest strikes to that time. Women were also prominent in the 1912 Lawrence, Massachusetts, textile workers' strike. Female trade-union membership swelled during the 1910s, but men monopolized national trade-union leadership, even in industries with large female work forces.

Women, however, did dominate one union: the Telephone Operators' Department of the International Brotherhood of Electrical Workers. Organized in Montana and San Francisco early in the twentieth century, the union spread throughout the Bell system, the nation's monopolistic telephone company and single largest employer of women. To promote solidarity, union leaders sponsored social and educational programs. Their primary focus, however, was on workplace issues. The union opposed scientific management techniques and tightening of supervision. In 1919 several militant union branches paralyzed the phone service of five New England states. The union collapsed after a failed strike in 1923, but not before women had proved that they could battle a powerful employer.

The first women's organization seeking to promote the interests of laboring women was the Women's Trade Union League (WTUL), founded in 1903. The WTUL sought protective legislation for female workers, sponsored educational activities, and campaigned for women's suffrage. Initially the union's highest offices were held by middle-class women who sympathized with female wage laborers, but control shifted in the 1910s to forceful working-class leaders, notably Agnes Nestor, a glove maker; Rose Schneiderman, a cap maker; and Mary Anderson, a shoe worker. The WTUL advocated changes such as opening apprenticeship programs to women so they could enter skilled trades and training female workers to assume leadership roles. It served as a vital link between the labor and women's movements into the 1920s.

Organized labor excluded most immigrant and African American workers. Some trade unions welcomed skilled immigrants, but only

Immigrants, African Americans, and Labor Unions

the Knights of Labor and the IWW had explicit policies of accepting immigrants and blacks. Blacks were prominent in the coal miners' union, and they were partially unionized in trades such as construction, barbering, and dock work. But they could belong only to segregated local unions in the South, and the majority of northern AFL unions had exclusion policies. Long-held prejudices were reinforced when blacks and immigrants, eager for any work they could get, worked as strikebreakers.

The dramatic labor struggles in the half-century following the Civil War make it easy to forget that only a small fraction of American wage workers belonged to unions. In 1900 about 1 million out of a total of 27.6 million workers were unionized. By 1920 total union membership had grown to 5 million, still only 13 percent of the work force. For many workers, getting and holding a job held priority over wages and hours.

For most American workers, then, the machine age had mixed results. Industrial wages rose between 1877 and 1914, boosting purchasing power and creating a mass market for standardized goods. Yet in 1900 most employees worked sixty hours a week at wages that averaged 20 cents an hour for skilled work and 10 cents an hour for unskilled. Moreover, as wages rose, living costs increased even faster.

Standards of Living

 Some Americans, like "S," distrusted machines, but few could resist the changes that mechanization brought to everyday life. Mass production and mass marketing made available myriad goods that previously had not existed or had been the exclusive property of the wealthy. The new material well-being, heralded by products such as ready-made clothes, canned foods, and home appliances, had a dual effect: it blended Americans of differing status into consumer communities defined not by place or class but by possessions, and it accentuated differences between those who could afford goods and services and those who could not.

If a society's affluence can be measured by how it converts luxuries into commonplace articles, the United States was indeed becoming affluent in the years between 1880 and 1920. In 1880, for instance, only wealthy women could afford silk stockings and only residents of Florida, Texas, and California could enjoy fresh oranges. By 1921 Americans bought 217 million pairs of silk stockings and ate 248 crates of oranges per 1,000 people.

New Availability of Products

What people can afford obviously depends on their resources and incomes. Data for the period show that incomes rose broadly. The expanding economy spawned massive fortunes and created a new industrial elite. By 1920 the richest 5 percent of the population received almost one-fourth of all earned income. Incomes also rose among the middle class. For example, average pay for clerical workers rose 36 percent between 1890 and 1910. At the turn of the century, employees of the federal executive branch averaged $1,072 a year, and college professors $1,100. With such incomes, the middle class could afford relatively comfortable housing. A six- or seven-room house cost around $3,000 to buy or build and from $15 to $20 per month to rent.

Though wages for industrial workers increased, their income figures were deceptive because jobs were not always stable and workers had to expend a disproportionate amount of income on necessities. On average, annual wages of factory workers rose from $486 in 1890 to $630 in 1910, about 30 percent. In industries with large female work forces, such as shoe and paper manufacturing, hourly rates remained lower than in male-dominated industries such as coal mining and iron production. Regional variations were also wide. Nevertheless, most wages moved upward.

Cost of Living

Wage increases mean little, however, if living costs rise as fast or faster. That is what happened. The weekly cost of living for a typical wage earner's family of four rose over 47 percent between 1889 and 1913. In few working-class occupations did income rise as fast as the cost of living.

Supplements to Family Income

How then could working-class Americans afford the new machine-age goods and services? Many could not. Still, a family could raise its income and partake modestly in consumer society by sending children and women into the labor market. In a household where the father made $600 a year, wages of other family members might lift total income, or the family wage, to $800 or $900. Many families also rented rooms to boarders and lodgers, a practice that could yield up to $200 a year. These means of increasing family income enabled people to spend more and save more.

Higher Life Expectancy

Science and technology eased some of life's struggles, and their impact on living standards grew after 1900. Advances in medical care, better diets, and improved housing sharply reduced death rates and extended the life span. Between 1900 and 1920, life expectancy rose by fully six years. During this period notable declines occurred in deaths from typhoid, diphtheria, influenza (except for a harsh pandemic in 1918 and 1919), tuberculosis, and intestinal ailments. There were, however, significantly more deaths from cancer, diabetes, and heart disease, afflictions of an aging population and of new environmental factors such as smoke and chemical pollution.

Not only were amenities and luxuries more available than in the previous half-century, but the means to upward mobility seemed more accessible as well. Education increasingly became the key to success. Public education, aided by construction of new schools and the passage of laws that required children to stay in school to age fourteen, equipped young people to achieve a standard of living higher than their parents'. Yet inequities that had pervaded earlier eras remained in place. Race, gender, religion, and ethnicity still determined access to opportunity.

The Quest for Convenience

The toilet stood at the vanguard of a revolution in American lifestyles. The chain-pull washdown water closet, invented in England around 1870, reached the United States in the 1880s. Shortly after 1900 the flush toilet appeared; thanks to mass production of enamel-coated fixtures, it became standard in American homes and buildings. The toilet brought about a shift in habits and attitudes.

Flush Toilets

Before 1880 only luxury hotels and estates had private indoor bathrooms. By the 1890s the germ theory of disease had raised fears about carelessly disposed human waste as a source of infection and water contamination. Much more rapidly than Europeans did, Americans combined a desire for cleanliness with an urge for convenience, and water closets became common, especially in middle-class urban houses. Bodily functions took on an unpleasant image, and the home bathroom became a place of utmost privacy. At the same time, the toilet and the private bathtub gave Americans new ways to use—and waste—water. Plumbing advances were part of a broader democratization of convenience that accompanied mass production and consumerism.

The tin can also altered lifestyles. Before the mid-nineteenth century, Americans typically ate only foods that were in season. By the latter part of the century, however, the combination of knowledge about the cooking-and-sealing process of canning and the mass production of tin cans made a wide variety of foods available throughout the year. Even people remote from mar-

Processed and Preserved Foods

kets, like sailors and cowboys, could readily consume tomatoes, milk, oysters, and other alternatives to previously monotonous diets. Moreover, refrigerated railroad cars enabled growers and meatpackers to ship perishables greater distances and to preserve them for longer periods. And home iceboxes enabled middle-class families to store fresh foods.

Even the working class enjoyed a more diversified diet. As in the past, the poorest people still ate cheap foods, heavy in starches and carbohydrates. Poor urban families seldom could afford meat. Now, though, many of them could purchase previously unavailable fruits, vegetables, and dairy products. Workers had to spend a high percentage of their income on food—almost half of the breadwinner's wages—but they never suffered the severe malnutrition that plagued other developing nations.

Just as tin cans and iceboxes made many foods widely available, the sewing machine brought about a revolution in clothing. Before 1850 nearly all the clothes Americans wore were made at home or by seamstresses and tailors, and a person's social status was apparent in what he or she wore. Then in the 1850s the sewing machine, invented in Europe but refined by Americans Elias Howe, Jr., and Isaac M. Singer, came into use in clothing and shoe manufacture. Mass production enabled manufacturers to turn out good-quality apparel at relatively low cost and to standardize sizes to fit different body shapes. By 1900 only the poorest families could not afford "ready-to-wear" clothes.

Ready-Made Clothing

Mass-produced clothing and dress patterns reinforced a concern for style. Restrictive Victorian fashions still dominated women's clothing, but as women's participation in work and leisure activities became more active, dress designers placed greater emphasis on comfort. In the 1890s long sleeves and skirt hemlines receded, and high-boned collars disappeared. Designers used less fabric; by the 1920s a dress required three yards of material instead of ten. Petite was still the ideal, however: the most desirable waist measurement was 18 to 20 inches, and corsets were big sellers.

Men's clothes, too, became more lightweight and stylish. Before 1900 men in the middle and affluent working classes would have owned no more than two suits, one for Sundays and special occasions and one for everyday wear. After 1900, however, manufacturers began to produce garments from fabrics of different weights and for different seasons. Even for males of modest means, clothing was becoming something to be bought instead of made and remade at home.

Department stores and chain stores helped to create and serve this new consumerism. Between 1865 and 1900, Macy's in New York, Wanamaker's in Philadelphia, and Rich's in Atlanta became urban landmarks.

Department and Chain Stores

Previously, working classes had bought their goods in stores with limited inventories, and wealthier people had patronized fancy shops. Now department stores, with their open displays of clothing, housewares, and furniture, caused a merchandising revolution. They offered not only a wide variety but also home deliveries, exchange policies, and charge accounts.

A society of scarcity does not need advertising: when demand exceeds supply, producers have no trouble selling what they market. But in a society of abundance such as industrial America, supply frequently outstrips demand, necessitating a means to increase and create demand. Thus advertising assumed a new scale and function. Between 1865 and 1919, the amount of money retailers spent on advertising increased from $9.5 million to nearly $500 million.

Advertising

Advertisers aim to invent needs and persuade large groups of people to buy a specific product—a brand of cigarettes, a particular cosmetic, a company's canned foods. In the late nineteenth century, large companies

This photograph of the food counter at R. H. Macy's Department Store in 1902 indicates the large number of processed and preserved foods that became available to Americans at the end of the nineteenth century. The use of tin cans and glass bottles permitted food producers to sell products previously available only at limited times of the year.   (Museum of the City of New York, The Byron Collection)

that mass-produced consumer goods charged advertisers to create "consumption communities," bodies of consumers loyal to a particular brand name.

In 1881 Congress passed a trademark law enabling producers to register and protect brand names. Thousands of companies registered products as varied as Hires Root Beer and Carter's Little Liver Pills. Advertising agencies—a service industry pioneered by N. W. Ayer & Son of Philadelphia—in turn offered expert advice to companies that wished to cultivate brand loyalty.

Newspapers served as the prime vehicle for advertising. In the mid-nineteenth century, publishers began to pursue higher revenues by selling more ad space. Wanamaker's placed the first full-page ad in 1879, and advertisers began to print pictures of products. Such attention-getting techniques transformed advertising into news. More than ever before, people read newspapers to find out what was for sale as well as what was happening.

The Corporate Consolidation Movement

 Neither new products nor new marketing techniques could mask certain unsettling factors in the American economy. In the last decades of the nineteenth century, financial panics afflicted the economy, ruining businesses and destroying workers' security. Economic declines that began in 1873, 1884, and 1893 lingered for several years. Business leaders disagreed on what caused them. Some blamed overproduction; others pointed to underconsumption; still others blamed lax credit and investment practices. Whatever the explanation, businesspeople began seeking ways to combat the uncertainty of boom-and-bust business cycles. Many adopted centralized forms of business organization, notably corporations, pools, trusts, and holding companies.

Corporations proved to be the best instruments to raise capital for industrial expansion, and by 1900 two-thirds of all goods manufactured in the United States were produced by corporate firms. Moreover, corporations won judicial protection in the 1880s and 1890s when the Supreme Court ruled that they, like individuals, are protected by

Rise of Corporations

the Fourteenth Amendment. That is, states could not deny corporations equal protection under the law and could not deprive them of rights or property without due process of law. Such rulings insulated corporations against government interference in their operations.

As downward swings of the business cycle threatened profits, corporation managers sought greater stability in new and larger forms of economic concentration. Between the late 1880s and early 1900s, an epidemic of business consolidation swept the United States, resulting in massive conglomerates that have since dominated the nation's economy. At first such alliances were tentative and informal, consisting mainly of cooperative agreements among firms that manufactured the same product or offered the same service. Through these arrangements, called pools, competing companies tried to control the market by agreeing how much each should produce and sharing profits. Such "gentlemen's agreements" worked during good times when there was enough business for all; but during slow periods, the desire for profits often tempted pool members to evade their commitments by secretly reducing prices or by selling more than the agreed quota.

Pools

John D. Rockefeller, boss of Standard Oil, disliked pools, calling them weak and undependable. In 1879 one of his lawyers, Samuel Dodd, devised a more stable means of dominating the market. Since state laws prohibited one corporation from holding stock in another corporation, Dodd adapted an old device called a trust, a legal arrangement whereby responsible individuals would manage the financial affairs of a person unwilling or unable to handle them alone. Dodd reasoned that one company could control an industry by luring or forcing stockholders of smaller companies in that industry to yield control of their stock "in trust" to the larger company's board of trustees. This device allowed Rockefeller to achieve horizontal integration of the petroleum industry in 1882 by combining his Standard Oil Company of Ohio with other refineries he bought up.

Trusts

In 1888 New Jersey adopted new laws allowing corporations chartered there to own property in other states and to own stock in other corporations. This liberalization facilitated the creation of the holding com-

Holding Companies

pany, which owned a partial or complete interest in other companies. Holding companies could in turn merge their companies' assets as well as their management. Under this arrangement, Rockefeller's holding company, Standard Oil of New Jersey, merged forty refining companies. Holding companies also encouraged vertical integration. This allowed companies to control all aspects of their operations, including raw materials, production, and distribution.

Mergers provided an answer to industry's search for order and profits. Between 1889 and 1903, some three hundred combinations were formed, most of them trusts and holding companies. The most spectacular was U.S. Steel Corporation, financed by J. P. Morgan in 1901. This enterprise, made up of iron-ore properties, freight carriers, wire mills, plate and tubing companies, and other firms, was capitalized at over $1.4 billion. Other mammoth combinations included the Amalgamated Copper Company, American Sugar Refining Company, and U.S. Rubber Company.

Financiers

The merger movement created a new species of businessman, one whose vocation was financial organizing rather than producing a particular good or service. Shrewd operators sought opportunities for combination, formed a holding company, then persuaded producers to sell their firms to the new company. These financiers raised money by selling stock and borrowing from banks. Investment bankers like J. P. Morgan and Jacob Schiff piloted the merger movement, inspiring awe with their financial power and organizational skills.

The Gospel of Wealth and Its Critics

Business leaders used corporate consolidation not to promote competition but to minimize it. To justify their tactics to a public committed to the free market, they called on the doctrine of Social Darwinism. This philosophy loosely grafted Charles Darwin's theory of the survival of the fittest onto laissez faire, the doctrine that government should not interfere in private economic affairs. Social Darwinists reasoned that, in an uncon-

Social Darwinism

strained economy, power and wealth would flow naturally to the most capable people. Acquisition and possession of property were sacred and well-deserved rights. Monopolies thus represented the natural accumulation of economic power by those best suited for wielding it.

Social Darwinists reasoned, too, that wealth carried moral responsibilities to provide for those less fortunate or less capable. Steel baron Andrew Carnegie asserted what he called "the Gospel of Wealth"—that he and other industrialists were guardians of society's wealth and that they had a duty to fulfill their obligation in humane ways. Such philanthropy, however, also implied a right for benefactors like Rockefeller and Carnegie to define what was good and necessary for society; it did not translate into paying workers decent wages.

Government Assistance to Business

In contradiction, business leaders who extolled individual initiative and independence also pressed for government assistance. While denouncing efforts to legislate maximum working hours or regulate factory conditions as interference with natural economic laws, they lobbied governments for subsidies, loans, and tax relief to encourage business growth. Grants to railroads were one form of such assistance. Tariffs, which raised the prices of foreign products by placing an import tax on them, were another. When Congress imposed high tariffs on foreign goods, American producers could raise prices on their own comparable products. Industrialists argued that tariff protection encouraged the development of new products and the founding of new enterprises. But tariffs also forced consumers to pay artificially high prices for many goods.

Dissenting Voices

While defenders insisted that trusts and other forms of big business were a natural and efficient outcome of economic development, critics charged that these forms were unnatural because they stifled opportunity and originated from greed.

Such charges emanating from farmers, workers, and intellectuals voiced an ardent fear of monopoly, the domination of an economic activity by one powerful company. Those who feared monopoly believed—with considerable justification—that large corporations fixed prices, exploited workers by cutting wages, destroyed opportunity by crushing small businesses, and threatened democracy by corrupting politicians.

Many believed in a better path to progress. By the mid-1880s, a number of intellectuals began to challenge Social Darwinism and laissez-faire economics. Sociologist Lester Ward attacked the application of evolutionary theory to social and economic relations. In *Dynamic Sociology* (1883), Ward argued that human control of nature, not natural law, accounted for the advance of civilization. A system that guaranteed survival only to the fittest was wasteful and brutal; instead, Ward reasoned, cooperative activity fostered by government intervention was more moral.

While academics such as Ward endorsed intervention in the natural economic order, others more directly

Utopian Economic Schemes

questioned why the United States had to have so many poor people while a few became fabulously wealthy. Henry George, the author of *Progress and Poverty* (1879), believed that inequality stemmed from the ability of a few to profit from rising land values. George argued that such profits made speculators rich simply because of increased demand for living and working space, especially in cities. To prevent profiteering, George proposed to replace all taxes with a "single tax" on the "unearned increment"—the rise in property values caused by increased market demand rather than by owners' improvements.

Novelist Edward Bellamy believed competitive capitalism promoted waste. His solution was the establishment of a state in which government owned the means of production. Bellamy outlined his dream in *Looking Backward* (1888). This novel, which sold over a million copies, depicted Boston in the year 2000 as a peaceful community where everyone had a job and a technological elite managed the economy according to scientific principles. Though a council of elders ruled and ordinary people could not vote in this utopia, Bellamy tried to convince readers that a "principle of fraternal cooperation" could replace vicious competition and wasteful monopoly.

Few people supported the universal government ownership envisioned by Bellamy, but several states took steps to prohibit monopolies and regulate business. By the end of the nineteenth century, fifteen

Antitrust Legislation

states had constitutional provisions outlawing trusts, and twenty-seven had laws forbidding pools. Most of these were agricultural states in the South and West that were responding to antimonopolistic pressure from farm organizations. But state authorities lacked the staff and judicial support for an effective attack on big business. Only national legislation, it seemed, could work.

Congress moved hesitantly toward such legislation and in 1890 finally passed the Sherman Anti-Trust Act. The law made illegal "every contract, combination in the form of trust or otherwise, or conspiracy in the restraint of trade." However, the law was left purposely vague so as to attract broad support. It did not clearly define "restraint of trade" and consigned interpretation of its provisions to the courts, which at the time were strong allies of business.

Judges used the law's vagueness to blur distinctions between reasonable and unreasonable restraints of trade. When in 1895 the federal government prosecuted the so-called Sugar Trust for owning 98 percent of the nation's sugar-refining capacity, eight of the nine Supreme Court justices ruled that control of manufacturing did not necessarily mean control of trade (*U.S. v. E. C. Knight Co.*). According to the Court, the Constitution empowered Congress to regulate interstate commerce, but manufacturing did not fall under congressional control.

Summary

 Mechanization and new inventions thrust the United States into the vanguard of industrial nations and immeasurably altered daily life between 1877 and 1920. But in industry, as in farming and mining, massive size and aggressive consolidation engulfed the individual, changing the nature of work from individual activity undertaken by producers to mass production undertaken by wage earners. Laborers fought to regain control of their work but struggled to develop well-organized unions that could meet their needs. The outpouring of products created a new mass society based on consumerism, but even the democratization of consumption did not benefit all social groups.

The problems of enforcing the Sherman Anti-Trust Act reflected the uneven distribution of power. Corporations consolidated to control resources, production, and politics. Farmers, laborers, and reformers benefited from the material gains that technology and mass production provided, but they charged that business was acquiring too much influence and profiting at their expense.

LEGACY FOR A PEOPLE AND A NATION
Rockefeller and Standard Oil

For a generation after he founded his oil trust in 1882, John D. Rockefeller and Standard Oil evoked awe and fear of their power and wealth. Then, in 1911, the U.S. Supreme Court enforced anti-trust law and broke the company into thirty-four pieces. After the breakup, the Rockefeller family and the oil business drifted apart, but both left legacies to American society, though in different ways.

John D. Rockefeller personified the big-business "Robber Baron." His wealth inspired dreams, with sayings and song lyrics expressing a person's hope of becoming "rich as Rockefeller." For years he regularly gave away millions of dollars for educational and humanitarian purposes, and in 1913 he permanently endowed a philanthropic foundation "to promote the well-being of mankind throughout the world." Since then, the Rockefeller Foundation has disbursed over $2 billion for education, the eradication of disease, food production, population research, and the arts and humanities. Rockefeller's only son, John, Jr., oversaw the foundation while he withdrew the family from the oil business in the 1920s and 1930s. A grandson, John III, continued to give away money made by his grandfather.

Meanwhile, the business of oil refining became a critical element of everyday life, not just for the production of gasoline, but also for the plastics industry that provides so many modern products. In 1998, at the height of another era of corporate consolidation, the two largest segments of the former Standard Oil Trust—Exxon Corporation and Mobil Corporation (formerly Standard Oil of New Jersey and Standard Oil of New York)—negotiated an $83 billion merger that reunited them into the world's largest oil company, with 123,000 employees and $200 billion in annual revenues. But the newly created Exxon Mobil did not presage the revival of a monopolistic trust. While in his day the senior Rockefeller controlled 90 percent of American refining capacity, the Exxon-Mobil combination would control 21 percent.

The closest modern replica of Rockefeller might be William H. Gates, founder and chairman of Microsoft, the giant computer software firm. Also the target of anti-trust prosecution, Gates, like Rockefeller, drove rivals out of business through aggressive pricing and continually innovated to maintain a competitive edge. Gates also amassed a vast fortune, reputed to be the largest of any American, and gave away huge sums for humanitarian and educational purposes.

For Further Reading, see the Appendix. For Web resources, go to history.college.hmco.com/students.

THE VITALITY AND TURMOIL OF URBAN LIFE

1877–1920

It sounds like a movie story line. Rahel Gollop grew up in a village in western Russia. Her father, driven to desperation by persecution and poverty, left his family in 1890 to find a better life. Arrested by Russian soldiers, he escaped into Germany and found passage on a steamship bound for New York City. After two and a half years in the United States, he had saved enough to purchase tickets so Rahel and her aunt could join him in America. A year later, her mother, brothers, and sisters arrived.

Like other immigrant families, the Gollops struggled and coped with this urban world where a family could not afford their own house and where, without a garden, they had to pay for everything. To help her parents and enable her brothers to attend school, Rahel,

only twelve years old, went to work in a garment sweatshop. She witnessed—and went through—many of the travails suffered by other immigrants, including the beating of eastern European Jews on election night and the harassment of street vendors by drunken nativists. Like other immigrants, Rahel sought security by associating with her own kind, rarely mingling with strangers.

But gradually Rahel broke away. Health problems brought her into a Protestant hospital, where she was exposed to another culture. She learned to read English and acquired an education. Rejecting the man whom her parents had selected for her husband, she married a grocer and became a writer. She published her autobiography in 1918 and died in 1925 at the age of forty-five, possibly of suicide.

IMPORTANT EVENTS

1867 First law regulating tenements passes, in New York State

1870 One-fourth of Americans live in cities

1876 National League of Professional Baseball Clubs founded

1880s "New" immigrants from eastern and southern Europe begin to arrive in large numbers

1883 Pulitzer buys *New York World* and creates a major vehicle for yellow journalism

1886 First settlement house opens, in New York City

1889 Edison invents the motion picture and viewing device

1890s Electric trolleys replace horse-drawn mass transit

1893 Columbian Exposition opens in Chicago

1898 Race riot erupts in Wilmington, North Carolina

1900–10 Immigration reaches peak
Vaudeville rises in popularity

1903 Boston beats Pittsburgh in first baseball World Series

1905 Intercollegiate Athletic Association, forerunner of National College Athletic Association (NCAA), is formed and restructures rules of football

1906 Race riot erupts in Atlanta, Georgia

1915 Griffith directs *Birth of a Nation*, one of the first major technically sophisticated movies

1920 Majority (51.4 percent) of Americans live in cities

The experiences of Rahel Gollop illustrate many themes characterizing urban life in America in the late nineteenth and early twentieth centuries. Where to live, where to work, how to support the family, the cash-based economy, ethnic consciousness and bigotry, the quest for individual independence and respectability—all these things and more made cities places of hope, frustration, satisfaction, and conflict.

Cities had exerted significant influence on the nation's history since its inception, but not until the 1880s did the United States begin to become a truly urban nation. By 1920 a milestone of urbanization was passed: that year's census showed that, for the first time, a majority of Americans (51.2 percent) lived in cities (settlements with more than 2,500 people). This new fact of national life was as symbolically significant as the disappearance of the frontier in 1890.

Cities served as marketplaces and forums, bringing together the people, resources, and ideas responsible for many of the changes that American society was experiencing. By 1900 a network of small, medium, and large cities spanned every section of the country. Some people relished the opportunities and excite-

ment cities offered; others found American cities disquieting and threatening. But whatever people's personal impressions, the city had become central to American life. ◼

Industrial Growth and Transportation in the Modern City

Though their initial functions had been commercial, cities became the main arenas for industrial growth in the late nineteenth century. As centers of labor, transportation, and communication, cities provided everything factories needed. Capital accumulated by the cities' mercantile enterprises fed industrial investment. Urban populations also furnished consumers for myriad new products. Thus urban growth and industrialization wound together in a mutually advantageous spiral. The further industrialization advanced, the more opportunities it created for work and investment. Increased opportunity in turn

Urban Industrial Development

drew more people to cities; as workers and as consumers, they fueled yet more industrialization.

Urban and industrial growth transformed the national economy and freed the United States from dependence on European capital and manufactured goods. Imports and foreign investments still flowed into the United States. But by the early 1900s, cities and their factories, stores, and banks were converting America from a debtor agricultural nation into an industrial, financial, and exporting power.

Late in the nineteenth century, the compact city of the early nineteenth century, where residences mingled among shops, factories, and warehouses, burst open. From Boston to Los Angeles, the built environment sprawled several miles beyond the original central core. No longer did walking distance determine a city's size. No longer did different social groups live close together, poor near rich, immigrant near native-born, black near white. Instead, cities subdivided into distinct districts: working-class and ethnic neighborhoods, downtown, a ring of suburbs. Two forces— mass transportation and economic change—were responsible for this new arrangement.

Birth of the Modern City

Mass transportation moved people faster and farther. By the 1870s, horse-drawn vehicles were disappearing from city streets, replaced by motor-driven conveyances. Cable cars (carriages that moved by clamping onto a moving underground wire) came first. By the 1880s, cablecar lines operated in Chicago, San Francisco, and many other cities. Then in the 1890s, electric-powered streetcars began replacing horse cars and cable cars. Between 1890 and 1902, the total extent of electrified track grew from 1,300 to 22,000 miles. In a few cities, companies raised track onto trestles, enabling vehicles to travel without interference above jammed downtown streets. In Boston, New York, and Philadelphia, transit firms dug underground passages for their cars, also to avoid traffic congestion. Because elevated railroads and subways were extremely expensive to construct, they appeared in only a few cities.

Mechanization of Mass Transportation

Another form of mass transit, the electric interurban railway, helped link nearby cities. Interurban railways operated between cities in areas with growing suburban populations and furthered urban development by making outer regions attractive for home buyers and businesses. The extensive network of the Pacific Electric Railway in southern California, for example, facilitated both travel and economic development in that region.

Mass-transit lines launched millions of urban dwellers into outlying neighborhoods and created a commuting public. Those who could afford the fare—usually a nickel a ride—could live beyond the crowded central city and commute there for work, shopping, and entertainment. Working-class families, whose incomes rarely topped a dollar a day, found streetcar fares unaffordable. But the growing middle class could escape to quiet neighborhoods on the urban outskirts and live in bungalows with their own yards. Between 1890 and 1920, for example, real-estate developers in the Chicago area opened 800,000 new lots.

Beginnings of Urban Sprawl

Urban sprawl was essentially unplanned, but certain patterns did emerge. Investors paid little attention to the need for parks, traffic control, and public services. Construction of mass transit was guided by the profit motive and thus benefited the urban public unevenly. Streetcar lines serviced mainly those districts that promised the most riders—those whose fares would increase company profits.

Streetcars, elevateds, and subways altered commercial as well as residential patterns. When consumers moved outward, businesses followed. Branches of department stores and banks joined groceries, theaters, taverns, and shops to create neighborhood shopping centers, the forerunners of today's suburban malls. Meanwhile, the urban core became the work zone, filled with offices and stores.

Peopling the Cities: Migrants and Immigrants

Between 1870 and 1920, the number of Americans living in cities increased from 10 million to 54 million. During this period, the number of cities with more than 100,000 people grew from fifteen to sixty-eight; the number with more than 500,000 swelled from two to twelve (see Map 19.1). These figures, dramatic in themselves, represent millions of stories of dreams and frustration, coping and confusion, success and failure.

A city can increase its population in three ways: by natural increase (an excess of births over deaths); by extending its borders to annex land and people; and by net migration (an excess of in-migrants over out-migrants). Between the 1870s and early 1900s, natural increase did not account for urban population growth. Many cities, however, annexed nearby territory, thereby instantly increasing their populations. But by far the greatest contribution to urban population growth was in-migration from the countryside and immigration from abroad, especially Europe.

How Cities Grew

Despite land rushes in the West, rural populations declined as urban populations burgeoned. Low crop prices and high debts dashed white farmers' hopes and drove them off the land toward the opportunities that cities seemed to offer. Such migration affected not only major cities such as Detroit, Chicago, and San Francisco but also secondary cities such as Indianapolis, Nashville, and San Diego. The thrill of city life beckoned especially to young people.

Migration from the Countryside

In the 1880s and 1890s, thousands of rural African Americans also moved cityward, seeking better employment and fleeing crop liens, ravages of the boll weevil on cotton crops, racial violence, and political oppression. Though black urban dwellers grew more numerous after 1915, thirty-two cities already had more than ten thousand black residents by 1900. These urban newcomers resembled other migrants in their rural backgrounds and economic motivations, but they differed in several important ways. Because few factories would employ African Americans, most found jobs in the service sector—cleaning, cooking, and driving—rather than in industrial trades. Also, because most service openings were traditionally female jobs, black women outnumbered black men in cities such as New York, Baltimore, and New Orleans.

African American and Hispanic Migration to Cities

In the West, many Hispanics, who once had been a predominantly rural population, moved into cities.

They took over unskilled construction and grading jobs once held by Chinese laborers who were driven from southern California cities, and in some Texas cities native Mexicans (called *Tejanos*) held the majority of all unskilled jobs.

Even more newcomers were immigrants from Europe who had fled foreign villages and cities for American shores. Smaller numbers from Asia, Canada, and Latin American came for the same reasons. The dream of many was not to stay but to make enough money to return home and live in greater comfort and security. For every hundred foreigners who entered the country, around thirty later left. Still, most of the 26 million immigrants who arrived between 1870 and 1920 remained, and the great majority settled in cities, where they helped reshape American culture.

Immigration from Other Lands

Immigrants from northern and western Europe had long made the United States their main destination, but after 1880 economic and demographic changes propelled a second wave of immigrants from other regions. Northern and western Europeans continued to arrive, but the new wave brought more people from eastern and southern Europe, plus smaller contingents from Canada, Mexico, and Japan (see Figure 19.1). Two-thirds of the newcomers who arrived in the 1880s came from Germany, England, Ireland, and Scandinavia; between 1900 and 1909, two-thirds came from Italy, Austria-Hungary, and Russia. By 1910 arrivals from Mexico were beginning to outnumber arrivals from Ireland, and large numbers of Japanese had moved to the West Coast and Hawai'i. Foreign-born blacks, chiefly from the West Indies, also increased in number.

The New Immigrants

Many Americans feared the customs, Catholic and Jewish faiths, and poverty of "new" immigrants, considering them less desirable than "old" immigrants, whose languages and beliefs seemed less alien. In reality, however, old and new immigrants closely resembled each other. The majority of both groups came from societies that made the family the focus of all undertakings. As Rahel Gollop's case illustrates, whether and when to emigrate was decided in light of the family's needs, and family bonds continued to prevail after immigrants reached the New World. New arrivals

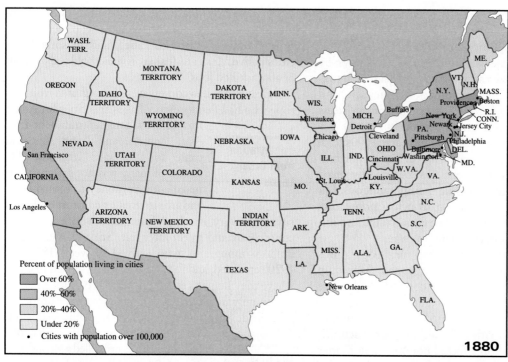

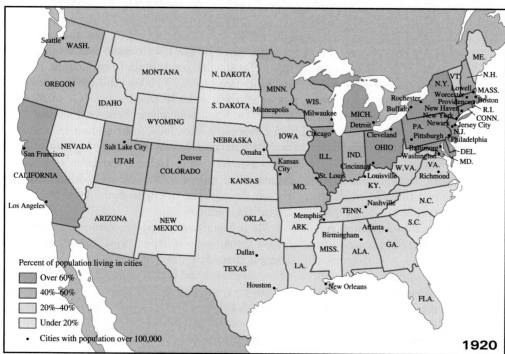

Map 19.1   Urbanization, 1880 and 1920   In 1880 the vast majority of states still were heavily rural. By 1920 only a few had less than 20 percent of their population living in cities.

The Caribbean as well as Europe sent immigrants to the United States. Proud and confident on arrival from their homeland of Guadeloupe, these women perhaps were unprepared for the double disadvantage they faced as both blacks and foreigners. (Augustus Sherman William Williams Papers, Manuscripts & Archives Division, The New York Public Library, Astor, Lenox and Tilden Foundations)

usually knew where they wanted to go and how to get there because they received aid from relatives who had already immigrated.

The migration streams moving into American cities were only part of an extraordinary amount of movement because, once settled, in-migrants and immigrants rarely stayed put. Each year millions of families packed up and moved elsewhere. The urge to move affected every region, every city. From Boston to San Francisco, from Minneapolis to San An-

Residential Mobility

tonio, no more than half of the families residing in a city at any one time were still there ten years later.

In addition to movement between cities, countless numbers of people moved within the same city. In American communities today, one in every five families changes residence in a given year. A hundred years ago, the proportion was closer to one in four or one in three. Population turnover affected almost every neighborhood, every ethnic and occupational group.

Thus the peopling of American cities was a very dynamic process. Americans of all groups, native and

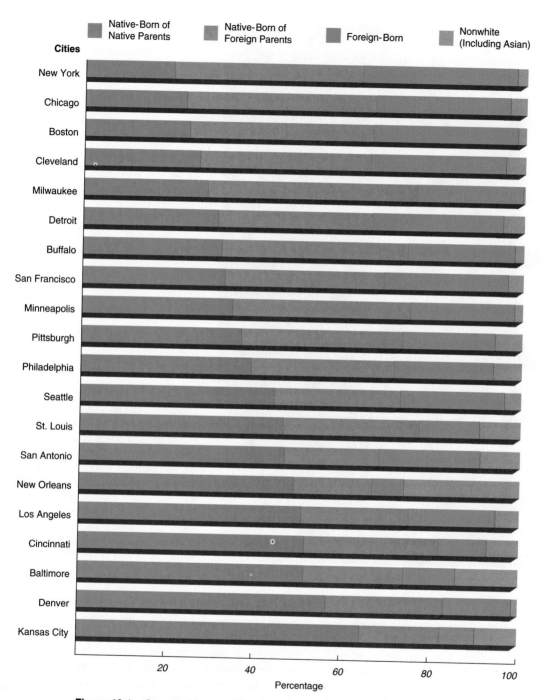

Figure 19.1 Composition of Population, Selected Cities, 1920 Immigration and migration made native-born whites of native-born parents minorities in almost every major city by the early twentieth century. Moreover, foreign-born residents and native-born whites of foreign parents (combining the green and purple segments of a line) constituted absolute majorities in numerous places.

foreign, were always seeking a better life, and hope for improved conditions elsewhere acted as a safety valve, relieving some of the tensions and frustrations that simmered inside the city. Sometimes families moved a short distance to another home or another neighborhood; sometimes they simply picked up and left town.

Urban Neighborhoods

 In their new surroundings—where the language was a struggle, the workday followed the clock rather than the sun, and housing and employment often were uncertain—immigrants first anchored their lives to the rock they knew best: their cultures. Old World customs persisted in immigrant enclaves of Italians from the same province, Japanese from the same island district, or Russian Jews from the same *shtetl* (village). People practiced religion as they always had, held traditional feasts and pageants, married within their group, and pursued old feuds with people from rival villages.

Immigrant Cultures

Yet, as Rahel Gollop discovered, the diversity of American cities forced immigrants to modify their attitudes and habits. Few newcomers could avoid contact with people different from themselves, and few could prevent such contacts from altering their traditional ways of life. Although many foreigners identified themselves by their village or region of birth, native-born Americans categorized them by nationality.

In most large cities, immigrants inhabited multiethnic neighborhoods, places one historian has called "urban borderlands" where a diversity of people, identities, and lifestyles coexisted. Even within districts identified with a certain group, such as Little Italy, Jewtown, or Polonia, rapid mobility constantly undermined residential stability. Seldom did a single ethnic group predominate. Rather, an area's businesses and institutions, such as its bakeries, butcher shops, churches, and club headquarters, gave the neighborhood its identity.

Ethnic and Racial Borderlands

Nevertheless, though different groups jointly inhabited these urban borderlands, various ethnic and racial groups insulated themselves culturally, or were isolated by outside forces, from other immigrants and from the majority population. Some groups, such as Italians, Jews, and Poles, deliberately tried to maintain their separate religious, linguistic, and cultural lifestyles. For such European immigrants, their neighborhoods acted as havens until individuals were ready to cross from the borderland into the majority society.

Mass transportation and the outward movement of factories benefited those wanting to leave the borderlands for other neighborhoods. In the new neighborhoods, they interspersed with families of their own socioeconomic class but not necessarily of their own ethnicity. For people of color, however—African Americans, Asians, and Mexicans—the borderlands had a more persistent character that, because of discrimination, became less multiethnic over time.

Though African Americans originally may have lived in multiethnic, multiracial communities, by the early twentieth century institutionalized racial discrimination was forcing them into relatively permanent, highly segregated ghettos. By 1920 in Chicago, Detroit, Cleveland, and other cities outside the South, two-thirds or more of the total African American population lived in only 10 percent of the residential area. Circumscribed within color-line boundaries, blacks found it increasingly difficult to find jobs as well as housing outside the ghettos. The only way blacks could relieve the pressure resulting from increasing migration was to expand the ghetto borders into surrounding, previously white neighborhoods, a process often resulting in harassment and attacks on black families.

Ghettos

Within the ghettos, African Americans, like other urban people, nurtured cultural institutions that helped them cope with urban life. Churches, particularly those of the Baptist and African Methodist Episcopal (AME) branches of Protestantism, were especially influential. In virtually all cities, black religious activity not only dominated ghetto life but also represented cooperation of blacks across class, cultural, and regional lines.

Asians encountered similar kinds of discrimination and ghetto experience. Although these immigrants often preferred to live in Chinatowns and Japanese sections, Anglos made every effort to keep them separated. In the 1880s, San Francisco's school board, for example, tried to isolate Japanese and Chinese children in Chinatown schools.

Mexicans in southwestern cities experienced somewhat more complex patterns. In some places, such as

Barrios

Los Angeles, Santa Barbara, and Tucson, Mexicans had been the original inhabitants and Anglos were migrants who overtook the city, pushing Mexicans into adjoining areas. Here, Mexicans became increasingly isolated in residential and commercial districts called *barrios*. Frequently, real-estate covenants, by which property owners pledge not to sell homes to Mexicans (or to African Americans, or to Jews, or to some other ethnic group), kept Mexican families confined in *barrios* of Los Angeles, Albuquerque, and San Antonio. To a considerable extent, then, race, more than any other factor, made the urban experiences of nonwhites unique compared to those of whites.

Everywhere, Old World culture mingled with New World realities. Immigrants struggled to maintain

Americanization

their native languages and to pass them down to younger generations, but English was taught in the schools and needed on the job. Foreigners modified many traditional folkways in light of the American experience. Music especially revealed adaptations. Polka bands entertained at Polish social gatherings, but their repertoires soon blended American and Polish folk music; once dominated by violins, the bands added accordions, clarinets, and trumpets so they could play louder. Mexican ballads acquired new themes that described the adventures of border crossing and the hardship of labor in the United States.

The influx of so many immigrants between 1870 and 1920 transformed the United States from a basi-

Accommodation of Religion

cally Protestant nation into one composed of Protestants, Catholics, Orthodox Christians, and Jews. Newcomers from Italy, Hungary, Polish lands, and Slovakia joined Irish and Germans to boost the proportion of Catholics in many cities. Catholic Mexicans constituted over half of the population of El Paso. German and Russian immigrants gave New York one of the largest Jewish populations in the world.

Partly in response to Protestant charges that they could not retain Old World religious beliefs and still assimilate into American society, many Catholics and Jews tried to accommodate their faiths to the new environment. Catholic and Jewish leaders from more established immigrant groups supported liberalizing trends—the use of English in sermons, the phasing out of Old World rituals such as saints' feasts, and a preference for public over religious schools. Newcomers, however, resisted such changes and usually held on to familiar practices, whether the folk Catholicism of southern Italy or the Orthodox Judaism of eastern Europe.

Each of the three major migrant groups that peopled American cities—native-born whites, foreigners of various races, and native-born blacks—helped to mold modern American culture. The cities nurtured rich cultural variety: American folk music and literature, Italian and Mexican cuisine, Irish comedy, Yiddish theater, African American jazz and dance, and much more. Newcomers in the late nineteenth century changed their environment as much as they were changed by it.

Living Conditions in the Inner City

Urban population growth created intense pressures on the public and private sectors. The masses of people who jammed inner-city districts were recognized more for their problems than for their cultural contributions. American cities seemed to harbor all the afflictions that plague modern society: poverty, disease, crime, and other unpleasant conditions that occur when large numbers of people live close together. City dwellers coped as best they could. Although technology, private enterprise, and public authority could not solve every problem, city officials and engineers achieved some remarkable successes. In the late nineteenth and early twentieth centuries, construction of buildings, homes, streets, sewers, and schools proceeded at a furious pace. American cities set world standards for fire protection and water purification. But many problems still await solution.

One of the most persistent shortcomings—the failure to provide adequate housing for all who need it—

Housing

has its origins in nineteenth-century urban development. In spite of massive construction in the 1880s and early 1900s, population growth outpaced housing supplies. Scarcity of inexpensive housing especially afflicted working-class families who, because of low wages, had to rent their living quarters. As cities grew, landlords took advantage of shortages in low-cost rental housing by splitting up existing buildings to house more people, constructing multiple-unit tenements, and hiking rents. Low-income families adapted to high costs and short supply by sharing space and expenses. Thus it became common in many big cities for a one-family apartment to be occupied by two or three families or by a single family plus several boarders. The result was unprecedented crowding. In 1890 New York City's immigrant-packed Lower East Side averaged 702 people per acre.

Inside these buildings, conditions were harsh. The largest rooms were barely ten feet wide, and interior rooms either lacked windows or opened onto narrow shafts that bred vermin and rotten odors. Few buildings had indoor plumbing; the only source of heat was dangerous, polluting coal-burning stoves.

Housing problems aroused reform campaigns in several places. New York State took the lead by legislating light, ventilation, and safety codes for new tenement buildings in 1867, 1879, and 1901. A few reformers, such as journalist Jacob Riis and humanitarian Lawrence Veiller, advocated housing low-income families in "model tenements," with more spacious rooms and better facilities. Model tenements, however, required landlords to accept lower profits—a sacrifice few were willing to make. Both reformers and public officials opposed government financing of better housing, fearing that such a step would undermine private enterprise.

Housing Reform

Housing reforms for the poor had only limited success, but scientific and technological advances eventually

Inner-city dwellers used not only indoor space as efficiently as possible but also what little outdoor space was available to them. Scores of families living in this cramped block of six-story tenements in New York strung clotheslines behind the buildings. Notice that there is virtually no space between buildings, so only rooms at the front and back received daylight and fresh air.   (Library of Congress)

Sanitation and Construction Technology

enabled city dwellers and the entire nation to live in greater comfort and safety. By the 1880s, some doctors had begun to accept the theory that microorganisms (germs) cause disease. In response, cities established more efficient systems of water purification and sewage disposal. Although tuberculosis and other respiratory ills continued to plague inner-city districts, public health regulations as applied to water purity, sewage disposal, and food quality helped to control dread diseases such as cholera, typhoid fever, and diphtheria.

Meanwhile, street paving, modernized firefighting equipment, and electric street lighting spread rapidly across urban America. Steel-frame construction made possible the erection of skyscrapers, and steel-cable suspension bridges linked metropolitan sections more closely. None of these improvements, however, lightened the burden of poverty.

Since colonial days, Americans have disagreed about how much responsibility the public should assume for poor relief. According to traditional beliefs, still widespread at the turn of the century, anyone could escape poverty through hard work and clean living; indigence existed only because some people were morally weaker than others. Such reasoning bred fear that aid to poor people would encourage paupers to rely on public support rather than their own efforts. As the business cycle fluctuated and poverty increased, this attitude hardened, and city governments discontinued direct grants of food, fuel, and clothing to needy families. Instead, cities provided relief in return for work on public projects and sent special cases to state-run almshouses, orphanages, and homes for the blind, deaf, and mentally ill.

Urban Poverty

Close observation of the poor, however, prompted some humanitarians to conclude that people's environments, not their personal shortcomings, caused poverty. In turn, they had faith that poverty could be prevented and eliminated by improving housing, education, sanitation, and job opportunities rather than admonishing the poor to be more moral. This attitude, which had been gaining ground since the mid-nineteenth century, fueled drives for building codes, factory regulations, and public health measures. Still, most middle- and upper-class Americans continued to endorse the creed that in a society of abundance only

the unfit were poor and that poverty relief should be tolerated but never encouraged.

More than crowding and pauperism, crime and disorder nurtured fears that urban growth, especially the slums, threatened the nation. The more cities grew, it seemed, the more they shook with violence. While homicide rates declined in industrialized nations such as England and Germany, those in America rose alarmingly: 25 murders per million people in 1881; 107 per million in 1898. Pickpockets, swindlers, and burglars roamed every city.

Crime and Violence

Despite fears of robberies and violence, urban crime may simply have become more conspicuous and sensational, rather than more prevalent. To be sure, concentrations of wealth and the mingling of different peoples provided opportunities for larceny, vice, and assault. But urban lawlessness and brutality probably did not exceed that of backwoods mining camps. Nativists were quick to blame immigrants for urban crime and disorder, but there is little evidence that more foreigners than native-born Americans populated the rogues' gallery.

The cityward movement of African Americans especially roused white fears, and as the twentieth century dawned, a series of race riots spread across the nation. In 1898 white citizens of Wilmington, North Carolina, resenting the success of African Americans in local politics, rioted and killed dozens of blacks. In the wake of the fury, whites expelled all black officeholders and instituted restrictions to prevent blacks from voting. In Atlanta in 1906, a series of newspaper accounts alleging attacks by black men on white women provoked a wave of shooting and killing that left twelve blacks dead and over seventy injured. An influx of African American unskilled laborers and strikebreakers into the industrial city of East St. Louis, Illinois, heightened racial tensions that erupted in 1917, leaving nine whites and thirty-nine blacks dead.

Promises of Mobility

The persistence of poverty, crime, and violence undercut the image of cities as places of opportunity, yet as locales of economic progress, cities could provide avenues by which people might achieve some modicum of success. The story of urban social mobility is not one of rags to riches but rather one of countless small triumphs mixed with dashed hopes, discrimination, and failure. Basically, there were two ways a person could get ahead: occupational advancement and acquisition of property. These options were open chiefly to white men.

Many women held paying jobs, owned property, and migrated, but their economic standing was usually defined by the men in their lives—usually their husbands or fathers. Women could improve their status by marrying men with wealth or potential, but other avenues were mostly closed. Educational institutions blocked their training in professions such as medicine and law, and prevailing assumptions attributed higher aptitude for manual skills and business to men. For African Americans, American Indians, Mexican Americans, and Asian Americans, opportunities were even fewer.

For white men, however, occupational mobility was a reality, thanks to urban and industrial expansion.

Occupational Mobility

Thousands of businesses were needed to supply goods and services to burgeoning urban populations. As corporations grew and centralized their operations, they required new managerial personnel. To be sure, only a very few traveled the rags-to-riches path, but considerable movement occurred along the road from poverty to moderate success.

Rates of occupational mobility were slow but steady between 1870 and 1920. Although some men slipped from a higher to a lower rung on the occupational ladder, rates of upward movement were usually double those of downward movement. While patterns were not consistent, immigrants generally experienced less upward and more downward mobility than the native-born did. Still, regardless of birthplace, the chances for a white male to rise occupationally over the course of his career or to hold a higher-status job than his father had were relatively good.

In addition to advancing occupationally, a person might achieve social mobility by acquiring property such as a building or a house. But

Acquisition of Property

property was not easy to acquire. Banks and savings-and-loan institutions had far stricter lending practices than they did after the 1930s, when the federal government began to insure real-estate financing. Before then, mortgage loans carried high interest rates and short repayment periods. Thus

renting, even of single-family houses, was common, especially in big cities. A general rise in wage rates nevertheless enabled many families to amass savings, which they could use as down payments on property. Ownership rates varied regionally—higher in western cities, lower in eastern cities—but 36 percent of all urban American families owned their homes in 1900, the highest homeownership rate of any Western nation except for Denmark, Norway, and Sweden.

The possibilities of upward mobility seemed to temper people's dissatisfaction. Although the gap between the very rich and the very poor widened, the expanding economies of American cities created room in the middle of the socioeconomic scale. Few could become another Rockefeller, but many did become respectable shopkeepers, foremen, clerks, and agents. Some also used politics and management of the city as routes to status and success.

Managing the City

 Cities faced daunting challenges in the late nineteenth century. Burgeoning populations, business expansion, and technological change created urgent needs for sewers, police and fire protection, schools, parks, and other services. Such needs strained municipal resources beyond their capacities. Furthermore, city governments approached these needs in a disorganized fashion.

Since the mid-nineteenth century, city dwellers had gradually overcome their resistance to professional law enforcement and increas-

Role of the Police

ingly depended on the police to protect life and property. By the early 1900s, however, law enforcement had become complicated and controversial because various groups differed in their views of the law and how it should be enforced. As the chief urban law enforcers, police forces were caught between pressures for swift and severe action on one hand and leniency on the other. Some people clamored for crackdowns on drunkenness, gambling, and prostitution at the same time that others favored loose law enforcement so they could indulge in these customer-oriented crimes. Achieving a balance between the idealistic intentions of criminal law and people's desire for individual freedom grew increasingly difficult, and it has remained so to this day.

Out of the apparent confusion surrounding urban management arose political machines, organizations whose main goals were the rewards—money, influence, and prestige—of getting and keeping political power.

The Machine

Machine politicians routinely used bribery and graft to further their ends. But machines needed popular support, and they could not have succeeded if they had not provided relief, security, and services to large numbers of people. By meeting those needs, machine politicians accomplished things that other agencies had been unable or unwilling to attempt.

Machines bred leaders—bosses—who were adept at satisfying special-interest groups while simultaneously catering to the urban working classes. Bosses and machines established power bases among new immigrant voters and used politics to solve important urban problems. Most bosses had immigrant backgrounds and had grown up in the inner city, so they knew their constituents' needs firsthand. Machines made politics a full-time profession. To be sure, fraud, bribery, and thievery tainted the system, but machines were rarely as dictatorial or corrupt as critics charged.

The system rested on a popular base and was held together by loyalty and service. Machines usually were coalitions of smaller organizations that derived power directly from inner-city working-class neighborhoods. In return for votes, bosses provided jobs, built parks and bathhouses, distributed food and clothing to the needy, and helped when someone ran afoul of the law. Such personalized service cultivated mass attachment to the boss; never before had public leaders assumed such responsibility for people in need.

To finance their activities and campaigns, bosses exchanged favors for votes or money. Power over local government enabled machines to control the awarding of public contracts, the granting of utility or streetcar franchises, and the distribution of city jobs. Recipients of city business and jobs were expected to repay the machine with a portion of their profits or salaries and to cast supporting votes on election day. Critics called this process graft; bosses called it gratitude.

The Boss

Machine-led city governments constructed public buildings, sewer systems, and mass-transit lines that otherwise might not have been built; but bribes and kickbacks made such projects costly to taxpayers. In addition, machines dispensed favors to legal and illegal businesses. Payoffs from gambling, prostitution, and illicit liquor traffic became important sources of machine revenue.

Bosses held power because they tended to problems of everyday life. Martin Lomasney, boss of Boston's South End, explained, "There's got to be in every ward somebody that any bloke can come to—no matter what he's done—and get help. Help, you understand, none of your law and justice, but help." The boss system, however, was neither neutral nor fair. Racial minorities and new immigrant groups received only token jobs and nominal favors, if any. But bosses were no more guilty of self-interest and discrimination than were business leaders who exploited workers, spoiled the landscape, and manipulated government in pursuit of profits.

While bosses were consolidating their power, others were attempting to destroy them. Many middle- and upper-class Americans feared that immigrant-based political machines menaced the republic and that unsavory alliances between bosses and businesses wastefully depleted municipal finances. Anxious over the poverty, crowding, and disorder that accompanied population expansion, and convinced that urban services were making taxes too high, civic reformers organized to install more responsible leaders at the helm of urban administrations.

Urban Reform

Urban reform arose in part from the industrial system's emphasis on eliminating inefficiency. Business-minded reformers believed government should be run like a company. The way to achieve this goal, they believed, was to elect officials who would hold down expenses and prevent corruption. Thus they advocated reducing city budgets, making public employees work more efficiently, and cutting taxes.

To implement business principles in government, civic reformers supported structural changes such as the city-manager and commission forms of government, which would place administration in the hands of experts rather than politicians, and nonpartisan, citywide election of officials. Armed with such strategies, reformers believed they could cleanse party politics and

Structural Reform in Government

weaken bosses' power bases in the neighborhoods. They rarely realized, however, that bosses succeeded because they used government to meet people's needs.

A few reform mayors moved beyond structural changes to address social problems. Hazen S. Pingree of Detroit, Samuel "Golden Rule" Jones of Toledo, and Tom Johnson of Cleveland worked to provide jobs for poor people, reduce charges by transit and utility companies, and promote governmental responsibility for the welfare of all citizens. They also supported public ownership of gas, electric, and telephone companies, a quasi-socialist reform that alienated their business allies. But few reformers could match the bosses' political savvy and soon found themselves out of power.

A different type of reform arose outside politics. Driven by an urge to improve as well as manage society, social reformers—mostly young **Social Reform** and middle class—embarked on campaigns to identify and solve urban problems. Housing reformers pressed local governments for building codes to ensure safety in tenements. Educational reformers sought to use public schools as a means of preparing immigrant children for citizenship by teaching them American values.

Perhaps the most ambitious and inspiring feature of urban reform movements was the settlement house. Located in slum neighborhoods and run mostly by women, settlement houses were buildings where middle-class young people went to live and work in order to bridge the gulf between social classes. The first American settlement, patterned after London's Toynbee Hall, opened in New York City in 1886, and others quickly appeared in cities across the country. Early settlement leaders such as Jane Addams and Florence Kelley wanted to improve the lives of slum dwellers by helping them obtain education, appreciation of the arts, better jobs, and decent housing. Though sometimes mistrusted, settlement workers achieved important successes with activities such as vocational classes, childcare, and ethnic pageants.

As they broadened their scope to fight for school nurses, building and factory safety codes, and public playgrounds, settlement workers became reform leaders in cities and in the nation. Their efforts to involve national and local governments in the solution of social problems later made them the vanguard of early-twentieth-century reform. Moreover, the activities of settlement houses created new professional opportunities for women in social work, public health, and child welfare. These professions enabled female reformers to build a dominion of influence over social policy independent of male-dominated professions and to make valuable contributions to national as well as inner-city life.

A contrast developed, however, between white female reformers and black female reformers. Middle-class white women lobbied for government programs to aid needy people, mostly white immigrant and native-born working classes. Black women, barred by their race from political institutions, raised funds from private donors and focused on helping members of their own race. African American women were especially active in founding schools, old-age homes, and hospitals, but they also worked for advancement of the race and protection of black women from sexual exploitation. Their ranks included women such as Jane Hunter, who founded a home for unmarried black working women in Cleveland in 1911, and Modjeska Simkins, who organized a program to address health problems among blacks in South Carolina.

Regardless of their focus, urban reformers wanted to save cities, not abandon them. They believed they could improve urban life by restoring cooperation among all citizens. They often failed to realize, however, that cities were places of great diversity and that different people held very different views about what reform actually meant. To civic reformers, distributing city jobs on the basis of civil service exams rather than party loyalty meant progress, but to working-class men civil service signified reduced employment opportunities. Moral reformers believed that prohibiting the sale of alcoholic beverages would prevent working-class breadwinners from squandering their wages, but immigrants saw such crusades as interference in their private lives. Thus urban reform merged idealism with naiveté and insensitivity.

At the same time, efforts of still a different sort were making cities more livable. Providing sanitation, street lighting, bridge and street **Engineers** construction, and other such needs required technological creativity, not political or humanitarian action. In addressing these critical urban issues, the American engineering profession developed new systems and standards of worldwide significance.

Take, for example, the problems associated with refuse. To solve these problems, by 1900 engineers were devising systems for incinerating refuse, dumping trash while safeguarding water supplies, constructing efficient sewers, and providing for regular street cleaning and snow removal. Engineers had similar influence in matters of street lighting, parks, and fire protection, and they also advised officials on budget and contracts. City officials, whether bosses or reformers, came to depend on the expertise of engineers, who generally carried out their responsibilities efficiently and with little fanfare and made some of the most lasting contributions to urban management.

Family Life

Although the overwhelming majority of Americans continued to live within families, this basic social institution suffered strain during the era of urbanization and industrialization. New institutions—schools, social clubs, political organizations, and others—increasingly competed with the family to provide nurture, education, and security. Clergy and journalists warned that rising divorce rates, the growing separation between home and work, the entrance of numerous women into the work force, and loss of parental control over children spelled peril for home and family. Yet the family retained its fundamental role as a cushion in a hard, uncertain world.

Throughout modern Western history, most people have lived in two overlapping social units: household and family. A household is a group of people, related or unrelated, who share the same residence. A family is a group related by kinship, some members of which typically live together. In the late nineteenth and early twentieth centuries, different patterns characterized the two institutions.

Family and Household Structures

Since colonial times, the vast majority of American households (75 to 80 percent) have consisted of nuclear families—usually a married couple, with or without children. About 15 to 20 percent of households have consisted of extended families—usually a married couple, with or without children, plus one or more relatives such as parents, adult siblings, grandchildren, aunts, and uncles. About 5 percent of households have consisted of people living alone.

The average size of nuclear families changed over time. In 1880 the birth rate was 40 live births per 1,000 people; by 1920 it had dropped to 28. Several factors explain this decline. First, the United States was becoming an urban nation, and birth rates are historically lower in cities than in rural areas. On farms, each child represented a new set of hands for the family work force. In the wage-based urban economy, children could not contribute significantly to the family income for many years, and a new child represented another mouth to feed. Second, infant mortality fell as diet and medical care improved, and families did not have to bear many children just to ensure that some would survive. Third, awareness that smaller families meant improved quality of life seems to have stimulated decisions to limit family size. Although fertility was higher among blacks, immigrants, and rural people than among white native-born city dwellers, birth rates of all groups fell. Families with six or eight children became rare; three or four became more usual.

Declining Birth Rates

The household tended to expand and contract over the lifetime of a given family. Its size increased as children were born, and it shrank as children left home. The process of leaving home altered household composition; huge numbers of young people—and some older people—lived as boarders and lodgers. Middle- and working-class families commonly took in boarders to occupy rooms vacated by grown children and to get additional income. Indeed, by 1900 as many as 50 percent of city residents had lived either as or with boarders at some point during their lifetime. Though criticized by housing reformers, for people on the move, boarding was a transitional stage, providing them with a quasi-family environment until they set up their own households.

Boarding

At a time when welfare agencies were rare, the family was the institution to which people could turn in times of need. Families took in widowed parents or unmarried siblings who otherwise would have lived alone, and newlyweds sometimes lived temporarily

The Hedlund family of St. Paul, Minnesota, celebrates the Fourth of July together in 1911 with flags and fireworks. Consisting of two parents and three children, the family represents the modern household of two generations and limited family size.   (Minnesota Historical Society)

Importance of Kinship

with one spouse's parents. Even when relatives did not live together, they often lived nearby and aided one another with childcare, meals, shopping, advice, and consolation. They also obtained jobs for one another.

But obligations of kinship were not always welcome. Immigrant families often pressured last-born children to stay at home to care for aging parents, a practice that stifled opportunities for education, marriage, and economic independence. Tensions also developed between generations, such as when immigrant parents and American-born children clashed over the abandonment of Old World ways or the amount of money employed children should contribute to the household. Nevertheless, for better or worse, kinship provided people a means of coping with the stresses caused by an urban-industrial society. Social and economic change did not sever family ties.

Large numbers of city dwellers lived beyond the haven of traditional family relationships, however. In

Unmarried People

1890 almost 42 percent of adult American men and 37 percent of women were single, almost twice as high as the figures for 1960. Mostly young, these men and women constituted a separate subculture that helped support institutions like dance halls, saloons, cafés, and the YMCA and YWCA. Some of these unmarried people numbered among the homosexual population that thrived especially in large cities like New York and Boston. Though their numbers are difficult to estimate, gay men had their own subculture complete with clubs, restaurants, coffeehouses, theaters, and support networks. A number of gay couples, especially women, formed lasting marriage-type relationships, sometimes called "Boston marriages." Some men cruised in the sexual underground of the streets and bars. Gay women were more cautious, and a lesbian subculture of clubs and commercial establishments seldom existed until the 1920s. The gay world, then, was a complex one that included a variety of relationships and institutions.

By the early 1900s, family life and functions were both changing and holding firm. New institutions were assuming tasks formerly performed by the family. Schools were making education a community responsibility. Employment agencies, personnel offices, and labor unions were taking responsibility for employee recruitment and job security. In addition, migration and a soaring divorce rate seemed to be splitting families apart. Yet in the face of these pressures, the family adjusted by expanding and contracting to meet temporary needs, and kinship remained a dependable though not always appreciated institution.

Change in Family Life and Functions

The New Leisure and Mass Culture

On December 2, 1889, as hundreds of workers paraded through Worcester, Massachusetts, in support of shorter working hours, a group of carpenters hoisted a banner proclaiming "Eight Hours for Work, Eight Hours for Rest, Eight Hours for What We Will." That last phrase was significant, for it laid claim to a special segment of daily life that belonged to the individual. Increasingly, among all urban social classes, leisure activities filled this time segment.

American inventors had long tried to create labor-saving devices, but not until the late 1800s did technology become truly time-saving. Mechanization and assembly-line production helped to cut the average workweek in manufacturing from sixty-six hours in 1860 to sixty in

Increase in Leisure Time

1890 and forty-seven in 1920. These reductions meant shorter workdays and freer weekends. To be sure, thousands of laborers still endured twelve- or fourteen-hour shifts in steel mills and sweatshops and had no time or energy for leisure. But as the nation's economy shifted from one of scarcity and production to one of surplus and consumption, more Americans began to engage in a variety of diversions, and a substantial segment of the economy began providing for—and profiting from—leisure.

After the Civil War, amusement became an organized, commercial activity. The production of games, toys, and musical instruments for indoor family entertainment expanded. Games such as checkers and backgammon had existed for decades, but the rise of new manufacturers such as Milton Bradley and Parker Brothers increased the popularity of board games markedly. Significantly, the content of board games shifted from moral lessons to topics involving transportation, finance, and sports.

The vanguard of new leisure pursuits, however, was sports, and baseball was the most popular organized sport. An outgrowth of older bat, ball, and base-circling games, baseball was formalized in 1845 by a group of wealthy New Yorkers—the Knickerbocker Club—who codified the rules of play. By the 1880s, professional baseball was a big business. In 1903 the National League (founded in 1876) and the American League (formed in 1901) began a World Series between their championship teams, entrenching baseball as the national pastime. The Boston Red Socks beat the Pittsburgh Pirates in that first series.

Baseball

Baseball appealed mostly to men. But croquet, which also swept the nation, attracted both sexes. Middle- and upper-class people held croquet parties and outfitted wickets with candles for night contests. In an era when the departure of paid work from the home had separated men's from women's spheres, croquet increased opportunities for social contact between the sexes.

Croquet and Cycling

Meanwhile, cycling achieved a popularity rivaling that of baseball. Like croquet, cycling brought men and women together, combining opportunities for courtship and exercise. Moreover, the bicycle played an influential role in freeing women from the constraints of Victorian fashions. In order to ride the dropped-frame female models, women had to wear divided skirts and simple undergarments. Gradually, cycling costumes influenced everyday fashions. As the 1900 census declared, "Few articles . . . have created so great a revolution in social conditions as the bicycle."

Other sports had their own patrons. Tennis and golf attracted both sexes but remained pastimes of the wealthy. Played mostly at private clubs, these sports lacked baseball's team competition and cycling's informality. American football also began as a sport for people of high social rank. As an intercollegiate competition, football attracted players and spectators wealthy enough to have access to higher education. By the end of the century, however, the game was appealing to a broader audience. The 1893 Princeton-Yale game drew fifty thousand spectators.

Football

At the same time, college football became a national scandal because of its violence and its use of "tramp athletes," nonstudents whom colleges hired to help their teams win. The scandals climaxed in 1905, when 18 players died from game-related injuries and over 150 were seriously injured. President Theodore Roosevelt, a strong advocate of athletics, convened a White House conference to discuss ways to eliminate brutality and foul play. The conference founded the Intercollegiate Athletic Association (renamed the National College Athletic Association in 1910) to police college sports. In 1906 the association altered the game to make football less violent and more open.

As more women enrolled in college, they began to pursue physical activities besides croquet and cycling. Believing that intellectual success required active and healthy bodies, college women participated in sports such as rowing, track, and swimming. Eventually women made basketball their most popular intercollegiate sport. Invented in 1891 as a winter sport for men, basketball was given women's rules (which limited dribbling and running and encouraged passing) by Senda Berenson of Smith College in the 1890s.

Paralleling the rise of sports, American show business also became a mode of leisure created by and for common people. Circuses—traveling shows of acrobats and animals—had existed since the 1820s. But after the Civil War, railroads enabled them to

Circuses

reach cities and towns across the country. Circuses offered two main attractions: so-called freaks of nature, both human and animal, and the temptation and conquest of death. At the heart of their appeal was the astonishment that trapeze artists, lion tamers, acrobats, and clowns aroused.

Three branches of American show business— popular drama, musical comedy, and vaudeville— matured with the growth of cities. Theatrical performances offered audiences an escape from the harshness of urban-industrial life into melodrama, adventure, and comedy. Plots were simple, the heroes and villains recognizable. For urbanized people unfamiliar with the frontier, popular plays brought to life the mythical Wild West and Old South through stories of Buffalo Bill and Civil War romances. Virtue, honor, and justice always triumphed in melodramas, reinforcing faith that in an uncertain and disillusioning world, goodness would prevail.

Popular Drama and Musical Comedy

Musical comedies entertained audiences with song, humor, and dance. American musical comedy grew out of lavishly costumed operettas common in Europe. By introducing American themes (often involving ethnic groups), folksy humor, and catchy tunes, these shows featured the nation's most popular songs and entertainers. Comic opera, too, became popular. The first American comic operas imitated European musicals, but by the early 1900s composers like Victor Herbert were writing for American audiences. Shortly thereafter Jerome Kern began to compose more sophisticated musicals, and American musical comedy came into its own.

Vaudeville was probably the most popular entertainment in early-twentieth-century America. Shows included, in rapid succession, acts of jugglers, dancing bears, pantomimists, storytellers, magicians, puppeteers, acrobats, comedians, singers, and dancers. Around 1900, the number of vaudeville theaters and troupes skyrocketed. The famous promoter Florenz Ziegfeld brilliantly packaged shows in a stylish format—the Ziegfeld Follies—and gave the nation a new model of femininity, the Ziegfeld Girl, whose graceful dancing and alluring costumes suggested a haunting sensuality.

Vaudeville

Show business provided new opportunities for female, African American, and immigrant performers, but it also encouraged stereotyping and exploitation. Comic opera diva Lillian Russell, vaudeville singer-comedienne Fanny Brice, and burlesque queen Eva Tanguay attracted intensely loyal fans, commanded handsome fees, and won respect for their talents. But lesser female performers were often exploited by male promoters and theater owners, many of whom wanted only to titillate the public, for a price, with the sight of scantily clad women.

Before the 1890s, the chief form of commercial entertainment open to African American performers was the minstrel show, but vaudeville opened new opportunities to them. As stage settings shifted from the plantation to the city, music shifted from folk tunes to ragtime. Pandering to the prejudices of white audiences, composers and performers of both races ridiculed blacks. Even Burt Williams, a talented and highly paid black comedian and dancer who achieved success by playing stereotypical roles of darky and dandy, was tormented by the humiliation he had to suffer.

An ethnic flavor gave much of American mass entertainment its uniqueness. Indeed, immigrants occupied the core of American show business. Vaudeville in particular utilized ethnic humor, exaggerating dialects and other national traits. Skits and songs reinforced ethnic stereotypes and made fun of ethnic groups, but such distortions were more self-conscious and sympathetic than those directed at blacks.

Shortly after 1900, live entertainment began to yield to a more accessible form of amusement: moving pictures. Perfected by Thomas Edison in the 1880s, movies began as slot-machine peepshows in penny arcades and billiard parlors. Eventually images were projected onto a screen so that large audiences could view them, and a new medium was born.

Movies

Producers soon discovered that a film could tell a story in exciting ways. Thanks to creative directors like D. W. Griffith, motion pictures became a distinct art form. Griffith's *Birth of a Nation* (1915), an epic film about the Civil War and Reconstruction, fanned racial prejudice by depicting African Americans as threats to white moral values. The National Association for the Advancement of Colored People (NAACP), formed in 1909, led an organized protest against it. But the film's

innovative techniques—close-ups, fade-outs, and battle scenes—heightened the drama.

The still camera, modernized by inventor George Eastman, enabled ordinary people to record their own visual images, especially useful for preserving family memories. The phonograph, another Edison invention, brought musical performances into the home. The spread of movies, photography, and phonograph records meant that access to live performances no longer limited people's exposure to art and entertainment. By making it possible to mass-produce sound and images, technology made entertainment a highly desirable consumer good.

News also became a consumer product. Joseph Pulitzer, a Hungarian immigrant who bought the *New York World* in 1883, pioneered journalism as a branch of mass culture. He filled the *World* with stories of disasters, crimes, and scandals. Sensational headlines, set in large bold type like that used for advertisements, screamed from every page. Pulitzer's journalists not only reported news but sought it out and even created it. *World* reporter Nellie Bly (real name, Elizabeth Cochrane), for instance, faked her way into an insane asylum and wrote a brazen exposé of the sordid conditions she found. Pulitzer also popularized comics, and the yellow ink they were printed in gave rise to the term *yellow journalism* as a synonym for sensationalism. Because of *World*'s success, other publishers adopted Pulitzer's techniques. Soon, yellow journalism became a nationwide phenomenon, feeding interest in bizarre aspects of the human condition.

Yellow Journalism

Pulitzer and his rivals boosted circulation further by emphasizing sports and women's news. Newspapers had previously reported sporting events, but yellow-journalism papers gave such stories far greater prominence by printing separate, expanded sports pages. Publishers also added special sections devoted to household tips, fashion, decorum, and club news to capture female readers. Like crime and disaster stories, sports and women's sections helped to make news a mass commodity.

By the early twentieth century, mass-circulation magazines were overshadowing the expensive elitist journals of earlier eras. Publications such as *McClure's* and *Ladies' Home Journal* offered human-interest sto-

Magazines ries, muckraking exposés, titillating fiction, photographs, and eye-catching ads to a growing mass market. Meanwhile, the total number of books published more than quadrupled between 1880 and 1917. This rising popular consumption of news and books reflected growing literacy.

Other forms of communication also expanded. In 1891 there was fewer than one telephone for every 100 people in the United States; by 1921 the number had swelled to 12.6. In 1900 Americans used 4 billion postage stamps; in 1922 they used 14.3 billion. The term *community* took on new dimensions, as people used the media, mail, and telephone to extend their horizons far beyond their immediate localities. More than ever before, people in different parts of the country knew about and discussed the same news event. America was becoming a mass society.

To some extent, the cities' new amusements and pastimes had a homogenizing influence, bringing together ethnic and social groups to share a common experience. Yet different groups of consumers often used these amusements to reinforce their own cultural habits. In some cities, for example, working-class immigrants occupied parks and amusement areas as sites for family and ethnic gatherings. To the dismay of reformers who hoped that recreation would assimilate newcomers and teach them habits of restraint, immigrants used picnics and Fourth of July celebrations as occasions for boisterous drinking and sometimes violent behavior.

Mass Culture and Americanization

Summary

Much of what American society is today originated in the urbanization of the late nineteenth and early twentieth centuries. This was an era when native inventiveness met the traditions of European, African, and Asian cultures. The result was the forging of a new kind of society.

American cities exhibited bewildering diversity. Fearful and puzzled, native-born whites tried to Americanize and uplift immigrants, but newcomers stubbornly strained to protect their cultures. Optimists had envisioned the American nation as a melting pot, where various nationalities would blend to become a unified people. Instead, the United States became a culturally pluralistic society—not so much a melting pot as a salad bowl, where ingredients retained their original flavor and occasionally blended.

Pluralism and interest-group loyalties enhanced the importance of politics. If America was not a melting pot, then different groups were competing for power, wealth, and status. Some people carried polarization to extremes and tried to suppress everything allegedly un-American. Efforts to enforce homogeneity generally failed, however. By 1920, immigrants and their offspring outnumbered the native-born in many cities, and the national economy depended on these new workers and consumers. Migrants and immigrants transformed the United States into an urban nation. They gave American culture its rich and varied texture, and they laid the foundations for the liberalism that characterized American politics in the twentieth century.

LEGACY FOR A PEOPLE AND A NATION
Ethnic Food

Today, an ordinary American might eat a bagel for breakfast, a gyro sandwich for lunch, and wonton soup, shrimp creole, and rice pilaf for dinner, followed by chocolate mousse and espresso. These items, each identified with a different ethnic group, serve as tasty reminders that immigrants made important and lasting contributions to the nation's culinary culture. Yet also, the American diet represents one of the few genuine ways that the multicultural nation has served as a melting pot.

The American taste for ethnic food has a complicated history. Since the nineteenth century, the food business has offered immigrant entrepreneurs lucrative opportunities, many of which involved products unrelated to their own ethnic background. The industry is replete with success stories linked to names of immigrants such as Hector Boiardi (Chef Boyardee), William Gebhardt (Eagle Brand chili and tamales), and Jeno Paulucci (Chun-King). But Americans have also supported unheralded immigrant merchants and restaurateurs who have offered special and regional fare—German, Chinese, Italian, Tex-Mex, "soul food," or Thai—in every era.

Unlike the strife that occurred over housing, jobs, schools, and politics when different nationalities collided, the evolution of American eating habits has been extremely peaceful. Occasionally, criticisms developed, such as when dietitians and reformers in the early twentieth century charged that Mexican immigrants were harming their digestion by overusing tomatoes and peppers and that the rich foods of eastern European Jews made them overly emotional and less capable of assimilating. But as historian Donna Gabaccia has observed, relatively conflict-free sharing and borrowing have characterized American foodways far more than "food fights" and intolerance.

As each wave of immigrants has entered the nation, food has given them certain ways of becoming American, of finding some form of group acceptance, while also giving them a means of confirming their identity. At the same time, those who already thought of themselves as Americans have willingly made the cuisine of the newcomers a part of the existing culture and a part of themselves.

For Further Reading, see the Appendix. For Web resources, go to history.college.hmco.com/students.

20

GILDED AGE POLITICS

1877–1900

Associates called him "Pitchfork Ben" because when he ran for the U.S. Senate in 1894, he promised to "stick a pitchfork" into Grover Cleveland to make the president more receptive to his ideas. A former slaveholder, he epitomized southern extremism. He never wavered in his belief that African Americans were inferior to whites, and he worked to exclude them from voting and advocated lynching in cases of rape. Yet Benjamin Tillman, two-term governor and four-term senator from South Carolina, also helped his state open new colleges, supported laws to regulate railroads, accused steelmakers of profiting at public expense, equalized state taxes, increased the education budget, helped secure direct primaries for nomination of state officers, and fought tirelessly on behalf of embattled farmers.

Tillman's turbulent career paralleled an eventful era, one that can be characterized by three themes: special interests, legislative accomplishment, and political exclusion. When he attacked those whom he accused of exploiting farmers, Tillman expressed the growing dissatisfaction with the ways in which powerful private interests—manufacturers, railroad managers, bankers, and wealthy men in general—were exercising monumental greed in large corporations across the continent. The era's venality seemed so widespread that when, in 1874, Mark Twain and Charles Dudley Warner satirized America as a land of shallow money grubbers in their novel, *The Gilded Age*, the name stuck. Historians have used the expression "Gilded Age" to characterize the late nineteenth century.

347

At the same time, Tillman's economic and political reforms reflected the era's accomplishments not just at the state level, but also at the national level. Between 1877 and 1900, industrialization, urbanization, and the commercialization of agriculture altered national politics and government as much as they shaped everyday life. Congress achieved legislative landmarks in railroad regulation, tariffs, currency, civil service, and other important issues. Even so, exclusion—the third phenomenon—prevented the majority of Americans—including women, southern blacks, Indians, uneducated whites, and unnaturalized immigrants—from voting and from access to the tools of democracy.

Until the 1890s, the three phenomena of special interests, accomplishment, and exclusion existed within a delicate political equilibrium characterized by a stable party system and a balance of power among the country's geographical sections. Then in the 1890s rural discontent erupted in the West and South, and a deep economic depression bared flaws in the industrial system. Though he stood on the fringes of the mass agrarian reform movement, Tillman helped awaken the rural masses with his fiery rhetoric. Amid the economic and political disruption, a presidential campaign in 1896 stirred Americans as they had not been stirred for a generation. ◼

The Nature of Party Politics

At no other time in the nation's history was public interest in elections more avid than between 1870 and 1896. Consistently, 80 to 90 percent of eligible voters cast ballots in local and national elections. (Under 50 percent typically do so today.) Politics served as a form of recreation, more popular than baseball or circuses. Actual voting was only the final stage in a process that included parades, picnics, and speeches.

Party loyalty in part reflected American pluralism. As different groups competed for power, wealth, and status, they formed coalitions to achieve their goals. With some exceptions, groups who opposed government interference in matters of personal liberty identified with the Democratic Party, and those who believed government could be an agent of moral reform identified with the Republican Party. Democrats in-

Cultural-Political Alignments

cluded immigrant Catholics and Jews and would restrict government power. Republicans, most of them native-born Protestants, believed in direct government action.

At state and local levels, adherents of these two cultural traditions battled over how much control government should exercise over people's lives. The most contentious issues were use of leisure time and celebration of Sunday, the Lord's day. Protestant Republicans tried to keep the Sabbath holy through legislation that prohibited bars, stores, and commercial amusements from being open on Sundays. Immigrant Democrats, accustomed to feasting and playing after church, fought saloon closings and other restrictions on the only day they had free from work. Similar splits developed over public versus parochial schools and prohibition versus the free availability of liquor.

Allegiances to national parties and candidates were so evenly divided that no faction gained control for any sustained period of time. Between 1877 and 1897, Republicans held the presidency for three terms, Democrats for two. Rarely did the same party control both the presidency and Congress simultaneously.

Moreover, internal quarrels split both the Republican and Democratic Parties. Among Republicans, a faction known as the "Stalwarts" was led by New York's pompous Senator Roscoe Conkling. Conkling worked the spoils system to win government jobs for his supporters. The Stalwarts' rivals were the "Half Breeds," led by James G. Blaine of Maine, who pursued influence as blatantly as Conkling did. On the sidelines stood more idealistic Republicans, or "Mugwumps," such as Senator Carl Schurz of Missouri, who believed that only righteous, educated men like themselves should govern. Meanwhile, Democrats tended to subdivide into white-supremacy southerners, immigrant-stock and working-class urban political machines, and business-oriented advocates of low tariffs. Like Republicans, Democrats eagerly pursued the spoils of office.

Party Factions

At the state level, one party usually dominated, and within that party a few men typically held dictatorial power. Often the state "boss" was a senator. Until the Seventeenth Amendment to the Constitution was ratified in 1913, state legislatures elected U.S. senators, and a senator could wield enormous influence with his command of federal jobs.

IMPORTANT EVENTS

1873 Congress ends coinage of silver dollars

1874 Twain and Warner's *The Gilded Age* appears and gives a name to its era

1873–78 Economic hard times hit

1876 Hayes elected president

1877 Georgia passes poll tax and begins legislative movement to disfranchise African Americans in the South
Munn v. Illinois upholds principle of state regulation

1878 Bland-Allison Act requires Treasury to buy between $2 and $4 million in silver each month
Anthony-backed woman suffrage amendment defeated in Congress

1880 Garfield elected president

1881 Garfield assassinated; Arthur assumes the presidency

1883 Pendleton Civil Service Act creates Civil Service Commission to oversee competitive examinations for some government positions
Supreme Court strikes down 1875 Civil Rights Act

1884 Cleveland elected president

1886 *Wabash* case declares that only Congress can limit interstate commerce rates

1887 Farm prices collapse
Farmers' Alliances form
Interstate Commerce Act creates commission to regulate rates and practices of interstate shippers

1888 B. Harrison elected president

1890 Sherman Silver Purchase Act commits Treasury to buying 4.5 million ounces of silver each month
"Mississippi Plan" uses poll taxes and literacy tests to prevent African Americans from voting
National American Woman Suffrage Association formed

1892 Populist convention in Omaha draws up reform platform
Cleveland elected president

1893–97 Major economic depression hits U.S.

1893 Sherman Silver Purchase Act repealed

1894 Wilson-Gorman Tariff attempts to reduce rates; Senate Republicans restore House cuts
Eugene V. Debs arrested and turns to socialism
Coxey's army marches on Washington, D.C.

1895 Cleveland cuts deal with bankers to save gold reserves

1896 McKinley elected president
Plessy v. Ferguson establishes "separate-but-equal" doctrine, allowing segregation of African Americans in public accommodations

1897 Dingley Tariff raises duties

1898 Louisiana implements "grandfather clause" that keeps blacks from voting

1899 *Cummins v. County Board of Education* applies separate-but-equal doctrine to schools

1900 Gold Standard Act requires all paper money to be backed by gold
McKinley reelected president

Politics in the Industrial Age

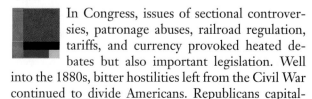 In Congress, issues of sectional controversies, patronage abuses, railroad regulation, tariffs, and currency provoked heated debates but also important legislation. Well into the 1880s, bitter hostilities left from the Civil War continued to divide Americans. Republicans capital-ized on war memories by "waving the bloody shirt" at Democrats. In the South, Democratic candidates also waved the bloody shirt, calling Republicans traitors to white supremacy and states' rights.

Other Americans also sought advantages by invoking war memories. The Grand Army of the Republic, an organization of 400,000 Union Army veterans, allied with the Republican Party and cajoled Congress

into providing generous pensions for former Union soldiers and their widows. Many pensions were deserved, but for some veterans, the war's emotional memories furnished an opportunity to profit at public expense.

Few politicians dared oppose Civil War pensions, but some attempted to dismantle the spoils system.

Civil Service Reform

The practice of awarding government jobs to party workers, regardless of their qualifications, had taken root before the Civil War and flourished after it. As the postal service, diplomatic corps, and other government agencies expanded, so did the public payroll. Between 1865 and 1891, the number of federal jobs tripled, from 53,000 to 166,000. Elected officials scrambled to control these jobs as a means of cementing support for themselves and their parties. In return for comparatively short hours and high pay, appointees to federal positions pledged their votes and a portion of their earnings to their patrons.

Shocked by such corruption, some reformers began advocating appointments and promotions based on merit rather than political connections. Civil service reform accelerated in 1881 with the formation of the National Civil Service Reform League. The same year, the assassination of President James Garfield by a demented job seeker hastened the drive for change. The Pendleton Civil Service Act, passed by Congress in 1882 and signed by President Chester Arthur in 1883, created the Civil Service Commission to oversee competitive examinations for government positions. The act gave the commission jurisdiction over only 10 percent of federal jobs, though the president could expand the list.

Veterans' pensions and civil service reform were not representative issues of the Gilded Age, however. Rather, economic policymaking occupied congressional business more than ever before. Railroad expansion had become a particularly controversial issue. As the rail network spread, so did competition. In their quest for customers, railroad lines reduced rates to outmaneuver rivals, but rate wars cut into profits and wildly fluctuating rates angered shippers and farmers. On noncompetitive routes, railroads often boosted charges as high as possible to compensate for unprofitably low rates on competitive routes. Charges on short-distance shipments served by only one line could exceed those on long-distance shipments served by competing lines. Railroads also reduced rates to large shippers and provided free passenger passes to preferred customers and politicians.

Such favoritism stirred farmers, small merchants, and reform politicians to demand public regulation of

Railroad Regulation

railroad rates. Their efforts occurred first at the state level. By 1880 fourteen states had established commissions to limit freight and storage charges of state-chartered lines. Railroads fought these measures, arguing that the Constitution guaranteed them freedom to acquire and use property without government restraint. But in 1877, in *Munn v. Illinois*, the Supreme Court upheld the principle of state regulation.

State legislatures, however, could not regulate interstate lines, a limitation affirmed by the Supreme Court in the *Wabash* case of 1886, in which the Court declared that only Congress could limit rates involving interstate commerce. Congress responded in 1887 by passing the Interstate Commerce Act. The law prohibited pools, rebates, and long-haul/short-haul rate discrimination, and it created the Interstate Commerce Commission (ICC) to investigate railroad rate-making methods, issue cease-and-desist orders against illegal practices, and seek court aid to enforce compliance. The legislation's lack of provisions for enforcement, however, left railroads room for evasion, and federal judges chipped away at ICC powers. In the *Maximum Freight Rate* case (1897), the Supreme Court ruled that the ICC did not have power to set rates; and in the *Alabama Midlands* case (1897), the Court overturned prohibitions against long-haul/short-haul discrimination. Even so, the principle of government regulation, though weakened, remained in force.

The economic issue of tariffs carried strong political implications. Congress initially had created tariffs

Tariff Policy

to protect American manufactured goods and agricultural products from European competition. But tariffs quickly became a tool by which special interests could protect and enhance their profits. By the 1880s these interests had succeeded in having tariffs applied to more than four thousand items.

The Republican Party, claiming credit for economic growth, put protective tariffs at the core of its political agenda. Democrats opposed tariffs that made prices artificially high by keeping out less expensive foreign goods, thereby benefiting manufacturers while hurting farmers whose crops were not protected and consumers who had to buy manufactured goods. While Democrats acknowledged a need for tariff protection of some manufactured goods and raw materials, they favored lower rates to encourage foreign trade and to reduce a Treasury surplus created by taxes, tariffs, and other levies.

Manufacturers and their congressional allies maintained control over tariff policy. The McKinley Tariff of 1890 boosted already-high rates by another 4 percent. When House Democrats supported by President Grover Cleveland passed a bill to reduce tariff rates in 1894, Senate Republicans, aided by southern Democrats eager to protect their region's infant industries, added six hundred amendments restoring most of the cuts (Wilson-Gorman Tariff). In 1897 the Dingley Tariff raised rates further.

Monetary policy aroused even stronger emotions than tariffs did. When increased industrial and agricultural production caused prices to fall after the Civil War, debtors and creditors had opposing reactions. Farmers suffered because the prices they received for their crops were dropping, but they had to pay high interest rates on money they borrowed to pay off their mortgages and other debts. They favored schemes like the coinage of silver to increase the amount of currency in circulation. An expanded money supply, they reasoned, would reduce interest rates, making their debts less burdensome, and their costs would be lower relative to the prices they received for their crops. Creditors believed that overproduction had caused prices to decline. They favored a more stable, limited money supply backed only by gold as the best means to protect their wealth and maintain investors' confidence in the U.S. economy.

Monetary Policy

Arguments over the quantity and quality of money, however, transcended economics. Creditor-debtor tension translated into class divisions between haves and have-nots. The debate also represented sectional cleavages: western silver-mining areas and agricultural regions of the South and West against the more conservative industrial Northeast.

By the 1870s, the currency controversy had boiled down to gold versus silver. Previously, the government had bought both gold and silver to back the national currency, setting a ratio that made a gold dollar worth sixteen times the value of a silver dollar. Mining discoveries after 1848, however, increased the supply of gold and lowered its market price relative to that of silver. As a result, silver dollars disappeared from circulation—because of their inflated value relative to gold, owners hoarded them—and in 1873 Congress officially stopped coining silver dollars, an act that silver partisans later called the "Crime of '73." Europeans also stopped buying silver, and the United States and many of its trading partners unofficially adopted the gold standard, meaning that their currency was backed chiefly by gold.

Within a few years, new mines in the American West began to flood the market with silver, and its price dropped. Gold then became worth more than sixteen times the value of silver, and it became profitable to spend rather than hoard silver dollars. Silver producers wanted the government to resume buying silver at the old sixteen-to-one ratio, which amounted to a subsidy because it would let them sell silver to the government for more than the market price. Debtors, hurt by falling prices and the economic hard times of 1873–1878, saw silver as a means of expanding the currency supply. They joined with silver producers to denounce the "Crime of '73" and to press for resumption of silver coinage at the old sixteen-to-one ratio.

With both parties split into silver and gold factions, Congress at first tried to compromise. The Bland-Allison Act of 1878 authorized the Treasury to buy between $2 million and $4 million worth of silver each month, and the Sherman Silver Purchase Act of 1890 increased the government's monthly purchase of silver by specifying weight (4.5 million ounces) rather than dollars. Neither act satisfied the different interest groups. The government paid for the silver with Treasury notes, not with gold dollars as silver interests wanted. Moreover, the acts failed to expand the money supply as substantially as debtors had hoped and failed to erase the impression that the government favored creditors' interests.

National politics was not a glamorous field of endeavor in the Gilded Age. Senators and representatives received small salaries and usually had the financial burden of maintaining two homes: one in their home districts and one in Washington. Most members of Congress had

Legislative Accomplishments

no private office space, only a desk. They worked long hours responding to constituents' requests, wrote their own speeches, and had to pay for staff out of their own pockets. Yet, cynics to the contrary, most politicians were principled and dedicated and managed to deal with important issues and pass significant legislation.

The Presidency Restrengthened

 Operating under the cloud of Andrew Johnson's impeachment, Grant's scandals, and doubts about the legitimacy of the election of 1876, American presidents between 1877 and 1900 moved gingerly to restore the authority of their office. Proper and honest, Presidents Rutherford Hayes (1877–1881), James Garfield (1881), Chester Arthur (1881–1885), Grover Cleveland (1885–1889 and 1893–1897), Benjamin Harrison (1889–1893), and William McKinley (1897–1901) tried to act as legislative as well as administrative leaders. Moreover, each of these presidents initiated legislation and used the veto to guide national policy.

Rutherford B. Hayes, a former Ohio congressman, emphasized national harmony over sectional rivalry and opposed violence of all kinds. He tried to overhaul the spoils system by appointing civil service reformer Carl Schurz to his cabinet and by battling New York's patronage king, Senator Conkling. Though he was too cautious to use government power to do so, Hayes believed society was obligated to help the oppressed, including American Chinese and Indians.

Hayes, Garfield, and Arthur

When Hayes declined to run for reelection in 1880, Republicans nominated another Ohio congressman and Civil War hero, James A. Garfield. A solemn and cautious man, Garfield defeated Democrat Winfield Scott Hancock, also a Civil War hero, by just forty thousand votes out of 9 million cast.

Garfield spent most of his brief presidency trying to secure an independent position among party potentates. He hoped to reduce the tariff and develop economic relations with Latin America but had to spend most days dealing with hordes of men seeking government jobs. His chance to make lasting contributions ended in July 1881 when Charles Guiteau, a disappointed patronage seeker, shot him in a Washington railroad station. Garfield lingered for seventy-nine days, but then succumbed to infection and died on September 19.

Garfield's successor was Vice President Chester A. Arthur, a New York spoilsman whom Hayes had fired in 1878. Republicans had nominated Arthur for vice president only to help Garfield carry New York State. Though his elevation to the presidency made reformers shudder, Arthur became a dignified and temperate executive. He signed the Pendleton Civil Service Act, urged Congress to modify outdated tariff rates, and supported federal regulation of railroads. He wielded the veto aggressively, killing several bills that excessively benefited railroads and corporations. But congressional partisans frustrated his plans for reducing the tariff and strengthening the navy. Arthur wanted to run for reelection in 1884 but lost the nomination to James G. Blaine.

To oppose Blaine, Democrats named New York's governor Grover Cleveland. On election day Cleveland beat Blaine by only 29,000 popular votes; his tiny margin of 1,149 votes in New York gave him that state's 36 electoral votes, enough for a 219-to-182 victory in the electoral college. Cleveland may have won New York thanks to last-minute remarks of a local Protestant minister, who equated Democrats with "rum, Romanism, and rebellion." Democrats eagerly publicized the slur among New York's large Irish-Catholic population, urging voters to protest by supporting Cleveland.

Cleveland, the first Democratic president since James Buchanan (1857–1861), expanded civil service, vetoed hundreds of private pension bills, and urged Congress to cut tariffs on raw materials and manufactured goods. When advisers warned that his stand might weaken his chances for reelection, the president retorted, "What is the use of being elected or reelected, unless you stand for something?" But the Mills tariff bill of 1888, passed by the House in response to Cleveland's wishes, died in the Senate.

Cleveland and Harrison

Republicans in 1888 nominated Benjamin Harrison, grandson of President William Henry Harrison (1841), to oppose Cleveland. During the campaign, both parties engaged in political chicanery. Both parties also indulged in bribery and vote fraud, but in this election Republicans proved more successful at such deceits. Bribery and multiple voting helped Harrison carry Indiana by 2,300 votes and New York by 14,000. Those states ensured Harrison's victory. Though Cleveland outpolled Harrison by 90,000 popular votes, Harrison carried the electoral vote by 233 to 168.

Harrison was the first president since 1875 whose party had majorities in both houses of Congress. Using a variety of methods, ranging from threats of vetoes to informal dinners and consultations, Harrison influenced the course of legislation. He also showed support for civil service by appointing the reformer Theodore Roosevelt a civil service commissioner, but yielded to pressure by signing the Dependents' Pension Act. The law doubled the number of welfare recipients by providing pensions for Union veterans who had suffered war-related disabilities and granted aid to their widows and minor children.

The Pension Act and other appropriations pushed the federal budget past $1 billion in 1890 for the first time in the nation's history. Democrats blamed the "Billion-Dollar Congress" on spendthrift Republicans. Seeking to capitalize on voter unrest, Democrats nominated Cleveland to run against Harrison again in 1892. This time Cleveland attracted large contributions from business and beat Harrison.

In office again, Cleveland moved boldly to address problems of currency, tariffs, and labor unrest. But his actions reflected a narrow orientation toward interests of business and bespoke political weakness. During his campaign Cleveland had promised sweeping tariff reform, but he made little effort to line up support in the Senate. And during the Pullman strike of 1894, Cleveland bowed to requests from railroad managers and Attorney General Richard Olney to send in troops. Throughout Cleveland's second term an economic downturn and agrarian ferment seemed to overwhelm the president.

Limits of Gilded Age Politics

Though the scope and size of government activity expanded during the Gilded Age, policies of discrimination and exclusion continued. In the South poor whites, facing economic losses, feared that newly enfranchised African Americans would challenge whatever political

and social superiority (real and imagined) they enjoyed. Wealthy white landowners and merchants fanned these fears, using racism to divide whites and blacks and to distract poor whites from protesting their own economic subjugation.

The majority of the nation's African Americans lived in the South. The abolition of slavery had not markedly improved their economic opportunities. In 1880, 90 percent of all southern blacks depended for a living on farming or personal and domestic service—the same occupations they had held as slaves. The New South, moreover, proved to be as violent for blacks as the Old South had been. Between 1889 and 1909, more than seventeen hundred African Americans were lynched in the South. Most lynchings occurred in sparsely populated districts, and most victims were accused of an assault—rarely proved—on a white woman.

Violence Against African Americans

With slavery dead, white supremacists fashioned further ways to keep blacks in a position of inferiority. Southern leaders, embittered by northern interference in race relations during Reconstruction and eager to reassert authority over people whom they believed to be inferior, instituted measures to prevent blacks from voting and to segregate them legally from whites.

After Reconstruction blacks continued to vote and remained the backbone of the southern Republican Party. White politicians sought to discourage the "Negro vote" by imposing restrictions that appeared neutral but actually barred blacks from the polls. Beginning with Georgia in 1877, southern states levied taxes of $1 to $2 on all citizens wishing to vote. These poll taxes proved prohibitive to poor black voters.

Disfranchisement Begins

Disfranchisement was accomplished in other devious ways as well. The Supreme Court affirmed in *U.S. v. Reese* (1876) that the Fifteenth Amendment prohibited states from denying the vote only "on account of race, color, or previous condition of servitude." This narrow interpretation cleared a path for states to find ways to exclude black voters without mentioning race, color, or servitude. For instance, an 1890 state constitutional convention established the "Mississippi Plan," requiring all voters to pay a poll tax eight months before each election, to present the tax receipt at election

In the years after Reconstruction, lynchings of African American men occurred with increasing frequency, chiefly in sparsely populated areas where whites looked on strangers, especially black strangers, with fear and suspicion. (Index Stock Photography)

acy requirements. Thus the total number of eligible voters in Mississippi shrank from 257,000 in 1876 to 77,000 in 1892.

Racial discrimination also stiffened in social affairs. In a series of cases during the 1870s, the Supreme

Legal Segregation

Court opened the door to discrimination by ruling that the Fourteenth Amendment protected citizens' rights only against infringement by state governments. The federal government, according to the Court, lacked authority over what individuals or organizations might do. If blacks wanted legal protection, the Court said, they must seek it from the states.

These rulings climaxed in 1883 when in the *Civil Rights* cases the Court struck down the 1875 Civil Rights Act, which had prohibited segregation in public facilities such as streetcars, hotels, theaters, and parks. Subsequent lower court rulings established the principle that blacks could be restricted to "separate but equal" facilities. The Supreme Court upheld the separate-but-equal doctrine in *Plessy v. Ferguson* (1896) and applied it to schools in *Cummins v. County Board of Education* (1899).

Thereafter, segregation laws—known as Jim Crow laws—multiplied throughout the South, confronting African Americans with daily reminders of their inferior status. State and local laws restricted them to the rear of streetcars, to separate public drinking fountains and toilets, and to separate sections of hospitals and cemeteries. Atlanta even mandated separate Bibles for the swearing-in of black witnesses in court.

As African American men were being pushed out of public life, African American women began using their traditional roles as mothers, educators, and moral guardians to seek services and reforms that reflected subtle yet important political activity. They participated in successful lobbying of local and state governments in the South for reforms such as cleaner city streets, better public health, expanded charity services, and vocational education. In less threatening means than casting ballots, black women found ways to join with white women in campaigns to improve the general community and to negotiate with the white male power structure to achieve their goals.

Women also contended head-on with male power structures. During the twenty years following the ex-

time, and to prove that they could read and interpret the state constitution. In 1898 Louisiana enacted the first "grandfather clause," which established literacy and property qualifications for voting but exempted sons and grandsons of those eligible to vote before 1867, the year the Fifteenth Amendment had gone into effect. Other southern states initiated similar measures.

By the 1900s African Americans had effectively lost political rights in every southern state except Tennessee. Disfranchisement also affected poor whites, few of whom could meet poll tax, property, and liter-

Woman Suffrage

tension of the vote to black men, two organizations—the National Woman Suffrage Association (NWSA) and the American Woman Suffrage Association (AWSA)—battled for female suffrage. The NWSA, led by militants Elizabeth Cady Stanton and Susan B. Anthony, advocated comprehensive women's rights in courts and workplaces as well as at the ballot box. The AWSA, led by former abolitionists Lucy Stone and Thomas Wentworth Higginson, focused more narrowly on suffrage.

In 1878 Susan B. Anthony persuaded Senator A. A. Sargent of California to introduce a constitutional amendment stating that "the right of citizens of the United States to vote shall not be denied or abridged by the United States or by any state on account of sex." A Senate committee killed the bill, but the NWSA had it reintroduced repeatedly over the next eighteen years. On the few occasions when the bill reached the

Senate floor, it was voted down by senators who claimed that suffrage would interfere with women's family obligations.

While the NWSA fought for suffrage on the national level, the AWSA worked to amend state constitutions. (The groups merged in 1890 to form the National American Woman Suffrage Association.) Women did win partial victories. Between 1870 and 1910, eleven states (mostly in the West) legalized woman suffrage. By 1890 nineteen states allowed women to vote on school issues, and three granted suffrage on tax and bond issues.

Agrarian Unrest and Populism

 While voting concerned those suffering from political exclusion, inequities in the economic order sparked a mass movement that would shake American society. The

Livingstone College in North Carolina was one of several institutions of higher learning established by and for African Americans in the late nineteenth century. With a curriculum that emphasized training for educational and religious work in the South and in Africa, these colleges were coeducational, operating on the belief that both men and women could have public roles. (Courtesy of Heritage Hall, Livingstone College, Salisbury, North Carolina)

agrarian revolt began in Grange organizations in the early 1870s. The revolt accelerated when Farmers' Alliances, first formed in Texas in the late 1870s, spread across the Cotton Belt and Great Plains in the 1880s. The Alliance movement had appeal chiefly in areas where tenancy, debt, railroads, weather, and insects threatened the well-being of hopeful farmers. Once under way, the agrarian rebellion inspired visions of a truly cooperative and democratic society.

Agricultural expansion in the West and Great Plains exposed millions of people to the hardships of rural life. Farmers who had moved into these areas knew life would be hard, but they had hoped that the rewards would be more promising than they turned out to be.

Following the Civil War, landlords who employed sharecroppers and tenants dominated southern agriculture. Sharecropping and tenant

Sharecropping and Tenant Farming in the South

farming entangled millions of black and white southerners in a web of debt and humiliation, at whose center stood the crop lien. Most farmers, too poor to have cash on hand, borrowed in order to buy necessities. They could offer as collateral only what they could grow. A farmer in need of supplies dealt with a nearby "furnishing merchant," who would exchange supplies for a lien, or legal claim, on the farmer's forthcoming crop. After the crop was harvested and brought to market, the merchant collected his debt. All too often the debt exceeded the crop's value and the farmer— still in need of food and supplies for the coming year— had no choice but to sink deeper into debt by reborrowing and giving the merchant a new lien on his next crop.

Merchants frequently took advantage of indebted farmers' powerlessness by inflating prices and charging them interest ranging from 33 to 200 percent on the advances they received. Suppose, for example, that a cash-poor farmer needed a 20-cent bag of seed. The furnishing merchant would sell him the seed on credit but would boost the price to 28 cents. At year's end that 28-cent loan would have accumulated interest, raising the farmer's debt to 42 cents—more than double the item's original cost. The farmer, having pledged more than his crop's worth against scores of such debts, fell behind on payments and never recovered. If he fell too far behind, he could be evicted.

Because the holders of crop liens insisted that debtors grow cotton, the system trapped farmers in the backcountry as well as the old plantation South. Prior to the Civil War, backcountry yeomen had practiced diversified farming. Now, when they fell into debt, they had to plant cotton and buy foods they had formerly grown.

In the Midwest, as growers cultivated more land, as mechanization boosted productivity, and as foreign competition increased, supplies

Hardship in the Midwest and West

exceeded national and worldwide demand for agricultural products. Consequently, prices for staple crops dropped steadily. A bushel of wheat that sold for $1.45 in 1866 brought only 49 cents by the mid-1890s. Meanwhile, transportation and storage fees remained high relative to other prices. Expenses for seed, fertilizer, manufactured goods, taxes, and mortgage interest trapped many farm families in troubling and sometimes desperate circumstances. In order to buy necessities and pay bills, farmers had to produce more. But the spiral wound ever more tightly: the more farmers produced, the lower prices for their crops dropped.

The West suffered from special hardships. Charges of monopolistic control by railroads echoed among farmers, miners, and stockmen in Wyoming and Montana. In California, Washington, and Oregon, wheat and fruit growers found their opportunities reduced by railroads' control of transportation and storage rates.

Even before they felt the full impact of these developments, farmers began to organize. With aid from

Grange Movement

Oliver H. Kelley, a clerk in the Department of Agriculture, farmers in almost every state during the 1860s and 1870s founded local organizations called Granges. By 1875 the Grange had twenty thousand branches and a million members. Strongest in the Midwest and South, Granges at first served a chiefly social function, sponsoring meetings and educational events to relieve the loneliness of farm life.

As membership flourished, Granges turned to economic and political action. Local branches formed cooperative associations to buy supplies and to market crops and livestock. In a few instances, Grangers operated farm-implement factories and insurance companies. Most of these enterprises failed, however, because farmers lacked capital for cooperative buying and because competition from large manufacturers and dealers undercut them.

Grangers had some political successes, convincing states to establish agricultural colleges, electing sympathetic legislators, and pressing for so-called Granger laws to regulate transportation and storage rates. But these efforts faltered when corporations won court support to overturn Granger laws. Thus after a brief assertion of economic and political influence, Granges again became farmers' social clubs.

In the Southwest, the movement of English-speaking ranchers into communal pastureland used by Mexican farmers and villagers sparked another kind of agrarian protest. In the late 1880s, a group calling itself *Las Gorras Blancas*, or White Hats, believed that they should have control of lands that their Mexican ancestors had once held. They harassed Anglo ranchers and destroyed the fences that they had erected on public land. In 1889, *Las Gorras Blancas* proclaimed "Our purpose is to protect the rights and interest of the people in general and especially those of the helpless classes." Their cause, however, could not keep Anglos from legally buying and using public land, and by 1900 many Hispanics had given up farming on their own to work as agricultural laborers or to migrate into the cities.

The White Hats

By 1890 rural activism shifted to the Farmers' Alliances. The first Farmers' Alliances arose in Texas, where hard-pressed small farmers rallied against crop liens, merchants, and railroads in particular, and against money power in general. Using traveling lecturers to recruit members, Alliance leaders extended the movement into other southern states. By 1889 the Southern Alliance boasted 2 million members, and a separate Colored Farmers' National Alliance claimed over 1 million black members. A similar movement flourished in the Plains, which by the late 1880s organized 2 million members in Kansas, Nebraska, and the Dakotas.

Farmers' Alliances

Farmers' Alliances advocated cooperative buying and selling agreements and proposed the subtreasury plan to relieve shortages of cash and credit. The plan, originating in 1890, had two parts. One called for the federal government to construct warehouses where farmers could store nonperishable crops while awaiting higher prices; the government would then loan farmers Treasury notes amounting to 80 percent of the market price that the stored crops would bring. Farmers could use these notes as legal tender to pay debts and make purchases. Once the stored crops were sold, farmers would repay the loans plus small interest and storage fees. The second part of the subtreasury plan would have the government provide low-interest loans to farmers who wanted to buy land.

Subtreasury Plan

If all Farmers' Alliances had been able to unite, they would have made a formidable political force, but sectional and racial differences thwarted early attempts at merging. Differences on issues also prevented unity. Northern farmers, mostly Republicans, wanted protective tariffs to keep out foreign grain. White southerners, mostly Democrats, wanted low tariffs to hold down costs of foreign manufactured goods. Northern and Southern Alliances both favored government regulation of transportation and communications, equitable taxation, currency reform, and prohibition of landownership by foreign investors.

Growing membership and rising confidence drew Alliances more deeply into politics. By 1890 farmers had elected several officeholders sympathetic to their programs, especially in the South. In the Midwest, Alliance candidates often ran on third-party tickets and achieved some success in Kansas, Nebraska, and the Dakotas. During the summer of 1890, the Kansas Alliance held a "convention of the people" and nominated candidates who swept the state's fall elections. Formation of this People's Party, whose members were called Populists (from *populus*, the Latin word for "people"), gave a title to Alliance political activism. Two years later, after overcoming sectional differences, Northern and Southern Alliance leaders summoned a People's Party convention in Omaha on July 4 to draft a platform and nominate a presidential candidate.

Rise of Populism

The new party's Omaha platform was an extraordinary reform document that addressed three central sources of rural unrest: transportation, land, and money. Frustrated with weak state and federal regulation, Populists demanded government ownership of railroad and telegraph lines. They urged the federal government to reclaim all land owned for speculative purposes by railroads and foreigners. The monetary plank called on the government to expand the currency by printing money to be made available for farm loans and by basing the money on free and unlimited coinage of silver. Other planks advocated a graduated income tax, postal savings banks, direct election of U.S. senators, and a shorter workday. As its presidential candidate, the People's Party nominated James B. Weaver of Iowa, a former Union general and supporter of an increased money supply.

Weaver garnered 8 percent of the popular vote in 1892, majorities in four states, and twenty-two electoral votes. Not since 1856 had a third party done so well in its first national effort. Nevertheless, the party faced a dilemma of whether to uphold its principles at all costs or compromise in order to gain power. The election had been successful for Populists only in the West. The vote-rich Northeast had ignored Weaver, and Alabama was the only southern state that gave Populists as much as one-third of its votes.

Although Populists were flawed egalitarians—they mistrusted blacks and foreigners—they sought change in order to fulfill their version of American ideals. Amid hardship and desperation, millions of people began to believe that a cooperative democracy in which government would ensure equal opportunity could overcome corporate power.

The Depression of the 1890s

In 1893, shortly before Grover Cleveland's second presidency, the Philadelphia and Reading Railroad, once a thriving and profitable line, went bankrupt. Like other railroads, the Philadelphia and Reading had borrowed heavily to lay track and build stations and bridges. But overexpansion cut into profits, and ultimately the company was unable to pay its debts.

The same problem beset manufacturers. For example, output at McCormick farm machinery factories was nine times greater in 1893 than in 1879, but revenues had only tripled. To compensate, the company bought more factory equipment and squeezed more work out of fewer laborers. This strategy, however, only enlarged debt and unemployment. Jobless workers found themselves in the same plight as employers:

they could not pay their creditors. Banks suffered, too, when their customers defaulted. The failure of the National Cordage Company in May 1893 accelerated a chain reaction of business and bank closings. The failures signaled the onset of a devastating depression that lasted from1893 to late 1897 and left nearly 20 percent of the population jobless.

As the depression deepened, the currency problem reached a crisis. The Sherman Silver Purchase Act of 1890 had committed the government to issue Treasury notes (silver certificates) to buy 4.5 million ounces of silver each month. These certificates could be redeemed in gold, at the ratio of one ounce of gold for every sixteen ounces of silver. But a western mining boom made silver more plentiful, causing its market value relative to gold to fall and prompting holders of Sherman silver notes and greenback currency issued during the Civil War to cash in their notes in exchange for gold, whose worth remained fairly constant. As a result, the nation's gold reserve soon dwindled, falling below the psychologically significant $100 million level in early 1893.

Continuing Currency Problems

Vowing to protect the gold reserve from redeemers of silver certificates, President Cleveland called a special session of Congress to repeal the Sherman Silver Purchase Act. Repeal passed in late 1893, but the run on the Treasury continued through 1894. In early 1895 gold reserves fell to $41 million. In desperation, Cleveland accepted an offer of 3.5 million ounces of gold in return for $65 million worth of federal bonds from a banking syndicate led by financier J. P. Morgan. When the bankers resold the bonds to the public, they made about $2 million in profits. Cleveland claimed that he had saved the gold reserves, but many saw only humiliation in the president's deal with big businessmen. "When Judas betrayed Christ," charged Senator Tillman, "his heart was not blacker than this scoundrel, Cleveland, in betraying the [Democratic Party]."

Like previous hard times, the depression ultimately ran its course. But the downturn of the 1890s hastened the crumbling of the old economic system and the emergence of a new one. Since the 1850s, railroads had steered American economic development, opening new markets,

Effects of a New Economic System

boosting steel production, and invigorating banking. The central features of a new business system—consolidation and a trend toward bigness—were beginning to solidify just when the depression hit.

The American economy had become national rather than sectional; the fate of a large business in one part of the country had repercussions elsewhere. Before the depression many companies had expanded too rapidly. When contraction occurred, their reckless debts dragged them down, and they pulled other industries with them. In early 1893, for example, five hundred banks and sixteen thousand other businesses filed for bankruptcy. European economies also slumped, and more than ever before the fortunes of one country affected the fortunes of other countries. The downward spiral ended late in 1897, but the depression exposed problems that demanded reform and set an agenda for future years.

Depression-Era Protests

The depression exposed fundamental tensions in the industrial system. Technological and organizational changes had been widening the gap between employees and employers for half a century. By the 1890s workers' protests against exploitation were threatening to spark an economic and political explosion. In 1894, the year the economy plunged into depression, there were over thirteen hundred strikes and countless riots. Contrary to accusations of business leaders, few protesters were anarchists or communists come from Europe to sabotage American democracy. Rather, the disaffected included thousands of men and women who believed that in a democracy their voices should be heard.

The era of protest began with the railroad strikes of 1877 (see page 316). The vehemence of those strikes, and the support they drew from working-class people, raised fears that the United States would experience a popular uprising like one in Paris six years earlier, which had briefly overturned the government and introduced communist principles. The Haymarket riot of 1886, a general strike in New Orleans in 1891, and a prolonged strike at the Carnegie Homestead Steel plant in 1892 (see page 317) heightened anxieties. In the West, embittered workers also took action. In 1892 violence erupted at a silver mine in Coeur d'Alene, Idaho. Angered by wage cuts and a lockout, striking miners seized the mine and battled federal troops sent to subdue them. Such defiance convinced some businessmen that only force could counter the radicalism allegedly promoted by socialists and anarchists.

Socialists

Small numbers of socialists did participate in the era's strikes, riots, and other confrontations. Furthermore, personal experience convinced many workers who never became socialists to agree with Karl Marx (1818–1883), the German philosopher and father of communism, that whoever controls the means of production holds the power to determine how well people live. Marx wrote that industrial capitalism generates profits by paying workers less than the value of their labor and that mechanization and mass production alienate workers from their labor. Marx predicted that workers throughout the world would become so discontented that they would revolt and seize factories, farms, banks, and transportation lines. This revolution would establish a socialist order of justice and equality.

In America, socialism suffered from lack of strong leadership and disagreement over how to achieve Marx's vision. Moreover, American socialist leaders failed to attract the mass of unskilled laborers, in part because they often focused on fine points of doctrine while ignoring workers' everyday needs. Social mobility and the philosophy of individualism also undermined socialist aims. Workers hoped that they or their children would benefit through education and acquisition of property or by becoming their own bosses; thus most workers sought individual advancement rather than the betterment of all.

Events in 1894 triggered changes within the socialist movement. That year an inspiring new leader arose in response to the government's quashing of the Pullman strike and of the newly formed American Railway Union. Eugene V. Debs, the union's intense and animated president, converted to socialism while serving a six-month prison term for defying an injunction against the strike. Once released, Debs became the leading spokesman for American socialism. Though never good at organizing, Debs captivated audiences with passionate eloquence and indignant attacks on the free-enterprise system.

Eugene V. Debs

In 1894 Debs shared public attention with Jacob S. Coxey, a quiet businessman from Massillon, Ohio.

Coxey's Army Like Debs, Coxey had a vision. He was convinced that, to aid debtors, the government should issue $500 million of "legal tender" paper money, make low-interest loans to local governments, and use the loans and money to pay the unemployed to build roads and other public works. He planned to publicize his scheme by leading a march from Massillon to Washington, D.C., gathering a "petition in boots" of unemployed workers along the way.

Coxey's army, about two hundred strong, left Ohio in March 1894 and, after being joined by other marchers on the road, numbered five hundred as it entered Washington on April 30. The next day (May Day, a date traditionally associated with socialist demonstrations), the group, armed with "war clubs of peace," marched to the Capitol. When Coxey and a few others vaulted the wall surrounding the Capitol grounds, mounted police moved in and routed the crowd. Coxey tried to speak from the Capitol steps, but police dragged him away. As arrests and clubbings continued, Coxey's dream of a demonstration of 400,000 jobless workers dissolved. Like the strikes, the first people's march on Washington yielded to police muscle.

Coxey's troops merely wanted more jobs and better living standards. Today, in an age of union contracts, regulation of business, and government-sponsored unemployment relief, their goals do not appear radical. The brutal reactions of officials, however, reveal how threatening dissenters such as Coxey and Debs seemed to defenders of the existing social order.

Populists, the Silver Crusade, and the Election of 1896

Populists encountered roadblocks just when their political goals seemed attainable. As late as 1894, Populist candidates made good showings in elections in the West and South. Like earlier third parties, though, Populists were underfinanced and underorganized. They had strong and colorful candidates but not enough of them to effectively challenge the major parties.

Issues of race also permeated politics. The possibility of biracial political action posed by Farmers' Al-

Stifling of Biracial Dissent liances in the early 1890s failed for two reasons. First, southern white Democrats had succeeded in creating restrictions on voting rights that prevented African Americans from becoming a political force. Second, raw racism impeded the acceptance of blacks by white Populists. Some Populists did seek to unite distressed black and white farmers, but poor white farmers could not forgo their racism. Thus few Populists addressed the needs of black farmers, and many used white-supremacist rhetoric to guard against accusations that they encouraged race-mixing.

In the national arena, the Populist crusade against "money power" settled on the issue of silver. Many people saw silver as a simple solution to the nation's complex ills. To them, free coinage of silver meant the end of special privileges for the rich and the return of government to the people. Populists agreed and made free coinage of silver their political battle cry. But as the election of 1896 approached, Populists had to decide how to translate their few previous electoral victories into larger success. Should they join with sympathetic factions of the major parties, thus risking a loss of identity, or should they remain an independent third party and settle for minor wins at best?

The 1896 presidential election climaxed a generation of political turbulence. Each party was divided.

Republican Nomination of McKinley Republicans, directed by Marcus A. Hanna, a prosperous Ohio industrialist, had only minor problems. For a year, Hanna had been maneuvering to win the nomination for Ohio's governor, William McKinley. By the time the party convened in St. Louis, Hanna had corralled enough delegates to succeed. The Republicans' only distress occurred when they adopted a moderate platform supporting gold, rejecting a prosilver stance proposed by Colorado's Senator Henry M. Teller. Teller, who had been among the party's founders forty years earlier, walked out of the convention in tears, taking a small group of silver Republicans with him.

At the Democratic convention, prosilver delegates wearing silver badges and waving silver banners paraded through the Chicago Amphitheatre. A *New York World* reporter remarked that "All the silverites need is a Moses." They soon found one in William Jennings Bryan.

A former Nebraska congressman and silverite, the thirty-six-year-old Bryan was highly distressed by the depression's impact on midwestern farmers. As a member of the party's resolutions committee, Bryan helped write a platform calling for free coinage of silver. When the committee presented the platform to the full convention, Bryan rose to speak on its behalf. Bryan's now-famous closing words ignited the delegates:

William Jennings Bryan

> Having behind us the producing masses of this nation and the world, supported by the commercial interests, the laboring interests, and the toilers everywhere, we will answer [the wealthy classes'] demand for a gold standard by saying to them: You shall not press down upon the brow of labor this crown of thorns, you shall not crucify mankind upon a cross of gold.

The speech could not have been better timed. Delegates who backed Bryan for president now had no trouble enlisting support. The "Boy Orator" proved irresistible and won the nomination, but a minority of gold Democrats withdrew and nominated their own candidate.

Bryan's nomination presented the Populist party (as it was now called) with a dilemma. Should Populists join Democrats in support of Bryan, or should they nominate their own candidate? Tom Watson of Georgia, expressing opposition to fusion with Democrats, warned that "the Democratic idea of fusion [is] that we play Jonah while they play whale." Others reasoned that supporting a different candidate would split the anti-McKinley vote and guarantee a Republican victory. In the end the convention compromised, first naming Watson as its vice-presidential nominee to preserve party identity and then nominating Bryan for president.

The election results revealed that the political standoff had finally ended. McKinley, symbol of Republican pragmatism and corporate ascendancy, beat Bryan by over 600,000 popular votes and won in the electoral college by 271 to 176. It was the most lopsided presidential election since 1872.

Election Results

Bryan worked hard to rally the nation, but obsession with silver undermined his effort and prevented Populists from building the urban-rural coalition that would have expanded their political appeal. Urban workers, who might have benefited from Populist goals, shied away from the silver issue out of fear that free coinage would reduce the value of their wages. Labor leaders would not commit themselves fully because they viewed farmers as businessmen, not workers. And socialists denounced Populists as "retrograde" because they, unlike socialists, believed in free enterprise. Thus the Populist crusade collapsed.

As president, McKinley signed the Gold Standard Act (1900), requiring that all paper money be backed by gold. He also supported the Dingley Tariff of 1897, which raised duties even higher. Domestic tensions subsided during McKinley's presidency; an upward swing of the business cycle and a money supply enlarged by gold discoveries in Alaska, Australia, and South Africa helped restore prosperity. A believer in opening new markets abroad to sustain prosperity at home, McKinley encouraged imperialistic ventures. Good times and victory in the Spanish-American-Cuban-Filipino War enabled him to beat Bryan again in 1900, using the slogan "The Full Dinner Pail."

The McKinley Presidency

Summary

Government during the Gilded Age succeeded in making many modest, and some major, accomplishments. Guided by well-meaning, generally competent people, much of what occurred in statehouses, the halls of Congress, and the White House prepared the nation for the twentieth century. Laws encouraging economic growth with some principles of regulation, measures expanding government agencies while reducing crass patronage, federal intervention in trade and currency issues, and a more active presidency all evolved during the 1870s and 1880s. Still, disfranchisement of African Americans and continued discrimination against both blacks and women continued to pollute politics, and the system vehemently rejected the radical views expressed by socialists, Coxey, or Populists.

The 1896 election realigned national politics. The Republican Party became the majority party by emphasizing active government aid to business expansion, expanding its social base to include urban workers, and playing down its moralism. The Democratic Party miscalculated on the silver issue and held its traditional support only in the South. After 1896, however, party loyalties weakened and a new kind of politics was brewing.

In retrospect, it is easy to see that the Populists never had a chance. Nevertheless, by 1920 many Populist goals were achieved, including regulation of railroads, banks, and utilities; shorter workdays; a variant of the subtreasury plan; a graduated income tax; direct election of senators; and the secret ballot. These reforms succeeded because a variety of groups united behind them. Immigration, urbanization, and industrialization had transformed the United States into a pluralistic society in which compromise among interest groups had become a political fact of life. As the Gilded Age ended, business was still in the ascendancy, but the winds of dissent and reform had begun to blow more strongly.

LEGACY FOR A PEOPLE AND A NATION
Politics and Popular Culture

The Wizard of Oz, one of the most popular movies of all time, began as a Populist fable penned by journalist L. Frank Baum in 1900. Originally titled "The Wonderful Wizard of Oz," the story used memorable characters to represent the conditions of overburdened farmers and laborers. Dorothy symbolized the well-intentioned common person; the Scarecrow, the struggling farmer; the Tin Man, the industrial worker. Hoping for a better life, these new friends, along with the Cowardly Lion (William Jennings Bryan with a loud roar but little power), followed a yellow brick road (the gold standard) that led nowhere. Along their journey, they encountered the Wicked Witch of the East, who, Baum wrote, kept the little people (Munchkins) "in bondage, . . . making them slaves for her night and day." They also met the Wicked Witch of the West, who symbolized industrial corporations. The Emerald City they find is presided over by the Wizard of Oz, who rules from behind a screen. A typical politician, the Wizard tries to be all things to all people, but Dorothy and her friends reveal him as a fraud, just "a little man, with a bald head and a wrinkled face." Dorothy is able to leave this muddled society and return to her simple Kansas farm family of Aunt Em and Uncle Henry by using her magical silver slippers (coinage of silver).

Baum used his tale to argue that powerful leaders were deceiving and manipulating ordinary people. He believed that if *Oz* exposed what really was going on, the people—no longer ignorant—would be outraged by the greed and deceit of politicians and industrialists, and would act. But this message disappeared when Metro Goldwyn Mayer (MGM) bought Baum's story and made it into a 1939 motion picture to showcase their new child star, Judy Garland.

The saga of *The Wizard of Oz* shows how modern popular culture can subsume politics. The adventures of four endearing characters came to have more appeal than their political symbolism. The rise of movies, television, and sports also altered the nature of fame. Whereas in the Gilded Age politicians held the spotlight as the nation's chief celebrities, by the twentieth century they had been bumped into the background. And instead of popular culture, such as Baum's fable, influencing politics, the legacy to a people and a nation has been the opportunity of some celebrities to use popular culture to become politicians. Thus the nation has seen movie stars and sports personalities become governors, senators, representatives, and even president.

For Further Reading, see the Appendix. For Web resources, go to history.college.hmco.com/students.

21

THE PROGRESSIVE ERA

1895–1920

The Varied Progressive Impulse
Governmental and Legislative Reform
New Ideas in Education, Law, and Religion
Challenges to Racial and Sexual Discrimination
Theodore Roosevelt and the Revival of the Presidency
Woodrow Wilson and the Extension of Reform

LEGACY FOR A PEOPLE AND A NATION
Women and Social Work

Once described as a "guerrilla warrior" in the "wilderness of industrial wrongs," Florence Kelley accomplished as much as anyone in guiding the United States out of the tangled swamp of unregulated industrial capitalism into the uncharted seas of the twentieth-century welfare state.

The daughter of a Republican congressman, Kelley graduated from Cornell in 1883. She prepared to study law, but the University of Pennsylvania denied her admission to its graduate school because of her gender. Instead, she traveled to Europe. In Zurich, Kelley joined a group of socialists who alerted her to the plight of the underprivileged. She married a Russian socialist and returned to New York City in 1886. When the marriage collapsed, Kelley took her three

children to Chicago in 1891. Later that year she moved into Hull House, a residence in the slums where middle-class reformers went to live in order to help and learn from working-class immigrants. There her transforming work truly began. At Hull House, Kelley entered a female-dominated environment, where women sought to apply helping skills to the betterment of society. This environment encouraged Kelley to assert her powerful abilities.

Over the next decade, Kelley became the nation's most ardent advocate of improved conditions for working-class women and children. She lobbied for laws to prohibit child labor and regulate women's working hours, and she served as Illinois's first factory inspector. Her work helped create new professions for women in social service, and her strategy of investigating, publicizing, and crusading for action became a model for reform. Perhaps most significant, she and fellow reformers enlisted government to aid in the solution of social problems.

During the 1890s economic depression, labor violence, political upheaval, and foreign entanglements shook the nation. By 1900, however, the political tumult of the previous decade had died down, and the economic depression seemed to be over. The nation emerged victorious from a war, and a new era of dynamic political leaders such as Theodore Roosevelt and Woodrow Wilson was dawning. A sense of renewal raised hopes that social and political problems could be fixed.

By the 1910s many reformers were calling themselves "Progressives"; in 1912 they formed a political party by that name to embody their principles. Historians have uniformly used the term *Progressivism* to refer to the era's reformist spirit. The era between 1895 and 1920 included a series of movements, each aiming in one way or another to renovate or restore American society, values, and institutions.

The reform impulse had many sources. Industrial capitalism had created awesome technology, unprecedented productivity, and a cornucopia of consumer goods. But it also brought harmful overproduction, domineering monopolies, labor strife, and the spoiling of natural resources. Burgeoning cities facilitated the amassing and distribution of goods, services, and cultural amenities; they also bred poverty, disease, and crime. Inflows of immigrants and the rise of a new class of managers and professionals reconfigured the social order. And the depression of the 1890s forced many leading citizens to realize what working people had known for some time: equality of opportunity was a myth.

Progressives organized their ideas and actions around three goals. First, they sought to end abuses of power. Thus trustbusting, consumers' rights, and good government became compelling political issues. Second, they aimed to supplant corrupt power with humane institutions such as schools, charities, and medical clinics. They acknowledged that society had responsibility and power to improve individual lives, and they believed that government, acting for society at large, must intervene to protect the common good. Third,

Progressives wanted to apply scientific principles and efficient management to economic, social, and political institutions. Their aim was to establish bureaus of experts that would end wasteful competition and promote social and economic order. Science and the scientific method—planning, control, and predictability—were their central values. Just as corporations applied scientific management techniques to achieve economic efficiency, Progressives advocated expertise and planning to achieve social and political efficiency.

Befitting their name, Progressives had deep faith in the ability of humankind to create a better world and believed, as expressed by Judge Ben Lindsey of Denver, that "in the end the people are bound to do the right thing, no matter how much they fail at times." ▧

The Varied Progressive Impulse

Progressive reformers addressed vexing issues that had surfaced in the previous half-century, but they did so in a new political climate. As the twentieth century dawned, party loyalty eroded and voter turnout declined. Moreover, parties and elections, it seemed, were losing influence over government policies. At the same time, the political system was opening to new interest groups, each of which championed its own cause. These new nationwide organizations included professional associations such as the American Bar Association; women's organizations such as the National American Woman Suffrage Association; issue-oriented groups such as the National Consumers League; civic clubs such as the National Municipal League; and minority-group associations such as the National Negro Business League and the Society of American Indians. Because they usually acted independently of either of the established political parties, such groups made politics more fragmented and issue-focused than in earlier eras.

Also, American politics became receptive to foreign models and ideas for reorganizing society. A variety of programs and proposals traveled across the Atlantic; some were introduced by Americans such as Florence Kelley, others by foreigners traveling in the United States. Such reforms as old-age insurance, subsidized workers' housing, city

Foreign Influences

IMPORTANT EVENTS

1893 Anti-Saloon League founded

1895 Washington gives Atlanta Compromise
speech
National Association of Colored Women
founded

1896 *Holden v. Hardy* upholds limits on miners'
working hours

1900 McKinley reelected

1901 McKinley assassinated; T. Roosevelt
assumes the presidency

1904 T. Roosevelt elected president
Northern Securities case dissolves railroad trust

1905 Niagara Conference promotes African
American rights
Lochner v. New York removes limits on
bakers' working hours

1906 Hepburn Act tightens control over railroads
Sinclair's *The Jungle* exposes poor condi-
tions in meatpacking plants
Meat Inspection Act passed
Pure Food and Drug Act passed

1907 Reckless speculation causes economic panic

1908 Taft elected president
Muller v. Oregon upholds limits on women's
working hours

1909 NAACP founded
Payne-Aldrich Tariff passed

1910 Mann-Elkins Act reinforces ICC powers
White Slave Traffic Act prohibits transportation of women for "immoral purposes"

Ballinger-Pinchot controversy angers conservationists

1911 Society of American Indians founded

1912 T. Roosevelt runs for president on the
Progressive (Bull Moose) ticket
Wilson elected president

1913 Sixteenth Amendment ratified, legalizing
federal income tax
Seventeenth Amendment ratified, providing
for direct election of U.S. senators
Underwood Tariff institutes income tax
Federal Reserve Act establishes central banking system

1914 Federal Trade Commission created to
investigate unfair trade practices
Clayton Anti-Trust Act outlaws monopolistic
business practices
Sanger indicted for sending articles on contraception through the mail

1916 Wilson reelected
Federal Farm Loan Act provides credit to
farmers
Adamson Act mandates eight-hour workday
for railroad workers

1919 Eighteenth Amendment ratified, establishing
prohibition of alcoholic beverages

1920 Nineteenth Amendment ratified, giving
women the vote in federal elections

1921 Sanger founds American Birth Control
League

planning, and rural reconstruction originated abroad and were adopted or modified in America.

Although the goals of the rural-based Populist movement—moral regeneration, political democracy, and antimonopolism—lingered, the Progressive quest for social justice, educational and legal reform, and government streamlining had a largely urban bent. Between 1890 and 1920 the proportion of the nation's population living in cities swelled from 35 percent to 51 percent. By utilizing advances in mail, telephone, and telegraph communications, urban reformers exchanged information and coordinated efforts to alleviate the consequences of this change.

Organizations and individuals intent on achieving Progressive goals—ending the abuse of power, reforming social institutions, and promoting bureaucratic and scientific efficiency—existed in almost all levels of society. But the new middle class—men and women in the

Urban Middle-Class Reformers and Muckrakers

professions of law, medicine, engineering, social work, religion, teaching, and business—formed the vanguard of reform. Offended by inefficiency and immorality in business, government, and human relations, these people set out to apply rational techniques they had learned in their professions to problems of the larger society.

Their indignation motivated many middle-class Progressive reformers to seek an end to abuses of power. Their views were voiced by journalists whom Theodore Roosevelt dubbed muckrakers (after a character in the Puritan allegory *Pilgrim's Progress* who, rather than looking heavenward at beauty, looked downward and raked the muck to find what was wrong with life). Muckrakers fed the public taste for scandal and sensation by exposing social, economic, and political wrongs. Their investigative articles attacked adulterated foods, fraudulent insurance, prostitution, and other offenses. Lincoln Steffens's articles in *McClure's*,

later published as *The Shame of the Cities* (1904), epitomized the muckraking style. Steffens hoped his exposés of bosses' misrule would inspire mass outrage and, ultimately, reform. Other well-known muckraking efforts included Upton Sinclair's *The Jungle* (1906), a novel that disclosed crimes of the meatpacking industry, and Ida M. Tarbell's critical history of Standard Oil (1904).

To improve politics, Progressives advocated nominating candidates through direct primaries instead of party caucuses and holding nonpartisan elections to prevent the fraud and bribery bred by party loyalties. To make officeholders more responsible, Progressives pressed for three reforms: the initiative, which permitted voters to propose new laws; the referendum, which enabled voters to accept or reject a law; and the recall, which allowed voters to remove offending officials and judges from office before their terms expired. Their goal was to reclaim government by replacing the boss system with accountable managers chosen by a responsible electorate.

Though their objectives sometimes differed from those of middle-class Progressive reformers, socialists also became a more active force in the early twentieth century. Socialist parades on May Day, such as this one in 1910, were meant to express the solidarity of all working people. (Library of Congress)

The Progressive spirit also stirred some elite business leaders. Several executives supported some government regulation and political reforms

Upper-Class Reformers

to protect their interests from more radical reformers. Others were humanitarians who worked unselfishly for social justice. Business-dominated organizations like the Municipal Voters League and U.S. Chamber of Commerce thought that running schools, hospitals, and local government like efficient businesses would help stabilize society. Elite women often led organizations like the Young Women's Christian Association (YWCA) and the Women's Christian Temperance Union (WCTU), which supported numerous causes besides abstinence from drinking.

Not all Progressives were middle- or upper-class. Vital elements of what became modern American liberalism derived from working-class

Working-Class Reformers

urban experiences. By 1900 many urban workers were pressing for government intervention to ensure safe factories, shorter workdays, workers' compensation, better housing, and health safeguards. Often these were the same people who supported political bosses, supposedly the enemies of reform. In fact, bossism was not necessarily at odds with humanitarianism.

After 1900, voters from urban working-class districts elected several Progressive legislators who had trained in the trenches of machine politics. They opposed reforms such as prohibition, Sunday closing laws, civil service, and nonpartisan elections, which conflicted with their constituents' interests. Their goal, instead, was to have government take the responsibility for alleviating hardships that resulted from urban-industrial growth.

Some disillusioned people moved beyond Progressive reform; they wanted a different society altogether. Such individuals turned to the socialist movement. The majority of socialists

Socialists

united behind Eugene V. Debs, the American Railway Union organizer. As the Socialist Party's presidential candidate Debs won 400,000 votes in 1904, and in 1912, at the pinnacle of his and his party's career, he polled over 900,000.

With stinging rebukes of exploitation and unfair privilege, socialist leaders made compelling overtures to reform-minded people. Some, such as Florence Kelley, joined the Socialist Party. But most Progressives had too much at stake in the capitalist system to want to overthrow it. Municipal ownership of public utilities represented their limit of drastic change.

It would be a mistake to assume that a Progressive spirit captured all of American society. Large numbers of people, heavily represented in

Opponents of Progressivism

Congress, disliked government interference in economic affairs and found no fault with existing power structures. Government interference, they contended, contradicted the natural law of survival of the fittest. For tycoons like J. P. Morgan and John D. Rockefeller, progress would result only from maintaining the profit incentive and an economy unfettered by government regulation.

Progressive reformers occupied the center of the ideological spectrum. They believed on one hand that the laissez-faire system was obsolete and on the other that a radical shift away from free enterprise was dangerous. Like Thomas Jefferson, they expressed faith in the conscience and will of the people; like Alexander Hamilton, they desired strong central government to act in the interests of conscience.

Governmental and Legislative Reform

A mistrust of tyranny had traditionally prompted American theorists and ordinary citizens to believe that democratic government should be small and unobtrusive and should interfere in private affairs only in unique circumstances. But in the late 1800s this point of view weakened when problems resulting from economic change seemed to overwhelm individual effort. Corporations pursued government aid and protection for their enterprises. Discontented farmers sought government regulation of railroads and other monopolistic businesses. And city dwellers, accustomed to favors performed by political machines, came to expect government to act on their behalf.

Progressive reformers supported the assumption that government should ensure justice and well-being. Increasingly aware that a simple, inflexible government was inadequate in a complex industrial age, they

Restructuring Government

reasoned that public authority needed to counteract inefficiency and exploitation. But before activists could effectively use such power, they would have to reclaim government from politicians whose greed had soiled the democratic system. Thus eliminating corruption from government was a central thrust of Progressive activity.

Prior to the Progressive era, opponents of boss politics had tried to restructure government through reforms such as civil service and nonpartisan elections. A few reformers had advocated poverty relief, housing improvement, and prolabor laws, but most worked for efficient—meaning economical—government. After 1900 reform campaigns installed city manager and commission forms of government (in which urban officials were chosen for professional expertise, rather than political connections) and public ownership of utilities (to prevent monopolistic gas, electric, and transit companies from profiting at public expense).

Reformers, however, found the city too small an arena for the changes they sought. State and federal governments offered better opportunities for enacting needed legislation. Their goals tended to vary regionally. In the Great Plains and Far West, they rallied behind railroad regulation and government control of natural resources. In the South, reformers crusaded against big business and autocratic politicians. In the Northeast and Midwest, they attacked corrupt politics and unsafe labor conditions.

Faith in a strong, fair-minded executive prompted Progressives to support a number of skillful and charismatic governors. The most forceful Progressive governor was Wisconsin's Robert M. La Follette, who rose through the state Republican Party and won the governorship in 1900. As governor he initiated a reform program that included direct primaries, more equitable taxes, and regulation of railroad rates. He also appointed commissions staffed by experts, who supplied him with the facts and figures he used in fiery speeches to arouse public support for his policies. After three terms as governor, La Follette was elected to the U.S. Senate and carried his ideals into national politics.

Robert M. La Follette

The South experienced a brand of Progressive reform that in many ways resembled that of other re-

Southern Progressivism

gions. It also led the way in political reform; the direct primary originated in North Carolina, the city commission plan arose in Galveston, Texas, and the city manager plan began in Staunton, Virginia.

But racial bitterness tainted southern Progressive politics, largely excluding former slaves from many benefits of reform. The exclusion of black men from voting meant that electoral reforms affected only whites—and then only white men with enough cash and education to satisfy voting prerequisites. And all too often southern reformers rested their power on appeals to white supremacy. Racism was not unique to the South, however; Governor Hiram Johnson of California, a leading western Progressive, promoted discrimination against Japanese Americans, and New Jersey's Woodrow Wilson had no sympathy for African Americans.

At the same time, however, southern women, white and black, made notable contributions to Progressive causes. Southern white women crusaded against child labor, ran social service organizations, and challenged unfair wage rates. African American women, using a nonpolitical guise as homemakers and religious leaders, attempted to serve their communities by acting as spokespersons for street cleaning, better education, and health reforms. Thus, though much of southern Progressivism was racist, it would have been even more so without the reformist efforts of women, especially black women.

In all regions, crusades against corrupt politics produced notable changes. By 1916 all but three states had direct primaries, and many had adopted the initiative, referendum, and recall. Political reformers achieved a major goal in 1913 with adoption of the Seventeenth Amendment, which provided for direct election of U.S. senators (they previously had been elected by state legislatures). Such measures did not always help. Party bosses, better organized and more experienced than reformers, were still able to control elections, and courts usually aided rather than reined in entrenched power.

State laws to improve labor conditions had greater impact than did political reforms. Many states used their constitutional powers to protect public health and safety (police power) and to enact factory inspection laws, and by 1916 nearly two-thirds of the states

Labor Reform

required compensation for victims of industrial accidents. And under pressure from the National Child Labor Committee, nearly every state set a minimum age for employment (varying from twelve to sixteen) and prohibited employers from working children more than eight or ten hours a day. Such laws had limited effect, though, because they were hard to enforce and were often violated.

Several groups united to achieve restricted working hours for women. After the Supreme Court upheld Oregon's ten-hour limit in 1908, more states passed laws protecting female workers. Meanwhile, in 1914 efforts of the American Association for Old Age Security showed signs of success when Arizona established old-age pensions. The courts struck down the law, but demand for pensions continued, and in the 1920s many states enacted laws to provide for needy elderly people.

Reformers themselves did not always agree about what was Progressive, especially in human behavior.

Moral Reform

The main question was whether state intervention was necessary to enforce purity, especially in drinking habits and sexual behavior. For example, the Anti-Saloon League, formed in 1893, allied with the Women's Christian Temperance Union (founded in 1873) to publicize the role of alcoholism in liver disease and other health problems. The League was especially successful in shifting attention from the individual's responsibility for temperance to the alleged link between the drinking that saloons encouraged and the accidents, poverty, and poor productivity that were consequences of drinking.

The war on saloons prompted many states and localities to restrict consumption of liquor. By 1900 almost one-fourth of the nation's population lived in "dry" communities (which

The War on Alcohol

prohibited the sale of liquor). Finally, in 1918 Congress passed the Eighteenth Amendment (ratified in 1919 and implemented in 1920) outlawing the manufacture, sale, and transportation of intoxicating liquors.

Moral outrage erupted also when muckraking journalists charged that international gangs were kidnapping young women and forcing them into prostitution, a practice called white slavery. The charges were

Prostitution and White Slavery

more imagined than real, but they alarmed some moralists who falsely perceived a link between immigration and prostitution. Those fearful about the social consequences of prostitution prodded governments to investigate the problem and pass corrective legislation.

In 1910 Congress passed the White Slave Traffic Act, known as the Mann Act, prohibiting interstate and international transportation of a woman for immoral purposes. By 1915 nearly every state had outlawed brothels and solicitation of sex. Such laws ostensibly protected young women from exploitation, but in reality they failed to address the more serious problem of sexual violence that women suffered at the hands of family members and presumed friends and at the workplace. The Mann Act, like prohibition, reflected growing sentiment that government could improve behavior by restricting it.

New Ideas in Education, Law, and Religion

In addition to legislative paths, reform impulses opened new vistas in ideas. Preoccupation with efficiency and scientific management infiltrated the realms of education, law, religion, and science. Darwin's theory of evolution had challenged traditional beliefs in a God-created world; immigration had caused confusing social diversity; and technology had made old habits of production and consumption obsolete. Thoughtful people in a number of professions grappled with how to respond to the new era yet preserve what was best from the past.

Before the Civil War, school curricula had consisted chiefly of moralistic pieties from *McGuffey's Reader*. But in the late nineteenth century, psychologist G. Stanley Hall and philosopher John Dewey asserted that modern education ought to prepare children differently. They insisted that personal development, not subject matter, should be the focus of the curriculum. Education, argued Dewey, must relate directly to experience; children should be encouraged to discover knowledge for themselves. Learning relevant to

John Dewey and Progressive Education

students' lives should replace rote memorization and outdated subjects.

A more practical curriculum became the driving principle behind reform in higher education as well.

Growth of Colleges and Universities

Previously, the purpose of American colleges and universities had been to train a select few for careers in law, medicine, teaching, and religion. But in the late 1800s, institutions of higher learning multiplied, aided by land grants and an increase in the number of people who could afford tuition. Curricula expanded as educators sought to make learning more appealing and to keep up with technological and social changes. Harvard University, under President Charles W. Eliot, pioneered in substituting electives for required courses and experimenting with new teaching methods.

Southern states, in keeping with their separate-but-equal policies, set up segregated land-grant colleges for blacks in addition to the public institutions for whites. Separate was a more accurate description of these institutions than equal. African Americans continued to suffer from inferior educational opportunities and facilities in both state institutions and private all-black colleges. Nevertheless, African American men and women found intellectual stimulation in all-black colleges and hoped to use their educations to promote better race relations.

As higher education expanded, so did female enrollments. Between 1890 and 1920 the number of women in colleges and universities swelled from 56,000 to 283,000, accounting for 47 percent of total enrollment. But discrimination lingered in admissions and curriculum policies. Women were encouraged to take home economics and education courses rather than science and mathematics, and most medical schools, including Harvard and Yale, refused to admit women. Barred from such institutions, women continued to attend their own schools, places such as Women's Medical College of Philadelphia and women's colleges such as Smith, Mount Holyoke, and Wellesley.

The legal profession also embraced new emphases on experience and scientific principles. Oliver Wendell Holmes, Jr., associate justice of the Supreme Court between 1902 and 1932, led the attack on the traditional view of law as universal and unchanging. His opinion that law should reflect society's needs challenged the

Progressive Legal Thought

practice of invoking inflexible legal precedents that often obstructed social legislation. Louis D. Brandeis, a lawyer who later joined Holmes on the Supreme Court, insisted that judges' opinions be based on factual, scientifically gathered information about social realities.

The new legal thinking met with some resistance. Judges raised on laissez-faire economics and strict construction of the Constitution continued to overturn laws Progressives thought necessary for effective reform. Thus despite Holmes's forceful dissent, in 1905 the Supreme Court, in *Lochner v. New York*, revoked a New York law limiting bakers' working hours. As in similar cases, the Court's majority argued that the Fourteenth Amendment protected an individual's right to make contracts without government interference and that this protection superseded police power.

Courts did uphold some regulatory measures, however, particularly those protecting public safety. A string of decisions beginning with *Holden v. Hardy* (1898), in which the Supreme Court sustained Utah's mining regulations, confirmed the use of state police power to protect health, safety, and morals. Judges also affirmed federal police power and Congress's authority over interstate commerce by supporting federal legislation such as the Pure Food and Drug Act, the Meat Inspection Law, and the Mann Act.

But the concept of general welfare often conflicted with the concept of equal rights when the will of local majorities was imposed on minorities. The United States was a mixed nation; gender, race, religion, and ethnicity deeply influenced law. In many localities a native-born Protestant majority imposed Bible reading in public schools (offending Catholics and Jews), required businesses to close on Sundays, limited women's rights, restricted religious practices of Mormons and other groups, prohibited interracial marriage, and enforced racial segregation. Justice Holmes asserted that laws should be made for "people of fundamentally differing views," but were such laws possible in a nation of so many different interest groups? The debate continues to this day.

In public health, organizations like the National Consumers League (NCL) joined physicians and social scientists to bring about some of the most far-reaching Progressive reforms. Founded by Florence

Public Health
Kelley in 1899, NCL activities included women's suffrage, protection of female and child laborers, and elimination of potential health hazards. The organization was also active in sponsoring court cases on behalf of women workers and worked with reform lawyers in support of these cases. Local branches united with women's clubs to advance consumer protection measures such as the licensing of food vendors and inspection of dairies. And they also urged city governments to fund neighborhood clinics that provided health education and medical care to the poor.

Much of Progressive reform rested on religious underpinnings. The distresses of modern society especially sparked new thoughts about fortifying social relations with moral

The Social Gospel
principles. In particular, a movement known as the Social Gospel, led by Protestant ministers Walter Rauschenbusch, Washington Gladden, and Charles Sheldon, would counter the brutality of competitive capitalism by interjecting Christian churches into practical, worldly matters such as arbitrating industrial harmony and improving the environment of the poor. Believing that service to fellow humans provided the way both to securing individual salvation and to creating God's kingdom on earth, Social Gospelers actively participated in social reform and governed their lives by asking, "What would Jesus do?"

Thus a new breed of men and women pressed for institutional change as well as political reform in the two decades before the First World War. Largely middle class, trained in new professional standards, confident that new ways of thinking could bring about progress, these people helped broaden government's role to meet the needs of a mature industrial society. But their questioning of prevailing assumptions also unsettled conventional attitudes toward race and gender.

Challenges to Racial and Sexual Discrimination

The Progressive era, dominated as it was by white reformers, often ignored issues directly affecting former slaves, nonwhite immigrants, Indians, and women. Yet activists among these groups caught the Progressive spirit and strove for change in this time of challenge to entrenched ideas and customs. Their efforts, however, posed a dilemma. Should women and nonwhites aim to become just like white men, with white men's values as well as their rights? Or was there something unique about racial and sexual cultures that they should preserve at the risk of sacrificing some gains?

African Americans began to move northward in the 1880s, accelerating their migration after 1900.

Disadvantages of African Americans
The conditions they found represented a relative improvement over the rural sharecropping existence, but job discrimination, inferior schools, and segregated housing existed in northern as well as southern cities. White authorities perpetuated segregation by maintaining separate and inferior institutions, such as hospitals and schools, for blacks. Long after slavery's abolition, most whites still agreed with historian James Ford Rhodes, who wrote that blacks were "innately inferior and incapable of citizenship."

African American leaders differed sharply over how—and whether—to pursue assimilation. In the wake of emancipation, ex-slave Frederick Douglass urged "ultimate assimilation through self-assertion, and on no other terms." Others favored separation from white society and supported migration to Africa or the establishment of all-black communities in Oklahoma Territory and Kansas. Still others advocated militancy.

Most blacks, however, could neither escape nor conquer white society. They sought other routes to economic and social improvement.

Booker T. Washington and Self-Help
Self-help, a strategy articulated by educator Booker T. Washington, offered one popular alternative. Born to slave parents in 1856, Washington obtained an education and in 1881 founded Tuskegee Institute in Alabama, a vocational school for blacks. There he developed a philosophy that blacks' best hopes for assimilation lay in at least temporarily accommodating to whites. Rather than fighting for political rights, Washington said, blacks should work hard, acquire property, and prove they were worthy of respect. Washington voiced his views in a speech at the Atlanta Exposition in 1895. In this speech—which became known as the Atlanta

Booker T. Washington's Tuskegee Institute helped train young African Americans in useful crafts such as shoemaking and shoe repair, as illustrated here. At the same time, however, Washington's intentions and the Tuskegee curriculum reinforced what many whites wanted to believe: that blacks were unfit for anything except manual labor. (Tuskegee University Library)

Compromise—Washington observed that "in all things that are purely social we can be as separate as the fingers, yet one as the hand in all matters essential to mutual progress." Whites welcomed Washington's accommodation policy because it urged patience and reminded black people to stay in their place.

Though Washington had never argued that African Americans were inferior to whites, some blacks thought that he favored a degrading second-class citizenship. His southern-based philosophy did not appeal to educated northern African Americans. In 1905 a group of "anti-Bookerites" convened near Niagara Falls and pledged militant pursuit of rights such as unrestricted voting, economic opportunity, integration, and equality before the law. The spokesperson for the Niagara movement was W. E. B. Du Bois, an outspoken critic of the Atlanta Compromise.

A New Englander and the first black to receive a Ph.D. from Harvard, Du Bois was both a Progressive

W. E. B. Du Bois and the Niagara Movement

and a member of the black elite. He held an undergraduate degree from all-black Fisk University and had studied in Germany, where he learned about scientific investigation. Du Bois compiled fact-filled sociological studies of black ghetto dwellers and wrote poetically in support of civil rights. He treated Washington politely but could not accept white domination.

Dissatisfied with Washington's strategy, Du Bois in 1905 organized a conference of blacks who favored more active opposition to racism. Meeting at Niagara Falls, the group took the name Niagara Conference and began meeting annually. Then, in 1909, Du Bois joined with a group of white liberals who also were discontented with Washington's accommodationism to form the National Association for the Advancement of Colored People (NAACP), which aimed to end racial discrimination and obtain voting rights by pursuing legal redress in the courts. By 1914 the NAACP had fifty branch offices and six thousand members.

Whatever their views, African Americans faced continued oppression. Those who managed to acquire property and education encountered white resentment, especially when they fought for equality. The federal government only aggravated biases. During Woodrow Wilson's presidency, southern cabinet members supported racial separation in restrooms, restaurants, and government office buildings and balked at hiring black workers.

African Americans still sought to fulfill the dream of success, but many wondered whether their goals should include membership in a corrupt white society. Du Bois voiced these doubts poignantly, observing that "one ever feels his twoness—an American, a Negro, two souls, two thoughts, two unreconciled strivings, two warring ideals in one dark body." Somehow blacks had to reconcile that "twoness" by combining racial pride with national identity. As Du Bois put it, blacks' desire was for it to become "possible for a person to be both a Negro and an American." That simple desire would haunt the nation for decades to come.

The dilemma of identity bedeviled Native Americans as well, but it had an added tribal dimension.

Society of American Indians

Since the 1880s, Native American reformers had belonged to white-led Indian organizations. In 1911 educated, middle-class Indians formed their own association, the Society of American Indians (SAI), to work for better education, civil rights, and healthcare. It also sponsored "American Indian Days" to cultivate pride.

The SAI's emphasis on racial pride, however, was squeezed between pressures for assimilation from one side and tribal allegiance on the other. Its small membership did not genuinely represent the diverse and unconnected Indian nations, and its attempt to establish a governing body fizzled. Some tribal governments no longer existed to select representatives, and most SAI members simply promoted their own self-interest. At the same time, the goal of achieving acceptance in white society proved elusive, and attempts to redress grievances through legal action faltered for lack of funds. Torn by internal disputes, the association folded in the early 1920s.

The challenges to established social assumptions also raised questions of identity among women. What

"The Woman Movement"

tactics should women use to achieve equality? What should be their role in society? Could women achieve equality with men and at the same time change male-dominated society?

The answers that women found involved a subtle but important shift in women's politics. Before about 1910, crusaders for women's rights referred to themselves as "the woman movement." This label applied to middle-class women striving to move beyond the household into social welfare activities, higher education, and paid labor. They argued that legal and voting rights were indispensable to such moves. These women's rights advocates based their claims on the theory that women's special, even superior, traits as guardians of family and morality would humanize all of society.

Women's clubs represented a unique dimension of the woman movement. Originating as middle-class lit-

Women's Clubs

erary and educational organizations, women's clubs began taking stands on public affairs in the late 1800s. Because female activists were excluded from holding office, they were drawn less to government reform than to social betterment. Thus these women worked for factory inspection, regulation of children's and women's labor, housing improvement, upgrading of education, and consumer protection.

Such efforts were not confined to white women. African American women had their own club movement, including the Colored Women's Federation, which sought to establish a training school for "colored girls." Founded in 1895, the National Association of Colored Women was the nation's first African American social service organization; it concentrated on establishing nurseries, kindergartens, and retirement homes.

Around 1910 some of those concerned with women's place in society began using a new term, *feminism*, to refer to their ideas. Whereas

Feminism

the woman movement spoke generally of duty and moral purity, feminists—more explicitly conscious of their identity as women—emphasized rights and self-development. Feminism focused primarily on economic and sexual independence. Charlotte Perkins Gilman articulated feminist goals in *Women and Economics* (1898), declaring that domesticity and female innocence were obsolete and attacking the male monopoly on economic opportunity. Gilman argued that modern women must take jobs in industry and the professions and that paid employees should handle domestic chores such as cooking, cleaning, and childcare.

Feminists also supported "sex rights"—a single standard of behavior for men and women—and several

Margaret Sanger's Crusade

feminists joined the birth-control movement led by Margaret Sanger. As a visiting nurse in New York City's immigrant neighborhoods, Sanger distributed information about contraception to help poor women prevent unwanted pregnancies. Though Sanger later gained

acceptance among middle-class women, her actions initially aroused opposition from those who saw birth control as a threat to family and morality. In 1914 Sanger's opponents caused her to be indicted for defying an 1873 law that prohibited the sending of obscene literature (articles on contraception) through the mails, and she fled the country for a year. Sanger persevered and in 1921 formed the American Birth Control League, enlisting physicians and social workers to convince judges to allow distribution of birth-control information.

During the Progressive era, a generation of feminists, represented by Harriot Stanton Blatch, who was the daughter of nineteenth-century suffragist Elizabeth Cady Stanton, carried on women's battle for the vote (see Map 21.1). Blatch made the improvement of work-

Map 21.1 Woman Suffrage Before 1920 Before Congress passed and the states ratified the Nineteenth Amendment, woman suffrage already existed, but mainly in the West. Several midwestern states allowed women to vote only in presidential elections, but legislatures in the South and Northeast generally refused such rights until forced to do so by constitutional amendment.

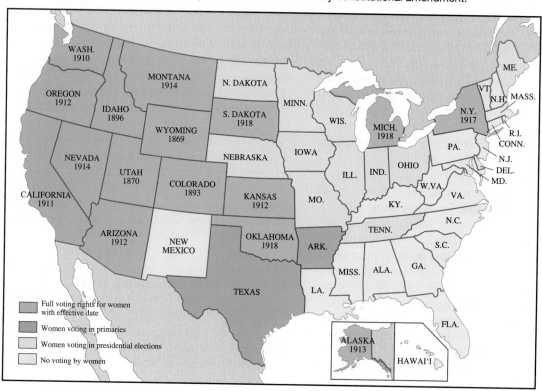

Woman Suffrage

ing conditions for women a primary goal and agreed with those who saw the vote as the means by which women could effect such improvement. Declaring that all women worked, whether they performed paid labor or unpaid housework, Blatch argued that women should exercise the vote to promote and protect their economic roles.

Despite internal differences, suffragists united behind their single goal and achieved some successes. Nine states, all in the West, allowed women to vote in state and local elections by 1912, and women continued to press for national suffrage. Their tactics ranged from the moderate but persistent letter-writing and publications of the National American Woman Suffrage Association, led by Carrie Chapman Catt, to the spirited meetings and militant marches of the National Woman's Party, led by Alice Paul. All these activities heightened public awareness. More decisive, however, were women's performances during the First World War as factory laborers, medical volunteers, and municipal workers (see pages 407–408). Women's wartime shouldering of public responsibilities gave final impetus to passage of the national suffrage amendment in 1920.

The activities of women's clubs, feminists, and suffragists failed to create an interest group united or powerful enough to overcome men's political, economic, and social control. Like blacks, women knew that voting rights would mean little until society's attitudes changed. The Progressive era helped women to clarify issues that concerned them, but major reforms were not achieved until a later era.

Theodore Roosevelt and the Revival of the Presidency

The Progressive era's theme of reform—in politics, institutions, and social relations—drew attention to government, especially the federal government, as the foremost agent of change. Though the federal government had made some notable accomplishments during the preceding Gilded Age, its role mainly had been to support rather than control economic expansion, as when it transferred western public lands and resources to private ownership. Then, in September 1901, the political climate suddenly shifted. The assassination of President William McKinley vaulted Theodore Roosevelt, the vigorous young vice president, into the White House.

Political manager Mark Hanna had warned fellow Republicans against running Roosevelt for vice president in 1900. "Don't any of you realize," Hanna asked after the nominating convention, "that there's only one life between that madman and the presidency?" As governor of New York, Roosevelt had angered Republican bosses by showing sympathy for regulatory legislation, so they rid themselves of their pariah by pushing him into national politics.

As president, Roosevelt concurred with Progressives that a small, uninvolved government would not suffice in the industrial era. Instead, economic development necessitated a government powerful enough to guide national affairs broadly. Especially in economic matters, he wanted the government to act as an umpire, deciding when big business was good and when it was bad. But his brash patriotism and dislike of weakness and indecisiveness, qualities he considered effeminate, also recalled earlier eras of unbridled expansion when raw power prevailed in social and economic affairs.

Theodore Roosevelt

The federal regulation of the economy that characterized twentieth-century American history began with Roosevelt's presidency. Roosevelt turned his attention first to big business, where consolidation had created massive, monopolistic trusts. Although Roosevelt was labeled a "trustbuster," he actually considered consolidation the most efficient means to achieve material progress. He believed in distinguishing between good and bad trusts and preventing bad ones from manipulating markets. Thus he instructed the Justice Department to use antitrust laws to prosecute railroad, meatpacking, and oil trusts, which he believed were unscrupulously exploiting the public. Roosevelt's policy triumphed in 1904 when the Supreme Court, convinced by the government's arguments, ordered the breakup of Northern Securities Company, the huge railroad combination created by J. P. Morgan and his business allies (*Northern Securities* case).

Regulation of Trusts

Theodore Roosevelt (1858–1919) liked to think of himself as a great outdoorsman. He loved most the rugged countryside and believed that he and his country should serve as examples of "manliness." (Keystone-Mast Collection, UCR/California Museum of Photography, University of California, Riverside)

Despite the image created by his trustbusting activities, Roosevelt did not favor prosecution at every turn. Instead, he urged the Bureau of Corporations (part of the newly created Department of Labor and Commerce) to assist companies with mergers and other forms of expansion. Through investigation and cooperation, the administration cajoled businesses to regulate themselves.

Roosevelt also supported regulatory legislation, especially after his resounding electoral victory in 1904. After a year of wrangling, Roosevelt persuaded Congress to pass the Hepburn Act (1906), which gave the Interstate Commerce Commission (ICC) more authority to set railroad freight and storage rates, though it did allow the courts to overturn rate decisions. To ensure passage of the bill, Roosevelt compromised with congressional business allies.

Roosevelt showed similar willingness to compromise on legislation to ensure the purity of food and drugs. For decades reformers had been urging government regulation of processed meat and patent medicines. Public outrage at fraud and adulteration was heightened in 1906 when Upton Sinclair published *The Jungle*, a fictionalized exposé of Chicago meatpacking plants. After reading the novel, Roosevelt ordered an investigation. Finding Sinclair's descriptions accurate, he supported the Meat Inspection Act, which passed in 1906. Like the Hepburn Act, this law reinforced the principle of government regulation. But as part of a compromise to pass the bill, the government, rather than the meatpackers, had to finance inspections, and meatpackers could appeal adverse decisions in court.

Pure Food and Drug Laws

The Pure Food and Drug Act (1906) not only prohibited dangerously adulterated foods but also addressed abuses in the patent medicine industry. Makers of tonics and pills had long been making undue claims about their products' effects and liberally using alcohol and narcotics as ingredients. Although the law did not ban such products as a "Brain Stimulator and Nerve Tonic," it did require that the labels list the ingredients—a goal consistent with Progressive confidence that if people knew the truth they would make wiser purchases.

Roosevelt's approach to labor resembled his stance toward business. When the United Mine Workers struck against Pennsylvania coal mine owners in 1902 over an eight-hour workday and higher pay, the president employed Progressive tactics of investigation and arbitration. Owners, however, stubbornly refused to recognize the union or arbitrate grievances. As winter approached and fuel shortages threatened, Roosevelt roused public opinion. He threatened to use federal troops to reopen the mines, thus forcing management to accept arbitration of the dispute by a special commission. The commission decided in favor of higher wages and reduced hours and required management to deal with grievance committees elected by the miners, but it did not mandate recognition of the union. The decision, according to Roosevelt, provided a "square deal" for all. The settlement also embodied Roosevelt's belief that the president or his representatives should have a say in which labor demands were legitimate and which were not.

Roosevelt did not originate government involvement in modern resource conservation; important developments in this area, especially the establishment of national parks, had begun in the late nineteenth century. But he did combine the Progressive impulse for efficiency with his love for the great outdoors to advance conservation policy. Prior to Roosevelt, the government had habitually transferred ownership and control of natural resources on federal land to the states and to private interests. Roosevelt, however, believed the most efficient way to use and conserve these resources would be for the government to retain public management over those lands that remained in the public domain.

Conservation

Roosevelt took steps to exert federal power over resources in several ways. He tried, though unsuccessfully, to revise an 1873 law under which the government sold western coal and oil lands at very cheap prices to private concerns. Roosevelt wanted to retain government ownership and charge producers lease fees (such a policy was instituted in 1920). He did succeed in protecting waterpower sites from sale and instead charged permit fees for users who wanted to produce hydroelectricity. He also supported the Newlands Reclamation Act of 1902, which controlled the sale of irrigated federal land in the West. He tripled the number and acreage of national forests and supported conservationist Gifford Pinchot in creating the U.S. Forest Service. Pinchot advocated scientific management of the nation's woodlands to protect the land and water from overuse by timber cutters, farmers, and herders. Like Roosevelt, Pinchot did not seek to lock up resources permanently, but rather to guarantee their efficient use.

During his last year in office, Roosevelt retreated from the Republican Party's traditional friendliness to big business. He lashed out at the irresponsibility of "malefactors of great wealth" and supported stronger business regulation and heavier taxation of the rich. Having promised that he would not seek reelection, Roosevelt backed his friend Secretary of War William Howard Taft for the Republican nomination in 1908, hoping that Taft would continue his initiatives. Democrats nominated William Jennings Bryan for the third time, but the "Great Commoner" lost again.

Early in 1909 Roosevelt traveled to Africa to shoot game, leaving Taft to face political problems that his predecessor had managed to postpone. Foremost among them was the tariff; rates had risen to excessive levels. Honoring Taft's pledge to cut rates, the House passed a bill sponsored by Representative Sereno E. Payne that provided for numerous reductions. Protectionists in the Senate prepared, as in the past, to amend the House bill and revise rates upward. But Senate Progressives, led by La Follette, organized a stinging attack on the tariff for benefiting special interests, trapping Taft between reformers who claimed to be preserving Roosevelt's antitrust campaign and protectionists who still dominated the Republican Party. In the end, Senator Nelson W. Aldrich and other protectionists restored many of the cuts the Payne bill had made, and Taft

Taft Administration

signed what became known as the Payne-Aldrich Tariff (1909). In the eyes of Progressives, Taft had failed the test of filling Roosevelt's shoes.

Progressive and conservative wings of the Republican Party were rapidly drifting apart. Soon after the tariff controversy, a group of insurgents in the House challenged Speaker "Uncle Joe" Cannon of Illinois, whose power over committee assignments and the scheduling of debates could make or break a piece of legislation. Taft first supported then abandoned the insurgents, who nevertheless managed to liberalize procedures by enlarging the influential Rules Committee and removing selection of its members from Cannon's control. In 1910 Taft also angered conservationists by firing Gifford Pinchot, who had protested Secretary of the Interior Richard A. Ballinger's plan to reduce federal supervision of western waterpower sites and his sale of coal lands in Alaska.

In reality Taft was as sympathetic to reform as Roosevelt was. He prosecuted more trusts than Roosevelt, expanded national forest reserves, signed the Mann-Elkins Act (1910), which bolstered the regulatory powers of the ICC, and supported labor reforms such as the eight-hour workday and mine safety legislation. The Sixteenth Amendment, which legalized the federal income tax, and the Seventeenth Amendment, which provided for direct election of U.S. senators, were initiated during Taft's presidency (and ratified in 1913).

In 1910, when Roosevelt returned from Africa, he found his party torn and tormented. Reformers, angered by Taft's apparent insensitivity to their causes, formed the National Progressive Republican League and rallied behind Robert La Follette for president in 1912. Another wing of the party remained loyal to Taft. Disappointed by Taft's performance (particularly his firing of Pinchot), Roosevelt began to speak out. He filled his speeches with references to "the welfare of the people" and stronger regulation of business. When La Follette became ill early in 1912, Roosevelt, proclaiming himself fit as a "bull moose," threw his hat into the ring for the Republican presidential nomination.

The Bull Moose Party

Taft's supporters controlled the Republican convention and nominated him for a second term. In protest, Roosevelt's supporters bolted the convention to form a third party—the Progressive, or Bull Moose, Party—and nominated the fifty-three-year-old former president. Meanwhile, Democrats took forty-six ballots to select their candidate, New Jersey's Progressive governor Woodrow Wilson. Socialists again nominated Eugene V. Debs.

Woodrow Wilson and the Extension of Reform

Wilson won the election with 42 percent of the popular vote. He was a minority president, though he did capture 435 out of 531 electoral votes. Roosevelt received 27 percent of the popular vote. Taft finished third, polling 23 percent of the popular vote and only 8 electoral votes. Debs won 901,000 votes, 6 percent of the total, but no electoral votes. Fully three-quarters of the electorate thus supported some alternative to the view of restrained government that Taft represented.

Sharp debate over Progressive fundamentals had characterized the campaign. Roosevelt offered voters the "New Nationalism." He foresaw an era of national unity in which government would coordinate and regulate economic activity. He would not destroy big business, which he viewed as an efficient organizer of production. Instead, he would establish regulatory commissions of experts who would protect citizens' interests and ensure wise use of economic power.

New Nationalism and New Freedom

Wilson offered a more idealistic scheme, the "New Freedom." He argued that concentrated economic power threatened individual liberty and that monopolies had to be broken up so the marketplace could become genuinely open. Like Roosevelt, Wilson would enhance government authority to protect and regulate, but he stopped short of advocating the cooperation between business and government inherent in Roosevelt's New Nationalism.

Roosevelt and Wilson stood closer together than their rhetoric implied. Both men strongly supported equality of opportunity (chiefly for white males), conservation of natural resources, fair wages, and social betterment for all. Neither would hesitate to expand government activity through strong personal leadership and bureaucratic reform. Thus even though Wilson received a minority of the total vote in 1912, he could interpret the election results as a mandate to subdue trusts and broaden the federal government's role in social reform.

As president, Wilson found it necessary to blend New Freedom competition with New Nationalism regulation; in so doing, he set the direction of future federal economic policy. The corporate merger movement had proceeded so far that restoration of open competition proved impossible. Wilson could only try to prevent corporate abuses by expanding government's regulatory powers. His administration moved toward that end with passage in 1914 of the Clayton Anti-Trust Act and a bill creating the Federal Trade Commission (FTC). The Clayton Act corrected deficiencies of the Sherman Anti-Trust Act of 1890 by outlawing monopolistic practices such as price discrimination (efforts to destroy competition by lowering prices in some regions but not in others) and interlocking directorates (management of two or more competing companies by the same executives). The FTC would investigate companies and issue cease-and-desist orders against unfair trade practices. Accused companies could appeal FTC orders in court; nevertheless, the FTC represented another step toward consumer protection.

Wilson's Policy on Business Regulation

Wilson expanded regulation of banking with the Federal Reserve Act (1913), which established the nation's first central banking system since 1836, when the Second Bank of the United States expired. The act created twelve district banks to hold reserves of member banks throughout the nation. The district banks, supervised by the Federal Reserve Board, would lend money to member banks at a low interest rate called the discount rate. By adjusting this rate (and thus the amount a bank could afford to borrow), district banks could increase or decrease the amount of money in circulation. In other words, in response to the nation's needs, the Federal Reserve Board could loosen or tighten credit. Monetary affairs no longer would depend on the gold supply, and interest rates would be fairer, especially for small borrowers.

Wilson attempted to restore competition in commerce with the Underwood Tariff, passed in 1913. By

Tariff and Tax Reform

the 1910s, prices for some consumer goods had become unnaturally high because tariffs had discouraged the importation of cheaper foreign materials and manufactured goods. By reducing or eliminating certain tariff rates, the Underwood Tariff encouraged imports. To replace revenues lost because of tariff reductions, the act levied a graduated income tax on U.S. residents—an option that had been made possible when the Sixteenth Amendment was ratified earlier that year. The income tax was tame by today's standards. Incomes under $4,000 were exempt; thus almost all factory workers and farmers escaped taxation. Individuals and corporations earning between $4,000 and $20,000 had to pay a 1 percent tax; thereafter rates rose gradually to a maximum of 6 percent on earnings over $500,000.

The outbreak of the First World War and the approaching presidential election campaign prompted Wilson to support stronger reforms in 1916. Concerned that farmers needed a better system of long-term mortgage credit, the president backed the Federal Farm Loan Act. This measure created twelve federally supported banks that would lend money at moderate interest to farmers who belonged to credit institutions.

To forestall railroad strikes that might disrupt transportation at a time of national emergency, Wilson pushed passage of the Adamson Act, which mandated an eight-hour workday and time-and-a-half overtime pay for railroad laborers. Finally, Wilson courted support from social reformers by backing laws that regulated child labor and provided workers' compensation for federal employees who suffered work-related injuries or illness.

In selecting a candidate to oppose Wilson in 1916, Republicans snubbed Theodore Roosevelt in favor of Charles Evans Hughes, a Supreme Court justice and former reform governor of New York. Acutely aware of the First World War's impact on national affairs (Europe had been ablaze since 1914), Wilson ran for reelection on a platform of peace, Progressivism, and preparedness; his supporters used the campaign slogan "He Kept Us Out of War." Hughes and his fractured party could not muzzle Roosevelt, whose bellicose speeches suggested that Republicans

Election of 1916

would drag Americans into war. Wilson received 9.1 million votes to Hughes's 8.5 million, and the president barely won in the electoral college, 277 to 254. Because of the war in Europe, and America's eventual entry into the conflict, foreign policy issues dominated Wilson's second term (see Chapter 23).

Summary

By 1920, government, economy, and society as they had existed in the nineteenth century were gone forever. In their efforts to achieve their goals of ending abuses of power, reforming institutions, and applying scientific principles and efficient management, Progressives established the principle of public intervention to ensure fairness, health, and safety. Concern over poverty and injustice reached new heights. However, with the nation's growing affluence, reformers were unable to sustain the reform impulse. Although Progressive values lingered after the First World War, a mass consumer society began to refocus people's attention from reform to materialism.

The Progressive era was characterized by multiple and sometimes contradictory goals. By no means was there a single Progressive movement. Reform programs on the national level ranged from Roosevelt's faith in big government as a coordinator of big business to Wilson's promise to dissolve economic concentrations and legislate open competition. At state and local levels, reformers pursued causes as varied as neighborhood improvement, government reorganization, public ownership of utilities, betterment of working conditions, and control of morality.

In spite of the Progressives' remarkable successes, the outright failure of many Progressive initiatives indicates the strength of the opposition, as well as weaknesses within the reform movements themselves. Courts asserted constitutional and liberty-of-contract doctrines in striking down key Progressive legislation, notably the federal law prohibiting child labor. In states and cities, adoption of the initiative, referendum, and recall did not encourage greater participation in government as had been hoped. On the federal level, regulatory agencies rarely had enough resources for thorough investigations; they had to depend on information from the very companies they policed. Progressives thus failed in many respects to redistribute power. In 1920 as in 1900, government remained under the influence of business and industry.

Yet the reform movements that characterized the Progressive era reshaped the nation's future. Trust-busting, however faulty, forced industrialists to become more sensitive to public opinion, and insurgents in Congress partially diluted the power of dictatorial politicians. Progressive legislation equipped government with tools to protect consumers against price fixing and dangerous products. The income tax, created to redistribute wealth, also became a source of government revenue. And perhaps most important, Progressives challenged old ways of thinking and made the nation acutely aware of its principles and promises.

LEGACY FOR A PEOPLE AND A NATION
Women and Social Work

By the year 2000, human services—occupations catering to people's personal needs in the areas of health, education, housing, income, and justice and public safety—constituted the sixth-fastest-growing career field in the United States. Social workers dominated this profession, and over three-fourths of social workers were female, a legacy from the actions of concerned women during the Progressive era.

Jane Addams, the indomitable founder and leader of the Hull House settlement, laid the groundwork for the social work profession. Almost all early social work pioneers who aided her were women, including Florence Kelley, Alice Hamilton, and Edith and Grace Abbott. These and other women used the field of social welfare to create occupations for other educated, ambitious, and service-minded women not only in social work but also in the areas of child welfare, juvenile justice, and healthcare.

In 1898 formal organization of the profession began with the establishment of The New York School of Philanthropy, later named the Columbia University School of Social Work. Thereafter, programs for educating social workers appeared in other cities. Women continued to dominate the profession. Of 111 individuals listed as "social work pioneers" by the National

Association of Social Workers over the past one hundred years, 77 are female. These leaders and the profession in general served critical functions in bringing public resources to people in need, especially during major periods of social action such as the New Deal of the 1930s, the Great Society of the 1960s, and today—especially in the area of assisting new immigrants.

Women's activities in social service have had drawbacks as well as successes. Throughout the twentieth century, men have held most of the top administrative positions in social work organizations and schools. Women in the profession still tend toward casework, while men more frequently are involved in social welfare policymaking. And women social workers receive lower salaries than men and are less likely to be promoted. Moreover, psychological principles, which have become central to social work theory, carry a sexist tone in that they are likely to define "normal" social behavior in male-oriented terms, making it more probable that social workers will view female clients with social problems as having "abnormal" traits. Thus the pioneer efforts by women in social service dating from the Progressive era have still not erased gender-based biases in American culture.

For Further Reading, see the Appendix. For Web resources, go to history.college.hmco.com/students.

22

THE QUEST FOR EMPIRE

1865–1914

evil!" they angrily shouted at Lottie Moon. "Foreign devil!" The Southern Baptist missionary braced herself against the antiforeign Chinese "rabble" she had vowed to convert to Christianity. On a day in the 1880s, she walked "steadily and persistently" through the village hecklers, vowing to win their acceptance and then their souls.

Born in 1840 in Virginia and educated at what is now Hollins College, Charlotte Diggs Moon volunteered in 1873 for "woman's work" in northern China. There she taught and proselytized, largely among women and children because women seldom preached to men and men were forbidden to preach to women. This compassionate, pious, and courageous single woman, "putting love into action," worked in China until her death in 1912.

Lottie Moon (Mu Ladi or 幕拉第) made bold and sometimes dangerous evangelizing trips in the 1870s and 1880s to isolated Chinese hamlets. Then in the 1890s a "storm of persecution" against foreigners swept China. Missionaries, because they were upending traditional ways and authority, became hated targets. In the village of Shaling in early 1890, Lottie Moon's Christian converts were beaten and the "foreign devils" ordered to move out. Fearing for her life, she had to flee. For several months in 1900, during the violent Boxer Rebellion, she had to leave China altogether as a multinational force (that included U.S. troops) intervened to save foreign missionaries, diplomats, and merchants.

Like so many other Americans who went overseas in the late nineteenth and early twentieth centuries,

IMPORTANT EVENTS

1861–69	Seward sets expansionist course
1866	Transatlantic cable completed
1867	Alaska and Midway acquired
1868	Burlingame Treaty with China regulates immigration
1871	Anglo-American treaty sends *Alabama* claims issue to tribunal
1874	U.S. foreign trade shifts to favorable balance
1876	Pro-U.S. Díaz begins long rule in Mexico
1880	Treaty limits Chinese immigration to the United States
1883	Congress votes funds for New Navy
1885	Strong's *Our Country* celebrates Anglo-Saxons
1887	U.S. gains naval rights to Pearl Harbor, Hawai'i
1889	First Pan-American Conference
1890	Mahan's *The Influence of Sea Power upon History* published
1893	Severe economic depression begins Turner sets forth frontier thesis Hawaiian Queen Lili'uokalani overthrown
1894	Wilson-Gorham Tariff imposes duty on Cuban sugar
1895	Olney blasts Britain in Venezuelan crisis Cuban revolution against Spain begins Japan defeats China in war
1898	Publication of de Lôme letter Sinking of the *Maine* Spanish-American-Cuban-Filipino War Hawai'i annexed by the United States

1899	Treaty of Paris enlarges U.S. empire First Open Door note calls for equal trade opportunity in China Philippine insurrection breaks out
1900	Second Open Door note issued during Boxer Rebellion in China U.S. exports total $1.5 billion
1901	Hay-Pauncefote Treaty allows U.S. canal
1903	Panama grants canal rights to U.S. Platt Amendment subjugates Cuba
1904	Roosevelt Corollary declares U.S. a hemispheric "police power"
1905	Taft-Katsura Agreement gains Japanese pledge to respect Philippines Portsmouth Conference ends Russo-Japanese War U.S. financial supervision of Dominican Republic begins
1906	San Francisco school board segregates Asian schoolchildren U.S. invades Cuba to quell revolt
1907	"Great White Fleet" makes world tour "Gentleman's agreement" with Japan restricts immigration
1908	Root-Takahira Agreement with Japan reaffirms Open Door in China
1910	Mexican revolution threatens U.S. interests
1911	Treaty bans pelagic sealing in Bering Sea
1912	U.S. troops invade Cuba again U.S. troops occupy Nicaragua
1914	U.S. troops invade Mexico First World War begins Panama Canal opens

Lottie Moon helped spread American culture and implant U.S. influence abroad. In this complex process, other peoples sometimes adopted and sometimes rejected American ways. At the same time, American participants in this cultural expansion, and the cultural collisions it generated, became transformed. Lottie Moon, for example, strove to understand the Chinese people and learn their language. She even assumed their dress. She reminded other less sensitive missionaries that the Chinese rightfully took pride in their own ancient history and thus had no reason to "gape in astonishment at Western civilization."

Lottie Moon also changed—again, in her own words—from "a timid self-distrustful girl into a brave self-reliant woman." As she questioned the Chinese confinement of women, most conspicuous in arranged marriages, footbinding, and sexual segregation, she advanced women's rights. She understood that she could not convert Chinese women unless they had the freedom to listen to her appeals.

Critics over the decades have labeled as "cultural imperialism" the activities of Lottie Moon and other missionaries, accusing the missionaries of seeking to subvert indigenous traditions and sparking destructive cultural clashes. Defenders of missionary work, on the other hand, have celebrated their efforts to break down cultural barriers and to bring the world's peoples closer together. Either way, Lottie Moon's story illustrates how Americans interacted with the world in diverse ways, how through their experiences the categories "domestic" and "foreign" intersected, and how they expanded abroad not only to seek land, trade, investments, and strategic bases but also to promote American culture, including the Christian faith.

Between the Civil War and the First World War, Americans ranked as unabashed expansionists and imperialists. The expansionistic impulse that the Civil War interrupted was rekindled after that conflict, and Americans began building, managing, and protecting an overseas empire. In that imperialistic age of "living" and "dying" nations, as British prime minister Lord Salisbury observed, the international system witnessed an assertive Germany challenge an overextended Great Britain, an economic and military giant becoming, said one diplomat, the "weary titan" of the world. Japan expanded in Asia at the expense of both China and Russia. As for the "living" United States, it emerged as a great power with particular clout in Latin America, especially as the "dying" Spain declined and Britain disengaged from the hemisphere.

The United States's imperialist surge, however, sparked considerable opposition. Abroad, native nationalists, commercial competitors, and other imperial nations tried to block the spread of U.S. influence, while anti-imperialists at home stimulated a momentous debate over the fundamental course of American foreign policy. Most Americans applauded expansionism—the outward movement of goods, ships, dollars, people, and ideas—as a traditional feature of their nation's history. But many became uneasy whenever expansionism gave way to imperialism—the imposition of control over other peoples, undermining their sovereignty and usurping their freedom to make their own decisions. Imperial control could be imposed either formally (by military occupation, annexation, or colonialism) or informally (by economic domination, political manipulation, or the threat of intervention). As the informal methods indicate, imperialism meant far more than the taking of territory.

Critics in the late nineteenth century disparaged territorial imperialism as unbefitting the United States. Would not an overseas territorial empire, incorporating people of color living far from the United States, weaken institutions at home, threaten American culture, invite perpetual war, and violate honored principles? Most Americans endorsed economic expansion as essential to the nation's prosperity and security, but anti-imperialists drew a line between expansionism and imperialism: profitable and fair trade relationships, yes; exploitation, no.

In the late nineteenth century the federal government sometimes failed to fund adequately the vehicles of expansion (such as the navy until the 1880s), and most businessmen ignored foreign commerce in favor of the domestic marketplace. Still, the direction of U.S. foreign policy after the Civil War became unmistakable: Americans intended to exert their influence beyond the continental United States. ■

Imperial Promoters: The Foreign Policy Elite and Economic Expansion

 Foreign policy has always sprung from the domestic setting of a nation—its needs, wants, moods, ideology, and culture. The leaders who guided America's expansionist foreign relations were the same people who guided the economic development of the machine age, forged the transcontinental railroad, built America's bustling cities and giant corporations, and shaped a mass culture. They unabashedly espoused the idea that the United States was an exceptional nation.

"The people" may influence domestic policy, but they seldom shape foreign policy. Most Americans simply do not follow international relations or express themselves on foreign issues. The making of foreign policy, then, is usually dominated by what scholars have labeled the "foreign policy elite"—opinion leaders in politics, business, labor, agriculture, religion, journalism, education, and the military. In the post–Civil War era, this small group—better read and better traveled than most Americans, more cosmopolitan in outlook, and politically active—believed that U.S. prosperity and security depended on the exertion of U.S. influence abroad. Theodore Roosevelt, appointed assistant secretary of the navy in 1897, was among them; so were Senator Henry Cabot Lodge, who joined the Foreign Relations Committee in 1896, and the corporate lawyer Elihu Root, who later would serve as both secretary of war and secretary of state. Increasingly in the late nineteenth century, and especially in the 1890s, the expansionist-minded elite urged both formal and informal imperialism.

Foreign Policy Elite

These American leaders believed that selling, buying, and investing in foreign marketplaces were important to the United States. Why? One reason was profits from foreign sales. Fear also helped make the case for foreign trade because the nation's farms and factories produced more than Americans could consume, especially during the 1890s depression. Foreign commerce might serve as a safety valve to relieve overproduction, unemployment, economic depression, and the social tension that arose from them. Moreover, in an era when the most powerful nations in the world were also the greatest traders, vigorous foreign economic expansion symbolized national stature.

Foreign trade figured prominently in the tremendous economic growth of the United States after the Civil War. Foreign commerce, in turn, stimulated the building of a larger protective navy, the professionalization of the foreign service, calls for more colonies, and a more interventionist foreign policy. In 1865 U.S. exports totaled $234 million; by 1914 they had reached $2.5 billion (see Figure 22.1). In 1874 the United States reversed its historically unfavorable balance of trade (importing more than it exported) and began to enjoy a

Foreign Trade Expansion

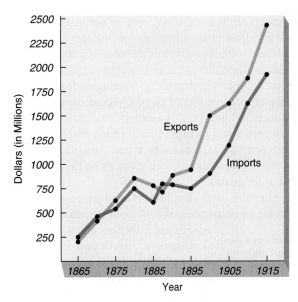

Figure 22.1   U.S. Trade Expansion, 1865–1914   This figure illustrates two key characteristics of U.S. foreign trade: first, that the United States began in the 1870s to enjoy a favorable balance of trade (exporting more than it imported); second, that U.S. exports expanded tremendously, making the United States one of the world's economic giants.   (Source: Thomas G. Paterson, J. Garry Clifford, and Kenneth J. Hagan, *American Foreign Relations: A History,* 5th ed. Copyright © 2000 by Houghton Mifflin Company.)

long-term favorable balance (exporting more than it imported).

Agricultural goods accounted for about three-fourths of total exports in 1870 and about two-thirds in 1900. In 1913, when the United States outranked both Great Britain and Germany in manufacturing production, manufactured goods led U.S. exports for the first time. Meanwhile, direct American investments abroad reached $3.5 billion by 1914, placing the United States among the top four investor countries.

Ideology, Culture, and Empire

In the American march toward empire, ideology and culture figured prominently. An intertwined set of ideas conditioned U.S. foreign relations. Nationalism, exceptionalism, capitalism, Social Darwinism, paternalism, and the categorization of foreigners in derogatory race-, age-, and gender-based terms—all influenced American leaders. Fear and prejudice infused many American ideas about the world and foreign peoples—fear of the social disorder stirred by revolution, fear of economic depression, fear of racial and ethnic mixing, fear of women's rights, fear of a closed frontier, fear of losing international stature. To calm their fears and promote their values, leaders exported American culture and sought to remake other societies in the image of the United States.

After the Civil War, leaders championed a nationalism based on notions of American supremacy. Some

Race Thinking

Americans placed people with darker skin, such as blacks and Indians, at the bottom of a racial hierarchy, calling them "uncivilized." At the top sat "civilized" white Anglo-Saxon Americans. Near the top, but beneath Anglo-Saxons, came European peoples—"aggressive" Germans followed by "peasant" Slavs, "sentimental" French and Italians, and "Shylock" Jews. In the middle rank came Latinos, the Spanish-speaking people of Latin America. Also midway in the hierarchy were East Asian peoples, the "Orientals" or "Mongolians."

Reverend Josiah Strong's popular and influential *Our Country* (1885) celebrated an Anglo-Saxon race destined to lead others. Strong believed that "to be a Christian and an Anglo-Saxon and an American . . . is to stand at the very mountaintop of privilege." Social Darwinists saw Americans as a superior people certain to overcome all competition.

The magazine *National Geographic*, which published its first issue in 1888, chronicled with photographs America's new overseas possessions. The editors chose pictures that reflected prevailing American ethnocentric attitudes toward foreigners. Even when smiling faces predominated, the image portrayed was that of strange, exotic, premodern people who had not become "Western." Emphasizing this point, National Geographic regularly pictured women with naked breasts.

Race thinking—popularized in world's fairs, magazine cartoons, postcards, school textbooks, and political orations—reinforced notions of American greatness, influenced the way U.S. leaders dealt with other peoples, and obviated the need to think about the subtle textures of other societies. Such racism

downgraded diplomacy and justified domination and war because self-proclaimed superiors do not negotiate with people ranked as inferiors.

A masculine ethos also characterized American views of foreigners. The language of U.S. leaders was

Male Ethos

weighted with words such as *manliness* and *weakling*. The warrior and president Theodore Roosevelt, along with his imperialist cohorts, often described other nations (and the American peace movement) as effeminate—unable, in contrast to a masculine Uncle Sam, to cope with the demands of world politics. The gendered imagery prevalent in U.S.-foreign relations joined race thinking to place women, people of color, and nations weaker than the United States in the low ranks of the hierarchy of power and, hence, in a necessarily dependent status justifying U.S. hegemony.

Issues of race and gender also marked the experiences of religious missionaries, many of whom were

Missionaries

single women (like Lottie Moon) or wives of clergymen. Missionaries dispatched to Asia and Africa helped spur the transfer of American culture and power abroad. In China by 1915 more than 2,500 American Protestant missionaries—most of them female—labored to preach the gospel, to teach school, and to administer medical care. But as they struggled to win converts, women missionaries also critiqued the Chinese gender system. When they judged non-Christian foreign societies as more exploitative of women than the United States was, in essence they perpetuated cultural stereotypes of Anglo-Saxon superiority that undergirded imperialism.

Expansionists believed that empire benefited both Americans and those who came under their control.

The "Civilizing" Impulse

When the United States intervened in other lands or lectured weaker states, Americans claimed that in remaking foreign societies they were extending liberty and prosperity to less fortunate people. To critics at home and abroad, however, American paternalism appeared hypocritical—a violation of cherished principles. To impose on Filipinos an American-style political system, for example, U.S. officials censored the press, jailed critics, and picked candidates for public office. From this coercive experience, Filipinos may have learned more about how to fix elections than about how to make democracy work.

Ambitions Abroad, 1860s–1880s

The U.S. empire grew gradually, sometimes haltingly, as American leaders defined guiding principles and built institutions to support overseas ambitions. William H. Seward, one of its chief architects, argued relentlessly for extension of the American frontier as senator from New York (1849–1861) and secretary of state (1861–1869). Seward envisioned a large, coordinated U.S. empire encompassing Canada, the Caribbean, Cuba, Central America, Mexico, Hawai'i, Iceland, Greenland, and Pacific islands. This empire would be built not by war but by a natural process of gravitation toward the United States. Commerce would hurry the process, as would a canal across Central America, a transcontinental American railroad to link up with Asian markets, and a telegraph system to speed communications.

Most of Seward's grandiose plans did not reach fruition in his own day. Political foes and anti-imperialists such as Senator Carl Schurz and

William H. Seward's Quest for Empire

E. L. Godkin, editor of the magazine *The Nation*, blocked some of his expansion schemes. They argued that the country already had enough unsettled land and that creating a showcase of democracy and prosperity at home would best persuade other peoples to adopt American institutions and principles.

Seward did enjoy some successes. In 1866, citing the Monroe Doctrine, he sent troops to the border with Mexico and demanded that France abandon its puppet regime there. Also facing angry Mexican nationalists, Napoleon III abandoned the Maximilian monarchy that he had installed by force three years earlier. In 1867 Seward paid Russia $7.2 million for the 591,000 square miles of Alaska—land twice the size of Texas. Some critics lampooned "Seward's Icebox," but the Senate voted overwhelmingly for the treaty. That same year, Seward laid claim to the Midway Islands in the Pacific Ocean.

Seward also realized his dream of a world knit together into a giant communications system. In 1866 an underwater transatlantic cable linked European

International Communications

and American telegraph networks. Telegraph lines to Latin America reached Chile in 1890, and in 1903 a submarine cable crossed the Pacific to the Philippines; three years later it extended to Japan and China. Information about markets, crises, and war flowed steadily and quickly.

Gradually through the late nineteenth century, despite frequent squabbles over such issues as fishing rights along the North Atlantic coast,

Anglo-Canadian-American Relations

Britain and the United States worked to negotiate rather than fight over their differing interests. Seward's successor, Hamilton Fish (1869–1877), inherited the knotty problem of the *Alabama* claims. The *Alabama* and other vessels built in Great Britain for the Confederacy during the Civil War had preyed on Union shipping. Senator Charles Sumner demanded that Britain pay $2 billion in damages or cede Canada to the United States, but Fish favored negotiations. In 1871 Britain and America signed the Washington Treaty, whereby the British apologized and agreed to the creation of a tribunal, which later awarded the United States $15.5 million. Bitter controversy over sealing also ended in a peaceful settlement. Beginning in the late 1860s the United States sought to curb pelagic (open sea) sealing—especially the harvesting of fur seals as they swam in the Bering Sea. Pelagic poachers ignored the law, and despite U.S. seizures of ships, many of them Canadian, the seals faced extermination by the end of the century. Finally, in 1911, Great Britain, the United States, Russia, and Japan banned pelagic sealing altogether and limited land kills.

In China, missionaries became targets of nationalist anger. At the same time, American oil and textile companies sent their wares into a

Sino-American Troubles

China market they dreamed was boundless but actually was limited. American religious leaders and business executives throughout the late nineteenth century appealed for official U.S. protection. At home, although the Burlingame Treaty (1868) provided for free immigration between the United States and China and pledged Sino-American friendship, Sinophobia in the American West led to frequent riots against Chinese immigrants. Moreover, a new treaty in 1880 permitted Congress to suspend Chinese immigration to the United States, and it did so two years later.

In Latin America, meanwhile, the convening in 1889 of the first Pan-American Conference in Washington, D.C., demonstrated growing U.S. influence in the Western Hemisphere. Conferees from Latin America toured U.S. factories and then pledged support for reciprocity treaties to improve hemispheric trade. To encourage inter-American cooperation, they founded the Pan-American Union.

Pan-American Conference

With eyes on all parts of the world, ardent expansionists embraced navalism—the campaign to build an imperial navy. They argued for a bigger, modernized navy. Captain Alfred T. Mahan became a major popularizer for this "New Navy." Because foreign trade was vital to the United States, he argued, the nation required an efficient navy to protect its shipping; in turn, a navy required colonies for bases. Mahan's widely read book *The Influence of Sea Power upon History* (1890) sat on every serious expansionist's shelf, and foreign leaders turned the book's pages. Theodore Roosevelt and Henry Cabot Lodge eagerly consulted Mahan, sharing his belief in the links between trade, navy, and colonies.

Alfred T. Mahan, Navalism, and the New Navy

Moving toward naval modernization, Congress in 1883 authorized construction of the first steel-hulled warships. American factories went to work to produce steam engines, high-velocity shells, powerful guns, and precision instruments. The navy shifted from sail power to steam and from wood construction to steel. Often named for states and cities to kindle patriotism and local support for naval expansion, New Navy ships such as the *Maine*, *Oregon*, and *Boston* thrust the United States into naval prominence.

Crises in the 1890s: Hawai'i, Venezuela, and Cuba

In the depression-plagued 1890s, crises in Hawai'i, Venezuela, and Cuba gave expansionist Americans opportunities to act on their zealous arguments for what Senator Lodge called a "large policy." Belief that the frontier at home had closed accentuated the expansionist case. In 1893 the historian Frederick Jackson Turner postulated that an ever-expanding continental frontier had shaped the American character. That "frontier has gone," Turner pronounced. He did not explicitly say that a new frontier had to be found overseas, but he did claim that "American energy will continually demand a wider field for its exercise."

Hawai'i emerged as a new frontier for Americans. The Hawaiian Islands had long commanded American attention—commercial, religious missionary, naval, and diplomatic. In 1881 Secretary of State James Blaine had declared the Hawaiian Islands "essentially a part of the American system." By 1890 Americans, who represented only 2.1 percent of the population, owned about three-quarters of Hawai'i's wealth and subordinated its economy to that of the United States. Two years later the American elite on the islands formed the subversive Annexation Club.

Annexation of Hawai'i

The annexationists struck in January 1893 in collusion with John L. Stevens, the chief American diplomat in Hawai'i, who dispatched troops from the U.S.S. *Boston* to occupy Honolulu. Queen Lili'uokalani, who had sought to roll back the political power of the foreigners, was arrested and confined, surrendered, and relinquished authority to the U.S. government. Up went the American flag. Against the queen's protests and those of Japan, President Benjamin Harrison hurriedly sent an annexation treaty to the Senate. Incoming President Grover Cleveland, however, ordered an investigation, which confirmed a conspiracy by the economic elite in league with Stevens and noted that most Hawaiians opposed annexation. Down came the American flag. But when Hawai'i gained renewed attention as a strategic and commercial way station to Asia and the Philippines during the Spanish-American-Cuban-Filipino War, President William McKinley maneuvered annexation through Congress on July 7, 1898.

The Venezuelan crisis of 1895 also saw the United States in an expansive mood. For decades Venezuela and Great Britain had quarreled over the border between Venezuela and British Guiana. The disputed territory contained rich gold deposits and the mouth of the Orinoco River, a commercial gateway to northern South America. Venezuela asked for U.S. help. Presi-

Venezuelan Boundary Dispute

Queen Lili'uokalani (1838–1917), ousted from her throne in 1893 by wealthy revolutionaries, vigorously protested in her autobiography and diary, as well as in interviews, the U.S. annexation of Hawai'i in 1898. For years she defended Hawaiian nationalism and emphasized that American officials in 1893 had conspired with Sanford B. Dole and others to overthrow the native monarchy.   (Courtesy of the Lili'uokalani Trust)

dent Cleveland decided that the British had to be warned away. In July 1895, Secretary of State Richard Olney brashly lectured the British that the Monroe Doctrine prohibited European powers from denying self-government to nations in the Western Hemisphere. The British, seeking international friends to counter intensifying competition from Germany, quietly retreated from the crisis. In 1896 an Anglo-American arbitration board divided the disputed territory between Britain and Venezuela. The Venezuelans were barely consulted. Thus the United States displayed a trait common to imperialists: disregard for the rights and sensibilities of small nations.

In 1895 came yet another crisis, this one in Cuba. From 1868 to 1878 the Cubans had battled Spain

U.S. Interests and Revolution in Cuba

for their independence. Slavery was abolished but independence denied. While the Cuban economy suffered depression, repressive Spanish rule continued. Insurgents committed to *Cuba Libre* waited for another chance. José Martí, one of the heroes of Cuban history, collected money, arms, and men in the United States. This was but one of the many ways the lives of Americans and Cubans intersected, the settling of Cubans of all classes in Baltimore, New York, Boston, and Philadelphia being another. Prominent Cubans on the island sent their children to schools in the United States.

The Cuban and U.S. economies also became linked. American investments of $50 million, most in sugar plantations, dominated the Caribbean island. More than 90 percent of Cuba's sugar was exported to the United States, and most island imports came from the United States. A change in U.S. tariff policy hastened the Cuban revolution against Spain and the island's further incorporation into "the American system." The Wilson-Gorman Tariff (1894) imposed a duty on Cuban sugar, which had been entering the United States duty-free. The Cuban economy, highly dependent on exports, plunged into deep crisis.

From American soil, Martí launched a revolution in 1895 that mounted in human and material costs. Rebels burned sugar-cane fields and razed mills, conducting an economic war and using guerrilla tactics to avoid head-on clashes with Spanish soldiers. To separate the insurgents from their supporters among the Cuban people, Spanish general Valeriano Weyler instituted a policy of "reconcentration." Some three hundred thousand Cubans were herded into fortified towns and camps, where hunger, starvation, and disease led to tens of thousands of deaths. As reports of atrocity and destruction became headline news in the American yellow press, Americans sympathized increasingly with the insurrectionists. In late 1897 a new government in Madrid modified reconcentration and promised some autonomy for Cuba, but the insurgents continued to gain ground.

Events in early 1898 caused President William McKinley to lose faith in Madrid's ability to bring peace to Cuba. In January, when antireform pro-Spanish loyalists and army personnel rioted in Havana, Washington ordered the battleship *Maine* to Havana harbor to demonstrate U.S. concern and to protect

Sinking of the Maine

American citizens. On February 15 an explosion ripped the *Maine*, killing 266 of 354 American officers and crew. Just a week earlier, William Randolph Hearst's inflammatory *New York Journal* had published a stolen private letter written by the Spanish minister in Washington, Enrique Dupuy de Lôme, who belittled McKinley and suggested that Spain would fight on. Congress soon complied unanimously with McKinley's request for $50 million in defense funds. The naval board investigating the *Maine* disaster then reported that a mine had caused the explosion. (Later, official and unofficial studies attributed the sinking to an accidental internal explosion.)

The impact of these events narrowed McKinley's diplomatic options. He decided to send Spain an ultimatum. In late March the United

McKinley's Ultimatum and War Decision

States insisted that Spain accept an armistice, end reconcentration altogether, and designate McKinley as arbiter. Madrid made concessions. It abolished reconcentration and rejected, then accepted, an armistice. The weary president hesitated, but he would no longer tolerate chronic disorder just 90 miles off the U.S. coast. On April 11 McKinley asked Congress for authorization to use force against Spain. Congress acted and on April 19 declared Cuba free and independent and directed the president to use force to remove Spanish authority from the island. The legislators also passed the Teller Amendment, which disclaimed any U.S. intention to annex Cuba or "control" the island "except for the pacification thereof." McKinley beat back a congressional amendment to recognize the rebel government. Believing that the Cubans were not ready for self-government, he argued that they needed a period of American tutoring.

The Spanish-American-Cuban-Filipino War and the Debate over Empire

The motives of Americans who favored war were mixed and complex. McKinley's April message expressed a humanitarian impulse to stop the bloodletting, a concern for com-

Motives for War

A

merce and property, and the psychological need to end the nightmarish anxiety once and for all. Republican politicians advised McKinley that their party would lose the upcoming congressional elections unless he solved the Cuban question. Many businesspeople, who had been hesitant before the crisis of early 1898, joined many farmers in the belief that ejecting Spain from Cuba would open new markets for surplus production.

Inveterate imperialists saw war as an opportunity to fulfill expansionist dreams. Naval enthusiasts could prove the worth of the New Navy. Some religious leaders also saw merit in war; one leader remarked that "in saving others we may save ourselves." Conservatives, alarmed by Populism and violent labor strikes, welcomed war as a national unifier. Sensationalism also figured in the march to war, with the yellow press exaggerating stories of Spanish misdeeds. Some too young to remember the bloody Civil War looked on war as adventure and used masculine rhetoric to trumpet the call to arms. Anglo-Saxon supremacists such as the politician Albert Beveridge shouted, "God's hour has struck." Overarching all explanations for the 1898 war were expansionism and imperialism.

More than 263,000 regulars and volunteers served in the army and another 25,000 in the navy during

The U.S. Military at War

B

the war. Most of them never left the United States. Deaths numbered 5,462—but only 379 in combat. The rest fell to yellow fever and typhoid. About 10,000 African American troops, assigned to segregated regiments, found no relief from racism and Jim Crow. For all, food, sanitary conditions, and medical care were bad.

To the surprise of most Americans, the first war news actually came from faraway Asia, from the Spanish colony of the Philippine Islands.

Dewey in the Philippines

C

On May 1, 1898, Commodore George Dewey's New Navy ship *Olympia* led an American squadron into Manila Bay and wrecked the outgunned Spanish fleet. Dewey and his sailors had been on alert in Hong Kong since February, when he received orders from imperial-minded Washington to attack the islands if war broke out. Manila ranked with Pearl Harbor as a choice harbor, and the Philippines sat significantly on the way to China and its potentially huge market.

American troops saw their first ground-war action on June 22, the day several thousand of them landed near Santiago de Cuba and laid siege to the city. On July 3 U.S. warships sank the Spanish Caribbean squadron in Santiago harbor. American forces then assaulted the Spanish colony of Puerto Rico. Losing on all fronts, Madrid sued for peace.

On August 12 Spain and the United States signed an armistice to end the war. In Paris, in December 1898, American and Spanish negotiators agreed on the peace terms: independence for Cuba from Spain; cession of the Philippines, Puerto Rico, and Guam (an island in the Pacific) to the United States; and American payment of $20 million to Spain for the territories. The U.S. empire now stretched deep into Asia; and the annexation of Wake Island (1898), Hawaiʻi (1898), and Samoa (1899) gave American traders, missionaries, and naval promoters other steppingstones to China.

Treaty of Paris

D

During the war with Spain, the *Washington Post* detected "a new appetite, a yearning to show our strength. . . . The taste of empire is in the mouth of the people." But as the nation debated the Treaty of Paris, anti-imperialists such as Mark Twain, William Jennings Bryan, Jane Addams, Andrew Carnegie, and Senator George Hoar of Massachusetts argued vigorously against annexation of the Philippines. They were disturbed that a war to free Cuba had led to empire.

Some critics appealed to principle, citing the Declaration of Independence and the Constitution: the conquest of people against their wills violated the right of self-determination. Other anti-imperialists argued that the United States could acquire markets without having to subjugate foreign peoples. Some white anti-imperialists, believing in a racial hierarchy, warned that annexing people of color would undermine Anglo-Saxon purity and supremacy at home. Others claimed that to maintain empire, the president would repeatedly have to dispatch troops overseas. Because he could do so as commander-in-chief, he would not have to seek congressional approval, thus subverting the constitutional checks-and-balances system.

Anti-imperialist Arguments

E

The anti-imperialists entered the debate with many handicaps and never launched an effective campaign. Although they organized the Anti-Imperialist League in November 1898, they differed so profoundly on domestic issues that they found it difficult to speak with one voice on a foreign question. They also appeared inconsistent: Carnegie would accept colonies if they were not acquired by force; Hoar voted for annexation of Hawaiʻi but not of the Philippines. Finally, possession of the Philippines was an established fact, very hard to undo.

The imperialists answered their critics with appeals to patriotism, destiny, and commerce. They sketched a scenario of American greatness: merchant ships plying the waters to boundless Asian markets; naval vessels cruising the Pacific to protect American interests; missionaries uplifting inferior peoples. Furthermore, Germany and Japan, two powerful international competitors, were snooping around the Philippines, apparently ready to seize them if the United States's grip loosened. National honor dictated that Americans keep what they had shed blood to take.

Imperialist Arguments

F

In February 1899, by a 57-to-27 vote, the Senate passed the Treaty of Paris ending the war with Spain. Most Republicans voted "yes" and most Democrats "no." The Democratic presidential candidate Bryan carried the anti-imperialist case into the election of 1900, warning that repudiation of self-government in the Philippines would weaken the principle at home. But the victorious McKinley refused to apologize for American imperialism.

Asian Encounters: Open Door in China, Philippine Insurrection, and Japan

In 1895, the same year as the Venezuelan crisis and the outbreak of the Cuban revolution, Japan claimed victory over China in a short war. Outsiders had been pecking away at China since the 1840s, but the Japanese onslaught intensified the international scramble. Taking advantage of the Qing (Manchu) dynasty's weakness, the major powers carved out spheres of influence (regions

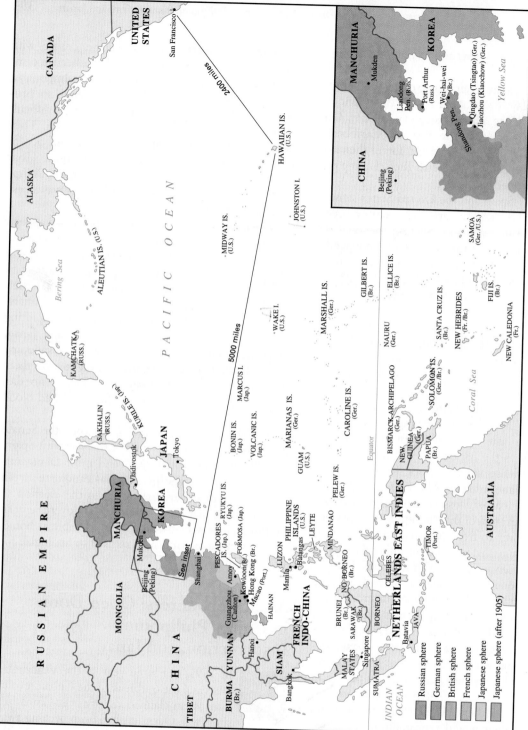

Map 22.1 Imperialism in Asia: Turn of the Century China and the Pacific region had become imperialist hunting grounds by the turn of the century. The European powers and Japan controlled more areas than the U.S., which nonetheless participated in the imperial race by annexing the Philippines, Wake, Guam, Hawai'i, and Samoa; announcing the Open Door policy; and expanding trade. As the spheres of influence in China demonstrate, that besieged nation succumbed to outsiders despite the Open Door policy.

over which the outside powers claimed political control and exclusive commercial privileges): Germany in Shandong; Russia in Manchuria; France in Yunnan and Hainan; Britain in Kowloon and Hong Kong. Japan controlled Formosa and Korea as well as parts of China proper (see Map 22.1). American religious and business leaders petitioned Washington to halt the dismemberment of China before they were closed out.

Secretary of State John Hay knew that the United States could not force the imperial powers out of China, but he was determined to

Open Door Policy

A

protect American commerce and missionaries such as Lottie Moon. In September 1899 Hay sent the imperial nations active in China a note asking them to respect the principle of equal trade opportunity—an Open Door. The recipients sent evasive replies, privately complaining that the United States was seeking for free in China the trade rights that they had gained at considerable military and administrative cost. The next year, a Chinese secret society called the Boxers incited riots that killed foreigners, including missionaries. The Boxers laid siege to the foreign legations in Beijing. The United States joined the imperial powers in sending troops to lift the siege. Hay also sent a second Open Door note in July that instructed other nations to preserve China's territorial integrity and to honor "equal and impartial trade."

Though Hay's foray into Asian politics settled little, the Open Door policy became a cornerstone of U.S. diplomacy. The "open door" had actually been a long-standing American principle, for as a trading nation the United States opposed barriers to international commerce and demanded equal access to foreign markets. After 1900, however, the Open Door policy became an instrument first to pry open markets and then to dominate them, not just in China but throughout the world. The Open Door also developed as an ideology with several tenets: first, that America's domestic well-being required exports; second, that foreign trade would suffer interruption unless the United States intervened abroad to implant American principles and keep markets open; and third, that the closing of any area to American products, citizens, or ideas threatened the survival of the United States itself.

In the Philippines, meanwhile, U.S. occupation authorities soon antagonized their new "wards," as McKinley labeled them. Emilio Aguinaldo, the Philip-

Philippine Insurrection and Pacification

B

pine nationalist leader who had been battling the Spanish for years, believed that American officials had promised independence for his country. But after the victory, U.S. officers ordered Aguinaldo out of Manila and isolated him from decisions affecting his nation. In January 1899, feeling betrayed by the Treaty of Paris, he proclaimed an independent Philippine Republic and took up arms.

Before the Philippine insurrection was suppressed in 1902, more than 200,000 Filipinos and 5,000 Americans lay dead. Resistance to U.S. rule, however, did not abate. The fiercely independent, vehemently anti-Christian, and often violent Muslim Filipinos of Moro Province refused to knuckle under. The U.S. military ordered them to submit or be exterminated. In 1906 the Moros finally met defeat; six hundred of them, including many women and children, were slaughtered at the Battle of Bud Dajo.

U.S. officials, with a stern military hand, soon tried to Americanize the Philippines. American teachers were imported; English was declared the official language. The University of the Philippines was founded in 1908 to train a pro-American elite. The Philippine economy grew as an American satellite, and a sedition act silenced critics of U.S. authority by sending them to prison. In 1916 the Jones Act vaguely promised independence to the Philippines, but independence did not come until 1946.

As the United States disciplined the Filipinos, Japan rose as the dominant power in Asia and as a U.S.

Japanese Expansion

C

rival. Many race-minded Japanese interpreted the U.S. advance into the Pacific as an attempt by whites to gain ascendancy over Asians. Because of Japan's increased power, the U.S. gradually made concessions to it in order to protect the vulnerable Philippines and to sustain the Open Door policy. Japan continued to plant interests in China and then smashed the Russians in the Russo-Japanese War (1904–1905). President Roosevelt mediated the crisis at the Portsmouth Conference in New Hampshire and won the Nobel Peace Prize for this ultimately vain effort to preserve a balance of power in Asia.

In 1905, in the Taft-Katsura Agreement, the United States conceded Japanese hegemony over Korea in return for Japan's pledge not to undermine the

U.S. position in the Philippines. Three years later, in the Root-Takahira Agreement, the United States recognized Japan's interests in Manchuria, whereas Japan again pledged the security of the United States's Pacific possessions and endorsed the Open Door in China. In late 1907 Roosevelt sent on a world tour the navy's "Great White Fleet" (so named because the ships were painted white for the voyage). Duly impressed, the Japanese began to build a bigger navy of their own.

President William Howard Taft thought he might counter Japanese advances in Asia through dollar diplomacy—the use of private funds to serve American diplomatic goals and at the same time to garner profits for American financiers. In this case, Taft induced American bankers to join an international consortium to build a railway in China. Taft's venture seemed only to embolden Japan.

Japanese-American relations also became tense over the treatment of Japanese citizens living in the United States. In 1906 the San Francisco School Board, reflecting the anti-Asian bias of many West Coast Americans, ordered the segregation of all Chinese, Koreans, and Japanese in special schools. Tokyo protested the discrimination against its citizens. The following year, President Roosevelt quieted the crisis by striking a "gentleman's agreement" with Tokyo restricting the inflow of Japanese immigrants; San Francisco then rescinded its segregation order.

Anti-Japanese Bias in California

In 1914, when the First World War broke out in Europe, Japan seized Shandong and some Pacific islands from the Germans. In 1915 Japan issued its Twenty-One Demands, virtually insisting on hegemony over all of China. The Chinese door was being slammed shut, but the United States lacked adequate countervailing power in Asia to block Japan's imperial thrusts.

Latin America, Europe, and International Rivalry

Intense international rivalry also characterized U.S. relations with Latin America, where U.S. economic and strategic interests and power towered (see Map 22.2), and with Europe, where repeated political and military disputes persuaded Americans to develop friendlier relations with Great Britain while avoiding entrapment in the continent's troubles.

As U.S. economic interests expanded in Latin America, so did U.S. political influence. Exports to Latin America, which exceeded $50 million in the 1870s, rose to $300 million in 1914. Investments by U.S. citizens in Latin America climbed to a commanding $1.26 billion in 1914.

Economic Hegemony in Latin America

After the destructive war in Cuba, U.S. citizens and corporations continued to dominate the island's economy, controlling the sugar, mining, tobacco, and utilities industries; most of the rural lands; and foreign trade. The Teller Amendment outlawed the annexation of Cuba, but officials in Washington soon used the document's call for "pacification" to justify U.S. control. American troops remained there until 1902, and American officials forced the Cubans to append to their constitution a frank avowal of U.S. hegemony known as the Platt Amendment. This statement prohibited Cuba from making a treaty with another nation that might impair its independence; in practice, this meant that all treaties had to have U.S. approval. Most important, another Platt Amendment provision granted the United States "the right to intervene" to preserve the island's independence and to maintain domestic order. Cuba also had to lease a naval base (at Guantánamo Bay). Formalized in a 1903 treaty, the amendment governed Cuban-American relations until 1934.

Cuba and the Platt Amendment

The Cubans, like the Filipinos, chafed under U.S. mastery. Widespread demonstrations protested the Platt Amendment, and a rebellion against the Cuban government in 1906 prompted Roosevelt to order another invasion of Cuba. The marines stayed until 1909, returned briefly in 1912, and occupied the island again from 1917 to 1922.

Panama, meanwhile, became the site of a bold U.S. expansionist venture. In 1869 the world had marveled at the completion of the Suez Canal, a waterway that greatly facilitated travel between the Indian Ocean and Mediterranean Sea and enhanced the power of the British Empire. Surely that feat could

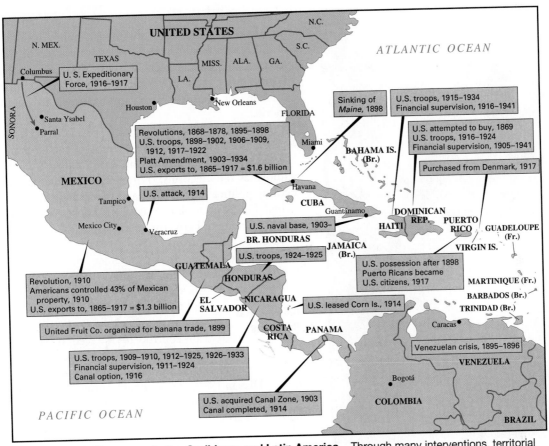

Map 22.2   U.S. Hegemony in the Caribbean and Latin America   Through many interventions, territorial acquisitions, and robust economic expansion, the United States became the predominant power in Latin America in the early twentieth century. The United States often backed up the Roosevelt Corollary's declaration of a "police power" by dispatching troops to Caribbean nations, where they met nationalist opposition.

Panama Canal

be duplicated in the Western Hemisphere, possibly in Panama, a province of Colombia. Daunting obstacles had to be overcome. The Clayton-Bulwer Treaty with Britain (1850) provided for joint control of a canal. However, the British, recognizing their diminishing influence in the region and cultivating friendship with the United States as a counterweight to Germany, stepped aside in the Hay-Pauncefote Treaty (1901) to permit a solely U.S.-run canal. When Colombia hesitated to meet Washington's terms, Roosevelt encouraged Panamanian rebels to declare independence and ordered American warships to the isthmus to back them. In 1903 the new Panama awarded the United

States a canal zone and long-term rights to its control. The completion of the Panama Canal in 1914 marked a major technological achievement.

As for the rest of the Caribbean, Roosevelt resisted challenges to U.S. hegemony. Worried that Latin American nations' defaults on debts owed to European banks were provoking European intervention (England, Germany, and Italy sent warships to Venezuela in 1902), the president in 1904 issued the Roosevelt Corollary to the Monroe Doctrine. He warned Latin Americans to stabilize their politics and finances. "Chronic wrongdoing," the corollary lectured, might require

Roosevelt Corollary

The Panama-Pacific Exposition in San Francisco in 1915 celebrated the opening of the Panama Canal with this official poster by Perham Nahl, "The Thirteenth Labor of Hercules." The artist commemorates the ten-year construction feat by using symbols that reflect the imperialism and male hegemony of that time: a gigantic, muscular Hercules (the powerful United States) forcibly opens the land (a yielding Panama) to make space for the canal. When President Theodore Roosevelt asked Secretary of War Elihu Root whether he had adequately defended himself against charges that the United States had acted imperialistically in helping to sever Panama from Colombia in 1903, Root replied: "You have shown that you were accused of seduction and you have conclusively proved that you were guilty of rape." (Courtesy of the Oakland Museum of California)

"intervention by some civilized nation," and "in flagrant cases of such wrongdoing or impotence," the United States would have to assume the role of "an international police power." Laced with presumptions of superiority, Roosevelt's declaration provided the rationale for frequent U.S. interventions in Latin America.

Between 1900 and 1917, the presidents ordered U.S. troops to Cuba, Panama, Nicaragua, the Dominican Republic, Mexico, and Haiti (see Map 22.2). U.S. authorities ran elections, trained national guards that became politically powerful, and renegotiated foreign debts. They also took over customs houses to control tariff revenues and government budgets (as in the Dominican Republic, from 1905 to 1941).

In neighboring Mexico, under the long-time (1876–1910) dictator Porfirio Díaz, American capitalists came to own Mexico's railroads and mines and invested heavily in petroleum and banking. By 1910 Americans controlled 43 percent of Mexican property and produced more than half of the country's oil. The Mexican revolutionaries who ousted Díaz in 1910, like nationalists elsewhere in Latin America, set out to reclaim their nation's sovereignty by ending their economic dependency on the United States.

U.S.-Mexico Relations

As the United States reaffirmed the Monroe Doctrine and demonstrated the power to enforce it, European nations reluctantly honored U.S. hegemony in Latin America. In turn, the United States held to its tradition of standing outside European embroilments. The balance of power in Europe was precarious, and seldom did an American president involve the United States directly.

A special feature of American-European relations was the flowering of the Anglo-American cooperation that had been growing throughout the late nineteenth century. One outcome of the intense German-British rivalry and the rise of the United States to world power was London's quest for friendship with Washington. The growing friendship benefited Great Britain in 1917 when the United States threw its weapons and soldiers into the First World War on the British side against Germany.

Anglo-American Rapprochement

Summary

In the years from the Civil War to the First World War, expansionism and imperialism elevated the United States to world power status. By 1914 Americans held extensive economic, strategic, and political interests in a world made smaller by modern technology. The victory over Spain in 1898 was but the most dramatic moment in the long process. The outward reach of U.S. foreign policy from Seward to Wilson sparked opposition from domestic critics, other imperial nations, and foreign nationalists, but expansionists prevailed and the trend toward empire endured.

From Asia to Latin America, economic and strategic needs and ideology motivated and justified expansion and empire. The belief that the United States needed foreign markets to absorb surplus production to save the domestic economy joined missionary zeal to reform other societies through the promotion of American products and culture. Notions of racial and male supremacy and appeals to national greatness also fed the appetite for foreign adventure and commitments.

Revealing the great diversity of America's intersection with the world, missionaries, generals, navy captains, companies, and politicians carried American ways, ideas, guns, and goods abroad to a mixed reception. The conspicuous declarations of Olney, Hay, Roosevelt, and other leaders became the guiding texts for U.S. principles and behavior in world affairs. A world power with far-flung interests to protect, the United States had to face a tough test of its self-proclaimed greatness and reconsider its political isolation from Europe when a world war broke out in August 1914.

LEGACY FOR A PEOPLE AND A NATION
The Status of Puerto Rico

Ever since the U.S. invasion of their island in July 1898 and their transfer under the Treaty of Paris from Spain to the United States, Puerto Ricans have debated their status, their very identity. Colony? territory? nation? state? or the "Commonwealth of Puerto Rico" that the U.S. Congress designated in 1952? A small Caribbean island with 3.8 million people (another 2.5 million Puerto Ricans live in the United States), Puerto Rico has held nonbinding plebiscites in 1967, 1993, and 1998, each time rejecting both statehood and independence in favor of commonwealth. The U.S. Congress, which holds the constitutional authority to set the rules by which Puerto Ricans live, stands as sharply divided as the islanders, rejecting independent nationhood, unwilling to force statehood if Puerto Ricans do not want it, yet uneasy with the ambivalence that commonwealth status promotes.

Although a plurality of Puerto Ricans have narrowly endorsed commonwealth status, they remain troubled by their incomplete self-government. They are U.S. citizens who can and do move freely between the island and the mainland and who are subject to the military draft, but they cannot vote in U.S. presidential elections. Although they send a delegate to the U.S. Congress, this representative cannot vote. Puerto Ricans pay Medicare and Social Security taxes, but not federal income taxes, and they receive benefits under federal programs. They also take pride in the symbols of nationalism, such as their own Olympic team, but the symbols do not signify independence.

The issue of cultural nationalism dominates the debate over Puerto Rico's political status. A majority of Puerto Ricans have rejected statehood because they fear it would mean giving up their Latin American culture and Spanish language. Most Puerto Ricans today, although bilingual, prefer Spanish over English, and many oppose the mandatory school courses in English. Puerto Rico's uncertain status persists as a legacy of turn-of-the-century empire building; then, as now, the issue centered on the rights of self-determination—in this case, the right to sustain a people's own culture.

For Further Reading, see the Appendix. For Web resources, go to history.college.hmco.com/students.

23

AMERICANS IN THE GREAT WAR

1914–1920

The medical case files listed him as "A.P.," an eighteen-year-old Marine Corps private who had volunteered to fight in the Great War. In June 1918, A.P.'s company trudged forward to the battle lines in France, past the bodies of French soldiers dismembered by the big guns. His commanding officer detailed A.P. to bury the mangled corpses. For several nights thereafter the young man could not sleep. Artillery fire frightened him. During one bombardment, he began to tremble uncontrollably. Evacuated to a hospital, A.P. suffered horrifying dreams.

Doctors who treated military casualties saw many such patients, whom they diagnosed as having a mental illness known as war neurosis or war psychosis—shell shock, for short. The symptoms: a fixed empty stare, violent tremors, paralyzed limbs, listlessness, blubbering, screaming, and haunting dreams.

Their nervous systems shattered, some one hundred thousand victims went to special military hospitals staffed by psychiatrists. A regimen of rest, military discipline, recreation, exercise, counseling, and reminders about patriotic duty restored many shell-shock victims to health. Some returned to the front lines; the very ill went home to the United States. Even cured shell-shocked soldiers had lingering mental problems—flashbacks, nightmares, and a persistent disorientation that made it difficult for them to make decisions or organize their lives. Thousands of the most severely afflicted remained in veterans' hospitals.

Many Progressive era professionals and reformers found rewards and opportunities in the wrenching national emergency of World War I. The psychiatrists who treated the shell-shock victims, for example, hoped to use their wartime medical experience later, at

IMPORTANT EVENTS

1914 U.S. troops invade revolutionary Mexico
First World War begins in Europe

1915 *Lusitania* sinks
Secretary of State Bryan resigns

1916 Congress rejects Gore-McLemore resolution limiting travel on belligerent ships
U.S. troops invade Mexico again
After torpedoing *Sussex*, Germany pledges not to attack merchant ships without warning
National Defense Act expands military
Wilson reelected on platform of peace, progressivism, and preparedness

1917 Germany declares unrestricted submarine warfare
Zimmermann telegram aggravates U.S.-Mexico troubles
Russian Revolution ousts the czar
United States enters First World War
Selective Service Act creates the draft
Espionage Act limits First Amendment rights
War Industries Board created to manage the economy
War Revenue Act raises taxes to control war profiteering
Fuel crisis during severe winter

1918 Wilson announces Fourteen Points for new world order
Sedition Act further limits free speech
Debs imprisoned for antiwar speech
U.S. troops at Château-Thierry help blunt German offensive
U.S. troops intervene in Russia against Bolsheviks
Influenza pandemic
Republicans hand Wilson a setback by winning congressional elections
Armistice ends the First World War

1919 Paris Peace Conference punishes Germany and launches League of Nations
May Day bombings help instigate Red Scare
Chicago race riot
Steelworkers strike
Communist Party of the United States of America founded
Wilson suffers stroke after speaking tour
Senate rejects Treaty of Versailles and U.S. membership in League
Schenck v. U.S. upholds Espionage Act

1920 Palmer Raids round up suspected radicals

home, to improve care for the mentally ill. For them, the cataclysm of foreign crisis and the opportunity for domestic social betterment went hand in hand.

The outbreak of the Great War in Europe in 1914 at first stunned Americans. For years their nation had participated in the international competition for colonies, markets, and weapons supremacy. But full-scale war seemed unthinkable. The new machine guns, howitzers, submarines, and dreadnoughts were such awesome death engines that leaders surely would not use them. When they did, moaned one social reformer, "civilization is all gone, and barbarism come."

For almost three years President Woodrow Wilson kept America out of the war. During this time, he lectured the belligerents to rediscover their humanity and to respect international law. But American property, lives, and neutrality fell victim to British and German naval warfare. In April 1917, when the president finally asked Congress for a declaration of war, he did so with his characteristic crusading zeal. America entered the battle not just to win the war but to reform the postwar world.

Even after more than a decade of Progressive reform, Americans remained a heterogeneous and fractious people at the start of the Great War. Headlines still trumpeted labor-capital confrontations. Racial antagonisms were evident in Wilson's decision to segregate federal buildings in Washington and in continued lynchings of African Americans (fifty-one in 1914). Nativists protested the pace of immigration. Ethnic groups eyed one another suspiciously. Activist women argued for equality between the sexes and at the ballot box, but many men preferred restrictive traditions.

The war experience accentuated and intensified the nation's social divisiveness. Whites who did not like the northward migration of southern blacks to work in defense plants incited race riots. War hawks harassed pacifists and German Americans. The federal government itself, eager to stimulate patriotism, trampled on civil liberties to silence critics. And as communism implanted itself in Russia, a postwar Red Scare repressed radicals.

America's participation in the war wrought massive changes and accelerated ongoing trends. Wars are emergencies, and during such times normal ways of doing things surrender to the extraordinary and exaggerated. The U.S. government, more than ever before, became a manager—of people, prices, production, and minds. The presidency assumed greater powers. Unprecedented centralization and integration of the economy and unusual cooperation between government and business also characterized the times. Moreover the war experience helped splinter the Progressive movement.

The United States emerged from the war a major power in an economically hobbled world. Yet Americans who had marched to battle as if on a crusade grew disillusioned with the peace process. They recoiled from the spectacle of the victors squabbling over the spoils, and they chided Wilson for failing to deliver the "peace without victory" he promised. After negotiating the Treaty of Versailles at Paris, the president urged U.S. membership in the new League of Nations, which he touted as a vehicle for reforming world politics. The Senate rejected his appeal because many Americans feared that the League might entangle Americans in Europe's problems, threaten the U.S. empire, and compromise the country's traditional unilateralism, or nonaligned course in foreign relations. On many fronts, then, Americans during the era of the First World War were at war with themselves. ■

Precarious Neutrality

 The war that erupted in August 1914 grew from years of European competition over trade, colonies, allies, and armaments. Two powerful alliance systems had formed: the Triple Alliance of Germany, Austria-Hungary, and Italy, and the Triple Entente of Britain, France, and Russia. All had imperial holdings and ambitions for more, but Germany seemed particularly bold as it rivaled Great Britain for world leadership. Many Americans viewed Germans as an excessively militaristic people who embraced autocracy and spurned democracy.

Strategists said that Europe enjoyed a balance of power, but crises in the Balkan countries of southeastern Europe triggered a chain of events that shattered the "balance." Slavic nationalists sought to enlarge Serbia, an independent Slavic nation, by annexing regions such as Bosnia, then a province of the Austro-Hungarian Empire. On June 28, 1914, at Sarajevo, Bosnia, a member of a Serbian terrorist group in collusion with Serbian officials assassinated the heir to the Austro-Hungarian throne. Alarmed by the prospect of an engorged Serbia on its border, Austria-Hungary consulted its Triple Alliance partner Germany, which urged toughness. When Serbia called on its Slavic friend Russia for help, Russia in turn looked for backing from its ally France. In late July, Austria-Hungary declared war against Serbia. Russia then began to mobilize its armies.

Outbreak of the First World War

Germany, believing war inevitable, struck first, declaring war against Russia on August 1 and against France two days later. Britain hesitated, but when German forces slashed into neutral Belgium to get at France, London declared war against Germany on August 4. Eventually Turkey (the Ottoman Empire) joined Germany and Austria-Hungary as the Central Powers, and Italy (switching sides) and Japan teamed up with Britain, France, and Russia as the Allies.

President Wilson at first sought to distance America from the conflagration by issuing a proclamation of neutrality. He also asked Americans to refrain from taking sides. The president's lofty appeal for American neutrality and unity at home collided with several realities. First, ethnic groups in the United States did take sides. Many German Americans and anti-British Irish Americans (Ireland was then trying to break free from British rule) cheered for the Central Powers. Americans of British and French ancestry and others with roots in Allied nations championed the Allied cause. Germany's attack on Belgium

Taking Sides

confirmed in many people's minds the idea that Germany had become the archetype of unbridled militarism.

The pro-Allied sympathies of Wilson's administration also weakened the U.S. neutrality proclamation. Both Wilson and his key advisers shared the British leaders' conviction that a German victory would destroy free enterprise and government by law. If Germany won the war, he prophesied, "it would change the course of our civilization and make the United States a military nation."

U.S. economic links with the Allies also rendered neutrality difficult. England had long been one of the nation's best customers. Now the British flooded America with new orders, especially for arms. Between 1914 and 1916, American exports to England and France grew 365 percent, from $753 million to $2.75 billion. In the same period, however, largely because of Britain's naval blockade, exports to Germany dropped by more than 90 percent. Loans from private American banks—totaling $2.3 billion during the neutrality period—financed much of U.S. trade with the Allies. Germany received only $27 million in the same period. The Wilson administration, which at first frowned on these transactions, came to see them as necessary to the economic health of the United States.

Trade and Loans

From Germany's perspective, the linkage between the American economy and the Allies meant that the United States had become the Allied arsenal and bank. Under international law, Britain—which controlled the seas—could buy both contraband (war-related goods) and noncontraband from neutrals. It was Germany's responsibility, not America's, to stop such trade in ways that international law prescribed—that is, by an effective blockade of the enemy's territory, by the seizure of contraband from neutral (American) ships, or by the confiscation of goods from belligerent (British) ships. Germans, of course, judged the huge U.S. trade with the Allies an act of unneutrality that had to be stopped.

The president and his aides believed, finally, that Wilsonian principles stood a better chance of international acceptance if Britain, rather than Germany, sat astride the postwar world. "Wilsonianism," the cluster of ideas Wilson espoused, consisted of traditional

Wilsonianism

American principles and an ideology of internationalism and exceptionalism. The central tenet was that only the United States could lead the convulsed world into a new, peaceful era of unobstructed commerce, free-market capitalism, democratic politics, and open diplomacy. Empires had to be dismantled to honor the principle of self-determination. Armaments had to be reduced. Critics charged that Wilson often violated his own credos in his eagerness to force them on others—as his military interventions in Mexico in 1914, Haiti in 1915, and the Dominican Republic in 1916 testified. All agreed, though, that such ideals served the American national interest; in this way idealism and realism were married.

To say that American neutrality was never a real possibility given ethnic loyalties, economic ties, and Wilsonian preferences is not to say that Wilson sought to enter the war. He emphatically wanted to keep the United States out. Time and again he tried to mediate the crises. But go in the United States finally did. Why?

Americans got caught in the Allied–Central Power crossfire. The British, "ruling the waves and waiving the rules," declared a blockade of Germany. They also harassed neutral shipping by seizing cargoes and defined a broad list of contraband (including foodstuffs) that they prohibited neutrals from shipping to Germany. American vessels bearing goods for Germany seldom reached their destination. Furthermore, to counter German submarines, the British flouted international law by arming their merchant ships and flying neutral (sometimes American) flags. Wilson frequently protested British violations of neutral rights, but London often deftly defused Washington's criticism by paying for confiscated cargoes, and German provocations made British behavior appear less offensive by comparison.

British Violations of Neutral Rights

Unable to win the war on land and determined to lift the blockade and halt American-Allied commerce, Germany looked for victory at sea by using submarines. In February 1915 Berlin created a war zone around the British Isles, warned neutral vessels to stay out so as not to be attacked by mistake, and advised passengers from

The German Submarine and International Law

neutral nations to stay off Allied ships. Wilson informed Germany that the United States was holding it to "strict accountability" for any losses of American life and property.

Wilson was interpreting international law in the strictest possible sense. The law that an attacker had to warn a passenger or merchant ship before attacking, so that passengers and crew could disembark safely into lifeboats, predated the emergence of the submarine as a major weapon. When Wilson refused to make adjustments, the Germans thought him unfair. As they saw the issue, the slender, frail, and sluggish *unterseebooten* (U-boats) should not be expected to surface to warn ships. Berlin protested that Wilson was denying it the one weapon that could break the British economic stranglehold, disrupt the Allies' substantial connection with U.S. producers and bankers, and win the war.

Submarine Warfare and Wilson's Decision for War

Over the next few months the U-boats sank ship after ship. In May 1915 the swift, luxurious British passenger liner *Lusitania* left New York City carrying more than twelve hundred passengers and a cargo of food and contraband, including 4.2 million rounds of ammunition. Before "Lucy's" departure, the German embassy warned in a newspaper announcement that travelers on British vessels should know that Allied ships in war-zone waters "are liable to destruction." Few passengers paid attention. On May 7, off the Irish coast, submarine U-20 torpedoed the *Lusitania*, killing 1,198 people, 128 of them Americans. Even if the ship was carrying armaments, argued Wilson, the sinking was a brutal assault on innocent people. But he ruled out a military response. Secretary of State William Jennings Bryan advised that Americans be prohibited from travel on belligerent ships and that passenger vessels be prohibited from carrying war goods.

The president rejected Bryan's counsel, insisting on the right of Americans to sail on belligerent ships

Secretary Bryan's Resignation

and demanding that Germany cease its inhumane submarine warfare. When Wilson refused to ban American travelers from belligerent ships, Bryan resigned in protest. The pro-Allied Robert Lansing took Bryan's place. When criticized for pursuing a double standard in favor of the Allies, Wilson responded that the British were taking cargoes and violating property rights but the Germans were taking lives and violating human rights.

Seeking to avoid war with America, Germany ordered U-boat commanders to halt attacks on passenger liners. But in August another British vessel, the *Arabic*, was sunk off Ireland and three Americans died. The Germans hastened to pledge that an unarmed passenger ship would never again be attacked without warning. Meanwhile, Wilson's critics asked, why not require Americans to sail on American craft?

In early 1916 Congress began to debate the Gore-McLemore resolution to prohibit Americans from traveling on armed merchant vessels

Gore-McLemore Resolution

or on ships carrying contraband. The resolution, its sponsors hoped, would prevent incidents such as the *Lusitania* sinking from hurtling the United States into war. But Wilson would tolerate no interference in the presidential making of foreign policy and no restrictions on American travel. After heavy politicking, Congress tabled the resolution, effectively killing it.

In March 1916 a U-boat attack on the *Sussex*, a French vessel crossing the English Channel, took the United States a step closer to war. Four Americans were injured on that ship, which the U-boat commander mistook for a minelayer. Stop the marauding submarines, Wilson lectured Berlin, or the United States will sever diplomatic relations. Again the Germans retreated, pledging not to attack merchant vessels without warning.

As the United States became more entangled in the Great War, many Americans urged Wilson to keep the nation out. Antiwar advocates such as

Peace Advocates

Jane Addams and the Women's Peace Party emphasized several points: that war drained a nation of its youth, resources, and reform impulse; that it fostered repression at home; that it violated Christian morality; and that wartime business barons reaped huge profits at the expense of the people. The peace movement carried political and intellectual weight that Wilson could not ignore, and it articulated several ideas that he shared. In fact, he campaigned on a peace platform in the 1916 presidential election. After his triumph, Wilson futilely labored once again to bring the belligerents to the conference table. In early 1917 he advised them to temper their acquisitive war aims, appealing for "peace without victory."

Germany rejected Wilson's overture in early February 1917, when it launched unrestricted submarine warfare. All vessels—belligerent or neutral, warship or merchant—in the declared war zone would be attacked. This bold decision represented a calculated risk that submarines could impede American munitions shipments to England and permit Germany to defeat the Allies before U.S. troops could be ferried across the Atlantic. Wilson quickly broke diplomatic relations with Berlin.

Unrestricted Submarine Warfare

This German challenge to American neutral rights and economic interests was soon followed by a German threat to U.S. security. In late February, British intelligence intercepted and passed to U.S. officials a telegram addressed to the German minister in Mexico from German Foreign Secretary Arthur Zimmermann. Its message: If Mexico joined a military alliance against the United States, Germany would help Mexico recover the territories it had lost in 1848, including several western states. Zimmermann hoped to "set new enemies on America's neck—enemies which give them plenty to take care of over there."

U.S. officials took the message seriously because Mexican-American relations had deteriorated recently. The Mexican revolution, which began in 1910, had deteriorated into a bloody civil war with strong anti-Yankee overtones, and the Mexican government intended to nationalize extensive American-owned properties. Wilson had twice ordered troops onto Mexican soil: in 1914, at Veracruz, to avenge a slight to the U.S. uniform and flag and to overthrow the nationalistic government of President Victoriano Huerta; and again in 1916, in northern Mexico, where General John J. "Black Jack" Pershing futilely sought to capture Pancho Villa after the Mexican rebel had raided an American border town.

Zimmermann Telegram and Mexican Revolution

Soon after learning of Zimmermann's ploy, Wilson asked Congress for "armed neutrality" to defend American lives and commerce. He requested authority to arm American merchant ships. In the midst of the debate, Wilson released Zimmermann's telegram to the press. Americans expressed outrage. Still, antiwar senators saw the armed-ship bill as a blank check for the president to move the country to war, and they filibustered it to death. Wilson armed America's commercial vessels anyway. The action came too late to prevent the sinking of several American ships. War cries echoed across the nation.

On April 2, 1917, the president stepped before a hushed Congress. Passionately and eloquently, Wilson enumerated U.S. grievances: Germany's violation of freedom of the seas, disruption of commerce, fomenting trouble with Mexico, and breach of human rights by killing innocent Americans. The "Prussian autocracy"

War Message and War Declaration

Jeannette Rankin (1880–1973) of Montana was the first woman to sit in the House of Representatives (elected in 1916) and the only member of Congress to vote against U.S. entry into both world wars (in 1917 and 1941). A lifelong pacifist, she led a march in Washington, D.C.—at age eighty-seven—against U.S. participation in the Vietnam War. (Brown Brothers)

had to be punished by "the democracies." Congress declared war against Germany on April 6 by a vote of 373 to 50 in the House and 82 to 6 in the Senate. The first woman ever to sit in Congress, Montana's Jeannette Rankin, cast a ringing "no" vote. "Peace is a woman's job," she declared.

For principle, for morality, for honor, for commerce, for security, for reform—for all of these reasons, Wilson took the United States into World War I. The submarine was certainly the culprit that drew a reluctant president and nation into the maelstrom. Yet critics did not attribute the U.S. descent into war to the U-boat alone. They emphasized Wilson's rigid definition of international law, which did not take account of the submarine's tactics. They faulted his contention that Americans should be entitled to travel anywhere, even on a belligerent ship loaded with contraband. They criticized his policies as unneutral. But they lost the debate.

America went to war to reform world politics, not to destroy Germany. By early 1917 Wilson concluded that America would not be able to claim a seat at the postwar peace conference unless it became a combatant. At the peace conference, Wilson intended to promote the principles he thought essential to a stable world order, to advance democracy and the Open Door, and to outlaw revolution and aggression.

Taking Up Arms and Winning the War

Even before the U.S. declaration of war, the Wilson administration had been beefing up the military under the banner of "preparedness." The National Defense Act of 1916 provided for increases in the army and National Guard and for summer training camps modeled on the one in Plattsburgh, New York, where a slice of America's social and economic elite had trained in 1915 as "citizen soldiers." The Navy Act of 1916 started the largest naval expansion in American history.

To raise an army after the declaration of war, Congress in May 1917 passed the Selective Service Act, requiring all males between the ages of twenty-one and thirty (later changed to eighteen and forty-five) to register. National service, proponents believed, would not

The Draft and the Soldier

only prepare the nation for battle but instill respect for order, democracy, and personal sacrifice. Critics feared that "Prussianism," not democratization, would be the likely outcome. By war's end, 24 million men had been registered by local draft boards. Of this number, 4.8 million had served in the armed forces, 2 million of that number in France. Approximately 3 million men evaded draft registration. Some were arrested and others fled to Mexico or Canada, but most stayed at home and were never discovered. Another 338,000 men who had registered and been summoned by their draft boards failed to show up for induction.

The typical soldier was a draftee in his early twenties, white, single, American-born, and poorly educated (most had not attended high school and perhaps 30 percent could not read or write). Some 400,000 African Americans also served in the military. Although some southern politicians feared arming African Americans, the army drafted them into segregated units and assigned them to menial labor. One hope of African Americans was that a war to "make the world safe for democracy" might blur the color line at home. And tens of thousands of women enlisted in the Army Nurse Corps, served as "hello girls" in the Army Signal Corps, and became clerks in the Navy and Marine Corps.

Some 15,000 Native Americans served, too. Most of them were enlistees who sought escape from restrictive Indian schools and lives of poverty, opportunities to develop new skills, and chances to prove their patriotism, which might later earn white respect. James McCarthy, a Papago from an Arizona reservation, volunteered because he wanted adventure; he got it: gas that blistered his body, a grenade wound, and German capture and imprisonment.

Indian Enlistees

American leaders worried that the young soldiers, once away from home, would be tempted by vice—especially by the saloons and houses of prostitution that quickly surrounded training camps. To protect the supposed novices with "invisible armor," the government created the Commission on Training Camp Activities to coordinate the work of the Young Men's Christian Association (YMCA) and other groups that dispensed

Commission on Training Camp Activities

food, showed movies, held athletic contests, and distributed books. Men in uniform were not permitted to drink. Alarmed by the spread of venereal disease, commission officials declared "sin-free" zones around military bases and exhorted soldiers to abstain from sex.

General John J. Pershing, head of the American Expeditionary Forces (AEF), insisted that his "sturdy rookies" remain a separate, independent army. He was not about to turn over his "doughboys" to Allied commanders, who had become wedded to unimaginative and deadly trench warfare, producing a military stalemate and ghastly casualties on the western front. Zigzag trenches fronted by barbed wire and mines stretched across France. Between the mud-

Trench Warfare

dy, stinking trenches lay "no man's land," denuded by artillery fire. When ordered out, soldiers would charge the enemy's trenches. Machine guns mowed them down; gas poisoned them. Little was gained.

The first American units landed in France on June 26, 1917. They soon learned about the horrors caused by advanced weaponry. Poison gases (chlorine, phosgene, and mustard), first used by the Germans in spring 1915, blistered, incapacitated, and killed. Many men, like A.P., suffered shell shock. Providing some relief were Red Cross canteens, staffed by women volunteers, which gave soldiers way stations in a strange land and offered haircuts, food, and recreation. Some ten thousand Red Cross nurses also cared for the young warriors.

A U.S. soldier of Company K, 110th Infantry Regiment, receives aid during fighting at Verennes, France.   (National Archives)

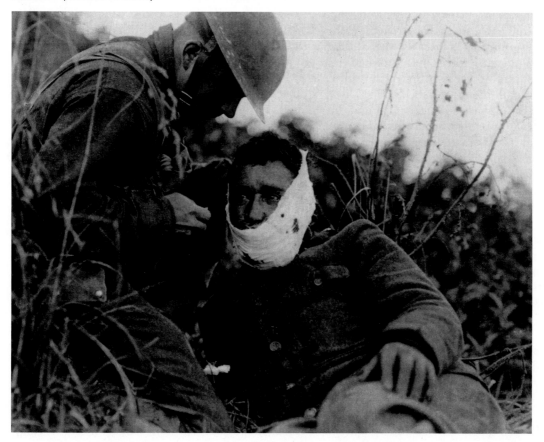

In Paris, where houses of prostitution thrived, it became commonplace to hear that the British were drunkards, the French were whore-mongers, and the Americans were both. Venereal disease became a serious problem. By war's end, about 15 percent of America's soldiers had contracted venereal disease, costing the army $50 million and 7 million days of active duty.

Problem of Venereal Disease

The influx of American men and materiel decided the outcome of the First World War. With both sides virtually exhausted, the Americans tipped the balance toward the Allies. On the high seas, the U.S. Navy battled submarines and escorted troop carriers. Pilots in the U.S. Air Service saw limited action, but the aerial "dogfights" of such "aces" as Edward V. Rickenbacker helped advance the cause of military aviation. U.S. ground troops actually did not engage in much combat until early 1918.

The Germans launched a major offensive in March 1918, after Russia left the war, permitting the shift of German troops from the eastern front to France. By May, Kaiser Wilhelm's forces had stormed to within 50 miles of Paris. Late that month, troops of the U.S. First Division helped blunt the German advance at Cantigny. In June the Third Division and French forces held positions along the Marne River at Château-Thierry, and the Second Division soon attacked the Germans in the Belleau Wood. American soldiers won the battle, but thousands died or were wounded after they made almost sacrificial frontal assaults against German machine guns.

AEF Battles in France

Allied victory in the Second Battle of the Marne in July 1918 seemed to turn the tide against the Germans. In September French and American forces took St. Mihiel, a ferocious battle in which American gunners fired 100,000 rounds of phosgene gas shells. Then the Allies began their massive Meuse-Argonne offensive. More than 26,000 Americans died before the Allies claimed the Argonne Forest on October 10. For Germany—its ground war stymied, its submarine warfare failed, its troops and cities mutinous, and its allies Turkey and Austria dropping out—peace became imperative. The Germans accepted an armistice on November 11, 1918.

The belligerents counted 10 million soldiers and 6.6 million civilians dead and 21.3 million people wounded. Fifty thousand American soldiers died in battle, and another 62,000 died from disease—many from the influenza pandemic (see page 408). More than 200,000 Americans were wounded.

Casualties

Mobilizing and Managing the Home Front

The United States was a belligerent for only nineteen months, but the war had a tremendous impact at home. The federal government quickly created a command economy to meet war needs and intervened in American life as never before. The vastly enlarged Washington bureaucracy managed the economy, labor force, military, public opinion, and more. Federal expenditures increased tremendously as war expenses ballooned to $33.5 billion. The total cost of the war was probably triple that figure, since future generations would have to pay veterans' benefits and interest on loans.

The federal government and private business became partners during the war. Dollar-a-year executives flocked to the nation's capital from major companies; they retained their corporate salaries while serving in official administrative and consulting capacities. Early in the war, the government relied on several industrial committees for advice on purchases and prices. But evidence of self-interested businesspeople cashing in on the national interest aroused public protest. The committees were disbanded in July 1917 in favor of a single manager, the War Industries Board. But the government continued to work closely with business through trade associations. The federal government suspended antitrust laws and signed cost-plus contracts, which guaranteed companies a healthy profit and a means to pay higher wages to head off labor strikes. Competitive bidding was virtually abandoned. Under these wartime practices, big business grew bigger.

Business-Government Cooperation

Hundreds of new government agencies, staffed primarily by businesspeople, placed controls on the economy in order to shift the nation's resources to the

New Agencies for Economic Management

war effort. The Food Administration launched voluntary programs to increase production and conserve food; it also set prices and regulated distribution. The Railroad Administration took over the snarled railway industry, and the Fuel Administration controlled coal supplies and rationed gasoline.

The largest of the superagencies was the War Industries Board (WIB), headed by the financier Bernard Baruch. Designed as a clearing-house to coordinate the national economy, the WIB made purchases, allocated supplies, and fixed prices at levels that business requested. The WIB also ordered the standardization of goods to save materials and streamline production. The varieties of automobile tires, for example, were reduced from 287 to 3.

Economic Performance

The performance of the mobilized economy was mixed, but it delivered enough men and materiel to France to ensure the defeat of the Central Powers. About a quarter of all American production was diverted to war needs. Farmers enjoyed boom years of higher prices, put more acreage into production, and mechanized as never before. Some industries also realized substantial growth because of wartime demand. There were, of course, problems. Weapons deliveries fell short of demand; the bloated bureaucracy of the War Shipping Board failed to build enough ships. And in the severe winter of 1917–1918, millions of Americans could not get coal to heat their homes.

Inflation

Government officials failed to stem inflation. Clothing tripled in cost, and food prices rose dramatically. A quart of milk that cost 9 cents in 1914 climbed to 17 cents in 1920. Fuel prices also skyrocketed: the price for a 100-pound sack of coal rose 100 percent. Overall, the wholesale price index was 98 percent higher in 1918 than it had been in 1913.

Paying for the War

Tax policies during the war sought to pull some of the profits reaped from high prices and defense contracts into the Treasury, reflecting the belief that wealth as well as labor should be conscripted. The Revenue Act in 1916 started the process by raising the surtax on high incomes and corporate profits, and significantly increasing the tax on munitions manufacturers. Still, the government financed only one-third of the war through taxes. The other two-thirds came from loans, including Liberty bonds sold to the American people through aggressive campaigns. The War Revenue Act of 1917 provided for a more steeply graduated personal income tax, a corporate income tax, an excess-profits tax, and increased excise taxes on alcoholic beverages, tobacco, and luxury items. Although these taxes did curb excessive corporate profiteering, several loopholes tempted the unscrupulous. Sometimes companies inflated costs to conceal profits or paid high salaries and bonuses to their executives.

Labor Unions and the War

For unions, the war seemed to offer opportunities for recognition and better pay through partnership with government. Samuel Gompers threw the AFL's loyalty to the Wilson administration, promising to deter strikes. Gompers and other moderate labor leaders accepted appointments to federal agencies. The National War Labor Board (NWLB), instituted by Wilson in 1918, discouraged strikes and lockouts and urged management to negotiate with existing unions. Membership in unions climbed from roughly 2.5 million in 1916 to more than 4 million in 1919. The AFL, however, could not curb strikes by the radical Industrial Workers of the World (IWW) or by rebellious AFL locals, especially those controlled by labor activists and socialists. In the nineteen war months, more than six thousand strikes expressed workers' demands for a "living wage" and improved working conditions (including an eight-hour workday). Exploiting Wilsonian wartime rhetoric, workers and their unions also sought to create "industrial democracy," a more representative workplace with a role for labor in determining job categories and content and with workplace representation through shop committees.

Women in the Work Force

When immigration dropped off and when 16 percent of the male work force entered the military, business targeted women to fill vacancies. Although the total number of women in the work force increased slightly, the real story was that many changed jobs, sometimes moving into formerly male domains. Some white women left domestic service for factories or departed from textile mills for employment in firearms plants. At least 20 percent of all workers in the wartime electrical-machinery, air-plane, and food industries were women. Some one hundred thousand women worked in the railroad in-dustry. As white women took advantage of these new opportunities, black women took some of their places in domestic service and in textile factories. Most work-ing women were single and remained concentrated in sex-segregated occupations, serving as typists, nurses, teachers, and domestic servants.

Some male workers, unaccustomed to working be-side women, complained that women destabilized the work environment with their higher productivity and acceptance of lower pay. Women pointed out that male-dominated companies discriminated against them and that unions largely denied them membership. Male em-ployees also resented the spirit of independence evident among women. These critics charged that working mothers neglected their children and their housework. Day nurseries were scarce and beyond the means of most working-class families. The war experience barely changed the attitude that women's proper sphere was the home, and most women workers lost their jobs to the returning veterans.

War mobilization wrought significant change for the African American community as southern blacks

African American Migration North

undertook a great migration to northern cities to work in railroad yards, packing houses, steel mills, shipyards, and coal mines. Between 1910 and 1920, about a half-million African Americans uprooted them-selves to move to the North. Families sometimes pooled savings to send one member; others sold their household goods to pay for the journey. Most of the migrants were males—young (in their early twenties), unmarried, and skilled or semiskilled. Wartime jobs in the North provided an escape from low wages, share-cropping, tenancy, crop liens, debt peonage, lynch-ings, and political disfranchisement.

But African Americans continued to experience discrimination in both North and South. When the United States entered the First World War, there was not one black judge in the entire country. Segregation remained social custom. The Ku Klux Klan was reviv-ing, and racist films such as D. W. Griffith's *The Birth*

of a Nation (1915) fed prejudice. Lynching statistics ex-posed the wide gap between wartime declarations of humanity and the American practice of inhumanity at home: between 1914 and 1920, 382 blacks were lynched, some of them in military uniform.

Urban whites who resented "the Negro invasion" vented their anger in riots. In August 1917, African

Race Riots

American soldiers in Houston faced white harassment and refused to obey segregation laws. Gunfire was exchanged and seventeen whites and two African Americans were killed. The army later sentenced thirteen black soldiers to death and forty-one to life imprisonment for mutiny. During the bloody "Red Summer" of 1919, race riots rocked two dozen cities and towns. The worst violence occurred in Chicago, a favorite destination for migrating blacks. In the very hot days of July 1919, a black youth swim-ming at a segregated white beach was hit by a thrown rock and drowned. Rumors spread, tempers flared, and soon blacks and whites were battling one another. Stabbings, burnings, and shootings went on for days until state police restored some calm. Thirty-eight people died, twenty-three African Americans and fif-teen whites.

Another home-front crisis cut across race, gender, and class lines: the influenza pandemic that engulfed

Influenza Pandemic

the world in 1918–1919. High fevers, aching muscles, and headaches stag-gered people. In many cases, severe pneumonia set in, and victims' lungs filled with fluid. Before the pandemic abated, as many as 40 million people died worldwide, including seven hundred thousand in the United States. The first case of the extremely contagious flu virus was reported at Camp Funston, in Kansas, on March 4, 1918. It quickly spread to most American cities and then to Europe, carried there by U.S. troops.

Emergence of the Civil Liberties Issue

"Woe be to the man that seeks to stand in our way in this day of high resolution," warned President Wilson. An official and unofficial campaign soon began to silence dissenters who questioned Wilson's decision for war or who protested the draft. The targets of governmental and quasi-vigilante repression were the hundreds of thousands of Americans and aliens who refused to support the war. In the wartime process of debating the question of the right to speak freely in a democracy, the concept of "civil liberties" for the first time in American history emerged as a major public policy issue.

Shortly after the declaration of war in 1917, the president appointed George Creel, a Progressive jour-

Committee on Public Information

nalist, to head the Committee on Public Information (CPI). The CPI used propaganda to shape and mobilize public opinion. Pamphlets and films demonized the Germans, and CPI "Four-Minute Men" spoke at movie theaters, schools, and churches to pump up a patriotic mood. The committee also urged the press to practice "self-censorship" and encouraged people to spy on their neighbors. Exaggeration, fear-mongering, distortion, half-truths—such were the stuff of the CPI's "mind mobilization."

The Wilson administration also guided through an obliging Congress the Espionage Act (1917) and

Espionage and Sedition Acts

the Sedition Act (1918). The first statute forbade "false statements" designed to impede the draft or promote military insubordination, and it banned from the mails materials considered treasonous. The Sedition Act made it unlawful to obstruct the sale of war bonds and to use "disloyal, profane, scurrilous, or abusive" language to describe the government, the Constitution, the flag, or the military uniform. These loosely worded laws gave the government wide latitude to crack down on critics. More than two thousand people were prosecuted under the acts, and many others were intimidated into silence.

The war emergency gave Progressives and conservatives alike an opportunity to throttle the Indus-

Imprisonment of Eugene V. Debs

trial Workers of the World and the Socialist Party. Government agents raided IWW meetings, and the army marched into western mining and lumber regions to put down IWW strikes. By the end of the war most of the union's leaders were in jail. The Socialist Party

fared little better. In summer 1918 Socialist Party leader Eugene V. Debs delivered a spirited oration extolling socialism and freedom of speech—including the freedom to criticize the Wilson administration for taking America into the war. He was arrested by federal agents, convicted, and given a ten-year sentence. Debs remained in prison until late 1921, when he received a pardon.

Intolerance knew few boundaries. Local school boards dismissed teachers who questioned the war. At Wellesley College, economics professor Emily Greene Balch was fired because of her pacifist views (she won the Nobel Peace Prize in 1946). A German American miner in Illinois was wrapped in a flag and lynched. In Hilger, Montana, citizens burned history texts that mentioned Germany. By the end of the war, sixteen states had banned the teaching of the German language. Because towns had Liberty Loan quotas to fill, they sometimes bullied "slackers" into purchasing bonds.

Prior to World War I, American citizens of good standing could freely express mainstream political

Roger Baldwin and Free Speech

views, whereas people more marginal to a community (such as recent immigrants) or local leaders with radical opinions sometimes met with harsh treatment. Before the war, few formally questioned these informal restrictions on political dissent. Yet the Wilson administration's vigorous suppression of dissidents led some Americans, most notably a conscientious objector named Roger Baldwin, to reformulate the traditional definition of allowable speech. Baldwin founded the Civil Liberties Bureau (forerunner of the American Civil Liberties Union) to defend the rights of those people accused under the Espionage and Sedition Acts. He was the first to advance the ideas that the content of political speech could be separated from the identity of the speaker and that a patriotic American could—indeed should—defend the right of someone to express political beliefs abhorrent to his or her own.

In unanimously upholding the Espionage Act in *Schenck v. U.S.* (1919), the Supreme Court adhered to the traditional view rather than Baldwin's. In time of war, Justice Oliver Wendell Holmes wrote, the First Amendment could be restricted: "Free speech would not protect a man falsely shouting fire in a theater and causing panic." If, according to Holmes, words "are of such a nature as to create a clear and present danger that they will bring about the substantial evils that Congress has a right to prevent," free speech could be limited. A few months later, however, Holmes and Louis Brandeis dissented when the Court similarly upheld the Sedition Act, in *Abrams v. U.S.* (1919). In the interim, pressed by friends to adopt Baldwin's approach to freedom of speech and of the press, Holmes had changed his mind and accepted the notion that active political dissent was essential to a democratic government.

The Bolshevik Revolution, Labor Strikes, and the Red Scare

The line between wartime suppression of dissent and the postwar Red Scare is not easily drawn. In the name of patriotism, both harassed suspected internal enemies and deprived them of their constitutional rights; both had government sanction. Together they stabbed at the Bill of Rights and wounded radicalism in America. In the last few months of the war, guardians of Americanism began to label dissenters not only pro-German but pro-Bolshevik. After the Bolshevik Revolution in fall 1917, American hatred for the Kaiser's Germany was readily transferred to communist Russia. When the new Russian government under V. I. Lenin made a separate peace with Germany in early 1918, Americans grew angry because the closing of the eastern front would permit the Germans to move troops west. Many lashed out at American radicals, casually applying the term "Red" (derived from the red flag used by communists) to discredit them.

The Wilson administration's ardent anti-Bolshevism became clear in mid-1918 when the president ordered

Intervention in Russia Against Bolsheviks

five thousand American troops to northern Russia and ten thousand more soldiers to Siberia, where they joined other Allied contingents. Wilson did not consult Congress. He said the military expeditions would guard Allied supplies and Russian railroads from German seizure and would also rescue a group of Czechs who wished to return home to fight the Germans. Worried that the Japanese were building influence in Siberia and closing the Open Door, Wilson also hoped

to deter Japan from further advances in Asia. Mostly he wanted to smash the infant Bolshevik government, a challenge to his new world order. Wilson also backed an economic blockade of Russia, sent arms to anti-Bolshevik forces, and refused to recognize the Bolshevik government. These interventions in Russia embittered Washington-Moscow relations for many decades.

At home, too, the Wilson administration moved against radicals and others imprecisely defined as Bolsheviks or communists. By the war's close, Americans had become edgy. The war had exacerbated racial tensions. It had disrupted the workplace and the family. Americans had suffered an increase in the cost of living, and postwar unemployment loomed. To add to their worries, Russians in 1919 created the Communist (Third) International (or Comintern) to promote world revolution. Already hardened by wartime violations of civil liberties, Americans found it easy to blame their postwar troubles on new scapegoats.

In 1919 a rash of labor strikes sparked the Red Scare. All told, more than thirty-three hundred strikes jolted the nation that year, including the Seattle general strike in January. On May 1, a day of celebration for workers around the world, bombs were sent through the mails to prominent Americans. Most of the devices were intercepted and dismantled, but police never captured the conspirators. Most people assumed, not unreasonably, that anarchists and others bent on the destruction of the American way of life were responsible. Next came the Boston police strike in September. Some sniffed a Bolshevik conspiracy, but others thought it ridiculous to label Boston's Irish-American Catholic cops "radicals."

Labor Strikes and the Red Scare

Unrest in the steel industry in September stirred more ominous fears. Many steelworkers worked twelve hours a day, seven days a week, and lived in squalid housing. When 350,000 workers walked off the job demanding the right to collective bargaining, a shorter workday, and a living wage, the steel barons hired strikebreakers and sent agents to club strikers. The companies won and the strike collapsed in early 1920.

One of the leaders of the steel strike was William Z. Foster, an IWW member and militant labor organizer who later joined the Communist Party. His presence in a labor movement seeking bread-and-butter goals permitted political and business leaders to dismiss the steel strike as a foreign threat orchestrated by American radicals. There was in fact no conspiracy, and the American left was badly splintered and posed no threat to the established order.

Wilson's attorney general, A. Mitchell Palmer, insisted that Americans think alike. A Progressive reformer, Quaker, and ambitious politician, Palmer declared that "revolution" was "eating its way into the homes of the American workmen, licking the altars of the churches, leaping into the belfry of the school bell." Palmer appointed J. Edgar Hoover to head the Radical Division of the Department of Justice. The zealous Hoover compiled index cards bearing the names of allegedly radical individuals and organizations. During 1919 agents jailed IWW members; Palmer also saw to it that 249 alien radicals, including the anarchist Emma Goldman, were deported to Russia.

Again, state and local governments took their cue from the Wilson administration. States passed peacetime sedition acts under which hundreds of people were arrested. Vigilante groups and mobs flourished once again, their numbers swelled by returning veterans. In November 1919, in Centralia, Washington, American Legionnaires broke from a parade to storm the IWW hall. A number of Wobblies were soon arrested, and one of them, an ex-soldier, was taken from jail by a mob, then beaten, castrated, and shot. The New York State legislature expelled five duly elected Socialist Party members in early 1920.

The Red Scare reached a climax in January 1920 in the Palmer Raids. Hoover planned and directed the operation; government agents in thirty-

Palmer Raids

three cities broke into meeting halls and homes without search warrants. More than four thousand people were jailed and denied counsel. Nearly six hundred were deported.

Palmer's disregard for elementary civil liberties drew criticism. Civil libertarians and lawyers charged that his tactics violated the Constitution. Many of the arrested "Communists" had committed no crimes. When Palmer called for a peacetime sedition act, he alarmed both liberal and conservative leaders. His dire prediction that serious violence would mar May Day 1920 proved mistaken; Palmer's power then waned.

The campaigns against free speech from 1917 through 1920 left casualties. Debate, so essential to democracy, was wounded. Reform suffered as reform-

ers either joined in the antiradicalism or became victims of it. Radical groups were badly weakened: the IWW became virtually extinct, and the Socialist Party became paralyzed. Wilson's intolerance of those who disagreed with him seemed to bespeak a fundamental distrust of democracy.

The Peace Conference, League Fight, and Postwar World

President Wilson seemed more focused on international relations than on the civil liberties issue at home. For the first time in its history, the United States offered a framework for world order, when, in January 1918, Wilson announced his Fourteen Points. The first five points called for diplomacy "in the public view," freedom of the seas, lower tariffs, reductions in armaments, and the decolonization of empires. The next eight points specified the evacuation of foreign troops from Russia, Belgium, and France and appealed for self-determination for nationalities in Europe, such as the Poles. For Wilson, the fourteenth point was the most important—the mechanism for achieving all the others: "a general association of nations" or League of Nations.

When the president departed for the Paris Peace Conference in December 1918, he faced obstacles erected by his political enemies, by

Obstacles to a Wilsonian Peace

the Allies, and by himself. During the 1918 congressional elections, Wilson had urged a vote for Democrats as a sign of support for his peace goals. But the American people did just the opposite. The Republicans gained control of both houses, signaling trouble for Wilson in two ways. First, a peace treaty would have to be submitted for approval to a potentially hostile Senate. Second, the election results at home diminished Wilson's stature in the eyes of foreign leaders. Wilson aggravated his political problems by not naming a senator to his advisory American Peace Commission. He also refused to take any prominent Republicans with him to Paris or to consult with the Senate Foreign Relations Committee before the conference.

Another obstacle in Wilson's way was the Allies' determination to impose a harsh, vengeful peace on the Germans. Georges Clemenceau of France, David

Lloyd George of Britain, and Vittorio Orlando of Italy—with Wilson, the Big Four—became formidable adversaries. They had signed secret treaties in 1915 to grab German- and Turkish-controlled territories, and they scoffed at the pious, headstrong, self-impressed president who wanted to deny them the spoils of war while he sought to expand U.S. power.

At the conference the victors demanded that Germany pay a huge reparations bill. Wilson instead called

Paris Peace Conference

for a small indemnity, fearing that a resentful and economically hobbled Germany might turn to Bolshevism. Unable to moderate the Allied position, the president reluctantly gave way, agreeing to a clause blaming the war on the Germans and to the creation of a commission to determine the amount of reparations (later set at $33 billion).

As for the breaking up of empires and the principle of self-determination, Wilson could deliver on only some of his goals. Creating a League-administered "mandate" system, the conferees placed former German and Turkish colonies under the control of other imperial nations. France and Britain, for example, obtained parts of the Middle East, and Japan gained authority over Germany's colonies in the Pacific. In other arrangements, Japan replaced Germany as the imperial overlord of China's Shandong Peninsula, and France was permitted occupation rights in Germany's Rhineland. Elsewhere in Europe, Wilson's prescriptions fared better. Out of Austria-Hungary and Russia came the newly independent states of Austria, Hungary, Yugoslavia, Czechoslovakia, and Poland. Wilson and his colleagues also built a *cordon sanitaire* (buffer zone) of new westward-looking nations (Finland, Estonia, Latvia, and Lithuania) around Russia to quarantine the Bolshevik contagion (see Map 23.1).

Wilson worked hardest on the charter for the League of Nations. In the long run, he believed, such

League of Nations and Article 10

an organization would moderate the harshness of the Allied peace terms and temper imperial ambitions. The League reflected the power of large nations such as the United States: it consisted of an influential council of five permanent members and elected delegates from smaller states, an assembly of all members, and a World Court. Wilson identified Article 10 as the "kingpin" of

the League covenant: "The Members of the League undertake to respect and preserve as against external aggression the territorial integrity and existing political independence of all Members of the League." This collective-security provision, along with the entire League charter, became part of the peace treaty.

In March 1919, thirty-nine senators (enough to deny the treaty the necessary two-thirds vote) had signed a petition stating that the League's structure did not adequately protect U.S. interests. Wilson denounced his critics as "pygmy" minds, but he persuaded the peace conference to exempt the Monroe Doctrine and domestic matters from League jurisdiction. Having made these concessions to senatorial advice, Wilson would budge no more.

The president's modifications failed to satisfy many and criticism of the peace process and the treaty

Critics of the Treaty

mounted: Wilson had bastardized his own principles. He had conceded the former German-held Shandong in China to Japan. He personally had killed a provision affirming the racial equality of all peoples. The treaty did not mention freedom of the seas, and tariffs were not reduced. And Article 10 raised serious questions: Would the United States be *obligated* to use armed force to ensure collective security?

Senator Henry Cabot Lodge of Massachusetts boldly disputed Wilson. Lodge packed the Foreign Relations Committee with critics and prolonged public hearings. The partisan Republican introduced several reservations to the treaty: one stated that Congress had to approve any obligation under Article 10.

In September 1919 Wilson embarked on a speaking tour of the United States. In Colorado, a day after delivering another passionate speech, the president awoke to nausea and uncontrollable facial twitching. A few days later, back in Washington, he suffered a massive stroke that paralyzed his left side. He became increasingly unable to conduct presidential business. Advised to placate senatorial critics so the treaty would have a chance of passing, Wilson rejected "dishonorable compromise." From Senate Democrats he demanded utter loyalty—a vote against all reservations.

Twice in November the Senate rejected the Treaty of Versailles and thus U.S. membership in the League. In the first vote, Democrats joined sixteen "Irreconcil-

Map 23.1   Europe Transformed by War and Peace   After President Wilson and the other conferees at the Paris Peace Conference negotiated the Treaty of Versailles, empires were broken up. In eastern Europe, in particular, new nations emerged.

Senate Rejection of the Treaty and League

ables," mostly Republicans who opposed any treaty whatsoever, to defeat the treaty with reservations (39 for and 55 against). In the second vote, Republicans and Irreconcilables turned down the treaty without reservations (38 for and 53 against). In March 1920 the Senate again voted; this time a majority (49 for and 35 against) favored the treaty with reservations, but the tally fell short of the two-thirds needed. Had Wilson permitted Democrats to compromise—to accept reservations—he could have achieved his fervent goal of membership in the League.

At the core of the debate over Article 10 lay a basic issue in American foreign policy: whether the United States would endorse collective security or continue to travel the path of unilateralism articulated in George Washington's Farewell Address and in the Monroe Doctrine. In a world dominated by imperialist states unwilling to subordinate their selfish ambitions to an international organization, Americans preferred their traditional nonalignment and freedom of choice over binding commitments to collective action. That is why so many of Wilson's critics targeted Article 10 and why the president was so adamant in defending it.

Collective Security Versus Unilateralism

In the end, Woodrow Wilson failed to create a new world order through reform. He promised more than he could deliver. Still, the United States emerged from the First World War an even greater world power. By 1920 the United States had become the world's economic power, producing 40 percent of its coal, 70 percent of its petroleum, and half of its pig iron. It also rose to first rank in world trade and became the world's leading banker.

The international system born in these years was unstable and fragmented. Espousing decolonization and taking to heart the Wilsonian principle of self-determination, nationalist leaders active during the First World War, such as Ho Chi Minh of Indochina and Mohandas K. Gandhi of India, vowed to achieve independence for their peoples. Communism became a disruptive force in world politics, and the Soviets

Unstable International System

bore a grudge against those invaders who had tried to thwart their revolution. The new states in central and eastern Europe proved weak, dependent on outsiders for security. Germans bitterly resented the harsh peace settlement, and the war debts and reparations problems dogged international order for years.

Summary

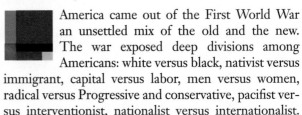

America came out of the First World War an unsettled mix of the old and the new. The war exposed deep divisions among Americans: white versus black, nativist versus immigrant, capital versus labor, men versus women, radical versus Progressive and conservative, pacifist versus interventionist, nationalist versus internationalist.

During the war the federal government intervened in the economy and influenced people's everyday lives as never before. Centralization of control in Washington, D.C., and mobilization of the home front served as a model for the future. The partnership of government and business in managing the wartime economy advanced the development of a mass society through the standardization of products and the promotion of efficiency. Wilsonian wartime policies also nourished the continued growth of oligopoly through the suspension of antitrust laws. Business power dominated the next decade. American labor, by contrast, entered lean years.

Although the disillusionment evident after Versailles did not cause the United States to adopt a policy of isolationist withdrawal, skepticism about America's ability to right wrongs abroad marked the postwar American mood. The war was grimy and ugly. People recoiled from photographs of shell-shocked faces. American soldiers, tired of idealism, craved the latest baseball scores and their regular jobs. Those Progressives who had believed that entry into the war would deliver the millennium, later marveled at their naiveté. Many lost their enthusiasm for crusades.

Woodrow Wilson himself had remarked, soon after taking office in 1913 and before the Great War, that "there's no chance of progress and reform in an administration in which war plays the principal part." Wilson was right; progress and reform took a beating.

LEGACY FOR A PEOPLE AND A NATION

Remembering War at the Tomb of the Unknown Soldier

The much visited Tomb of the Unknown Soldier is a solemn place. At the marble plaza in Virginia's Arlington National Cemetery, overlooking Washington, D.C., stern-faced military guards stiffly march back and forth, twenty-four hours a day. Buried there are the remains of three (until mid-1998, four) unidentified American soldiers "known but to God."

After World War I, U.S. leaders declared that the ceremonial burial of an anonymous hero would remind Americans of the war and symbolize national unity while saluting diversity, for it could not be determined whether the "Unknown Soldier" was white or nonwhite, immigrant or native, rich or poor, young or old, Protestant, Catholic, or Jewish. In fall 1921, four unknowns were exhumed from graves in France; one was selected. On Armistice Day, November 11, American dignitaries reburied the unidentified combatant. On Memorial Day, May 26, 1958, an unknown from World War II and an unknown from the Korean War were interred in crypts beside the World War I soldier.

On May 28, 1984, U.S. leaders buried a fourth unknown, this one from the Vietnam War. Controversy ensued. Military authorities had initially classified the remains as those of twenty-four-year-old Lieutenant Michael J. Blassie, a pilot shot down in South Vietnam. But officials then changed their designation to unidentified. The Blassie family pressed for reconsideration. In 1998 a reluctant Department of Defense finally agreed to disinter the Vietnam War unknown. A DNA sample was removed from the pelvis and successfully matched to blood from Blassie's mother, Jean. Blassie's remains were shipped to Missouri for reburial.

One crypt at Arlington now sits empty, and will remain so given the use of DNA testing by forensic scientists. Since 1994, moreover, the Pentagon has compiled DNA "prints" of all military personnel, making certain the identification of killed, badly mangled U.S. soldiers separated from their ID tags. Watching the changing of the guards at Arlington and musing about the role of science in changing how Americans remember war, a history teacher from Kentucky recently remarked that "we are losing our sense of meaning. I guess this memorial will have to stand for more than soldiers that are unknown. We are going to have to look deeper now." And perhaps look to new labels, such as "missing-in-action soldier," to sustain a legacy for a people and a nation.

For Further Reading, see the Appendix. For Web resources, go to history.college.hmco.com/students.

THE NEW ERA OF THE 1920S

Eager to win the $25,000 offered by a hotel owner to the first person to fly an airplane non-stop between New York and Paris, three different aircraft crews stood ready to go at Roosevelt Airfield in the spring of 1927. One man, Charles A. Lindbergh, the only one piloting his plane solo, decided to risk drizzly weather and start the trip May 20. For thirty-three hours, his craft, *The Spirit of St. Louis*, bounced across the Atlantic skies. The flight seized the attention of practically every American, as newspaper and telegraph reports followed Lindbergh's progress. He reached the Irish coast! He crossed over England! He entered France! And when he landed at Le Bourget Airfield, the nation rejoiced.

Charles Lindbergh was one of the most revered heroes in American history. One newspaper exclaimed that Lindbergh had accomplished "the greatest feat of a solitary man in the history of the human race." Among countless medals, Lindbergh received the Distinguished Flying Cross and the Congressional Medal of Honor. Promoters offered him millions of dollars to tour the world by air and $700,000 for a movie contract.

Through it all, Lindbergh, nicknamed "The Lone Eagle," remained dignified, even aloof. His flight and its aftermath, however, open insights into his era. The burst of publicity and the thrill of celebration point to the impact of commercialism, new technology, and mass entertainment. But Lindbergh himself epitomized individual achievement, high moral character, and patriotism—old-fashioned values that also vied for public allegiance in an era contemporaries themselves identified as "new."

Big Business Triumphant **417**

IMPORTANT EVENTS

1920 Nineteenth Amendment ratified, legalizing the vote for women in federal elections
Harding elected president
KDKA transmits first commercial radio broadcast

1920–21 Postwar deflation and depression occurs

1921 Federal Highway Act funds national highway system
Johnson Act establishes immigration quotas
Sacco and Vanzetti convicted
Sheppard-Towner Act allots funds to states to set up maternity and pediatric clinics

1922 Economic recovery raises standard of living
Coronado Coal Company v. United Mine Workers rules that strikes may be illegal actions in restraint of trade
Bailey v. Drexel Furniture Company voids restrictions on child labor
Federal government ends strikes by railroad shop workers and miners

1923 Harding dies; Coolidge assumes the presidency
Adkins v. Children's Hospital overturns a minimum-wage law affecting women
Ku Klux Klan activity peaks

1923–24 Government scandals (Teapot Dome) exposed

1924 Johnson-Reid Act revises immigration quotas
Coolidge elected president

1925 Scopes trial highlights battle between religious fundamentalists and modernists

1927 Sacco and Vanzetti executed
Lindbergh pilots solo transatlantic flight
The Jazz Singer, the first movie with sound, is released

1928 Stock market soars
Hoover elected president

1929 Stock market crashes; Great Depression begins

During the 1920s, consumerism flourished. Although poverty beset small farmers, workers in declining industries, and nonwhites in inner cities, most other people enjoyed a high standard of living relative to previous generations. Spurred by advertising and installment buying, Americans eagerly acquired radios, automobiles, real estate, and stocks. As in the Gilded Age, government maintained a favorable climate for business. Yet important reforms occurred at the state and local levels of governments.

It was an era of contrast and complexity. Fads and frivolities coincided with new creativity in the arts and notable advances in science and technology. Changes in work habits, family responsibilities, and healthcare fostered new uses of time and new attitudes about behavior. While material bounty and leisure enticed Americans into new amusements, winds of change also stirred up waves of reaction. Liberal ideas repelled those who held tight to traditional beliefs.

An unseen storm lurked on the horizon, however. The glitter of consumer culture that dominated everyday life blinded Americans to rising debts and uneven prosperity. Just before the decade ended, a devastating depression brought the era to a brutal close. ■

Big Business Triumphant

 The 1920s began with a jolting economic decline. Shortly after the First World War ended, industrial output dropped, unemployment rose as wartime orders dried up, and farm income plunged. Unemployment, around 2 percent in 1919, passed 12 percent in 1921.

Aided by electric energy, a recovery began in 1922 and continued unevenly until 1929. By decade's end, factories using electric motors dominated American industry, increasing productivity and sending thousands

Landing in France on May 21, 1927, Charles Lindbergh completed a flight across the Atlantic Ocean and instantly became one of the nation's most revered heroes. His accomplishment and the publicity surrounding it represented much of what made the 1920s a New Era.   (Picture Research Consultants & Archives)

of steam engines to the scrap heap. Electric power helped manufacturers produce new metal alloys such as aluminum and synthetic materials such as rayon. As well, most urban households now had electric lighting and could utilize new appliances such as refrigerators, toasters, and vacuum cleaners.

The economic expansion brought a continuation of the corporate consolidation movement that had cre-

Business Consolidation and Lobbying

ated trusts and holding companies in the late nineteenth century. Although trustbusting had reined in big business, it had not eliminated control of an entire industry by a few large firms. By the 1920s such oligopolies dominated not only production but also marketing, distribution, and even finance.

Business and professional organizations that had come into being around 1900 also expanded in the 1920s. Retailers and manufacturers formed trade associations to swap information and coordinate planning. Farm bureaus promoted scientific agriculture and tried to stabilize markets. These and other special-interest groups participated in what has been called the "new lobbying." In a complex society in which government was playing an increasingly influential role, hundreds of organizations sought to convince federal and state legislators to support their interests.

Government assistance helped business thrive, and legislators came to depend on the expertise of lobbyists in making decisions. Prodded by lobbyists, Congress reduced taxes on corporations and wealthy individuals in 1921 and the next year raised tariff rates.

Presidents Warren G. Harding, Calvin Coolidge, and Herbert Hoover appointed cabinet officers who pursued policies favorable to business. Regulatory agencies such as the Federal Trade Commission and Interstate Commerce Commission cooperated with corporations more than they regulated them.

The Supreme Court protected business and private property as aggressively as in the Gilded Age. In *Coronado Coal Company v. United Mine Workers* (1922), the Court ruled that a striking union, like a trust, could be prosecuted for illegal restraint of trade. The Court also voided restrictions on child labor (*Bailey v. Drexel Furniture Company*, 1922) and overturned a minimum-wage law affecting women because it infringed on liberty of contract (*Adkins v. Children's Hospital*, 1923).

Organized labor suffered other setbacks during the 1920s. Fearful of communism, public opinion turned against workers who disrupted every-

Fate of Organized Labor

day life with strikes. Perpetuating tactics used during the Red Scare, the Harding administration in 1922 obtained a sweeping court injunction to quash a strike by 400,000 railroad shop workers. Meanwhile, some large corporations countered the appeal of unions by offering pensions, profit sharing, and company-sponsored picnics and sporting events—a policy known as welfare capitalism. State legislators aided employers by prohibiting closed shops (workplaces where union membership was mandatory). Concerned about job security, workers in turn shied away from unions; union membership fell from 5.1 million in 1920 to 3.6 million in 1929.

Politics and Government

A series of Republican presidents in the 1920s extended Theodore Roosevelt's notion of government-business cooperation, but they made government a compliant coordinator rather than the active director Roosevelt had advocated. A symbol of government's goodwill toward business was President Warren G. Harding, elected in 1920 when the populace no longer desired national or international crusades.

A small-town newspaperman and senator from Ohio, Harding appointed some capable assistants, notably Secretary of State Charles Evans Hughes, Secre-

Harding Administration

tary of Commerce Herbert Hoover, Secretary of the Treasury Andrew Mellon, and Secretary of Agriculture Henry C. Wallace. Harding also backed some reforms. His administration helped streamline federal spending with the Budget and Accounting Act of 1921, supported antilynching legislation (rejected by Congress), and approved bills assisting farm cooperatives and liberalizing farm credit.

Harding's problem was that he had some predatory friends who saw officeholding as an invitation to personal gain. Charles Forbes of the Vet-

Teapot Dome

erans Bureau went to federal prison, convicted of fraud and bribery in connection with government contracts. Attorney General Harry Daugherty was implicated in bribery and other fraudulent schemes; he escaped prosecution by refusing to testify against himself. Most notoriously, a congressional inquiry in 1923 and 1924 revealed that Secretary of the Interior Albert Fall had accepted bribes to lease oil-rich government property to private oil companies. For his role in the affair—called the Teapot Dome scandal after a Wyoming oil reserve that had been turned over to Mammoth Oil Company—Fall was fined $100,000 and spent a year in jail, the first cabinet officer ever to be so disgraced.

By mid-1923, Harding had become disillusioned. Amid rumors of mismanagement and crime, he told a journalist, "My God, this is a hell of a job. I have no trouble with my enemies. . . . But my friends, my God-damned friends . . . they're the ones that keep me walking the floor nights." On a speaking tour that summer, Harding became ill and died in San Francisco on August 2.

Vice President Calvin Coolidge succeeded Harding. This somber former governor of Massachusetts had attracted national attention in 1919 with his active stand against striking Boston policemen. Coolidge's opposition to the strike had won him business support and the vice-presidential nomination in 1920.

Coolidge's presidency coincided with business prosperity. Respectful of private enterprise and aided by Andrew Mellon, whom he retained as secretary of the treasury, Coolidge's administration reduced government debt, lowered income-tax rates (especially for the rich), and began construction of a national highway system. Congress took little initiative

Coolidge Prosperity

during these years, with the exception of farm policy. Responding to farmers' complaints of falling prices, Congress twice passed bills to establish government-backed price supports for staple crops (the McNary-Haugen Bills of 1927 and 1928). The bills provided for the government to buy surplus farm products and either hold them until prices rose or sell them abroad. Coolidge vetoed the measure both times as improper government interference in the market economy.

"Coolidge prosperity" was the decisive issue in the presidential election of 1924. Both major parties ran candidates who favored private initiative. Republicans nominated Coolidge with little dissent. At their national convention, Democrats first debated whether to condemn the newly aroused Ku Klux Klan, voting 542 to 541 against condemnation. They then endured 103 ballots before nominating John W. Davis, a New York corporation lawyer. Remnants of the Progressive movement, along with various farm, labor, and socialist groups, formed a new Progressive Party and nominated Robert M. La Follette, the aging Wisconsin reformer. Coolidge easily defeated Davis; La Follette finished third.

Impressed by the triumph of business influence, political analysts claimed that Progressivism had died.

State and Local Reform

They were partly right. The urgency for political and economic reform faded in the 1920s. Much reform, however, occurred at state and local levels. Following initiatives begun before the First World War, thirty-four states instituted or expanded workers' compensation laws in the 1920s. Many states established employee-funded old-age pensions and welfare programs for the indigent. In cities, social workers strived for better housing and poverty relief, and planning and zoning commissions aimed to harness physical growth to the common good. The nation's statehouses, city halls, and universities trained a new generation of reformers who later influenced national affairs.

The federal government's generally apathetic Indian policy disturbed some reformers. Organizations such as the Indian Rights Association, the Indian Defense Association, and the General Federation of Women's Clubs worked to obtain justice and social services, including better education and return of

Indian Affairs

tribal lands. But Native Americans, no longer a threat to whites' ambitions, were treated by the general population like other minorities: as objects of discrimination who were expected to assimilate. Severalty, the policy created by the Dawes Act of 1887 of allotting land to individuals rather than to tribes, had failed to make Indians self-supporting. Indian farmers had to endure poor soil, lack of irrigation, scarce medical care, and cattle thieves. Deeply attached to their land, they showed little inclination to move to cities. Whites still ignored indigenous cultures.

Meanwhile, the federal government struggled to clarify Indians' citizenship status. The Dawes Act had conferred citizenship on all Indians who accepted allotments of land but not on those who remained on reservations. After several court challenges, Congress finally passed a law in 1924 granting full citizenship to all Indians who previously had not received it. Also, the administration of President Herbert Hoover reorganized the Bureau of Indian Affairs and increased expenditures for health, education, and welfare. Much of the money, however, went to enlarge the bureaucracy rather than into Indian hands.

Even after achieving suffrage in 1920 with final ratification of the Nineteenth Amendment, politically active women remained excluded from local and national power structures, but their voluntary organizations used tactics that contributed to modern pressure-group politics. Whether the issue was birth control, peace, education, Indian affairs, or opposition to lynching, women in these associations publicized their causes and lobbied legislators rather than trying to elect their own candidates.

Women and Politics

Action by women's groups persuaded Congress to pass the Sheppard-Towner Act (1921), which allotted funds to states to set up maternity and pediatric clinics. (The measure ended in 1929 when Congress, under pressure from private physicians, canceled funding.) The Cable Act of 1922 reversed the law under which an American woman who married a foreigner assumed her husband's citizenship; under the new law such a woman could retain U.S. citizenship. At the state level, women achieved other rights, such as the ability to serve on juries.

As new voters, however, women accomplished relatively little. The National Woman's Party remained the champion of feminism, but women pursued a variety of interests. African American women, for example, fought for the rights of minority women and men. Some groups, such as the National Woman's Party, pressed for an equal rights amendment, to ensure women's equality with men under the law. But such activity alienated the National Consumers League, the Women's Trade Union League, the League of Women Voters, and other groups that supported protective legislation to limit the hours and improve conditions for employed women. And like men, women of all types seemed preoccupied by the new era's materialism.

Materialism Unbound

Between 1919 and 1929, the gross national product—the total value of all goods and services produced in the United States—swelled by 40 percent. Wages and salaries also grew (though not as drastically), while the cost of living remained relatively stable. People had more purchasing power, and they spent as Americans had never spent.

Technology's benefits were reaching more people than ever before. By 1929 two-thirds of all Americans lived in dwellings that had electricity, compared with one-sixth in 1912. In 1929 one-fourth of all families owned vacuum cleaners, and one-fifth had toasters. Many could afford goods such as radios, washing machines, and movie tickets only because more than one family member earned wages or because the breadwinner took a second job. Nevertheless, these goods were available to more than just the rich.

Expansion of Consumer Society

The automobile stood as vanguard of all the era's material wonders. During the 1920s automobile registrations soared from 8 million to 23 million. Mass production and competition brought down prices, making cars affordable even by some working-class families. A Ford Model T cost less than $300 and a Chevrolet sold for $700 by 1926—when factory workers earned about $1,300 a year and clerical workers about $2,300.

Effects of the Automobile

The car altered American life as much as the railroad had seventy-five years earlier. City streets became much cleaner as autos replaced the numerous horses that had dumped tons of manure every day. Women who learned to drive achieved newfound independence, taking touring trips by themselves or with female friends. By 1927 most autos were enclosed (they had previously been open), creating a new private space for courtship and sex. Most importantly, the car was the ultimate symbol of social equality.

Americans' passion for driving necessitated extensive construction of roads and abundant supplies of fuel. In 1921 Congress passed the Federal Highway Act, providing money for state roads, and in 1923 the Bureau of Public Roads planned a national highway system. The oil industry, already vast and powerful, shifted its emphasis from illumination and lubrication to propulsion. The automobile also forced public officials to pay more attention to safety regulations and traffic control.

Advertising whetted demand for automobiles and other goods and services. By 1929 more money was spent on advertising than on all types of formal education. Advertising became a new gospel for business-minded Americans. In his best-selling *The Man Nobody Knows* (1925), advertising executive Bruce Barton called Jesus "the founder of modern business" because he "picked up twelve men from the bottom ranks of business and forged them into an organization that conquered the world."

Advertising

As newspaper circulation declined, other media assumed vital advertising functions. Radio became one of the era's most influential agents. By 1929 over 10 million families owned radios, which bombarded them with advertisements. Station KDKA in Pittsburgh pioneered broadcasting in 1920. Soon stations began airing advertisements, and by 1922 there were 508 such stations. In 1929 the National Broadcasting Company began to assemble a network of stations and soon was charging advertisers $10,000 to sponsor an hour-long show. Highway billboards and commercials projected during intermissions at movie houses also reminded viewers to buy.

Radio

Cities, Migrants, and Suburbs

Consumerism signified not merely an economically mature nation but an urbanized one. The 1920 federal census revealed that for the first time a majority of Americans lived in urban areas (defined as places with 2,500 or more people); the city had become the focus of national experience. Growth in manufacturing and services helped propel urbanization. Industries such as steel, oil, and auto production energized cities like Birmingham, Houston, and Detroit; services and retail trades boosted expansion in Seattle, Atlanta, and Minneapolis. Explosive growth also occurred in warm-climate cities—notably Miami and San Diego.

During the 1920s, 6 million Americans left their farms for the city. Midwestern migrants moved to re-

Farm-to-City Migration

gional centers like Kansas City and Indianapolis or to the West. African Americans, involved in what has been called the Great Migration, made up a sizable portion of people on the move. Pushed from cotton farming by a boll weevil plague and lured by industrial jobs, 1.5 million blacks moved city-ward during the 1920s, doubling the African American populations of New York, Chicago, Detroit, and Houston. Forced by low wages and discrimination to seek the cheapest housing, newcomers squeezed into low-rent ghettos from which escape was difficult at best.

In response to discrimination, threats, and violence, thousands of urban blacks joined movements that glorified racial independence.

Marcus Garvey

The most influential of these nationalist groups was the Universal Negro Improvement Association (UNIA), headed by Marcus Garvey, a Jamaican immigrant who believed blacks should separate themselves from corrupt white society. Proclaiming "I am the equal of any white man," Garvey cultivated racial pride with mass meetings and parades. He also promoted black-owned businesses. *Negro World*, Garvey's newspaper, refused to publish ads for hair straightening and skin-lightening cosmetics, and he set up the Black Star shipping line to help blacks emigrate to Africa.

The UNIA declined in the mid-1920s after ten UNIA leaders were arrested on charges of anarchism, and Garvey was deported for mail fraud involving the bankrupt Black Star line—though the company's main problem was that unscrupulous dealers had sold it dilapidated ships. Although middle-class black leaders like W. E. B. Du Bois opposed the UNIA, the organization attracted a large following, and Garvey's speeches instilled many African Americans with a heightened sense of race pride.

The newest immigrants to American cities came from Mexico and Puerto Rico. Most Mexicans migrated

Mexican and Puerto Rican Immigrants

to work as agricultural laborers in the Southwest, but many also were drawn to growing cities like Denver, San Antonio, Los Angeles, and Tucson. Like other immigrant groups, they generally lacked resources and skills, and men outnumbered women. Mexicans crowded into low-rent districts plagued by poor sanitation, poor police protection, and poor schools.

The 1920s influx of Puerto Ricans to the mainland began when a shift in the island's economy from sugar to coffee production created a surplus of workers. Attracted by contracts from employers seeking cheap labor, most Puerto Rican migrants moved to New York City, where they created *barrios* (communities).

Within their communities, both Puerto Ricans and Mexicans maintained traditional customs and values and developed businesses and social organizations to help themselves adapt to American society. Educated elites—doctors, lawyers, business owners—tended to become community leaders.

As urban growth peaked, suburban growth accelerated. Although towns had clustered around cities since the nation's earliest years, pros-

Growth of Suburbs

perity and automobile transportation made the suburbs more accessible to those wishing to flee crowded urban neighborhoods in the 1920s. Between 1920 and 1930, suburbs of Chicago, Cleveland, and Los Angeles grew five to ten times faster than did the central cities. Most suburbs were middle- and upper-class bedroom communities whose residents wanted to escape big-city crime, dirt, and taxes. They fought to preserve control over their own police, schools, and water and gas services.

Cities and suburbs fostered the mass culture that gave the decade its character. Most of the consumers who jammed shops, movie houses, and sporting arenas and who embraced fads like crossword puzzles, miniature golf, and marathon dancing lived in or around cities. These were the places where people defied law and morality by patronizing speakeasies (illegal saloons), wearing outlandish clothes, and listening to jazz. Yet the ideal of small-town society survived. While millions thronged cityward, Americans reminisced about the innocence and simplicity of a world gone by. This was the dilemma the modern nation faced: how does one anchor oneself in a world of rampant materialism and rapid social change?

New Rhythms of Everyday Life

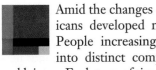 Amid the changes of modern society, Americans developed new ways of using time. People increasingly split their daily lives into distinct compartments: work, family, and leisure. Each type of time was altered in the 1920s. For many people, time on the job shrank as increased mechanization and higher productivity enabled employers to shorten the workweek for many industrial laborers from six days to five and a half. White-collar employees often worked a forty-hour week and enjoyed a full weekend off. Annual vacations became a standard job benefit for white-collar workers.

Family time is harder to measure, but certain trends are clear. Family size decreased between 1920 and 1930. Meanwhile, the divorce rate rose. In 1920 there was 1 divorce for every 7.5 marriages; by 1929 the national ratio was 1 in 6. In conjunction with longer life expectancy, lower birth rates and more divorce meant that adults were devoting a smaller portion of their lives to raising children.

Family Time

Housewives still worked long hours cleaning, cooking, and raising children, but machines now lightened some of their tasks. However, while a wife was no

Wide highways, cheap land, and affordable housing allowed automobile commuters to move to the urban periphery. In this photo, young women wearing 1920s flapper-style outfits celebrate the phenomenal growth of Culver City, outside Los Angeles. Notice the strong presence of the motor car. (Security Pacific National Bank Collection, Los Angeles Public Library)

Household Management
longer a producer of food and clothing as her predecessors had been, she now became the chief shopper, responsible for making sure the family spent its money wisely. And the automobile made the wife a family's chief chauffeur. One survey found that urban housewives spent on average 13 percent of their work time, seven and a half hours per week, driving to shop and transport children.

A new emphasis on nutrition added a scientific dimension to housewives' responsibilities. With the discovery of vitamins between 1915 and 1930, nutritionists began advocating the consumption of certain foods to prevent illness. Giant food companies scrambled to advertise their products as filled with vitamins and minerals beneficial to growth and health. C. W. Post, for example, claimed that his Grape-Nuts contained "iron, calcium, phosphorus, and other mineral elements that are taken right up as vital food by the millions of cells in the body."

Nutrition

Better diets and improved sanitation made Americans generally healthier. Life expectancy at birth increased from fifty-four to sixty years between 1920 and 1930. Research in bacteriology and immunology combined with better nutrition to reduce the risks of life-threatening diseases such as tuberculosis and diphtheria. Medical progress did not benefit all groups—especially nonwhites—equally. Nevertheless, Americans in general were living longer: the total population over age sixty-five grew 35 percent between 1920 and 1930, while the rest of the population increased only 15 percent.

Longer life spans and the worsening economic status of the elderly stirred interest in government pensions and other forms of old-age assistance. Recognizing the needs of aging citizens, most European countries established state-supported pension systems in the early 1900s. Many Americans, however, believed that individuals should prepare for old age by saving in their youth; pensions, they felt, smacked of socialism.

Older Americans and Retirement

Yet conditions were alarming. Most inmates in state poorhouses were older people, and almost one-third of Americans age sixty-five and older depended financially on someone else. Few employers offered pension plans. Resistance to pension plans finally broke at the state level in the 1920s, when reformers persuaded voluntary associations, labor unions, and legislators to endorse the principle of old-age assistance through pensions, insurance, and retirement homes. By 1933 almost every state provided at least minimal assistance to needy elderly people.

As people were exposed to new influences in their time away from work and family, new habits and values were inevitable. Clothes became a means of self-expression and personal freedom. Both men and women wore more casual and gaily colored styles than their parents would have considered. The line between acceptable and inappropriate behavior blurred as smoking, drinking, swearing, and frankness about sex became fashionable. Birth-control advocate Margaret Sanger, who a decade earlier had been accused of promoting race suicide, gained a large following in respectable circles. Newspapers, magazines, motion pictures, and popular songs (such as "Burning Kisses") made certain that Americans did not suffer from "sex starvation."

Social Values

Other modern trends helped to weaken inherited customs. Because child-labor laws and compulsory-attendance rules kept children in school longer than ever before, peer groups played a more influential role in socializing children. In earlier eras, different age groups had shared the same activities: children had worked with older people in fields and kitchens, and young apprentices had toiled in workshops beside older journeymen and craftsmen. Now, graded school classes, sports, and clubs constantly brought together children of the same age, separating them from the company and influence of adults. Meanwhile, parents tended to rely less on family traditions of childcare and more on manuals on how best to raise children.

After the First World War, women continued to stream into the labor force. By 1930, 10.8 million women held paying jobs, an increase of over 2 million since the war's end. The sex segregation that had long characterized workplaces persisted, and wherever women were employed, their wages seldom exceeded half of those paid to men.

Employment for Women

For many women, employment outside the home represented an extension of family roles. Although women worked for a variety of reasons, their families' economic needs were paramount. The consumerism of the 1920s tempted working-class and middle-class families to satisfy their wants by living beyond their means or by sending women into the labor force. In previous eras, most extra-wage earners had been young and single. In the 1920s, even though the vast majority of married women remained outside the work force (only 12 percent were employed in 1930), the number of employed married women swelled from 1.9 million to 3.1 million.

Women of racial minorities were the exception; the proportions of these women who worked for pay were double those of white women.

Jobs for Minority Women

Often they entered the labor force because their husbands were unemployed or underemployed. The vast majority of African American women held domestic jobs, doing cooking, cleaning, and laundry. The few who held factory jobs, such as in cigarette factories and meatpacking plants, performed the least desirable, lowest-paying tasks.

Economic necessity also drew thousands of Mexican women into wage labor, although their tradition resisted the employment of women. Exact figures are difficult to uncover, but it is certain that many Mexican women in the Southwest worked as field laborers, operatives in garment factories, and domestic servants. Next to black women, Japanese American women were the most likely to hold paying jobs. They too worked as field hands and domestics. And, like Mexican American and African American women, Japanese American women encountered racial bias and low pay.

Employed or not, some women were remaking the image of femininity. The short skirts and bobbed hair of the 1920s "flapper" symbolized independence and sexual freedom. Though few women lived the flapper life, the new look became fashionable among office workers and store clerks as well as college coeds. As models of female behavior, chaste, modest heroines were eclipsed by movie temptresses like Clara Bow, known as the "It Girl," and Gloria Swanson, notorious for her torrid love affairs on and off the screen. Many women were asserting a new social equality with men.

The New Woman

The era's openness regarding sexuality also enabled the underground homosexual culture to emerge a little more than in previous eras. In nontraditional city neighborhoods cheap rents and an apparent toler-

Gay and Lesbian Culture

ance of alternative lifestyles attracted gay men and lesbians. Commercial establishments that catered to a gay clientele remained targets for police raids, however, demonstrating that homosexual men and women could not expect tolerance from the rest of society.

Lines of Defense

Early in 1920 the leader of a newly formed organization hired two public relations experts to recruit members. The experts canvassed communities in the South, Southwest, and Midwest, where they found thousands of men eager to pay a $10 membership fee and another $6 for a white uniform. By 1923 the organization, a revived version of the Ku Klux Klan, had 5 million members.

Reconstituted in 1915 by William J. Simmons, an Atlanta evangelist and insurance salesman, the Klan was the most sinister reactionary movement of the 1920s. It revived the hoods, intimidating tactics, and mystical terminology of its forerunner (its leader was the Imperial Wizard, its book of rituals the Kloran). But the new Klan had broader membership, including a female auxiliary group, and objectives than the old. It fanned outward from the Deep South and for a time wielded frightening power in places as diverse as Oregon, Oklahoma, and Indiana. Unlike the original Klan, which directed terrorist tactics at emancipated blacks, the new Klan targeted a variety of racial and religious groups. One phrase summed up Klan goals: "Native, white, Protestant supremacy."

Ku Klux Klan

Using threatening assemblies, violence, and political pressure, the Klan menaced many communities in the early 1920s. Klansmen meted out vigilante justice to suspected bootleggers, wife beaters, and adulterers; forced schools to adopt Bible reading and to stop teaching the theory of evolution; campaigned against Catholic and Jewish political candidates; and fueled racial tensions against Mexicans in Texas border cities. By 1925, however, the Invisible Empire was on the wane, as scandal undermined its moral base.

The Ku Klux Klan had no monopoly on bigotry in the 1920s; intolerance pervaded American society. Nativists had been urging an end to free immigration since the 1880s. They charged that Catholic and

Jewish immigrants clogged city slums, flouted community norms, and stubbornly held to alien religious and political beliefs.

Guided by such sentiments, the movement to restrict immigration gathered support. With encouragement from labor leaders and business executives, Congress drastically restructured immigration policy by setting yearly quotas for each nationality. The limits favored northern and western Europeans, reflecting nativist prejudices against immigrants from southern and eastern Europe. By stipulating that annual immigration of a given nationality could not exceed 3 percent of the number of immigrants from that nation residing in the United States in 1910, the Quota (Johnson) Act of 1921 discriminated against immigrants from southern and eastern Europe, whose numbers were small in 1910 relative to those from northern Europe.

Immigration Quotas

The Johnson Act did not satisfy restrictionists, so Congress replaced it with the Immigration Act (Johnson-Reid Act) of 1924. This law set quotas at 2 percent of each nationality residing in the United States in 1890. It limited total immigration to 165,000 people and further restricted southern and eastern Europeans, since fewer of those groups lived in the United States in 1890 than in 1910. In 1929 the National Origins Act apportioned new quotas, totaling 150,000 possible immigrants, among European countries in proportion to the "national-origins" (country of birth or descent) of American people in 1920. People from Canada, Mexico, and Puerto Rico did not fall under the quotas, and soon they became the largest immigrant groups (see Figure 24.1).

Fear of immigrant radicalism fueled antiforeign flames. Heated debate occurred in 1921, when a court convicted Nicola Sacco and Bartolomeo Vanzetti, two immigrant anarchists, of murdering a guard and paymaster during a robbery in South Braintree, Massachusetts. Sacco and Vanzetti's main offenses seem to have been their political beliefs and Italian origins. Though the evidence failed to prove their guilt, Judge Webster Thayer openly sided with the prosecution and privately called the defendants "anarchist bastards." Both were executed in 1927 after a series of failed appeals.

Sacco and Vanzetti Case

While nativists lobbied for racial purity, the pursuit of spiritual purity stirred religious fundamentalists. Deeply disturbed by what they perceived as a hedonistic society, fundamentalists sought salvation by following evangelical denominations of Protestantism that accepted a literal interpretation of the Bible. Resolutely believing that God's miracles created life and the world, they were convinced that Darwin's theory of evolution was just that, a theory, and that if fundamentalists constituted a majority of a community, as they did throughout the South, they should be able to determine what would be taught in schools. Their enemies were "modernists," those who interpreted "truths" critically, using reasoning from psychology and anthropology.

Fundamentalism

In 1925 Christian fundamentalism clashed with modernism in a celebrated case in Dayton, Tennessee. Early that year the state legislature passed a law forbidding public school instructors to teach the theory that humans had evolved from lower forms of life rather than descended from Adam and Eve. Shortly thereafter, high school teacher John Thomas Scopes volunteered to serve in a test case and was arrested for violating the law. Scopes's trial that summer became a headline event. Three-time presidential candidate William Jennings Bryan argued for the prosecution, and a team of civil liberties lawyers headed by Clarence Darrow represented the defense. News correspondents crowded into town, and radio stations broadcast the trial from coast to coast.

Scopes Trial

Although Scopes was convicted—clearly he had broken the law—modernists claimed victory. The testimony, they believed, showed fundamentalism to be illogical. Nevertheless, fundamentalists were undeterred. They succeeded in getting many school boards to limit the teaching of evolution and influenced the content of high school biology books. As well, they created an independent subculture, with their own schools, camps, radio ministries, and missionary societies.

Klan rallies, immigration restriction, and fundamentalist literalism might appear as last gasps of a rural society yielding to modern urban-industrial values. Yet city dwellers swelled the ranks of all these movements. Nearly half the Klan's members lived in cities. And even urban reformers backed immigration

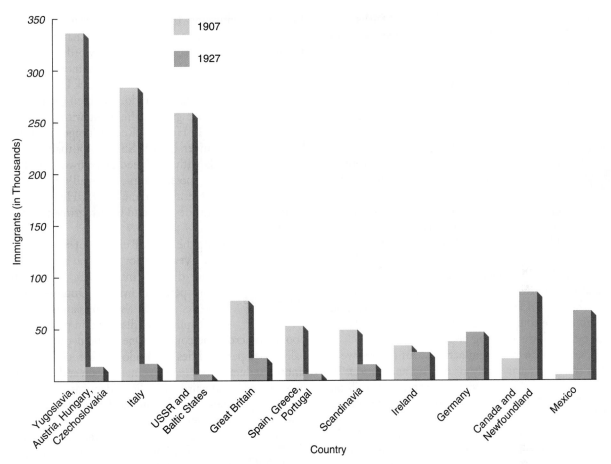

Figure 24.1   Sources of Immigration, 1907 and 1927   Immigration peaked in 1907 and 1908, when newcomers from southern and eastern Europe poured into the United States. After immigration restriction laws were passed in the 1920s, the greatest number of immigrants came from the Western Hemisphere (Canada and Mexico), which was exempted from the quotas, and the number coming from eastern and southern Europe shrank.

restriction as a means of controlling poverty and quickening the assimilation of immigrants.

Cities also housed hundreds of Pentecostal churches, which attracted both blacks and whites struggling with economic insecurity and swayed by the pageantry and closeness to God that such churches offered. Using modern advertising techniques and elaborately staged services broadcast live on radio, magnetic preachers such as flamboyant Aimee Semple McPherson of Los Angeles, former baseball player Billy Sunday, and Father Divine

Revivalism

(George Baker, an African American who amassed a huge interracial following especially in eastern cities) stirred revivalist fervor. And many urban dwellers supported prohibition, believing that eliminating the temptation of drink would help win the battle against poverty, vice, and corruption.

These emotional responses represented an attempt to sustain old-fashioned values in a fast-moving and materialistic world. Some Americans lashed out at "different" cultures and hedonistic trends in behavior. Millions of Americans firmly believed that nonwhites and immigrants were inferior people who imperiled national welfare. Clergy and teachers of all faiths condemned drinking, dancing, new dress styles, and sex on the movie screen and in parked cars. Yet even while mourning a lost past, most Americans tried to adjust to the modern order in one way or another.

The Age of Play

Americans in the 1920s engaged in commercial entertainment as never before, and entrepreneurs responded quickly to an appetite for fads, fun, and "ballyhoo"—a blitz of publicity that lent exaggerated importance to some person or event. Games and fancies particularly attracted newly affluent middle-class families. Mahjong, a Chinese tile game, was the rage in the early 1920s. In the mid-1920s people popularized crossword puzzles. Next, fun seekers adopted miniature golf as their new fad. Dance crazes like the Charleston riveted public attention throughout the country, aided by live and recorded music on radio and the growing popularity of jazz.

In addition to indulging actively, Americans were avid spectators, particularly of movies and sports. In

Movies

1922 movies attracted 40 million viewers weekly; by 1930 the number reached 100 million—at a time when the nation's population was 120 million and total weekly church attendance was 60 million. The introduction of sound in *The Jazz Singer* in 1927, and of color a few years later, made movies even more exciting and realistic.

Spectator sports also boomed. Each year millions packed stadiums and parks to watch athletic events. In an age when technology and mass production had robbed experiences and objects of their uniqueness, sports provided an unpredictability and drama that people craved. Baseball's drawn-out suspense, variety of plays, and potential for keeping statistics attracted a huge following. Newspapers and radio magnified the drama of sports, feeding news to an eager public and glorifying events with unrestrained narrative.

Sports, movies, and the news created a galaxy of heroes. As technology and mass society made the indi-

Sports Heroes

vidual less significant, people clung to heroic personalities as a means of identifying with the unique. Names such as Bill Tilden in tennis, Gertrude

Ederle in swimming (in 1926 she became the first woman to swim across the English Channel), and Bobby Jones in golf became household words. But boxing, football, and baseball produced the most popular sports heroes. Heavyweight champion Jack Dempsey, a brawler from Manassa, Colorado, attracted the first of several million-dollar gates in his fight with Georges Carpentier in 1921. Harold "Red" Grange, running back for the University of Illinois football team, thrilled thousands with his speed and power and became the idol of sportswriters. Baseball's foremost hero was George Herman "Babe" Ruth. His prowess on the field, defiant lifestyle, and boyish grin endeared him to millions.

While admiring the physical exploits of sports stars, Americans fulfilled a yearning for romance and adven-

Movie Stars

ture through movie stars. The films and personal lives of Douglas Fairbanks, Gloria Swanson, and Charlie Chaplin were discussed in parlors and pool halls across the country. One of the decade's most ballyhooed personalities was Rudolph Valentino, whose smooth seductiveness made women swoon and men imitate his pomaded hairdo and slick sideburns.

In their quest for fun and self-expression, some Americans became lawbreakers by refusing to give up

Prohibition

drinking. The Eighteenth Amendment (1919) and the federal law (1920) that prohibited the manufacture, sale, and transportation of alcoholic beverages worked well at first. Per capita consumption of liquor dropped. But after 1925 the so-called noble experiment broke down as thousands of people made their own wine and bathtub gin, and bootleg importers along the country's borders and shorelines easily evaded the few patrols that attempted to curb them.

Drinking, like gambling and prostitution, was a business with willing customers, and criminal organi-

Al Capone

zations quickly capitalized on public demand. The most notorious of such mobs belonged to Al Capone, a burly tough who seized control of illegal liquor and vice in Chicago and maintained his grip on both politicians and the vice business through intimidation, bribery, and violence. But Capone contended, in a statement revealing of the era, "Prohibition is a business. All I do is supply a public demand."

Babe Ruth had widespread appeal as one of the country's first sports superstars. Here a photograph of his mighty home run swing appears on a school notebook, showing the new link between sports and consumerism. (Private collection)

Cultural Currents

Literature of Alienation

During the decade, serious writers and artists felt at odds with society, and their rejection of materialism and conformity was both biting and bitter. Several writers of the so-called Lost Generation, including novelist Ernest Hemingway and poets Ezra Pound and T. S. Eliot, left the United States for Europe. Others, such as novelists William Faulkner and Sinclair Lewis, remained in America but, like the expatriates, expressed disillusionment with the materialism and hypocrisy that they witnessed. F. Scott Fitzgerald's novels and Eugene O'Neill's plays exposed and derided Americans' preoccupation with money.

Edith Wharton explored the clash of old and new moralities in novels such as *The Age of Innocence* (1921). Ellen Glasgow, one of the South's leading literary figures, lamented the trend toward impersonality in *Barren Ground* (1925). John Dos Passos's *Three Soldiers* (1921) and Hemingway's *A Farewell to Arms* (1929) interwove antiwar sentiment with critiques of the emptiness in modern relationships.

Harlem Renaissance

Spiritual discontent quite different from that of white writers inspired a new generation of African American artists. Middle class, well educated, and proud of their African heritage, these writers rejected white culture and exalted the militantly assertive "New Negro." Most of them lived in New York's Harlem; in this "Negro Mecca" black intellectuals and artists celebrated black culture during what became known as the Harlem Renaissance.

The popular 1921 musical comedy *Shuffle Along* is often credited with launching the Harlem Renaissance. The musical showcased talented African American artists such as lyricist Noble Sissle, composer Eubie Blake, and singers Florence Mills, Josephine Baker, and Mabel Mercer. Harlem in the 1920s also fostered a number of gifted writers, among them poets Langston Hughes, Countee Cullen, and Claude McKay; novelist Jean Toomer; and essayist Alain Locke. As well, the movement included visual artists such as Aaron Douglas and Augusta Savage.

Issues of identity troubled the Harlem Renaissance. Although intellectuals and artists cherished their African heritage, they realized that blacks had to come to terms with themselves as Americans. Thus Alain Locke urged that the New Negro should become "a collaborator and participant in American civilization."

The Jazz Age, as the 1920s is sometimes called, owes its name to music that derived from black culture. Evolving from African and black American folk music, early jazz communicated an exuberance, humor, and authority that African Americans seldom expressed in their public and political lives. With emotional rhythms and emphasis on improvisation, jazz blurred the distinction between composer and performer and created intimacy between performer and audience. More important, jazz endowed America with its most distinctive art form.

Jazz

In many ways the 1920s were the most creative years the nation had yet experienced. Painters such as Georgia O'Keeffe and John Marin tried to forge a uniquely American style of painting. European composers and performers still dominated classical music, but American composers such as Henry Cowell pioneered electronic music, and Aaron Copland built orchestral works around native folk motifs. George Gershwin blended jazz rhythms, classical forms, and folk melodies in his serious compositions, musical dramas, and hit tunes. In architecture the skyscraper boom drew worldwide attention, and Frank Lloyd Wright's "prairie-style"

Experiments in Art and Music

houses, churches, and schools celebrated the American landscape.

The Election of 1928 and the End of the New Era

Intellectuals' uneasiness about materialism seldom affected the confident rhetoric of politics. Herbert Hoover voiced that confidence in his speech accepting the Republican nomination for president in 1928. "We in America today," Hoover boasted, "are nearer to the final triumph over poverty than ever before in the history of any land."

Hoover was an apt Republican candidate in 1928 (Coolidge had chosen not to seek reelection) because he fused the traditional value of individual hard work with modern emphasis on collective action. A Quaker from Iowa, orphaned at age ten, Hoover worked his way through Stanford University and became a wealthy mining engineer. During and after the First World War, he distinguished himself as U.S. food administrator and head of food relief for Europe.

Herbert Hoover

As Hoover's opponent, Democrats chose New York's governor Alfred E. Smith, whose background contrasted sharply with Hoover's. Hoover had rural, native-born, Protestant, business roots and had never run for public office. Smith was an urbane, gregarious politician of immigrant stock with a career rooted in New York City's Tammany Hall. Smith was the first Roman Catholic to run for president on a major party ticket. His religion enhanced his appeal among urban ethnics, who were voting in increasing numbers, but intense anti-Catholic sentiments lost him southern and rural votes.

Al Smith

Smith waged a spirited campaign, but Hoover, who stressed national prosperity under Republican administrations, won the popular vote by 21 million to 15 million, the electoral vote by 444 to 87. Smith's candidacy nevertheless had beneficial effects on the Democratic Party. He carried the nation's twelve largest cities, which formerly had given majorities to Republican candidates, and he lured millions of foreign-stock voters to the polls for the first time. From 1928 onward, the Democratic Party solidified this urban base, which in conjunction with its traditional strength in the South would make the party a formidable force in national elections.

At his inaugural, Hoover proclaimed a New Day, "bright with hope." His cabinet, composed mostly of businessmen committed to the existing order, included six millionaires. To the lower ranks of government Hoover appointed young professionals who agreed with him that scientific methods could solve national problems. If Hoover was optimistic, so were most Americans. The belief was widespread that individuals were responsible for their own success and that unemployment or poverty suggested personal failing. Prevailing opinion also held that the ups and downs of the business cycle were natural and therefore not to be tampered with by government.

Hoover's Administration

This confidence dissolved in the fall of 1929 when stock prices suddenly plunged. Analysts explained the drop as temporary. But on October 24, "Black Thursday," panic selling set in. Prices of many stocks hit record lows. Stunned crowds gathered outside the frantic New York Stock Exchange. At noon, leading bankers met at the headquarters of J. P. Morgan and Company. To restore faith, they put up $20 million and ceremoniously began buying stocks. The mood changed and some stocks rallied.

Stock Market Crash

But as news of Black Thursday spread, panicked investors decided to sell their stocks rather than risk further losses. On "Black Tuesday," October 29, stock prices plummeted again. Hoover, who never had approved of what he called "the fever of speculation," assured Americans that the economy was sound. He shared the popular assumptions that the stock market's ills could be quarantined and that the economy was strong enough to endure until the market righted itself. Instead, the crash ultimately helped to unleash a devastating depression.

The economic weakness that underlay the Great Depression had several interrelated causes. One was declining demand. Since mid-1928, demand for new housing construction had faltered, leading to declining demand for building materials and unemployment among construction workers. Growth industries such as automobiles and electric appliances had been able to expand as long as consumers bought their products. Frenzied expansion, however, could not continue unabated. When demand leveled off, unsold inventories stacked up in warehouses, and laborers were laid off. Farm prices continued to sag, leaving farmers with less income to use in purchasing new machinery and goods. As wages and purchasing power stagnated, the workers who produced consumer products could not afford to buy them. Thus by 1929 a sizable population of underconsumers was causing serious repercussions.

Declining Demand

Underconsumption also resulted from the widening divisions in income distribution. As the rich grew richer, middle- and lower-income Americans made modest gains at best. Though average per capita disposable income rose about 9 percent between 1920 and 1929, the income of the wealthiest 1 percent rose 75 percent, accounting for most of the increase. Moreover, many people threw their new wealth into stock market investments instead of spending it on consumer goods.

Furthermore, in their eagerness to expand and increase profits, many businesses overloaded themselves with debt. To obtain loans, they manipulated or misrepresented their assets in ways that weakened their ability to repay if forced to do so. Such practices put the nation's banking system on a precarious footing. When one part of the edifice collapsed, the entire structure crumbled.

Corporate Debt

The depression also derived from risky speculation on the stock market. Not only had corporations invested huge sums in stocks, but individuals also bought heavily on margin, meaning that they purchased stock by placing a down payment of only a fraction of the stock's actual price and then used stocks they had bought but not fully paid for as collateral for more stock purchases. When stock values collapsed, brokers demanded full payment for stocks bought on margin. Investors attempted to comply by withdrawing savings from banks or selling stocks at a loss for whatever

Speculation on the Stock Market

they could get. Bankers in turn needed cash and put pressure on brokers to pay back their loans, tightening the vise further. The more obligations went unmet, the more the system tottered. Inevitably, banks and investment companies collapsed.

International Economic Troubles

International economic troubles also contributed to the crash and depression. During the First World War and postwar reconstruction, Americans had loaned billions of dollars to European nations. By the late 1920s, however, American investors were keeping their money at home, investing instead in the more lucrative U.S. stock market. Europeans, unable to borrow more funds and unable to sell their goods in the American market because of high tariffs, began to buy less from the United States. Moreover, the Allied nations depended on German war reparations to pay war debts to the United States. The German government depended on American bank loans to pay war reparations. When the depression choked off American loans, the Germans were unable to pay reparations debts, and in turn the Allies were unable to pay war debts. The world economy ground to a halt.

Drawbacks of Federal Policies

Government policies also contributed to the crash and depression. The federal government refrained from regulating wild speculation. Indeed, the Federal Reserve Board pursued easy credit policies before the crash, charging low discount rates (interest rates on its loans to member banks) even though easy money was financing the speculative mania.

Partly because of optimism and partly because of the relatively undeveloped state of economic analysis, neither the experts nor people on the street realized what really had happened in 1929. Conventional wisdom, based on experiences from previous depressions, held that little could be done to correct economic problems; they simply had to run their course.

Summary

Two disturbing events, the First World War and the Great Depression, marked the boundaries of the 1920s. In the war's aftermath, traditional customs weakened as women and men sought ways to balance new liberation with old-fashioned mores. Moreover, the decade's general prosperity and free-wheeling attitudes enabled countless Americans to emulate wealthier people not only by consuming more but also by trying to get rich through stock market speculation.

Beneath the "era of excess" lurked two important phenomena rooted in previous eras. One was the continued resurfacing of prejudice and intolerance that had long tainted the American dream. Meanwhile, the distinguishing forces of twentieth-century life—technological change, bureaucratization, and the growth of the middle class—accelerated, making the decade truly a "new era."

LEGACY FOR A PEOPLE AND A NATION
Intercollegiate Athletics

In 1924 scandals involving brutality, academic fraud, and illegal payments to recruits prompted the Carnegie Foundation for the Advancement of Higher Education to undertake a five-year investigation of college sports. Its 1929 report condemned coaches and alumni supporters for violating the amateur code. The report had minimal effect, however. College sports, especially football, had become big-time during the 1920s. Colleges and universities built stadiums and arenas to attract spectators, bolster alumni allegiance, and promote school spirit.

For most of the twentieth century, intercollegiate athletics ranked as one of the nation's major commercial entertainments. Highly paid coaches and highly recruited student-athletes have been common ever since the 1920s. At the same time, American colleges and universities have struggled to reconcile conflicts between the commercialism of athletic competition on one hand and the restraints of educational objectives and athletic amateurism on the other. Supposedly, cultivation of the mind is the main objective of higher education. But the economic potential of college sports has created programs that compete with and sometimes overshadow the academic operations of the institutions that sponsor intercollegiate athletics.

Since the 1920s, recruiting scandals, cheating incidents, and accusations of academic fraud in college sports have sparked continual controversy and criticism. In 1952, after revelations of point-shaving (fixing the outcome) of college basketball games, the American Council on Education undertook a study of all college sports. Its recommendations, including the abolition of bowl games, went largely unheeded. Then, in 1991, further abuses, especially in academics, prompted the Knight Foundation Commission on Intercollegiate Athletics to conduct a study that ultimately urged college presidents to take the lead in reforming intercollegiate athletics. Again, few significant changes resulted.

The most sweeping reforms followed court rulings in the 1990s that mandated expenditures for women's sports in proportion to women's share of a school's total enrollment (mandated under Title IX of the Educational Amendments Act of 1972). But given the millions of dollars involved and the fact that sports have remained a vital component of college as well as national culture, the system established in the 1920s has withstood most pressures for change.

For Further Reading, see the Appendix. For Web resources, go to history.college.hmco.com/students.

THE GREAT DEPRESSION AND THE NEW DEAL

1929–1941

In late 1937 on a farm near Stigler, Oklahoma, Marvin Montgomery counted up his assets: $53 and a car—a 1929 Hudson that he had just bought to take himself, his wife, and their four children to California. Times in Oklahoma had been tough for Montgomery's family. Across the Plains the combined disasters of soil exhaustion, drought, and dust storms were driving farm families from their homes. In addition, machines were replacing the labor of men, women, and children in the cotton fields. Finally, farm policies under the New Deal of President Franklin D. Roosevelt often benefited landowners at the expense of tenant farmers and sharecroppers.

Marvin Montgomery believed that he could have held out, but he wanted more than that. Above all, he wanted work, and newspaper advertisements held out the promise of jobs aplenty in the fields of California. The Montgomerys thus became part of the approximately four hundred thousand Americans—mostly from Oklahoma, Arkansas, Texas, Missouri, and Kansas—who made the westward trek.

There was never any doubt that the Montgomery family's destination would be California, where their married daughter and oldest son had already moved. "Yes, sir. I knew right where I was coming to," Marvin Montgomery told a congressional committee that in

IMPORTANT EVENTS

1929 Stock market crash (Oct.); Great Depression begins

Agricultural Marketing Act establishes Federal Farm Board to support crop prices

1930 Hawley-Smoot Tariff raises rates on imports

1931 Nine African American men arrested in Scottsboro affair

Hoover declares moratorium on First World War debts and reparations

1932 Reconstruction Finance Corporation established to make loans to banks, insurance companies, and railroads

Bonus Expeditionary Force marches on Washington

Roosevelt elected president

Revenue Act raises corporate, excise, and personal income taxes

1933 13 million Americans unemployed

National bank holiday suspends banking activities

Agricultural Adjustment Act (AAA) encourages decreased farm production

Civilian Conservation Corps provides jobs to young men

Tennessee Valley Authority established

Banking Act creates Federal Deposit Insurance Corporation

National Industrial Recovery Act (NIRA) attempts to spur industrial growth

Twentieth (Lame Duck) Amendment sets presidential inaugurations at January 20

Twenty-first Amendment repeals Eighteenth (Prohibition) Amendment

1934 Long starts Share Our Wealth Society

Indian Reorganization (Wheeler-Howard) Act restores lands to tribal ownership

Taylor Grazing Act closes grasslands to further settlement

1935 Emergency Relief Appropriation Act authorizes establishment of public works programs

Works Progress Administration creates jobs in public works projects

Schechter v. U.S. invalidates NIRA

National Labor Relations (Wagner) Act grants workers the right to unionize

Social Security Act establishes insurance for the aged, the unemployed, and needy children

Committee for Industrial Organization established

Congress passes Public Utility Holding Company Act

Revenue (Wealth Tax) Act raises taxes on business and the wealthy

1936 9 million Americans unemployed

U.S. v. Butler invalidates AAA

Roosevelt defeats Landon

United Auto Workers hold sit-down strike against General Motors

1937 Roosevelt's court-packing plan fails

NLRB v. Jones & Laughlin upholds Wagner Act

Memorial Day Massacre of striking steelworkers

Farm Security Administration established to aid farm workers

National Housing Act establishes United States Housing Authority

1937–39 Business recession

1938 10.4 million Americans unemployed

AFL expels CIO unions

Fair Labor Standards Act establishes minimum wage

Missouri ex rel. Gaines v. Canada orders law school established for African Americans

1939 Social Security amendments add benefits for spouses and widows

1940 Roosevelt defeats Willkie

1941 African Americans threaten to march on Washington to protest unequal access to defense jobs

Fair Employment Practices Committee prohibits discrimination in war industries and government

1940 held hearings in a migratory labor camp in California's San Joaquin valley. But the trip had not been easy.

The Montgomerys were relieved to be able to live in the housing provided for farm workers by the federal government through the Farm Security Administration (FSA). The FSA camp at Shafter in Kern County had 240 tents and forty small houses. For nine months the Montgomery family of six lived in a tent 14 by 16 feet. Then they proudly moved into an FSA house, "with water, lights, and everything, yes sir; and a little garden spot furnished."

Statistics suggest the magnitude of the Great Depression's human tragedy. Between 1929 and 1933, a hundred thousand businesses failed, corporate profits fell from $10 billion to $1 billion, and the gross national product was cut in half. Banks failed by the thousands, and the savings of Americans disappeared with the banks. Americans lost jobs as well. Thousands of men and women received severance slips every day. At the beginning of 1930 the number of jobless reached at least 4 million; by 1933, about one-fourth of the labor force was idle—13 million workers—and millions more were underemployed, working only part-time.

Elected amid prosperity and optimism, Herbert Hoover spent the years from late 1929 to his departure from office in March 1933 presiding over a gloomy and sometimes angry nation. Although he activated more of the federal government's resources than had any of his predecessors in an economic crisis, he opposed direct relief payments for the unemployed, and voters turned him out of office in 1932. His successor was Franklin D. Roosevelt, who promised hope and vigorous action.

From the first days of his presidency, Roosevelt displayed a willingness to experiment. He acted not only to reform the banks and stock markets but also to provide central planning for industry and agriculture and direct government relief for the jobless. This sweeping emergency legislation was based on the concept of "pump priming," or pouring billions of federal dollars into the economy to generate business and industrial activity, thereby stimulating employment and consumer spending. Roosevelt's New Deal vastly expanded the scope of the federal government and in the process initiated America's welfare system.

During these years several million workers seized the chance to organize for better wages and working conditions. Blacks registered political and economic gains, too, though they benefited less from the New Deal than did whites. Two and a half million additional women workers joined the labor force during the 1930s, but mostly in low-paying jobs that were not covered by New Deal legislation. Thus many women lacked Social Security coverage and minimum-wage protection.

The New Deal transformed the United States. The elderly and disabled still collect Social Security payments. The Federal Deposit Insurance Corporation still insures bank deposits. The Securities and Exchange Commission still monitors the stock exchanges. But the New Deal failed to put back to work all the people who wanted jobs. The Second World War did that. ■

Hoover and Hard Times: 1929–1933

As the Great Depression deepened in the early 1930s, its underlying causes—principally overproduction and underconsumption—grew in severity. So too did instability in the banking industry. What happened to America's banks illustrates the cascading nature of the depression. Banks that had invested depositors' money in the stock market or foreign investments were badly weakened. When nervous Americans made runs on banks to salvage their threatened savings, a powerful momentum—panic—set in. In 1929, 659 banks folded; in 1930 the number of failures more than doubled to 1,350. The Federal Reserve Board blundered after the crash, drastically raising interest rates and thus tightening the money supply when just the opposite was needed: lowering interest rates to spur borrowing and spending. In 1931, 2,293 banks shut their doors, and another 1,453 failed in 1932. When banks failed, depositors lost everything.

In the cities, some people quietly lined up at soup kitchens or in bread lines. Others scratched through garbage cans for bits of food. Millions of Americans were also cold. Unable to afford fuel, they huddled in unheated tenements and shacks. Families doubled up

No Food, No Home

in crowded apartments, and those unable to pay the rent were evicted. The homeless created shantytowns, called "Hoovervilles," where they lived in shacks made of everything from egg crates to discarded boards.

In the countryside, economic hardship deepened. Between 1929 and 1933 farm prices dropped 60 percent. At the same time, production decreased only 6 percent as individual farmers tried to make up for lower prices by producing more, thus adding to the surplus and depressing prices even further. Drought, foreclosure, clouds of hungry grasshoppers, and bank failures also plagued American farmers.

Hard times also affected marriage patterns and family life. People postponed marriage, and married couples postponed having children. Out-of-work fathers felt frustrated and ashamed. Divorces declined, but desertions rose as husbands unable to provide for their families simply took off.

Most Americans met the crisis with bewilderment. Some people were angry, though, and scattered protests raised the specter of popular revolt. Farmers in the Midwest prevented evictions and slowed foreclosures on farm properties by harassing sheriffs, judges, and lawyers. In Nebraska, Iowa, and Minnesota, farmers protesting low prices stopped trucks, smashed headlights, and dumped milk and vegetables in roadside ditches. Some of these demonstrations were organized by the Farmers' Holiday Association, which encouraged farmers to take a "holiday"—a strike that would keep farm products off the market until they commanded better prices. Elsewhere in the nation there were protests involving miners, unemployed urban workers, and World War I veterans.

Farmers' Holiday Association

The most spectacular confrontation shook Washington, D.C., in the summer of 1932. Congress was considering a bill to authorize the immediate issuance of $2.4 billion in bonuses promised to First World War veterans but not due for payment until 1945. To lobby for the bill, fifteen thousand unemployed veterans and their families converged on the nation's capital, calling themselves the Bonus Expeditionary

Bonus Expeditionary Force

Force (BEF), or "Bonus Army," and camping on vacant lots and in empty government buildings. President Hoover threw his weight against the bonus bill, and after much debate the Senate voted it down.

Much of the BEF left Washington, but several thousand stayed on during the summer. Hoover carelessly labeled them "insurrectionists" and refused to meet with them. Then, in July, General Douglas MacArthur, assisted by Major Dwight D. Eisenhower and Major George S. Patton, confronted the veterans and their families with cavalry, tanks, and bayonet-wielding soldiers. What followed shocked the nation. Men and women were chased down by horsemen; children were tear-gassed; shacks were set afire. When presidential hopeful Franklin D. Roosevelt heard about the attack on the Bonus Army, he turned to his friend Felix Frankfurter and remarked, "Well, Felix, this will elect me."

With capitalism on its knees, American Communists encouraged the jobless to join "unemployment councils," which led urban demonstrations, agitated for jobs and food, and sought to raise class consciousness. In resisting efforts to evict jobless people, the unemployment councils often clashed with local police. Such confrontations publicized the human tragedy of the depression. Still, total party membership in 1932 remained small at twelve thousand. The Socialist Party, which took issue with both capitalists and Communists, fared better. Few Americans, however, looked to left-wing doctrines. They turned instead to their local, state, and federal governments.

Communists and Socialists

But when urgent daily appeals for government relief for the jobless reached the White House, Hoover at first became defensive, if not hostile, rejecting direct relief in the belief that it would undermine character and individualism. To a growing number of Americans, Hoover seemed heartless and inflexible. True to his beliefs, the president urged people to help themselves and their neighbors. He applauded private voluntary relief through charities, but as the need increased, donations declined. State and urban officials found their treasuries drying up, too.

Hoover's Response

As the depression intensified, Hoover's opposition to federal action gradually diminished. He hesitantly energized the White House and federal agencies to take action. He won pledges from business and labor leaders to maintain wages and production and to avoid strikes. He urged state governors to increase their expenditures on public works. And he created the President's Organization on Unemployment Relief (POUR) to generate private contributions for relief of the destitute.

Though POUR proved ineffective, Hoover's spurring of federal public works projects (including Hoover and Grand Coulee Dams) did provide some jobs. Help also came from the Federal Farm Board, created under the Agricultural Marketing Act of 1929, which supported crop prices by lending money to cooperatives to buy crops and keep them off the market. To retard the collapse of the international monetary system, Hoover in 1931 announced a moratorium on the payment of First World War debts and reparations.

The president also asked Congress to charter the Reconstruction Finance Corporation (RFC). Created

Reconstruction Finance Corporation

in 1932, the RFC was designed to make loans to banks, insurance companies, and railroads and later to state and local governments. In theory, the RFC would lend money to large entities at the top of the economic system, and benefits would filter down to people at the bottom. It did not work.

Despite warnings from prominent economists, Hoover also signed into law the Hawley-Smoot Tariff (1930). The tariff raised duties by

Hawley-Smoot Tariff

about one-third and further weakened the economy by making it even more difficult for foreign nations to sell their products and thus to earn dollars to buy American products.

Like most of his contemporaries, Hoover believed that a balanced budget was sacred and deficit spending sinful. In 1931 he therefore appealed for a decrease in federal expenditures and an increase in taxes. The Revenue Act of 1932 raised corporate, excise, and personal income taxes. Hoover seemed tangled in a contradiction: he urged people to spend to spur recovery, but his tax policies deprived them of spending money.

Although Hoover expanded public works projects and approved loans to some institutions, he vetoed a variety of relief bills. In rejecting a public power project for the Tennessee River, he argued that its inexpensive electricity would compete with power from

Hoover's Traditionalism

private companies. Hoover's traditionalism also was well demonstrated by his handling of prohibition. Although the law was not and could not be enforced, Hoover resisted mounting public pressure for repeal. Opponents of prohibition argued that its repeal would stimulate economic recovery by reviving the nation's breweries and distilleries. But the president refused. After Hoover left office in 1933, prohibition was repealed through ratification of the Twenty-first Amendment.

Still, President Hoover stretched governmental activism as far as he thought he could without violating his cherished principles. He also mobilized the resources of the federal government as never before. By doing so Hoover prepared the way for massive federal activity by giving private enterprise the opportunity to solve the depression—and to fail in the attempt.

Franklin D. Roosevelt and the Election of 1932

Herbert Hoover and the Republican Party faced dreary prospects in 1932. What soured public opinion most was that Hoover did not offer leadership when the times required it. So unpopular had he become by 1932 that Republicans who did not want to be associated with a loser ran independent campaigns.

Franklin D. Roosevelt enjoyed quite a different reputation. Though born into the upper class of old

Franklin D. Roosevelt

money and privilege, the smiling, ingratiating governor of New York appealed to people of all classes, races, and regions, and he shared the American penchant for optimism. After serving as assistant secretary of the navy under Woodrow Wilson and running as the Democratic Party's vice-presidential candidate in 1920, Roosevelt was stricken with polio and left totally paralyzed in both legs. Throughout the 1920s Franklin Roosevelt and his wife, Eleanor, contended with his handicap. Rejecting self-pity, Roosevelt worked to rebuild his body.

For her part, Eleanor Roosevelt—who had grown up shy and sheltered—launched her own career in public life. She worked hard to become an effective public speaker and participated in the activities of the

In November 1930 Franklin D. Roosevelt (1882–1945) read the good news. Reelected governor of New York by 735,000 votes, he immediately became a leading contender for the Democratic presidential nomination. Notice Roosevelt's leg braces, rarely shown in photographs because of an unwritten agreement by photographers to shoot him from the waist up.   (Corbis-Bettmann)

Eleanor Roosevelt

League of Women Voters, the Women's Trade Union League, and the Democratic Party. In a short time, she became a leading figure in a network of women activists. She became deeply committed to equal opportunity for women and for African Americans and wanted to alleviate the suffering of the poor. On these issues, she served as her husband's conscience.

Roosevelt was elected governor of New York in 1928 and reelected in 1930; his terms coincided with Hoover's presidency. But whereas Hoover appeared hardhearted and unwilling to help the jobless, Roosevelt supported direct relief payments for the unemployed, declaring that such aid "must be extended by Government, not as a matter of charity, but as a matter of social duty." To prepare a national political platform, Roosevelt surrounded himself with a "Brain Trust" of lawyers and university professors. These experts reasoned that bigness was unavoidable in the modern American economy. It thus followed that the cure for the nation's ills was not to go on a rampage of trustbusting but to place large corporations, monopolies, and oligopolies under effective government regulation.

Roosevelt's "Brain Trust"

Roosevelt and his Brain Trust also agreed that it was essential to restore purchasing power to farmers, blue-collar workers, and the middle classes, and that the way to do so was to cut production. If demand for a product remained constant and the supply were cut, they reasoned, the price would rise. Producers would make higher profits, and workers would earn more. This method of combating a depression has been called "the economics of scarcity," which the Brain Trust at the time saw as the preferred alternative to pump priming through deficit spending, in which the government borrowed money to prime the economic pump and thereby revive purchasing power.

Roosevelt and Hoover both campaigned as fiscal conservatives committed to a balanced budget. But Roosevelt, unlike Hoover, also advocated immediate and direct relief to the unemployed. And Roosevelt demanded that the federal government engage in centralized economic planning and experimentation to bring about recovery.

Upon accepting the Democratic nomination, Roosevelt called for a "new deal for the American people."

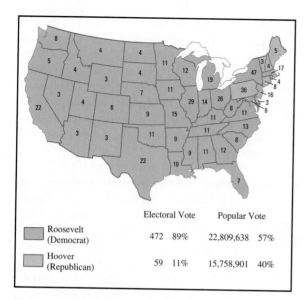

	Electoral Vote	Popular Vote
Roosevelt (Democrat)	472 89%	22,809,638 57%
Hoover (Republican)	59 11%	15,758,901 40%

Map 25.1   Presidential Election, 1932   One factor above all decided the 1932 presidential election: the Great Depression. Roosevelt won forty-two states, Hoover six.

1932 Election Results

The presidential election of 1932 was never much of a contest: Roosevelt won forty-two states to Hoover's six (see Map 25.1). Democrats also won overwhelming control of the Senate and the House.

On March 2, 1933, President-elect Roosevelt and his family and friends boarded a train for Washington, D.C., and the inauguration ceremony. (The Twentieth Amendment—ratified in 1933—changed the inauguration date to January 20.) Roosevelt was carrying with him rough drafts of two presidential proclamations, one summoning a special session of Congress, the other declaring a national bank holiday, suspending banking transactions throughout the nation.

Launching the New Deal and Restoring Confidence

"First of all," declared the newly inaugurated president, "let me assert my firm belief that the only thing we have to fear is fear itself." In his inaugural address Roosevelt scored his first triumph as president, instilling hope and courage in the American people. He invoked "the analogue of war," asserting that, if need be, "I shall ask the Congress for the one remaining instrument to meet the crisis—broad Executive power to wage a war against the emergency, as great as the power that would be given to me if we were in fact invaded by a foreign foe."

The next day, Roosevelt declared a four-day national bank holiday and summoned Congress to an emergency session, beginning March 9, that would launch the New Deal. Roosevelt's first measure, the Emergency Banking Relief Bill, was introduced that very day, passed by Congress, and signed into law by the president that evening. The new law provided for the reopening, under Treasury Department license, of banks that were solvent and for the reorganization and management of those that were not. It also prohibited the hoarding and export of gold.

Launching the New Deal

On March 12, a Sunday evening, the president broadcast the first of his "fireside chats," and 60 million people heard his reassuring words on their radios. His message: banks were once again safe places for depositors' savings. On Monday morning the banks opened their doors to people who were waiting outside to deposit their money instead of withdrawing it. The bank runs were over; Roosevelt had reestablished people's confidence in their political leadership, their banks, even their economic system.

First Fireside Chat

Roosevelt next pursued a measure, the Beer-Wine Revenue Act, that was deflationary because it actually took money out of people's pockets by imposing new taxes. The act, which legalized the sale of low-alcohol wines and beers, levied taxes on these products. (Congress had proposed repeal of prohibition in February 1933 in the Twenty-first Amendment, and the states ratified it by December 1933.)

Beer-Wine Revenue Act

In mid-March Roosevelt sent to Congress the Agricultural Adjustment Bill to restore farmers' purchasing power. If overproduction was the cause of farmers' problems, then the government had to en-

Agricultural Adjustment Act

courage farmers to grow less. Under the domestic allotment plan, the government would pay farmers to reduce their acreage or plow under crops already in the fields. Farmers would receive payments based on *parity*, a system of regulated prices for corn, cotton, wheat, rice, hogs, and dairy products that would provide them the same purchasing power they had had during the prosperous period of 1909 to 1914. The subsidies would be funded by taxes levied on the processors of agricultural commodities.

After overcoming vehement opposition to the domestic allotment plan, Roosevelt secured passage of the Agricultural Adjustment Act (AAA) on May 12. A month later the Farm Credit Act was passed, providing short- and medium-term loans that enabled many farmers to refinance their mortgages and hang onto their homes and land. Another New Deal measure assisted homeowners in the towns and cities; the Home Owners Refinancing Act provided $2 billion in bonds to refinance nonfarm home mortgages.

Meanwhile, other relief measures became law. On March 21 the president requested direct cash grants to

Other Relief Measures

the states for relief payments to needy citizens and two federal programs that would create jobs. Ten days later Congress approved the Civilian Conservation Corps (CCC), a job agency that ultimately put 2.5 million young men aged eighteen to twenty-five to work planting trees, clearing camping areas and beaches, and building bridges, dams, reservoirs, fish ponds, and fire towers. Then on May 12 Congress passed the Federal Emergency Relief Act, which authorized $500 million in aid to state and local governments. Finally, on June 16 Title II of the National Industrial Recovery Act established the Public Works Administration (PWA) and appropriated $3.3 billion for hiring the unemployed to build roads, sewage and water systems, public buildings, and a host of other projects. The key purpose of the PWA was to pump federal money into the economy.

If the AAA was the agricultural cornerstone of the New Deal, the National Industrial Recovery Act was the industrial cornerstone. The act, which established the National Recovery Administration (NRA), was a testimony to the New Deal belief in national economic planning as opposed to a laissez-faire economy. It was

National Recovery Administration

essential, planners argued, for businesses to cooperate in ending cutthroat competition and to raise prices by limiting production. Under NRA auspices, competing businesses met with each other, as well as with representatives of workers and consumers, to draft codes of fair competition, which limited production and established prices. Section 7(a) of the National Industrial Recovery Act guaranteed workers the right to unionize and to bargain collectively.

The New Deal also strengthened public confidence in the stock exchanges and banks. Roosevelt signed the Federal Securities Act, which compelled brokers to tell the truth about new securities issues, and the Banking Act of 1933, which set up the Federal Deposit Insurance Corporation (FDIC) for insuring bank deposits. In June Roosevelt also took the United States off the gold standard, no longer guaranteeing the gold value of the dollar abroad. Freed from the requirement that all paper money be backed by gold, the Federal Reserve Board could expand the supply of currency in circulation, thus enabling monetary policy to become another weapon for economic recovery.

One of the boldest programs enacted by Congress addressed the badly depressed Tennessee River valley, which runs through Virginia, North Carolina, Tennessee, Georgia, Alabama, Mississippi, and Kentucky. An expansion of a Progressive proposal, Roosevelt's Tennessee Valley Authority (TVA) was to build dams to both control floods and generate hydroelectric power. In constructing public power facilities, the TVA would provide a yardstick for determining fair rates for privately produced electric power. Most important, the goal of the TVA was nothing less than enhancement of the economic well-being of the entire Tennessee River valley.

TVA

The TVA achieved its goals but, in the process, became a major polluter. TVA strip mining caused soil erosion. Its coal-burning generators released sulfur oxides, which combined with water vapor to produce acid rain. Above all, the TVA degraded the water by dumping untreated sewage, toxic chemicals, and metal pollutants into streams and rivers.

The special session of Congress adjourned on June 16, 1933. In just over three months, Roosevelt

End of the First Hundred Days had delivered fifteen messages to Congress proposing major legislation, and Congress had passed fifteen significant laws (see Table 25.1). The United States had rebounded from hysteria and near collapse. Journalists called this period of remarkable achievement the Hundred Days.

Throughout the remainder of 1933 and the spring and summer of 1934, more New Deal bills became law, benefiting farmers, the unemployed, investors, homeowners, workers, and the environment. In 1934

Other Legislation additional hundreds of millions of federal dollars were appropriated for unemployment relief and public works. Legislation that year also established the Securities and Exchange Commission, the National Labor Relations Board, the Federal Housing Administration, and the Grazing Service (later to become the Bureau of Land Management). The Grazing Service established federal supervision of most of the remaining public domain, and it closed 80 million acres of grasslands to further settlement and use.

Table 25.1   New Deal Achievements

Year	Labor	Agriculture and Environment	Business and Industrial Recovery	Relief	Reform
1933	Section 7(a) of NIRA	Agricultural Adjustment Act Farm Credit Act	Emergency Banking Relief Act Economy Act Beer-Wine Revenue Act Banking Act of 1933 (guaranteed deposits) NIRA	Civilian Conservation Corps Federal Emergency Relief Act Home Owners Refinancing Act Public Works Administration Civil Works Administration	TVA Federal Securities Act
1934	National Labor Relations Board	Taylor Grazing Act			Securities Exchange Act
1935	National Labor Relations (Wagner) Act	Resettlement Administration Rural Electrification Administration		Works Progress Administration National Youth Administration	Social Security Act Public Utility Holding Company Act Revenue Act (wealth tax)
1937		Farm Security Administration		National Housing Act	
1938	Fair Labor Standards Act	Agricultural Adjustment Act of 1938			

Source: Adapted from Charles Sellers, Henry May, and Neil R. McMillen, *A Synopsis of American History*, 6th ed. Copyright © 1985 by Houghton Mifflin Company. Reprinted by permission.

New Deal legislation seemed to promise something for every group. This was interest-group democracy at work. In the midst of this

Interest-Group Democracy

coalition of special interests was President Roosevelt, the artful broker, who pointed to the economy as proof that this approach was working. As the New Deal became law, unemployment fell steadily from 13 million in 1933 to 9 million in 1936. Net farm income rose from just over $3 billion in 1933 to $5.85 billion in 1935. Manufacturing salaries and wages also increased, from $6.25 billion in 1933 to almost $13 billion in 1937.

Opposition to the New Deal

With the arrival of partial economic recovery, many businesspeople and conservatives became vocal critics of the New Deal. Some charged that there was too much taxation and government regulation. Others condemned the deficit financing of relief and public works. In 1934 the

Conservative Critics of the New Deal

leaders of several major corporations joined with Alfred E. Smith, John W. Davis, and disaffected conservative Democrats to establish the American Liberty League. Members of the Liberty League contended that the New Deal welfare payments were subverting individual initiative and self-reliance.

While businesspeople considered the government their enemy, others thought the government favored business too much. Critics argued

Farmers and Laborers

that NRA codes favored industry's needs over those of workers and consumers. Farmers, labor unions, and individual entrepreneurs complained that the NRA set prices too high and favored large producers over small businesses.

The AAA also came under attack for its encouragement of cutbacks in production. Farmers had plowed under 10.4 million acres of cotton and slaughtered 6 million pigs in 1933—a time when people were ill clothed and ill fed. Although for landowning farmers the program was successful, few tenant farmers and sharecroppers, especially African Americans, received the government payments they were entitled to for

taking crops out of cultivation. Furthermore, the AAA's hopes that landlords would keep their tenants on the land even while cutting production were not fulfilled. In the South the number of sharecropper farms dropped by 30 percent between 1930 and 1940. The result was a homeless population, dispossessed Americans heading to cities and towns in all parts of the country.

Joining the migration to the West Coast were "Okies," such as Marvin Montgomery, and "Arkies" from Arkansas. Many of them had been evicted from their tenant farms

The Dust Bowl

during the depression, but thousands (including Montgomery) also took to the road to escape the drought that plagued the southern plains states of Kansas, Colorado, New Mexico, Oklahoma, Arkansas, and Texas. The region, known in the mid-1930s as the Dust Bowl, was an ecological disaster. In the 1920s farmers on the southern plains had bought tens of thousands of tractors and plowed millions of acres. Then the rain stopped, and strong winds caused enormous dust storms. Farmers shuttered their homes against the dust as tightly as possible, but, as a woman in western Kansas recounted in 1935, "those tiny particles seemed to seep through the very walls."

Some farmers blamed the government for their woes; others blamed themselves. As dissatisfaction mounted, so too did the appeal of

Demagogic Attacks

various demagogues who presented an analysis of American society that people understood: the wealthy and powerful were ruling people's lives. One of the best-known demagogues was Father Charles Coughlin, a Roman Catholic priest who in his weekly radio sermons criticized the New Deal. Coughlin increasingly blamed the nation's woes on an international conspiracy of Jewish bankers.

Another challenge to the New Deal came from Dr. Francis E. Townsend, a public health officer in Long Beach, California. Disturbed by the plight of old people, Townsend devised the Old Age Revolving Pensions plan, under which the government would pay monthly pensions of $200 to all citizens older than sixty on condition that they spent the money in the same month they received it. The plan was fiscally impossible but recognized the real needs of elderly Americans.

Then there was Huey Long, perhaps the most successful demagogue in American history. Long was elected governor of Louisiana in 1928 with the slogan "Every Man a King, but No One Wears a Crown." As a U.S. senator, Long at first supported the New Deal, but he began to believe that Roosevelt had fallen captive to big business. Long countered in 1934 with the Share Our Wealth Society, which advocated the seizure by taxation of all incomes greater than $1 million and all inheritances of more than $5 million. With the resulting funds, the government would furnish each family a homestead allowance of $5,000 and an annual income of $2,000. By mid-1935 Long's movement claimed 7 million members, and few doubted that Long aspired to the presidency. An assassin's bullet extinguished his ambition in September 1935.

Some politicians, like Governor Floyd Olson of Minnesota, declared themselves socialists in the 1930s.

Left-Wing Critics

In Wisconsin the left-wing Progressive Party reelected Robert La Follette, Jr., to the Senate in 1934. And the old muckraker and socialist Upton Sinclair won the Democratic gubernatorial nomination in California in 1934 with the slogan "End Poverty in California."

Perhaps the most controversial alternative to the New Deal was the Communist Party of the United States of America. In 1935 the party leadership changed its strategy. Proclaiming "Communism Is Twentieth Century Americanism," the Communists disclaimed any intention of overthrowing the U.S. government and began to cooperate with left-wing labor unions, student groups, and writers' organizations in a "Popular Front" against fascism abroad and racism at home. In 1938, at its high point for the decade, the party had fifty-five thousand members.

In addition to challenges from the right and the left, the New Deal was also subject to challenge by

Supreme Court Decisions Against the New Deal

the Supreme Court. The majority of the justices feared that New Deal legislation had vested too much power in the presidency. In 1935 the Court unanimously struck down the NIRA (*Schechter v. U.S.*), asserting that it granted the White House excessive legislative power and that the commerce clause of the Constitution did not give the federal govern-

ment authority to regulate intrastate businesses. Roosevelt's industrial recovery program was dead. In early 1936 his farm program met a similar fate when the Court invalidated the AAA (*U.S. v. Butler*).

The Second New Deal and Roosevelt's Second Term

As Roosevelt looked ahead to the presidential election of 1936, he foresaw the danger of losing his capacity to lead and to govern. His broad coalition of special interests was breaking up, radicals and demagogues were offering Americans alternative programs, and the Supreme Court was dismantling the New Deal. In early 1935 Roosevelt took the initiative and launched what historians call the Second New Deal.

The Second New Deal differed in important ways from the first. When the chief legislative goal had been

Emergency Relief Appropriation Act

economic recovery, Roosevelt had cooperated with business. Beginning in 1935, however, he denounced business leaders for placing their own selfish interests above the national welfare. The first triumph of the Second New Deal was the Emergency Relief Appropriation Act, which authorized the president to establish massive public works programs for the jobless. Among the programs funded by the Emergency Relief Appropriation Act were the Rural Electrification Administration, which brought electricity to isolated rural areas, and the National Youth Administration, which sponsored work-relief programs for young adults and part-time jobs for students.

Perhaps the best-known program funded by the Emergency Relief Appropriation Act was the Works Progress Administration (WPA), later renamed the Work Projects Administration. The WPA ultimately employed more than 8.5 million people and built 650,000 miles of highways and roads, 125,000 public buildings, and 8,000 parks. The WPA also built or renovated 5,900 schools and 2,500 hospitals, operated nurseries for preschool children, and established schools to combat adult illiteracy.

The WPA also sponsored a multitude of cultural programs, which not only provided employment for

The New Deal's Cultural Programs

artists, musicians, writers, and actors, but brought art in myriad forms to the people. The WPA's Federal Theater Project brought vaudeville, circuses, and theater, including African American and Yiddish plays, to cities and towns across the country; its Arts Project hired painters and sculptors to teach their crafts in rural schools; and its Federal Music Project sponsored 225,000 concerts by symphony orchestras, jazz groups, and folk musicians. Perhaps the most ambitious of the New Deal's cultural programs was the WPA's Federal Writers Project, which hired talented authors such as John Steinbeck and Richard Wright to write local guidebooks and regional and folk histories.

Roosevelt also wanted new legislation aimed at controlling the activities of big business. Business-

Control of Business

people had become increasingly critical of Roosevelt and the New Deal. If big business would not cooperate with government, Roosevelt decided, government should "cut the giants down to size" through antitrust suits and heavy corporate taxes. In 1935 he asked Congress to enact a labor bill, a Social Security bill, and a "soak-the-rich" tax bill.

When the summer of 1935, which constituted the Second Hundred Days, was over, the president had everything he had requested. First,

National Labor Relations Act

the National Labor Relations (Wagner) Act granted workers the right to unionize and bargain collectively with management. The act also created a new National Labor Relations Board empowered to guarantee democratic union elections and to penalize unfair labor practices by employers, such as firing workers for union membership.

The Social Security Act established old-age insurance under which workers who paid Social Security taxes out of their wages, matched by

Social Security Act

their employers, would receive retirement benefits beginning at age sixty-five. The act also created a co-operative federal-state system of unemployment compensation and Aid to Dependent Children (later renamed Aid to Families with Dependent Children, AFDC).

Social Security was in some ways a conservative measure. First, the government did not pay for old-age benefits; workers and their bosses did. Second, the tax was regressive in that the more workers earned, the less they were taxed proportionally. Third, it was deflationary because it took out of people's pockets money that it did not repay for years. Finally, the law had a disparate impact on Americans, as it excluded agricultural labor, domestic service, and "casual labor not in the course of the employer's trade or business." Thus a disproportionally high number of women and people of color, who worked as farm laborers, as domestic servants, and in service jobs in hospitals and restaurants, received no benefits. Nevertheless, the Social Security Act was a milestone. With its passage, the federal government took responsibility for the aged, the temporarily jobless, dependent children, and disabled people.

The Wealth Tax Act was seen by some critics as the president's attempt to "steal Huey Long's thunder." The tax act helped achieve a slight redistribution of income by raising the income taxes of the wealthy. It also imposed a new tax on excess business profits and increased taxes on inheritances, large gifts, and profits from the sale of property.

The Second Hundred Days made it unmistakably clear that the president was once again in charge and

Election of 1936 and the New Deal Coalition

preparing to run for reelection. Roosevelt won by a landslide, easily defeating the Republican nominee, Governor Alf Landon of Kansas, by a margin of 27.8 million votes to 16.7 million.

By 1936 Roosevelt and the Democrats had forged what observers have called the "New Deal coalition." This new alliance consisted of the urban masses—especially immigrants from southern and eastern Europe and their sons and daughters—organized labor, the white South, and northern blacks. With the New Deal coalition, the Democratic Party came to dominate the two-party system.

But even Roosevelt's buoyant optimism and landslide victory could not sustain forward momentum in his second term. Some of Roosevelt's own actions, in fact, helped bring about the end of the New Deal.

Concerned that the Supreme Court would invalidate much of the Second Hundred Days legislation, as it had done to the First Hundred Days, Roosevelt

Roosevelt's Court-Packing Plan

concluded that what the federal judiciary needed was a more progressive world-view. His Judiciary Reorganization Bill of 1937 requested the authority to add a federal judge whenever an incumbent failed to retire within six months of reaching age seventy; the president also wanted the power to name up to fifty additional federal judges, including six to the Supreme Court. Roosevelt frankly envisioned using the reorganization to create a Supreme Court sympathetic to the New Deal. Liberals joined Republicans and conservative Democrats in resisting the bill, and the president had to concede defeat. The bill he signed into law provided pensions to retiring judges but denied him the power to increase the number of federal judges.

The episode had a final, ironic twist. During the public debate over court packing, swing-vote justices on the Supreme Court began to vote in favor of liberal, pro–New Deal rulings. In short order the Court upheld both the Wagner Act (*NLRB v. Jones & Laughlin Steel Corp.*) and the Social Security Act. Moreover, the new pensions encouraged judges older than seventy to retire, and the president was able to appoint seven new associate justices in the next four years.

Another New Deal setback was the renewed economic recession of 1937–1939. Roosevelt had never abandoned his commitment to a balanced budget. In 1937, confident that the depression had largely been cured, he began to order drastic cutbacks in government spending. At the same time the Federal Reserve Board tightened credit. The two actions sent the economy into a tailspin: unemployment climbed from 7.7 million in 1937 to 10.4 million in 1938. Soon Roosevelt resumed deficit financing.

Recession of 1937–1939

In 1939, with concern over events in Europe commanding more and more of the nation's attention, the New Deal came to an end. Roosevelt sacrificed further domestic reforms in return for conservative support for his programs of military rearmament and preparedness. The last significant New Deal laws enacted were the National Housing Act (1937), which established the United States Housing Authority and built housing projects for low-income families; a new Agricultural Adjustment Act (1938); and the Fair Labor Standards Act (1938), which forbade labor by children younger than sixteen and established a minimum wage and forty-hour workweek for many workers.

Industrial Workers and the Rise of the CIO

New Deal legislation that gave workers the right to organize unions and bargain collectively invigorated the labor movement. By taking advantage of the new environment, unions increased their membership from 3.6 million in 1929 to more than 7 million in mid-1938. The gains, however, did not always come easily. Management resisted vigorously in the 1930s, relying on the police or hiring armed thugs to intimidate workers and break up strikes.

Labor confronted yet another obstacle in the American Federation of Labor (AFL) craft unions' traditional hostility toward industrial unions. Craft unions typically consisted of skilled workers in a particular trade, such as carpentry or plumbing. Industrial unions represented all the workers, skilled and unskilled, in a given industry. The organizational gains of the 1930s were impressive in industrial unions, as hundreds of thousands of workers organized in industries such as autos, garments, rubber, and steel.

Rivalry Between Craft and Industrial Unions

Attempts to reconcile the craft and industrial union movements failed, and in 1935 John L. Lewis, a leading industrial unionist and head of the United Mine Workers, resigned as vice president of the AFL. He and other industrial unionists then formed the Committee for Industrial Organization (CIO). The AFL responded by suspending the CIO unions, and in 1938 the CIO held its first national convention, calling itself the Congress of Industrial Organizations. By that time CIO membership had reached 3.7 million, slightly more than the AFL's 3.4 million.

The CIO evolved during the 1930s into a pragmatic, bread-and-butter labor organization that brought together millions of workers, including nu-

Sit-Down Strikes

merous women and African Americans who never before had had an opportunity to join a union. One union, the United Auto Workers (UAW), scored a major victory in late 1936. The UAW demanded recognition from General Motors (GM), Chrysler, and Ford. When GM refused, workers at the Fisher Body plant in Flint, Michigan, launched a sit-down strike and refused to leave the building.

The strike lasted for weeks. General Motors obtained a court order to evacuate the plant, but the strikers stood firm, risking imprisonment and fines. With the support of their families and neighborhoods, and a women's "emergency brigade" that picketed and delivered food and supplies to the strikers, the UAW prevailed. GM agreed to recognize the union. Chrysler signed a similar agreement, but Ford held out for four more years. Workers in the textile, glass, and rubber industries later used the sit-down strike tactic.

In 1937 the Steel Workers Organizing Committee (SWOC) signed a contract with the nation's largest steelmaker, U.S. Steel, that guaranteed an eight-hour workday and a forty-hour workweek. Other steel companies, including Republic Steel, refused to go along. On Memorial Day, strikers and their families joined sympathizers on the picket line in front of the Republic Steel plant in Chicago. Violence erupted; the police opened fire, and ten strikers were killed and forty suffered gunshot wounds. The police explained that the marchers had attacked them with clubs and bricks and that they had responded with reasonable force to defend themselves. The strikers saw it differently; the police, they argued, without provocation had brutally attacked citizens who were peacefully asserting their constitutional rights.

Memorial Day Massacre

Though senseless, the Memorial Day Massacre was not surprising. During the 1930s industries had hired private police agents and accumulated large stores of arms and ammunition for use in deterring workers from organizing and joining unions. Meanwhile, the CIO continued to enroll new members. By the end of the decade the CIO had succeeded in organizing most of the nation's mass-production industries.

Mixed Progress for People of Color

In 1930 about three-fourths of all African Americans lived in the South, where they continued to face disfranchisement, segregation from the cradle to the grave, exclusion, and poverty. Their life expectancy was ten years less than that of whites. Moreover, the specter of the lynch mob was a continuing threat in the South: in 1929, seven black men were lynched; in 1930, twenty; in 1933, twenty-four.

Racism also plagued African Americans living in the North. Black unemployment rates ran high; in Pittsburgh 48 percent of black workers were jobless in 1933, compared with 31 percent of white laborers. In northern industries in the 1930s, African Americans were the last hired and the first fired.

As African Americans were aware, President Herbert Hoover shared prevailing white racial attitudes. In 1930 the president demonstrated his racial insensitivity by nominating Judge John J. Parker of North Carolina to the Supreme Court. Ten years earlier Parker had endorsed the disfranchisement of blacks. Pressure from the NAACP and the AFL helped to defeat Parker's nomination in the Senate.

Hoover and African Americans

Shortly thereafter, a celebrated trial revealed the ugliness of race relations in the depression era. In March 1931 nine African American teenagers who were riding a freight train near Scottsboro, Alabama, were arrested and charged with roughing up some white hoboes and throwing them off the train. Two white women removed from the same train claimed the nine men had raped them. Medical evidence later showed that the women were lying. But within two weeks, eight of the so-called Scottsboro boys were convicted of rape by all-white juries and sentenced to death. After the failure of several appeals, the first defendant, Haywood Patterson,

Scottsboro Trials

was condemned to die. A Supreme Court ruling intervened, however, on the ground that African Americans were systematically excluded from juries in Alabama. Patterson was found guilty again in 1936 and was given a seventy-five-year jail sentence. Four of the other youths were sentenced to life imprisonment. Not until 1950 were all five out of jail—four by parole and Patterson by escaping from a work gang.

African Americans coped with their white-circumscribed environment and battled racism in a variety of ways. The Brotherhood of Sleeping Car Porters, under the astute leadership of A. Philip Randolph, fought for the rights of black workers. In Harlem the militant Harlem Tenants League fought rent increases and evictions, and African American consumers began to boycott white merchants who refused to hire blacks as clerks. And lawyers for the NAACP sued state universities for providing blacks with facilities that were sep-

Organized Opposition

arate but decidedly unequal. The NAACP was victorious in 1938, when the Supreme Court ruled (*Missouri ex rel. Gaines v. Canada*) that Missouri, by offering a legal education only to qualified white law students, gave whites a "privilege" that was "denied to Negroes by reason of their race." Thus the Supreme Court ordered Missouri to establish a separate law school for its qualified African Americans.

With the election of Franklin D. Roosevelt, blacks' attitudes toward government changed, as did their political affiliation. For African Americans Franklin D. Roosevelt would become the most appealing president since Abraham Lincoln. They were heartened by photographs of African American visitors at the White House and by news stories about Roosevelt's black advisers. Most important, the New Deal programs aided black people in their struggle for economic survival.

Roosevelt's "Black Cabinet," or black brain trust, was unique in U.S. history. Never before had there

Mary McLeod Bethune, pictured here with her friend and supporter Eleanor Roosevelt, became the first African American woman to head a federal agency as director of the Division of Negro Affairs of the National Youth Administration.   (Corbis-Bettmann)

Black Cabinet been so many African American advisers at the White House. Among the consultants were black lawyers, journalists, and Ph.D.'s and black experts on housing, labor, and social welfare. William H. Hastie and Robert C. Weaver, holders of advanced degrees from Harvard, served in the Department of the Interior. Mary McLeod Bethune, educator and president of the National Council of Negro Women, was director of the Division of Negro Affairs of the National Youth Administration. Also among the New Dealers were some whites who had committed themselves to first-class citizenship for African Americans. Foremost among these people was Eleanor Roosevelt.

The president himself, however, remained uncommitted to African American civil rights. Fearful of alienating southern white Democrats, he never endorsed two key goals of the civil rights struggle: a federal law against lynching and abolition of the poll tax. Moreover, many New Deal programs functioned in ways that were definitely damaging to African Americans. Rather than benefiting black tenant farmers and sharecroppers, the AAA had the effect of forcing many of them off the land. The Federal Housing Administration (FHA) refused to guarantee mortgages on houses purchased by blacks in white neighborhoods, the CCC was racially segregated, and the TVA followed local custom in handing out skilled jobs to whites first. Also, Social Security coverage and the minimum-wage provisions of the Fair Labor Standards Act of 1938 excluded janitors, farm workers, and domestics, many of whom were African Americans.

Racism in the New Deal

In short, although African Americans benefited from the New Deal, they did not get anything approaching their fair share. Even so, the large majorities they gave Roosevelt at election time demonstrated their appreciation for the aid they did receive. Not all African Americans, however, trusted the mixed message of the New Deal. Some concluded that they could depend only on themselves and organized self-help and direct-action movements.

Nowhere was the trend toward direct action more evident than in the March on Washington Movement in 1941. That year, billions of federal dollars flowed into American war industries as the nation rearmed for the possibility of another world war. Thousands of new jobs were created, but discrimination deprived blacks of a reasonable proportion of them.

March on Washington Movement

A. Philip Randolph, leader of the porters' union, proposed that blacks march on the nation's capital to demand equal access to jobs in defense industries.

By early summer thousands were ready to march. Fearing that the march might provoke riots and that communists might infiltrate the movement, Roosevelt announced that he would issue an executive order prohibiting discrimination in war industries and in the government if the march was canceled. The result was Executive Order No. 8802, which established the Fair Employment Practices Committee (FEPC). The March on Washington Movement anticipated future trends in the civil rights movement: it was all-black, and its tactic was direct action.

Another group, American Indians, sank further into malnutrition and disease during the Hoover administration. At the heart of the problem was a 1929 ruling by the U.S. comptroller general that landless tribes were ineligible for federal aid. Not until 1931 did the Bureau of Indian Affairs take steps to relieve the suffering.

A New Deal for Native Americans

The New Deal approach to Native Americans differed greatly from that of earlier administrations; as a result, Indians benefited more directly than blacks from the New Deal. For the post of commissioner of Indian affairs, Roosevelt appointed John Collier, founder of the American Indian Defense Association, who sought an end to the allotment policy established by the Dawes Severalty Act of 1887. The Indian Reorganization (Wheeler-Howard) Act (1934) aimed to reverse the increasing landlessness of Native Americans by restoring lands to tribal ownership and forbidding future division of Indian lands into individual parcels. Other provisions of the act enabled tribes to obtain loans for economic development and to establish self-government. Under Collier, the Bureau of Indian Affairs also encouraged the perpetuation of Indian religions and cultures.

Mexican Americans also suffered extreme hardship during the Great Depression, but no government

Depression Hardships of Mexican Americans

programs benefited them. During these years many Mexicans and Mexican Americans packed up their belongings and moved south of the border; some did so willingly, but others were either deported by immigration officials or given one-way tickets to Mexico by California officials eager to purge them from the relief rolls. In addition, many employers changed their minds about the desirability of hiring Mexican American farm workers. Before the 1930s farmers had boasted that Mexican Americans were an inexpensive, docile labor supply and that they would not join unions. But in the 1930s Mexican Americans overturned the stereotype by engaging in prolonged and sometimes bloody strikes.

The New Deal offered Mexican Americans little help. The AAA was created to assist property-owning farmers, not migratory farm workers. The Wagner Act did not cover farm workers' unions, nor did the Social Security Act or the Fair Labor Standards Act cover farm laborers. One New Deal agency, the Farm Security Administration (FSA), was established in 1937 to help farm workers, in part by setting up migratory labor camps. But the FSA came too late to help Mexican Americans, most of whom had by then been replaced in the fields by dispossessed white farmers from the Dust Bowl states.

Women, Work, and the Great Depression

In *It's Up to the Women* (1933), Eleanor Roosevelt wrote that "women know that life must go on and that the needs of life must be met." Wives and mothers followed the maxim "Use it up, wear it out, make it do, or do without." Women bought day-old bread and cheap cuts of meat; they relined old coats with blankets. Many families were able to maintain their standard of living only because of astute spending and because women substituted their own labor for goods and services they had once purchased.

While they were cutting corners to make ends meet, women were also seeking paid work outside the home. In 1930 approximately 10.5 million women

Women at Work Outside the Home

were paid workers; ten years later, the female labor force exceeded 13 million. Many women were their families' sole providers. Despite these social realities, most Americans believed that women should not take jobs outside the home, that they should strive instead to be good wives and mothers, and that women who worked were doing so for "pin money" to buy frivolous extras.

These attitudes resulted in severe job discrimination. Most insurance companies, banks, railroads, and public utilities had policies against hiring married women. The same was true of many public school districts. And from 1932 to 1937, federal law prohibited more than one family member from working for the civil service. Because wives usually earned less than their husbands, they were the ones who quit their government jobs.

Job Discrimination Against Married Women

Although the preponderance of working women were single, married women too went to work during the depression. By 1940 married women constituted 35 percent of the female work force, up from 29 percent in 1930 and 15 percent in 1900. They worked to keep their families from slipping into poverty, but their assistance with family expenses did not improve their status. Their husbands, including those without jobs, still expected to rule the roost and to remain exempt from childcare and housework.

Wives and Husbands Face Hard Times

The New Deal did take women's needs into account, but only when forcefully reminded to do so by the activist women who advised the administration. These women, mainly government and Democratic Party officials, formed a network united by their commitment to social reform, to protective laws for women's health and safety on the job, and to the participation of women in politics and government. The network's most prominent member was Eleanor Roosevelt, who was her husband's valued adviser. Secretary of Labor Frances Perkins was the nation's first woman cabinet officer. Other historic New Deal appointments included the first woman federal appeals judge and the first women ambassadors.

Women in the New Deal

Even with increased participation by women, however, New Deal provisions for women were mixed. The maximum-hour and minimum-wage provisions mandated by the NRA helped women workers in the lowest-paying jobs, many of whom labored under sweatshop conditions. Some NRA codes mandated pay differentials based on gender, however, making women's minimum wages lower than men's. Moreover, federal relief agencies hired only one woman for every eight to ten men placed in relief jobs, the Civilian Conservation Corps was limited to young men, and women in agriculture and domestic service were not protected by the 1938 Fair Labor Standards Act. Most important, the 1935 Social Security Act excluded not only agricultural labor and domestic service, as already noted, but also occupations in the public sector. That meant that many teachers, nurses, librarians, and social workers, the majority of whom were women, went uncovered.

The Election of 1940 and the Legacy of the New Deal

No president had ever served more than two terms, and as the presidential election of 1940 approached, many Americans speculated about whether Franklin Roosevelt would run for a third term. Roosevelt seemed undecided until the spring of 1940, when Adolf Hitler's military advances in Europe apparently convinced him to stay on.

The Republican candidate was Wendell Willkie, a utilities executive who had become a prominent business opponent of Roosevelt's agenda and campaigned vigorously against the New Deal. He also criticized the government's lack of military preparedness. But Roosevelt preempted the defense issue by expanding military and naval contracts. As workers streamed into the factories to fill new orders, unemployment figures dropped as well. When Willkie reversed his approach and accused Roosevelt of warmongering, the president promised Americans, "Your boys are not going to be sent into any foreign wars." On election day Roosevelt received 27 million popular votes to Willkie's 22 million.

Wendell Willkie

Any analysis of the New Deal must begin with Franklin Delano Roosevelt himself. Most historians consider him a truly great president, citing his courage, his willingness to experiment, and his capacity to inspire the nation during the most somber days of the depression. Those who criticize him charge that he lacked vision and failed to formulate a bold and coherent strategy of economic recovery and political and economic reform. Essentially Roosevelt was a pragmatist whose goal was to preserve the capitalist system while at the same time alleviating suffering.

Roosevelt and the New Deal Assessed

Even scholars who criticize Roosevelt's performance agree that he transformed the presidency. "Only Washington, who made the office, and Jackson, who remade it, did more than Roosevelt to raise it to its present condition of strength, dignity, and independence," according to political scientist Clinton Rossiter. Other scholars, however, have charged that it was Roosevelt who initiated "the imperial presidency." Whether for good or ill, Roosevelt strengthened not only the presidency but the whole federal government. As the historian William Leuchtenburg has written, "the federal government became an institution that was directly experienced. More than state and local governments, it came to be the government."

During the Roosevelt years, the federal government for the first time assumed a responsibility to offer relief to the jobless and the needy. In doing so, it laid the foundation of the nation's welfare system. To fund the programs and to stimulate the economy the government engaged in deficit spending. However, the economy itself continued to be capitalistic. There was some redistribution of wealth, but the wealthy remained as a class (see Figure 25.1).

Origins of America's Welfare System

Summary

The New Deal brought about limited change in the nation's power structure. Beginning in the 1930s, business interests had to share their political clout with others. Labor gained influence in Washington, and farmers got more of what they wanted from Congress and the

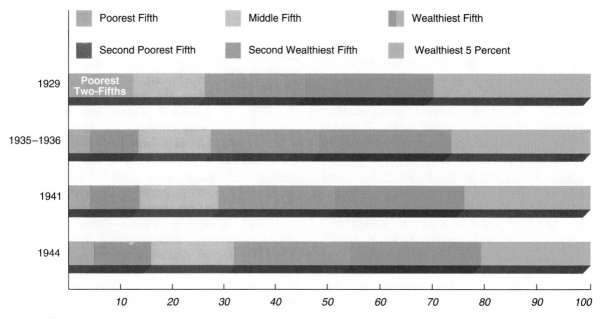

Figure 25.1   Distribution of Total Family Income Among the American People, 1929–1944 (Percentage)   Although the New Deal provided economic relief to the American people, it did not, as its critics so often charged, significantly redistribute income downward from the rich to the poor.   (Source: Adapted from U.S. Bureau of the Census, *Historical Statistics of the United States, Colonial Times to 1970,* 2 parts [Washington, D.C.: U.S. Government Printing Office, 1975], Part 1, p. 301.)

White House. If people wanted their voices to be heard, they had to organize into labor unions, trade associations, or other special-interest lobbies. Not everybody's voice was heard, however. Because of the persistence of racism, there was no real increase in the power of African Americans and other minorities.

The New Deal failed in one fundamental purpose: to put people back to work. As late as 1939, more than 10 million men and women were still jobless. That year, unemployment was 19 percent. In the end it was not the New Deal but massive government spending during the Second World War that put people back to work. In 1941, as a result of mobilization for war, unemployment declined to 10 percent, and in 1944, at the height of the war, only 1 percent of the labor force was jobless.

The New Deal's most lasting accomplishments were its programs to ameliorate the suffering of unemployed people. The United States has suffered several economic recessions since 1945, but even Republican presidents have primed the pump during periods of slump. Before the New Deal, the United States had experienced a major depression every fifteen to twenty years. The Great Depression was the last of its kind. Since the New Deal, thanks to unemployment compensation, Social Security, and other measures, the United States has not experienced another such national nightmare.

LEGACY FOR A PEOPLE AND A NATION
Social Security for Retired Americans

In breaking with historical precedent by authorizing old-age insurance, as well as unemployment compensation and aid to dependent children, the Social Security Act of 1935 became the single most important piece of social welfare legislation in American history. Under Social Security, working Americans today still make monthly payments for old-age, survivors, and disability insurance (OASDI). Although Social Security initially excluded some of America's neediest citizens from participation in OASDI, such as people working in low-paying menial jobs, amendments to the law eased eligibility requirements. Twenty-four million Americans made monthly payments to the OASDI fund in 1939; ten years later, the figure had risen to 34 million. By 1970, 69 million Americans were covered under OASDI; by 1997 the figure had ballooned to 172 million. Prior to the enactment of Social Security, millions of elderly Americans had lived in poverty. But a 1999 study showed that Social Security benefits kept a third of the nation's elderly from slipping into poverty and helped significantly to narrow the income disparities between women and men in old age.

Today, Americans worry about the future of Social Security. They fear that the tens of millions of baby boomers born in the 1940s, 1950s, and early 1960s will bankrupt the system when they retire. Many also know that in the 1980s and 1990s the federal government raided the Social Security trust fund, diverting billions of dollars to pay for the skyrocketing national debt. Some reduction of the system's responsibilities has also occurred; in 1996, reflecting Americans' hostility to welfare, Congress passed and President Bill Clinton signed a law eliminating aid to families with dependent children and greatly tightening eligibility requirements for public assistance. The future of Social Security is hotly debated today, both in and out of government. Two of the most important proposals are, first, to allow Americans to invest their retirement contributions in the stock market and, second, to impose a federal "lock box" law that would safeguard Social Security's trust funds from future federal tampering.

For Further Reading, see the Appendix. For Web resources, go to history.college.hmco.com/students.

PEACESEEKERS AND WARMAKERS: AMERICANS IN THE WORLD
1920–1941

In 1921 the Rockefeller Foundation declared war on the mosquito in Latin America. As the carrier of yellow fever, the *Aedes aegypti* mosquito transmitted a deadly virus that caused severe headaches, vomiting, jaundice (yellow skin), and, for many, death. Encouraged by the U.S. Department of State, the foundation dedicated several million dollars for projects to control yellow fever in Latin America.

Nothing less than U.S. hegemony in the hemisphere seemed at stake. U.S. diplomats, military officers, and business executives agreed with foundation officials that the disease threatened public health, which in turn disturbed political and economic order. When outbreaks occurred, ports were closed and

quarantined, disrupting trade. The infection struck down American officials, merchants, investors, and soldiers stationed abroad. Workers became incapacitated, reducing productivity. Throughout Latin America, insufficient official attention to yellow-fever epidemics stirred public discontent against regimes the United States supported.

In Veracruz, a Mexican province of significant U.S. economic activity, a yellow-fever outbreak in 1920 killed 235 people. The next year Rockefeller personnel painstakingly inspected breeding places in houses and deposited larvae-eating fish in public waterworks. In 1924 La Fundación Rockefeller declared yellow fever eradicated in Mexico. In Latin America,

IMPORTANT EVENTS

1921–22 Washington Conference limits naval arms
Rockefeller Foundation begins battle
against yellow fever in Latin America

1922 Mussolini comes to power in Italy

1924 Dawes Plan eases German reparations
U.S. troops leave Dominican Republic

1926 U.S. troops occupy Nicaragua

1927 Jiang breaks with Communists in China

1928 Kellogg-Briand Pact outlaws war

1929 Great Depression begins
Young Plan reduces German reparations

1930 Hawley-Smoot Tariff raises duties

1931 Japan seizes Manchuria

1932 Stimson Doctrine protests Japanese
control of Manchuria
Roosevelt elected president

1933 Hitler establishes Nazi regime in
Germany
U.S. recognizes Soviet Union
Good Neighbor policy for Latin
America

1934 Batista comes to power in Cuba
Export-Import Bank founded to expand
trade
Johnson Act forbids loans to debt-
defaulting countries
Reciprocal Trade Agreements Act lowers
tariffs
U.S. troops withdraw from Haiti

1935 Italy invades Ethiopia
Neutrality Act stops U.S. arms
shipments

1936 U.S. votes for nonintervention
at Pan-American Conference
Germany reoccupies the Rhineland
Spanish Civil War breaks out between
Loyalists and Franco's fascists
Neutrality Act forbids U.S. loans to
belligerents

Rome-Berlin Axis created
Germany and Japan unite against Soviet
Union in the Anti-Comintern Pact

1937 Neutrality Act creates cash-and-carry trade
with warring nations
Sino-Japanese War breaks out
Quarantine speech against aggressors
Ponce Massacre in Puerto Rico

1938 Mexico nationalizes American-owned oil
companies
Munich Conference grants part of Czechoslovakia to Germany

1939 Nazi-Soviet Pact carves up eastern Europe
Germany invades Poland
Second World War begins
U.S. repeals arms embargo to help
Allies

1940 Soviet Union invades Finland
Germany invades Denmark, Belgium, the
Netherlands, and France
Committee to Defend America by Aiding the
Allies formed
Germany, Italy, and Japan join in Tripartite
Pact
U.S. and Great Britain swap destroy-
ers for military bases
Isolationists form America First Committee
Selective Training and Service Act starts first
peacetime draft

1941 Lend-Lease Act gives aid to Allies
Germany attacks Soviet Union
U.S. freezes Japanese assets
Atlantic Charter produced at Roosevelt-
Churchill meeting
Roosevelt exploits *Greer* incident
Japanese flotilla attacks Pearl Harbor, Hawai'i
U.S. enters Second World War

the foundation's antimosquito campaign proved successful in maritime and urban areas. The foundation's work also carried political effects: strengthening central governments by providing a national public health infrastructure and helping diminish anti-U.S. sentiment.

The Rockefeller Foundation's drive to eradicate the mosquito exemplifies Americans' fervent but futile effort to build a stable international order between the First and Second World Wars. After World War I, Americans did not cut themselves off from international affairs, despite the tag "isolationist" that is sometimes still applied to U.S. foreign relations during the interwar decades. They remained very active in world affairs in the 1920s and 1930s. President Wilson had said after the First World War that the United States had "become a determining factor in the history of mankind, and after you have become a determining factor you cannot remain isolated, whether you want to or not." He was right.

The most apt description of interwar U.S. foreign policy is "independent internationalism." That is, the United States was active on a global scale but retained its independence of action, its traditional unilateralism. American interests abroad were far-flung and vast—colonies, client states, naval bases, investments, trade, missionaries, humanitarian projects. Nevertheless, many Americans did think of themselves as isolationists, by which they meant that they wanted no part of Europe's political squabbles, military alliances and interventions, or the League of Nations, which might drag them unwillingly into war. Americans, then, were isolationists in their desire to avoid war but independent internationalists in their activities to shape the world to their liking.

In the aftermath of the First World War, Americans had grown disenchanted with military methods of achieving order and protecting American prosperity and security. American diplomats thus increasingly sought to exercise the power of the United States through conferences, humanitarian programs, cultural penetration ("Americanization"), moral lectures and calls for peace, nonrecognition of disapproved regimes, arms control, and economic and financial ties under the Open Door principle. In Latin America, for example, U.S. leaders downgraded military interventions to fashion a Good Neighbor policy.

But a stable world order proved elusive. The debts and reparations bills left over from the First World War bedeviled the 1920s, and the Great Depression of the 1930s shattered world trade and finance. The depression spawned revolutions in Latin America and political extremism, militarism, and war in Europe and Asia. As Nazi Germany marched toward world war, the United States tried to protect itself from the conflict by adopting a policy of neutrality. At the same time, the United States sought to defend its interests in Asia against Japanese aggression by invoking the Open Door policy.

In the late 1930s, and especially after the outbreak of European war in September 1939, many Americans came to agree with President Franklin D. Roosevelt that Germany and Japan imperiled the national interest because they were building exclusive, self-sufficient spheres of influence based on military power and economic domination. Roosevelt pushed first for American military preparedness and then for the abandonment of neutrality in favor of aiding Britain and France. To deter Japanese expansion in China and in the Pacific, the United States ultimately cut off supplies of vital American products such as oil. But economic warfare only intensified antagonisms. Japan's surprise attack on Pearl Harbor, Hawai'i, in December 1941 finally brought the United States into the Second World War. ■

Searching for Peace and Order in the 1920s

 The First World War left Europe in shambles. Between 1914 and 1921, Europe suffered 60 million casualties from world war, civil war, massacre, epidemic, and famine. Germany and France both lost 10 percent of their workers. Crops, livestock, factories, trains, forests, bridges—little was spared. The American Relief Administration and private charities delivered food to needy Europeans, including Russians wracked by famine in 1921 and 1922.

The League of Nations, envisioned as a peacemaker, proved feeble, not just because the United States refused to join but because its members failed to utilize the new organization to settle important disputes. And, starting in the mid-1920s, American officials participated discreetly in League meetings on public health, prostitution, drug and arms trafficking, counterfeiting of currency, and other issues. American jurists served on the Permanent Court of International Justice (World Court), though the United States also refused to join that League body.

American peace societies working for international stability drew widespread popular support.

Peace Groups

Women within the movement often gravitated to their own organizations, such as the National Conference on the Care and Cause of War, because they lacked influence in the male-dominated groups and because of the popular assumption that women—as life givers and nurturing mothers—had a unique aversion to violence and war. Most peace groups pointed to the carnage of the First World War and the futility of war as a solution to international problems, but they differed over strategies to ensure world order. Some urged cooperation with the League and World Court. Others championed the arbitration of disputes, disarmament and arms reduction, the outlawing of war, and strict neutrality during wars.

The Washington Conference of November 1921–February 1922 seemed to mark a substantial step toward peace through arms control.

Washington Conference on the Limitation of Armaments

At the invitation of the United States, delegates from Britain, Japan, France, Italy, China, Portugal, Belgium, and the Netherlands joined U.S. diplomats to discuss limits on naval armaments. Britain, the United States, and Japan were facing a naval arms race whose huge military spending endangered economic rehabilitation.

The conference produced three treaties. The Five-Power Treaty set a ten-year moratorium on the construction of capital ships (battleships and aircraft carriers) and established total tonnage limits of 500,000 for Britain and the United States, 300,000 for Japan, and 175,000 for France and Italy. They also pledged not to build new fortifications in their Pacific possessions. In the Nine-Power Treaty, the conferees reaffirmed the Open Door in China, recognizing Chinese sovereignty. In the Four-Power Treaty, the United States, Britain, Japan, and France agreed to respect one another's Pacific possessions. The three treaties did not limit submarines, destroyers, or cruisers; nor did they provide enforcement powers for the Open Door declaration.

Peace advocates also welcomed the Kellogg-Briand Pact of 1928. In this document, sixty-two na-

Kellogg-Briand Pact

tions agreed to "condemn recourse to war for the solution of international controversies, and renounce it as an instrument of national policy." Although weak, the Kellogg-Briand Pact reflected popular opinion that war was barbaric and wasteful.

The World Economy, Cultural Expansion, and Great Depression

While Europe struggled to recover from the ravages of the First World War, the international economy wobbled and then, in the early 1930s, collapsed. The Great Depression set off a political chain reaction that carried the world to war. Cordell Hull, secretary of state under President Franklin D. Roosevelt from 1933 to 1944, often pointed out that political extremism and militarism sprang from maimed economies.

Hull believed that American economic expansion would stabilize world politics. Because of World War I, the United States became a creditor nation and the financial capital of the world (see Figure 26.1). Moreover, by the late 1920s the United States produced nearly half of the world's industrial goods and ranked first among exporters. For example, General Electric invested heavily in Germany, American companies began to exploit Venezuela's rich petroleum resources, and U.S. firms began to challenge British control of oil resources in the Middle East.

U.S. Trade and Investment

America's economic prominence facilitated the export of American culture. Hollywood movies saturated the global market and stimulated interest in American ways and products. Although some foreigners warned against "Americanization," others aped American mass-production methods and emphasis on efficiency and modernization. Coca-Cola opened a bottling plant in Essen, Germany, and Ford built an automobile assembly plant in Cologne. Germans marveled at Henry Ford's economic success and industrial techniques ("Fordismus"). Indeed, in the 1930s, Adolf Hitler sent German car designers to Detroit before he launched the Volkswagen.

Cultural Expansion

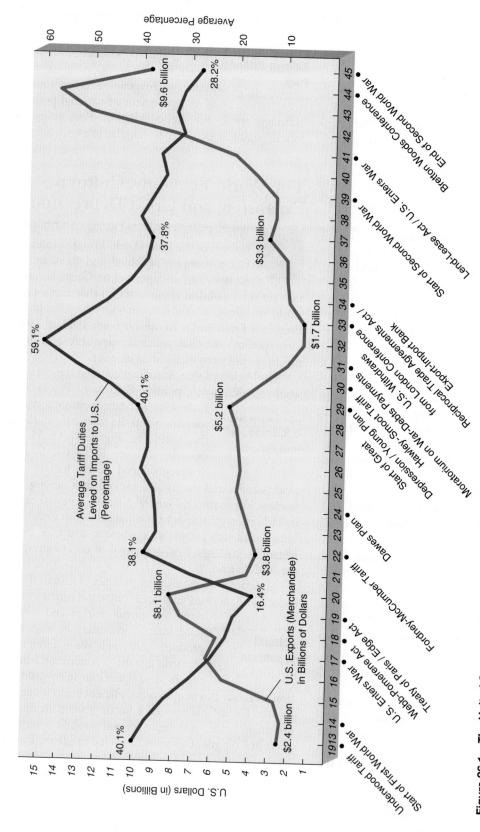

Figure 26.1 The United States in the World Economy In the 1920s and 1930s, global depression and war scuttled the United States's hope for a stable economic order. This graph suggests, moreover, that high American tariffs meant lower exports, further impeding world trade. The Reciprocal Trade Agreements program initiated in the early 1930s was designed to ease tariff wars with other nations. (Source: U.S. Bureau of the Census, *Historical Statistics of the United States, Colonial Times to 1970*, 2 parts [Washington, D.C.: U.S. Government Printing Office, 1975].)

The U.S. government assisted this cultural and economic expansion. The Webb-Pomerene Act (1918) excluded from antitrust prosecution those combinations set up for export trade; the Edge Act (1919) permitted American banks to open foreign branch banks; and the overseas offices of the Department of Commerce gathered and disseminated valuable market information.

Europeans watched American economic expansion with wariness and branded the United States stingy for its handling of World War I debts and reparations. Twenty-eight nations became entangled in the web of inter-Allied government debts, which totaled $26.5 billion ($9.6 billion of it owed to the U.S. government). Europeans also owed private American creditors another $3 billion. Europeans urged Americans to erase the government debts as a magnanimous contribution to the war effort, but American leaders insisted on repayment.

War Debts and German Reparations

The debts question became linked to Germany's $33 billion reparations bill. Hobbled by inflation and economic disorder, Germany began to default on its payments. To keep the nation afloat and to forestall the radicalism that might thrive on economic troubles, American bankers loaned millions of dollars. A triangular relationship developed: American investors' money flowed to Germany, Germany paid reparations to the Allies, and the Allies then paid some of their debts to the United States. The American-crafted Dawes Plan of 1924 greased the financial tracks by reducing Germany's annual payments, extending the repayment period, and providing still more loans. The United States also gradually scaled down Allied obligations, cutting the debt by half during the 1920s.

But the triangular arrangement depended on continued German borrowing in the United States, and in 1928 and 1929 American lending abroad dropped sharply in the face of more lucrative opportunities in the stock market at home. The U.S.-negotiated Young Plan of 1929, which reduced Germany's reparations, salvaged little as the world economy sputtered and collapsed. By 1931, when Hoover declared a moratorium on payments, the Allies had paid back only $2.6 billion. Staggered by the Great Depression—an international catastrophe—they defaulted on the rest.

As the depression accelerated, tariff wars revealed a reinvigorated economic nationalism. By 1932 some twenty-five nations had retaliated against rising American tariffs (created in the Fordney-McCumber Act of 1922 and the Hawley-Smoot Act of 1930) by imposing higher rates on foreign imports. From 1929 to 1933, world trade declined in value by some 40 percent. Exports of American merchandise slumped from $5.2 billion to $1.7 billion.

Tariffs and Economic Nationalism

Many nations contributed to the worldwide economic cataclysm. The United States might have lowered its tariffs so that Europeans could sell their goods in the American market and thus earn dollars to pay off their debts. Vengeful Europeans might have trimmed Germany's huge indemnity. The Germans might have borrowed less from abroad and taxed themselves more. The Soviets might have agreed to pay rather than repudiate Soviet Russia's $4 billion debt.

Calling the protective tariff the "king of evils," Hull successfully pressed Congress to pass the Reciprocal Trade Agreements Act in 1934. This important legislation empowered the president to reduce U.S. tariffs by as much as 50 percent through special agreements with foreign countries. The central feature of the act was the most-favored-nation principle, whereby the United States was entitled to the lowest tariff rate set by any nation with which it had an agreement.

Reciprocal Trade Agreements Act

In 1934 Hull also helped create the Export-Import Bank, a government agency that provided loans to foreigners for the purchase of American goods. The bank stimulated trade and became a diplomatic weapon, allowing the United States to exact concessions through the approval or denial of loans. But in the short term, Hull's ambitious programs—examples of America's independent internationalism—brought only mixed results.

U.S. Hegemony in Latin America

Through the Platt Amendment, Roosevelt Corollary, Panama Canal, military intervention, and economic preeminence, the United States had thrown an imperial net over

Map 26.1 The United States and Latin America Between the Wars The United States often intervened in other nations to maintain its hegemonic power in Latin America, where nationalists resented outside meddling in their sovereign affairs. The Good Neighbor policy decreased U.S. military interventions, but U.S. economic interests in the hemisphere remained strong.

The labels within the map read:

CANADA
Ottawa★
UNITED STATES
ATLANTIC OCEAN
San Francisco
Washington, D.C.★

Roosevelt's Good Neighbor Policy, 1933

U.S. upholds right of intervention at Pan-American Conference, 1928

U.S. troops, 1917–1922
U.S. investors dominate sugar industry
Revolution of 1933
U.S. abrogates Platt Amendment, 1934
Batista era, 1934–1959

U.S. troops, 1915–1934
Financial supervision, 1916–1941

MEXICO

Constitution of 1917 challenges U.S. interests
Nationalization of foreign oil companies, 1938
U.S.-Mexico agreement settles oil dispute, 1942

U.S. financial supervision, 1905–1941
U.S. troops withdrawn, 1924
Trujillo era, 1930–1961

Gulf of Mexico
Miami
THE BAHAMAS
Nassau
Guantánamo
Havana CUBA
JAMAICA
Mexico City
Belmopan
BELIZE
Kingston
HONDURAS
Tegucigalpa
Port-au-Prince
Santo Domingo
DOMINICAN REP.
HAITI
San Juan
PUERTO RICO (US)
VIRGIN IS. (US,UK)
U.S. colony since 1917
GUATEMALA
Guatemala City
EL SALVADOR
San Salvador
NICARAGUA
Managua
Caribbean Sea

U.S. colony
Jones Act grants U.S. citizenship, 1917

U.S. invasion, 1924
United Fruit Company active

San José
COSTA RICA
Panama
PANAMA
Caracas
VENEZUELA
Bogotá
COLOMBIA
GUYANA
SURINAM
Georgetown
Paramaribo
Cayenne
FRENCH GUIANA (FR.)

U.S. financial supervision, 1911–1924
U.S. military occupation, 1912–1925
U.S. war against Sandino, 1926–1933
Somoza era, 1936–1979

U.S. control of Canal Zone
Declaration of Panama, 1939

ECUADOR
Quito

U.S. oil investments

PERU
Lima
BRAZIL
La Paz
Brasília
BOLIVIA

U.S. copper interests

CHILE
PARAGUAY
Asunción
PACIFIC OCEAN

Santiago
Buenos Aires
URUGUAY
Montevideo
ARGENTINA

U.S. votes for nonintervention pledge at Pan-American Conference, 1936

0 500 1000 Km.
0 500 1000 Mi.

Latin America in the early twentieth century. U.S. hegemony in the hemisphere grew apace after the First World War. A prominent State Department officer patronizingly remarked that Latins were incapable of political progress because of their "low racial quality." They were, however, "very easy people to deal with if properly managed." And managed they were. American-made schools, roads, telephones, and irrigation systems dotted Caribbean and Central American nations. American "money doctors" in Colombia and Peru helped reform tariff and tax laws and invited U.S. companies to build public works. U.S. soldiers occupied Cuba, the Dominican Republic, Haiti, Panama, and Nicaragua. U.S. authorities maintained Puerto Rico as a colony (see Map 26.1).

Criticisms of U.S. Interventionism

Criticism of U.S. imperialism in the region mounted in the interwar years. Senator William Borah of Idaho urged that Latin Americans be granted the right of self-determination. Some charged that U.S. presidents were usurping constitutional power by ordering troops abroad without a congressional declaration of war. Businesspeople feared that Latin American nationalists would direct their anti-Yankee feelings against American-owned property. And Hoover's secretary of state, Henry L. Stimson, acknowledged a double-standard problem in 1932 when he was protesting Japanese incursions in China: "If we landed a single soldier among those South Americans now . . . it would put me absolutely in the wrong in China, where Japan has done all this monstrous work under the guise of protecting her nationals with a landing force."

Good Neighbor Policy

Renouncing unpopular military intervention, the United States shifted to other methods to maintain its influence in Latin America: Pan-Americanism, support for strong local leaders, the training of national guards, economic and cultural penetration, Export-Import Bank loans, financial supervision, and political subversion. Franklin D. Roosevelt gave this general approach a name in 1933: the Good Neighbor policy. It meant that the United States would be less blatant in its domination—less willing to defend exploitative business practices, less eager to launch military expeditions, and less reluctant to consult with Latin Americans.

National Guards and Dictators

To avoid military interventions and occupations, the United States trained Latin American national guards and supported dictators. For example, before the United States withdrew its troops from the Dominican Republic in 1924, U.S. personnel created a guard. One of its first officers was Rafael Leonidas Trujillo, who became head of the national army in 1928 and became president two years later. Trujillo ruled the Dominican Republic with an iron fist until his assassination in 1961. "He may be an S.O.B.," Roosevelt supposedly remarked, "but he is our S.O.B."

Nicaraguans endured a similar experience. U.S. troops occupied Nicaragua from 1912 to 1925 and returned in late 1926 during a civil war. Nationalistic, anti-imperialist Nicaraguan opposition, led by César Augusto Sandino, prompted Washington to end the occupation and move toward the Good Neighbor policy. In 1933 the marines departed, but they left behind a powerful national guard headed by General Anastasio Somoza, who "always played the game fairly with us," recalled a top U.S. officer. With backing from the United States, the Somoza family ruled Nicaragua from 1936 to 1979 through corruption, political suppression, and torture.

Marine Occupation of Haiti

The marine occupation of black, French-speaking Haiti from 1915 to 1934 also left a negative legacy. U.S. officials censored the Haitian press, manipulated elections, wrote the constitution, jailed or killed protesters, managed government finances, and created a national guard. The National City Bank of New York became the owner of the Haitian Banque Nationale, and the United States became Haiti's largest trading partner. When U.S. troops withdrew in 1934, Haiti had Latin America's highest illiteracy rate, lowest per capita income, and poorest health, as well as police-state repression.

Backing Batista in Cuba

The Cubans, too, grew restless under North American domination. By 1929 North American investments in Cuba totaled $1.5 billion, including two-thirds ownership of the sugar industry. The U.S. military uniform remained conspicuous at the Guantánamo naval base. And

travel?
adventure?
answer– **join the Marines!**
ENLIST TO-DAY FOR 2-3 or 4 YEARS

This U.S. government recruiting poster captured the post-war American mood of independent internationalism by offering overseas duty to prospective marines.   (Library of Congress)

American influences continued to permeate Cuban culture. In 1933 Cubans rebelled against the dictator and U.S. ally Gerardo Machado. In open defiance of U.S. warships cruising offshore, Professor Ramón Grau San Martín became president and declared the Platt Amendment null and void. His government also seized some North American–owned mills, refused to repay American bank loans, and debated land reform. Unsettled by this nationalistic "social revolution," U.S. officials plotted with army sergeant Fulgencio Batista to overthrow Grau in 1934.

During the Batista era, which lasted until Fidel Castro dethroned Batista in 1959, Cuba attracted and protected U.S. investments while it aligned itself with U.S. foreign policy goals. In return, the United States

provided military aid and Export-Import Bank loans, abrogated the unpopular Platt Amendment, and gave Cuban sugar a favored position in the U.S. market. Cuba also became further incorporated into the North American consumer culture through American tourism. Nationalistic Cubans protested that their nation had become a mere extension of the United States.

In Puerto Rico, U.S. officials disparaged Puerto Ricans as people of color unfit to govern themselves.

Control over Puerto Rico

The Jones Act of 1916 had granted Puerto Ricans U.S. citizenship, but the United States rejected calls for the colony's independence or statehood. Under U.S. paternalism, schools and roads were improved, but 80 percent of the island's rural folk remained landless, and others crowded into urban slums. New Deal relief programs fell far short of need. Students, professors, and graduates of the Universidad de Puerto Rico formed the nucleus of islanders critical of U.S. tutelage. Some founded the Nationalist Party under the leadership of Pedro Albizo Campos, who eventually advocated the violent overthrow of U.S. rule. Police fired on a Nationalist Party march in 1937; nineteen people died in the Ponce Massacre. Other Puerto Ricans followed the socialist Luis Muñoz Marín, whose Popular Democratic Party ultimately settled for the compromise of commonwealth status (officially conferred in 1952).

Mexico stood as a unique case in inter-American relations. In 1917 the Mexicans openly threatened American-owned landholdings and oil interests by adopting a new constitution specifying that all "land and waters" and all subsoil raw materials (such as petroleum) belonged to the Mexican nation. U.S. officials worried that if Mexico succeeded in restricting the ownership of private property, other Latin Americans might also defy U.S. hegemony.

Clash with Mexican Nationalism

In 1938, during a petroleum workers' strike, the Mexican government led by President Lázaro Cárdenas boldly expropriated the property of all foreign-owned petroleum companies. The United States countered by reducing purchases of Mexican silver and promoting a multinational business boycott against the nation. But President Roosevelt decided to compromise because he feared that the Mexicans would increase oil sales to Germany and Japan. In a 1942 agreement the United States conceded that Mexico owned its raw materials and could treat them as it saw fit, and Mexico compensated the companies for their lost property.

Roosevelt's movement toward nonmilitary methods—the Good Neighbor policy—was also expressed in Pan-Americanism. In 1936, at the Pan-American Conference in Buenos Aires, U.S. officials endorsed nonintervention. The new policy marked a distinct change from the Roosevelt Corollary and marine expeditions. One payoff was the Declaration of Panama (1939), in which Latin American governments drew a security line around the hemisphere and warned aggressors away. In exchange for more U.S. trade and foreign aid, Latin Americans also reduced their sales of raw materials to Germany, Japan, and Italy and increased shipments to the United States. On the eve of the Second World War, then, the U.S. sphere of influence in the hemisphere seemed intact, and most Latin American regimes backed U.S. diplomatic objectives.

Pan-Americanism

Nazi Germany, the Soviet Union, and War in Europe

In depression-wracked Germany, Adolf Hitler came to power in 1933. Like Benito Mussolini, who had gained control of Italy in 1922, Hitler was a fascist. Fascism (called Nazism, or National Socialism, in Germany) celebrated supremacy of the state over the individual; of dictatorship over democracy; of authoritarianism over freedom of speech; of a regulated, state-oriented economy over a free-market economy; and of militarism and war over peace. The Nazis vowed not only to revive German power but also to cripple communism and "purify" the German "race" by destroying Jews and other people, such as homosexuals and Gypsies, whom Hitler disparaged as inferiors.

Resentful of the punitive terms of the 1919 Treaty of Versailles, Hitler immediately withdrew Germany from the League of Nations, ended reparations payments, and began to rearm. While secretly laying plans for the conquest of neighboring states, he watched admiringly as Mussolini's troops invaded the African nation of Ethiopia in 1935. The next year Hitler ordered his troopers into the demilitarized Rhineland, and France did not resist.

German Aggression Under Hitler

Soon the aggressors joined hands. In 1936 Italy and Germany formed an alliance called the Rome-Berlin Axis. Shortly thereafter Germany and Japan united against the Soviet Union in the Anti-Comintern Pact. To these events Britain and France responded with a policy of appeasement, hoping to curb Hitler's expansionist appetite by permitting him a few territorial nibbles. The policy proved disastrous.

In those hair-trigger times, a civil war in Spain soon turned into an international struggle. Beginning in 1936, the Loyalists defended Spain's elected republican government against Francisco Franco's fascist movement. About three thousand American volunteers, known as the Abraham Lincoln Battalion of the "International Brigades," joined the fight on the side of the Loyalist republicans, which also had the backing of the Soviet Union. Hitler and Mussolini sent military aid to Franco, who won in 1939.

Early in 1938 Hitler sent soldiers into Austria to annex the nation of his birth. Then in September he seized the Sudeten region of Czechoslovakia. Appeasement reached its apex that month when France and Britain, without consulting the Czechs, agreed at Munich to allow Hitler this territorial bite. In March 1939 Hitler swallowed the rest of Czechoslovakia.

The Nazi leader next eyed Poland. Scuttling appeasement, London and Paris announced that they would stand by their ally Poland. Undaunted, Berlin signed the Nazi-Soviet Pact with Moscow in August. A top-secret protocol attached to the pact carved eastern Europe into German and Soviet zones and permitted the Soviets to grab half of Poland and the three Baltic states of Lithuania, Estonia, and Latvia, formerly part of the Russian empire. On September 1 Hitler launched *blitzkrieg* (lightning war) attacks against Poland. Britain and France declared war on Germany two days later. So started the Second World War.

Poland and the Outbreak of World War II

As the world hurtled toward war, Soviet-American relations remained embittered. During the 1920s the

United States refused to open diplomatic relations with the Soviet government, which had failed to pay $600 million for confiscated American-owned property and had repudiated preexisting Russian debts. American businesses nonetheless entered the Soviet marketplace, and by 1930 the Soviet Union had become the largest buyer of American farm and industrial equipment.

In the early 1930s, when trade began to slump, some American business leaders lobbied for diplomatic recognition of the Soviet Union.

U.S. Recognition of the Soviet Union President Roosevelt himself concluded that nonrecognition had failed to alter the Soviet system, and he speculated that closer Soviet-American relations might deter Japanese expansion. In 1933 Roosevelt granted U.S. diplomatic recognition to the Soviet Union in return for Soviet agreement to discuss the debts question, to forgo subversive Communist activities in the United States, and to grant Americans in the Soviet Union religious freedom and legal rights. However, Stalin's brutalities against his people and the Nazi-Soviet Pact outraged many Americans.

Isolationism, Neutrality Acts, and Roosevelt's Cautious Foreign Policy

 As conditions deteriorated in Europe, Americans began embracing isolationism, whose key elements were abhorrence of war, limited military intervention abroad, and freedom of action in international relations. Isolationism was a nationwide phenomenon that cut across socioeconomic, ethnic, party, and sectional lines and attracted a majority of the American people. Conservative isolationists feared higher taxes and increased executive power if the nation went to war again. Liberal isolationists worried that domestic problems might go unresolved as the nation spent more on the military. The vast majority of isolationists opposed fascism and condemned aggression, but they did not think the United States should have to do what Europeans themselves refused to do: block Hitler.

Some isolationists charged that corporate "merchants of death" had promoted war and were assisting

Nye Committee Hearings the aggressors. Such allegations led Senator Gerald P. Nye to take up the issue. A congressional committee held hearings from 1934 to 1936 on the role of business and financiers in the U.S. decision to enter the First World War. The Nye committee did not prove that American munitions makers had dragged the nation into that war, but it did uncover evidence that corporations practicing "rotten commercialism" had bribed foreign politicians to bolster arms sales in the 1920s and 1930s, had lobbied against arms control, and had signed contracts with companies in Nazi Germany and fascist Italy.

Reflecting the popular desire for distance from Europe's disputes, President Roosevelt signed a series of neutrality acts. Congress sought to

Neutrality Acts protect the nation by outlawing the kinds of contacts that had compromised U.S. neutrality during World War I. The Neutrality Act of 1935 prohibited arms shipments to either side in a war once the president had declared the existence of belligerency. The Neutrality Act of 1936 forbade loans to belligerents. After a joint resolution in 1937 declared the United States neutral in the Spanish Civil War, Roosevelt embargoed arms shipments to both sides. The Neutrality Act of 1937 introduced the cash-and-carry principle: warring nations wishing to trade with the United States would have to pay cash for their nonmilitary purchases and carry the goods from U.S. ports in their own ships. The act also forbade Americans from traveling on the ships of belligerent nations.

President Roosevelt shared isolationist views in the early 1930s. In a passionate speech delivered in

Roosevelt's Evolving Views August 1936 at Chautauqua, New York, Roosevelt expressed prevailing isolationist opinion and made a pitch for the pacifist vote in the upcoming election: "I have seen war. . . . I have seen blood running from the wounded. I have seen men coughing out their gassed lungs. . . . I have seen the agony of mothers and wives. I hate war." The United States, he promised, would remain unentangled in the European conflict.

All the while, Roosevelt grew troubled by the arrogant behavior of Germany, Italy, and Japan—aggressors he tagged the "three bandit nations." Because he worried that the United States was ill prepared to confront the aggressors, his New Deal public works programs included millions for the construction of new warships. In 1935 the president requested the largest peacetime defense budget in American history. Three years later, in the wake of Munich, he asked Congress for funds to build up the air force, which he believed essential to deter aggression. In January 1939 the president secretly decided to sell bombers to France, saying privately that "our frontier is on the Rhine."

In early 1939 the president lashed out at the international lawbreakers. He also tried and failed to get Congress to repeal the arms embargo and permit the sale of munitions to belligerents on a cash-and-carry basis. When Europe descended into the abyss of war in September 1939, Roosevelt declared neutrality and pressed again for repeal of the arms embargo. After much debate, Congress in November lifted the embargo on contraband and approved cash-and-carry exports of arms. Using "methods short of war," Roosevelt thus began to aid the Allies. Hitler sneered that a "half Judaized, half negrified" United States was "incapable of conducting war."

Repeal of the Arms Embargo

Japan, China, and a New Order in Asia

While Europe succumbed to political turmoil and war, Asia suffered the aggressive march of Japan. The United States had interests at stake in Asia: the Philippines and Pacific islands, religious missions, trade and investments, and the Open Door in China. In traditional missionary fashion, Americans also believed that they were China's special friend and protector. By contrast, the aggressive Japan loomed as a threat to American attitudes and interests. The Tokyo government seemed bent on subjugating China and unhinging the Open Door doctrine of equal trade and investment opportunity.

In the late 1920s, civil war broke out in China when Jiang Jieshi (Chiang Kai-shek) ousted Mao Zedong and his Communist followers from the ruling Guomindang Party. Americans applauded this display of anti-Bolshevism and Jiang's conversion to Christianity in 1930. Warming to Jiang, U.S. officials abandoned one imperial vestige by signing a treaty in 1928 restoring control of tariffs to the Chinese. U.S. gunboats and marines still remained in China to protect American citizens and property.

Jiang Jieshi

The Japanese grew increasingly suspicious of U.S. ties with China. In the early twentieth century, Japanese-American relations steadily deteriorated as Japan gained influence in Manchuria, Shandong, and Korea. The Japanese sought not only to oust Western imperialists from Asia but also to dominate Asian territories that produced the raw materials that their import-dependent island nation required. The Japanese also resented the discriminatory immigration law of 1924, which excluded them from emigrating to the United States. And despite the Washington Conference treaties, naval competition continued.

Relations further soured in 1931 after the Japanese military seized Manchuria in China. Although the seizure of Manchuria violated the Nine-Power Treaty and the Kellogg-Briand Pact, the United States did not have the power to compel Japanese withdrawal, and the League of Nations did little but debate. The American response came as a moral lecture known as the Stimson Doctrine: the United States would not recognize any impairment of China's sovereignty or of the Open Door policy.

Manchurian Crisis

Japan continued to harry China. In mid-1937 the Sino-Japanese War erupted. Japanese forces seized cities and bombed civilians. In an effort to help China by permitting it to buy American arms, Roosevelt refused to declare the existence of war, thus avoiding activation of the Neutrality Acts. And in a speech denouncing the aggressors on October 5, 1937, the president called for a "quarantine" to curb the "epidemic of world lawlessness." People who thought Washington had been too gentle with Japan cheered. Isolationists warned that the president was edging toward war.

Roosevelt's Quarantine Speech

Japan's declaration of a "New Order" in Asia, in the words of one American official, "banged, barred, and bolted" the Open Door. Alarmed, the Roosevelt administration during the late 1930s gave loans and sold military equipment to the Chinese. Secretary Hull declared a moral embargo on the shipment of airplanes to Japan. Meanwhile, the U.S. Navy continued to grow, aided by a billion-dollar congressional appropriation in 1938. In mid-1939 the United States abrogated its trade treaty with Tokyo, yet Americans continued to ship oil, cotton, and machinery to Japan. The administration hesitated to initiate economic sanctions because such pressure might spark a Japanese-American war at a time when Germany posed a more serious threat and the United States was unprepared for war. When war broke out in Europe in fall 1939, Japanese-American relations were stalemated.

On a Collision Course with Japan and Germany, 1939–1941

President Roosevelt remarked in 1939 that the United States could not insulate itself from world war. Polls showed that Americans strongly favored the Allies and that most supported aid to Britain and France, but the great majority emphatically wanted the United States to remain at peace. Troubled by this conflicting advice—oppose Hitler, aid the Allies, but stay out of the war—the president gradually moved the nation from neutrality to undeclared war against Germany and then, after the Japanese attack on Pearl Harbor, to full-scale war itself.

Because the stakes were so high, unprecedented numbers of Americans spoke out on foreign affairs and joined organizations that addressed the issues. The American Legion, the League of Women Voters, labor unions, and local chapters of the Committee to Defend America by Aiding the Allies and the isolationist America First Committee (both organized in 1940) provided outlets for citizen participation in the national debate.

Foreign Policy Debate

In March 1940 the Soviet Union invaded Finland. In April Germany invaded Denmark and Norway (see Map 26.2). In May, Germany attacked Belgium, the Netherlands, and France. German divisions ultimately pushed French and British forces back to the English Channel.

The Fall of France

At Dunkirk, France, between May 26 and June 6, more than three hundred thousand Allied soldiers frantically escaped to Britain on a flotilla of small boats. The Germans occupied Paris a week later. With France knocked out of the war, the German Luftwaffe (air force) launched massive bombing raids against Great Britain. Stunned Americans asked, Could Washington or New York be the Luftwaffe's next target?

After Roosevelt tried futilely to draw the belligerents to the peace table, he told his advisers that he was "not willing to fire the first shot" but was waiting for some incident to bring the United States into the war. In the meantime, Roosevelt began to aid the beleaguered Allies to prevent the fall of Britain. In May 1940 he ordered the sale of old surplus military equipment to Britain and France. In July he cultivated bipartisan support by naming Republicans Henry L. Stimson and Frank Knox, ardent backers of aid to the Allies, secretaries of war and the navy respectively. In September, by executive agreement, the president traded fifty over-age American destroyers for leases to eight British military bases, including Newfoundland, Bermuda, and Jamaica. Two weeks later Roosevelt signed into law the hotly debated and narrowly passed Selective Training and Service Act, the first peacetime military draft in American history.

Roosevelt claimed that the United States could stay out of the war by enabling the British to win. The United States, he said, must become the "great arsenal of democracy." In January 1941 Congress debated the president's Lend-Lease bill. Because Britain was broke, the president explained, the United States should lend rather than sell weapons, much as a neighbor lends a garden hose to fight a fire. In March 1941, Congress passed the Lend-Lease Act with an initial appropriation of $7 billion. By the end of the war the amount had reached $50 billion, more than $31 billion of it for Britain.

Lend-Lease Act

To ensure the safe delivery of Lend-Lease goods, Roosevelt ordered the U.S. Navy to patrol halfway across the Atlantic, and he sent American troops to Greenland. In July, arguing that Iceland was also essential to the defense of the Western Hemisphere, the president dispatched marines there. He also sent Lend-Lease aid to the Soviet Union, which Hitler had attacked in June.

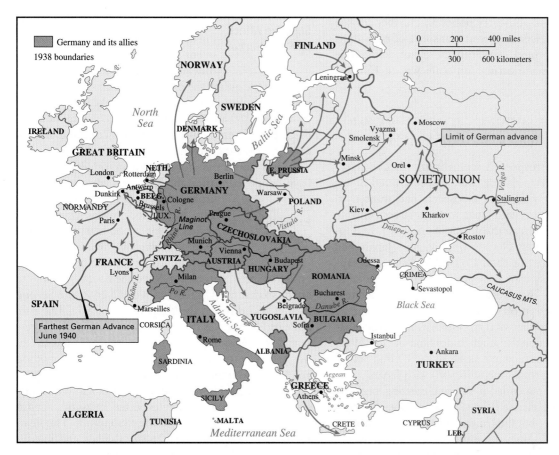

Map 26.2   The German Advance, 1939–1942   Hitler's drive to dominate Europe pushed German troops deep into France and the Soviet Union. Great Britain took a beating but held on with the help of American economic and military aid before the United States itself entered the Second World War in late 1941.

In August 1941, British prime minister Winston Churchill and Roosevelt met for four days on a British battleship off the coast of New-

Atlantic Charter

foundland. The two leaders issued the Atlantic Charter, a set of war aims reminiscent of Wilsonianism: collective security, disarmament, self-determination, economic cooperation, and freedom of the seas. Churchill later recalled that the president told him in Newfoundland that he could not ask Congress for a declaration of war against Germany but "he would wage war" and "become more and more provocative."

On September 4, 1941, came an incident that Roosevelt could exploit. In the Atlantic, a German

Greer Incident

submarine launched torpedoes at (but did not hit) the American destroyer _Greer_, after it had cooperated with British patrol bombers that dropped depth charges on the submarine. Roosevelt declared that the German vessel, without warning, had fired first. Henceforth, he said, the U.S. Navy would shoot on sight. He also announced a policy he already had promised Churchill in private: American warships would convoy British merchant ships across the ocean.

Thus the United States entered into an undeclared naval war with Germany. In October, when the destroyer _Reuben James_ went down with the loss of more than one hundred American lives, Congress scrapped the cash-and-carry policy and further revised the Neutrality Acts to permit transport of munitions to Britain on armed American merchant ships. The United States was nearing full-scale war in Europe.

Why War Came: Pearl Harbor and U.S. Entry into World War II

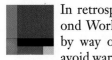

In retrospect, it seems ironic that the Second World War came to the United States by way of Asia. Roosevelt had wanted to avoid war with Japan in order to concentrate American resources on the defeat of Germany. In September 1940, after Germany, Italy, and Japan had signed the Tripartite Pact, Roosevelt slapped an embargo on shipments of aviation fuel and scrap metal to Japan. Because the president believed the Japanese would consider a cutoff of oil a life-or-death matter, he did not embargo that vital commodity. But after Japanese troops occupied French Indochina in July 1941, Washington froze Japanese assets in the United States, virtually ending trade (including oil) with Japan.

Tokyo recommended a summit meeting between President Roosevelt and Prime Minister Prince Konoye, but the United States rejected the idea. American officials insisted that the Japanese first agree to respect China's sovereignty and territorial integrity and to honor the Open Door policy—in short, to get out of China. Though Europe was Roosevelt's first priority, he supported Hull's hard-line policy against Japan's pursuit of the Greater East Asia Co-Prosperity Sphere—the name Tokyo gave to the vast Asian region it intended to dominate.

U.S. Demands on Japan

By breaking the Japanese diplomatic code and deciphering intercepted messages through Operation MAGIC, American officials learned that Tokyo's patience with diplomacy was fast dissipating. In late November the Japanese rejected American demands that they withdraw from Indochina. An intercepted message that American experts decoded on December 3 instructed the Japanese embassy in Washington to burn codes and destroy cipher machines—a step suggesting that war was coming.

The Japanese plotted a daring raid on Pearl Harbor in Hawai'i. An armada of sixty Japanese ships, with a core of six aircraft carriers, crossed 3,000 miles of the Pacific Ocean. In the early morning of December 7, Japanese airplanes swept down on the unsuspecting American naval base and nearby airfields. In the attack the invaders sank or damaged eight battleships and many smaller vessels and smashed more than 160 aircraft on the ground. A total of 2,403 died; 1,178 were wounded. By chance, three aircraft carriers at sea escaped the disaster.

Surprise Attack on Pearl Harbor

How could the stunning attack on Pearl Harbor have happened? After all, American cryptanalysts had broken the Japanese diplomatic code. The intercepts, however, never revealed naval or military plans and never specifically mentioned Pearl Harbor. Roosevelt did not, as some critics charged, conspire to leave the fleet vulnerable to attack so that the United States could enter the Second World War through the "back door" of Asia. The base at Pearl Harbor was not on red alert because a message sent from Washington warning of the imminence of war had been too casually transmitted by a slow method and had arrived too late. Base commanders were too relaxed, believing Hawai'i too far from Japan to be a target for all-out attack. They expected an assault against British Malaya, Thailand, or the Philippines. The Pearl Harbor calamity stemmed from mistakes and insufficient information, not from conspiracy.

Explaining Pearl Harbor

On December 8, referring to the previous day as "a date which will live in infamy," Roosevelt asked Congress for a declaration of war against Japan. A unanimous vote in the Senate and a 388-to-1 vote in the House thrust America into war. Representative Jeannette Rankin of Montana voted "no," repeating her vote against entry into the First World War. Three days later, Germany and Italy, honoring the Tripartite Pact they had signed with Japan in September 1940, declared war against the United States. On January 1, 1942, the United States was among the twenty-six nations that signed the Declaration of the United Nations, pledging allegiance to the Atlantic Charter.

A fundamental clash of systems explains why war came. Germany and Japan preferred a world divided into closed spheres of influence. The United States sought a liberal capitalist world order in which all nations enjoyed freedom of trade and investment. American principles manifested respect for human rights; fascists in Europe and militarists in Asia defiantly tram-

The stricken U.S.S. *West Virginia* was one of eight battleships caught in the surprise Japanese attack at Pearl Harbor, Hawai'i, on December 7, 1941. In this photograph, sailors on a launch attempt to rescue a crew member from the water as oil burns around the sinking ship.   (U.S. Army)

Clash of Systems

pled such rights. The United States prided itself on its democratic system; Germany and Japan embraced authoritarian regimes backed by the military.

Summary

In the 1920s and 1930s, Americans proved unable to create a peaceful and prosperous world order. The Washington Conference treaties failed to curb a naval arms race or to protect China; the Dawes Plan collapsed; the Kellogg-Briand Pact proved ineffective; philanthropic activities fell short of need; the process of cultural "American-

ization" provided no panacea; the aggressors Germany and Japan ignored repeated U.S. protests, from the Stimson Doctrine onward; recognition of the Soviet Union barely improved relations; U.S. trade policies, shifting from protectionist tariffs to reciprocal trade agreements, only minimally improved U.S. or international commerce in the era of the Great Depression; and the Neutrality Acts did not prevent U.S. entanglements in Europe. Even where American power and policies seemed to work to satisfy Good Neighbor goals—in Latin America—nationalist resentments simmered and Mexico challenged U.S. hegemony.

During the late 1930s and early 1940s, President Roosevelt hesitantly but steadily moved the United

States from neutrality to aid for the Allies, to belligerency, and finally to a declaration of war after the attack on Pearl Harbor. Congress gradually revised and retired the Neutrality Acts in the face of growing danger and receding isolationism. Independent internationalism and economic and nonmilitary means to peace gave way to alliance-building and war.

The Second World War offered yet another opportunity for Americans to set things right in the world. As the publisher Henry Luce wrote in *American Century* (1941), the United States must "exert upon the world the full impact of our influence, for such purposes as we see fit and by such means as we see fit." As they had so many times before, Americans flocked to the colors. Isolationists joined the president in spirited calls for victory.

LEGACY FOR A PEOPLE AND A NATION
Presidential Deception of the Public

Before U-652 launched two torpedoes at the *Greer*, heading for Iceland on September 4, 1941, the U.S. destroyer had stalked the German submarine for hours. Twice the *Greer* signaled the U-boat's location to British patrol bombers, one of which dropped depth charges on the submarine. In a dramatic radio "fireside chat" on September 11, President Roosevelt protested German "piracy" as a violation of the principle of freedom of the seas.

Throughout the twentieth century, presidents have exaggerated, distorted, withheld, or even lied about the facts of foreign relations in order to shape a public opinion favorable to their policies. One result: the growth of the "imperial presidency"—the president's grabbing of power from and supremacy over Congress, and the president's use of questionable means to reach his objectives. Franklin D. Roosevelt provided a telling example in the *Greer* incident. The president deliberately misrepresented the encounter in order to whip up anti-German passions, to discredit isolationists, to announce his policy to convoy com-

mercial ships across the Atlantic, and to issue an order to the navy to shoot German ships on sight.

In his radio message, Roosevelt described the clash as an unprovoked German attack. He never mentioned that the U.S. ship had been cooperating with British warplanes, and he failed to note that the *Greer* had been tracking the submarine for hours. Roosevelt's words amounted to a call to arms, yet he never asked Congress for a declaration of war against Germany. The president believed that he had to deceive the public in order to move hesitant Americans toward noble positions. Public opinion polls soon demonstrated that the practice worked, as most Americans approved the shoot-on-sight policy.

Several years later, in his book *The Man in the Street* (1948), Thomas A. Bailey defended Roosevelt. The historian argued that "because the masses are notoriously shortsighted, and generally cannot see danger until it is at their throats, our statesmen are forced to deceive them into an awareness of their own long-term interests." Roosevelt's critics, on the other hand, have seen in his methods a danger to the democratic process, which cannot work in an environment of dishonesty and usurped powers. In the 1960s, during America's descent into the Vietnam War, Senator J. William Fulbright of Arkansas recalled the *Greer* incident: "FDR's deviousness in a good cause made it easier for LBJ to practice the same kind of deviousness in a bad cause." Indeed, during the Tonkin Gulf crisis of 1964, President Lyndon B. Johnson shaded the truth in order to gain from Congress wide latitude in waging war. In the 1980s Reagan administration officials, in the Iran-contra affair, consciously and publicly lied about U.S. arms sales to Iran and about covert aid to Nicaraguan terrorists. Practicing deception of the public and Congress—advancing the imperial presidency—was one of Roosevelt's legacies for a people and a nation.

For Further Reading, see the Appendix. For Web resources, go to history.college.hmco.com/students.

THE SECOND WORLD WAR AT HOME AND ABROAD

1941–1945

In 1942, when recruiters from the U.S. Marine Corps came to the Navajo reservation in Shiprock, New Mexico, William Dean Wilson was only sixteen years old. The marines came seeking young men who spoke both English and Navajo. Fewer than thirty non-Navajos, none of them Japanese, could understand the language at the outbreak of the war. The Navajo recruits of 1942 would become not only U.S. Marines but also "code talkers" in the war against the Japanese.

Wilson volunteered. "I said I was eighteen," he recalled. His parents had opposed his decision, but he removed a note from his file that read "Parents will not consent" and was inducted. Wilson was among an initial group of thirty Navajos chosen for a project with an important goal: to prevent the Japanese from deciphering radio messages sent by American troops landing on the shores of Pacific islands.

By the time Wilson's seventeenth birthday arrived, he was fighting in the Pacific. Beginning with the Battle of Guadalcanal, he and others from the corps of 420 Navajo code talkers took part in every assault the marines conducted in the Pacific from 1942 to 1945. Usually, two code talkers were assigned to a battalion, one going ashore and the other remaining aboard ship. Those who went ashore quickly began transmitting, reporting sightings of enemy forces and directing shelling by American detachments.

As it did for millions of other American fighting men and women, wartime service changed the Navajo code talkers' lives, broadening their horizons and often deepening their ambitions. Many became community leaders. William Dean Wilson, for example, became a tribal judge. But in 1945 most Navajo war veterans were happy to return to their homes and traditional culture. And in accordance with Navajo ritual, the returning veterans participated in purification ceremonies to dispel the ghosts of the battlefield and invoke blessings for the future.

The Second World War marked a turning point in the lives of millions of Americans, as well as in the history of the United States. Most deeply affected were those who fought the war. For forty-five months Americans fought abroad to subdue the German, Italian, and Japanese aggressors. The Nazis capitulated in May 1945. In the Pacific, Americans drove the Japanese back from one island to another before turning to the just-tested atomic bombs, which demolished Hiroshima and Nagasaki in August and helped spur a Japanese surrender.

Throughout the war the Allies—Britain, the Soviet Union, and the United States—stuck together to defeat Germany. But they squabbled over many issues: when to open a second front; how to structure a new international organization; how eastern Europe would be reconstructed; how Germany and Japan would be governed after defeat. At the end of the war, Allied leaders seemed more intent on retaining and expanding their own nations' spheres of influence than on building a community of mutual interest, and the advent of the atomic age frightened everyone.

The war transformed America's soldiers and sailors. Horizons expanded for the more than 16 million men and women who ultimately served in the armed forces. But at war's end they were older than their years, both physically and emotionally. Many felt they had sacrificed the best years of their lives.

During the war nearly one of every ten Americans moved permanently to another state. Most headed for war-production centers, especially cities in the North and on the West Coast. Japanese Americans moved, too, but involuntarily, as they were rounded up by the army and placed in internment camps. And while the war offered new economic and political opportunities for numerous African Americans, competition for jobs

and housing created the conditions for an epidemic of race riots. The war offered women new job opportunities. For some, work was an economic necessity; for others, it was a patriotic obligation; for all, it brought financial independence and enhanced self-esteem.

The American people united behind the war effort, but more than national unity was required to win. Essential to victory was the mobilization of all sectors of the economy—industry, finance, agriculture, labor. America's big businesses got even bigger, as did its central government, labor unions, and farms. The federal government had the monumental task of coordinating activity in these spheres, as well as in two new ones: higher education and science. For this war was a scientific and technological war, supported by the development of new weapons such as radar and the atomic bomb. For all these reasons, the Second World War transformed America. ∎

Winning the Second World War

Two days after the surprise attack on Pearl Harbor, President Franklin D. Roosevelt spoke to the American people: "We are now in the midst of a war . . . for a world in which this Nation, and all that this Nation represents, will be safe for our children." Americans agreed with Roosevelt that they were defending their homes, families, and way of life.

Wartime relations among the United States, Great Britain, and the Soviet Union ran hot and cold. Allied leaders knew that military decisions had political consequences. For instance, the positions of troops at the end of the war might determine the politics of the regions they occupied. Thus an undercurrent of mutual suspicion ran just beneath the surface of Allied cooperation. Early on, however, Allied leaders agreed on a "Europe first" formula—knock out Germany and then concentrate on an isolated Japan.

Roosevelt, British prime minister Winston Churchill, and Soviet premier Joseph Stalin differed vehemently over the opening of a second, or western, front in Europe. After Germany conquered France in 1940 and invaded the Soviet Union in 1941, the Soviets bore the brunt of the war until mid-1944, suffering millions of casual-

Second-Front Controversy

IMPORTANT EVENTS

1941 Germany invades Russia
Roosevelt issues Executive Order No. 8802, forbidding racial discrimination by defense industry employers
Japan attacks Pearl Harbor
U.S. enters Second World War

1942 National War Labor Board created to deal with labor-management conflict
War Production Board begins to oversee conversion to military production
West Coast Japanese Americans interned in prison camps
War Manpower Commission created to manage labor supply
Office of Price Administration created to control inflation
U.S. defeats Japanese forces at Battles of the Coral Sea and Midway
Office of War Information created to maintain support for the war at home
Manhattan Project set up to produce atomic bomb
Synthetic-rubber program begins
Allies invade North Africa
Republicans gain in Congress

1943 Red Army defeats German troops at Stalingrad
Congress passes War Labor Disputes (Smith-Connally) Act
Race riots break out in Detroit, Harlem, and forty-five other cities
Allies invade Italy

Hirabayashi v. U.S. upholds restrictions on personal liberties of Japanese Americans because of their race
Roosevelt, Churchill, and Stalin meet at Teheran Conference

1944 Roosevelt requests Economic Bill of Rights
War Refugee Board established to set up refugee camps in Europe
GI Bill of Rights provides educational benefits for veterans
Allied troops land at Normandy on D-Day
Dumbarton Oaks Conference approves charter for United Nations
Roosevelt reelected
U.S. retakes the Philippines
Korematsu v. U.S. upholds removal of Japanese Americans from the West Coast

1945 Roosevelt, Stalin, and Churchill meet at Yalta Conference
Battles of Iwo Jima and Okinawa result in heavy American and Japanese losses
Roosevelt dies; Truman becomes president
United Nations founded
Germany surrenders
First atomic bomb explodes in test at Alamogordo, New Mexico
Potsdam Conference calls for Japan's "unconditional surrender"
Atomic bombs devastate Hiroshima and Nagasaki
Japan surrenders

ties. Stalin pressed for a British-American landing on the western coast to draw German troops away from the eastern front, but Churchill would not agree. The Red Army therefore did most of the fighting and dying on land, while the British and Americans concentrated on getting Lend-Lease supplies across the Atlantic and harassing the Germans from the air.

Roosevelt was both sensitive to the Soviets' burden and fearful that the Soviet Union might be knocked out of the war, leaving Hitler free to invade England. In 1942 he told the Soviets that they could expect the Allies to cross the English Channel and invade France later that year. But Churchill balked. Fearing heavy losses in a premature cross-Channel invasion, Churchill favored a series of small jabs at the enemy's Mediterranean forces.

Churchill won the debate. Instead of attacking France, the British and Americans invaded North Africa in November 1942 (see Map 27.1). The news from the Soviet Union buoyed Roosevelt. In the battle

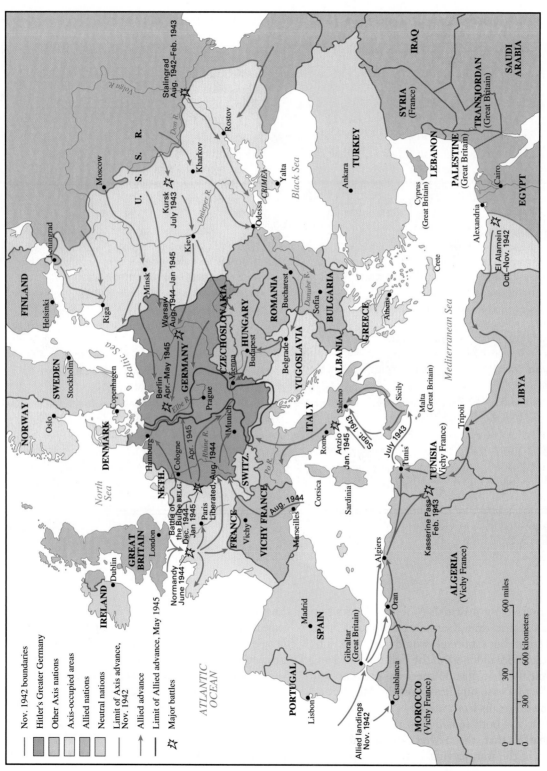

Map 27.1 The Allies on the Offensive in Europe, 1942–1945 The United States pursued a "Europe first" policy: first defeat Germany, then focus on Japan. American military efforts began in North Africa in late 1942 and ended in Germany in 1945 on May 8 (V-E Day).

for Stalingrad (September 1942–January 1943)—probably the turning point of the European war—the Red Army defeated the Germans. But shortly thereafter, the president once again angered the Soviets by declaring another delay in launching the second front. Stalin was not mollified by the Allied invasion of Italy in the summer of 1943. Italy surrendered in September to American and British officers; Soviet officials were not invited to participate. Stalin grumbled that the arrangement smacked of a separate peace.

With the alliance badly strained, the three Allied leaders met in Teheran, Iran, in December 1943.

Teheran Conference

Stalin dismissed Churchill's repetitious justifications for further delaying the second front. Roosevelt sided with Stalin, and the three finally agreed to launch Operation Overlord—the cross-Channel invasion of France—in early 1944.

The second front opened on June 6, 1944—D-Day—with the largest amphibious landing in history. The invading force of two

D-Day

hundred thousand troops immediately encountered the enemy. Although heavy aerial and naval bombardment and the clandestine work of saboteurs had softened the German defenses, the fighting was ferocious.

Allied troops soon spread across the countryside, liberating France and Belgium and entering Germany itself in September. In December, German armored divisions counterattacked in Belgium's Ardennes Forest, hoping to push on to Antwerp to halt the flow of Allied supplies through that Belgian port. After weeks of heavy fighting in what has come to be called the Battle of the Bulge, the Allies pushed the enemy back once again. Meanwhile, battle-hardened Soviet troops marched through Poland and cut a path to Berlin. American forces crossed the Rhine River in March 1945 and captured the heavily industrial Ruhr valley. As the Americans marched east, a new president took office in Washington: Franklin D. Roosevelt died on April 12, and Harry S Truman became president and commander-in-chief. Eighteen days later, in bomb-ravaged Berlin, Adolf Hitler killed himself. On May 8 Germany surrendered.

The war in the Pacific was largely America's to fight, and at first, it did not go well. By mid-1942

The War in the Pacific

Japan had seized the Philippines, Guam, Wake, Hong Kong, Singapore, Malaya, and the Dutch East Indies (Indonesia). In the Philippines in 1942, Japanese soldiers forced American and Filipino prisoners weakened by insufficient rations to walk 65 miles, clubbing, shooting, or starving to death about ten thousand of them. The Bataan Death March intensified American hatred of the Japanese.

In April 1942 Americans began to hit back, initially by bombing Tokyo. In May, in the momentous Battle of the Coral Sea, carrier-based

Battle of Midway

American planes halted a Japanese advance toward Australia (see Map 27.2). The next month American forces defeated the Japanese at Midway, sinking four of the enemy's aircraft carriers. The Battle of Midway was a turning point in the Pacific war, breaking the Japanese momentum and relieving the threat to Hawai'i.

American strategy was to "island-hop" toward Japan, skipping the most strongly fortified islands whenever possible and taking the weaker ones. In an effort to strand the Japanese armies on their island outposts and to cut off the supply of raw materials being shipped from Japan's home islands, Americans also set out to sink the Japanese merchant marine. The first U.S. offensive—at Guadalcanal in the Solomon Islands in mid-1942—gave American troops their first taste of jungle warfare. In 1943 and 1944 American troops attacked the enemy in the Gilbert, Marshall, and Mariana islands. And in October 1944, General Douglas MacArthur landed at Leyte to retake the Philippines for the United States.

In February 1945 both sides took heavy losses at Iwo Jima, an island less than 5 miles long. Stationed

Battles of Iwo Jima and Okinawa

on the island were 21,000 Japanese troops living in pillboxes and miles of caves, trenches, and connecting tunnels. After twenty days of fighting, victory finally came to the Americans. In this bitter battle, 6,821 Americans were killed along with all but 200 of the Japanese troops.

A month later, American troops landed on Okinawa, an island 350 miles from Japan. Fighting raged for two months. At Okinawa almost the entire Japanese

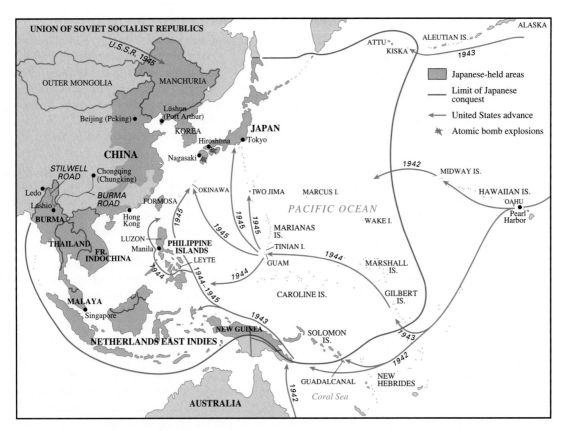

Map 27.2 The Pacific War The strategy of the United States was to "island-hop"—from Hawai'i in 1942 to Iwo Jima and Okinawa in 1945. Naval battles were also decisive, notably the Battles of the Coral Sea and Midway in 1942. The war in the Pacific ended with Japan's surrender on August 15, 1945 (V-J Day). (Source: Thomas G. Paterson, J. Garry Clifford, Kenneth J. Hagan, *American Foreign Policy: A History,* vol. 2, 3d ed. Copyright © 1991 by D. C. Heath Company. Used by permission of Houghton Mifflin Company.)

garrison of 100,000 was killed, and there were 80,000 civilian casualties. The American military lost 7,374 men. At sea, the supporting fleet reported almost 5,000 seamen killed or missing; most were the victims of *kamikaze* (suicide) attacks, in which Japanese pilots crashed their bomb-laden planes directly into American ships.

Still, Japanese leaders refused to admit defeat. Hoping to avoid a humiliating unconditional surrender (and to preserve the emperor's sovereignty), they hung on even while American bombers leveled their cities. In one staggering attack on Tokyo on May 23, 1945, American planes dropped bombs that engulfed the city in a firestorm, killing 83,000 people.

With victory in sight, American leaders began to plan a fall invasion of Japan's home islands, an expedition that was sure to incur high casualties. The invasion became unnecessary because American scientists working on the secret Manhattan Project developed the atomic bomb. On August 6, the Japanese city of Hiroshima was destroyed by a bomb dropped from an American B-29 plane called the *Enola Gay*. Much of the city was leveled almost instantly. Approximately 130,000 people were killed. Three days later another atomic attack flattened Nagasaki, killing at least 60,000 people. Five days later the Japanese, who had been sending out

The Atomic Bomb

peace feelers since June, surrendered. The victors promised that the Japanese emperor could remain as the nation's titular head. Formal surrender ceremonies were held September 2 aboard the battleship *Missouri*. The Second World War was over.

Most Americans agreed with President Truman that the atomic bombing of Hiroshima and Nagasaki was necessary to end the war as quickly as possible and to save American lives. At the highest government levels and among atomic scientists, alternatives had been discussed: detonating the bomb on an unpopulated Pacific island, with international observers as witnesses; blockading and bombing Japan conventionally; following up on Tokyo's peace feelers. Truman, however, had rejected these options because he believed they would take too long and would not convince the tenacious Japanese that they had been beaten.

The Decision to Use the Atomic Bomb

Diplomatic considerations also influenced the decision to use the bomb. American leaders wanted to take advantage of the real and psychological power the bomb would bestow on the United States. It might serve as a deterrent against aggression; it might intimidate the Soviet Union into making concessions in eastern Europe; it might end the war in the Pacific before the Soviet Union could claim a role in the postwar management of Asia.

Mobilizing the American Home Front

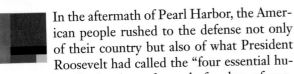

In the aftermath of Pearl Harbor, the American people rushed to the defense not only of their country but also of what President Roosevelt had called the "four essential human freedoms"—freedom of speech, freedom of worship, freedom from want, and freedom from fear. Women in war-production work, as well as men on the battlefields, believed they were fighting for both democracy and the American family.

No wartime agency better exemplified Americans' willingness to sacrifice to win the war than the Office of Price Administration (OPA). Established by Congress in 1942 with the power to control inflation by fixing price ceilings on commodities, and by controlling rents in defense areas, the OPA instituted nationwide rationing for automobile tires and issued rationing books with coupons for sugar, coffee, and gasoline; meat, butter and cheese, shoes, and other commodities were added later. Consumers became skilled at handling food ration stamps. Most Americans abided by the rules, but some hoarded sugar and coffee or bought beef on the "black market."

Office of Price Administration

Women consumers were central to OPA's success. They enlisted in the "food fight for freedom" by signing "The Home Front Pledge" and promising to pay "no more than Ceiling Prices." The OPA was active in every community through its 5,525 local War Price and Rationing Boards, operated largely by women volunteers, which allocated coupons for each family. Some of the volunteers were veterans of labor unions and consumer groups, while others were ordinary shoppers determined to sacrifice for the war effort. But the OPA's successes in enforcing price ceilings provoked opposition from businesses, large and small, which even in wartime wanted to charge whatever the market would bear.

While the guns boomed in Europe and Asia, the war was changing American lives and institutions. One month after Pearl Harbor, President Roosevelt established the War Production Board (WPB) and assigned to it the task of converting the economy from civilian to military production. Factories had to be expanded and new ones built. The wartime emergency also spurred the establishment of totally new industries, most notably synthetic rubber. The Japanese, in their conquest of the South Pacific, had captured 90 percent of the world's supply of crude rubber. Also established in 1942, the War Manpower Commission (WMC) recruited new workers for the nation's factories.

War Production Board and War Manpower Commission

The industrial mobilization was so successful that the production of durable goods more than tripled. Since this was the world's first massive air war, fighter planes and bombers were crucial, and America's factories responded to the need: the manufacture of military aircraft, which had totaled 6,000 in 1940, jumped to 85,000 in 1943. Women workers made a major contribution to the rapidly expanding aircraft industry, whose female work force increased from 4,000 in December 1941 to 310,000 two years later.

To gain the cooperation of business, the government guaranteed profits in the form of cost-plus-fixed-fee contracts, generous tax write-offs, and exemptions from antitrust prosecution. Such concessions made sense for a nation that wanted vast quantities of war goods manufactured in the shortest possible time. From mid-1940 through September 1944 the government awarded contracts totaling $175 billion, no less than two-thirds of which went to the top one hundred corporations.

Government Incentives in Business

In science and higher education, too, the big got bigger as federal contracts mobilized science and technology for the war effort. Massachusetts Institute of Technology was a major recipient for its development of radar. MIT received $117 million, followed by the California Institute of Technology, Harvard, and Columbia. The most spectacular result of government contracts with universities was the atomic bomb. The Manhattan Project, run by the army, financed research at the University of Chicago, which in 1942 was the site of the world's first sustained nuclear chain reaction. The University of California at Berkeley had a contract to operate the Los Alamos Scientific Laboratory in New Mexico, where the atomic bomb was tested.

University Research and Weapons Development

Wartime contracts with universities also accelerated medical progress. Indeed, because of the development of antibiotics and sulfa drugs, which greatly reduced deaths from infected war wounds, the survival rate among injured soldiers was 90 percent, compared with 10 percent in the First World War. Penicillin made its debut in America in 1942, saving the life of a woman suffering from a once-fatal bacterial infection.

Organized labor also grew during the war. Membership in unions ballooned from 8.5 million in 1940 to 14.75 million in 1945. To minimize labor-management conflict, in 1942 President Roosevelt created the National War Labor Board (NWLB). Unions were permitted to enroll as many new members as possible, but workers could not be required to join a union. Thus the NWLB forged a temporary compromise between

Unions and Wartime Labor Strikes

the unions' demand for a closed shop, in which only union members could be hired, and management's interest in open shops.

But when the NWLB attempted in 1943 to limit wage increases to cost-of-living pay hikes, workers responded with strikes. To discourage work stoppages, Congress passed the War Labor Disputes (Smith-Connally) Act in June 1943. The act gave the president authority to seize and operate any strike-bound plant deemed necessary to the national security, and it established a mandatory thirty-day cooling-off period before any new strike could be called.

Agriculture also made an impressive contribution to the war effort. Before the war, farming had been in the midst of a transition from the family-owned and -operated farm to the large-scale, mechanized agribusiness dominated by banks, insurance companies, and farm co-ops. The Second World War accelerated the trend, for wealthy financial institutions were better able than family farmers to pay for expensive new machinery. Thus from 1940 to 1945, the farm population fell from 30.5 million to 24.4 million people.

Wartime Changes in Agriculture

At the apex of the burgeoning national economy stood the federal government, the size and importance of which was mushrooming. The executive branch grew most dramatically. Besides raising the armed forces, mobilizing industrial production, and pacifying labor and management, the executive branch also had to manage the labor supply and control inflation. Although government-business-labor relations were sometimes bitter, Americans were generally ready to make personal sacrifices. They knew the war would be costly and long. Indeed, the cost of the war was such that the national debt increased from $49 billion in 1941 to $259 billion in 1945.

Growth in the Federal Government

The Military Life

America's men and women responded eagerly to their nation's call to arms. In 1941, only 1.8 million people were serving on active duty. By the end of the war, more than 16.3 million women and men had served in the armed forces. American troops served overseas for an average of sixteen months. Some never returned: total deaths exceeded 405,000.

Military service demanded enormous personal adjustments. Soldiers and sailors who had never been more than a few miles from home became homesick.

The Ordeal of Combat

But loneliness was inconsequential compared with the intense fear that soldiers admitted to feeling in battle. Some would return home with what the American Psychiatric Association would much later name post-traumatic stress disorder. The symptoms included nightmares and flashbacks to the battlefield, depression and anger, and widespread alcoholism.

Some of those who served in the armed forces were men and women who had experienced homosexual attraction in peacetime. Freed of their familial environments and serving in sex-segregated units, many acted on their feelings.

Homosexuals on Active Duty

The military court-martialed homosexuals, but gay relationships usually went unnoticed by the heterosexual world. For lesbians in the armed forces, the military environment offered friendships and a positive identity. "For many gay Americans," the historian John D'Emilio has written, "World War II created something of a nationwide coming out situation."

Wartime service not only broadened horizons but also fostered soldiers' ambitions. Many GIs returned to civilian life with new skills they had learned in the military's technical schools.

Postwar Ambitions

Still others took advantage of the educational benefits provided by the GI Bill of Rights (1944) to study for a college degree. Still, after two or three years abroad, men and women in the service returned to the United States not knowing what to expect from civilian life.

Enemy Aliens, Conscientious Objectors, and Japanese American Internees

After the United States entered the war, American leaders had to consider whether enemy agents were operating within the nation's borders. An early response of the government was to take into custody thousands of Germans, Italians, and other Europeans as suspected spies and potential traitors. During the war, the government interned 14,426 Europeans in Enemy Alien Camps. It was also clear that not all Americans were enthusiastic supporters of the nation's participation in the war.

Some Americans had conscientious objections to war. Conscientious objectors (COs) had to have a religious (as opposed to a moral or an ethical) reason for refusing military service. About 12,000 COs were sent to civilian public service camps, where they worked on conservation projects or as orderlies in hospitals. Approximately 5,500, three-fourths of whom were Jehovah's Witnesses, refused to participate in any way; they were imprisoned.

Compared with the First World War, the nation's wartime civil liberties record was generally creditable.

"An Enemy Race"

But there was one enormous exception: the internment in "relocation centers" of, ultimately, 120,000 Japanese Americans. Of these people, 77,000 were Nisei—native-born citizens of the United States. Their imprisonment was based not on suspicion or evidence of treason; their crime was solely that they were of Japanese descent.

During the war, charges of criminal behavior were never brought against any Japanese Americans; none was ever indicted or tried for espionage, treason, or sedition. Nevertheless in 1942 all the 112,000 Japanese Americans living in California, Oregon, and the state of Washington were rounded up and imprisoned. "It was really cruel and harsh," recalled Joseph Y. Kurihara, a citizen and a veteran of the First World War. "Seeing mothers completely bewildered with children crying from want and peddlers taking advantage and offering prices next to robbery made me feel like murdering those responsible."

The internees were sent to flood-damaged lands at Relocation, Arkansas; to the intermountain terrain of Wyoming and the desert of western Arizona; and to other arid and desolate spots in the West. Behind barbed wire stood tarpapered wooden barracks where entire families lived in a single room furnished only with cots, blankets, and a bare light bulb. Toilets and dining and bathing facilities were communal. Japanese Americans lost their positions in the truck-garden, floral,

Life in the Internment Camps

and fishing industries. Indeed, their economic competitors were among the most vocal proponents of their relocation.

The Supreme Court upheld the government's policy of internment. In wartime, the Court ruled in *Hirabayashi v. U.S.* (1943), "residents having ethnic affiliations with an invading enemy may be a greater source of danger than those of different ancestry." In *Korematsu v. U.S.* (1944), the Court, with three justices dissenting, approved the removal of the Nisei from the West Coast.

In 1983 Fred Korematsu had the satisfaction of hearing a federal judge rule that he—and by implication all detainees—had been the victim of "unsubstantiated facts, distortions and misrepresentations." A year earlier, the government's special Commission on Wartime Relocation and Internment of Civilians had recommended compensating the victims of this policy. Finally, in 1988, Congress voted to award $20,000 and a public apology to each of the surviving sixty thousand Japanese American internees.

Jobs and Racism on the Home Front

Prior to America's entry into the war, the Selective Service System and the War Department agreed to increase the number of African Americans in uniform by drafting blacks in proportion to their presence in the population: about 10 percent. At the height of the war, the army had more than 700,000 African American troops. An additional 187,000 black men and women enlisted in the navy, the Coast Guard, and the once all-white Marine Corps.

Although they served in segregated units, African Americans fought on the front lines. For the first time the War Department sanctioned the training of blacks as pilots. After instruction at Tuskegee Institute in Alabama, pilots saw heroic service in all-black units such as the Ninety-ninth Pursuit Squadron, winner of eighty Distinguished Flying Crosses. In 1940 Colonel Benjamin O. Davis was the first African American to be promoted to brigadier general.

African Americans in Combat

Serious failures in race relations, however, undercut these accomplishments. Race riots instigated by whites broke out on military bases, and white civilians assaulted black soldiers and sailors throughout the South. The worst racist outrage occurred at a munitions depot named Port Chicago in California. With a lack of training and a shocking disregard for safety by the navy, all-black squads of sailors were ordered to load explosives onto ships. On July 17, 1944, a tremendous ammunition explosion obliterated two vessels and killed 320 people, including 202 African Americans. When the surviving black sailors were ordered to resume loading ammunition, fifty refused; the men were arrested, found guilty of mutiny by an all-white panel, dishonorably discharged, and sentenced to fifteen years at hard labor.

Experiences such as these caused African Americans to wonder what, in fact, they were fighting for. They noted that the Red Cross separated blood according to the race of the donor, as if there were some difference. And although some African Americans argued that American racism was little different from German racism, persuasive reasons existed for blacks to participate in the war effort. Perhaps, as the NAACP believed, this was an opportunity "to persuade, embarrass, compel and shame our government and our nation . . . into a more enlightened attitude toward a tenth of its people." Proclaiming that in the Second World War they were waging a "Double V" campaign (for victory at home and abroad), blacks were more militant than before and readier than ever to protest. Membership in civil rights organizations soared.

Civil Rights Movement

The war also created opportunities in industry. Roosevelt's Executive Order No. 8802, issued in 1941, required employers in defense industries to make jobs available "without discrimination because of race, creed, color or national origin." To secure defense jobs, 1.5 million black Americans migrated from the South to the industrial cities of the North and West in the 1940s. More than half a million became active members of CIO unions. African American voters in northern cities were beginning to constitute a vital swing vote in local, state, and presidential elections.

African American War Workers

The benefits of urban life, however, came with a high price tag. Migrants from the rural South had to

Race Riots of 1943

adjust to life in big cities, and white hostility made the adjustment more difficult. Southern whites who had migrated north brought with them the racial prejudices of the Deep South. Northern whites were also hostile. In 1942 more than half of them believed that African Americans should be segregated in separate schools and neighborhoods. Such attitudes, and the competition between blacks and whites for jobs and housing, created tensions which in 1943 erupted in racial conflicts in forty-seven cities. Outright racial warfare bloodied the streets of Detroit in June. At the end of thirty hours of rioting, twenty-five blacks and nine whites lay dead.

The federal government did practically nothing to prevent further racial violence. From President Roosevelt on down, most federal officials put the war first, domestic reform second. But this time government neglect could not discourage African Americans. By war's end they were ready—politically, economically, and emotionally—to wage a struggle for voting rights and for equal access to public accommodations and institutions.

Racial violence was not directed exclusively against blacks. Some whites judged people of Mexican origin as undesirable as those whose

Bracero Program

roots were African. In 1942 American farms and war industries needed workers, and the United States and Mexico had agreed to the *bracero* program, whereby Mexicans were admitted to the United States on short-term work contracts. Although the newcomers suffered racial discrimination and segregation, they seized the economic opportunities that had become available. In Los Angeles, seventeen thousand people of Mexican descent found shipyard jobs where before the war none had been available to them.

Ethnic and racial animosities intensified during the war. In 1943 Los Angeles witnessed the "zoot-suit riot," in which whites, most of them sailors and soldiers, wantonly attacked Mexican Americans. White racist anger focused on Mexican American street gangs (*pachucos*). For four days mobs invaded Mexican American neighborhoods. Not only did white police officers look the other way during these assaults, but the city of Los Angeles passed an ordinance that made wearing a zoot suit within city limits a crime.

Women and Children in the War Effort

 During the war large numbers of American women patriotically responded to their nation's call for help. The WACs (Women's Army Corps) enlisted 140,000 women, while 100,000 served in the navy's WAVES (Women Accepted for Volunteer Emergency Service) and 39,000 in the Marine Corps and Coast Guard. Another 75,000 women served in the army and navy's Nursing Corps, where they saw duty during the invasions of North Africa, Italy, and France. Women also served as pilots in the WASP (Women Air Service Pilots), teaching basic flying, towing aerial targets for gunnery practice, ferrying planes across the country, and serving as test pilots. WASP flying duty was often hazardous; thirty-eight women lost their lives.

During the Great Depression public opinion had been hostile to the hiring of women, but the war brought about a rapid increase in employment. Just when men were going off to war, industry had to recruit millions of new workers to supply the rapidly expanding need for military equipment. Filling these new jobs were African Americans, southern whites, Mexican Americans, and, above all, women.

No matter how impressive, statistics tell only part of the story. Changes in people's attitudes were also

Women in War Production

important. Until early in the war, employers had insisted that women were not suited for industrial jobs. As labor shortages began to threaten the war effort, however, employers did an about-face. Women now became basic to the labor force and worked as riveters, welders, crane operators, tool makers, shell loaders, lumberjacks, and police officers.

During the war years, the number of working women increased by 57 percent. The economist Claudia Goldin has observed that labor-force participation rates increased most for women over age forty-five, and that "married, rather than single women, were the

Women workers mastered numerous job skills during the war. In 1942 crews of women cared for Long Island commuter trains like this one.   (Corbis-Bettmann)

primary means of bolstering the nation's labor force." By 1945 more working women were married than single, and more were over age thirty-five than under.

New employment opportunities also increased women's occupational mobility. Especially noteworthy were the gains made by African American women; over 400,000 quit work as domestic servants to enjoy the better working conditions, higher pay, and union benefits of industrial employment. To take advantage of the new employment opportunities, over 7 million women willingly moved to war-production areas.

As public opinion shifted to support women's war work, newspapers and magazines, radio, and movies proclaimed Rosie the Riveter a war hero. But few people asserted that women's war work should bring about a permanent shift in sex roles. Once the victory was won, women should go back to nurturing their husbands and children, relinquishing their jobs to returning GIs. Wartime surveys, however, showed that many of the women wanted to remain in their jobs—80 percent of New York's women workers felt that way.

Although women's wages rose when they acquired better jobs, they still received lower pay than men.

Discrimination Against Women

In 1945 women in manufacturing earned only 65 percent of what men were paid. Working women, particularly working mothers, suffered in other ways as well. Early in the war, childcare centers were in short supply in war-boom areas. And even as mothers were being encouraged to work in the national defense, there was still opposition to their doing so. One form this campaign took was a series of exaggerated articles in mass-circulation magazines about the suffering of "eight-hour orphans" or "latchkey children," left alone or deposited in all-night movie theaters while their mothers worked eight-hour shifts in war plants.

By and large, however, the home-front children of working women were not neglected or abused during the war. Families made their own childcare arrangements, which often involved leaving children in the care of their grandmothers. Some families benefited from the Lanham Act of 1940, which provided federal aid, including funds for childcare centers, to communities that had to absorb large war-related populations. In mid-1944, 130,000 children were enrolled in Lanham Act childcare centers.

Childcare in Wartime

While millions of women were entering the work force, hundreds of thousands of women were also getting married. The number of marriages rose from 73 per 1,000 unmarried women in 1939 to 93 in 1942. Some couples scrambled to get married so they could live together before the man was sent overseas; others doubtless married and had children to qualify for military deferments. Many of these hasty marriages did not survive long military separations, and divorces soared, too—from 25,000 in 1939 to 485,000 in 1945. As might be expected, the birth rate also climbed. Many births were "goodbye babies," conceived as a guarantee that the family would be perpetuated if the father died in battle overseas.

Increase in Marriage, Divorce, and Birth Rates

Ironically, women's efforts to hold their families together during the war posed problems for returning fathers. Women war workers had brought home the wages; they had taken over the budgeting of expenses and the writing of checks. In countless ways they had proved they could hold the reins in their husbands' absence. Many husbands returned home to find that the lives of their wives and children seemed complete without them. And what of the women who wanted to remain in the labor market? In 1945 many such women were pushed out of the factories and shipyards to make way for returning veterans; often they could find only low-paying jobs in restaurants and laundries.

The Decline of Liberalism and the Election of 1944

Even before Pearl Harbor, political liberals had suffered major defeats. Some Democrats hoped to revive the reform movement during the war, but Republicans and conservative Democrats were on guard against such a move. In the 1942 elections, the Republicans scored impressive gains. Part of the Democrats' problem was that once people acquired jobs and gained some economic security, they began to be more critical of New Deal policies. The New Deal coalition had always been a fragile alliance: southern white farmers had little in common with northern blacks or white factory workers. In northern cities, blacks and whites who had voted for Roosevelt in 1940 were competing for jobs and housing and soon would collide in race riots.

But though New Deal liberalism was enfeebled, it was far from dead. At its head still stood Franklin D. Roosevelt, and it had a program to present to the American people. The liberal agenda began with a pledge to secure full employment. Roosevelt emphasized the concept in his Economic Bill of Rights, delivered as part of his 1944 State of the Union address. Every American, the president declared, had a right to a decent job, to sufficient food, shelter, and clothing, and to financial security in unemployment, illness, and old age. To attain these goals, Roosevelt had to be reelected.

Wartime Liberalism

In 1944 Franklin D. Roosevelt looked like an exhausted old man, and rumors of his ill health abounded. Whether or not Roosevelt expected to survive his fourth term, he selected a running mate who was inexperienced in international affairs: Senator Harry S Truman of Missouri. There was little evidence that Truman possessed the capacities for national and world leadership that he would need as president. Nor did Roosevelt take Truman into his confidence, failing even to inform his running mate about the atomic bomb project.

Roosevelt and Truman

Roosevelt won a fourth term, defeating his Republican opponent, New York's Governor Thomas E. Dewey. It was Roosevelt's narrowest-ever margin of victory. Dewey's stiff manner and bland personality

Roosevelt's Fourth-Term Victory

hurt him, but the city vote was the Republican's undoing. Wartime population shifts had enhanced the Democrats' urban political clout: southern whites who had been lifelong Democrats, along with southern blacks who had never voted before, had migrated to the urban industrial centers and cast Democratic ballots.

Added to the Democrats' urban vote was a less obvious factor. Many voters seemed to be exhibiting what has been called "depression psychosis." Fearful that hard times would return once war contracts were terminated, they remembered New Deal relief programs and voted for Roosevelt. With victory within grasp, many Americans wanted Roosevelt's experienced hand to guide both the nation and the world to a lasting international peace. Roosevelt's death in April 1945, however, meant that Harry Truman would deal with the postwar world.

Planning for Peace

American leaders vowed to make a peace that would ensure a postwar world free from economic depression, totalitarianism, and war. Their goals included the Open Door policy and lower tariffs; self-determination for liberated peoples; avoidance of the debts-reparations fiasco that had plagued Europe after the First World War; expansion of the United States's sphere of influence; gradual and orderly decolonization; and management of world affairs by what Roosevelt once called the Four Policemen: the Soviet Union, China, Great Britain, and the United States.

Although the Allies concentrated on defeating the aggressors, their suspicions of one another undermined cooperation. Questions about eastern Europe proved the most difficult. The Soviet Union sought to fix its boundaries where they had stood before Hitler attacked in 1941. This meant that the part of Poland that the Soviets had invaded and captured in 1939 would become Soviet territory. The British and Americans hesitated, preferring to deal with eastern Europe at the end of the war. Yet in an

Allied Disagreement over Eastern Europe

October 1944 agreement, Churchill and Stalin struck a bargain: the Soviet Union would gain Romania and Bulgaria as a sphere of influence; Britain would have the upper hand in Greece; and the two countries would share authority in Yugoslavia and Hungary.

Poland stood as a special case. In 1943 Moscow had broken off diplomatic relations with the conservative Polish government-in-exile in London. The Poles had angered Moscow by asking the International Red Cross to investigate German charges, later substantiated, that the Soviets had massacred thousands of Polish army officers in the Katyn Forest in 1940. Then an uprising in Warsaw in 1944 complicated matters still further. Encouraged by approaching Soviet troops to expect assistance, the Warsaw underground rose against the occupying Germans. To the dismay of the world community, Soviet armies stood by as German troops slaughtered 166,000 people and devastated the city. The Soviets then set up a pro-Communist government in Lublin. Thus near the end of the war Poland had two competing governments: one in London, recognized by America and Britain, and another in Lublin.

Early in the war the Allies had begun talking about a new international peacekeeping organization. At Teheran in 1943 Roosevelt called for an institution controlled by the Four Policemen. The next year, at a Washington, D.C., mansion called Dumbarton Oaks, American, British, Soviet, and Chinese representatives approved a preliminary charter for a United Nations Organization, providing for a supreme Security Council dominated by the great powers and a weak General Assembly. The Security Council would have five permanent members, each with veto power (Britain had insisted that France be one of the permanent members). Meanwhile, the Soviet Union, hoping to counter pro-American and pro-British blocs in the General Assembly, asked for separate membership in the General Assembly for each of the sixteen Soviet republics. This issue remained unresolved, but the meeting was still a success.

Creation of the United Nations

Diplomatic action on behalf of the European Jews, however, proved to be a tragic failure. By war's end, about 6 million Jews had been forced into concentration camps and systematically murdered. The

Jewish Refugees

Nazis also exterminated as many as 250,000 Gypsies and about 60,000 gay men. During the depression, the United States and other nations had refused to relax their immigration restrictions to save Jews fleeing persecution. Because of anti-Semitism, American immigration officials applied the rules so strictly—requiring legal documents that fleeing Jews could not possibly provide—that otherwise-qualified refugees were kept out of the country.

Even the tragic voyage of the *St. Louis* did not change government policy. The vessel left Hamburg in mid-1939 carrying 930 desperate Jewish refugees who lacked proper immigration documents. Denied entry to Havana, the *St. Louis* headed for Miami, where Coast Guard cutters prevented it from docking. The ship was forced to return to Europe.

The Holocaust

As evidence mounted that Hitler intended to exterminate the Jews, British and American representatives met in Bermuda in 1943 but came up with no plans. Secretary of State Hull submitted a report to the president that emphasized "the unknown cost of moving an undetermined number of persons from an undisclosed place to an unknown destination." Appalled, Secretary of the Treasury Henry Morgenthau, Jr., charged that the State Department's foot-dragging made the United States an accessory to murder. Early in 1944, stirred by Morgenthau's well-documented plea, Roosevelt created the War Refugee Board, which set up refugee camps in Europe and played a crucial role in saving 200,000 Jews from death.

The Yalta Conference

With the war in Europe nearing an end, Roosevelt called for another summit meeting. The three Allied leaders met at Yalta, in the Russian Crimea, in early February 1945. Controversy has surrounded the conference ever since. Roosevelt was obviously ill, and critics of the Yalta agreements later charged that he was too weak to resist Stalin's cunning and that he struck a poor bargain. The evidence suggests, however, that Roosevelt was mentally alert and managed to sustain his strength during negotiations.

Each of the Allies arrived at Yalta with definite goals. Britain sought to make France a partner in the postwar occupation of Germany, to curb Soviet influence in Poland, and to ensure protection for the vulnerable British Empire. The Soviet Union wanted reparations from Germany to assist in the massive task of rebuilding at home, possessions in Asia, continued influence in Poland, and a permanently weakened Germany. The United States lobbied for the United Nations Organization, a Soviet declaration of war against Japan, recognition of China as a major power, and a compromise between rival factions in Poland.

Military positions at the time of the conference helped to shape the final agreements. Soviet troops occupied much of eastern Europe, including Poland. Stalin insisted on a Polish government friendly to Moscow—the Lublin regime. He also demanded boundaries that would give Poland part of Germany in the west and the Soviet Union part of Poland in the east. Churchill wanted the London government-in-exile to return to Poland.

With Roosevelt's help, a compromise was reached: a boundary favorable to the Soviet Union in the east; postponement of the western boundary issue; the creation of a "more broadly based" coalition government that would include members of the London regime; and free elections to be held sometime in the future. The agreement was vague but, given Soviet occupation of Poland, Roosevelt considered it "the best I can do."

As for Germany, the Big Three agreed that it would be divided into four zones, the fourth zone to be administered by France. Berlin, within the Soviet zone, also would be divided among the four victors. On the question of reparations, Stalin wanted a precise figure, but Churchill and Roosevelt insisted on determining Germany's ability to pay. With Britain abstaining, the Americans and Russians agreed that an Allied committee would consider the sum of $20 billion as a basis for discussion in the future.

Other issues led to tradeoffs. Stalin promised to declare war on Japan two or three months after Hitler's defeat. The Soviet premier also agreed to sign a treaty of friendship and alliance with Jiang Jieshi (Chiang Kai-shek), America's ally in China, rather than with the Communist Mao Zedong (Mao Tsetung). In return, the United States agreed that the Soviets could take the southern part of Sakhalin Island

The three Allied leaders—Winston Churchill, Franklin D. Roosevelt, and Joseph Stalin—met at Yalta in February 1945. Having been president for twelve years, Roosevelt showed signs of age and fatigue. Two months later, he died of a massive cerebral hemorrhage.   (Franklin D. Roosevelt Library)

and the Kurile Islands. Regarding the new world organization, Roosevelt and Churchill granted the Soviets three votes in the General Assembly. Finally, the conferees issued the Declaration of Liberated Europe, a pledge to establish order and to rebuild economies by democratic methods.

Yalta marked the high point of the Grand Alliance. But as the great powers jockeyed for influence at the close of the war, the alliance began to break up. The crumbling became evident almost immediately, at

Potsdam Conference

the Potsdam Conference, which began in mid-July. Roosevelt had died in April, and Truman—a novice at international diplomacy—was less patient with the Soviets. Truman also was emboldened by learning during the conference that the atomic test in New Mexico had been successful.

Despite major differences at Potsdam, the Big Three did agree on general policies toward Germany: complete disarmament, dismantling of industry used for military production, dissolution of Nazi institutions and laws, and war crimes trials. In a compromise over reparations, they decided that each occupying nation should extract reparations from its own zone.

Potsdam left much undone. As the war drew to a close, there was little that bound the Allies together. Roosevelt's cooperative style was gone. And the United States, with the awesome atomic bomb in the offing to force defeat on Japan, no longer needed or even wanted the Soviet Union in the Pacific war. Moreover, each of the victors was seeking to preserve and enlarge its sphere of influence. Britain claimed authority in Greece and parts of the Middle East; the Soviet Union already dominated much of eastern Europe; and the United States retained its hegemony in Latin America. The United States also seized several Pacific islands as strategic outposts and laid plans to dominate a defeated Japan.

Summary

Hitler once prophesied, "We may be destroyed, but if we are, we shall drag a world with us—a world in flames." Indeed, *rubble* was the word most often invoked to describe the European landscape at the end of the war. In Asia as well as in Europe, ghostlike people wandered about, searching desperately for food and mourning those who would never come home. The Soviet Union had suffered by far the greatest losses: more than 21 million military and civilian war dead. The Chinese calculated their war losses at 10 million, the Germans and Austrians at 6 million, and the Japanese at 2.5 million. And 6 million Jews had been killed during the Holocaust. In all, the Second World War caused the deaths of 55 million people.

Only one major combatant escaped such grisly statistics: the United States. Its cities were not burned and its fields were not trampled. American deaths from the war—405,399—were few compared with the losses of other nations. In fact, the United States emerged from the Second World War more powerful than it had ever been. It alone had the atomic bomb. The U.S. Air Force and Navy were the largest anywhere. What is more, only the United States had the capital and economic resources to spur international recovery.

For many Americans life in 1945 was fundamentally different from what it had been before Pearl Harbor. The Academy Award for 1946 went to *The Best Years of Our Lives*, a painful film about the postwar readjustments of three veterans and their families and friends. Many men returned home suffering flashbacks, nightmares, and deep emotional distress. "Dad came home a different man," recalled one girl; "he didn't laugh as much and he drank a lot."

On another front, the Second World War stimulated the trend toward bigness, not only in business and labor but also in government, agriculture, higher education, and science. The seeds of the military-industrial complex were also sown during these years. Moreover, with the advent of what would become known as the Cold War, millions of young men would be inducted into the armed forces during the next thirty years. War and the expectation of war would become part of American life.

At the same time, the Second World War was a powerful engine of social change in the United States. The gains made during the war by African Americans and women were overdue. And by blending New Deal ideology and wartime urgency, the government assumed the responsibility of ensuring prosperity and stepping in when capitalism faltered. Americans emerged from the war fully confident that theirs was the greatest country in the world. The United States, they boasted, had preserved democracy and freedom around the globe. Clearly, the Second World War was a turning point in the nation's history.

LEGACY FOR A PEOPLE AND A NATION
Atomic Waste

Although victory in the Second World War tasted sweet to the American people, the war's environmental legacy proved noxious, toxic, and deadly. New industries brought with them hazardous pollutants. The production of synthetic rubber spewed forth sulfur dioxide, carbon monoxide, and other dangerous gases. War industries fouled the water and the soil with both solid and petrochemical wastes. Air pollution—smog—was first detected in Los Angeles in 1943. Although these were ominous signs, few people at the time worried about human-made threats to America's seemingly endless supplies of fresh air, water, and soil.

No wartime, or postwar, weapons program became more threatening to the natural environment than the project to develop the atomic bomb. Many of the bomb's ingredients, notably plutonium, beryllium, and mercury, are highly toxic and contaminate the environment. The storing of radioactive waste began during the war at Oak Ridge, Tennessee, and Hanford, Washington, where plutonium was produced. During the postwar nuclear arms race with the Soviet Union, the United States opened other production facilities, for example, at Rocky Flats in Colorado and on the Savannah River in South Carolina. At these sites, radioactive waste seeped from leaky barrels into the soil and water, threatening human life and killing fish, birds, and other wildlife. Moreover, between 1945 and 1963, nuclear testing, which was done above ground, killed an estimated 800,000 Americans from cancer attributable to radioactive fallout.

In the twenty-first century, the environmental legacy of the atomic bomb continues to threaten the American people. The biggest problem is how to dispose of radioactive materials. In 1999 the federal government opened the nation's first nuclear dump in New Mexico. Scientists, however, are skeptical that current technology is up to the task of cleaning soil and water at the nuclear weapons sites. "The technology . . . used to remediate contaminated sites," said the chairman of a National Research Council task force that studied the problem, "is simply ineffective and unable to accomplish the massive job that needs to be done."

For Further Reading, see the Appendix. For Web resources, go to history.college.hmco.com/students.

28

POSTWAR AMERICA: COLD WAR POLITICS, CIVIL RIGHTS, AND THE BABY BOOM

1945–1961

On May 2, 1945, Bob Bush, a U.S. Navy medical corpsman, was attached to a marine rifle company fighting on the Japanese island of Okinawa. Firing from heavily fortified positions, the Japanese were inflicting heavy casualties on the Americans. Bush was constantly on the run, patching up one wounded marine after another. Lying in the open was a critically wounded officer; Bush rushed to the man's side and began giving him blood plasma just as the enemy opened fire again. Holding the bottle of plasma high in one hand, he drew his pistol with the other. According to a citation Bush, "fired into the enemy ranks until his ammunition was expended. Quickly seizing a discarded carbine, he trained his fire on the Japanese charging

point blank over the hill," killing six men, "despite his own serious wounds and the loss of one eye. . . ."

Recovering from his wounds in a hospital in Hawai'i, Bob Bush thought about his future. And in the navy plane carrying him back to the United States, he promised himself that he would put the war behind him. "I was eighteen. I had to get back to school in the fall. I had the girlfriend back home in [the state of] Washington." Her name was Wonda Spooner, and she too was eighteen. Bob wanted to ask her to marry him, and he was pleased when she said yes; that summer they were married. For their honeymoon, the couple boarded a train for Washington, D.C., where President Harry S Truman awarded Bush the Medal of Honor.

489

Back home, Bush completed his high-school requirements and, under the GI Bill, enrolled in business courses at the University of Washington. Anticipating a postwar housing boom, Bush and another veteran then decided to buy a small lumberyard. As Tom Brokaw describes in *The Greatest Generation* (1998), Bush was ambitious and hard working, and in the 1940s and 1950s, his business boomed.

Like many veterans, Bush had one overriding goal: to build a happy life for his family. While he was busy succeeding in business, Wonda was busy at home raising their baby-boom children, three boys and a girl. The Bushes were not alone in having babies after the war. From 1946 until 1964, births hit record highs. Parents of Bob and Wonda's generation had grown up during the Great Depression and were determined that their children's lives would be better than theirs had been.

Material comfort was the hallmark for millions of middle-class families. Often, however, both parents worked to pay for a new home and a second car. This meant that women had at least two jobs, for they still were expected to do the housework and cooking. In postwar America, "family togetherness" took on almost religious significance, including evenings watching television in the "family room" and family vacations.

Postwar America was not only prosperous, but also proud and boastful. From 1945 to the 1960s, the American people were in the grip of "victory culture"—that is, the belief that unending triumph was the nation's birthright and destiny. Americans believed that their nation was the greatest in the world, not only the most powerful but the most righteous.

As evidence of the nation's perfectibility, Americans pointed to the postwar economic boom. The cornerstones of the boom, which began in 1945 and lasted twenty-five years, were the automobile, construction, and defense industries. As the gross national product (GNP) grew, income levels rose and property ownership spread. New houses and schools sprang up throughout the country. More and more people bought homes in the suburbs.

Although the postwar years constituted an age of consensus, Cold War politics were often volatile. When Harry Truman became president in 1945, his initial response to the challenge was a deep feeling of inadequacy. Nevertheless, he had to deal with the closing months of the war, the onset of the Cold War, and the nation's reconversion from war back to peace.

In 1948, Truman seemed politically vulnerable, but he confounded experts by winning the presidency in his own right. His victory demonstrated the volatility of politics. The key domestic issues of the postwar period—civil rights for African Americans and the anti-Communist crusade to be called McCarthyism—were both highly charged. Later, the outbreak of the Korean War in 1950 intensified discontent. The war, inflation, and corruption in the White House caused Truman's popularity to plummet. After twenty years of Democratic presidents, Americans in 1952 elected the Republican nominee, General Dwight D. Eisenhower.

Eisenhower's major goal was to promote economic growth, and he pursued staunchly Republican goals: a balanced budget, reduced taxes and government spending, low inflation, and a return of power to the states. During Eisenhower's presidency, Americans celebrated the American Dream and their economic system for providing a high standard of living.

It was the infant civil rights movement that challenged the national consensus. Most African Americans were at the bottom of the economic ladder and were being denied constitutional rights such as the right to vote. How would blacks be incorporated into the consensus? The president, Congress, southern whites, and black civil rights activists all gave different answers as they debated *Brown v. Board of Education of Topeka*, the Supreme Court's momentous decision of 1954 invalidating racial segregation in public schools.

Still, however fragile, the age of consensus remained basically intact. In 1961 Democratic senator John F. Kennedy of Massachusetts succeeded President Eisenhower. During his brief presidency, the nation began dealing with problems it had postponed addressing for too long. ■

Cold War Politics: The Truman Presidency

After the initial joyous reaction to the end of the Second World War, Americans faced a number of important questions. What would be the effect of reconversion—the

IMPORTANT EVENTS

1945 Roosevelt dies; Truman becomes president
12 million GIs demobilized
Truman's economic message to Congress

1946 Baby boom begins
Spock's *Baby and Child Care* changes child-rearing practices
More than 1 million GIs enroll in colleges
Coal miners strike
Inflation reaches 18.2 percent
Republicans win both houses of Congress

1947 Truman institutes employee loyalty program
Taft-Hartley Act limits power of unions
To Secure These Rights issued by the President's Committee on Civil Rights

1948 Truman appoints committee to oversee racial desegregation of the armed forces
Truman elected president
Kinsey's *Sexual Behavior in the Human Male* published

1949 Soviet Union explodes an atomic bomb
Communists win revolution in China
National Housing Act promises decent housing for all Americans

1950 Fuchs arrested as an atomic spy
Hiss convicted of perjury
McCarthy alleges Communists in government
Korean War begins
Rosenbergs charged with conspiracy to commit treason
Internal Security (McCarran) Act requires members of "Communist front" organizations to register with the government

1951 Supreme Court upholds the Alien Registration (Smith) Act in *Dennis et al. v. U.S.*

1952 Ellison's *Invisible Man* shows African Americans' exclusion from the American Dream
Eisenhower elected president
Republicans win both houses of Congress

1953 Korean War ends
Rosenbergs executed

Congress adopts termination policy for Native Americans
Kinsey causes further public uproar with *Sexual Behavior in the Human Female*

1954 *Brown* decision reverses "separate-but-equal" doctrine
Communist Control Act makes Communist Party membership illegal
Senate condemns McCarthy

1955 AFL and CIO merge
Rebel Without a Cause idealizes youth subculture
Montgomery bus boycott begins

1956 Highway Act launches interstate highway system
Eisenhower reelected
Ginsberg's poem *Howl*, anthem of the Beat generation, published
Presley releases his first single

1957 King elected first president of the Southern Christian Leadership Conference
Little Rock, Arkansas, desegregation crisis
Congress passes Civil Rights Act
Soviet Union launches *Sputnik*
Kerouac criticizes white middle-class conformity in *On the Road*

1958 Congress passes National Defense Education Act to improve education in mathematics, foreign languages, and science
Adams resigns over scandal
St. Lawrence Seaway opens

1960 Sit-in in Greensboro, North Carolina
Student Nonviolent Coordinating Committee formed
Kennedy elected president

1961 Eisenhower warns against "military-industrial complex"

1962 Harrington's *The Other America* creates awareness of America's poor
Carson's *Silent Spring* warns of dangers of DDT

cancellation of war contracts, termination of wage and price controls, and expiration of wartime labor agreements? Would depression recur? Or would Americans spend their wartime savings on a buying spree?

Even before the war's end, cutbacks in production had caused layoffs. At Ford Motor Company's massive

Postwar Job Layoffs

Willow Run plant outside Detroit, where nine thousand Liberator bombers had been produced, most workers were let go in the spring of 1945. Ten days after the victory over Japan, 1.8 million people nationwide received pink slips. The employment picture was made more complex by the return of millions of discharged GIs in 1945 and 1946.

Despite high unemployment immediately after the war, the United States was hardly on the brink of depression. In fact, after a brief period of readjustment, the economy

Beginnings of the Postwar Economic Boom

embarked on a quarter-century of unprecedented boom. People had plenty of savings to spend in 1945 and 1946, and, in time, there were new houses and cars for them to buy. Easy credit also promoted the buying binge. As a result, the nation's most immediate postwar economic problem was not depression but inflation. Prices skyrocketed, and inflation exceeded 18 percent in 1946.

As prices spiraled upward, many people were earning less in real income (actual purchasing power) than they had earned during the war. Indus-

Upsurges in Labor Strikes

trial workers complained that the end of war production had eliminated much of their overtime work, and as their incomes fell in 1946, net profits reached all-time highs. Indignant that they were not sharing in the prosperity, unions forced nationwide shutdowns in the coal, automobile, steel, and electric industries and halted railroad and maritime transportation.

By 1946 there was no doubt about the growing unpopularity of labor unions and their leadership. In May, when a nationwide railroad strike was threatened, Truman made a dramatic appearance before a joint session of Congress. If strikers in an industry deemed vital to the national security refused to honor a presidential order to return to work, he would "request the Congress immediately to authorize the President to draft into the Armed Forces of the United States all workers who are on strike against their government." Truman's speech alienated union members in general, who vowed to defeat him in the 1948 presidential election.

Truman fared little better in his direction of the Office of Price Administration (OPA). Now that the war was over, powerful interests wanted

Consumer Discontent

price controls lifted. Consumers grew impatient with shortages and black-market prices, and manufacturers and farmers wanted to raise prices legally. Yet when most controls expired in mid-1946 and inflation rose further, consumers grumbled. Republicans made the most of public discontent. "Got enough meat?" asked Republican congressman John M. Vorys of Ohio. "Got enough houses? Got enough OPA? . . . Got enough inflation? . . . Got enough debt? . . . Got enough strikes?" In 1946 the Republicans won a majority in both houses of the Eightieth Congress, and the White House in 1948 seemed within their grasp.

But the politicians who dominated the Eightieth Congress were committed conservatives, and if Truman had alienated labor and consumers, the Eightieth Congress made them livid. Particularly unpopular with workers was the Taft-Hartley Act, which Congress approved over Truman's veto in 1947. The bill prohibited the closed shop, a workplace where membership in a particular union was a prerequisite for being hired. It also permitted the states to enact right-to-work laws banning union-shop agreements, which required all workers to join if a majority voted in favor of a union shop. In addition, the law forbade union contributions to political candidates in federal elections, required union leaders to swear in affidavits that they were not Communists, and mandated an eighty-day cooling-off period before carrying out strikes that imperiled the national security. Truman's veto vindicated him in the eyes of labor.

Not since 1928 had Republicans been so confident of capturing the presidency, and most political experts agreed. At their national convention, Republicans strengthened their position by nominating the governors of two of the nation's most populous states: Thomas E. Dewey of New York for president and Earl Warren of California for vice president.

Democrats were up against more than Republicans in 1948. Two years before, Henry A. Wallace, the only remaining New Dealer in the cabinet, had been fired by Truman for publicly criticizing U.S. foreign policy. In 1948 Wallace ran for president on the Progressive Party ticket, which advocated friendly relations with the Soviet Union, racial desegregation, and nationalization of basic industries. A fourth party, the Dixiecrats (States' Rights Democratic Party), was organized by southerners who walked out of the 1948 Democratic convention when it adopted a pro–civil rights plank; they nominated Governor Strom Thurmond of South Carolina.

But Truman had a few ideas of his own. He called the Eightieth Congress into special session and challenged it to enact all the planks in the Republican platform. After two weeks of Congress accomplishing nothing of significance, Truman took to the road,

Truman's Upset Victory

delivering scores of speeches denouncing the "do-nothing" Eightieth Congress. Truman confounded the experts. He received 24 million popular votes and 303 electoral votes; Dewey had 22 million popular votes and 189 electoral votes. Peace, prosperity, and the endurance of the New Deal brought Truman his victory.

Truman began his new term brimming with confidence. It was time, he believed, for government to fulfill its responsibility to provide economic security for the poor and the elderly. As he worked on his 1949 State of the Union message, he penciled in an expression of his intentions: "I expect to give every segment of our population a fair deal." Little of Truman's Fair Deal came to fruition, however, and he would leave office a highly unpopular president. One reason for the president's unpopularity was the Korean War.

So few pollsters predicted that President Harry S Truman (1884–1972) would win in 1948 that the *Chicago Tribune* announced his defeat before all the returns were in. Here a victorious Truman pokes fun at the newspaper for its premature headline.   (Corbis-Bettmann)

In June 1950, following the invasion of South Korea by North Korea, President Truman ordered

Korean War Discontent on the Home Front

American troops to fight in Korea (see Chapter 29). Americans, fearing wartime shortages, flocked to their grocery stores for sugar, coffee, and canned goods. Fueled by panic buying, inflation began to rise again. Moreover, people disliked the draft, and many reservists and national guardsmen resented being among those called to active duty. Thanks to an unpopular war and charges of influence peddling by some of Truman's cronies, the president's public approval rating slumped to an all-time low of 23 percent.

Although Truman was highly unpopular when he left office in 1953, historians now rate him among the

Truman's Historical Standing

nation's ten best presidents. Truman was president at the beginning of the Cold War, and in eight years he strengthened the powers of the presidency. He fought for programs to benefit workers, African Americans, farmers, homeowners, retired persons, and people in need of healthcare. Little of Truman's Fair Deal was enacted during his presidency; much of it became law as part of the Great Society in the 1960s.

Consensus and Conflict: The Eisenhower Presidency

In the 1952 presidential election, the fate of the Democratic Party was sealed when the Republicans nominated General Dwight D. Eisenhower. A bona fide war hero, "Ike" had a friendly smile and seemed to embody the virtues Americans most admired: integrity, decency, and lack of pretense. Eisenhower's unlucky Democratic opponent was Adlai Stevenson, the governor of Illinois. It was never much of a contest, especially after Eisenhower promised to "go to Korea," implying he would end the war. The result was a landslide: Eisenhower and his running mate, Senator Richard M. Nixon of California, won almost 34 million votes to the Democrats' 27 million votes. The Republicans even carried four states in the once-solid Democratic South, and with Eisenhower's long coattails gained control of both houses of Congress.

Smiling Ike, with his folksy style, garbled syntax, and frequent escapes to the golf course, provoked Democrats to charge that he failed to lead. But Dwight D. Eisenhower was not that simple. His low-key style was a way of playing down his role as politician and highlighting his role as chief of state. Eisenhower relied heavily on staff work, delegating authority to cabinet members. Sometimes he was not well informed on details and gave the impression that he was out of touch with his own government. In fact, he was not.

During Eisenhower's presidency most Americans clung to the status quo. It was an era of both self-

The "Consensus Mood"

congratulation and constant anxiety, especially over communism. Demand for reform at such a time seemed to most Americans unnecessary, if not unpatriotic. A weak minority on the American left advocated checks on the political power of corporations, and a noisy minority on the right accused the government of a wishy-washy campaign against communism. But both liberal Democrats and moderate Republicans avoided extremism, satisfied to be occupying what the historian Arthur M. Schlesinger, Jr., called "the vital center."

President Eisenhower approached his duties with a philosophy he called "dynamic conservatism." He

"Dynamic Conservatism"

meant being "conservative when it comes to money and liberal when it comes to human beings." Eisenhower's was unabashedly "an Administration representing business and industry," as Interior Secretary Douglas McKay acknowledged. The president and his appointees gave priority to reducing the federal budget, but they did not always succeed; and they recognized that dismantling New Deal and Fair Deal programs was politically impossible. The administration did try to remove the federal government from agriculture, but the effort failed.

Eisenhower made headway in other spheres. In 1954 Congress passed legislation to construct the St. Lawrence Seaway between Montreal and Lake Erie. This inland waterway, which opened in 1958, was intended to spur the economic development of the Midwest by linking the Great Lakes to the Atlantic Ocean. Also in 1954 Eisenhower signed into law amendments to the Social Security Act that raised benefits and added 7.5 million workers, mostly self-employed farmers, to the program's coverage. Congress also obliged the president with tax reform that raised business depreciation allowances and with the Atomic Energy Act of 1954, which granted private companies the right to own reactors and nuclear materials for the production of electricity.

Eisenhower also presided over a dramatic change in the lives of Native Americans. In 1953 Congress adopted a policy known as *termination*: the forced assimilation of Native Americans into the dominant culture by terminating the Indian reservations, as well as by ending tribal sovereignty and federal services to Indians. Another act of the same year made Indians subject to state laws.

Termination Policy for Native Americans

Between 1954 and 1960, the federal government withdrew its benefits from sixty-one tribes. About one in eight Indians abandoned the reservations; many joined the ranks of the urban poor in low-paying jobs. The policy of termination and relocation was motivated largely by land greed. The Klamaths of Oregon, for example, lived on a reservation rich in ponderosa pine, which lumber interests coveted. Enticed by cash payments, almost four-fifths of the Klamaths accepted termination and voted to sell their shares of the forestland. With termination, their way of life collapsed.

In the 1954 congressional elections, most Americans revealed that, though they still liked Eisenhower, they remained loyal to the Democratic Party. The voters gave the Democrats control of both houses of Congress. Lyndon B. Johnson of Texas became the Senate's new majority leader. Johnson worked with the Republican White House to pass legislation, including the Highway Act of 1956, which authorized the construction over the next thirteen years of an interstate highway system. In 1955 Eisenhower suffered a heart attack, but he regained his strength and declared his intention to run again. The Democrats nominated Adlai E. Stevenson once more. Eisenhower won by a landslide, but the Democrats continued to dominate Congress.

Election of 1956

Eisenhower faced rising federal expenditures in his second term, in part because of the tremendous expense of America's global activities. In 1959 federal expenditures climbed to $92 billion, about half of which went to the military. Though opposed to deficit spending, Eisenhower balanced only three of his eight budgets. The administration's resort to deficit spending also was fueled by the need to cushion the impact of three recessions.

Setbacks in 1958 made that year a low point for the Eisenhower administration. Scandal unsettled the White House when the president's chief aide, Sherman Adams, resigned under suspicion of influencing government regulatory decisions in exchange for luxury gifts such as a fur coat. Then came large Republican losses in the 1958 congressional elections. The Democrats took the Senate by 64 seats to 34 and the House by 283 seats to 153.

Assessments of the Eisenhower administration used to emphasize its conservatism, passive style, limited achievements, and reluctance to confront difficult issues. Current evaluations, however, often stress Eisenhower's command of policymaking, sensibly moderate approach to most problems, political savvy, and great popularity. Eisenhower is now viewed as a competent, pragmatic leader.

Eisenhower Presidency Assessed

The record of Eisenhower's presidency is nonetheless mixed. At home he failed to deal with poverty, urban decay, and blatant denials of civil rights. He kept military budgets under control and managed crises adroitly so that the United States avoided major military ventures abroad. But he authorized the Central Intelligence Agency (CIA) to undertake covert actions to overthrow elected governments in Iran and Guatemala. At home the Eisenhower administration curbed inflation, strengthened the infrastructure by building an interstate highway system, and expanded Social Security coverage. Eisenhower brought dignity to the presidency.

Just before leaving office in early 1961, Eisenhower went on national radio and television to deliver his farewell address to the nation. Because of the Cold War, he observed, the United States had been "compelled to create a permanent industry of vast proportions," as well as a standing army of 3.5 million. "This conjunction of an immense military establishment and a large arms industry is new in the American experience," Eisenhower noted. "The total influence . . . is felt in every city, every statehouse, every office of the

The "Military-Industrial Complex"

federal government." So powerful was this influence, the president declared, that it threatened the nation's democratic processes. Then Eisenhower issued a direct warning, urging Americans to "guard against . . . the military-industrial complex." They did not.

McCarthyism

 One of the most volatile political issues in postwar America was the anti-Communist crusade known as McCarthyism. Both Truman and Eisenhower overreacted to the alleged threat of Communist subversion in government.

It is a misconception that anticommunism began in 1950 with the furious speeches of Senator Joseph R. McCarthy of Wisconsin. Actually, anticommunism had been a prominent strand in the American political fabric ever since the First World War and the Red Scare of 1919 and 1920. The Cold War heightened anti-Communist fears. In manipulating these fears to his own advantage, Joe McCarthy became the most successful and frightening redbaiter the country had ever seen.

Was there reason to fear Communist influence in the United States in the 1940s and 1950s? During the Second World War the United States voluntarily supplied valuable military intelligence to its Soviet ally. In addition, however, documents selectively released in the 1990s from Russian archives suggest not only that Soviet spies had penetrated America's top-secret Manhattan Project to build the atomic bomb, but also that a handful of Americans working in sensitive government departments had provided classified documents to Soviet espionage agents. Was the Communist Party of the United States of America a tool of the Soviet Union? Its leaders were, but as the historian Ellen Schrecker has observed, the party "was both subservient to the Kremlin and genuinely dedicated to a wide range of social reforms," such as the elimination of racism in America.

President Truman shared responsibility for initiating the postwar anti-Communist crusade. He was bothered by the revelation in 1945 that classified government documents had been found in a raid on the offices of *Amerasia*, a little-known magazine whose editors sympathized with the Communist revolution in China. Who had supplied the documents to the maga-

zine, and why? Similar concerns greeted the release of a Canadian royal commission report in 1946, which asserted that Soviet spies were operating in Canada.

Spurred by these revelations, Truman in 1947 ordered investigations into the loyalty of the more than 3 million employees of the U.S. government. In 1950 the government began discharging people deemed "security risks," among them alcoholics, homosexuals, and debtors thought to be susceptible to blackmail. Others became victims of guilt by association. Their loyalty was considered questionable because they either knew or were related to people thought to be subversive or disloyal. Soon Americans of many political persuasions were using allegations of being "soft on communism" to discredit their opponents.

Truman's Loyalty Probe

Finger pointing spread across the land. Hollywood film personalities who had been ardent left-wingers such as Will Geer and Zero Mostel were blacklisted and could not find work in the movies; and ten screenwriters and directors (the "Hollywood Ten") were sent to prison for contempt of Congress when they refused to provide names of alleged Communists. Schoolteachers and college professors were fired for expressing dissenting viewpoints. Even the CIO expelled eleven unions, with a combined membership of over 900,000, for alleged communist domination. Anti-Communists also exploited the hysteria to drive homosexuals from their jobs. "Sexual perverts have infiltrated our government in recent years," warned the Republican national chairman in 1950.

Victims of Anti-Communist Hysteria

Despite the rampant false accusations, there was cause for anxiety. In 1949 a former State Department official, Alger Hiss, was on trial for perjury for swearing to a grand jury that he had never passed classified documents to his accuser, former American Communist spy Whittaker Chambers, and that he in fact had not seen Chambers since 1936. When Truman and Secretary of State Dean Acheson came to Hiss's defense, some people began to suspect that the Democrats had something to hide. In early 1950 Hiss was convicted of perjury. At the same time, a British court sentenced and sent to prison Klaus

Hiss Case

Fuchs, a nuclear scientist and Nazi refugee, for turning over to Soviet agents secrets from the atomic bomb project at Los Alamos, New Mexico.

It was in this bedeviled atmosphere that Senator Joseph McCarthy mounted a rostrum in Wheeling, West Virginia, in February 1950 and gave a name to the hysteria: McCarthyism. "The State Department," he asserted, was "thoroughly infested with Communists." The senator claimed to have a list of 205 Communists working in the department; McCarthy later lowered the figure to "57 card-carrying members," then raised it to 81. But the number did not matter. What McCarthy needed was a winning campaign issue, and he had found it. Republicans, distraught over losing the 1948 presidential election, were eager to support his attack.

McCarthy's Attack on the State Department

McCarthy and McCarthyism gained momentum throughout 1950. Nothing seemed to slow the senator down, not even attacks by other Republicans. Seven Republican senators, led by Maine's Margaret Chase Smith, broke with their colleagues in 1950 and publicly condemned McCarthy for his "selfish political exploitation of fear, bigotry, ignorance, and intolerance"; a Senate committee reported that his charges against the State Department were "a fraud and a hoax." But McCarthy had much to sustain him, including Julius and Ethel Rosenberg's 1950 arrest for conspiracy to commit espionage. During the war, they allegedly had recruited and supervised a spy who worked at the Los Alamos atomic laboratory. Perhaps even more helpful to McCarthy than the Rosenberg case was the outbreak of the Korean War in June 1950.

Widespread support for anti-Communist measures was also apparent in the adoption, over Truman's veto, of the Internal Security (McCarran) Act of 1950, which required members of "Communist-front" organizations to register with the government and prohibited them from holding defense jobs or traveling abroad. In a telling decision in 1951 (*Dennis et al. v. U.S.*), the Supreme Court upheld the Smith Act of 1940, under which eleven Communist Party leaders had been convicted and imprisoned.

The conduct of Senator Joseph R. McCarthy was one of the most vexing problems facing Eisenhower's first administration. The Wisconsin senator's search

Eisenhower's Reluctance to Confront McCarthy

for subversives in government turned up none and was an affront to political fair play, decency, and civil liberties. However, Eisenhower, fearing that a showdown would splinter the Republican Party, avoided confronting McCarthy. Instead, he hoped the media and Congress would bring McCarthy down.

Meanwhile, the Eisenhower administration practiced its own brand of anticommunism. A new executive order in 1953 expanded the criteria under which federal workers could be dismissed as "security risks." One of Eisenhower's most controversial decisions was his denial of clemency to Julius and Ethel Rosenberg, who had two young sons. The Rosenbergs, having been sentenced to death, were executed in 1953. In 1954 both liberals and conservatives helped enact the Communist Control Act, which in effect made membership in the Communist Party illegal.

As for Senator McCarthy, he made a crucial mistake by taking on the U.S. Army in front of millions of television viewers. At issue was the senator's wild accusation that the army was shielding and promoting Communists. The so-called Army-McCarthy hearings, held by a Senate subcommittee in 1954, became a showcase for the senator's abusive treatment of witnesses. McCarthy, apparently drunk, alternately ranted and slurred his words. Finally, after he maligned a young lawyer who was not even involved in the hearings, army counsel Joseph Welch protested, "Have you no sense of decency, sir?" The gallery erupted in applause, and McCarthy's career as a witch-hunter was over. The Senate finally condemned McCarthy for sullying the dignity of the Senate. He remained a senator, but exhaustion and alcohol took their toll. McCarthy died in 1957 at the age of forty-eight.

Army-McCarthy Hearings

Eisenhower's reluctance to discredit McCarthy publicly had given the senator, other right-wing members of Congress, and some private and public institutions enough rein to divide the nation and destroy the careers of many innocent people. The anti-Communist campaigns of the 1950s also discouraged people from freely expressing themselves and hence from debating critical issues. Fear, in short, helped sustain the Cold War consensus.

The Civil Rights Movement in the 1940s and 1950s

Ironically, Cold War pressures benefited the civil rights movement. The United States, after all, could hardly pose as the leader of the free world or condemn the denial of human rights in the Soviet sphere while practicing segregation at home. Nor could the United States convince new African and Asian nations of its dedication to human rights if African Americans were subjected to segregation, discrimination, disfranchisement, and racial violence. To win the support of nonaligned nations, the United States would have to live up to its own ideals.

African Americans who had helped win the Second World War were determined to improve their lives in postwar America. And because in the 1940s more than a million African Americans migrated from the South to the North and West, they had in some urban-industrial states begun to control the political "balance of power." Harry Truman and other politicians knew they would have to compete for the growing African American vote in California, New York, Illinois, Michigan, Pennsylvania, and other large states.

African Americans' Political "Balance of Power"

President Truman also felt a moral obligation to do something, for he genuinely believed it was only fair that every American should enjoy the full rights of citizenship. Truman also was disturbed by the resurgence of a revived Ku Klux Klan. But what really horrified Truman was the report that police in Aiken, South Carolina, had gouged out the eyes of a black sergeant just three hours after he had been discharged from the army. Several weeks later, in December 1946, Truman signed an executive order establishing the President's Committee on Civil Rights.

The committee's report, *To Secure These Rights* (1947), would become the agenda for the civil rights movement for the next twenty years. Among its recommendations were the enactment of federal antilynching and antisegregation legislation. *To Secure These Rights* also called for laws guaranteeing voting rights and

President Truman's Committee on Civil Rights

equal employment opportunity and for the establishment of a permanent commission on civil rights. Although Congress failed to act, Truman's action was still significant. For the first time since Reconstruction, a president had acknowledged the federal government's responsibility to protect blacks and strive for racial equality.

Truman took this responsibility seriously, and in 1948 he issued two executive orders declaring an end to racial discrimination in the federal government. One proclaimed a policy of "fair employment throughout the federal establishment" and created the Employment Board of the Civil Service Commission to hear charges of discrimination. The other ordered the racial desegregation of the armed forces.

African Americans also benefited from a series of Supreme Court decisions. The trend toward judicial support of civil rights had begun in the late 1930s, when the NAACP established its Legal Defense Fund. In the 1940s and 1950s, NAACP attorneys set out to destroy the separate-but-equal doctrine by insisting on its literal interpretation. In higher education, the NAACP calculated, the cost of true equality in racially separate schools would be prohibitive. As a result of NAACP lawsuits, African American students won admission to professional and graduate schools at a number of state universities. In *Smith v. Allwright* (1944), the Supreme Court also outlawed the whites-only primaries held by the Democratic Party in some southern states, branding them a violation of the Fifteenth Amendment's guarantee of the right to vote. Two years later the Court struck down segregation in interstate bus transportation (*Morgan v. Virginia*). And in *Shelley v. Kraemer* (1948), the Court held that racially restrictive covenants (private agreements among white homeowners not to sell to blacks) violated the equal protection clause of the Fourteenth Amendment.

Supreme Court Decisions on Civil Rights

A change in social attitudes accompanied these gains in black political and legal power. Books like Gunnar Myrdal's social science study *An American Dilemma* (1944) and Richard Wright's novels *Native Son* (1940) and *Black Boy* (1945) were increasing white awareness of the social injustices that plagued African Americans. A new black middle class was emerging, composed of college-educated activists, war veterans, and union workers. Blacks and whites also worked together in CIO unions and service organizations such as the National Council of Churches. In 1947 a black baseball player, Jackie Robinson, broke the major league color barrier.

In 1954 the NAACP won a historic victory that stunned the white South and energized African Americans. *Brown v. Board of Education of Topeka* incorporated cases from several states, all involving segregated schools. Written by chief justice Earl Warren, the Court's unanimous decision concluded that "in the field of public education the doctrine of 'separate but equal' has no place. Separate educational facilities are inherently unequal." Such facilities, Warren wrote, deprived black children of "the equal protection of the laws guaranteed by the Fourteenth Amendment." But the Court's implementation decree in 1955 ordered desegregation to proceed "with all deliberate speed." The lack of a timetable encouraged the southern states to resist.

Brown v. Board of Education of Topeka

Some communities quietly implemented the order, and many southern moderates advocated a gradual rollback of segregation. But the forces of white resistance urged southern communities to defy the Court. The Klan experienced another resurgence, and business and professional people created White Citizens' Councils for the express purpose of resisting the order. Known familiarly as "uptown Ku Klux Klans," the councils brought their economic power to bear against black civil rights activists. One of the most effective resistance tactics was enactment of state laws that paid the private-school tuition of white children who had left public schools to avoid integration. In some cases, desegregated public schools were ordered closed.

White Resistance to Civil Rights

President Eisenhower wanted to avoid dealing with civil rights, preferring instead gradual and voluntary change in race relations. Although he personally disapproved of segregation, he objected to "compulsory federal law" in the belief that race relations would improve "only if it starts locally." He also feared that the ugly public confrontations likely to follow rapid desegregation would jeopardize Republican inroads in the South. Thus Eisenhower did not state forthrightly that the federal government would enforce the Court's decision and thereby tacitly encouraged white noncompliance.

Events in Little Rock, Arkansas, forced the president to stop sidestepping the issue. In September 1957 Governor Orval E. Faubus intervened to defy a court-ordered desegregation plan for Little Rock's Central High School. Faubus ordered the Arkansas National Guard to block the entry of black students. Eisenhower made no effort to impede Faubus's actions. Later that month, bowing to a federal judge's order, Faubus withdrew the guardsmen. As hundreds of jeering whites threatened to storm the school, eight black teenagers entered Central High. The next day, fearing violence, Eisenhower dispatched army paratroopers to Little Rock to ensure the black students' safety. In 1958 and 1959 Little Rock officials closed all public high schools rather than desegregate them.

Crisis in Little Rock, Arkansas

Elsewhere, African Americans did not wait for Supreme Court or White House decisions to claim equal rights. In 1955 Rosa Parks, a department store seamstress and active member of the NAACP, was arrested for refusing to give up her seat to a white man on a public bus in Montgomery, Alabama. Local black women's organizations and civil rights groups decided to boycott the city's bus system, and they elected Martin Luther King, Jr., a recently ordained minister who had just arrived in Montgomery, as their leader.

Montgomery Bus Boycott

Martin Luther King, Jr., was a twenty-six-year-old Baptist minister who recently had earned a Ph.D. at Boston University. Disciplined and analytical, he was committed to nonviolent protest in the spirit of India's leader Mohandas K. Gandhi. In 1957 King became the first president of the Southern Christian Leadership Conference, organized to coordinate civil rights activities.

Martin Luther King, Jr.

During the year-long Montgomery bus boycott, King urged perseverance, and, bolstered by a Supreme Court decision that declared Alabama's bus segregation laws unconstitutional, Montgomery blacks triumphed in 1956. They and others across the nation were further heartened when Congress passed the

Civil Rights Act of 1957, which created the United States Commission on Civil Rights to investigate systematic discrimination, such as voting discrimination. But this measure, like a voting rights act passed three years later, proved ineffective.

African Americans responded by launching a campaign of sit-ins in the South. In February 1960 four

Sit-ins

black students from North Carolina Agricultural and Technical College in Greensboro ordered coffee at a dime-store lunch counter. Told they would not be served, the students refused to budge. Thus began the sit-in movement. Inspired by the sit-ins, southern black college and high-school students met on Easter weekend in 1960 and organized the Stu-dent Nonviolent Coordinating Committee (SNCC). In the face of angry white mobs, SNCC members challenged the status quo.

King personally joined the sit-in movement, and in October 1960 he was arrested at a sit-in to desegre-

Civil Rights and the 1960 Election

gate an Atlanta snack bar. Sent to a cold, cockroach-infested state penitentiary where he faced four months at hard labor, he became ill. As an apathetic Eisenhower White House looked on, Senator John F. Kennedy, the Democratic presidential candidate, called King's wife, Coretta Scott King, to express support; and his brother, Robert F. Kennedy, persuaded the sentencing judge to release King on bond.

For leading the movement to gain equality for blacks riding city buses in Montgomery, Alabama, Martin Luther King, Jr. (1929–1968), and other African Americans, including twenty-three other ministers, were indicted by an all-white jury for violating an old law banning boycotts. In late March 1956 King was convicted and fined $500. A crowd of well-wishers cheered a smiling King (here with his wife, Coretta) outside the courthouse, where King proudly declared, "The protest goes on!" King's arrest and conviction made the bus boycott front-page news across America.   (Corbis-Bettmann)

The Postwar Booms: Babies, Business, and Bigness

 The postwar economic boom proved to be one of the longest periods of growth and prosperity the United States ever experienced. Its keys were increasing output and increasing demand. Despite occasional recessions the gross national product more than doubled between 1945 and 1961.

The Affluent Society

The Harvard economist John Kenneth Galbraith gave a name to the United States during the postwar economic boom: the "affluent society." As U.S. productivity increased in the postwar years, so did Americans' appetite for goods and services. In the flush postwar years, Americans bought as never before. Some families purchased two cars and equipped their new homes with the latest appliances and amusements, such as television. Easy credit was the economic basis of the consumer culture; when people lacked cash to buy what they wanted, they borrowed money.

Increased Purchasing Power

When the economy produced more, Americans generally brought home bigger paychecks and had more money to spend. Between the end of the war and 1950, per capita real income (based on actual purchasing power) rose 6 percent. In the 1950s it jumped another 15 percent, and in the 1960s the increase was 32 percent. The result was a noticeable increase in the standard of living. To the vast majority of Americans, such prosperity was a vindication of the American system of free enterprise.

Baby Boom

The baby boom was both a cause and an effect of prosperity. After the war the birth rate soared, and it continued to do so throughout the 1950s. During the 1950s, the number of births exceeded 4 million per year, reversing the downward trend in birth rates that had prevailed for 150 years. Births began to decline after 1961 but continued to exceed 4 million per year through 1964. The baby-boom generation was the largest by far in the nation's history.

The baby boom meant business for builders, manufacturers, and school systems. "Take the 3,548,000 babies born in 1950," wrote Sylvia F. Porter in her syndicated newspaper column. "Bundle them into a batch, bounce them all over the bountiful land that is America. What do you get?" Porter's answer: "Boom. The biggest, boomiest boom ever known in history."

Of the three cornerstones of the postwar economic boom—construction, automobiles, and defense—two were directly related to the upsurge in births. Demand for housing and schools for all these children generated a building boom, furthered by construction of shopping centers, office buildings, and airports. Much of this construction took place in the suburbs. The postwar suburbanization of America in turn would have been impossible without automobile manufacturing, for the car provided access to the sprawling new communities.

Housing Boom

Government funding helped new families to settle in the suburbs. Low-interest GI mortgages and Federal Housing Administration (FHA) mortgage insurance made the difference for people who otherwise would have been unable to afford a home. This easy credit, combined with postwar prosperity, produced a construction boom. From 1945 to 1946, housing starts climbed from 326,000 to more than 1 million; they approached 2 million in 1950 and remained above 1.3 million in 1961. Never before had new starts exceeded 1 million.

Highway Construction

As suburbia spread, pastures became neighborhoods with astounding rapidity. Highway construction was a central element in the transformation of rural land into suburbia. In 1947 Congress authorized construction of a 37,000-mile chain of highways, and in 1956 President Eisenhower signed the Highway Act, which approved funds for a 42,500-mile interstate highway system. Federal expenditures on highways swelled from $79 million in 1946 to $2.6 billion in 1961. State and local spending on highways also mushroomed. Highways both hastened suburbanization and homogenized the landscape. The high-speed trucking that highways made possible also accelerated the integration of the South into the national economy.

In the twenty-five years after the war, a mass movement was under way from the cities to the suburbs. By 1970 more people lived in suburbs than in

Growth of the Suburbs

cities or in rural areas. A combination of motives drew people to the suburbs. Some wanted to leave behind the noise and smells of the city. Some white families moved out of urban neighborhoods because African American families were moving in. Many wanted houses that had yards, family rooms, extra closets, and utility rooms. People were also looking for a place where they could have a measure of political influence, particularly on the education their children received.

Highway construction in combination with the growth of suburbia produced a new phenomenon, the *megalopolis*, a term coined in the early 1960s to refer to the almost uninterrupted metropolitan complex stretching from Boston 600 miles south through New York, Philadelphia, and Baltimore all the way to Washington, D.C. "Boswash" encompassed parts of eleven states and a population of 49 million people, all linked by interstate highways. Other megalopolises also took shape.

Millions of Americans began their search for affluence by migrating to the Sunbelt—roughly, the southern third of the United States. The

Growth of the Sunbelt

mass migration to the Sunbelt had started during the war, when GIs and their families were ordered to new duty stations and war workers moved to defense plants in the West and South. The economic bases of the Sunbelt's spectacular growth were defense contractors, such as the aerospace industry, agribusiness, the oil industry, real-estate development, and recreation. Industry was drawn to the southern rim by right-to-work laws, which outlawed closed shops, and by low taxes. Government policies—generous tax breaks for oil companies, siting of military bases, and awarding of defense and aerospace contracts—were crucial to the Sunbelt's development.

The third cornerstone of the postwar economic boom was military spending. Between 1947 and 1961

Military Spending

the annual defense budget increased from $10 billion to $98 billion. Many defense contracts went to industries and universities to develop weapons, and the government supported space research. Defense spending also helped stimulate rapid advances in the electronics industry. The ENIAC com-

puter, completed at the University of Pennsylvania in 1946, required 18,000 vacuum tubes. Then, in the 1950s, introduction of the transistor accelerated the computer revolution; the silicon microchip in the 1960s inaugurated even more stunning advances in electronics. The microchip facilitated the shift from heavy manufacturing to high-technology industries in fiber optics, lasers, video equipment, robotics, and genetic engineering.

The evolution of electronics meant a large-scale tradeoff for the American people. As industries automated, computerized processes replaced slower mechanical ones, increasing productivity but pushing people out of jobs. Electronic technology also promoted concentration of ownership in industry. Sophisticated technology was expensive, and small corporations were shut out of the market. Indeed, large corporations with capital and experience in high-tech fields expanded into related industries.

Corporate expansion was also marked by a third great wave of mergers. The first two such movements, in the 1890s and 1920s, had tended

Conglomerate Mergers

toward vertical and horizontal integration, respectively. The postwar era was distinguished by conglomerate mergers. A *conglomerate* brings together companies in unrelated industries as a hedge against instability in a particular market. International Telephone and Telegraph (IT&T), for instance, bought up companies in several fields, including suburban development, insurance, and hotels.

The labor movement also experienced a postwar merger. In 1955 the American Federation of Labor and the Congress of Industrial Orga-

Labor Merger

nizations finally put aside their differences and formed the AFL-CIO. Union membership grew slowly during the postwar years, increasing from 14.8 million in 1945 to 17.3 million in 1961. The main reason for the slow growth of union membership was a shift in employment patterns. Most new jobs were being created not in the heavy industries that hired blue-collar workers but in the union-resistant white-collar service trades.

The postwar economic boom was good for unionized blue-collar workers, many of whom won real increases in wages sufficient to enjoy a middle-class lifestyle that previously had been the exclusive province of white-collar workers and professionals. And they were more protected against inflation: in 1948 General Motors and the United Auto Workers agreed on automatic cost-of-living adjustments (COLAs) in workers' wages, a practice that spread to other industries.

The trend toward economic consolidation also changed agriculture. By the 1960s it took money—

Agribusiness

sometimes big money—to become a farmer. In many regions only banks, insurance companies, and large businesses could afford the necessary land, machinery, and fertilizer. The movement toward consolidation threatened the survival of the family farm. From 1945 to 1961 the nation's farm population declined from 24.4 million to 14.8 million.

Rapid economic growth also exacted environmental costs, to which most Americans were oblivious.

Environmental Costs

Steel mills, coal-powered generators, and internal-combustion car engines polluted the air and imperiled people's health. America's water supplies suffered as well. Human and industrial waste befouled many rivers and lakes. And the extraction of natural resources—strip mining of coal, for example—scarred the landscape, and toxic waste from chemical plants seeped deep into the soil.

Defense contractors and farmers were among the country's worst polluters. Refuse from nuclear weapons facilities polluted soil and water resources for years. Agriculture began employing massive amounts of pesticides and other chemicals. A chemical called DDT, for example, which had been used on Pacific islands during the war to kill mosquitoes and lice, was released for public use in 1945. During the next fifteen years, farmers eliminated chronic pests with DDT. In 1962, however, *Silent Spring* by Rachel Carson, a wildlife biologist, specifically indicted DDT for the deaths of mammals, birds, and fish. Because of Carson's book, many Americans finally realized that there were costs to human conquest of the environment. The federal government finally banned the sale of DDT in 1972.

But America had become a "throwaway" society. With its plastic cups, paper plates, disposable diapers, and products—especially cars—that were intentionally made less durable than they might have been, Americans used a disproportionate amount of the world's resources. By the 1960s the United States, with only 5 percent of the world's population, produced and consumed more than one-third of the world's goods and services.

Conformity and Consumerism

For the generation of adults in postwar America, the suburban home became a refuge, and family togetherness fulfilled a psychological need. But sociologists and other critics denounced the suburbs for breeding conformity and status seeking. William H. Whyte's *The Organization Man* (1956), a study of Park Forest, Illinois, pronounced these suburbanites mindless conservatives and extreme conformists. And the sociologist C. Wright Mills castigated white-collar suburbanites who "sell not only their time and energy but their personalities as well." Nonetheless, most residents of suburbia preferred their lifestyle to any other of which they were aware.

Education at all levels was a pressing concern for families in postwar America. Immediately after the

Pressures in Education

Second World War, for example, many former GIs took advantage of the Servicemen's Readjustment Act of 1944 (GI Bill of Rights) and enrolled in college. The law provided them living allowances and tuition payments. Over 1 million veterans enrolled in 1946—accounting for one out of every two students. The downside of this success story was that colleges made places for male veterans by turning away qualified women.

As the baby boom became a grade-school boom in the 1950s, American families became preoccupied with the education of their children. Convinced that success in school was a prerequisite for success in adult life, parents joined parent-teacher associations so they would have a voice in the educational process. Then in 1957 education became a matter of national security. In that year the Soviet Union launched *Sputnik*, the first earth-orbiting satellite. Congress responded in 1958 with the National Defense Education Act (NDEA), which funded enrichment of elementary and high-school programs in mathematics, foreign languages, and the sciences, and offered fellowships and loans to college students.

As education became intertwined with national security, so religion became a matter of patriotism.

Growth of Religion

As President Eisenhower put it, "Recognition of the Supreme Being is the first, the most basic expression of Americanism." In America's Cold War with an atheistic enemy, religious leaders emphasized traditional values like family togetherness. The Bible topped the bestseller list, and membership in religious congregations increased from 71.7 million in 1945 to 116 million in 1961.

The postwar religious revival was also spurred by the introduction of a revolutionary influence in American life: television. The evangelist

Television Togetherness

Billy Graham, who preached in stadiums throughout the country, and Catholic Bishop Fulton J. Sheen could reach mass audiences on television. Most important, television transformed family life in America. "More than a year passed before we again visited a movie theater. . . . Social evenings with friends became fewer and fewer still because we discovered we did not share the same television program interests," recalled a man whose parents bought their first television set in 1950.

Television was a crucial force in the evolution of both the consumer culture and family togetherness. TV told people what to buy; and as families strove to acquire the latest luxuries and conveniences, shopping became a form of recreation. TV's number-one product was entertainment, and situation comedies and action series were among the most popular shows. But as average TV-viewing time reached five hours a day in 1956, critics worried that TV's distorted presentation of the world would significantly define people's sense of reality.

In 1946 the anthropologist Margaret Mead reflected on society's contradictory expectations of

Women's Conflicting Roles and Dilemmas

American women. On the one hand, the home was premised on a full-time housewife who, with little regard for her own needs, provided her husband and children with a cozy haven from the outside world. On the other hand, women continued to

enter the labor force for a variety of reasons. Indeed, the female labor force rose from 19.3 million in 1945 to 31.6 million in 1970. Despite the cult of motherhood, most new entrants to the job market were married mothers (see Figure 28.1).

Women's responsibilities also increased at home after the war. Some of the change was due to the publication of Dr. Benjamin Spock's *Baby and Child Care* (1946). Spock urged mothers always to think of their children first (he assigned fathers little formal role in

Figure 28.1 Marital Distribution of the Female Labor Force, 1944–1970 The composition of the female labor force changed dramatically from 1944 to 1970. In 1944, 41 percent of women in the labor force were single; in 1970, only 22 percent were single. During the same years, the percentage of the female labor force that had a husband in the home jumped from 34 to 59. The percentage who were widowed or divorced remained about the same from 1944 to 1970. (Source: Adapted from U.S. Bureau of the Census, *Historical Statistics of the United States, Colonial Times to 1970*, 2 parts [Washington, D.C., U.S. Government Printing Office, 1975], p. 133.)

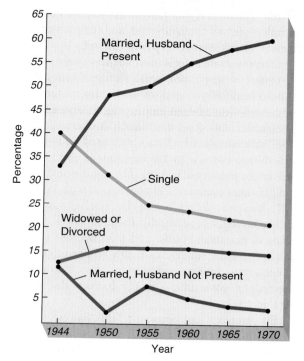

child rearing). Following Dr. Spock's advice, millions of women tried to be mother, teacher, psychologist, and playmate to their children. If they "failed" in any of these roles, guilt frequently was the outcome.

On the other hand, the social critic Philip Wylie denounced such selfless behavior as "Momism." In the guise of sacrificing for her children, Wylie wrote in *Generation of Vipers* (1942, revised 1955), Mom was pursuing "love of herself." She smothered her children with affection to make them emotionally dependent on her and reluctant to leave home. Other critics, however, considered women who pursued lives outside the home to be "feminist neurotics" or "imitation men."

In postwar America, there was a wide gap between sexual behavior and public discourse on the subject.

Sexuality

When Dr. Alfred Kinsey, director of the Institute for Sex Research at Indiana University, published his pioneering study *Sexual Behavior in the Human Male* (1948), the American public was shocked. Five years later Kinsey caused an uproar with *Sexual Behavior in the Human Female*, which claimed that 62 percent of his subjects masturbated and 50 percent had had intercourse before marriage.

Family, church, state, and media alike warned Americans that sex outside marriage was wrong and that premarital, extramarital, and homosexual behavior would bring "familial chaos and weaken the country's moral fiber." Women often were blamed for the impending disaster; despite any evidence of significant increases in women's sexual activity from the 1920s to the 1960s, female lust was perceived to pose a threat to the future of the family. Thus from Momism to promiscuity, American women were the victims of male-inspired stereotypes.

There was confusion for girls, too, in postwar America. Motherhood was venerated in American society, but a 1962 Gallup poll revealed that only 10 percent of mothers wanted their daughters to emulate them. Some urged their daughters to develop personally fulfilling and economically independent lives. It is clear that the seeds of feminist protest in the later 1960s and 1970s were planted during the postwar years.

During the postwar years, a distinctive youth subculture emerged. Bored with the era's syrupy music,

The Youth Subculture

young Americans were electrified by the driving energy and hard beat of Bill Haley and the Comets, Chuck Berry, Little Richard, and Buddy Holly. Although few white musicians acknowledged the debt, the roots of rock 'n' roll lay in African American rhythm and blues.

The motion picture industry also catered to teenagers. From 1946 to 1948, Americans had attended movies at the rate of nearly 90 million a week, but by 1960 the number had dropped to 40 million. The postwar years saw the steady closing of movie theaters. Teenagers were the one exception to the downturn in moviegoing. By the late 1950s the first wave of the postwar baby boom had reached adolescence, and teens and young adults were flocking to the theaters. Hollywood catered to this new audience with films portraying young people as sensitive and insightful, adults as boorish and hostile. *Rebel Without a Cause* (1955), starring James Dean, was one such movie. The cult of youth had been born.

Consumerism, which was crucial to the cult of youth, was also strikingly evident in Americans' postwar play and in the era's fads. Slinky began loping down people's stairs in 1947; Silly Putty was introduced in 1950; and 3-D movies and Hula-Hoops were all the rage. Another postwar activity was the family vacation. With more money and leisure time and a much-improved highway system, middle-class families took vacations that formerly had been restricted to the rich.

The consumer society was unreceptive to social criticism. Even serious artists tended to ignore the country's social problems. But there were exceptions. Ralph Ellison's *Invisible Man* (1952) gave white Americans a glimpse of the psychic costs to black Americans of exclusion from the American Dream. And one group of writers noisily repudiated the materialistic and self-congratulatory world of the middle class and the suburbs. Beat (for "beatific") writers rejected literary conventions and in the face of middle-class conformity flaunted their freewheeling sexuality and consumption of drugs. The Beats produced some memorable prose and poetry, including Allen Ginsberg's angry incantational poem *Howl* (1956) and Jack Kerouac's novel *On the Road* (1957).

Beat Generation

Although the Beats were largely ignored during the 1950s, millions of young Americans discovered their writings and imitated their lifestyle in the 1960s.

The Other America

In an age of abundance and rampant consumerism, most Americans dismissed poverty, if they noticed it at all, as the fault of poor people themselves. But by 1961 nearly one of every four Americans was poor. Age, race, gender, education, and marital status were all factors in their poverty. One-fourth of the poor were over age sixty-five. One-fifth were people of color. Two-thirds lived in households headed by a person with an eighth-grade education or less, one-fourth in households headed by a single woman. More than one-third were under age eighteen. Few of these people had much reason for hope.

A disproportionate number of the poor in postwar America were women. Occupational segregation was pervasive, relegating many women to low-paying jobs as laundresses, short-order cooks, and janitors. Median annual earnings for full-time women workers stood at 60 percent of men's earnings in 1960. Moreover, many women's jobs were not covered by either the minimum wage or Social Security. And if the family broke up, the woman was usually left with responsibility for the children. Many divorced fathers evaded their regular child-support payments. Single mothers and their children, dependent on welfare or low wages, more often than not slipped into poverty.

Women

While millions of Americans (most of them white) were settling in the suburbs, the poor were congregating in the inner cities, including African Americans who had migrated from the South. Joining African Americans in the exodus to the cities were poor whites from the southern Appalachians. Meanwhile, Latin Americans were arriving in growing numbers from Mexico, the Dominican Republic, Colombia, Ecuador, and Cuba. And New York City's Puerto Rican population exploded.

The Inner Cities

Second only to African Americans in numbers of urban newcomers were Mexican Americans. Millions came as farm workers during and after the Second World War. Despite the initiation in 1953 of Opera-

John F. Kennedy is surrounded by supporters and the press as he arrives for the 1960 Democratic National Convention in Los Angeles. Young, handsome, and articulate, Kennedy introduced new vitality, and perhaps superficiality, into political campaigning. On television and in person, Kennedy was a popular politician; when he became president, he became a media star as well. (Wide World Photos, Inc.)

tion Wetback, a federal program to find and deport illegal aliens, Mexicans continued to enter the country in large numbers, many of them illegally. Most settled in cities. According to the 1960 census, over a half-million Mexican Americans had migrated to the *barrios* of the Los Angeles–Long Beach area since 1940. Estimates of uncounted illegal aliens suggest that the actual total was far higher. The same was true in the *barrios* in southwestern and northern cities.

Native Americans, whose average annual income was barely half of the poverty level, were the country's poorest people. Many Native Americans moved to the cities in the 1950s and 1960s. Accustomed to semi-communal rural life on the reservation, many had difficulty adjusting to the urban environment. Like other migrant groups, they found cities to be dumping grounds for the poor.

Not all of the poor, however, lived in cities. In 1960, 30 percent of the poor still lived in small towns, 15 percent on farms. Tenant farmers **Rural Poverty** and sharecroppers, both black and white, continued to suffer severe economic hardship. Migratory farm workers lived in abject poverty. In postwar America, elderly people tended to be poor regardless of where they lived.

With the publication of Michael Harrington's *The Other America* in 1962, people became aware of the contradiction of poverty in their midst. America's poor, wrote Harrington, were "the strangest poor in the history of mankind," for they "exist within the most powerful and rich society the world has ever known."

The Election of 1960 and the Dawning of a New Decade

The election of 1960 was one of the closest and most hard-fought in the twentieth century. The forty-three-year-old Democratic candidate, Senator John F. Kennedy, injected new vigor and glamour into presidential politics. The Republican candidate was Richard M. Nixon, the forty-seven-year-old two-term vice president from California.

Kennedy's major liability with voters was his Roman Catholicism. He addressed the issue head-on by going to the Bible belt, where he told a group of Houston ministers that he respected the separation of church and state and would take his orders from the American people, not the pope. Seeing opportunity in the African American vote and calculating that his running mate Senator Lyndon B. Johnson of Texas could keep the white South loyal to the Democrats, Kennedy courted black voters. Foreign policy was another major issue. Nixon claimed that he alone knew how to deal with Communists, but Kennedy countered that Eisenhower and Nixon had let American prestige and power erode, and he promised victory instead of stalemate in the Cold War. Kennedy subscribed to the two

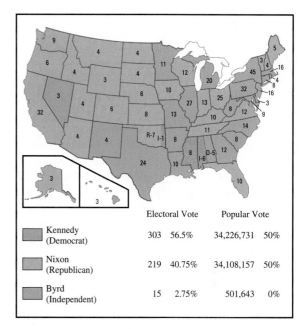

	Electoral Vote		Popular Vote	
Kennedy (Democrat)	303	56.5%	34,226,731	50%
Nixon (Republican)	219	40.75%	34,108,157	50%
Byrd (Independent)	15	2.75%	501,643	0%

Map 28.1   Presidential Election, 1960   In one of the closest presidential elections in twentieth-century America, John F. Kennedy defeated Richard Nixon. In fact, Nixon won the popular votes of twenty-six states to Kennedy's twenty-four. In the electoral college, fifteen southerners voted for neither Kennedy nor Nixon but cast protest votes for Harry F. Byrd, a conservative senator from Virginia.

fundamental tenets of the postwar consensus—economic growth and anticommunism—and asserted that he could expand the benefits of economic progress and win foreign disputes through more vigorous leadership. And in the nation's first televised presidential debates, Nixon looked unsavory. He came across as heavy-jowled and surly.

In an election characterized by the highest voter participation (63 percent) in a half-century, Kennedy defeated Nixon by the razor-slim margin of 118,000 votes (see Map 28.1). Slight shifts in the popular vote in Illinois and Texas—two states where electoral fraud helped produce narrow Democratic majorities—would have given Nixon enough electoral votes to win. Although Kennedy's Catholicism lost him some votes, religious bigotry did not decide the election, and Kennedy became the first Roman Catholic U.S. president.

Summary

In the fifteen years after the Second World War, Americans focused on their private lives. Those who had served their country believed they needed to make up for lost time. Millions of veterans used the GI Bill to attend college, buy homes, and start businesses. American families also had babies, and as their level of consumption rose in the 1940s and 1950s, business boomed.

During the Cold War presidencies of Truman and Eisenhower, the country was engaged in a mortal struggle with communism; and during such a crusade, people believed, citizens should support, not criticize, the government. Most white Americans believed that the United States was the greatest nation in the world and that its potential was boundless. For middle-class Americans, with their automobiles, televisions, and houses in suburbia, the American Dream seemed a reality. Still, the civil rights movement of the 1940s and 1950s and a renewed awareness of poverty in the 1960s reminded the country that not all Americans were first-class citizens.

LEGACY FOR A PEOPLE AND A NATION
The Eradication of Polio

No disease was more dreaded by postwar Americans, especially the nation's families with children, than infantile paralysis, or poliomyelitis. Children of all ages knew that polio seemingly struck out of nowhere (it is a water-borne virus), caused intense pain, and could be a lifelong affliction, leaving paralysis. During the Second World War, newspapers and magazines carried alarming stories about polio epidemics and gave advice on how to reduce the risks to children.

As frightening as the epidemics during the war had been, polio's most fearsome years came in 1949–1954, when the incidence of polio doubled the rate for the worst of the wartime epidemics. The year 1952 ranked as the worst ever, with 57,900 cases. The nation was in a panic in the early 1950s. Cities closed pools and beaches. Children were told not to jump in puddles or drink from water fountains.

Year by year, tests for a polio vaccine showed success. Then, in April 1955, the federal government approved a vaccine developed by Dr. Jonas E. Salk at the University of Pittsburgh. In the preceding forty years polio had killed or crippled 357,000 people in the United States alone, not to mention millions of others worldwide. But in spring 1955, American children lined up in schools and clinics, even on street corners, to be injected by needle with the vaccine; and in 1962 an oral vaccine was licensed by the federal government. Between 1969 and 1979 the United States counted only 179 new polio cases. In succeeding years, polio was also eliminated from most of the Western Hemisphere. Finally, in 1999, the World Health Organization announced that polio would be eradicated worldwide by the end of the year 2000—a triumphant legacy of medical research, government activism, and community cooperation.

For Further Reading, see the Appendix. For Web resources, go to history.college.hmco.com/students.

THE COLD WAR AND AMERICAN GLOBALISM

1945–1961

On July 16, 1945, the "Deer" Team leader parachuted into northern Vietnam. Colonel Allison Thomas and the other members of his Office of Strategic Services (OSS) unit knew their mission: to work with the Vietminh, a nationalist Vietnamese organization, to sabotage Japanese forces that in March had seized Vietnam from France. Ho Chi Minh, head of the Vietminh, cordially greeted the team and offered supper. The next day Ho denounced the French but remarked that "we welcome 10 million Americans." "Forget the Communist Bogy," Thomas radioed OSS headquarters in China.

A communist who had worked for decades to win his nation's independence from France, Ho helped supply information on Japanese military forces and rescue downed American pilots during the war. He also met in March 1945 with U.S. officials in Kunming, China. Receiving no aid from his ideological allies in the Soviet Union, Ho hoped that the United States would favor his nation's long quest for liberation from colonialism.

After other OSS personnel joined the "Deer" Team, the Americans, as a sign of friendship, named Ho "OSS Agent 19." During many conversations with the OSS members, Ho said that he hoped young Vietnamese could study in the United States and American technicians could help build an independent Vietnam. Citing history, Ho remarked that "your statesmen make eloquent speeches about . . . self-determination. We are self-determined. Why not help us? Am I any different from . . . your George Washington?"

A second OSS unit, the "Mercy" Team headed by Captain Archimedes Patti, arrived in the city of Hanoi on August 22. When Patti met Ho, the Vietminh leader applauded America's assistance and called for future "collaboration." But, unbeknownst to these OSS members, who believed that President Franklin D. Roosevelt's general sympathy for eventual Vietnamese independence remained U.S. policy, the new Truman administration in Washington had decided to let France, America's emerging Cold War ally, decide the fate of Vietnam.

On September 2, 1945, amid great fanfare in Hanoi, with OSS personnel present, an emotional Ho Chi Minh read his declaration of independence for the Democratic Republic of Vietnam: "All men are created equal; they are endowed by their Creator with certain unalienable Rights; among these are Life, Liberty, and the pursuit of Happiness." At one point in the ceremonies, two American P-38 aircraft swooped down over the crowded square. The Vietnamese cheered, interpreting the flyby as U.S. endorsement of their independence. Actually, the pilots just wanted to see what was happening.

By late September both OSS teams had departed Vietnam. In a last meeting with Captain Patti, Ho expressed his sadness that the United States had armed the French to reestablish their colonial rule in Vietnam. Sure, Ho said, U.S. officials in Washington judged him a "Moscow puppet" because he was a communist. But Ho claimed that he drew inspiration from the American struggle for independence and that he was foremost "a free agent," a nationalist. If necessary, Ho insisted, the Vietnamese would go it alone, with or without American or Soviet help. And they did—first against the French and eventually against more than half a million U.S. troops in what became America's longest war.

Because Ho Chi Minh was a communist, U.S. leaders rejected his appeal for recognition. Endorsing the containment doctrine to draw the line against communism everywhere, American presidents from Truman to George H. W. Bush believed that a ruthless Soviet Union was directing a worldwide communist conspiracy against peace, free-market capitalism, and political democracy. Soviet leaders from Joseph Stalin to Mikhail Gorbachev protested that a militarized, economically aggressive United States sought nothing less than world domination. This protracted contest between the United States and the Soviet Union acquired the name Cold War.

The primary feature of world affairs for more than four decades, the Cold War was fundamentally a bipolar contest between the United States and the Soviet Union over spheres of influence, over world power. Decisions made in Moscow and Washington dominated world politics, as the capitalist "West" squared off with the communist "East." The Cold War eventually took the lives of millions, cost trillions of dollars, spawned fears of doomsday, and destabilized one nation after another. On occasion the two superpowers signed agreements to temper their dangerous arms race; at other times they went to the brink of war and armed allies to fight vicious wars in the Third World.

Vietnam was part of the Third World, a general term for those nations that during the Cold War era wore neither the "West" (the "First World") nor the "East" (the "Second World") label. Third World nations on the whole were nonwhite, nonindustrialized, and located in the southern half of the globe—in Asia, Africa, the Middle East, and Latin America. Many of them had been colonies of European nations or Japan. The great-power Cold War rivalry intruded into the Third World. U.S. leaders often interpreted Third World anticolonialism, political instability, and restrictions on foreign-owned property as Soviet or communist inspired, rather than as expressions of profound indigenous nationalism.

Critics in the United States challenged the architects of the Cold War, questioning their exaggerations of threats from abroad, their meddlesome interventions in the Third World, and the expensive militarization of foreign policy. But when leaders such as Truman described the Cold War in extremist terms as a life-and-death struggle against a monstrous enemy, legitimate criticism became suspect and dissenters discredited. Cold Warriors charged the critics with being "soft on communism." ■

Why the Cold War Began

 After the Second World War, the international system was so unsettled that conflict became virtually inevitable. Much of Europe and Asia had been reduced to rubble, and the

IMPORTANT EVENTS

1945 Yalta Conference charts postwar order
 Roosevelt dies; Truman becomes president
 OSS cooperates with Vietminh
 Potsdam agreements on postwar Germany
 Atomic bombings of Japan; Tokyo surrenders
 Ho Chi Minh declares Vietnam independent
 World Bank and IMF begin operations

1946 Kennan's "long telegram" criticizes USSR
 Churchill's "iron curtain" speech
 Philippines gain independence
 Baruch Plan to control atomic weapons falters
 Truman fires Wallace from cabinet
 Vietnamese war against France erupts

1947 Truman Doctrine seeks aid for Greece
 and Turkey
 Communists take power in Hungary
 Marshall offers Europe economic assistance
 National Security Act reorganizes government
 "X" article posits containment doctrine
 Lippmann criticizes containment in *The
 Cold War*

1948 Fulbright Program initiates academic
 exchanges
 Communists take power in Czechoslovakia
 OAS founded as alliance in Latin America
 Marshall Plan aids European economic
 recovery
 Truman recognizes Israel
 U.S. organizes Berlin airlift

1949 Truman calls for Point Four technical
 assistance
 NATO founded as anti-Soviet alliance
 Soviet Union explodes atomic bomb
 Mao's Communists win power in China

1950 NSC-68 recommends major military buildup
 U.S. aids France in Vietnam
 Korean War starts in June; China enters in fall

1951 Truman fires General MacArthur
 Armistice talks open in Korea
 U.S. signs security treaty with Japan

1952 U.S. explodes first H-bomb

1953 Eisenhower becomes president
 Stalin dies
 U.S. helps restore shah to power in Iran
 USIA created as propaganda agency
 Korean War ends

1954 Siege of Dienbienphu in Vietnam
 Geneva accords partition Vietnam
 CIA overthrows Arbenz in Guatemala
 Crisis over islands of Jinmen and Mazu
 SEATO alliance formed for Southeast Asia

1955 Formosa Resolution to defend Taiwan
 Puerto Rico's Operation Bootstrap expands
 U.S.-USSR summit meeting at Geneva
 Soviets create Warsaw Pact
 U.S. backs Diem regime in Vietnam
 Bandung Conference of nonaligned nations

1956 Soviets crush uprising in Hungary
 Suez crisis sparks war in Middle East

1957 Eisenhower Doctrine for Middle East
 Soviets fire first ICBM and launch *Sputnik*

1958 U.S.-USSR cultural exchanges begin
 NASA created
 U.S. troops land in Lebanon
 Berlin crisis

1959 Castro ousts Batista in Cuba
 Nixon-Khrushchev "kitchen debate" in
 Moscow

1960 U.S. begins embargo against Cuba
 Soviets shoot down U-2 spy plane
 Vietcong organized in South Vietnam

1961 U.S. breaks relations with Cuba

United States and the Soviet Union offered very different approaches to postwar economic and political reconstruction. The collapse of Germany and Japan, moreover, had created power vacuums that drew the two major powers into collision as they sought influence in countries where the Axis aggressors once had held sway. And the political turmoil that many nations experienced after the war also spurred Soviet-American competition.

The international system also became unstable because empires were disintegrating, creating the new

Decolonization Third World. Financial constraints and nationalist rebellions forced the European imperial states to set their colonies free. As new nations emerged in Asia and the Middle East, America and the Soviet Union vied to win these new Third World states as allies that might provide military bases, resources, and markets. Some new nations chose nonalignment in the Cold War.

Driven by different ideologies and different economic and strategic needs in this volatile international climate, the United States and the Soviet Union downgraded diplomacy to build what Secretary of State Dean Acheson called "situations of strength." Both nations marched into the Cold War with convictions of righteousness, and each saw the other as the world's bully. While Americans feared "communist aggression," Soviets feared "capitalist encirclement."

U.S. officials vowed never to repeat the experience of the 1930s: they would accept no more Munichs, no more appeasement, and no more depressions that might spawn political extremism and war. To many Americans, it seemed that Soviet Russia had simply replaced Nazi Germany, that communism was simply "Red fascism."

U.S. leaders also knew that the nation's economic well-being depended on an activist foreign policy. After the Second World War, the United States stood as the largest supplier of goods to international markets. But that trade became jeopardized by the postwar economic paralysis of Europe and by discriminatory trade practices that violated the Open Door doctrine. Europe's economy was so prostrate that it could not earn dollars to buy American products (the "dollar gap"); if the gap were not closed, the United States might face a severe depression once again. In addition to the need to export American industrial and farm products, the U.S. also needed to import essential raw materials. Thus economic expansionism, so much a part of pre–Cold War history, remained a central feature of postwar foreign relations.

U.S. Economic and Strategic Needs

New strategic theory also propelled the United States toward an expansionist, globalist diplomacy. The shrinkage of the globe with the advent of the "air age" made nations more vulnerable to surprise attack from the air. The Americans and the Soviets collided as they strove to establish defensive positions, sometimes far from home. The United States sought overseas bases and air transit and landing rights to guard the approaches to the Western Hemisphere. These bases also would permit the United States to launch offensive attacks with might and speed.

President Truman, unlike the patient, ingratiating, and evasive Franklin Roosevelt, was brash, impatient, and direct. When Truman met the Soviet commissar of foreign affairs, V. M. Molotov, in 1945, the president sharply protested that the Soviets were not fulfilling the Yalta agreement on Poland. Molotov stormed out. Truman bragged after the encounter that "I gave it to him straight 'one-two to the jaw.'" Truman's display of toughness became a trademark of American Cold War diplomacy.

Truman's Get-Tough Style

Fearful of a revived Germany and a resurgent Japan, anticipating that capitalist nations would attempt to extinguish the communist flame, and facing a monumental task of economic reconstruction in their devastated nation, the Soviets made territorial gains in eastern Poland; the Baltic states of Lithuania, Latvia, and Estonia; and parts of Finland and Romania. In eastern Europe Soviet officials began to suppress noncommunists and install communist clients. The Americans, the steely premier Joseph Stalin protested, were surrounding the USSR with hostile bases and practicing atomic and dollar diplomacy.

Throughout the Cold War era, Americans debated Soviet intentions and capabilities. Some diplomats believed that the Soviet Union—well armed, opportunistic, and aggressive—could never be trusted. On the other hand, critics of U.S. policies charged that American officials exaggerated the Soviet/communist threat, imagining a bigger-than-life, troublemaking, monolithic archenemy.

Debate over Soviet Intentions and Behavior

In the immediate postwar years, in fact, the Soviet Union suffered a hobbled economy and, like the United States, undertook a major postwar demobilization of its armed forces. The Soviet Union was a regional power in eastern Europe, not a global menace. American leaders feared that the ravaging postwar economic and social unrest abroad would leave American strategic and economic interests vulnerable to political disorders that the Soviets might exploit, perhaps through subversion. In other words, Americans feared Soviet seizure of opportunities to challenge U.S. interests more than they feared a direct Soviet attack on western Europe.

The United States took advantage of the postwar power vacuum and economic supremacy to expand its overseas interests and shape a peace on American terms. The U.S. pursuit of nuclear superiority, outlying bases, raw materials and markets, supremacy in Latin America, and control of the Atlantic and Pacific Oceans aroused many opponents, in particular the Soviet Union. To Americans, Soviet opposition to U.S. globalism simply confirmed Moscow's wicked obstructionism.

Truman's Cold War: Europe and Global Containment

One of the first Soviet-American clashes came in Poland in 1945, when the Soviets refused to allow conservative Poles from London to join the communist government in Lublin. Truman officials argued that at the Yalta Conference, Stalin had agreed to a democratic government for Poland; Stalin disagreed and sustained the procommunist regime. The Soviets also snuffed out civil liberties in the former Nazi satellite of Romania. Moscow initially allowed free elections in Hungary and Czechoslovakia, but as U.S. influence in Europe expanded, the Soviets encouraged communist coups in Hungary (1947) and Czechoslovakia (1948). Yugoslavia stood as a unique case: its independent communist government, led by Josip Broz Tito, successfully broke with Stalin in 1948.

To defend their actions, the Soviets pointed out that the United States was reviving their traditional enemy, Germany. The Soviets also charged that the United States was pursuing a double standard—intervening in the affairs of eastern Europe but demanding that the Soviet Union stay out of Latin America and Asia.

The atomic bomb also divided the two major powers. The Soviets believed that the United States was practicing "atomic diplomacy"—maintaining a

Atomic Diplomacy

nuclear monopoly to scare the Soviets into diplomatic concessions. Secretary of State James F. Byrnes thought that the atomic bomb gave the United States bargaining power and could serve as a deterrent to Soviet expansion, but Secretary of War Henry L. Stimson thought otherwise in 1945. If Americans continued to have "this weapon rather ostentatiously on our hip," he warned Truman, the Soviets' "suspicions and their distrust of our purposes and motives will increase."

In this atmosphere of suspicion and distrust, Truman refused to turn over the weapon to an international control authority. In 1946 he backed the Baruch Plan, which provided for U.S. abandonment of its atomic monopoly only after the world's fissionable materials were brought under the authority of an international agency. The Soviets retorted that this plan would require them to shut down their atomic-bomb development project while the United States continued its own. Washington and Moscow soon became locked into an expensive and frightening nuclear arms race.

Soviets and Americans clashed on every front in 1946. When the United States turned down a Soviet request for a reconstruction loan but gave a loan to Britain, Moscow upbraided Washington for using its dollars to manipulate foreign governments. The two Cold War powers also backed different groups in Iran, where the United States helped bring the pro-West shah to the throne. Unable to agree on the unification of Germany, the Cold War antagonists built up their zones independently. Even the new World Bank and International Monetary Fund (IMF), created at the July 1944 Bretton Woods Conference by forty-four nations to stabilize trade and finance, became tangled in the Cold War. The Soviets refused to join because the United States so dominated both institutions.

After Stalin gave a speech in February 1946 that depicted the world as threatened by capitalist acquisitiveness, the American chargé d'affaires in Moscow, George F. Kennan, asserted that Soviet fanaticism made even a temporary understanding impossible. His "long telegram" fed a growing belief among American officials that only toughness would work

Kennan and Churchill Warn Against Soviet Power

with the Soviets. The following month, Winston Churchill delivered a stirring speech in Fulton, Missouri, in which he warned that a Soviet-erected "iron curtain" had cut off eastern European countries from the West.

The Cold War escalated further in early 1947, when the British requested American help in Greece

Truman Doctrine

to defend their conservative client government against a leftist insurgency. In his March 12, 1947, speech to Congress, Truman requested $400 million in aid to Greece and Turkey. The speech was laced with alarmist language intended to stake out the United States's role in the postwar world. Truman claimed that communism imperiled the world. "If Greece should fall under the control of an armed minority," he gravely concluded in an early version of the domino theory (see page 520), "the effect upon its neighbor, Turkey, would be immediate and serious. Confusion and disorder might well spread throughout the entire Middle East." At the time, civil war in which communists played a prominent role was rocking Greece. Turkey bordered the Soviet Union, considered by American leaders to be masterminding global communist expansion. At issue, Truman insisted, was the very security of the United States.

Especially momentous in the dramatic speech were the words, later known as the Truman Doctrine, that would guide American policymakers for almost a half-century: "I believe that it must be the policy of the United States to support free peoples who are resisting attempted subjugation by armed minorities or by outside pressures." Critics correctly pointed out that the Soviet Union was little involved in the Greek civil war, that the communists in Greece were more pro-Tito than pro-Stalin, and that the resistance movement had noncommunist as well as communist members. Nor was the Soviet Union threatening Turkey at the time. Nonetheless, the Senate approved Truman's request, and with U.S. dollars and military advisers, the Greek government defeated the insurgents in 1949. Turkey became a staunch U.S. ally on the Soviets' border.

Four months after Truman's speech, Kennan published an influential statement of the containment doctrine. Writing as "Mr. X" in the magazine *Foreign Affairs*, Kennan advocated a "policy of firm containment, designed to confront the Russians with unalter-

The "X" Article

able counterforce at every point where they show signs of encroaching upon the interests of a peaceful and stable world." Along with the Truman Doctrine, Kennan's "X" article became a key manifesto of Cold War policy. Veteran journalist Walter Lippmann, however, took issue with the containment doctrine in his book *The Cold War* (1947), calling it a "strategic monstrosity" that failed to distinguish between areas vital and peripheral to U.S. security.

Invoking the containment doctrine, the United States in 1947 and 1948 began to build an international economic and defensive network to protect American prosperity and security and to advance U.S. hegemony. In western Europe, the region of primary concern, American diplomats pursued several objectives: partnership with Great Britain; economic reconstruction; ouster of communists from governments, as occurred in 1947 in France and Italy; blockage of "third force" or neutralist tendencies; keeping the decolonization of European empires orderly; creation of a military alliance; and unification of the western zones of Germany. At the same time, American culture—consumer goods, music, consumption ethic, and production techniques—permeated European societies.

The first instrument designed to achieve U.S. goals in western Europe was the Marshall Plan. The

Marshall Plan

plan was unveiled in June 1947 when Secretary of State George C. Marshall announced that the United States would finance a massive European recovery program. Launched in 1948, without Soviet participation, the Marshall Plan sent $12.4 billion to western Europe before the program ended in 1951 (see Map 29.1). To stimulate business at home, the legislation provided that the foreign-aid dollars must be spent in the United States on American-made products. Partially designed to prevent the extremism bred by the global depression of the 1930s, the Marshall Plan proved a mixed success. The program caused inflation, failed to solve a balance-of-payments problem, took only tentative steps toward economic integration, and further divided Europe between "East" and "West." But the program spurred impressive western European industrial production and investment and started the region toward self-sustaining economic growth. From the American perspective,

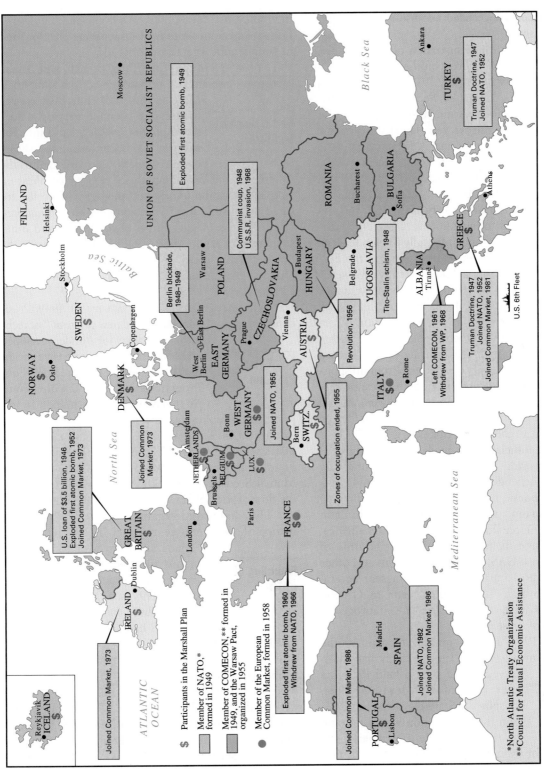

Map 29.1 Divided Europe   After the Second World War, Europe broke into two competing camps. When the United States launched the Marshall Plan in 1948, the Soviet Union countered with its own economic plan the following year. When the United States created NATO in 1949, the Soviet Union answered with the Warsaw Pact in 1955. On the whole, these two camps held firm until the late 1980s.

moreover, the plan succeeded because it helped contain communism.

To streamline the administration of U.S. defense, Truman worked with Congress on the National Security Act of July 1947. The act created

National Security Act

the Office of Secretary of Defense (which became the Department of Defense two years later), the National Security Council (NSC) to advise the president, and the Central Intelligence Agency (CIA) to conduct spy operations and information gathering. By the early 1950s the CIA had become a significant member of the national security state and had expanded its functions to include covert (secret) operations aimed at overthrowing unfriendly foreign leaders.

In 1948 the United States implemented the Fulbright Program. The brainchild of Democratic senator J. William Fulbright of Arkansas,

Fulbright Program and Cultural Expansion

this example of "public diplomacy" attempted to overcome cultural barriers to reach foreign peoples with a positive message about the United States. The Fulbright Program sponsored educational exchanges; professors and students from the United States went abroad to teach and study, and their counterparts from foreign countries came to the United States.

American officials also made military linkages around the world. The United States granted the Philippines independence in 1946 while retaining military and economic hegemony there. The following year, American diplomats created the Rio Pact in Latin America. To enforce this hemispheric military alliance, the United States helped found the Organization of American States (OAS) in 1948. Under this and other agreements the Truman administration sent several military missions to Latin America and to Greece, Turkey, Iran, China, and Saudi Arabia to improve the armed forces of those nations.

In May 1948 Truman quickly recognized the newly proclaimed state of Israel, which had been carved out of British-held Palestine after years of Arab-Jewish dispute.

Recognition of Israel

Despite the State Department objection that recognition would alienate oil-rich Arab nations, Truman made the decision for three reasons: he believed that, after

the Holocaust, Jews deserved a homeland; he desired Jewish-American votes in the upcoming election; and he sought another international ally.

In June 1948 the Americans, French, and British agreed to fuse their German zones, including their three sectors of Berlin. They sought

Berlin Blockade and Airlift

to integrate West Germany (the Federal Republic of Germany) into the western European economy. Fearing a resurgent Germany tied to the American Cold War camp, the Soviets cut off Western land access to the jointly occupied city of Berlin, located well inside the Soviet zone. Truman countered by ordering a massive airlift of food, fuel, and other supplies to Berlin. Their spoiling effort blunted, the Soviets finally lifted the blockade in May 1949 and founded the German Democratic Republic, or East Germany.

In his inaugural address of January 20, 1949, President Truman announced "a bold new program" of technical assistance for "underdeveloped

Point Four Program

areas." Seen as an inexpensive means to thwart communism, the Point Four Program began in 1950 with a comparatively meager $35 million to improve food supplies, public health, housing, and private investment in Third World countries that the United States sought to woo to its side in the Cold War. Point Four lost its identity in 1953 when it became part of the Mutual Security Agency and increasingly emphasized the flow of strategic raw materials to the United States.

The administration gave far more attention to formation of a Western security pact. The United States, Canada, and many western European

Founding of NATO

nations founded the North Atlantic Treaty Organization (NATO) in April 1949 (see Map 29.1). The treaty aroused considerable domestic debate, for not since 1778 had the United States entered a formal European military alliance. Administration officials contended that, should the Soviets ever probe westward, NATO would function as a "tripwire," bringing the full force of the United States to bear on the Soviet Union. Truman officials also hoped that NATO would keep western Europeans from embracing communism or even neutralism in the Cold War. The Senate ratified the treaty, and the United

States soon began to spend billions of dollars under the Mutual Defense Assistance Act.

In September 1949 the Soviets detonated an atomic bomb, ending the American nuclear monopoly.

NSC-68

That same year Mao Zedong's communist forces won the civil war in China. In response to the changed state of affairs, Truman ordered production of the hydrogen bomb. And in April 1950 the president received a top-secret report from the National Security Council. Tagged NSC-68, the report predicted continued tension with expansionistic communists. It appealed for a much enlarged military budget and the mobilization of public opinion to support such an increase. Officials worried about how to sell this prescription to voters and budget-conscious members of Congress. "We were sweating over it, and then—with regard to NSC-68—thank God Korea came along," recalled one U.S. official.

Asian Acrimony: Japan, China, and Vietnam

Asia, like Europe, became ensnared in the Cold War. The victors in the Second World War dismantled Japan's empire. The United States and the Soviet Union divided Korea into competing spheres of influence. Pacific islands (the Marshalls, Marianas, and Carolines) came under American control, and Formosa (Taiwan) was returned to China.

As for Japan itself, the United States monopolized its reconstruction through a military occupation directed by General Douglas Mac-Arthur, who envisioned turning the Pacific Ocean into "an Anglo-Saxon lake." Truman did not like "Mr. Prima Donna, Brass Hat" Mac-Arthur, but the general initiated "a democratic revolution from above," as the Japanese called it, that reflected Washington's wishes. MacArthur wrote a democratic constitution, gave women voting rights, revitalized the economy, and destroyed the nation's weapons. In 1951, against Soviet protests, the United States and Japan signed a separate peace that restored Japan's sovereignty and ended the occupation. A Mu-

Reconstruction of Japan

tual Security Treaty that year provided for the stationing of U.S. forces on Japanese soil, including a base on Okinawa.

Meanwhile, America's Chinese ally was faltering. The United States had long backed the Nationalists of Jiang Jieshi (Chiang Kai-shek) against Mao Zedong's communists. But Jiang became an unreliable partner who rejected U.S. advice. His government had become corrupt, inefficient, and out of touch with discontented peasants, whom the communists enlisted with promises of land reform. Still, seeing Jiang as the only alternative to Mao, Truman backed him to the end.

Communist Victory in Chinese Civil War

American officials divided on the question of whether Mao was a puppet of the Soviet Union. Some considered him an Asian Tito—communist but independent—but most believed him to be part of an international communist movement that might give the Soviets a springboard into Asia. Thus when the Chinese communists made secret overtures to the United States to begin diplomatic talks in 1945 and again in 1949, American officials rebuffed them. Mao then leaned to the Soviet side in the Cold War, but maintained a fierce independence that rankled the Soviets.

In fall 1949 Jiang fled to the island of Formosa, and Mao proclaimed the People's Republic of China (PRC). Truman refused to extend diplomatic recognition to the new government. U.S. officials had become alarmed by the 1950 Sino-Soviet treaty of friendship and by the harassment of Americans and their property in China. Truman also chose nonrecognition because a vocal group of Republican critics, the so-called China lobby, was winning headlines by charging that the United States had "lost" China. Future presidents followed Truman's nonrecognition policy. Not until 1979 did Sino-American relations resume.

U.S. Nonrecognition Policy

Mao's victory in China drew urgent American attention to Indochina (Vietnam, Cambodia, and Laos). Would the PRC attempt to exploit France's troubles with its rebellious colonies? As a colonial ruler, France had exploited Vietnam for its rice, rubber, tin, and tungsten. The French also had to beat back recurrent rebellions. Still, Vietnamese nationalists dedicated to

Vietnam's Quest for Independence

independence grew in strength. Their leader Ho Chi Minh, born in 1890, lived in France before the First World War; at the close of the war he joined the French Communist Party to use it as a vehicle for Vietnamese independence. For the next two decades, living in China, the Soviet Union, and elsewhere, Ho patiently planned and fought to free his nation from French colonialism.

The Truman administration rejected Vietnam's independence in the 1940s in favor of the restoration of French rule. Why? First, Americans wanted France's cooperation in the Cold War. Second, Southeast Asia was an economic asset: its rice could feed America's emerging ally Japan; it could provide markets for Japanese exports; and it was the world's largest producer of natural rubber. Third, the area seemed strategically vital to the defense of Japan and the Philippines. Finally, Ho Chi Minh, the State Department declared, was an "agent of international communism," who, it was assumed, would assist Soviet and Chinese expansionism. Overlooking the native roots of the nationalist rebellion against France, Washington officials took a globalist view of Vietnam, interpreting events through a Cold War lens.

After Jiang's regime collapsed in China, the Truman administration made two crucial decisions—both

U.S. Aid to France in the War Against the Vietminh

in early 1950, before the Korean War. First, Washington recognized the French puppet government of Bao Dai, a former emperor who had collaborated with the French and Japanese. In the eyes of the Vietnamese, the United States thus became in essence a colonial power, an ally of the hated French. Second, the administration agreed to send weapons, and ultimately military advisers, to sustain the French in Indochina. From 1945 to 1954, the United States gave $2 billion of the $5 billion that France spent to keep Vietnam within its empire.

The Korean War

In the early morning of June 25, 1950, a large military force of the Democratic People's Republic of Korea (North Korea) moved across the 38th parallel into the Republic of Korea (South Korea). Although the Soviets

had armed the North and the Americans had armed the South, the Korean War began as a civil war. Since August 1945, when Korea was hastily cut at the 38th parallel, the two parts had been skirmishing along their supposedly temporary border.

Both the North's communist leader Kim Il Sung and the South's president Syngman Rhee sought to reunify their nation. Kim's military especially gained strength when tens of thousands of battle-tested Koreans returned home in 1949 after serving in Mao's army. Displaying the Cold War mentality of the time, however, President Truman claimed that the Soviets had masterminded the North Korean attack.

Actually, Kim had to press a doubting Joseph Stalin, who only reluctantly approved the attack after

Origins of the War

Kim predicted an easy, early victory and after Mao backed Kim. The three communist leaders might have calculated that the United States would not come to South Korea's defense. In a public speech in early 1950, Secretary of State Acheson had drawn the American defense line in Asia through the Aleutians, Japan, and Okinawa to the Philippines. Formosa and Korea clearly lay beyond that line. Acheson did say, however, that those areas could expect U.N. (and hence U.S.) assistance if attacked. Two other thoughts probably convinced Stalin to support Kim: first, if he did not back North Korea, Mao might gain influence over Kim; second, if the United States rearmed Japan, South Korea might once again become a beachhead for Japanese (and American) expansion on the Asian continent.

Whatever Stalin's reasoning, his support for Kim's venture remained lukewarm. When the United Nations Security Council voted to defend South Korea, the Soviet representative was not even present to veto the resolution. And during the war, Moscow gave limited aid to North Korea and China, which grew angry at Stalin for reneging on promised Soviet airpower.

The president first ordered General Douglas MacArthur to send arms and troops to South Korea.

Truman Commits U.S. Forces

Worried that Mao might attempt to take Formosa, Truman also directed the Seventh Fleet to patrol the waters between the Chinese mainland and Jiang's sanctuary on Formosa, thus inserting the United States once again into Chinese politics. After the Security Council

CHILDREN'S CRUSADE AGAINST COMMUNISM

2. MacArthur Heads UN Forces

North Korean Reds attacked South Korea in what is believed to be part of a communist plan gradually to conquer the whole world. The United Nations pitched in to help the South Koreans, like your dad would help the folks next door if some bad men were beating them up. The troops sent to Korea for the UN were put under command of General Douglas MacArthur. "Mac" has a long military record. But you know him best as the general who led the Allied forces to victory in the Pacific during the second world war.

 FIGHT THE RED MENACE

Intensely anticommunist groups thrived in the United States during the Cold War. The "Children's Crusade Against Communism" distributed its exaggerated message of a global communist conspiracy in the early 1950s through bubble-gum cards such as this one. (The Michael Barson Collection/Past Perfect)

voted to assist South Korea, MacArthur became commander of U.N. forces in Korea (90 percent of them American). North Korean tanks and superior firepower sent the South Korean army into chaotic retreat. Within weeks of the invasion, the South Koreans and Americans had been pushed into the tiny Pusan perimeter at the base of South Korea.

General MacArthur planned a daring operation: an amphibious landing at heavily fortified Inchon, several hundred miles behind North Korean lines. After U.S. guns and bombs pounded Inchon, marines sprinted ashore on September 15, 1950. They soon liberated the South Korean capital of Seoul and pushed the North Koreans back to the 38th parallel.

In September Truman, with the intent of unifying the peninsula, authorized U.N. forces to cross the 38th parallel. These troops drove deep into North Korea, and American aircraft began strikes against bridges on the Yalu River, the border between North Korea and China. Mao publicly warned that China could not permit the bombing of its transportation links with Korea and would not accept the annihilation of North Korea itself. Both MacArthur and Washington officials shrugged off the warnings.

Chinese Entry into the War

On October 25, Mao sent Chinese soldiers into the war. Perhaps to lure American forces into a trap or to signal willingness to begin negotiations, they pulled back after a brief and successful offensive against South Korean troops. Then, after MacArthur sent the U.S. Eighth Army northward, tens of thousands of Chinese troops counterattacked on November 26, surprising American forces and driving them pell-mell southward.

By early 1951 the front had stabilized around the 38th parallel. Both Washington and Moscow welcomed negotiations, but MacArthur recklessly called for an attack on China and for Jiang's return to the mainland. Denouncing the concept of limited war (war without nuclear weapons, confined to one place), MacArthur hinted that the president was practicing appeasement. In April, backed by the Joint Chiefs of Staff, Truman fired MacArthur. Truman's popularity sagged, but he weathered demands for his impeachment.

Truman's Firing of General MacArthur

Armistice talks began in July 1951, but the fighting went on for two more years. The most contentious point in the negotiations was the fate of prisoners of war (POWs). Defying the Geneva Prisoners of War Convention (1949), U.S. officials announced that only those North Korean and Chinese POWs who wished to go home would be returned. Responding to the American statement that there would be no forced repatriation, the North Koreans denounced forced retention.

Dispute over POWs

Not until July 1953 was an armistice signed. Under its terms, the combatants agreed to hand over the

Costs and Consequences of the War

POW question to a special panel of neutral nations, which later gave prisoners their choice of staying or leaving. (In the end, 70,000 of about 100,000 North Korean and 5,600 of 20,700 Chinese POWs elected to return home; 21 American and 325 South Korean POWs of some 11,000 decided to stay in North Korea.) The North Korean–South Korean borderline was set near the 38th parallel, the prewar boundary, and a demilitarized zone was created between the two Koreas. American casualties totaled 54,246 dead and 103,284 wounded. Close to 5 million Asians died in the war, 3 million of whom were civilians.

The Korean War had major domestic political consequences. The failure to achieve victory and the public's impatience with a stalemated war undoubtedly helped to elect Eisenhower. The powers of the presidency grew as Congress repeatedly deferred to Truman. The president had never asked Congress for a declaration of war, believing that as commander-in-chief he had the authority to send troops wherever he wished.

The implementation of military containment worldwide became entrenched as U.S. policy. Increased American aid flowed to the French for their

Globalization of Containment

die-hard stand against nationalist insurgents in Vietnam. Because of heightened Sino-American hostility, South Korea and Formosa became major recipients of American foreign aid. The alliance with Japan strengthened. Australia and New Zealand joined the United States in a mutual defense agreement, the ANZUS Treaty (1951). The U.S. Army sent six divisions to Europe, and the military budget shot up from $14 billion in 1949 to $44 billion in 1953. In sum, Truman's legacy was a highly militarized U.S. foreign policy active on a global scale.

Eisenhower, Dulles, and Unrelenting Cold War

President Dwight D. Eisenhower largely sustained Truman's Cold War policies. Eisenhower brought considerable experience in foreign affairs to his presidency. As a

general during the Second World War, he had negotiated with world leaders. After the war, he served as army chief of staff and NATO supreme commander. Eisenhower accepted the Cold War consensus about the threat of communism and the need for global vigilance. At the same time, he tamed the more hawkish proposals of Vice President Richard Nixon and Secretary of State John Foster Dulles.

Eisenhower questioned Dulles's "practice of becoming a sort of international prosecuting attorney,"

John Foster Dulles

but the president relied heavily on the strong-willed secretary of state. Like the president, Dulles conceded much to the anticommunist McCarthyites, who claimed that the State Department was infested with communists. The State Department's chief security officer, a McCarthy follower, targeted homosexuals and other "incompatibles" and made few distinctions between New Dealers and Communists. Dulles thus forced many talented officers out of the Foreign Service with unsubstantiated charges that they were disloyal. Among them were Asia specialists whose expertise was thus denied to the American leaders who later plunged the United States into war in Vietnam.

Dulles considered containment too defensive a stance toward communism. He called instead for "lib-

Eisenhower-Dulles Policies

eration," although he never explained precisely how the countries of eastern Europe could be freed from Soviet control. "Massive retaliation" was the administration's phrase for the nuclear obliteration of the Soviet state or its assumed client, the People's Republic of China, if either one took aggressive actions. The ability of the United States to make such a threat was thought to provide "deterrence," the prevention of hostile Soviet behavior.

In their "New Look" for the American military, Eisenhower and Dulles emphasized airpower and nuclear weaponry. The president's preference for heavy weapons stemmed in part from his desire to trim the federal budget. During the Eisenhower presidency, the United States's stockpile of nuclear weapons grew from 1,200 to 22,229. Backed by its huge military arsenal, the United States practiced "brinkmanship": not backing down in a crisis, even if it meant taking the nation to the brink of war. Eisenhower also popularized the "domino theory": that small, weak neighboring nations would fall to communism like a row of dominoes if they were not propped up by the United States.

Eisenhower increasingly utilized the Central Intelligence Agency as an instrument of foreign policy.

CIA as Foreign Policy Instrument
The CIA put foreign leaders on its payroll; subsidized foreign labor unions, newspapers, and political parties; planted false stories in newspapers through its "disinformation" projects; and trained foreign military officers in counterrevolutionary methods. The CIA hired American journalists and professors, secretly funded the National Student Association to spur contacts with foreign student leaders, used business executives as "fronts," and conducted experiments on unsuspecting Americans to determine the effects of "mind control" drugs. The CIA also launched covert operations (including assassination schemes) to subvert or destroy governments in the Third World. The CIA helped overthrow the governments of Iran (1953) and Guatemala (1954) but failed in attempts to topple regimes in Indonesia (1958) and Cuba (1961).

The CIA and other components of the American intelligence community followed the principle of plausible deniability: covert operations should be conducted in such a way, and the decisions that launched them concealed so well, that the president could deny any knowledge of them. Thus Presidents Eisenhower and Kennedy denied that they had instructed the CIA to assassinate Cuba's Fidel Castro.

The Eisenhower administration also sought to interject American culture into the Soviet Union and its eastern European allies as a means to popularize democratic principles and to stimulate public discontent.

On July 22, 1959, in Moscow, the Soviet capital, Vice President Richard M. Nixon (1913–1994) (*hands clasped*) and Premier Nikita Khrushchev (*finger pointing*) toured the American National Exhibition, sponsored by the U.S. Information Agency. When they stopped at this display of a modern American kitchen, Khrushchev doubted Nixon's claim that average American workers owned such appliances. In the "kitchen debate" that followed, the two leaders sparred over comparative national strengths and over whether capitalism or communism best served people's needs.   (Howard Sochurek, Time-Life Agency © Time Inc.)

Propaganda and Cultural Infiltration

The primary propaganda tool was the United States Information Agency (USIA), founded in 1953. One of the USIA's agencies, Voice of America, broadcast news, editorials, and music worldwide. The CIA secretly funded Radio Free Europe, operated since 1950 by anticommunist eastern European émigrés headquartered in Munich, West Germany. In 1958 the United States and the Soviet Union attempted to regularize cultural relations through an agreement that provided for reciprocal exchange of radio and television broadcasts, films, students, professors, athletes, and civic groups.

Such expanded cultural relations did not calm the Cold War or temper the nuclear arms race. In November 1952 the United States detonated the first hydrogen bomb. The following year the Soviets tested their first H-bomb. Four years later, they shocked Americans by firing the world's first intercontinental ballistic missile (ICBM) and then propelling the satellite *Sputnik* into orbit in outer space. The United States soon tested its own ICBMs. It also enlarged its fleet of long-range bombers (B-52s) and deployed intermediate-range missiles in Europe, targeted against the Soviet Union. At the end of 1960 the United States began adding Polaris missile–bearing submarines to its navy. To foster future technological advancement, the National Aeronautics and Space Administration (NASA) was created in 1958.

Hydrogen Bomb, *Sputnik*, and Missiles

The CIA's U-2 spy planes collected information demonstrating that the Soviets had deployed very few ICBMs. Yet politically partisan critics charged that Eisenhower had allowed the United States to fall behind in the missile race. The much-publicized "missile gap" was actually not in the USSR's favor, but rather in America's. As the 1950s closed, the United States enjoyed overwhelming strategic dominance because of its air-sea-land triad of long-range bombers, submarine-launched ballistic missiles (SLBMs), and ICBMs.

President Eisenhower grew uneasy about the arms race and the deterrence policy that became known as "mutual assured destruction," or MAD. He feared nuclear war and doubted the need for more and bigger nuclear weapons. How many times, he once asked, "could [you] kill the same man?" Spurred by these

Eisenhower's Critique of Nuclear Arms

ideas, and by neutralist and Soviet appeals, Eisenhower cautiously initiated arms-control proposals.

Eisenhower's 1953 "atoms for peace" initiative recommended that fissionable materials be contributed to a U.N. agency for use in industrial projects. Two years later, to counter Soviet appeals for disarmament, the Eisenhower administration issued its own propaganda ploy—the "open skies" proposal: aerial surveillance of both Soviet and American military sites to reduce the chances of surprise attacks. In response to worldwide alarm over radioactive fallout, the two powers unilaterally suspended atmospheric testing from 1958 until 1961, when the Soviets resumed it. The United States also began testing again at the same time, but underground.

In May 1955, in a rare example of Cold War cooperation, the two great powers ended their ten-year occupation of Austria. But events in eastern Europe soon revived the customary acrimony of the Cold War. In 1956 Soviet premier Nikita Khrushchev called for "peaceful coexistence" between capitalists and communists, denounced Stalin who had died three years earlier, and suggested that Moscow would tolerate different brands of communism. Revolts against Soviet power erupted in Poland and Hungary, testing Khrushchev's new permissiveness. After a new Hungarian government in 1956 announced its withdrawal from the Warsaw Pact (the Soviet military alliance formed in 1955 with communist countries of eastern Europe), Soviet troops and tanks battled students and workers in the streets of Budapest and crushed the rebellion. Although the Eisenhower administration's propaganda had been encouraging liberation efforts, U.S. officials found themselves unable to aid the rebels without igniting a world war.

Rebellion in Hungary

Hardly had the turmoil subsided in eastern Europe when the divided city of Berlin once again became a Cold War flash point. The Soviets railed against the placement in West Germany of American bombers capable of carrying nuclear warheads, and they complained that West Berlin had become an escape route for disaffected East Germans. In 1958 Khrushchev announced that the Soviet Union would recognize East German control of all of Berlin unless the United States and its allies began talks on German reunification and rearmament. The United States refused to give up its hold on West Berlin or to break West German ties with NATO. Khrushchev backed away from his ultimatum.

Berlin and Germany were on the agenda of a summit meeting planned for Paris in mid-1960. On May 1,

U-2 Incident

two weeks before the conference, a U-2 spy plane carrying high-powered cameras crashed 1,200 miles inside the Soviet Union. Moscow claimed credit for shooting down the plane, which it put on display along with Francis Gary Powers, the captured CIA pilot. Khrushchev demanded an apology for the U.S. violation of Soviet airspace. When Washington refused, the Soviets walked out of the Paris summit.

While sparring over Europe, both sides kept a wary eye on the People's Republic of China, which denounced the Soviet call for peaceful

Jinmen-Mazu Crisis

coexistence. Despite evidence of a widening Sino-Soviet split, most American officials still treated communism as a unified world movement. The isolation separating Beijing and Washington made continued conflict between China and the United States likely. In a dispute over Jinmen (Quemoy) and Mazu (Matsu), two tiny islands off the Chinese coast, the United States and the People's Republic of China lurched toward the brink. Jiang used these islands as bases from which to raid the mainland. Communist China's guns bombarded the islands in 1954. Eisenhower decided to defend the outposts; he even hinted that he might use nuclear weapons.

Congress passed the Formosa Resolution (1955), authorizing the president to deploy American forces to defend Formosa and adjoining islands, and two years later the United States installed tactical nuclear weapons on Taiwan. War loomed again in 1958 over Jinmen and Mazu, but this time Washington strongly cautioned Jiang not to use force against the mainland. After Jiang withdrew some troops from the islands, China relaxed its bombardments. Eisenhower's nuclear threats, however, persuaded the Chinese that they, too, needed nuclear arms. In 1964 China exploded its first nuclear bomb.

As the United States went to the brink with China, it went to the market with Japan, rebuilding the

"Japanese Miracle"

nation with foreign aid as an anti-communist military partner and trader, all the while worrying China, the Soviet Union, and past victims of Japanese aggression. Huge U.S. purchases in Japan during the Korean War and American assistance in developing an export-oriented economy in the 1950s produced what many called the "Japanese miracle"—double-digit economic growth. Japan copied American technology, practiced trade protectionism, and gained a reputation for industrial efficiency and quality control. Before long, Japan became a major economic competitor with the United States.

At Odds with the Third World

A process of decolonization that began during the First World War accelerated after the Second World War, when the economically wracked imperial countries proved incapable of resisting their colonies' demands for freedom. A cavalcade of new nations cast off their colonial bonds (see Map 29.2). From 1943 to 1994 a total of 125 countries became independent (the figure includes the former Soviet republics that departed the USSR in 1991). The emergence of so many new states in the 1940s and after, and the instability associated with the transfer of authority, shook the foundations of the international system. In the United States's traditional sphere of influence, Latin America, nationalists once again challenged U.S. hegemony.

By the late 1940s, when Cold War lines were drawn fairly tightly in Europe, Soviet-American rivalry shifted increasingly to the

Interests in the Third World

Third World. Much was at stake. The new nations could buy American goods and technology, supply strategic raw materials, and invite investments. Both great powers, moreover, looked to these new states for votes in the United Nations and sought sites within their borders for military and intelligence bases.

To thwart nationalist, radical, and communist challenges, the United States directed massive resources—foreign aid, propaganda, development projects—toward the Third World. By 1961 more than 90 percent of U.S. foreign aid was going to developing

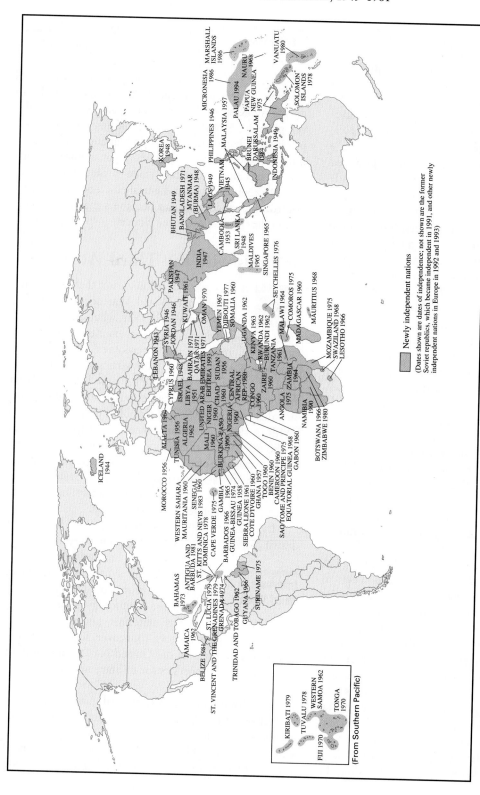

Map 29.2 The Rise of the Third World: Newly Independent Nations Since 1943 Accelerated by the Second World War, decolonization liberated many peoples from imperial rule. New nations emerged in the postwar international system dominated by the Cold War rivalry of the United States and the Soviet Union. Many newly independent states became targets of great-power intrigue but chose nonalignment in the Cold War.

nations. Washington also allied with native elites and with undemocratic but anticommunist regimes, meddled in civil wars, and unleashed CIA covert operations.

Many Third World states—notably India, Ghana, Egypt, and Indonesia—refused to take sides in the Cold War. To the dismay of both

Nonaligned Movement

Washington and Moscow, they declared themselves nonaligned, or neutral. In 1955 twenty-nine Asian and African nations met at the Bandung Conference in Indonesia and made nonalignment an organized movement. Secretary Dulles, however, denounced neutralism as a step on the road to communism. Both he and Eisenhower insisted that every nation should take a side in the life-and-death Cold War struggle.

American leaders argued that technologically "backward" Third World peoples needed Western-induced capitalist development and

American Images of Third World Peoples

modernization in order to enjoy economic growth, social harmony, and political moderation. U.S. policymakers ascribed stereotyped race-, age-, and gender-based characteristics to Third World peoples, seeing them as dependent, emotional, and irrational. American officials also used gendered language, suggesting that Third World countries were weak women—passive and servile, unable to resist the menacing appeals of communists and neutralists.

Race attitudes and segregation practices in the United States especially influenced relations. In 1955

Racism and Segregation as U.S. Handicaps

G. L. Mehta, the Indian ambassador to the United States, was refused service in the whites-only section of a restaurant at Houston International Airport. Fearing damaged relations with India, a large, neutralist nation whose allegiance the United States sought in the Cold War, John Foster Dulles apologized to Mehta. Dulles understood that racial segregation in the United States was spoiling American efforts to win friends in Third World countries and giving the Soviets a propaganda advantage. Thus when the U.S. attorney general appealed to the Supreme Court to strike down segregation in public schools, he underlined that the hu-

miliation of dark-skinned diplomats "furnished grist for the Communist propaganda mills."

The hostility of the United States toward revolution also obstructed its quest for influence in the Third

U.S. Hostility to Nationalist Revolution

World. In the twentieth century, the United States has openly opposed revolutions in Mexico, China, Russia, Cuba, Vietnam, Nicaragua, and Iran, among other nations. Americans celebrated the Spirit of '76 but grew intolerant of revolutionary disorder because many Third World revolutions arose against America's Cold War allies and threatened American investments, markets, and military bases. Indeed, by midcentury the United States stood as an established power in world affairs, eager for stability and order to protect American prosperity and security. During revolutionary crises, therefore, the United States usually supported its European allies or the conservative, propertied classes in the Third World.

Believing that Third World peoples craved modernization and that the American economic model was

Development and Modernization

best for them, American policymakers launched various "development" projects. Such projects held out the promise of sustained economic growth, prosperity, and stability, which the benefactors hoped would undermine radicalism. In the 1950s the Carnegie, Ford, and Rockefeller Foundations worked with the U.S. Agency for International Development (AID) to sponsor a Green Revolution—a dramatic increase in agricultural production, for example, by the use of hybrid seeds.

To persuade Third World peoples to abandon radical doctrines and neutralism, American leaders, often in cooperation with the business-sponsored Advertising Council, directed propaganda at the Third World. The U.S. Information Agency used films, radio broadcasts, the magazine *Free World*, exhibitions, exchange programs, and libraries (in 162 cities worldwide by 1961) to trumpet the theme of "People's Capitalism." The message showcased well-paid American workers, political democracy, and religious freedom.

Some Third World peoples did yearn to be like Americans—to enjoy their consumer goods, music, economic status, and educational opportunities. They also resented Americans for having so much and wasting so much while poorer peoples went without. The popular American novel *The Ugly American* (1958) spotlighted the "golden ghettoes" where American foreign diplomats lived in compounds separated from their poorer surroundings by high walls. The people of many countries, moreover, resented the ample profits that American corporations extracted from them. Americans often received blame for the persistent poverty of the Third World, even though the leaders of those nations made decisions that hindered their own progress, such as pouring millions of dollars into their militaries while their people craved food. Third World peoples also rejected unsavory aspects of American life, including racial segregation, political corruption, and drug abuse.

U.S. Interventions in the Third World

Anti-Yankee feelings grew in Latin America, where poverty, class warfare, overpopulation, illiteracy, and foreign exploitation fed discontent. In 1951 the leftist Jacobo Arbenz Guzmán was elected president of Guatemala, a poor country whose largest landowner was the American-owned United Fruit Company. United Fruit (UF) was an economic power throughout Latin America, where it owned 3 million acres of land and operated railroads, ports, ships, and telecommunications facilities. To fulfill his promise of land reform, Arbenz expropriated UF's uncultivated land and offered compensation. UF dismissed the offer and charged that Arbenz posed a communist threat.

The CIA, which was already concerned about Arbenz because he employed communists in his government, initiated a secret plot to overthrow him. Arbenz then turned to Moscow for military aid, thus reinforcing American suspicions. The CIA airlifted arms into Guatemala, dropping them at UF facilities, and in mid-1954 CIA-supported Guatemalans struck from Honduras. U.S. planes bombed the capital city, and the invaders drove Arbenz from power. The new pro-American regime

**CIA in
Guatemala**

returned land, but an ensuing civil war staggered the Central American nation into the 1990s.

The Cuban Revolution soon represented the greatest challenge to U.S. hegemony. In early 1959 Fidel Castro's rebels, driven by profound anti-American nationalism, ousted Fulgencio Batista, a long-time U.S. ally. Batista's corrupt, dictatorial regime had helped turn Havana into a haven for gambling and prostitution run by organized crime. Cubans resented U.S. domination, and curbing American influence became a rallying cry of the Cuban Revolution. From the start Castro sought to roll back the influence of American business and to break the U.S. grasp on Cuban trade.

**The Cuban
Revolution and
Fidel Castro**

Castro's increasing authoritarianism, anti-Yankee declarations, and growing popularity in the hemisphere alarmed Washington. In early 1960, after Cuba signed a trade treaty with the Soviet Union, Eisenhower ordered the CIA to organize an invasion force of Cuban exiles to overthrow the Castro government. The agency also began to plot an assassination of the Cuban leader. When the president drastically cut U.S. purchases of Cuban sugar, Castro seized all North American–owned companies that had not yet been nationalized. Castro also sought economic assistance from the Soviet Union. Just before leaving office in early 1961, Eisenhower broke diplomatic relations with Cuba and advised President-elect John F. Kennedy to advance plans for the invasion, which came in early 1961 (see page 551).

A different sort of U.S. intervention occurred in Puerto Rico—tourism and industrial development. Under the leadership of Teodoro Moscoso, Operation Bootstrap attracted investments from U.S. corporations with tempting tax benefits. As a General Electric officer remembered, Puerto Rico "offered many of the advantages of the Third World, such as an abundant, relatively low-cost and eager-to-work labor force, but none of the disadvantages," such as political instability and hostility to foreign investment. Tourism also expanded greatly in Puerto Rico, set off by a resort-building boom. Critics protested that Puerto Rico had spent millions on luxury hotels for North American tourists but little to combat poverty.

**Operation
Bootstrap in
Puerto Rico**

In the Middle East, the Eisenhower administration confronted challenges to U.S. influence from Arab nationalists (see Map 31.2 on page 560). American interests were conspicuous: survival of the Jewish state of Israel and extensive oil holdings. Oil-rich Iran had become a special friend. Its ruling shah had granted American oil companies a 40 percent interest in a new petroleum consortium in return for CIA help in the successful overthrow, in 1953, of his rival, Mohammed Mossadegh.

U.S. Interests in the Middle East

Egypt's Gamal Abdul Nasser became a towering figure in a pan-Arabic movement to reduce Western interests in the Middle East. Nasser vowed to expel the British from the Suez Canal and the Israelis from Palestine. The United States wished neither to anger the Arabs, for fear of losing valuable oil supplies, nor to alienate its ally Israel. But when Nasser declared neutrality in the Cold War, Dulles lost patience.

In 1956 the United States abruptly reneged on its offer to Egypt to help finance the Aswan Dam, a project to provide inexpensive electricity and water for thirsty Nile valley farmland. Nasser responded by nationalizing the British-owned Suez Canal. Fully 75 percent of western Europe's oil came from the Middle East, most of it transported through the Suez Canal. Fearing an interruption in this vital trade, the British and French conspired with Israel to bring down Nasser. On October 29, 1956, the Israelis invaded Suez, joined two days later by British and French forces.

Suez Crisis

Eisenhower fumed. America's allies had not consulted him. The president also feared that the invasion would cause Nasser to seek help from the Soviets, inviting them into the Middle East. Eisenhower sternly demanded that London, Paris, and Tel Aviv pull their troops out, and they did. Egypt took possession of the canal, the Soviets built the Aswan Dam, and Nasser became a hero to Third World peoples.

In an effort to improve the deteriorating Western position in the Middle East and to protect American interests there, the president proclaimed the Eisenhower Doctrine in 1957. The United States would intervene in the Middle East, he declared, if any government threatened

Eisenhower Doctrine

by a communist takeover asked for help. In 1958 fourteen thousand American troops scrambled ashore in Lebanon to quell an internal political dispute that Washington feared might be exploited by pro-Nasser groups or communists. By 1961, most analysts agreed, the Eisenhower administration had deepened Third World hostility toward the United States.

This was especially true in Vietnam. Despite substantial U.S. aid, the French lost steadily to the Vietminh. Finally, in early 1954, Ho's forces surrounded the French fortress at Dienbienphu in northwest Vietnam (see Map 31.1 on page 554). Although some of Eisenhower's advisers recommended a massive American air strike against Vietminh positions, the president moved cautiously. Worrying about a communist victory, Eisenhower compared the weak nations of the world to a row of dominoes, all of which would topple if just one fell. He pressed the British to help form a coalition to address the Indochinese crisis, but they refused. At home, influential members of Congress told the president to avoid any U.S. military commitment, especially in the absence of cooperation from U.S. allies. The issue became moot on May 7, when the weary French defenders at Dienbienphu surrendered.

Dienbienphu Crisis in Vietnam

Wanting out of the war, the French in April had entered into peace talks at Geneva with the United States, the Soviet Union, Britain, the People's Republic of China, Laos, Cambodia, and the competing Vietnamese regimes of Bao Dai and Ho Chi Minh. The 1954 Geneva accords, signed by France and Ho's Democratic Republic of Vietnam, temporarily divided Vietnam at the 17th parallel; Ho's government was confined to the North, Bao Dai's to the South. The 17th parallel was meant to serve as a military truce line, not a national boundary; the country was scheduled to be unified after national elections in 1956. In the meantime, neither North nor South was to join a military alliance or permit foreign military bases on its soil.

Geneva Accords

Certain that the Geneva agreements ultimately would mean communist victory, the United States and Bao Dai refused to accept the accords and set out to sabotage them. Soon after the conference, a CIA team entered Vietnam and undertook secret operations against the North. In fall 1954 the United States also joined Britain, France, Australia, New Zealand, the Philippines, Thailand, and Pakistan in the anticommunist Southeast Asia Treaty Organization (SEATO), one purpose of which was to protect the southern part of Vietnam.

In the South, the United States helped Ngo Dinh Diem push Bao Dai aside and inaugurate the Republic of Vietnam. A Catholic in a Buddhist nation, Diem had many enemies and no mass support. But he was a nationalist and an anticommunist. When Ho called for national elections in keeping with the Geneva agreements, Diem and Eisenhower refused, fearing that the popular Vietminh leader would win. From 1955 to 1961, the Diem government received more than $1 billion in American aid. It also received American military advisers. As American aid increased, South Vietnam became dependent on the United States for its existence, and the nation's culture became increasingly Americanized.

Backing the Diem Regime in South Vietnam

Diem proved a difficult ally. He acted dictatorially, abolishing village elections and jailing dissenters. Noncommunists and communists alike began to strike back at Diem's corrupt and repressive government. In 1959 Ho began sending aid to southern insurgents, whose tactics included assassinating hundreds of Diem's village officials. In late 1960 southern communists organized the National Liberation Front (NLF), known as the Vietcong. The war against imperialism had become a two-part civil war: Ho's North versus Diem's South, and NLF guerrillas versus the Diem government.

Summary

The United States emerged from the Second World War preeminent in power but fearful that the unstable international system, an unfriendly Soviet Union, and the decolonizing Third World threatened American plans for the postwar world. Locked with the Soviet Union in a "Cold War," U.S. leaders marshaled their nation's superior resources to influence and cajole other countries. Foreign economic aid, new international organizations, atomic threats, client states, development of new long-range missiles, military alliances, covert operations, interventions, propaganda, cultural infiltration—these and more became the instruments to wage the Cold War.

America's claim to international leadership sparked resistance. Communist countries condemned dollar and atomic diplomacy; Third World nations sought to undermine America's European allies and identified the United States as an imperial coconspirator; and even America's allies bristled at a United States that boldly proclaimed itself economic master and global policeman. Liberal and radical domestic critics protested that Presidents Truman and Eisenhower exaggerated the communist threat. Still, these presidents and their successors seldom hesitated to flex American muscle to enlarge the American sphere of influence and shape the world. In their years of nurturing allies and applying the containment doctrine worldwide, Truman and Eisenhower held the line—against the Soviet Union, the People's Republic of China, nonalignment, communism, nationalism, and revolution everywhere.

Putting itself at odds with the Third World, the United States usually stood with its European allies to slow decolonization. The globalist perspective of the United States prompted Americans to interpret many Third World troubles as Soviet-inspired or Soviet-backed conflicts. The intensity of the Cold War obscured for Americans the indigenous roots of most Third World troubles, as the wars in Korea and Vietnam attested. Nor could the United States abide Third World nations' drive to control their own raw materials and economies. The Third World, in short, challenged the United States's strategic power by forming a third force in the Cold War, and it challenged American economic power by demanding a new economic order of shared interests. Overall, the rise of the Third World introduced new actors to the world stage, challenging the bipolarity of the international system and diffusing power.

All the while, the threat of nuclear war unsettled Americans and foreigners alike. Stanley Kramer's popular but disturbing movie *On the Beach* (1959), based on Nevil Shute's 1957 novel, depicts a nuclear holocaust in which the last humans on earth choose to swallow government-issued poison tablets so that they could die before H-bomb radiation sickness kills them.

Such doomsday or Armageddon attitudes contrasted sharply with official U.S. government assurances that Americans would survive a nuclear war.

LEGACY FOR A PEOPLE AND A NATION
The National Security State

To build a cathedral, someone has observed, you first need a religion, and a religion needs inspiring texts that command authority. For decades, America's Cold War religion was national security; its texts the Truman Doctrine, "X" article, and NSC-68; and its cathedral the national security state. During the Cold War, embracing preparedness for total war, the U.S. government essentially transformed itself into a huge military headquarters that interlocked with corporations and universities. Preaching the doctrine of national security, moreover, members of Congress strove to gain lucrative defense contracts for their districts.

Overseen by the president and his advisory body, the National Security Council, the national security state has had as its core what the National Security Act of 1947 called the National Military Establishment; in 1949 it became the Department of Defense. This department ranked as a leading employer; its payroll by 1990 included almost 5 million persons. It operated 1,265 major installations, 375 of them abroad. Spending for national defense and veterans topped $328 billion, a quarter of the federal budget. In 1998, years after the Cold War ended, with the closing of some military facilities and downsizing of staffs, the figure still stood at $300 billion (about 16 percent of the budget).

Joining the Department of Defense as instruments of national security policy were the Joint Chiefs of Staff, Central Intelligence Agency, National Security Agency, U.S. Information Agency, Agency for International Development, and dozens more government bodies. The national security state also built ties to corporations such as General Electric and Raytheon, which received much of their income from defense contracts and even shared executives through a revolving military-industrial door. Scientists and engineers also joined the partnership. In the early 1970s, at least 50 percent of America's aeronautical engineers and 30 percent of its physicists worked on military-related projects.

In 1961 President Eisenhower warned against a "military-industrial complex," while others feared a "garrison state" or "warfare state." Despite the warnings, in the early twenty-first century, the national security state remains vigorous, a lasting legacy of the early Cold War period for a people and a nation.

For Further Reading, see the Appendix. For Web resources, go to history.college.hmco.com/students.

REFORM AND CONFLICT AT HOME: A TURBULENT ERA

1961–1974

Civil Rights and the New Frontier
The Great Society and the Triumph of Liberalism
Civil Rights Disillusionment, Race Riots, and Black Power
The New Left and the Counterculture
1968: A Year of Protest, Violence, and Loss
Rebirth of Feminism
Nixon and the Divided Nation
Nixon's Reelection and Resignation
LEGACY FOR A PEOPLE AND A NATION
Watergate and Political Reforms

In 1964 politics and civil rights were inextricably tied together. When the Democrats convened to pick a presidential candidate in that election year, they discovered the volatility of the civil rights issue. Two delegations had arrived from Mississippi. One was all white; the other was largely African American and called itself the Mississippi Freedom Democratic Party (MFDP). The MFDP asked the convention to honor its credentials instead of those of the state's segregationist regular Democratic organization.

In Mississippi, as a result of phony literacy tests, economic intimidation, and violence, less than 7 percent of the black population could vote. Civil rights activists had decided in 1963 to conduct their own

"freedom vote"—a mock election to prove, as one worker put it, "that politics is not just white folks' business." In 1964 more than a thousand northern students traveled south to Mississippi to work for the Freedom Summer Project, registering voters and organizing protests against segregation. White vigilantes responded by bombing and burning two dozen black churches. And in Philadelphia, Mississippi, sheriff's deputies murdered three young civil rights workers— one black and two white.

The Democratic Party's credentials committee met on August 22, 1964, to hear the contesting delegations. Speaking for the MFDP was an inspiring figure, Fannie Lou Hamer, a forty-six-year-old African

IMPORTANT EVENTS

1960 Sit-ins begin in Greensboro
Birth-control pill approved for use
Kennedy elected president

1961 Freedom Rides protest segregation in transportation
President's Commission on the Status of Women established

1962 SDS issues Port Huron Statement
Meredith enters University of Mississippi
Baker v. Carr establishes "one person, one vote" principle

1963 Friedan's *The Feminine Mystique* published
Civil rights advocates march on Washington
Baptist church in Birmingham bombed
Kennedy assassinated; Johnson becomes president

1964 Economic Opportunity Act allocates funds to fight poverty
Civil Rights Act outlaws discrimination in jobs and public accommodations
Twenty-fourth Amendment outlaws the poll tax in federal elections
Riots break out in first of the "long hot summers"
Hamer speaks on behalf of MFDP at Democratic convention
Free Speech movement begins at Berkeley
Johnson elected president

1965 Malcolm X assassinated
Voting Rights Act allows federal supervision of voting registration
Medicare and Medicaid programs begun
Elementary and Secondary Education Act provides federal aid to education
Watts race riot leaves thirty-four dead
Immigration and Nationality Act lowers barriers to certain ethnic and racial groups

1966 National Organization for Women founded
Miranda v. Arizona requires police to inform suspects of their rights

1967 Race riots erupt in Newark, Detroit, and other cities
Twenty-fifth Amendment establishes the order of presidential succession

1968 King assassinated
African Americans riot in 168 cities and towns
Civil Rights Act bans housing discrimination
Antiwar protests escalate
R. Kennedy assassinated
Violence erupts at Democratic convention
Nixon elected president

1969 Stonewall riot sparked by police harassment of homosexuals
Apollo 11 lands on moon
400,000 gather at Woodstock festival
Moratorium Day calls for end to war

1970 United States invades Cambodia
Students killed at Kent State and Jackson State Universities
First Earth Day celebrated
Environmental Protection Agency created

1971 *Pentagon Papers* published
Twenty-sixth Amendment extends vote to eighteen-year-olds
Inmates revolt at Attica prison
Swann v. Charlotte-Mecklenberg upholds North Carolina desegregation plan

1972 Nixon visits China and Soviet Union
Congress approves ERA
"Plumbers" break into Watergate
Revenue sharing distributes funds to states
Nixon reelected

1973 Watergate burglars tried
Ervin chairs Watergate hearings
Ehrlichman and Haldeman resign
Roe v. Wade legalizes abortion
War Powers Act passed
Agnew resigns; Ford named vice president
Saturday Night Massacre provokes outcry

1974 Supreme Court orders Nixon to release White House tapes
House Judiciary Committee votes to impeach Nixon
Nixon resigns; Ford becomes president
Ford pardons Nixon
Freedom of Information Act passed over Ford's veto

American organizer for the Student Nonviolent Coordinating Committee (SNCC). Hamer was the twentieth child of sharecropper parents, and at age six went to work chopping and picking in the cotton fields.

In the early 1960s Fannie Lou Hamer began to envision a better future through the direct action of the civil rights movement. In 1962 she lost her job on the plantation when she attempted to register to vote. The next year, Hamer was arrested with five other SNCC volunteers in Winona, Mississippi, taken to jail, and brutally assaulted by police swinging blackjacks. By 1964 she had become a field worker for SNCC, known for her courage.

At the televised hearings of the credentials committee, Hamer told the country about her experience in the Winona jail. She spoke of being beaten because she and others "wanted to register, to become first class citizens." She insisted that the MFDP—those who had fought for freedom—be seated, not those who opposed it. If "the Freedom Party is not seated now, I question America," she said.

The MFDP did not receive justice from the Democratic Party. Offered a consolation prize of two seats, the MFDP refused. In that election year, President Johnson would not alienate powerful southern white politicians by seating the civil rights delegation, but his action threw into question the Democrats' commitment to racial equality. Civil rights had become the most important political issue in the country, threatening to destroy the New Deal coalition in the South and the North.

The civil rights movement became a dynamic force in American society in the 1960s, helping to give birth in subsequent years to the antiwar movement, the New Left, a resurgent feminist movement, the environmental movement, and equality movements for other minorities. The civil rights movement also energized the presidential politics of John F. Kennedy and Lyndon B. Johnson. Kennedy's call for a New Frontier had inspired liberal Democrats, idealists, and brave young activists to work to eliminate poverty, segregation, and voting rights abuses. But Americans' dreams were shattered on November 22, 1963, when President Kennedy was assassinated in Dallas.

Lyndon Johnson, who asked for national unity in the wake of the Kennedy assassination, was a strong political leader. Johnson presided over what he called the Great Society, a flood of legislation designed to eradicate poverty in the United States and guarantee equal rights to all its citizens. But even during these years of liberal triumph, anger and social tension intermittently flared into violence. Beginning with Kennedy's assassination in 1963, ten years of bloodshed—race riots, the murders of other political and civil rights leaders, and the war in Vietnam—shattered the optimism of the Kennedy and Johnson eras.

The decade's turbulence, added to snowballing white opposition to the civil rights movement, prompted many Americans to shift to the right politically. In 1968 the Republican Richard M. Nixon was elected president, but his presidency polarized the nation still further. The presidencies of Nixon's two immediate predecessors had ended tragically: Dallas and Vietnam were the sites of their undoing. A third location, the Watergate apartment-office complex in Washington, D.C., marked Richard Nixon's downfall. ■

Civil Rights and the New Frontier

President John F. Kennedy was, as the writer Norman Mailer observed, "our leading man." Young, handsome, and vigorous, the new chief executive was the first president born in the twentieth century. Kennedy had a genuinely inquiring mind, and as a patron of the arts he brought wit and sophistication to the White House.

Kennedy's vitality and style captured the imagination of many Americans. In a departure from the Eisenhower administration's staid, conservative image, the new president surrounded himself with young men of intellectual verve who proclaimed that they had fresh ideas for invigorating the nation; the writer David Halberstam called them "the best and the brightest" (Kennedy appointed only one woman to a significant position). Secretary of Defense Robert McNamara (age forty-four) had been an assistant professor at Harvard at twenty-four and later the whiz-kid president of the Ford Motor Company. Kennedy's special assistant for national security affairs, McGeorge Bundy (age forty-one), had become a Harvard dean at thirty-four with only a bachelor's degree. Kennedy himself was only forty-three, and his brother Robert, the attorney general, was thirty-five.

"The Best and the Brightest"

Kennedy's ambitious program, the New Frontier, promised more than the president could deliver: an end to racial discrimination, federal aid to education, medical care for the elderly, and government action to halt the recession the country was suffering. Only eight months into his first year, it was evident that Kennedy lacked the ability to move Congress, which was dominated by a conservative coalition of Republicans and southern Democrats.

The New Frontier

Struggling to appease conservative southern members of Congress, the new president appointed five die-hard segregationists to the federal bench in the Deep South, and he pursued civil rights with a notable lack of vigor. Kennedy did establish the President's Committee on Equal Employment Opportunity to eliminate racial discrimination in government hiring. But he waited until late 1962 before honoring a 1960 campaign pledge to issue an executive order forbidding segregation in federally subsidized housing. The struggle for racial equality was the most important domestic issue of the time, and Kennedy's performance disheartened civil rights advocates.

Despite President Kennedy's lack of support, African American civil rights activists in the early 1960s continued their struggle through the tactic of nonviolent civil disobedience. Volunteers organized by SNCC and by the Southern Christian Leadership Conference (SCLC), headed by Reverend Martin Luther King, Jr., deliberately violated segregation laws by sitting in at whites-only lunch counters, libraries, and bus stations in the South. The Congress of Racial Equality (CORE) initiated the Freedom Rides in May 1961: an integrated group of thirteen people boarded a bus in Washington, D.C., and traveled into the South, where they braved attacks by white mobs for daring to desegregate interstate transportation. And many black high-school and college students in the South joined SNCC. These young people walked the dusty back roads of Mississippi and Georgia, encouraging African Americans to resist segregation and register to vote.

As the civil rights movement gained momentum, President Kennedy gradually made a commitment to first-class citizenship for blacks. In 1962 he ordered U.S. marshals to protect James Meredith, the first African American student to attend the University of Mississippi. And in June 1963 Kennedy finally re-

March on Washington

quested legislation to outlaw racial discrimination in employment and racial segregation in public accommodations. When more than 250,000 people, black and white, gathered at the Lincoln Memorial for a March on Washington that August, they did so with the knowledge that President Kennedy was at last on their side.

The television nightly news programs brought the civil rights struggles into Americans' homes. The story was sometimes grisly. In 1963 Medgar Evers, director

On July 20, 1969, American astronauts Neil A. Armstrong and Edwin E. (Buzz) Aldrin, Jr. (*shown below*), planted an American flag on the moon, thus fulfilling President John F. Kennedy's pledge to land a man on the moon by the end of the 1960s.   (NASA)

of the NAACP in Mississippi, was gunned down in his own driveway. The same year police in Birmingham, Alabama, attacked nonviolent civil rights demonstrators, including children, with snarling dogs, fire hoses, and cattle prods. Then two horrifying events helped to convince reluctant politicians that action on civil rights was long overdue. In September white terrorists exploded a bomb at Birmingham's Sixteenth Street Baptist Church. Sunday school was in session, and four black girls were killed. A little more than two months later, John Kennedy was assassinated in Dallas.

The first dreadful flash from Dallas clattered over newsroom Teletype machines across the country at 1:34 p.m. Eastern Standard Time, November 22, 1963. Broadcast immediately on radio and television, the news was soon on the streets. Time stopped for Americans, and they experienced what psychologists call flashbulb memory, the freeze-framing of an exceptionally emotional event down to the most incidental detail.

The Kennedy Assassination

Historians have wondered what John Kennedy would have accomplished had he lived. Although his legislative achievements were meager, he inspired genuine idealism in Americans. When Kennedy exhorted Americans in his inaugural address to "Ask not what your country can do for you; ask what you can do for your country," tens of thousands volunteered to spend two years of their lives in the Peace Corps. Kennedy also promoted a sense of national purpose through his vigorous support of the space program.

In recent years, writers have drawn attention to Kennedy's recklessness in world events, such as authorizing the Bay of Pigs invasion of 1961 (see page 551) and CIA attempts to assassinate Cuba's leader Fidel Castro. They also have criticized his timidity in civil rights. It is clear, however, that Kennedy had begun to grow as president during his last few months in office. He made a moving appeal for racial equality and called for reductions in Cold War tensions. And in a peculiar way he accomplished more in death than in life. In the postassassination atmosphere of grief and remorse, Lyndon Johnson pushed through Congress practically the entire New Frontier agenda.

Kennedy in Retrospect

The Great Society and the Triumph of Liberalism

In the aftermath of the assassination, President Lyndon Johnson resolved to unite the country behind the unfulfilled legislative program of the martyred president. More than that, he wanted to realize Roosevelt's and Truman's unmet goals. He called his new program the Great Society.

Johnson made civil rights his top legislative priority. "No memorial oration or eulogy," he told a joint session of Congress five days after the assassination, "could more eloquently honor President Kennedy's memory than the earliest passage of the civil rights bill." Within months Johnson had signed into law the Civil Rights Act of 1964, which outlawed discrimination on the basis of race, color, religion, sex, or national origin, not only in public accommodations but also in employment. The act also authorized the government to withhold funds from public agencies that discriminated on the basis of race, and it empowered the attorney general to guarantee voting rights and end school segregation. In 1964 African Americans gained two additional victories. First, President Johnson appointed an Equal Employment Opportunity Commission to investigate and judge complaints of job discrimination. Second, the states ratified the Twenty-fourth Amendment to the Constitution, which outlawed the poll tax as a prerequisite for voting in federal elections.

Civil Rights Act of 1964

Johnson enunciated another priority in his first State of the Union address: "The administration today, here and now, declares unconditional war on poverty." Eight months later, he signed into law the Economic Opportunity Act of 1964. The act became the opening salvo in Johnson's War on Poverty.

In the year following Kennedy's death, Johnson sought to govern by appealing to the shared values and aspirations of the majority of the nation for continued economic growth and social justice. His lopsided victory over his conservative Republican opponent in 1964, Senator Barry Goldwater of Arizona, indicates that he succeeded. Johnson gar-

Election of 1964

nered 61 percent of the popular vote, and the Democrats won large majorities in both the House and the Senate. Johnson recognized that the opportunity to push through further reform had arrived. Congress responded in 1965 and 1966 with the most sweeping reform legislation since 1935.

Three bills enacted in 1965 were legislative milestones: the Medicare program and Medicaid programs insured the elderly against medical and hospital bills and assisted the needy and disabled in paying for medical care; the Elementary and Secondary Education Act provided for general federal aid to education for the first time; and the Voting Rights Act empowered the attorney general to supervise voter registration in areas where fewer than half of the minority residents of voting age were registered. In 1960 only 29 percent of the South's African American population was registered to vote; when Johnson left office in 1969, the proportion was approaching two-thirds.

Voting Rights Act of 1965

The flurry of legislation enacted into law during Johnson's presidency was staggering: establishment of the Department of Housing and Urban Development, the Department of Transportation, and the National Endowments for the Arts and Humanities; water- and air-quality improvement acts; and appropriations for the most ambitious federal housing program since 1949, including rent supplements to low-income families. The Immigration and Nationality Act of 1965 lowered the barriers erected by the national origins quota system, which had severely restricted, or excluded altogether, certain ethnic and racial groups (see page 426). And the Civil Rights Act of 1968 banned racial and religious discrimination in the sale and rental of housing. Another provision of this legislation, known as the Indian Bill of Rights, extended those constitutional protections to Native Americans living under tribal self-government on reservations.

By far the most ambitious of Johnson's initiatives was the War on Poverty. Beginning with a $1 billion appropriation in 1964, the War on Poverty evolved in 1965 and 1966 to include the Job Corps, to provide marketable skills, work experience, and remedial education for young people; Project Head Start, to prepare preschoolers from low-income

War on Poverty

families for grade school; and Upward Bound, to help high-school students from low-income families to prepare for a college education. Other antipoverty programs were Legal Services for the Poor, Volunteers in Service to America (VISTA), and the Model Cities program, which channeled federal funds to upgrade employment, housing, education, and health in targeted urban neighborhoods.

In tandem with a rising gross national product (GNP), the War on Poverty substantially alleviated hunger and suffering in the United States. Its legislation directly addressed the debilitating housing, health, and nutritional deficiencies from which the poor suffered. Between 1965 and 1970, the GNP leaped from $685 billion to $977 billion, and federal spending for Social Security, health, welfare, and education more than doubled. Not only did some of this prosperity trickle down to the poor, but also—and more important—millions of new jobs were created. The result was a startling reduction in the number of poor people, from 25 percent of the population in 1962 to 11 percent in 1973 (see Figure 30.1).

Successes in Reducing Poverty

The period of liberal ascendancy represented by the War on Poverty was short-lived; most of the Great Society's legislative achievements occurred in 1964, 1965, and 1966. Disillusioned with America's deepening involvement in Vietnam and upset by the violence of urban race riots, many of Johnson's allies began to reject both him and his liberal consensus.

One branch of government, however, maintained the liberal tradition: the Supreme Court. Under the intellectual and moral leadership of Chief Justice Earl Warren, the Court in the 1960s was disposed by political conviction and a belief in judicial activism to play a central role in the resurgence of liberalism. In 1962 the Court began handing down a series of landmark decisions. *Baker v. Carr* (1962) and subsequent rulings established that the principle of "one person, one vote" must prevail at both the state and the national levels. This decision required the reapportionment of state legislatures by shifting seats from lightly populated rural areas to the burgeoning cities, so that each representative would serve the same number of constituents. The Court also

The Warren Court

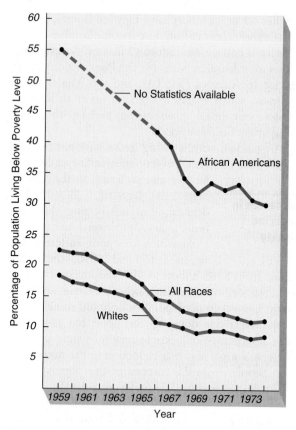

Figure 30.1 **Poverty in America for Whites, African Americans, and All Races, 1959–1974** Because of rising levels of economic prosperity, combined with the impact of Great Society programs, the percentage of Americans living in poverty in 1974 was half as high as in 1959. African Americans still were far more likely than white Americans to be poor. In 1959 more than half of all blacks (55.1 percent) were poor; in 1974 the figure remained high (30.3 percent). The government did not record data on African American poverty for the years 1960 through 1965.

Liberal Court Rulings

hibiting the use of contraceptives by married couples violated "a marital right of privacy" and was unconstitutional. The Court upheld the Civil Rights Act of 1964 and the Voting Rights Act of 1965. In other rulings that particularly upset conservatives, the Court decreed that books, magazines, and films could not be banned as obscene unless they were found to be "utterly without redeeming social value."

Perhaps most controversial of all was the Court's transformation of the criminal justice system. Beginning with *Gideon v. Wainwright* (1963), the Court ruled that a poor person charged with a felony had the right to a state-appointed lawyer. In *Escobedo v. Illinois* (1964), it decreed that the accused had a right to counsel during interrogation and a right to remain silent. *Miranda v. Arizona* (1966) established that police had to inform criminal suspects that they had these rights and that any statements they made could be used against them.

Despite conservatives' demands for Warren's removal, constitutional historians consider him one of the two most influential chief justices in the nation's history (the other was John Marshall). Whether or not one approved of the decisions of the Warren Court (which ended with Warren's retirement in 1969), its effect on the American people is undeniable.

Civil Rights Disillusionment, Race Riots, and Black Power

 Even while the civil rights movement was winning important victories in the mid-1960s, some activists began to grumble that the federal government was not to be trusted. The Mississippi Freedom Democratic Party felt betrayed by Lyndon Johnson and the Democrats, and evidence suggested that the Federal Bureau of Investigation was hostile to the civil rights movement. Indeed, one FBI informant was a member of the Ku Klux Klan and a terrorist who instigated violence against volunteers in the civil rights movement. FBI director J. Edgar Hoover was a racist, activists charged, and they were disturbed by rumors (later confirmed) that Hoover had wiretapped and bugged Martin Luther King, Jr.'s hotel rooms and planted allegations in the newspapers about his sexual improprieties.

outlawed required prayers and Bible reading in public schools, explaining that such practices imposed an "indirect coercive pressure upon religious minorities."

The Court also attacked the legal underpinning of the anti-Communist crusade, ruling in 1965 that a person need not register with the government as a member of a subversive organization. In *Griswold v. Connecticut* (1965), the Court ruled that a state law pro-

The year 1964 witnessed the first of the "long hot summers" of race riots in northern cities. In Harlem and Rochester in New York, and in several cities in New Jersey, brutal actions by white police officers sparked riots in black neighborhoods. African Americans deeply resented the unnecessary force that police sometimes used.

Explosion of Black Anger

Whites wondered why African Americans were venting their frustration violently at a time when they were making real progress in the civil rights struggle. The civil rights movement, however, had focused mostly on the South, aiming to abolish Jim Crow and black disfranchisement. In the North, African Americans could vote, but their median income was little more than half that of northern whites. Many African American families, particularly those headed by women, lived in perpetual poverty. The primary assistance program, Aid to Families with Dependent Children (AFDC), failed to provide payments that would cover a family's rent, utilities, household expenses, and food.

Northern blacks, surveying the economic and civil rights gains of the 1960s, wondered when they, too, would benefit from the Great Society. Concentrated in the inner cities, they looked around the ghettos in which they lived and knew their circumstances were deteriorating. Their neighborhoods were more segregated than ever; in increasing numbers during the 1960s, whites had responded to the continuing black migration from the South by fleeing to the suburbs. And as inner-city neighborhoods became all black, so did the neighborhood schools.

If 1964 was fiery and violent, 1965 was even more so. In August an altercation between blacks and police sparked rioting in the Watts section of Los Angeles; thirty-four people were killed. Between 1966 and 1968, other cities also exploded in riots. Instigated by blacks, the root causes were joblessness, lack of opportunity, and police brutality.

Race Riots

In 1968 the National Advisory Commission on Civil Disorders, chaired by Governor Otto Kerner of Illinois, released a report blaming white racism for the riots: "The nation is rapidly moving toward two increasingly separate Americas . . . a white society principally located in suburbs . . . and a Negro society largely concentrated within large central cities."

Clearly, many blacks, especially in the North, were beginning to question whether the nonviolent civil rights movement was serving their needs. In 1963 Martin Luther King, Jr., had appealed to whites' humanitarian instincts. Now another voice was beginning to be heard, one that urged blacks to seize their freedom "by any means necessary." It was the voice of Malcolm X, a one-time pimp and street hustler who had converted while in prison to the Nation of Islam faith, whose followers were commonly known as the Black Muslims.

A small sect that espoused black pride and separatism from white society, the Black Muslims condemned the "white devil" as the chief source of evil in the world. By the early 1960s Malcolm X had become the Black Muslims' chief spokesperson, and his advice was straightforward: "If someone puts a hand on you, send him to the cemetery." But Malcolm X was murdered in early 1965. His assassins were Black Muslims who believed he had betrayed their cause because he said he had met whites who were not devils and had expressed cautious support for the nonviolent civil rights movement. Still, for both blacks and whites, Malcolm X symbolized black defiance and self-respect.

Malcolm X

A year after Malcolm X's death, Stokely Carmichael, chairman of SNCC, called on African Americans to assert "Black Power." To be truly free from white oppression, Carmichael proclaimed, blacks had to elect black candidates, organize their own schools, and control their own institutions. After embracing Black Power, several organizations, including SNCC and CORE, expelled their white members and repudiated integration.

Black Power

To many white Americans, one of the most fearsome of the new groups was the Black Panther Party. Blending black nationalism and revolutionary communism, the Panthers dedicated themselves to destroying both capitalism and "the military arm of our oppressors," the police in the ghettos. The Panthers defied authority and carried rifles, but they also instituted free breakfast and healthcare programs for ghetto children, taught courses in African American history, and demanded jobs and decent housing for the poor. What particularly worried white parents was that some of

During award ceremonies at the 1968 Olympic Games in Mexico City, American sprinters Tommie Smith (*center*) and John Carlos (*right*) extend gloved hands skyward to protest racial inequality and express Black Power. In retaliation, Olympic officials suspended Smith and Carlos, but other African American athletes emulated them by repeating the clenched-fist salute on the victory stand.   (Wide World Photos, Inc.)

their own children agreed with the Panthers. Called the New Left, this vocal subset of the baby-boom generation set out to "change the system."

The New Left and the Counterculture

"I'm tired of reading history," Mario Savio, a graduate student at the University of California, complained in a letter to a friend in 1964. "I want to make it." Within a few months Savio realized his ambition as a leader of the campus Free Speech movement. After teaching in

SNCC's Mississippi Freedom Summer Project, Savio and others returned to Berkeley convinced that the power structure that dominated blacks' lives also controlled the bureaucratic machinery of the university.

In fact, the University of California at Berkeley was a model university in 1964, with a worldwide reputation for excellence and public service. At the time, Berkeley, with tens of thousands of students, was the largest single campus in the country. It was also hopelessly impersonal.

The struggle at Berkeley began when the university administration yielded to pressure from political conservatives and banned recruitment by civil rights and antiwar organizations in Sproul Plaza, the stu-

Free Speech Movement

dents' traditional gathering place. Militant students defied the ban, and the administration suspended them or had them arrested. In December the Free Speech movement seized and occupied the main administration building. Governor Pat Brown dispatched state police to Berkeley, and more than eight hundred people were arrested.

The willingness of those in positions of authority to mobilize the police against unruly but not violent students was radicalizing to many young people. Having grown up comfortable and even indulged, they soon found themselves treated like criminals for questioning authority and opposing what they considered a criminal war in Vietnam and racial injustice in America. Soon, the activism born at Berkeley spread to other campuses.

Two years earlier, another group of students met at Port Huron, Michigan, and founded the Students for a Democratic Society (SDS).

Students for a Democratic Society and the New Left

Like their leaders Tom Hayden and Al Haber, most SDS members were white, middle-class college students. In its Port Huron Statement, SDS condemned racism, poverty in the midst of plenty, and the Cold War. SDS sought nothing less than the revitalization of democracy by wresting power from the corporations, the military, and the politicians and returning it to the people.

Inspired by the Free Speech movement and SDS, a minority of students identified themselves as members of the "New Left." The New Left was united in its hatred of racism and the Vietnam War, but it divided along philosophical and political lines. Some radicals were Marxists, others black nationalists, anarchists, or pacifists. Some believed in pursuing social change through negotiation; others were revolutionaries.

As the slogan "Make Love, Not War" suggests, the New Left and the counterculture discovered a common cause as the war in Vietnam

Countercultural Revolution

escalated. Drugs and sexuality also were central to the "hippie" experience. Exhorted by Timothy Leary—a former Harvard instructor and advocate of expanded consciousness through use of LSD and other mind-altering drugs—to "turn on, tune in, drop out," millions of students experimented with marijuana and hallucinogenic drugs.

Music more than anything else expressed the countercultural assault on the status quo. Bob Dylan promised revolutionary answers "blowin'

Rock 'n' Roll

in the wind." Like sex and drugs, the music of the 1960s represented a quest to redefine reality and create a more just and joyful society. Rock festivals became cultural watersheds. In 1969 at Woodstock in upstate New York, more than four hundred thousand people ignored or reveled in rain and mud for days. A number of them began to dream of a peaceful "Woodstock nation" based on love, drugs, and rock music.

Some young people tried to construct alternative ways of life. In the Haight-Ashbury section of San Francisco, "flower children" created a distinct urban subculture. "Hashbury" inspired numerous other communal living experiments. The counterculture represented only a small proportion of American youth, but to middle-class parents, hippies seemed to be everywhere.

Most disturbing to parents were the casual sexual mores that young people were adopting. In 1960 the government approved the birth-control pill, and use of the pill accel-

Sexuality

erated among young people. For many young people, living together no longer equaled living in sin; and as attitudes toward premarital sex changed, so did notions about homosexuality and sex roles.

The militancy of the 1960s helped inspire the gay rights movement. Homosexuals had long feared that disclosing their sexual orientation would mean losing their jobs, friends,

Gay Rights Movement

and families. That attitude began to change in June 1969. When police raided the Stonewall Inn, a gay bar in New York City's Greenwich Village, they were greeted with a volley of beer bottles hurled by patrons tired of police harassment. The Stonewall riot, as historian John D'Emilio has written, "marked a critical divide in the politics and consciousness of homosexuals and lesbians. A small, thinly spread reform effort suddenly grew into a large, grass-roots movement for liberation."

During Lyndon Johnson's presidency, antiwar marches and demonstrations became a widespread

**Antiwar
Protests**

protest tactic (see Map 30.1), and students on campuses across the country held teach-ins—open forums for discussion of the war by students, professors, and guest speakers. Some young men fled the draft by moving abroad; others protested at local draft board offices. The Johnson administration charged that such acts threatened the nation's war-making powers.

President Johnson, after ordering American combat troops to Vietnam in 1965, claimed the United States was fighting for honorable reasons. By then, however, growing numbers of Americans had quit believing their elected leaders. Many people wondered what goal could justify the murder of Vietnamese women and children.

1968: A Year of Protest, Violence, and Loss

 As stormy and violent as the years from 1963 through 1967 had been, many Americans still tried to downplay the nation's distress in the hope that it would go away. But in 1968 a series of shocks hit them harder than ever. The first jolt came in January 1968, when the U.S.S. *Pueblo*, a navy intelligence ship, was captured by North Korea. A week later came the Tet Offensive in Vietnam (see page 557), and for the first time many Americans believed that America might lose the war.

Controversy over the war deepened within the Democratic Party, and two candidates rose to challenge Johnson for the 1968 presidential nomination. Senator

Map 30.1   Disturbances on College and University Campuses, 1967–1969   Students on campuses from coast to coast protested against the Vietnam War. Some protests were peaceful; others erupted into violent confrontations between protesters and police and army troops.

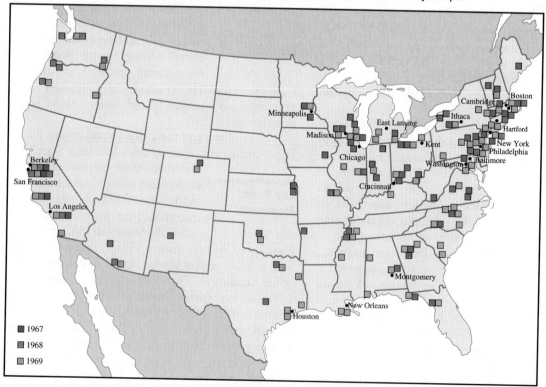

Eugene McCarthy of Minnesota entered the New Hampshire primary on March 12 solely to contest the Vietnam War; he won twenty of New Hampshire's twenty-four convention delegates. Soon another Democrat, Senator Robert F. Kennedy of New York, brother of the late president, entered the race. Then, on March 31, President Johnson went on national television to announce a scaling-down of the bombing in North Vietnam and his decision not to run for reelection.

Less than a week later, Martin Luther King, Jr., was murdered in Memphis by a white man. The mur-

Assassination of Martin Luther King, Jr.

der touched off massive grief and rage in the nation's ghettos. Riots erupted in 168 cities and towns, including the looting and burning of white businesses. Thirty-four blacks and five whites died in the violence. The terror provoked a white backlash. Tough talk was the response from Chicago mayor Richard Daley, who ordered police to shoot to kill arsonists.

Gallup polls in April and May reported Robert Kennedy to be the front-running Democratic presi-

Assassination of Robert Kennedy

dential candidate, and in June he won the California primary. After addressing his joyous supporters in a Los Angeles hotel, Kennedy took a shortcut through the kitchen to a press conference. A young man stepped forward with a .22-caliber revolver and fired. Sirhan Sirhan, the assassin, was an Arab nationalist who despised Kennedy for his unwavering support of Israel.

Violence erupted again in August at the Democratic national convention in Chicago. The Democrats

Violence at the Democratic Convention

were divided over the war, and thousands of antiwar protesters and members of the zany and anarchic Youth International Party (Yippies) had traveled to Chicago. The Chicago police force was still in the psychological grip of Mayor Daley's shoot-to-kill directive. Twelve thousand police were assigned to twelve-hour shifts, and another twelve thousand army troops were on call with rifles, bazookas, and flamethrowers. They attacked in front of the Hilton Hotel, wading into the ranks of demonstrators, reporters, and TV camera operators. Throughout the nation, viewers watched as club-swinging police beat protesters to the ground.

The Democratic convention nominated Vice President Hubert Humphrey for president and Senator Edmund Muskie of Maine for vice president. Humphrey was an unstinting supporter of the Vietnam War and a political liberal supported throughout his career by big-city bosses, African Americans, and union members. The Republicans selected as their presidential nominee Richard M. Nixon; his running mate was the tough-talking Governor Spiro Agnew of Maryland. Another tough-talking governor, George C. Wallace of Alabama, ran as the nominee of the American Independent Party. Wallace was a segregationist, a proponent of reducing North Vietnam to rubble with nuclear weapons, and an advocate of "law and order."

When the votes were tabulated, Nixon emerged the winner by the slimmest of margins. Wallace col-

Election of 1968

lected nearly 10 million votes, or almost 14 percent of the total. His strong showing made Nixon a minority president, elected with 43 percent of the popular vote. Moreover, the Democrats maintained control of the House and the Senate.

Still, given that the combined vote for Nixon and Wallace was 57 percent, the 1968 election was a tri-

Unraveling of the New Deal Coalition

umph for conservatism. The war had hurt the Democrats' appeal, but even more politically damaging was the party's identification with the cause of civil rights and welfare for the poor. In 1968 Humphrey received 97 percent of the black vote but only 35 percent of the white vote. Southern whites and northern blue-collar ethnic voters had defected from the New Deal coalition.

Rebirth of Feminism

Another liberation movement gained momentum during the turbulence of the 1960s. The women's rights movement had languished after the adoption of the Nineteenth Amendment in 1920. But in the 1960s feminism was reborn. Many women were dissatisfied with their lives, and in 1963 they found a voice with the publication of Betty Friedan's *The Feminine Mystique*. According to Friedan, most women had grown up believing that "all they had to do was devote their lives from earliest girlhood to finding a husband and bearing children." The problem was that this "mystique of feminine fulfillment" left many wives and mothers feeling empty and incomplete.

President Kennedy appointed only one woman, Esther Petersen, to a policymaking post in his administration. While serving as assistant secretary of labor and director of the Women's Bureau, Petersen encouraged Kennedy to establish the first President's Commission on the Status of Women, which he did in 1961.

National Organization for Women

Its report, *American Women* (1963), urged that every obstacle to women's full participation in society be removed. But little federal action followed the report, and the government was failing to enforce the gender-equality provisions of the Civil Rights Act of 1964. The need for action inspired the founding in 1966 of the National Organization for Women (NOW).

Not long after NOW's formation, a new generation of radical feminists emerged. Most radical feminists were white and well educated. The intellectual ferment of their movement produced a new feminist literature. Radical feminists focused not only on legal barriers but also on cultural assumptions and traditions. In the process they introduced the term *sexism* to signify a phenomenon far more pervasive and demeaning than lack of legal equality, and they challenged everything from women's economic and political inequality to sexual double standards and sex-role stereotypes.

Unlike NOW, the radical feminists practiced direct action, such as picketing the 1968 Miss America contest. One woman auctioned off an effigy of Miss America: "Gentlemen, I offer you the 1969 model. . . . She walks. She talks. She smiles on cue. *And* she does the housework." Into the "freedom trash can" the pickets dumped false eyelashes, hair curlers, girdles, and *Playboy* magazine to protest the prevailing view of women as domestic servants and sex objects.

"Personal Politics"

Many radical feminists were veterans of the struggles for black civil rights and against the Vietnam War. Even in these movements, however, women often found that instead of making policy, they were expected to make coffee, take minutes, and even provide sexual favors. Many of these feminists organized consciousness-raising groups to discuss sensitive matters such as homosexuality, abortion, and power relationships in romance and marriage. The issue of homosexuality caused a split in the women's movement. In 1969 and 1970 NOW forced lesbians to resign from membership and offices in the organization. The rift was healed in 1971, largely because lesbians as well as gay men had begun to fight back.

For working women in the 1960s, the most pressing problems were sex discrimination in employment, meager professional opportunities, low pay, lack of adequate daycare for children, and prohibitions against abortion. "Occupational segregation" forced women into low-paying positions. Thus in 1973 women earned 57 cents for every dollar earned by a man. Because many women with college educations earned less than men with eighth-grade educations, two of the most important women's goals of the 1960s were equal job opportunity and equal pay for equal work.

Working Women's Burdens

Despite setbacks, women were making impressive gains. They entered professional schools in record numbers: from 1969 to 1973, the number of women law students almost quadrupled, and the number of women medical students more than doubled. Under Title IX of the Educational Amendments of 1972, female college athletes gained the right to the same financial support as male athletes. The same year, Congress approved the Equal Rights Amendment (ERA)—"Equality of rights under the law shall not be denied or abridged by the United States or by any State on account of sex." But the number of states ratifying the ERA fell short of the number required.

Women's Educational and Professional Gains

The Supreme Court also ruled on several issues particularly pertinent to women. In *Roe v. Wade* (1973) the Court struck down laws that made abortion a crime. The Court at this time also addressed sex discrimination. In a 1971 ruling (*Reed v. Reed*), it held that legislation differentiating between the sexes "must be reasonable, not arbitrary," and in 1973 (*Frontiero v. Richardson*) the justices declared that job-related classifications based on sex, like those based on race, were "inherently suspect."

Roe v. Wade

Nixon and the Divided Nation

 Richard Nixon's presidency was born in chaos. Bloody confrontations occurred at Berkeley, Wisconsin, Cornell, Harvard, and scores of other colleges and universities in 1969. In October three hundred Weathermen (a splinter group of SDS) raced through downtown Chicago, smashing windows and attacking police officers. Violence was absent a month later, however, when a half-million people assembled peacefully at the Washington Monument on Moratorium Day to call for an end to the Vietnam War.

The following year was even more turbulent. President Nixon appeared on television on April 30 to announce that the United States had launched an "incursion" into Cambodia, a neutral country bordering Vietnam. Antiwar protest escalated. On May 4 national guardsmen in Ohio fired into a crowd of fleeing students at Kent State University, killing four young people. Ten days later, police and state highway patrolmen armed with automatic weapons blasted a women's dormitory at Jackson State, an all-black university in Mississippi, killing two students and wounding nine others. The police claimed they had been shot at, but no evidence of sniping could be found.

Kent State and Jackson State

Many Americans, though disturbed by the increasing ferocity of campus confrontations, felt more personally endangered by street crime than by student unrest. Sales of pistols, burglar alarms, and bulletproof vests soared. And conservatives accused liberals and the Supreme Court of causing the crime wave by coddling criminals.

Riots, protests, and violent crime convinced Nixon that the nation was plunging into anarchy. Worried that the antiwar movement was communist inspired, he ordered the FBI, the CIA, the National Security Agency, and the Defense Intelligence Agency to formulate a coordinated attack on "internal threats." Meanwhile, the administration also worked to put the Democratic Party on the defensive. The theme for the 1970 elections was to depict the Democrats "as being on the fringes: radical liberals who . . . excuse disorder, tolerate crime . . .

Politics of Divisiveness

and undercut the President's foreign policy." The strategy failed and the Democrats gained seats in the House.

Nixon's fortunes declined further in 1971. In June the *New York Times* began to publish the *Pentagon Papers*, a top-secret Defense Department study that revealed that the government had repeatedly lied to the American people about the Vietnam War (see page 558). Nixon also had to contend with inflation, a problem not entirely of his making. Lyndon Johnson's policy of "guns and butter"—massive deficit financing to support both the Vietnam War and the Great Society—had fueled inflation. By early 1971 the United States was suffering from a 5.3 percent inflation rate and a 6 percent unemployment rate. The word *stagflation* soon would be coined to describe this coexistence of economic recession (stagnation) and inflation.

Stagflation

Nixon shocked both critics and allies by declaring in early 1971 that "I am now a Keynesian." (According to the British economist John Maynard Keynes, governments could stimulate economic growth in the private sector by means of "pump priming," even if it necessitated deficit financing.) Nixon's budget for fiscal 1971 would have a built-in deficit of $23 billion. Then in August, in an effort to correct the nation's balance-of-payments deficit, Nixon announced that he would devalue the dollar and allow it to "float" in international money markets. Finally, to curb inflation, the president froze prices, wages, and rents for ninety days.

One of Nixon's chief legislative aims was revenue sharing, a program that distributed federal funds to the states to use as they saw fit. Invoking the federalism of the nation's founders, the president called this effort to shift responsibility back to state and local governments the New Federalism.

The environmental movement bore fruit during Nixon's first term. Alerted in 1962 to ecological hazards by Rachel Carson's *Silent Spring*, growing numbers of Americans began to heed warnings of impending disaster due to rapid population growth and rampant development. Environmental tragedies such as a 1969 oil spill that fouled the beaches and killed wildlife in Santa Barbara, California,

Environmental Issues

spurred citizen action. The Environmental Defense Fund (founded in 1967) successfully fought the use of DDT, and Greenpeace (founded in 1969) protested radioactive poisoning from nuclear-bomb testing. Although President Nixon was personally unsympathetic to the environmental movement, he acknowledged the movement's political appeal by reluctantly agreeing to the establishment of the Environmental Protection Agency in 1970 and by signing into law the Clean Air Act (1970), Clean Water Act (1972), and Pesticide Control Act (1972).

Nixon's Reelection and Resignation

Political observers believed that President Nixon would have a hard time running for reelection on his contrary first-term record. Having urged Americans to "lower our voices," he had ordered Vice President Agnew to denounce the press and student protesters. Having espoused unity, he had practiced the politics of polarization. Having campaigned as a fiscal conservative, he had authorized near-record budget deficits. And having promised peace, he had widened the war in Southeast Asia.

During Nixon's first term, the Democrats dominated both houses of Congress, and they continued to pursue a liberal agenda. Congress increased Social Security payments and food-stamp funding and established the Occupational Safety and Health Administration to reduce hazards in the workplace. Moreover, in 1971 the states quickly ratified the Twenty-sixth Amendment, which extended the vote to eighteen-year-olds.

Liberal Legislative Victories

In his campaign for reelection, Nixon continued to employ a "southern strategy" of political conservatism. A product of the Sunbelt, he was acutely aware of the growing political power of that conservative region. He thus appealed to the Silent Majority. And as in the 1970 congressional elections, Nixon equated the Republican Party with law and order and the Democrats with permissiveness, crime, drugs, pornography, the hippie lifestyle, student radicalism, black militancy, feminism, homosexuality, and dissolution of the family.

Nixon's "Southern Strategy"

The southern strategy also guided Nixon's nomination of Supreme Court justices. After appointing Warren Burger, a conservative federal judge, to succeed Earl Warren as chief justice, Nixon had selected two southerners to serve as associate justices, one of whom was a segregationist. When the Senate declined to confirm either nominee, Nixon protested angrily. By 1972, however, the president had managed to appoint three more conservatives to the Supreme Court. Ironically, the new appointees did not always vote as Nixon would have wished. In *Swann v. Charlotte-Mecklenberg* (1971), for instance, the justices upheld a desegregation plan that required a school system in North Carolina to work toward racial integration through massive cross-town busing. Nixon disagreed with this decision, as well as with Court rulings on abortion, wiretapping, and the death penalty.

Nixon and the Supreme Court

Nixon campaigned by assuming the elevated role of world statesman: in early 1972 he traveled to China and to the Soviet Union. But it was the inept campaign waged by the Democratic nominee, Senator George McGovern of South Dakota, that handed victory to the Republicans. When McGovern endorsed a $30 billion cut in the defense budget, people began to fear that he would reduce the United States to a second-rate power. McGovern's proposals split the Democrats between his supporters—antiwar activists, African Americans, feminists, young militants—and old-guard urban bosses, labor leaders, white southerners, and growing numbers of blue-collar workers.

Election of 1972

Nixon's victory in November was overwhelming: he polled 47 million votes, more than 60 percent. McGovern won just one state and the District of Columbia. Nixon's southern strategy had been supremely successful. He carried the entire once-Democratic Deep South. The president also carried a majority of the urban vote, including long-time Democrats such as blue-collar workers, Catholics, and white ethnics. Only blacks, Jews, and low-income voters stuck by the Democratic candidate. The Democrats did, however, retain control of both houses of Congress.

Little noticed during the campaign was a break-in at the Watergate apartment-office complex in Washington, D.C., on June 17, 1972. A watchman tele-

Watergate Break-in

phoned the police to report an illegal late-night entry into the building. At 2:30 A.M., police arrested five men who were attaching listening devices to telephones in the offices of the Democratic National Committee. The men had cameras and had been rifling through files.

One of those arrested was James W. McCord, a former CIA employee who had become security coordinator of the Committee to Re-Elect the President (CREEP). The other four were anti-Castro Cubans from Miami who had worked with the CIA before. Unknown to the police, two other men had been in the Watergate building at the time of the break-in. One was E. Howard Hunt, a one-time CIA agent who had become a White House consultant. The other was G. Gordon Liddy, a former FBI agent serving on CREEP's staff.

The Watergate fiasco actually began in 1971, when the White House established not only CREEP

White House Cover-up

but the Special Investigations Unit, known familiarly as the "Plumbers," to stop the leaking of secret government documents to the press. After publication of the *Pentagon Papers*, the Plumbers burglarized the office of Daniel Ellsberg's psychiatrist in an attempt to discredit Ellsberg, who had leaked the top-secret report to the press. It was the Plumbers who broke into the Democratic National Committee's headquarters, and money raised by CREEP was used to pay the Plumbers' expenses both before and after the break-ins.

The arrest of the Watergate burglars generated furious activity in the White House. Incriminating documents were shredded; E. Howard Hunt's name was expunged from the White House telephone directory; and President Nixon ordered his chief of staff, H. R. Haldeman, to discourage the FBI's investigation into the burglary on the pretext that it might compromise national security. Nixon also authorized CREEP "hush money" payments in excess of $460,000 to keep Hunt and others from implicating the White House in the crime. And he assured the press that no one in the administration "was involved in this very bizarre incident."

Had it not been for the diligent efforts of reporters, government special prosecutors, federal judges, and members of Congress, President Nixon might have suc-

Watergate Hearings and Investigations

ceeded in disguising his involvement in Watergate. Slowly, however, the truth emerged. In early 1973 U.S. District Judge John Sirica tried the burglars, one of whom implicated his superiors in CREEP and at the White House. From May until November, the Senate Select Committee on Campaign Practices, chaired by Senator Sam Ervin of North Carolina, heard testimony from White House aides. John W. Dean III, the White House counsel, acknowledged not only that there had been a cover-up but that the president had directed it. Another aide shocked the committee and the nation by disclosing that Nixon had had a voice-activated taping system installed in his White House office and that conversations about Watergate had been recorded.

In April 1973 Nixon tried to distance himself from the cover-up by announcing the resignations of his two chief White House aides. The ad-

Saturday Night Massacre

ministration then appointed Archibald Cox, a Harvard law professor with a reputation for uncompromising integrity, to fill the new position of special Watergate prosecutor. But when Cox sought in October to obtain the White House tapes by means of a court order, Nixon decided to have him fired. Both Attorney General Elliot Richardson and his deputy resigned rather than carry out the dismissal order. It thus fell to the third-ranking person in the Department of Justice to fire Cox. The public outcry provoked by the so-called Saturday Night Massacre compelled the president to agree to the appointment of a new special prosecutor, Leon Jaworski. When Nixon still refused to surrender the tapes, Jaworski took him to court.

In the same month as the Saturday Night Massacre, the Nixon administration was stung by another scandal. Vice President Spiro Agnew

Agnew's Resignation

resigned after pleading no contest to charges of income-tax evasion and acceptance of bribes when he was governor of Maryland. Under the provisions of the Twenty-fifth Amendment, Nixon nominated Gerald R. Ford, the House minority leader from Michigan, to replace Agnew. Congress confirmed the nomination.

Throughout 1973 and 1974, enterprising reporters uncovered more details of the break-in, the hush money, and the various people from Nixon on down who had taken part in the cover-up. White House aides and CREEP subordinates began to go on trial, and Nixon was cited as an "unindicted co-conspirator." *Washington Post* reporters Carl Bernstein and Bob Woodward found an informant, known as Deep Throat, who provided damning information about Nixon and his aides. As Nixon's protestations of innocence became less credible, his hold on the tapes became more tenuous. In late April 1974 the president finally released an edited transcript of the recorded conversations.

The edited transcript, however, had a lot of gaps. It swayed neither the public nor the House Judiciary Committee, which had begun to draft articles of impeachment against the president. Nixon still was trying to hang onto the original tapes when the Supreme Court in July, in *U.S. v. Nixon*, unanimously ordered him to surrender the recordings to Judge Sirica. At about the same time, the Judiciary Committee conducted nationally televised hearings. After several days of testimony, the committee voted for impeachment on three of five counts: obstruction of justice through the payment of hush money to witnesses, lying, and withholding evidence; defiance of a congressional subpoena of the tapes; and use of the CIA, the FBI, and the Internal Revenue Service to deprive Americans of their constitutional rights of privacy and free speech.

On August 6 the president finally handed over the complete tapes, which he knew would condemn him.

Nixon's Resignation

Three days later he became the first president to resign from office. Nixon's successor was Gerald Ford, whose first substantive act was to pardon Nixon. Some people concluded that Ford and Nixon had struck a deal.

The Watergate scandal prompted the reform of abuses that predated the Nixon administration. The executive's usurpation of legislative prerogatives, which historian Arthur M. Schlesinger, Jr., called "the imperial presidency," dated from Franklin D. Roosevelt's administration. To curtail presidential abuses of power, Congress enacted the War Powers Act (1973) and the Congressional Budget and Im-

Post-Watergate Restrictions on Executive Power

poundment Control Act (1974). The War Powers Act mandated that "in every possible instance" the president must consult with Congress before sending American troops into foreign wars. Under this law the president could commit American troops abroad for no more than sixty days, after which he had to obtain congressional approval. The Congressional Budget and Impoundment Control Act prohibited presidents from impounding federal money by requiring them to spend money appropriated by Congress for the purposes intended by Congress. Finally, to aid citizens who were victims of dirty-tricks campaigns, in 1974 Congress strengthened the Freedom of Information Act of 1966.

Summary

The thirteen years coinciding with the presidencies of John Kennedy, Lyndon Johnson, and Richard Nixon were a period of increasing disillusionment. As historian James T. Patterson observed, the period began with "grand expectations" about the attainability of "the Good Life." But riots in cities, violence on campus, diminished respect for government leaders, and growing economic uncertainty shattered Americans' illusions and supplanted earlier hopes for peaceful social change.

In 1961 John F. Kennedy challenged Americans to "pay any price, bear any burden, meet any hardship" to defend freedom and inspire the world. Twelve years later, Richard M. Nixon echoed that rhetoric: "Let us pledge to make these four years the best four years in America's history, so that on its 200th birthday America will be as young and vital as when it began, and as bright a beacon of hope for all the world." Largely because of his own actions, however, Nixon resigned the presidency before the nation could celebrate its bicentennial in 1976. Rather than young and vital, America seemed bruised and battered.

LEGACY FOR A PEOPLE AND A NATION
Watergate and Political Reforms

The legacy of Watergate has helped to undermine, if not destroy, many Americans' trust in their government. For more than twenty-five years, Watergate has contributed greatly to political cynicism, and it has cast a shadow over the presidencies of all of Nixon's successors. Its legacy is evident in the proliferation of special prosecutors, independent counsels, and congressional investigating committees, not to mention TV and newspaper reporters, who have examined political and personal behavior in the White House as never before. Both John F. Kennedy and Lyndon B. Johnson were widely known to be philanderers, yet the press subscribed to an unwritten code that held that such behavior was off-limits to reporters. This hands-off decorum all changed with Watergate. After 1974 even the smallest presidential mistakes were scrutinized and vilified.

In 1978 Congress passed the Ethics in Government Act authorizing the appointment of special prosecutors to investigate criminal wrongdoing in the White House. Sometimes, the controversial decisions and behavior were substantive, such as Ronald Reagan's Iran-contra affair and Bill Clinton's host of scandals, including a sexual relationship with a White House intern. Another special prosecutor, known as an independent counsel, Kenneth Starr, spent $48 million in more than five years of investigating scandals in the Clinton White House. In 1999 the independent counsel law expired and was not extended.

Watergate's legacy, however, is not limited to scandal-mongering. Soon after Nixon's resignation, Congress made a modest attempt to reduce campaign fundraising abuses, setting ceilings on campaign contributions. However, instead of limiting such abuses, this legislation provided new loopholes for electioneers to exploit. To circumvent the ceilings on contributions, special-interest groups established political-action committees (PACs). Moreover, Capitol Hill was crawling as never before with lobbyists from trade associations, corporations, labor unions, and single-issue groups such as the National Rifle Association. As the influence of money in politics has grown in the aftermath of Watergate, so too has political disillusionment.

For Further Reading, see the Appendix. For Web resources, go to history.college.hmco.com/students.

31

DISASTER AND DÉTENTE: THE COLD WAR, VIETNAM, AND THE THIRD WORLD

1961–1989

South Vietnam was "crumbling fast," Secretary of Defense Robert McNamara remarked. So the Joint Chiefs of Staff boldly recommended that another hundred thousand American troops be added to the eighty thousand already in Vietnam. In a tense meeting on July 21, 1965, President Lyndon B. Johnson asked his advisers, "Is there anyone here of the opinion we should not do what the [JCS] memorandum says?" Only Undersecretary of State George Ball spoke up: "I can foresee a perilous voyage." Johnson responded, "What other road can I go?" Ball answered, "Take our losses, let their government fall apart, negotiate, discuss, knowing full well there will be a probable takeover by the Communists." The president, imbued with the Cold War mentality, recoiled from the conclusion that what he once called a "damn little pissant country" could deny victory to the United States.

At an afternoon session, Ball again forthrightly argued a case few of his colleagues endorsed. "The war will be long and protracted. The most we can hope for is a messy conclusion." Ball doubted that "an army of Westerners can successfully fight Orientals in an Asian jungle," and he insisted that ultimately "the war will disclose our weakness, not our strength." Johnson listened but worried about U.S. credibility.

The next day Johnson met with top military officials. They told him that more men, more bombings, and more money were needed to save America's ally South Vietnam from defeat. "But if we put in 100,000 men," the president asked, "won't they put in an equal number, and then where will we be?" And have the

IMPORTANT EVENTS

1961 Kennedy becomes president
Peace Corps is initiated
Invasion at Cuba's Bay of Pigs fails
Alliance for Progress begins
Berlin Wall is built
Kennedy increases aid to South Vietnam

1962 Cuban missile crisis courts nuclear war

1963 Treaty bans atmospheric nuclear testing
U.S. cooperates in removal of Diem
Johnson becomes president

1964 Tonkin Gulf Resolution permits wider war

1965 Operation Rolling Thunder bombs North
Vietnam
Johnson increases troop strength in Vietnam
Antiwar teach-ins and demonstrations begin

1966 Fulbright's Senate hearings on Vietnam

1967 Six-Day War in the Middle East

1968 Tet Offensive sets back U.S. objectives
Dollar/gold crisis threatens U.S. economy
My Lai massacre leaves hundreds dead
U.S. invades Dominican Republic
Vietnam peace talks open in Paris

1969 Nixon becomes president; promotes détente
"Vietnamization" begins exit of U.S. troops
Nixon Doctrine calls for self-help by nations

1970 U.S. ratifies 1968 nuclear nonproliferation
treaty
Invasion of Cambodia sparks demonstrations

1971 *Pentagon Papers* reveal lies by U.S. leaders

1972 Nixon's trip to China thaws relations
SALT-I treaty limits nuclear weapons
"Christmas bombing" of North Vietnam

1973 Vietnam cease-fire agreement
Allende ousted in Chile

Arab-Israeli war and oil embargo
War Powers Act restricts president

1974 Ford becomes president
U.N. proposes "New International
Economic Order"

1975 Vietnam reunified under Communist rule

1977 Carter becomes president

1978 Senate approves Panama Canal treaties
Mideast peace accord made at Camp David

1979 SALT-II treaty recognizes nuclear parity
Hostages taken in Iran after shah falls
Soviets invade Afghanistan

1980 U.S. grain embargo and Olympics boycott
against USSR
Carter Doctrine for Persian Gulf

1981 Reagan becomes president
American hostages released in Iran
U.S. intervenes in Central America
Nuclear freeze movement grows worldwide

1982 U.S. troops intervene in Lebanon
START talks over nuclear forces begin
Law of the Sea Convention adopted, but not
by U.S.

1983 Reagan introduces SDI
U.S. deploys Pershing missiles in Europe
Terrorists kill U.S. Marines in Lebanon

1984 Reagan aids contras despite congressional ban

1985 Reagan Doctrine extols "freedom fighters"
Gorbachev promotes reforms in USSR

1986 Iran-contra scandal
U.S. economic sanctions against South Africa

1987 INF Treaty bans some missiles in Europe

1988 Negotiated settlement in Namibia

bombing raids hurt the enemy? Not really, the generals answered, but they would if more sites were added to the target list. Johnson wondered: "Isn't this going off the diving board?"

After asking searching questions and even revealing some doubts, Johnson nonetheless rejected a with-

drawal strategy and gave the Joint Chiefs of Staff what they wanted. He thought that America could win the war. A turning point in the Vietnam War, this decision meant that the United States was for the first time assuming primary responsibility for fighting the war. Fearing that he might spark a national debate about the deepening U.S. role, Johnson deliberately under-played the decision's importance when he announced it. He chose to deceive the American people because if the public focused its attention on the war, he argued, his Great Society reform legislation might be derailed.

By the end of 1965, nearly two hundred thousand American combat troops were at war in Vietnam. Yet Congress had not passed a declaration of war, and most of the American people remained ignorant of the venture. Ball later called Johnson's July decision "the greatest single error that America had made in its national history." McNamara, who vigorously challenged Ball's case in 1965, later wrote that he, McNamara, had been "wrong."

While the Vietnam War intensified, the Cold War became even more acrimonious, engulfing much of the world. Interventions and dangerous confrontations in the Third World, the nuclear arms race, and brinkmanship unsettled people everywhere. The Cuban missile crisis of 1962 brought the Soviet Union and the United States close to nuclear disaster. In its drive to win the Cold War, deter neutralism, and defuse revolutionary nationalism, the United States employed a host of instruments—foreign aid, CIA covert actions, military assaults, cultural penetration, economic sanctions, and diplomacy, among them. But the world did not become a safer place.

Ultimately the two great powers, the United States and the Soviet Union, weakened by the huge costs of their competition and challenged by other nations demanding that the Cold War end, faced an international system in which power became diffused. In an effort to stem their relative decline, the two adversaries began cautiously in the 1970s to embrace a process of détente, which soon sputtered. In the late 1980s, however, they took important steps toward ending the Cold War. ∎

Kennedy's Nation Building, Arms Buildup, and the Cuban Missile Crisis

 President John F. Kennedy's views owed much to the past. He criticized the appeasement policy of the 1930s, praised the containment doctrine of the 1940s, and vowed

to rout communism in the 1960s. Indeed, Kennedy's inaugural address suggested no halfway measures: "Let every nation know that we shall pay any price, bear any burden, meet any hardship, support any friend, oppose any foe to assure the survival and the success of liberty."

After Khrushchev endorsed "wars of national liberation" such as the one in Vietnam, Kennedy called for "peaceful revolution" based on the concept of nation building. The administration set out to help developing nations through the early stages of nationhood with aid programs aimed at improving agriculture, transportation, and communications. Kennedy thus initiated the Alliance for Progress in 1961 to spur economic development in Latin America. That year Kennedy also created the Peace Corps. This agency sent thousands of American teachers, agricultural specialists, and health workers into developing nations.

Nation Building and Counterinsurgency

Kennedy also relied on counterinsurgency to defeat revolutionaries who challenged Third World governments friendly with the United States. American military and technical advisers trained native troops and police forces to quell unrest. And American soldiers provided a protective shield against insurgents while American civilian personnel worked on economic projects.

Nation building and counterinsurgency seldom worked. Americans assumed that the U.S. model of capitalism and representative government could be transferred successfully to foreign cultures. But, although many foreign peoples welcomed U.S. economic assistance and craved U.S. material culture, they resented meddling by outsiders. And because aid was usually funneled through a self-interested elite, it often failed to reach the very poor. To people who preferred the relatively quick solutions of a managed economy, moreover, the American emphasis on private enterprise seemed inappropriate.

Under Kennedy, the CIA continued its covert operations, including training the Cuban exile brigade and Operation Mongoose against Cuba (see page 551). The agency also plotted in the Congo in 1960 and 1961 to poison Premier Patrice Lumumba. A CIA-backed Congolese political faction finally murdered Lumumba, who had turned to the Soviet Union for help during a civil war. In Brazil the CIA spent $20 million to influence the 1962 elections against President João Goulart, who had expropriated the property of the U.S.-based firm International Telephone and Telegraph and had refused to vote to oust Cuba from the Organization of American States. When Goulart's supporters won, the CIA helped organize opposition groups. In 1964, with U.S. complicity, the Brazilian military overthrew Goulart.

In fall 1961 the Soviet Union resumed aboveground nuclear testing by exploding a giant 50-megaton bomb. Khrushchev also bragged about Soviet ICBMs, raising American anxiety over Soviet capabilities. Intelligence data soon demonstrated that there was no "missile gap"—except the one in America's favor. Kennedy nonetheless sought to fulfill his campaign commitment to a military buildup based on the principle of flexible response: the capability to make any kind of war, from guerrilla combat to nuclear showdown. Thus the United States would be able to contain both the Soviet Union and revolutionary movements in the Third World. In 1961 the military budget shot up 15 percent; by mid-1964, U.S. nuclear weapons had increased by 150 percent. Although Kennedy inaugurated the Arms Control and Disarmament Agency and signed the Limited Test Ban Treaty with the Soviet Union (1963), which banned nuclear testing in the atmosphere, in outer space, and under water, his legacy was an accelerated arms race.

Military Expansion

In 1961 the Soviets again demanded negotiations to end Western occupation of West Berlin. Calling the city "the great testing place of Western courage and will," Kennedy rejected negotiations and asked Congress for an additional $3.2 billion for defense. In August the Soviets, at the urging of the East German regime, erected a concrete and barbed-wire barricade to halt the exodus of East Germans into West Berlin. The Berlin Wall inspired protests throughout the noncommunist world, but Kennedy privately sighed that "a wall is a hell of a lot better than a war."

Berlin Wall

U.S. hostilities with Cuba provoked Kennedy's most serious confrontation with the Soviet Union. When he took office in 1961, Kennedy inherited from Eisenhower a partially developed CIA plan to over-

Bay of Pigs Invasion

throw Fidel Castro (see page 526): Cuban exiles would land and secure a beachhead; the Cuban people would rise up against Castro and welcome a new government brought in from the United States. Because he felt uneasy over such a blatant attempt to topple a sovereign government, Kennedy ordered that the U.S. hand be kept hidden.

On April 17, 1961, directed by the CIA and escorted by U.S. warships, some fourteen hundred commandos scrambled ashore at the Bay of Pigs. A CIA scheme to assassinate Castro before the invasion had faltered. The Cuban people did not rise up against Castro. Within two days most of the invaders had been captured by Cubans loyal to Castro. Although Kennedy refused to order an air strike to aid the invaders when the landing was failing, the operation from the start never had much chance of success. As for Castro, the Bay of Pigs invasion helped him remain popular as a nationalist hero, as did his land reform and improvements in healthcare and education. Concluding that the United States might launch another invasion, the Cuban leader looked even more toward the Soviet Union.

Kennedy vowed to bring Castro down. The CIA soon hatched a project called Operation Mongoose to disrupt the island's trade, support raids on Cuba from Miami, and plot with organized-crime bosses to assassinate Castro. The United States also tightened its economic blockade, engineered Cuba's eviction from the Organization of American States, and undertook military maneuvers in the Caribbean.

Had there been no Bay of Pigs invasion, no Operation Mongoose, no assassination plots, and no program of diplomatic and economic isolation against Cuba, there would have been no missile crisis. For Castro, relentless U.S. hostility represented a real threat to Cuba's independence. For the Soviets, American actions challenged the only procommunist regime in Latin America. Premier Khrushchev also saw an opportunity to improve the Soviet position in the nuclear arms race. Castro and Khrushchev devised a risky plan to deter any new U.S. intervention. In mid-1962 they agreed to install in Cuba nuclear armed missiles capable of hitting the United States.

Cuban Missile Crisis

In mid-October 1962 a U-2 plane flying over Cuba photographed missile sites. The president immediately organized a special Executive Committee of advisers to find a way to force the missiles and their nuclear warheads out of Cuba. Some members advised a surprise air strike. The Joint Chiefs of Staff recommended a full-scale military invasion, an option that risked a prolonged war with Cuba, a Soviet attack against West Berlin, or even nuclear holocaust. Charles Bohlen, a U.S. expert on Soviet affairs, unsuccessfully urged quiet, direct negotiations with Moscow. McNamara proposed the formula that the president accepted: a naval quarantine of Cuba.

Kennedy addressed the nation on television on October 22 to demand that the Soviets retreat. U.S. warships began crisscrossing the Caribbean, while B-52s with nuclear bombs took to the skies. Khrushchev replied that the missiles would be withdrawn if Washington pledged never to attack Cuba. And he added that American Jupiter missiles aimed at the Soviet Union must be removed from Turkey. Edgy advisers predicted war, but on October 28 came a Soviet-American compromise. The United States promised not to invade Cuba and secretly pledged to withdraw the Jupiters from Turkey in exchange for the withdrawal of Soviet offensive forces from Cuba. Khrushchev agreed and the missiles departed Cuba.

Forcing Khrushchev to back down, many said, was Kennedy's finest hour. But critics then and now hold Kennedy responsible for provoking the crisis in the first place through his anti-Cuban projects. These critics also reject the view that Kennedy practiced an exemplary model of crisis management. His handling of the crisis actually courted disaster. Accidents, near misses, and inadequate information caused events to come close to spinning out of control. Finally, critics have argued that the strategic balance of power was not seriously altered by the missiles in Cuba; the United States still enjoyed a tremendous advantage over the Soviets in the nuclear arms race. Did Kennedy risk doomsday unnecessarily?

Kennedy's Handling of the Crisis

The Cuban missile crisis both calmed and accelerated the Cold War. In June 1963 Kennedy spoke at American University in conciliatory terms, urging cautious Soviet-American steps toward disarmament.

Aftermath

In August the adversaries signed a treaty banning nuclear tests in the atmosphere. They also installed a coded wire-telegraph "hot line." Both sides refrained from further confrontation in Berlin. Still, humiliated by the missile crisis, the Soviets determined to catch up in the nuclear arms race, sending the Cold War to a more dangerous stage. In mid-1963 Castro, seeking an accommodation with Washington, directed "feelers" toward U.S. diplomats. Kennedy authorized contacts with Cuban intermediaries, but also approved a new sabotage program against Cuba. The CIA at the same time revitalized assassination plots, all of which failed. After Kennedy's death, Johnson decided to put the cautious diplomatic contacts "on ice," words that well describe the years of Cuban-U.S. antagonism that followed.

Johnson and Americanization of the War in Vietnam

Lyndon B. Johnson held firmly to ideas about U.S. superiority and the menace of communism. A supreme can-do politician from Texas, Johnson saw the world in simple, bipolar terms: them against us. Invoking macho images of a fight-to-the-last-man Alamo, Johnson often exaggerated, went into rages, and lied. He opened a credibility gap with the American people. An old New Dealer and ardent liberal reformer, the president talked about building Tennessee Valley Authorities around the world.

Championing the global containment doctrine and holding a monolithic view of communism, Johnson drew the line not only in Southeast Asia but also in Latin America. In spring 1965, with the president fearing "another Cuba," twenty-three thousand U.S. troops landed in the Dominican Republic to prevent a leftist government from coming to power. Johnson's disparaging view of Dominicans and continued worries about anti-Americanism led to U.S. backing of a dictatorship on the island that lasted some thirty years.

As both the United States and the Soviet Union grew more alarmed by China's nuclear capability (the Chinese detonated their first atomic bomb in 1964), the Johnson administration in 1968 successfully com-

Nuclear Non-proliferation Treaty

pleted negotiations for the Treaty on the Non-proliferation of Nuclear Weapons. But many nonnuclear states saw discrimination because they had to renounce nuclear weapons while the nuclear states (United States, Soviet Union, Britain, France, and China) could keep them. The treaty ran into other obstacles. Both France and China refused to sign the agreement and supplied nonnuclear countries with nuclear fuel, and other nations defied the treaty by eventually developing their own nuclear weapons—Israel, South Africa, India, and Pakistan, among them. The Soviet invasion of Czechoslovakia in 1968 to block a nationalist movement caused Johnson to shelve further arms-control talks. And the war in Vietnam further diminished hopes for a relaxing of Cold War tensions.

Some observers called it "Johnson's War," but President Kennedy had significantly deepened U.S. engagement in Vietnam. Kennedy stepped up aid dollars to the Diem regime in the South, increased the airdropping of raiding teams into North Vietnam, and launched crop destruction by herbicides to starve the Vietcong and expose their hiding places. Under Project Beef-up, he sent more U.S. military personnel to South Vietnam; by late 1963 some 16,000 of these American "advisers" operated in Vietnam, and, that year, 489 of them were killed.

Kennedy's Legacy in Vietnam

Meanwhile, Diem's opponents grew in number. The U.S. Strategic Hamlet Program, which aimed to isolate peasants from the Vietcong by uprooting them into barbed-wire compounds, alienated villagers. Buddhist priests charged Diem with religious persecution. In the streets of Saigon, protesting monks poured gasoline over their robes and ignited themselves. Diem ran a corrupt government, handed out financial favors to family and friends, and jailed critics. U.S. officials, with Kennedy's approval, encouraged ambitious South Vietnamese generals to remove Diem. The generals struck on November 1, 1963, capturing and murdering Diem. A few weeks later Kennedy himself met death by an assassin's bullet.

With new governments in Saigon and in Washington, some leaders called for a coalition government in South Vietnam. But Lyndon Johnson vowed victory.

Tonkin Gulf Incident

On August 2, 1964, the U.S.S. *Maddox*, sailing in the Gulf of Tonkin off the coast of North Vietnam on an electronic intelligence–gathering patrol in an area where South Vietnamese commando raids recently had hit North Vietnam, came under attack from northern patrol boats (see Map 31.1). The unharmed *Maddox* repelled the attackers. Two days later, the *Maddox*, joined by another destroyer, moved toward the North Vietnamese shore once again. In bad weather on a moonless night, sonar technicians reported torpedo attacks; the two destroyers began firing ferociously. Johnson quickly informed his advisers that the United States would retaliate. But then the *Maddox* sent a flash message: "Review of action makes many reported contacts and torpedoes fired appear doubtful." Indeed, there was no attack that night.

President Johnson, aware at the time that the evidence was questionable, nonetheless pulled from his desk a resolution for Congress that he had had drafted months before. He announced on television that the United States would strike back against the "unprovoked" attack in the Tonkin Gulf by bombing North Vietnam. Congress passed the Tonkin Gulf Resolution, by 466 votes to 0 in the House and by 88 votes to 2 in the Senate. The resolution authorized the president to "take all necessary measures to repel any armed attack against the forces of the United States and to prevent further aggression." By passing the Tonkin Gulf Resolution, Congress essentially surrendered its powers in the foreign policy process by giving the president wide latitude to conduct the war as he saw fit.

Meanwhile, in Laos, Vietnam's neighbor, American bombers hit the "Ho Chi Minh Trail"—supply routes connecting the Vietcong with the North Vietnamese (see Map 31.1). The bombings were kept secret from Congress and the public. After winning the presidency in his own right in the fall of 1964, Johnson directed the military to plan stepped-up bombing of both Laos and North Vietnam.

Bombing Campaigns in Laos and Vietnam

In February 1965 the Vietcong, who controlled nearly half of South Vietnam, attacked the American airfield at Pleiku, killing nine Americans. In response, Johnson ordered a reprisal raid against North Vietnam. Shortly thereafter the U.S. initiated Operation

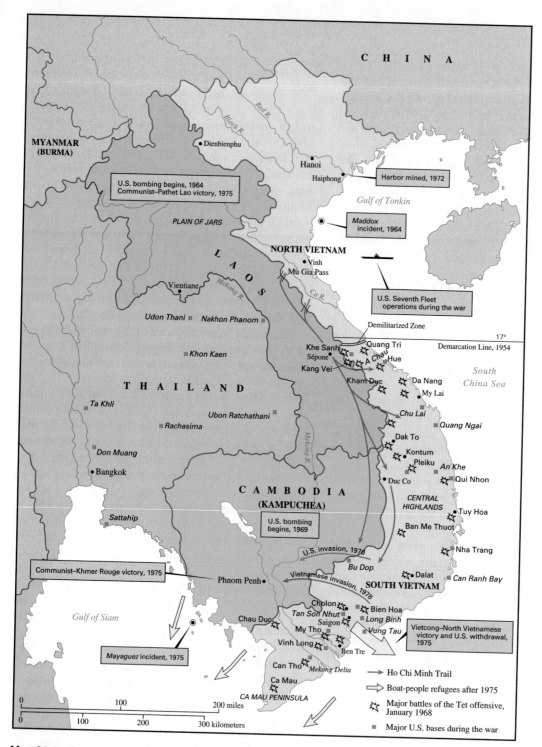

Map 31.1 Southeast Asia and the Vietnam War To prevent communists from coming to power in Vietnam, Cambodia, and Laos in the 1960s, the United States intervened massively in Southeast Asia. The interventions failed, and the remaining American troops made a hasty exit from Vietnam in 1975, when the victorious Vietcong and North Vietnamese took Saigon and renamed it Ho Chi Minh City.

Rolling Thunder, a sustained bombing program of the North (above the 17th parallel).

Then came Johnson's July decision to increase significantly U.S. ground forces. Month by month the war became Americanized. In 1966 American troops climbed to 385,000; the number peaked in 1969 at 543,400. The level of bombing also increased. In 1967 alone U.S. warplanes dropped 226,000 tons of bombs on North Vietnam. That same year the secret CIA-run Phoenix Program began to kill Vietcong leaders; probably 60,000 were assassinated. Undeterred, Ho increased the flow of arms and men to the rebels in the South. In this seemingly endless war of attrition, each American escalation begot a new Vietnamese escalation.

Troop Strength

Vietnam: Escalation, Carnage, and Protest

The Americanization of the war under Johnson troubled growing numbers of Americans, especially as television coverage brought the war into their homes every night. Innocent civilians were maimed and died, refugees straggled into "pacification" camps, and U.S. planes sprayed chemicals such as Agent Orange to kill crops and forests. The Vietcong and North Vietnamese contributed to the carnage and destruction, but American guns, bombs, and chemicals took by far the greater toll, and the Vietnamese people knew it.

Stories of atrocities made their way home. Most gruesome was the My Lai massacre. On March 16, 1968, a U.S. army unit led by Lieutenant William Calley entered the hamlet of My Lai and for four hours mutilated, raped, sodomized, and killed unarmed Vietnamese civilians, most of them women and children. The actual death toll numbered some 500.

My Lai Massacre

Calley and the other rapists and killers had lost their moral bearings. But the aftermath reveals that U.S. officials had lost theirs too. For twenty months the army covered up the massacre. And though Calley was court-martialed in 1971, President Nixon ordered him released from jail; three years later the mass murderer was paroled. Army juries acquitted and army officials dismissed murder and cover-up charges against all other personnel connected with the My Lai massacre.

Many incidents of deliberate shooting of civilians, torturing and killing of prisoners, and burning of villages have been recorded. Most American soldiers, however, were not committing atrocities. They were trying to save their own young lives (their average age was nineteen) and to serve the U.S. mission of defeating enemy troops. Less than 15 percent actually served in combat units; most made up the important rear-echelon supply and medical services that supported the "grunts" in the field. But wherever they were, the environment was inhospitable. Insects swarmed, and leeches sucked at weary bodies. Boots and human skin rotted from the rains, which alternated with withering suns. And no place in Vietnam was secure. Well-hidden booby traps blasted away body parts. And the phantom enemy was everywhere yet nowhere, often burrowed into elaborate underground tunnels or melded into the population, where any Vietnamese might be a Vietcong.

American Soldiers in Vietnam

As the war ground on to no discernible conclusion and became increasingly unpopular at home, growing numbers of GIs became cynical, believing either that the administration in Washington restrained them from clobbering the enemy or that the United States had no business being in Vietnam. Morale among U.S. forces sagged, and discipline sometimes lapsed. Disobedience, desertions, and absent-without-official-leave (AWOL) cases steadily increased. Racial tensions between whites and blacks intensified. Drug abuse became serious. Many soldiers smoked plentiful, cheap marijuana; 10 percent of the troops used heroin. "Fragging"—the murder of officers by enlisted men, usually using hand grenades—took at least a thousand lives between 1969 and 1972.

At home some young men were expressing their opposition to the war by fleeing the draft. By the end of 1972 more than thirty thousand draft resisters were living in Canada; thousands more had gone into exile in Sweden or Mexico or were living under false identities in the United States. During the war more than a half-million men committed draft violations, including

Wounded American soldiers after a battle in Vietnam.   (Larry Burrows/*Life* Magazine © Time Warner, Inc.)

a quarter-million who never registered and thousands who burned their draft cards. Others legally joined the National Guard to avoid the draft.

As American military engagement in Vietnam escalated, so did protest at home. Teach-ins at universities began in 1965, followed by years of campus and street demonstrations. In 1966 Senator J. William Fulbright held televised public hearings on whether the national interest was being served by pursuing the war in Asia. What exactly was the threat? senators asked. To the surprise of some, George F. Kennan testified that his containment doctrine was meant for Europe, not the volatile environment of Southeast Asia.

Growing Antiwar Sentiment

Disenchantment also rose in the administration itself. Defense Secretary Robert McNamara, once a vigorous advocate of prosecuting the war, became aghast over the Joint Chiefs' contemplating the use of nuclear

McNamara's Doubts

weapons in Vietnam and came to believe that continued bombing would not win the war. But, publicly, McNamara endorsed the war until early 1968, when he left office to head the World Bank. Much later, in his 1995 autobiography, he lamented that the decisions of the Kennedy and Johnson administrations on Vietnam "were wrong, terribly wrong."

Cheered by opinion polls that showed Americans favoring escalation over withdrawal, Johnson dug in. Though on occasion he halted the bombing to encourage Ho Chi Minh to negotiate and to disarm critics, such pauses often were accompanied by increases in American troop strength. And the United States sometimes resumed or accelerated the bombing just when a diplomatic breakthrough seemed imminent. The North demanded a complete suspension of bombing raids before sitting down at the conference table. And Ho could not accept American terms: nonrecognition of the Vietcong as a legitimate political organization, withdrawal of northern soldiers from the South, and an end to North Vietnamese military aid to the Vietcong—in short, abandonment of his lifelong dream of an independent, unified Vietnam.

In January 1968 a shocking event forced Johnson to reappraise his position. During Tet, the Vietnamese holiday of the lunar new year, Viet-

Tet Offensive

cong and North Vietnamese forces struck all across South Vietnam, capturing provincial capitals (see Map 31.1). Vietcong raiders even penetrated the American embassy compound in Saigon. U.S. and South Vietnamese units eventually regained much of the ground they lost, including the cities, and inflicted heavy casualties on the enemy.

The Tet Offensive jolted Americans. Although Tet counted as a U.S. military victory, it proved a psychological defeat for the U.S. war effort. Had not the Vietcong and North Vietnamese demonstrated that they could strike when and where they wished? If all of America's airpower and dollars and half a million troops could not defeat the Vietcong once and for all, could anything do so? Had the American public been deceived? The highly respected CBS television anchorman Walter Cronkite went to Vietnam to find out. When Cronkite somberly raised questions about the war on his evening telecasts, President Johnson sensed political trouble: "If I've lost Cronkite, I've lost middle America."

The new secretary of defense, Clark Clifford, told Johnson that the war—"a sinkhole"—could not be won, even if the 206,000 more sol-

Dollar/Gold Crisis

diers requested by the army were sent to Vietnam. The ultimate Cold Warrior, Dean Acheson—one of the "wise men" Johnson brought in to advise him—bluntly told the surprised president that the generals did not know what they were talking about. The wise men were aware that the nation was suffering a financial crisis prompted by rampant deficit spending, largely due to heavy U.S. expenditures abroad to sustain the war and other global commitments. Nervous foreigners were exchanging their U.S. dollars for gold at an alarming rate. On March 14 alone, foreigners—especially Europeans—redeemed $372 million for gold. A post-Tet effort to take the ini-

tiative in Vietnam would surely cost billions more and thus further derail the budget, panic foreign owners of dollars, and wreck the economy.

Strained by exhausting sessions with skeptical advisers, troubled by the economic implications of escalation, sensing that more soldiers

Johnson's Exit

and firepower would not bring victory, meeting protesters wherever he went, and faced with serious opposition within his own party (Senator Eugene McCarthy of Minnesota had just made a strong showing in the New Hampshire primary), Johnson changed course. On March 31 he announced that he had stopped the bombing of most of North Vietnam, and he asked Hanoi to begin negotiations. Then he stunned the television audience by dropping out of the presidential race. Peace talks began in May in Paris, but the war ground on.

Nixon, Vietnamization, and the Impact of America's Longest War

 In July 1969 the new president, Richard Nixon, announced the Nixon Doctrine: the United States will help those nations that help themselves. Washington knew that it no longer could afford to sustain its many overseas commitments and that the United States would have to rely more on regional allies to maintain an anticommunist world order. In Southeast Asia this doctrine translated into "Vietnamization" —building up South Vietnamese forces to replace U.S. forces. Nixon began to withdraw troops from Vietnam, decreasing their number to 156,800 by the end of 1971. But he also intensified the bombing of the North, hoping to pound Hanoi into concessions.

In April 1970 South Vietnamese and U.S. forces invaded Cambodia in search of arms depots and enemy forces using the neutral nation as a

Invasion of Cambodia

sanctuary. B-52 raids had been bombing Cambodia for more than a year, although Nixon never informed Congress or the American people. But the conspicuous venture into Cambodia could not be kept secret; it especially provoked angry demonstrations on college campuses (see page 543). In June the

Senate joined the outcry against Nixon's broadening of the war by terminating the Tonkin Gulf Resolution of 1964.

Nixon's troubles at home mounted in June 1971 when the *New York Times* began to publish the *Pentagon Papers*, a top-secret official study of U.S. decisions in the Vietnam War. Daniel Ellsberg, a former Defense Department official working at the RAND Corporation (a think tank for analyzing defense policy), leaked the report to the *Times*. The *Pentagon Papers* revealed that U.S. leaders frequently had lied to the American people.

The Nixon administration continued to expand the war. Johnson had lacked the will to "go to the brink," Nixon told Kissinger. "I have the *will* in spades." In December 1972 the United States launched a massive air strike on the North—the "Christmas bombing." Kissinger called the saturation air terror of 20,000 tons of bombs "brutal unpredictability." At the same time, the United States lost fifteen B-52 bombers.

In Paris, meanwhile, the peace talks begun in 1968 seemed to be going nowhere. But Kissinger was also meeting privately with Le Duc Tho, North Vietnam's chief delegate. On January 27, 1973, Kissinger and Le Duc Tho signed a cease-fire agreement. President Nguyen Van Thieu of South Vietnam objected to the agreement, but Nixon compelled him to accept it by threatening to cut off U.S. aid while at the same time promising to defend the South if the North violated the agreement. In the accord, the United States promised to withdraw all of its troops within sixty days. All Vietnamese troops would stay in place, and a coalition government that included the Vietcong eventually would be formed in the South.

Cease-Fire Agreement

The United States pulled its troops out of Vietnam, leaving behind some advisers. Soon, both North and South violated the cease-fire, and full-scale war erupted once more. The feeble South Vietnamese government could not hold out. On April 29, 1975, the South Vietnamese government collapsed. Shortly thereafter Saigon was renamed Ho Chi Minh City for the persevering patriot, who had died in 1969.

The overall costs of the war were immense. More than 58,000 Americans and some 1.5 million Vietnamese had died. Civilian deaths in Cambodia and Laos numbered in the millions. The war cost the United States at least $170 billion, and billions more would be paid out in veterans' benefits. The vast sums spent on the war became unavailable for investment at home to improve the infrastructure and quality of life. Instead, the nation suffered inflation and retreat from reform programs. The war also delayed accommodation with the Soviet Union and the People's Republic of China, fueled friction with allies, and alienated Third World nations.

Costs of the Vietnam War

In 1975 communists assumed control and instituted repressive governments in South Vietnam, Cambodia, and Laos, but the domino effect once predicted by U.S. officials never occurred. Acute hunger afflicted the people of those devastated lands. Soon refugees—"boat people"—crowded aboard unsafe vessels in an attempt to escape their battered homelands. Many emigrated to the United States, where they were received with mixed feelings by Americans reluctant to be reminded of defeat in Asia.

Americans seemed both angry and confused about the nation's war experience. For the first time in their history, the historian William Appleman Williams observed, Americans, having had their overseas sphere of influence violently pushed back, were suffering from a serious case of "empire shock." Hawkish leaders claimed that America's failure in Vietnam undermined the nation's credibility and tempted enemies to attack U.S. interests. They pointed to a "Vietnam syndrome"—a suspicion of foreign entanglements—that they feared would inhibit the exercise of U.S. power. Next time, they said, the military should be permitted to do its job free from the constraints of whimsical public opinion, stab-in-the-back journalists, and meddlesome politicians. America lost in Vietnam, they asserted, because Americans lost their guts at home.

Debate over the Lessons of Vietnam

Dovish leaders drew different conclusions, denying that the military had suffered undue restrictions. Some blamed the war on an imperial presidency that had permitted strong-willed men to act without restraint. Make the president adhere to the checks-and-balances system—make him go to Congress for a declaration of war—these critics counseled, and America would become less interventionist. This view found expression in the War Powers Act of 1973, which sought to limit the president's war-making freedom.

Other critics claimed that as long as the United States remained a major power with compelling ideological, strategic, economic, and political needs that could be satisfied only through activism abroad, the nation would continue to be interventionist. The United States was destined to intervene abroad, they argued, to sustain its hegemonic role as the world's policeman, teacher, social worker, banker, and merchant. Some critics blamed the containment doctrine. The containment doctrine could not work, they argued, if there were no political stability and no effective government in the country where it was being applied.

Public discussion of the lessons of the Vietnam War also was stimulated by veterans' calls for help in

Vietnam Veterans

dealing with post-traumatic stress disorder, which afflicted thousands of veterans. Doctors reported that the disorder of extreme nervousness and nightmares stemmed primarily from the soldiers' having seen so many children, women, and elderly people killed. Some GIs inadvertently killed these people; some killed them vengefully and later felt guilt. Other veterans heightened public awareness of the war by publicizing their deteriorating health from the effects of Agent Orange and other chemicals they had handled or were accidentally sprayed with in Vietnam. The Vietnam Veterans Memorial, erected in Washington, D.C., in 1982, has also kept the war before the public, as have many oral history projects of veterans conducted by school and college students in classes to this day.

Nixon, Kissinger, and Détente

Nixon's national security affairs adviser (1969–1973) and secretary of state (1973–1977), Henry Kissinger, often gets the credit (or blame) for the Nixon administration's grand strategy to promote a global balance of power. Nixon and Kissinger actually shared views about the need to boldly and repeatedly demonstrate U.S. power. The first part of the strategy was détente: measured cooperation with the Soviets through negotiations within a general environment of rivalry. Détente's primary purpose was to check Soviet expansion

and limit the Soviet arms buildup. The second part of the strategy sought to curb revolution and radicalism in the Third World so as to quash threats to American interests. The Cold War and limited wars like Vietnam were costing too much.

Nixon and Kissinger pursued détente with extraordinary energy and fanfare. They expanded trade

SALT

with the Soviet Union; a 1972 deal sent $1 billion worth of American grain to the Soviets at bargain prices. To slow the expensive arms race, they initiated the Strategic Arms Limitations Talks (SALT). In May 1972 Soviet and American negotiators produced two SALT I agreements. The first treaty limited antiballistic missile (ABM) systems for each nation to just two sites. ABM systems had accelerated the arms race because both sides built more missiles to overcome the ABM protection.

The other SALT I agreement imposed a five-year freeze on the number of offensive nuclear missiles each side could possess. At the time, the Soviets held an advantage in total strategic forces (ICBMs, SLBMs, and long-range bombers). But the United States had more warheads per missile because it could outfit each missile with MIRVs (multiple independently targeted reentry vehicles) that could send warheads to several different targets. In short, the United States had a two-to-one advantage in deliverable warheads (5,700 to 2,500). Because SALT did not restrict MIRVs, the nuclear arms buildup actually continued.

While cultivating détente with the Soviet Union, the United States took dramatic steps to end more

Opening to China

than two decades of Sino-American hostility. The Chinese welcomed the change because they wanted to spur trade and hoped that friendlier Sino-American relations would make their onetime ally and now enemy, the Soviet Union, more cautious. Nixon reasoned the same way. In early 1972 he made a historic trip to "Red China," where he and the venerable Chinese leaders Mao Zedong and Zhou Enlai agreed to disagree on a number of issues, except one: the Soviet Union should not be permitted to make gains in Asia. Official diplomatic recognition and the exchange of ambassadors came in 1979.

Events in the Third World—especially in the Middle East—revealed the fragility of the U.S. grand

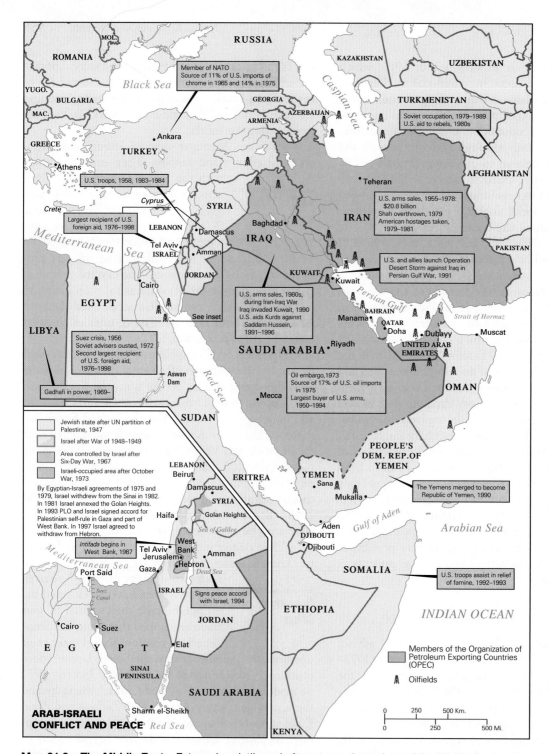

Map 31.2   The Middle East   Extremely volatile and often at war, the nations of the Middle East maintained precarious relations with the United States. To protect its interests, the United States extended large amounts of economic and military aid and sold huge quantities of weapons to the area. At times, Washington ordered American troops to the region. The Arab-Israeli dispute particularly upended order, although the peace process moved forward.

War in the Middle East

strategy. Israel, using American weapons, had scored victories against Egypt and Syria in the Six-Day War (1967), seizing the West Bank and the ancient city of Jerusalem from Jordan, the Golan Heights from Syria, and the Sinai Peninsula from Egypt (see Map 31.2), and thereby creating the enduring problem of the "occupied territories." A few years earlier Palestinians, many of them expelled from their homes in 1948 when the nation of Israel was created, had organized the Palestine Liberation Organization (PLO) and pledged to destroy Israel.

In October 1973 Egypt and Syria attacked Israel. In an attempt to push Americans into a pro-Arab stance, the Organization of Petroleum Exporting Countries (OPEC) embargoed shipments of oil to the United States. An energy crisis and dramatically higher oil prices rocked the nation. Soon Kissinger arranged a cease-fire, and in March 1974 OPEC lifted the oil embargo. The next year Kissinger persuaded Egypt and Israel to accept a U.N. peacekeeping force in the Sinai. But peace did not come to the region because Palestinian and other Arabs still vowed to destroy Israel, and Israelis insisted on building Jewish settlements in occupied lands.

In Latin America, meanwhile, the Nixon administration pursued the traditional antiradical course of the United States. In Chile, after

Chile

voters in 1970 elected a Marxist president, Salvador Allende, the CIA began secret operations to disrupt Chile and encouraged military officers to stage a coup. In 1973 a military junta ousted Allende and installed an authoritarian regime. Washington publicly denied any role in the affair, which implanted iron-fisted tyranny in Chile for two decades.

In Africa, Washington built economic ties with mineral-rich countries and sent arms to friendly black nations such as Kenya and Zaire.

Containing Radicalism in Africa

However, Nixon also backed the white-minority regime in Rhodesia (now Zimbabwe); activated the CIA in a failed effort to defeat a Soviet- and Cuban-backed faction in newly independent Angola's civil war; and in South Africa tolerated the white rulers who imposed the segregationist policy of apartheid on blacks. But gradually, the administration began to distance the United States

from the white governments of Rhodesia and South Africa. America had to "prevent the radicalization of Africa," said Kissinger.

The United States was interventionist in the Third World in part because the American economy was so intertwined with the world

United States in the World Economy

economy. American investments abroad totaled more than $133 billion by the mid-1970s. The United States also depended on imports of strategic raw materials such as manganese. American leaders read threats to markets, investments, and raw materials as stabs at the high American standard of living. Particularly alarming was the United Nations's 1974 call for a "New International Economic Order" for the Third World: low-interest loans, lower prices for technology, and higher prices for raw materials.

Global economic instability undercut the Nixon-Kissinger grand design. The worldwide economic downturn of the early 1970s was the worst since the 1930s. Inflation and high oil prices pinched rich and poor nations alike. Protectionist tendencies raised tariffs and impeded world trade. And debt-ridden Third World nations—sometimes called the "South"—insisted that countries of the industrial "North" share their wealth. In this turbulent setting, the United States began to suffer a trade deficit—importing more goods than it exported. A "dollar glut" abroad threatened to drain the U.S. gold supply as foreigners exchanged their dollars for the precious metal. In 1971 Nixon shocked foreign capitals when he devalued the dollar, suspended its convertibility into gold, and imposed a surtax on imports, seeking thereby to reduce the influx of Japanese and European goods.

Nixon's 1971 decisions shocked Japan, which enjoyed a favorable balance of trade with the United States ($3.2 billion in 1971) derived from an

Economic Competition with Japan

increasing share of the American market in motor vehicles and electronics and from sales to U.S. forces in Vietnam and for maintaining the 169 U.S. military bases in Japan. Although the Japanese agreed to limit some exports to the United States (such as color televisions), the two nations were "getting bogged down in economic arm-wrestling," as Kissinger feared. By 1980 the trade balance had jumped even more in Japan's favor to $10.4 billion; by

1989 it was $50 billion. Americans increasingly worried that in the contest between the two economic giants, Japan was winning. So it seemed in 1989 when the best-selling car in America was the Honda Accord and Sony bought Columbia Pictures. Still, by most measurements, Americans remained at the top of the economic hill.

Changes in the natural environment also earned a place on America's foreign policy agenda. Public discussion of environmental degradation and of the imbalance between food supplies and burgeoning populations, along with the work of nongovernmental organizations such as Greenpeace, formed in 1969, pressed Washington to act. In 1972 the United States agreed to participate in a U.N.-sponsored environmental conference in Stockholm, Sweden. The conferees especially spotlighted transborder pollution, the overkilling of whales to the point of endangerment, and goals for environmental protection that all nations should seek to meet.

International Environmental Issues

Carter, Preventive Diplomacy, and a Reinvigorated Cold War

When President Jimmy Carter took office in 1977, he asked Americans to put their "inordinate fear of Communism" behind them. With reformist zeal, Carter vowed to reduce the U.S. military presence overseas, to cut back arms sales, and to slow the nuclear arms race. He also promised to avoid new Vietnams through an activist preventive diplomacy in the Third World and to give more attention to North-South and environmental issues. Carter especially determined to improve human rights abroad—the freedom to vote, worship, travel, speak out, and get a fair trial.

Carter spoke and acted inconsistently, in part because in the post-Vietnam years no consensus existed in foreign policy and in part because his advisers squabbled among themselves. One source of the problem was the stern-faced Zbigniew Brzezinski, a Polish-born political scientist who became Carter's national security adviser. An old-fashioned Cold Warrior, Brzezinski blamed foreign

Carter's Divided Administration

crises on the Soviet Union. Carter gradually listened more to Brzezinski than to Secretary of State Cyrus Vance, an experienced public servant who advocated quiet diplomacy.

Under Carter, détente deteriorated and the Cold War deepened. Soviet leaders objected to Carter's insistence that their authoritarian regime respect human rights. They also reproached the U.S. for playing its "China card"—building up China in order to threaten the Soviet Union.

Despite this rocky start, a new treaty, SALT II, codified Soviet-American nuclear parity in 1979. The agreement placed a ceiling of 2,250 delivery vehicles on each side, capped MIRVed launchers at 1,200 for each, and limited the number of warheads per delivery vehicle. The treaty did not affect nuclear warheads, which stood at 9,200 for the United States and 5,000 for the Soviet Union. To win votes for the treaty from skeptical conservatives, Carter announced an expensive military expansion program and deployment of Pershing II missiles and cruise missiles in NATO countries.

SALT II

As Senate ratification of SALT II stalled and Moscow fumed over the Pershings, events in Afghanistan led to Soviet-American confrontation. In late 1979 the Red Army bludgeoned its way into Afghanistan to shore up a faltering Communist government under siege by Muslim rebels. Carter shelved SALT II (the two powers nonetheless unilaterally honored its terms later), suspended shipments of grain and high-technology equipment to the Soviet Union, and initiated an international boycott of the 1980 Summer Olympics in Moscow. The Soviets did not withdraw their forces from Afghanistan. The president also announced the Carter Doctrine: the United States would intervene, unilaterally and militarily if necessary, should Soviet aggression threaten the petroleum-rich Persian Gulf.

Carter markedly improved the Mideast peace process. Through tenacious personal diplomacy at a Camp David, Maryland, meeting in September 1978 with Egyptian and Israeli leaders, the president persuaded Israel and Egypt to sign a peace treaty, gained Israel's promise to withdraw from the Sinai Peninsula, and forged an agreement that provided for continued negotiations

Camp David Accords

On March 26, 1979, Egypt's president Anwar el-Sadat (1918–1981) on the left, Israel's prime minister Menachem Begin (1913–1992) on the right, and U.S. president Jimmy Carter (b. 1924) signed a peace treaty known as the Camp David accords. Studiously negotiated by Carter, the Egyptian-Israeli peace has held to this day—despite conflict in much of the rest of the Middle East.   (Jimmy Carter Presidential Library)

on the future status of the Palestinian people living in the occupied territories of Jordan's West Bank and Egypt's Gaza Strip (see Map 31.2). Other Arab states denounced the agreement for not requiring Israel to relinquish all occupied territories and for not guaranteeing a Palestinian homeland. But the treaty at least ended warfare along one frontier in that troubled area of the world.

Carter's toughest foreign policy test came in Iran, where the U.S.-backed shah was overthrown in 1979 by Iranian revolutionaries led by Ayatollah Ruhollah Khomeini, a bitterly anti-American Muslim cleric. Much of the revolutionaries' anti-Americanism stemmed from the CIA's training of the shah's ruthless secret police and the huge infusion of U.S. arms into their country. When the shah was overthrown and then admitted to the United States for medical treatment, mobs stormed the U.S. embassy

Iranian Hostage Crisis

in Teheran. They took American personnel as hostages, demanding the return of the shah to stand trial. Fifty-two Americans languished more than a year under Iranian guard.

Unable to gain the hostages' freedom through diplomatic intermediaries, Carter took steps to freeze Iranian assets in the United States. In April 1980, frustrated and at a low ebb in public opinion polls, Carter broke diplomatic relations with Iran and ordered a daring rescue mission. But the rescue effort miscarried after equipment failure in the sandy Iranian desert, and during the hasty withdrawal two aircraft collided, killing eight American soldiers. As for the hostages, they were not freed until January 1981, after Carter left office and the United States unfroze Iranian assets and promised not to intervene again in Iran's internal affairs.

In Latin America, Carter sought compromise with nationalists (see Map 31.3), even seeking to reduce

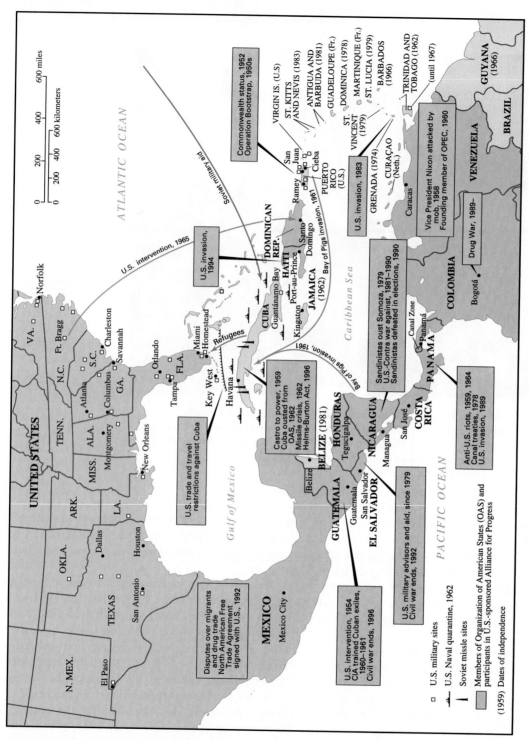

Map 31.3 The United States in the Caribbean and Central America The United States often has intervened in the Caribbean and Central America. Geographical proximity, economic stakes, political disputes, security links, trade in illicit drugs, and Cuba's alliance with the Soviet Union and defiance of the United States have kept North American eyes fixed on events in the region.

tensions with Castro's Cuba by establishing limited diplomatic links. But a crisis in 1980, during which the island regime allowed a hundred thousand Cubans (many of them mentally ill or prisoners freed from jail) to sail to Florida from the port of Mariel, poisoned relations once again.

In Panama, where citizens believed that the Canal Zone had been wrongfully taken from them in 1903, Carter reenergized negotiations that

Panama Canal Treaties

had begun after anti-American riots in 1964. The United States signed two treaties with Panama in 1977. One provided for the return of the Canal Zone to Panama in 2000, and the other guaranteed the United States the right to defend the canal after that time. The Senate narrowly endorsed both agreements in 1978.

Carter's record sparked considerable criticism from both left and right. Contrary to his goals, more American military personnel were stationed overseas in 1980 than in 1976, the defense budget climbed, and sales of arms abroad grew to $15.3 billion in 1980. On human rights, the president proved inconsistent. He practiced a double standard by applying the human-rights test to some nations (the Soviet Union, Argentina, and Chile) but not to U.S. allies (South Korea, the shah's Iran, and the Philippines). Carter's human-rights policy nonetheless popularized and institutionalized concern for human rights around the world. Carter did not satisfy Americans who wanted a post-Vietnam restoration of the economic hegemony and military edge the United States once enjoyed. In 1980 dissatisfaction with Carter's foreign policy helped elect the hawkish Ronald Reagan, former Hollywood actor and governor of California.

The Ups and Downs of Reagan's World

Reagan did not have a firm grasp of world issues, history, or geography. After returning from his first trip to South America, he commented, "Well, I've learned a lot. . . . You'd be surprised. They're all individual countries." Superficial and often mistaken about elementary facts, Reagan acted more on instinct than on analysis.

Embracing traditional American bipolar thinking, Reagan endorsed a devil theory: a malevolent Soviet Union, the "evil empire," would "commit any crime," "lie," and "cheat" to achieve a communist world. Because he attributed Third World disorders to Soviet intrigue, the president in 1985 declared the Reagan Doctrine: the United States would openly support anticommunist movements—"freedom fighters"—wherever they were battling the Soviets or Soviet-backed governments. Under this doctrine, the CIA funneled aid to insurgents in Afghanistan, Nicaragua, Angola, and elsewhere. In open defiance of the sovereignty of those nations, Reagan worked to overthrow their governments.

Reagan officials also championed free-market capitalism, evident in their enthusiasm for the 1988

Law of the Sea Convention

U.S.-Canada Free Trade Agreement, and in their rejection of the 1982 United Nations Convention on the Law of the Sea, patiently crafted through compromise over a ten-year period. Third World nations argued that rich sea-bed resources of petroleum and minerals should be shared under international supervision among all nations as a "common heritage of mankind." The industrial states preferred private exploitation with minimal international management. The Reagan administration shelved the convention on the grounds that it did not adequately protect private American companies.

Another Reagan tenet held that a substantial military buildup would thwart the Soviet threat and intimidate Moscow. CIA reports overestimating Soviet military strength reassured the president that he was on the right track. Assigning low priority to arms-control talks, Reagan announced in 1983 development of an antimissile defense system in space: the Strategic Defense Initiative (SDI) or "Star Wars."

Reagan's first decision affecting the Soviets was actually friendly. Fulfilling a campaign pledge to help American farmers, in 1981 he lifted the grain embargo. The Soviet Union soon bought grain worth $3 billion. But bitter hostility soon followed when Poland's pro-Soviet leaders cracked down on the Solidarity labor movement. In response, Washington placed restrictions on Soviet-American trade and hurled angry words at Moscow. In 1983 Reagan restricted commercial flights to the Soviet Union after a

Soviet fighter pilot mistakenly shot down a South Korean commercial jet that had strayed some 300 miles off course into Soviet airspace. The world was shocked by the death of 269 passengers, and Reagan exploited the tragedy to score Cold War points.

When he came to office, Reagan believed that the Soviets and Castro's Cuba were fomenting disorder in

Intervention in El Salvador

Central America (see Map 31.3). In El Salvador, revolutionaries challenged the government, which was dominated by the military and a landed elite. The regime used (or could not control) right-wing death squads, which killed thousands of dissidents and other citizens as well as several American missionaries who had been working with landless peasants. Reagan officials hoped for reform but intended to prevent revolution in El Salvador. By 1989 the United States had spent $6 billion there in a counterinsurgency war.

The U.S. intervention in the Salvadoran civil war sparked a debate much like the earlier one over Vietnam. Those who urged negotiations thought Reagan wrong to interpret the conflict as a Cold War contest; such civil wars stemmed not from Soviet meddling but from deep-seated economic instability, poverty, and class oppression. Resurrecting the discredited domino theory, Reagan retorted that the "Communists" would soon be at the Texas border if they were not stopped in El Salvador. After intense debate, Congress repeatedly gave Reagan the funds he wanted for El Salvador, while the death squads murdered at will, thwarting the radicals. In January 1992 the Salvadoran combatants finally negotiated a U.N.-sponsored peace.

In 1979 leftist insurgents in Nicaragua overthrew Anastasio Somoza, a long-time ally of the United

Contra War in Nicaragua

States. The revolutionaries, called Sandinistas, denounced the tradition of U.S. imperialism in their country. When the Sandinistas aided rebels in El Salvador, bought Soviet weapons, and invited Cubans to work in Nicaragua's hospitals and schools and to help reorganize their army, Reagan officials charged that Nicaragua was becoming a Soviet client. In 1981 the CIA began to train, arm, and direct more than ten thousand counterrevolutionaries, called contras, to overthrow the Nicaraguan government. From CIA bases in Honduras and Costa Rica, the contras crossed into Nicaragua to kill officials and destroy oil refineries, transportation facilities, and medical clinics.

In 1984 Congress voted to stop U.S. military aid to the contras ("humanitarian" aid was soon sent in its place). The Reagan administration secretly lined up other countries, including Saudi Arabia, Panama, and Korea, to funnel money and weapons to the contras, and in 1985 Reagan imposed an economic embargo against Nicaragua. The next year, Congress once again voted military aid for the contras. During the undeclared U.S. war against Nicaragua, Reagan rejected opportunities for diplomacy. But Central American presidents brokered a national election in 1990. The Sandinistas lost to a U.S.-funded party.

Scandal tainted the North American crusade against the Sandinistas. It became known in 1986 that

Iran-Contra Scandal

the president's national security adviser, John M. Poindexter, and an aide, Marine Lieutenant Colonel Oliver North, in collusion with CIA director William J. Casey, had covertly sold weapons to Iran and then diverted the profits to the contras so that they could purchase arms. The diversion occurred after Congress had prohibited military assistance to the contras. President Reagan lied when he said that he knew nothing of these activities. In late 1992 outgoing president George H. W. Bush pardoned several former government officials who had been convicted of lying to Congress. Critics smelled a cover-up, for Bush himself, as vice president, had participated in high-level meetings on Iran-contra deals.

Elsewhere in the Third World, the deeply divided Middle East continued to defy American solutions

U.S. Interests in the Middle East

(see Map 31.2). The United States had commitments (Israel), political friends (Saudi Arabia), and enemies (Libya and Iran). Mideast oil supplies fueled Western economies. An Iraqi-Iranian war, in which the United States aided Iraq, threatened Persian Gulf shipping. The Middle East was also a major source of the world's terrorism against U.S. citizens and property.

Even Israel gave the United States trouble. By the early 1980s many American supporters of Israel had become impatient with some of its provocative actions. In 1981, for instance, Israel annexed the Syrian territory of the Golan Heights. The following year, Israeli troops invaded civil war–torn Lebanon, reaching the

Crisis in Lebanon

capital Beirut and inflicting massive damage. The beleaguered Palestine Liberation Organization and various Lebanese factions called on Syria to contain the Israelis. Thousands of civilians died in the multifaceted conflict, and a million people became refugees. Reagan sent U.S. Marines to Lebanon to join a peacekeeping force, but in October 1983 terrorist bombs demolished a barracks, killing 241 American servicemen. Four months later, Reagan recognized failure and pulled the remaining marines out.

Washington, which openly sided with Israel, continued to propose peace plans designed to persuade the Israelis to give back occupied territories and the Arabs to give up attempts to push the Jews out of the Middle East. As the peace process stalled in 1987, Palestinians living in the West Bank began an uprising called *intifada* against Israeli forces. Israel refused to negotiate, but the United States decided to reverse its policy and talk with PLO chief Yasir Arafat after he renounced terrorism and accepted Israel's right to live in peace and security.

South Africa

In South Africa the Reagan administration at first followed a policy called "constructive engagement"— asking the white government to reform its repressive system. But many Americans demanded economic sanctions: cutting off imports from South Africa and pressing some 350 American companies to cease operations there. Some American cities and states passed divestment laws, withdrawing dollars (such as pension funds used to buy stock) from American companies active in South Africa. Public protest and congressional legislation forced the Reagan administration in 1986 to impose economic restrictions against South Africa. Within two years, about half of the American companies in South Africa had pulled out.

Third World Indebtedness

In the 1980s the Third World suffered economic setbacks that endangered American prosperity. Third World nations, having borrowed heavily in the 1970s, had staggering debts. By 1989 they owed creditors, including American banks, more than $1.2 trillion. Many Third World nations burdened with such debt had to cut back on imports of American goods. Hundreds of thousands of jobs in the United States were lost as a result, while economic instability spawned political unrest throughout the Third World.

Debate over Nuclear Weapons

Reagan's expansion of the U.S. military, his careless utterances about winning a limited nuclear war, and his quest for nuclear supremacy provoked worldwide debate. In 1981 hundreds of thousands of marchers in Europe demanded Soviet-American negotiations to prevent a nuclear holocaust. And in the largest peaceful protest in American history, a million people marched through New York City in June 1982 to support a freeze in the nuclear arms race. Towns across the nation and the House of Representatives passed resolutions to freeze the development, production, and deployment of new weapons. Meanwhile, scientists described the "nuclear winter" that would follow a nuclear war: the earth, cut off from the sun's rays, would turn cold, and food sources would disappear.

In 1982 Reagan substituted the Strategic Arms Reduction Talks (START) for the inactive SALT talks. At Reykjavik, Iceland, in 1986, he and the new Soviet leader Mikhail S. Gorbachev came very close to a major strategic weapons reduction agreement. SDI, however, stood in the way: Gorbachev insisted that it be shelved, and Reagan refused to part with it despite widespread scientific opinion that it would cost billions of dollars and never work. But Reagan and Gorbachev warmed toward one another, and the American president toned down his strident anti-Soviet rhetoric.

Gorbachev's Reforms

The turnaround in Soviet-American relations stemmed more from changes abroad than from Reagan's decisions. Under Gorbachev, a younger generation of Soviet leaders began to restructure and modernize the highly bureaucratized, decaying economy (a reform program called *perestroika*) and to liberalize the authoritarian political system (a reform program called *glasnost*). For these reforms to work, Soviet military expenditures had to be reduced and foreign aid decreased.

In 1987 Gorbachev and Reagan signed the Intermediate-range Nuclear Forces (INF) Treaty banning all land-based intermediate-range nuclear missiles in Europe. Soon the destruction of 2,800 missiles began. Gorbachev also unilaterally reduced his nation's armed forces, helped settle regional conflicts, and began the withdrawal of Soviet troops from Afghanistan. The Cold War was waning.

Summary

Secretary of State Henry Kissinger once observed that the international order was coming apart "politically, economically, and morally." Indeed, the emergence of the Third World in the 1950s and 1960s and growing independent decision making on the part of allies undermined the bipolar Cold War international system the United States and the Soviet Union had constructed at the end of the Second World War. By the 1980s power had become more diffused: great-power management of world affairs had diminished, and international relations had become more fluid and less predictable. In this changed setting, the United States and the Soviet Union moved haltingly toward détente and a winding down of the Cold War, as the INF Treaty demonstrated. But this superpower shift toward diplomacy and cooperation came only after dangerous crises, nuclear brinkmanship, international economic instability, monumental expenditures, and interventionism in the Third World.

For the United States, the Vietnam War proved the most damaging element. Determined to contain communism, Washington threw its young armed services personnel and its national wealth into a war it could not and did not win in a country it did not understand. Steeped in the Cold War mentality, American officials wrongheadedly saw the Soviet Union and the People's Republic of China—leaders of a supposed international communist conspiracy—maliciously at work in Vietnam, where the issue was actually more one of independence than of communism. The Vietnam War set off a major national debate about the fundamental purposes of American foreign policy—a debate that still resonates today when the United States dispatches its military forces into foreign disputes.

LEGACY FOR A PEOPLE AND A NATION
The Peace Corps

"How many of you are willing to work in the foreign service and spend your lives traveling around the world?" Democratic presidential candidate John F. Kennedy asked University of Michigan students on October 14, 1960. He was trying out an idea he inherited from others: overseas service "working for freedom." Some forty years later, a Peace Corps recruitment poster echoed the original challenge: "How far are you willing to go to make a difference?" Since the corps' founding in 1961 to promote world peace through cross-cultural understanding and economic development, more than 163,000 Americans have volunteered for service in 135 countries. Most volunteers are college educated, female, single, and white, and their average age is twenty-nine (2001 figures; for more recent data, see www.peacecorps.gov). Over the years, volunteers have built fish farms in Togo, water pumps in Kenya, sawmills in Peru, and bridges in Sierra Leone. They have served as nurses in Tanganyika and as English teachers in country after country.

Today, many host nations instead want Peace Corps volunteers to run computer workshops, create management models, teach free-market business skills, and design web pages. In its first decades, volunteers largely went to the Third World. Today increasing numbers serve in eastern Europe and in the former Soviet republics, helping them in the transition to market-oriented economies and political democracy.

From the beginning, not all Peace Corps projects have succeeded, and some volunteers have proved ill-suited for corps work. Also, during the Vietnam War, after volunteers protested U.S. intervention, President Nixon demanded that the Peace Corps serve, not question, U.S. Cold War goals and sharply cut its budget. As the Vietnam War and Watergate scandal spawned public cynicism, and as the military-minded era of the Reagan eighties marginalized the volunteers' way of promoting peace, the number of volunteers dropped, hitting an all-time low of 5,219 in 1987.

Today, the Peace Corps is highly respected as an institution where American ideals of humanitarian service, cultural understanding, and self-determination repose, even when U.S. leaders sometimes trample on such principles. In 1999 Congress voted to increase the corps to 10,000 volunteers by 2003, allocating a generous budget of $241 million. With such assistance, a legacy from the 1960s has been secured for a people and a nation—and the world.

For Further Reading, see the Appendix. For Web resources, go to history.college.hmco.com/students.

THE END OF THE POSTWAR BOOM
1974–1989

Economic Crisis and Ford's Response
Continuing Economic Problems and the Carter Presidency
Conservative Resurgence and Reagan
"Reaganomics"
People of Color and New Immigrants
Feminism, Antifeminism, and Women's Lives
A Polarized People: American Society in the 1980s
Economic Upturn and the Election of 1988

LEGACY FOR A PEOPLE AND A NATION
Ethnic America

Nguyet Thu Ha was twenty-two years old when South Vietnam capitulated to North Vietnamese and Vietcong forces in 1975. North Vietnamese soldiers were fighting close to her home, so she fled, taking along her four younger brothers and sisters, all teenagers, and a six-year-old nephew whose distraught parents had entrusted him to Ha for safekeeping. The six found their way onto a fishing ship dangerously overcrowded with refugees. After stops in Guam and a refugee camp in Arkansas, Nguyet Ha and the children went to Kansas City, Missouri.

Nguyet Ha obtained a job working seven days a week as a hotel housekeeper, and at night she made shirts and dresses. She next worked as a waitress, saving her tips to buy a house. Within eight months, she had saved enough for a down payment on a $16,000 house; she paid off the mortgage in three years. She married and had two daughters of her own, and in 1989 she bought a laundromat, five adjoining lots, and a vacant building to house her relatives, should they be allowed to emigrate to the United States. Ha also earned two associate of arts degrees and was hired as a paraprofessional at a magnet school for law and public service.

What sustained Nguyet Thu Ha was her dream of bringing her entire family to Kansas City. For ten years Ha failed in her attempts to bring her mother and older siblings to America. Then she received a call from the Immigration and Naturalization Service: Ha's mother, two brothers, a sister-in-law, and a niece would be arriving in a couple of days at Kansas City International Airport.

Nguyet Thu Ha and her family were part of the "new immigration," which began in the early 1970s, when record numbers of immigrants came to the United States from Asia, Mexico, Central and South America, and the Caribbean. Unlike earlier immigrants, most of the new arrivals were people of color, and race proved to be both a barrier and a spur to success for the new immigrants. Almost 70 percent of the new immigrants settled in six states: California, Florida, Texas, New York, New Jersey, and Illinois. The newcomers redefined urban areas such as Los Angeles, Chicago, and Miami, where nearly three-quarters of city residents spoke a language other than English at home.

Most of the newcomers found only low-paying jobs, and some suffered hostility and even violence from native-born Americans. Nevertheless, they persevered, pursuing their dreams in a country that was changing racially and ethnically. At the school where Nguyet Thu Ha found her first job as a teacher's aide, for example, the student body was richly diverse: white, black, Hispanic, Asian, and American Indian.

The American people experienced wrenching economic, political, and social change in the 1970s and 1980s. First, the new immigration touched millions of people's lives, immigrant and nonimmigrant alike. Second, in the 1970s, the postwar economic boom ended. The rate of economic growth slowed and sometimes stalled, and disquieting signs of inflation materialized. Third, economic inequality and social polarization grew in the 1970s and 1980s, widening the gap between rich and poor, between whites and people of color, and between the suburbs and the inner cities. Fourth, a host of new social problems emerged in the 1980s, notably AIDS and crack cocaine. Finally, although women made significant gains in the 1970s and 1980s, especially in education, the professions, and the job market, they also suffered setbacks, including the emergence of an antifeminist movement that opposed women's aspirations for gender equality.

After Vietnam and Watergate, the American people were cynical about politics and skeptical of their leaders. The presidency of Gerald R. Ford was a time of healing, not activism. Ford's successor as president, Jimmy Carter, scored notable domestic successes, but he was unpopular with the public. Moreover, neither Ford nor Carter was able to restore economic or social health to the nation. In response to their failures, there was a resurgence of conservatism, particularly among Americans who believed that the 1960s had been a period of immoral excesses, and who doubted that government had the capacity to solve major problems. Ronald Reagan became a hero to the conservatives, and after defeating Carter in 1980, he served as president for the next eight years. ■

Economic Crisis and Ford's Response

It was evident in the early 1970s that the United States was beginning to suffer economic decline. Recessions—which economists define as at least two consecutive quarters of no growth in the gross national product (GNP)—began to occur more frequently. Five recessions between 1969 and 1990 reflected the economy's weakening. America's economic vulnerability was confirmed by the Arab oil embargo of 1973 (see page 551). At the time, the United States was importing one-third of its oil supplies and was dependent for its survival on imported oil. Even before the embargo, the United States had suffered occasional shortages of natural gas, heating oil, and gasoline. But the American people, who had grown up on inexpensive and abundant energy, made few efforts to conserve.

In 1973 the American people also had to deal with the oil price increases ordered by the Organization of Petroleum Exporting Countries (OPEC). Oil prices rose 350 percent that year. As Americans grappled with the economic, social, and political costs of the price hikes, multinational oil companies prospered: their profits jumped 70 percent in 1973 and another 40 percent in 1974. Meanwhile, the steep rises in oil prices reverberated through the entire economy. Inflation jumped from 3 percent in 1972 to a frightening 11 percent in 1974.

OPEC Price Increases Fuel Inflation

In 1973 and 1974 sales of gas-guzzling American autos plummeted as consumers began to buy energy-efficient foreign subcompacts. Soon General Motors, Ford, and Chrysler, with their mostly large-car assembly plants, found themselves mired in a recession.

IMPORTANT EVENTS

1974 OPEC increases oil prices
Nixon resigns; Ford becomes president
Ford creates WIN program to fight
   inflation
Equal Credit Opportunity Act equalizes
   loan and credit card terms for men and
   women

1975 Nuclear accident occurs at Brown's Ferry
Antibusing agitation erupts in Louisville
   and Boston
Economic recession hits nation

1976 Hyde Amendment cuts off Medicaid funds
   for abortions
Carter elected president

1978 *Bakke v. University of California* outlaws
   quotas but upholds affirmative action
California voters approve Proposition 13

1979 Three Mile Island nuclear accident raises
   fears of meltdown
Moral Majority established
Federal Reserve Board tightens money
   supply
American hostages seized in Iran

1980 Economic recession recurs
Race riots break out in Miami and
   Chattanooga
Reagan elected president
Republicans gain control of Senate

1981 AIDS first observed in United States
Prime interest rate reaches 21.5 percent
Congress approves Reagan's budget and tax
   cuts
Reagan breaks air traffic controllers strike
Economic recession; unemployment hits 8
   percent

1982 Unemployment reaches 10 percent
Voting Rights Act of 1965 renewed

1983 More than half of adult women work outside
   the home
ERA dies for lack of ratification

1984 Reagan reelected

1985 Gramm-Rudman bill calls for balanced
   budget by 1991

1986 Tax Reform Act lowers personal income taxes
Immigration Reform and Control (Simpson-
   Rodino) Act provides amnesty to undocu-
   mented workers
Iran-contra scandal breaks
Republicans lose control of Senate

1987 Stock market prices drop 508 points in one
   day

1988 *Understanding AIDS* mailed to 107 million
   households
Bush elected president

Auto Industry Recession

Moreover, there was an accelerator effect because the ailing American auto companies quit buying steel, glass, rubber, and tool-and-die products. And as the recession in the auto industry spread, other manufacturers began laying off workers.

Unlike earlier postwar recessions, this one did not fade away in a year or two. Americans in the 1970s reeled under the one-two punch of *stagflation*. First, economic *stag*nation produced unemployment, particularly in heavy industry. Americans saw once-proud automobile and steel plants close. As a result of such "deindustrialization," many jobs were jeopardized,

while others disappeared forever. Second, *inflation* produced soaring prices, which eroded the purchasing power of workers' paychecks and forced them to raid their savings.

Stagflation also presented formidable problems to government policymakers. In earlier recessions, Republican as well as Democratic administrations had held to a policy of Keynesianism. To minimize the swings in the business cycle, they had manipulated federal policies—both fiscal policies (taxes and government spending) and monetary policies (interest rates and the money supply). They hoped by so doing to keep employment up and inflation down. Beginning in

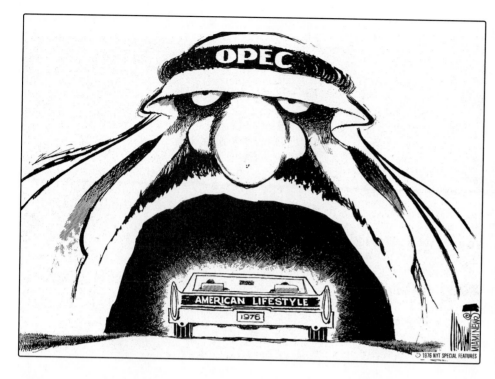

The Organization of Petroleum Exporting Countries (OPEC) raised oil prices several times in the 1970s. Each increase fueled the rise of inflation in the United States; and Americans, who had expected cheap energy to last forever, saw their expectations dashed. Long lines at the gas pumps were a reminder that an era of easy abundance had passed.   (Don Wright in the *Miami News,* 1976, Tribune Media Services)

the 1970s, however, joblessness and prices both began to rise sharply. Policies designed to correct one problem seemed only to worsen the other.

Even in the best of times, the economy would have been hard-pressed to produce jobs for the millions of baby boomers who joined the labor market in the 1970s. Moreover, deindustrialization was causing a shift in the occupational structure. As heavy industries collapsed, laid-off workers took jobs in the service sector, working in fast-food restaurants, all-night gas stations, and convenience stores—but at half of their former wages and without healthcare and other benefits. Workers who once had held high-paying blue-collar jobs saw their middle-class standards of living slipping away from them.

The Shifting Occupational Structure

A central economic problem was a slowing of growth in productivity—the average output of goods per hour of labor. Between 1947 and 1965, American industrial productivity had increased an average of 3.3 percent a year, raising manufacturers' profits and lowering the cost of prod-

Lagging Productivity

ucts to consumers. From 1966 to 1970, annual productivity growth averaged only 1.5 percent; it fell further between 1971 and 1975 and reached a mere 0.2 percent between 1976 and 1980. The result was that American goods cost more than those of foreign competitors.

The lag in productivity was not matched by a decrease in workers' expectations. Wage increases regularly exceeded production increases, and some economists blamed the raises for inflation. Indeed, wages that went up seldom came down again. Managers of the nation's basic industries—steel, autos, rubber—complained that the automatic cost-of-living adjustments in their labor contracts left them little margin to restrain price hikes.

Another spur to inflation was easy credit. More people had credit cards. And with their credit cards in hand, Americans went on a buying spree; between 1975 and 1979, household and business borrowing more than tripled (from $94 billion to $328 billion). The credit explosion helped bid up the price of everything, from houses to gold.

Easy Credit and Inflation

Every expert had a scapegoat to blame for the nation's economic doldrums. Labor leaders cited foreign competition and called for protective tariffs. Some businesspeople and economists blamed the cost of obeying federal health and safety laws and pollution controls. They urged officials to abolish the Environmental Protection Agency and the Occupational Safety and Health Administration. They also pressed for deregulation of the oil, airline, and trucking industries on the theory that competition would drive prices down. Above all, critics attacked the federal government's massive spending programs and mounting national debt.

By the time Gerald Ford became president in 1974, OPEC price increases had pushed the inflation rate to

President Ford's Response

11 percent. Appalled, Ford created Whip Inflation Now (WIN), a voluntary program that encouraged businesses, consumers, and workers to save energy and organize grassroots anti-inflation efforts. In the 1974 congressional elections, voters responded to WIN, Watergate, and Ford's pardon of Nixon by giving the Democrats fifty-two additional seats in the House and four in the Senate.

Ford's response to inflation was to curb federal spending and encourage the Federal Reserve Board to raise its interest rates to banks, thus tightening credit. But these actions prompted yet another recession—only this time it was the worst in forty years. Unemployment jumped to 8.5 percent in 1975, and because the economy had stagnated, the federal deficit for fiscal year 1976–1977 hit a record $60 billion.

Ford devised no lasting solutions to the energy crisis, but the crisis seemed to pass when OPEC ended the embargo—and the incentive to

Nuclear Power

prevent future shortages dissolved as well. The energy crisis, however, did intensify public debate over nuclear power. For the sake of energy independence, advocates asserted, the United States had to rely more on nuclear energy. Environmental activists countered that the risk of nuclear accident was too great and that there was no safe way to store nuclear waste. Accidents in the nuclear power reactors at Brown's Ferry, Alabama (1975), and Three Mile Island, Pennsylvania (1979), gave credence to the activists' arguments. By 1979, however, ninety-six reactors were under construction throughout the nation, and thirty more were on order.

In the 1970s the combined effects of the energy crisis, stagflation, and the flight of industry and the middle class to the suburbs and the Sunbelt were producing fiscal disaster in the nation's cities. Not since 1933 had a major American city gone bankrupt. But New York City was near financial collapse by late 1975. President Ford vowed "to veto any bill that has as its purpose a federal bailout of New York City," but he relented after the Senate and House Banking Committees approved loan guarantees, and the city was saved. Other Frostbelt cities were also in trouble, saddled with growing welfare rolls, deindustrialization, and a declining tax base. In 1978 Cleveland defaulted on its debts.

Throughout Ford's two-and-a-half-year presidential administration, relatively little was accomplished.

Gerald Ford's Presidency

Congress asserted itself and enjoyed new power, often overriding presidential vetoes. For the first time in the nation's history, furthermore, neither the president nor the vice president had been popularly elected. One of Ford's first acts as president had been to select Nelson Rockefeller, former governor of New York, as his vice president. But Republican prospects for retaining the presidency in the 1976 election seemed gloomy.

While Ford struggled, the Democratic Party geared up for the presidential election of 1976. Against

Election of 1976

the background of Watergate secrecy and corruption, one candidate in particular promised honesty and openness. "I will never lie to you," pledged Jimmy Carter, an obscure former one-term governor of Georgia. When this born-again Christian promised voters efficiency and decency in government, they believed him. Carter arrived at the convention with more than enough delegates to win the nomination. He chose Senator Walter Mondale of Minnesota as his running mate.

Neither Carter nor President Ford, the Republican nominee, inspired much interest, and on election day only 54 percent of the electorate voted. But as one political commentator observed, the vote nationwide was "fractured to a marked degree along the fault line separating the haves and have-nots." Although Carter won nearly 90 percent of the African American and Mexican American vote, he squeaked to victory by a slim 1.7 million votes out of 80 million cast. Ford's appeal was strongest among middle- and upper-middle-class white voters.

Continuing Economic Problems and the Carter Presidency

Economic troubles got worse, and by 1980 the economy was in a shambles. Inflation had jumped in 1979 to over 13 percent, and traders around the world had lost confidence in the dollar, causing unprecedented increases in the price of gold. To steady the dollar and curb inflation, the Federal Reserve Board took drastic measures. First, the board cut the money supply—partly by selling Treasury securities to take money out of circulation—thus forcing borrowers to bid up interest rates sufficiently to dampen the economy and reduce inflation. Second, it raised the rate at which the Federal Reserve loaned money to banks. As a result, mortgage-interest rates leaped beyond 15 percent, and the prime lending rate (the rate charged to businesses) hit an all-time high of 20 percent. Inflation fell, but only to 12 percent.

Worse still, by 1980 the nation was in a full-fledged recession. The 1980 unemployment rate of 7.5 percent, combined with the 12 percent inflation rate, had produced a staggeringly high "discomfort index" (the unemployment rate plus the inflation rate) of just under 20 percent (see Figure 32.1). Yet the government was unable to control the causes of the discomfort, and Americans blamed Carter for the nation's problems.

Economic Discomfort in 1980

Carter failed to inspire Americans, and he alienated Democratic Party members. Elected as an outsider, he remained one throughout his presidency. Moreover, Carter's support of deregulation and his opposition to wage and price controls and gasoline rationing ran counter to liberal Democratic principles. Seeing inflation as a greater threat to the nation's economy than either recession or unemployment, Carter announced that his top priority would be "to discipline the growth of government spending," even though doing so would add to the jobless rolls.

Carter's Flagging Popularity

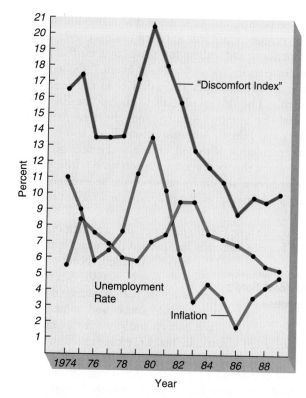

Figure 32.1 "Discomfort Index" (Unemployment Plus Inflation), 1974–1989 Americans' economic discomfort directly determined their political behavior. When the "discomfort index" was high in 1976 and 1980, Americans voted for a change in presidents. When economic discomfort declined in 1984 and 1988, Ronald Reagan and George Bush were the political beneficiaries. (Source: Adapted from *Economic Report of the President, 1992* [Washington, D.C., 1992], pp. 340, 365.)

Carter's problems were not entirely of his own making. In 1979 the shah of Iran's government fell to revolutionary forces. When Carter admitted the shah to the United States for medical treatment, mobs seized the American embassy in Teheran and held fifty-two Americans as hostages for 444 days. The new Iranian government also cut off oil supplies to the United States. The same year OPEC raised its prices again, and the cost of crude oil nearly doubled. With long lines at gasoline pumps and Americans held hostage, public approval of the president reached a new low.

Despite his flagging popularity and declining presidential authority, Carter scored noteworthy domestic accomplishments in energy, transportation, and conservation policy.

Carter's Domestic Accomplishments

To encourage domestic production of oil, he phased in decontrol of oil prices. To moderate the social effects of the energy crisis, he called for a windfall-profits tax on excessive profits resulting from decontrol, and for grants to the poor and elderly for the purchase of heating fuel. Carter also deregulated the airline, trucking, and railroad industries and persuaded Congress to ease federal control of banks. His administration established a $1.6 billion "superfund" to clean up abandoned chemical-waste sites and created two free-standing departments—the Departments of Energy and Education. Finally, he placed more than 100 million acres of Alaskan land under the federal government's protection as national parks, national forests, and wildlife refuges.

Conservative Resurgence and Reagan

Political and economic conservatives had long expressed doubt about whether big government programs can actually serve the people. At the state level, conservatives in the 1970s worked to repeal the social welfare system. California voters approved a 1978 tax-cutting referendum called Proposition 13, which reduced property taxes and put stringent limits on state spending for social programs. Proposition 13 set off shock waves: nearly a score of other states imposed similar ceilings on taxes and expenditures. On the national level, conservatives lobbied for a constitutional amendment to prohibit federal budget deficits. Perhaps most significant, tax revolts became political vehicles for conservative candidates to win elections.

In the 1970s and 1980s political and economic conservatives joined forces with cultural and religious conservatives and thereby changed the political landscape. In 1979 Reverend Jerry Falwell, a minister from Virginia, helped to found the Moral Majority, which advocated what it

Resurgence of Conservatism

called "family values," including opposition to abortion rights and homosexuality. Together with conservative think tanks and magazines, the Moral Majority and various church groups formed a flourishing network of potential supporters for conservative candidates. By the late 1970s, conservatism was becoming a potent political force.

Ronald Reagan, a former movie star and two-term governor of California, appealed mightily to both wings of the movement. A proponent of prayer in the

Ronald Reagan, the Republican presidential candidate in 1980, campaigned for "family values," an aggressive anti-Soviet foreign and military policy, and tax cuts. He also exuded optimism and appealed to Americans' patriotism. This poster issued by the Republican National Committee included Reagan's favorite campaign slogan, "Let's make America great again."   (Collection of David J. and Janice L. Frent)

public schools and an opponent of abortion, Reagan argued for a return to the morality that he believed had dominated American culture before the 1960s. He promised a balanced budget, and he blamed government for fettering American economic creativity. Reagan's 1980 presidential victory revealed that conservatism had become the dominant mood of the nation.

The 1980 federal census provided additional insights into the reasons for conservatism's resurgence in

A Shifting Population

the United States. First, the 1980 census revealed significant growth in the more politically conservative elderly population—up 24 percent since 1970. Second, the census documented the continuing shift of large numbers of people from

the politically liberal Frostbelt states of the Northeast and Midwest to the more conservative Sunbelt states of the South and West (see Map 32.1). The census findings also meant that seventeen seats in the House of Representatives would shift from the Frostbelt to the Sunbelt by the 1982 elections.

In the Republican primaries, Reagan triumphed easily over former CIA director George H. W. Bush

Reagan as the Republican Candidate

and Representative John Anderson, who ran as an independent. Reagan's appeal to the voters in the presidential campaign was much broader than experts had predicted. He promised economy in government and a balanced budget, and he committed himself to "supply-side" economics, or tax reductions to businesses to

Map 32.1   The Shift to the Sunbelt in the 1970s and 1980s   Throughout the 1970s and 1980s, Americans continued to leave economically declining areas of the North and East in pursuit of opportunity in the Sunbelt. States in the Sunbelt and in the West had the largest population increases.

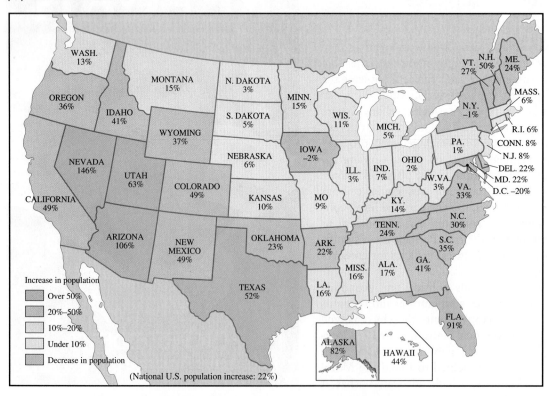

encourage capital investment. Although Reagan planned to slash federal spending, he also pledged to cut income taxes and boost the defense budget—a prescription that George Bush ridiculed as "voodoo economics." Reagan declared that he now opposed legalized abortion, and his stand against the Equal Rights Amendment (ERA) recommended him to social conservatives. Reagan's strength was his ability to unite the old political right wing with the new social conservative wing.

On election day, voters gave Reagan and his running mate George H. W. Bush 51 percent of the vote versus 41 percent for Carter and almost 7 percent for Anderson. The

Election of 1980

vote was both an affirmation of Reagan's conservatism and a signal of the nation's deep dissatisfaction with Jimmy Carter's management of both the economy and foreign policy. As startling as Reagan's sweep was the capture of twelve Senate seats by Republican candidates, giving the Republicans a majority in that house. Republicans also gained thirty-five seats in the House.

"Reaganomics"

Upon taking office, President Reagan immediately launched a double-barreled attack called "Reaganomics" on problems in the economy. First, he asked Congress to cut billions from domestic programs, including Medicare and Medicaid, food stamps, welfare subsidies for the working poor, and school meals. Congress endorsed most of Reagan's demands. Soon thereafter, Reagan initiated a second round of budget cuts, which trimmed a million food-stamp recipients from government rolls.

Tax cuts were the second facet of Reagan's economic plan. A fervent believer in supply-side economics, he called for reductions in the

Tax Cuts

income taxes of the affluent and of corporations in order to stimulate savings and investments. New capital would be invested, the argument went, and would produce new plants, new jobs, and new products. As prosperity returned, the profits at the top would "trickle down" to the middle classes and even to the poor. Congress responded with a five-year, $750 billion tax cut featuring a 25 percent reduction in personal in-

come taxes over three years. Other provisions increased business investment tax credits and depreciation allowances and lowered the maximum tax on income from 70 to 50 percent. The wealthy gained the most from these tax cuts.

A third item occupied Reagan's agenda: a vigorous assault on federal environmental, health, and safety regulations that, Reagan believed, ex-

Weakened Environmental Enforcement

cessively reduced business profits and discouraged economic growth. The president appointed opponents of the regulations to enforce them. Reagan officials explained that slackened enforcement was necessary to reduce business costs and make American goods competitive in world markets; critics countered that such policies invited environmental disaster.

Hard times hit labor unions in the 1980s. Faced with recession and unemployment, in the first three

Hard Times for Labor Unions

months of Reagan's term union negotiators settled for pay increases averaging only 2.2 percent, the biggest drop in wage settlements since the government began collecting such data in 1954. Unions had suffered large membership losses when unemployment hit heavy industry, and their efforts to unionize the high-growth electronics and service sectors of the economy were failing.

Reagan made the unions' hard times worse. He presided over the government's busting of the Professional Air Traffic Controllers Organization (PATCO) during the union's 1981 strike. His appointees to the National Labor Relations Board consistently voted against labor and for management. However, although Reagan appeared to be an enemy of labor, many union families responded positively to his genial personality, espousal of old-fashioned values, and vigorous anticommunist rhetoric.

Reagan enjoyed two notable economic successes during his first two years in office. First, the inflation rate plummeted, falling from 12 per-

Falling Inflation

cent in 1980 to less than 7 percent in 1982. Oil led the way in price declines; after eight years OPEC had at last increased its oil production, thus lowering prices. Moreover, as inflation fell, so too did the cost of borrowing money. Interest rates for bank loans dropped from 21.5 percent in early 1981 to 10.5 percent by 1983.

But there was a second, more sobering, explanation for the decline in inflation. By mid-1981 the nation was mired in a recession that not only persisted but deepened. During the last three months of the year, the GNP fell 5 percent, and unemployment soared to 8 percent, the highest level in almost six years.

A year later, in late 1982, unemployment had reached 10.8 percent, the highest rate since 1940.

Rising Unemployment

Most of the jobless were adult men, particularly African Americans, who suffered an unemployment rate of 20 percent. Many of the unemployed were blue-collar workers in ailing "smokestack industries" such as autos, steel, and rubber. Reagan and his advisers had promised that supply-side economics would produce demand-side results and that consumers would lift the economy out of the recession by spending their tax cuts. But as late as April 1983, unemployment still stood at 10 percent and people were angry. Agriculture, too, was faltering and near collapse from falling crop prices, floods and droughts, and burdensome debts. Many farmers lost their property through mortgage foreclosures and farm auctions. Others filed for bankruptcy.

As the recession deepened in 1982, poverty rose to its highest level since 1965. The Bureau of the Census

Resurgence of Poverty

reported that the number of Americans living in poverty increased from 26 million in 1979 to 34 million in 1982. The largest single category of poor families consisted of households headed by women (36 percent). With one exception, poverty continued its rise in 1983, returning to the level that had prevailed before the enactment of President Johnson's Great Society. That exception was the elderly; politicians had begun paying attention to this vocal and rapidly growing population.

President Reagan had announced that his administration would halt the expansion of social and health programs but would retain a "safety net" for the "truly needy." But he reneged on this promise. Facing a budget deficit in excess of $200 billion in mid-1982, Reagan had three choices. First, he could cut back on his rearmament plans to spend $1.7 trillion over five years. This he refused to do; in fact, the budget he signed raised defense spending another 13 percent.

Second, he could suspend or reduce the second installment of his tax cut. This choice, too, he found unacceptable. Third, he could—and did—cut welfare and social programs, pushing through Congress further cuts in Medicare and Medicaid, food stamps, federal pensions, and government-guaranteed home mortgages. Nevertheless, in the absence of budget cuts in other areas, or higher taxes, the federal debt continued to grow.

By 1984 the economy was showing strong signs of recovery. In that year the GNP rose 7 percent, the sharpest increase since 1951, and midyear unemployment fell to a four-year low of 7 percent. Moreover, the gains were made without sparking inflation. The resurging economy became one of Reagan's key reelection assets. A second factor in Reagan's favor was people's perception of him as a strong leader in foreign as well as national affairs. Third, Reagan was the enthusiastic choice of political conservatives of all kinds across the country.

The Election of 1984

Aiding Reagan was the Democrats' failure to field a convincing alternative. The Democratic nominee—former vice president Walter Mondale—did not inspire Americans. Even the policies he espoused seemed out of step with the nation's conservatism. Adding to Mondale's woes was the disarray of the Democratic Party; it had fragmented into separate caucuses of union members, African Americans, women, Jews, homosexuals, Hispanics, and other groups, each with its own agenda. The one bright spot for the Democrats was Mondale's historic selection of Representative Geraldine Ferraro of New York as the first woman vice-presidential candidate of a major political party. Ferraro showed herself to be an intelligent, indefatigable campaigner.

Mondale wanted to debate the federal deficit, but Reagan preferred to invoke the theme of leadership and rely on slogans. Mondale chastised Reagan for the mounting deficit, which had reached $175 billion in fiscal year 1984. But when Mondale announced that he would raise taxes to cut the deficit, he lost votes. Voters in 1984 had a clear choice, and in every state but Minnesota—Mondale's home state—they chose the Republican ticket. Many Reagan voters were Democrats who opposed the liberalized moral standards associated with their party. As holders of conservative views on welfare, abortion, homosexuality, and other social issues, these Democrats supported Ronald Reagan and the Republican Party. The election returns were thus the most convincing evidence yet that the nation had shifted to the right.

People of Color and New Immigrants

 Poverty was a growing problem in the 1970s and 1980s, particularly for people of color. Joblessness plagued blacks, Native Americans, and Hispanics, as well as many of the new immigrants. African Americans made up a disproportionate share of the poor. The overall poverty rate was 13 percent by 1980, but among blacks it was 33 percent and among Hispanics 26 percent, compared with 10 percent for whites. These figures had barely changed by the end of Ronald Reagan's presidency in 1989.

The weight of poverty fell most heavily on children, especially African American children, almost half of whom lived below the poverty line. A 1981 Children's Defense Fund survey reported that black children in the United States were four times more likely than whites to be born into poverty, twice as likely to drop out of school before twelfth grade, three times as likely to be unemployed, and five times as likely to be murdered. Many children lived in poor families headed by single women who earned meager incomes as domestic servants, laundresses, and kitchen helpers, supplemented by welfare assistance.

Some whites and even other blacks grumbled that poor blacks were responsible for their own poverty. But

Declining Job Opportunities for African Americans
the job market in the 1970s and 1980s was far different from that of twenty-five, fifty, or seventy-five years before. During periods of rapid industrialization, unskilled European immigrants and black migrants from the South had been able to find blue-collar jobs. Beginning in the 1970s, fewer such jobs were available; demand was greatest for skilled workers such as computer operators, bank tellers, secretaries, and bookkeepers. Most jobless people could not qualify.

But a historical anomaly was at work. For even as the plight of the African American poor worsened, the black middle class expanded. The number of black college students increased from 282,000 in 1966 to more

African American Middle Class
than 1 million in 1980; by 1980 about one-third of all black high-school graduates were going on to college, the same proportion as among white youths. By 1990 the number of black college students had increased further to 1.3 million. At least at the upper levels of black society, the dream of equality was being realized.

But as middle-class African Americans made gains, resentful whites complained that they were being victimized by "reverse discrimination."

White Backlash
To meet federal affirmative-action requirements, some schools and companies had established quotas for minorities and women; in some cases the standards were lower than those for whites. When Allan Bakke, a white man, was denied admission to medical school, he sued on the grounds that black applicants less qualified than he had been admitted. In a 5-to-4 ruling in 1978, the Supreme Court outlawed quotas but upheld the principle of affirmative action (*Bakke v. University of California*). Eleven years later, however, the Court ruled that past discrimination did not "justify a rigid racial quota" and that white workers could sue to re-open affirmative-action cases settled in federal courts years earlier (*Richmond v. Croson, Martin v. Wilks*).

White anger over affirmative action and busing combined with the effects of stagflation to produce an upsurge in racism. In Boston, where busing provoked numerous riots, a group of white students attacked a black passerby outside city hall. "Get the nigger; kill him!" they shouted as they ran at him with the sharp end of a flagstaff flying an American flag. Racial tension rose in cities across the nation.

African Americans were tense, and they showed their anger more openly than in the past. Charles Silberman wrote in *Criminal Violence,*

Black Anger
Criminal Justice (1978) that "black Americans have discovered that fear runs the other way, that whites are intimidated by their very presence. . . . The taboo against expression of antiwhite anger is breaking down, and 350 years of festering hatred has come spilling out." That hatred erupted several times in 1980, most notably in Miami and Chattanooga, after all-white juries acquitted whites in the killings of blacks. Miami's three days of rioting left eighteen dead and four hundred injured.

In the 1980s African American civil rights leaders denounced not only the judicial system but also the executive branch headed by President Reagan. Appointments were one issue: whereas 12 percent of President Carter's high-level appointees had been black and 12 percent women, Reagan's were 4 percent black and 8 percent women. (Reagan did appoint four women to his cabinet and made history by appointing Sandra Day O'Connor the first woman associate justice of the Supreme Court.) Moreover, Reagan's civil rights chief in the Justice Department opposed busing and affirmative action, and he was criticized for lax enforcement of fair housing laws and laws banning sexual and racial discrimination in federally funded education programs.

Every bit as angry as African Americans were Native Americans. For one thing, in the 1970s and 1980s they suffered the worst health of any group in the United States. American Indians suffered the highest incidence of tuberculosis, alcoholism, and suicide of any ethnic group in the country. Four in ten Native Americans were unemployed, and nine out of ten lived in substandard housing. Faced with deplorable conditions in the 1970s, Native American militants were prepared to struggle to improve the quality of life on the reservations.

Native Americans

In 1973 members of the militant American Indian Movement (AIM) called for "Red Power." Demanding the rights guaranteed Indians in treaties with the United States, they seized eleven hostages and a trading post on the Pine Ridge Reservation at Wounded Knee, South Dakota, where troops of the Seventh Cavalry had massacred three hundred Sioux in 1890. Their seventy-one-day confrontation with federal marshals ended with a government agreement to examine the treaty rights of the Oglala Sioux. For once, Congress listened to Native America, in 1974 passing the Indian Self-Determination Law, which provided Indians with greater control over federal programs, including schools, operating on reservations.

"Red Power": Indian Self-Determination

Native Americans also accused the federal government of breaking its treaty commitments—by seizing Indian lands, especially when they contained valuable minerals. In 1946 Congress established the Indian Claims Commission to compensate Indians for lands stolen from them. Under the legislation, lawyers for the Native American Rights Fund and other groups scored notable victories. In 1980, for instance, the Supreme Court ordered the government to pay $106 million plus interest to the Sioux nation for the Black Hills of South Dakota, stolen when gold was found there in the 1870s. Nevertheless, corporations and government agencies continued to covet Indian lands and disregard Indian religious beliefs: a coal company strip-mined a portion of the Hopi Sacred Circle, which according to tribal religion is the source of all life.

Indian Suits for Lost Lands

As Indians fought to regain old rights, Hispanic Americans struggled to make a place for themselves. An inflow of immigrants unequaled since the turn of the century, coupled with a high birth rate, made Hispanic peoples America's fastest-growing minority by the 1970s. Of the more than 20 million Hispanics living in the United States in the 1970s, 8 million were Mexican Americans concentrated in California, Texas, Arizona, New Mexico, and Colorado. Several million Puerto Ricans, Cubans, Dominicans, and other immigrants from the Caribbean also lived in the United States, clustered principally on the East Coast.

Hispanic Americans

These officially acknowledged Hispanic Americans were joined by millions of undocumented workers, or illegal aliens. Beginning in the mid-1960s, large numbers of poverty-stricken Mexicans began to cross the poorly guarded 2,000-mile border. The movement north continued in the 1970s and 1980s. By 1990 one out of three Los Angelenos and Miamians were Hispanic, as were 48 percent of the population of San Antonio and 70 percent of that of El Paso. Discrimination awaited many of these new immigrants, as it had previous groups of newcomers.

Most of these new Americans preferred their family-centered culture to Anglo culture and, for that reason, resisted assimilation. "We want to be here," explained Daniel Villanueva, a TV executive in Los Angeles, "but without losing our language and our culture."

Hispanic Cultural Pride

Like other minorities, Hispanics wanted political power—"brown power." In the 1960s César Chávez's United Farm Workers was the first Hispanic interest group to gain national attention. The militant Brown

Berets attracted notice for their efforts to provide meals to preschoolers and courses in Chicano studies and consciousness raising to older students. And throughout the 1970s the Mexican American political party *La Raza Unida* was a potent force in the Southwest and in East Los Angeles. Still, the group that was becoming the nation's largest minority exercised a disproportionately small share of political power.

During the 1970s and 1980s people of color immigrated to the United States in record numbers

New Flux of Immigrants

from Asia, Mexico, Central and South America, and the Caribbean. Between 1970 and 1980 the United States absorbed more than 4 million immigrants and refugees and uncounted numbers of illegal aliens. High as these figures were, they doubled again during the next decade, with almost 9 million new arrivals. Many of the new immigrants came in family units, and women and children accounted for two-thirds of all legal immigrants. Among the newcomers, Asian Americans seemed to be the most successful.

The arrival of so many newcomers put pressure on Congress to curtail the flow and perhaps offer amnesty

Immigration Reform

to aliens already living illegally in the United States. In 1978 Congress authorized a comprehensive reexamination of America's immigration policy. Eight years later Congress passed the Immigration Reform and Control (Simpson-Rodino) Act, which provided amnesty to undocumented workers who had arrived before 1982. The act's purpose was to discourage illegal immigration by imposing sanctions on employers who hired undocumented workers, but it failed to stem the flow of people fleeing Mexico's economic woes.

Feminism, Antifeminism, and Women's Lives

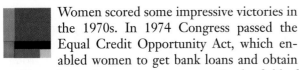

Women scored some impressive victories in the 1970s. In 1974 Congress passed the Equal Credit Opportunity Act, which enabled women to get bank loans and obtain credit cards on the same terms as men. In the field of criminal law, many states revised their statutes on rape, prohibiting defense lawyers from discrediting rape vic-

tims by revealing their previous sexual experience. Perhaps most significant were women's gains from affirmative action in hiring. As mandated by the Civil Rights Act of 1964 and the establishment of the Equal Employment Opportunity Commission, women and people of color applying for jobs had to receive the same consideration as white males.

Still, women continued to encounter opposition in their struggle for gender equality. Particularly formida-

Antifeminist Movement

ble was the antifeminist or "pro-family" movement, which contended that men should lead and women should follow, especially within the family, and that women should stay home and raise children. In defense of the patriarchal, or father-led, family, antifeminists campaigned against the Equal Rights Amendment, the gay rights movement, and abortion on demand. The conservative backlash against feminism became an increasingly powerful political force in the United States, especially in the Republican Party.

Antifeminists blamed the women's movement for the country's spiraling divorce rate; they charged that feminists would jettison their husbands and even their children in their quest for job fulfillment and gender equality. The number of divorces jumped 60 percent from 1970 to 1980, and remained near that level in the 1980s. Often, however, the decision to divorce was made not by the wives but by the husbands. According to Barbara Ehrenreich, a feminist scholar, men started walking out on their families in large numbers in the 1950s and 1960s, well before the rebirth of feminism. Tired of fulfilling the role of husband, many men came to see their wives as the agents of their entrapment; in "flight from commitment," they chose divorce.

Antifeminists successfully stalled ratification of the Equal Rights Amendment, which after quickly

Equal Rights Amendment

passing thirty-five state legislatures fell three states short of success in the late 1970s. Phyllis Schlafly's "Stop ERA" campaign claimed that the ERA would abolish alimony, legalize homosexual marriages, and subject women to single-sex bathrooms. Refusing to acknowledge gender-based discrimination, Schlafly derided ERA advocates as "a bunch of bitter women seeking a constitutional cure for their personal problems."

Many conservative women also participated in the anti-abortion or "prolife" movement, which sprang up almost overnight in the wake of the Supreme Court's 1973 decision in *Roe v. Wade*. Along with Catholics, Mormons, and other religious opponents of abortion, the anti-abortion movement supported the Hyde Amendment, the successful legislative effort of Representative Henry Hyde of Illinois in 1976 to cut off most Medicaid funds for abortions.

Feminists fought back, assailing Reagan for failing to reverse "the feminization of poverty" and for approving cuts in food stamps and school meals. The Reagan administration's opposition to federally subsidized childcare and the feminist goal of "comparable worth" also drew their ire. Because of persistent occupational segregation, 80 percent of all working women in 1985 were concentrated in low-paying "female" occupations such as clerking, selling, teaching, and waitressing. Recognizing this, feminists supplemented their earlier rallying cry of "equal pay for equal work" with a call for "equal pay for jobs of comparable worth." Why, women asked, should a grade-school teacher earn less than an electrician, if the two jobs require comparable training and skills and involve comparable responsibilities? In the 1970s female workers still took home only 60 cents to every male worker's dollar; by 1990 the figure had risen to 71 cents.

Women Opponents of Reagan's Conservatism

Activists in the women's struggle had to acknowledge certain harsh realities. One was the tight job market created by the economic recessions of the 1970s and 1980s. Other problems included a high teenage pregnancy rate and a rising divorce rate that left increasing numbers of women and their children with lower standards of living. Indeed, the tandem of divorce and teenage pregnancy meant that by 1990 about a quarter of all children lived with only one parent.

Increased Burdens on Women

Many single mothers, as well as other women, had to work. In 1983, for the first time in the nation's history, more than half of all adult American women (51 percent) held jobs outside the home. Working women usually had to contend with what came to be called "the Superwoman Squeeze." According to a report by the Worldwatch Institute, most working wives and mothers, even those with full-time jobs, "retained an unwilling monopoly on unpaid labor at home." Combining housework and outside employment, wives worked 71 hours a week; husbands worked 55 hours a week.

A Polarized People: American Society in the 1980s

 The United States became an increasingly polarized society in the 1980s. The rich got richer, while the poor sank deeper into despair (see Figure 32.2). Indeed, by 1989 the top 1 percent (834,000 households with $5.7 trillion in net worth) was worth more than the bottom 90 percent (84 million households with $4.8 trillion in net worth). The United States was also polarizing socially, and societal divisions were exacerbated by new problems: AIDS (acquired immune deficiency syndrome) and the cocaine-derived drug known as crack.

By the end of the 1980s, as many Americans were living in poverty as had been when President Johnson declared a War on Poverty in 1964. But the poor themselves were somewhat different. The poverty of the 1980s, explained the authors of a 1988 report of the Social Science Research Council, "is found less among the elderly and people living in nonurban areas and more among children living with one parent—in households headed principally by young women." As inequality grew, the gap widened between affluent whites and poor blacks, Indians, and Hispanics, and between the suburbs and the inner cities. And as inequality increased, so too did social pathology. Violent crime, particularly homicides and gang warfare, grew alarmingly, as did school dropout rates, crime rates, and child abuse.

Increasing Inequality

Poverty resulted not only from discrimination based on race and gender, but also from economic recessions and from the changing structure of the labor market. As deindustrialization took hold, the job market shifted from high-paying, unionized, blue-collar jobs to low-paying service jobs. By 1990, although 40 percent of the nation's poor were working, few had full-time, year-round jobs. At the same time, social workers reported that more and more of the nation's homeless were families.

Changing Job Market

Percentage Increase in Pretax Income, 1977–1989

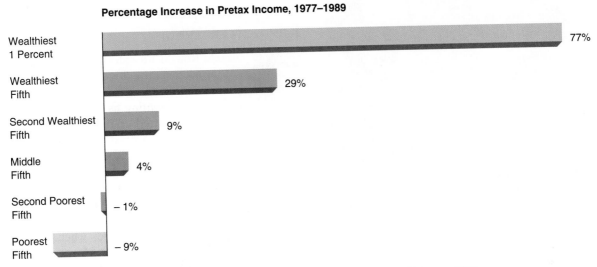

Figure 32.2   While the Rich Got Richer in the 1980s, the Poor Got Poorer   Between 1977 and 1989, the richest 1 percent of American families reaped most of the gains from economic growth. In fact, the average pretax income of families in the top percentage rose 77 percent. At the same time, the typical family saw its income edge up only 4 percent. And the bottom 40 percent of families had actual declines in income.   (Source: Data from the *New York Times*, March 5, 1992.)

About a third of the homeless were former psychiatric patients who found themselves living on the streets after hospitals emptied their psychiatric wards in a burst of enthusiasm for "deinstitutionalization." By 1985, 80 percent of the total number of beds in state mental hospitals had been eliminated on the premise that small neighborhood programs would be more responsive than large state hospitals to people's needs. Because local programs failed to materialize and few provisions were made for medical treatment, these troubled people increasingly found that they had nowhere to go except onto the streets.

Drugs and Violence

Another cause of homelessness was drug use. Mired in hopelessness, poverty-stricken men and women tried to find forgetfulness in hard drugs, especially cocaine and its derivative crack, which first struck New York City's poorest neighborhoods in 1985. Crack's legacy included destroyed families, abused children, and drug dealers too young for a driver's license but with access to state-of-the-art firearms. Gang shootouts over drugs were deadly: the toll in Los Angeles in 1987 was 387 deaths, with more than half of the victims innocent bystanders.

AIDS

Another lethal byproduct of the 1980s drug epidemic was the spread of AIDS. First observed in the United States in 1981, AIDS is a disease transmittable through the sharing of intravenous needles by drug users or through the exchange of infected body fluids, often during sexual contact. Caused by a virus that attacks cells in the immune system, AIDS makes its victims susceptible to deadly infections and cancers. In the United States, AIDS initially was confined to the sexual practices of male homosexuals, but the disease spread to heterosexuals and those receiving transfusions of tainted blood.

Between 1981 and 1988, of the 57,000 AIDS cases reported, nearly 32,000 resulted in death. But the worst had not yet revealed itself. A 1988 study reported that half of the gay men in San Francisco would develop AIDS and another 25 percent would develop the AIDS-related complex within about nine years of

A stunned nation watched in 1986 as the space shuttle *Challenger* exploded seventy-three seconds after lifting off. The *Challenger* explosion produces a flashbulb memory for many younger Americans who watched the tragedy on television at school (one of the *Challenger* crew, Christa McAuliffe, was an elementary school teacher).   (NASA)

infection. Some religious leaders and politicians heartlessly blamed the victims.

AIDS divided American communities, and AIDS—along with other sexually transmitted diseases such as genital herpes and chlamydia—affected Americans' sexual behavior. Caution replaced the sexual revolution. "Safe sex" campaigns urged the use of condoms. But conservative Protestant sects joined the Roman Catholic Church in warning that condom advertising implicitly sanctioned contraception and encouraged promiscuity. Sex education should not be offered in the schools, they contended, citing their deep belief that any sexual activity other than heterosexual matrimonial monogamy was wrong. Although gay men expected little assistance from the conservative executive branch, they were partly wrong. In 1988 the federal government mailed a booklet entitled *Understanding AIDS* to 107 million households. Nevertheless, AIDS continued to be one of several unsolved social problems dividing the nation in the late 1980s.

Economic Upturn and the Election of 1988

Despite Ronald Reagan's overwhelming re-election victory in 1984, for much of 1985 the president was on the defensive. One reason was the mounting fiscal deficit. A fiscal conservative long committed to balanced budgets, Ronald Reagan nonetheless oversaw the accumulation of more new debt than all previous American presidents put together.

Republicans blamed the deficit on the Democrats, but almost half of the national debt derived from fiscal

Mounting Fiscal Deficit

years 1982 through 1986. During this five-year period, when Reagan occupied the White House and the Republicans controlled the Senate, the national debt grew by $955 billion. In response, Reagan and Congress reluctantly agreed to the 1985 Gramm-Rudman bill, which called for a balanced federal budget by fiscal 1991 through a gradual reduction of the annual deficit. The deficit did drop, but for the three fiscal years from 1987 to 1989, it still totaled $457 billion. Another important bill, the Tax Reform Act of 1986, lowered personal income taxes while closing some flagrant loopholes and eliminating 6 million poor people from the tax rolls.

During his second term, Reagan realized one of his most important goals: putting more conservative

A Conservative Supreme Court

justices on the Supreme Court. After Warren Burger's decision to retire from the Supreme Court in 1986, Reagan nominated conservative William Rehnquist to serve as chief justice and conservative Antonin Scalia to fill Rehnquist's seat; the Senate confirmed both choices.

Reagan's place in history was secure until 1986, when the Iran-contra disclosures caused his aura to

Iran-Contra Scandal

fade. On election day 1986, the Republicans lost control of the Senate, stripping the president of a crucial power base. Then from Lebanon came a bizarre story that the president's national security adviser had traveled to Iran with a Bible, a cake, and a planeload of weapons seeking the release of Americans held hostage in the Middle East. "No comment," Reagan told reporters, but details of the Iran-contra scandal soon began to surface (see page 566).

On a personal level, President Reagan had taken on the appearance of a tired, bumbling old man. "Who's in Charge Here?" asked a *Time* magazine headline. The Iran-contra hearings focused attention on President Reagan's hands-off management style. Some observers, both outsiders and insiders, argued that Reagan was unengaged and uninformed. Donald T. Regan described his experience: "In the four years that I served as Secretary of the Treasury I never saw President Reagan alone and never discussed economic philosophy or fiscal and monetary policy with him one-on-one."

Reagan's Decline

Reagan's problems continued in 1987 and 1988. Congress overrode his veto of a massive highway construction bill, and twice his choices for the Supreme Court failed to win confirmation by the Senate. Still, as the 1988 elections approached, Republicans took heart over some excellent political and economic news for their party. First, Reagan had moderated his anti-Soviet rhetoric and in 1988, to the applause of most Americans, had traveled to the Soviet Union—the first American president to visit Moscow since 1972. Second—and of greater importance to voters—after the economic recession of 1981 and 1982, the United States had embarked on a six-year business recovery. The discomfort index, which had risen alarmingly in the 1970s and early 1980s, dropped to more comfortable levels in the later 1980s. And although unemployment dropped to a decade-low 5.4 percent in April 1988, it did so without refueling inflation (see Figure 32.1).

Continuing Economic Recovery

The Reagan administration pointed to the economy as proof of the success of supply-side economics. Critics retorted that Reagan's policy of pursuing massive tax cuts while greatly increasing the defense budget was just another form of Keynesianism—deficit financing to stimulate the economy. But the average American, caring little about this kind of debate, was content to enjoy the economic recovery. It was true that the poor had little to rejoice over and that Americans viewed the economic future with uncertainty. But it was also true that in the 1980s most Americans had jobs and were living very comfortably.

Had Reagan been allowed by the Constitution to run for a third term, he would probably have ridden both his personal popularity and the economic boom to victory. But the 1988 election was for his successor, and the competition in both parties was intense. On the Republican side the candidates included Vice President George H. W. Bush, Senate minority leader Bob Dole, and Pat Robertson, a television evangelist. Bush emerged with the nomination after bitter Republican infighting in state primaries.

George H. W. Bush

On the Democratic side, the race narrowed to a two-person contest between Michael Dukakis, under whose governorship Massachusetts had seemed a model of economic recovery and welfare reform, and Jesse Jackson, a former colleague of Reverend Martin Luther King, Jr., who campaigned on his dream of forming a "Rainbow Coalition" of the "rejected"— African Americans, women, Hispanics, the disabled. Jackson was the first African American to win mass support in seeking the presidential nomination of a major political party. But Dukakis won the Democratic nomination.

Both Bush and Dukakis avoided serious debate of the issues: drugs, environmental collapse, poverty, rising medical and educational costs, childcare, and the fiscal and trade deficits. Despite the gravity of the problems, the candidates relied on clichés and negative attack advertising. Television dominated the presidential election as never before. Bush aimed his appeals at the "Reagan Democrats" by pushing emotional "hot buttons" such as patriotism and the death penalty. A Republican advertisement for television appealed to racism and fear by accusing Dukakis of being soft on crime for furloughing Willie Horton, a black convicted murderer who while on weekend leave had stabbed a white man and raped a white woman.

Presidential Campaign of 1988

But with America at peace and inflation and unemployment both low, Bush's victory was seldom in doubt. His margin over Dukakis was substantial: 53 percent of the popular vote to 46 percent. Significantly, Bush was the beneficiary of the Reagan political legacy. The 1988 election

Bush's Victory in 1988

confirmed that the "Solid South," once a Democratic stronghold, had become solidly Republican. Bush won every state in the region. In both South and North, race was a key factor, as it had been in every presidential election since 1964: for twenty-five years, the Republican vote had been almost exclusively white, and almost all blacks had voted Democratic. Another political constant was low voter turnout. Only 50 percent of Americans who were eligible to vote in 1988 voted, compared with 63 percent in 1960.

Many Americans seemed unconcerned as they confronted the new decade. College students in the 1980s, unlike many of their predecessors in the 1960s, aspired to join the system. They yearned not to save the world but to scramble up the corporate ladder, and many educated young people worked long hours in pursuit of that goal. But many baby boomers and their younger sisters and brothers reported frustration in their efforts to replicate their parents' standard of living, particularly because of high housing costs.

Still, polls in 1989 reported that Americans were generally happy with their lives. Many expressed pleasure with their new toys and amenities. Especially noteworthy were the sales of videocassette recorders (VCRs). Between 1980 and 1984, the number of videotapes rented by Americans for viewing movies at home jumped from 26 million to 304 million. Even more impressive was the phenomenal spread of computers, which revolutionized not only communications but also people's workplaces and lifestyles. In 1981 the number of personal computers in use in America numbered 2 million; in 1988 the figure was 45 million.

Summary

The United States changed in fundamental ways between 1974 and 1989. The spread of technological developments was part of that change. So too was the new immigration, which in the 1970s and 1980s not only swelled tremendously but shifted in origin. People came from Mexico, Central and South America, and the Caribbean, as well as from the Philippines, Korea, Taiwan, and India. Refugees of the Vietnam War also arrived. Another change was the country's shift to the right po-

litically. The champion of this change was President Ronald Reagan, whose supporters included both economic and social conservatives and both Republicans and disillusioned Democrats.

Reagan enjoyed successes, but when he left office in 1989, the country faced unsolved economic, social, and political issues of great importance. "Ronald Reagan leaves no Vietnam War, no Watergate, no hostage crisis," reported the *New York Times*. "But he leaves huge question marks—and much to do." First, inequality had escalated in the 1980s, as the poor got poorer and the rich got richer. Second, the rise of the federal debt continued unabated. In 1981 the debt stood at $994 billion; by the time Reagan left office, it had jumped to almost $2.9 trillion. Third, the effects of mismanagement and outright fraud were beginning to show in certain industries, forcing the federal government to consider massive bailouts and threatening greater fiscal deficits.

When George H. W. Bush was inaugurated as the forty-first president of the United States on January 20, 1989, the American people prepared to greet not only a new presidency but also a new decade. It was clear that Americans and their leaders would have to make difficult economic, social, and political choices in the 1990s.

LEGACY FOR A PEOPLE AND A NATION
Ethnic America

The legacy of the new immigration of the 1970s and 1980s is evident in cities and towns across America. Mexican newcomers, for example, have opened restaurants, started Spanish-language newspapers and cable television channels, and flocked to the concerts of Latino superstars. Meanwhile, Mexican culinary culture is being consumed by millions of Americans of all cultural backgrounds. Among Asian American immigrants, Korean greengrocers own shops on Manhattan's Upper West Side, and Chinese workers assemble integrated circuits in California's Silicon Valley. Wherever they have settled, America's newcomers have established their own communities with their own distinctive cultures.

The legacy of America's new immigration resembles that of its predecessor one hundred years ago.

With almost 9 million immigrants arriving in the 1980s, that decade surpassed the historic high mark set by the 8.7 million immigrants who had reached American shores between 1900 and 1909. In addition to the documented immigrants, another 300,000 enter the country each year as undocumented, or illegal, aliens. Like the earlier immigration, the new influx has also provoked a nativist reaction. A *Newsweek* poll in 1993 reported that 60 percent of Americans believed that immigration was "bad for the country."

Immigrants have arrived from all over the world, bringing their cultures not merely from Latin America and Asia, but also from Europe, Africa, and the Middle East. Like the immigrants of a century before, these newcomers crave education and flock to public libraries to learn. The branch library in Flushing, New York, for example, has been inundated with Chinese, Korean, Indian, Russian, Colombian, and Afghan immigrants. "Watch Your Belongings" signs are displayed in several languages, and librarians are available who speak Russian, Hindi, Chinese, Korean, Gujarati, and Spanish. The legacy of the new immigration has permanently altered, and deeply enriched, the United States.

For Further Reading, see the Appendix. For Web resources, go to history.college.hmco.com/students.

33

PROSPERITY, POWER, AND PERIL: AMERICA TO 2002

We have lost a mighty rare friend and have suffered greatly. From the New York Fire Dept. to the homeless he loved so much—immigrants, prisoners, New York's lesbian and gay community, people with AIDS, people in recovery. . . . Mychal walked with us, touched our lives, & lifted us up!" As Brendan Fay, the writer of these words knew, Mychal Judge was a much-loved individual who put himself in harm's way on September 11, 2001. Judge was a chaplain for the New York Fire Department who died while administering the last rites of the Catholic Church to a fireman who was a victim of the terrorist attacks of that fateful morning.

The tragic events of September 11 began shortly before 9:00 A.M. (EDT), when terrorists who had seized control of American Airlines Flight 11 flew the plane into the north tower of the World Trade Center.

Minutes later United Airlines Flight 175 crashed into the World Trade Center's south tower. Both flights, having just departed from Boston's Logan International Airport, were fully fueled. So was another terrorist-seized plane, American Airlines Flight 77, which left Dulles International Airport in the nation's capital and crashed into the Pentagon at 9:43 in the morning. Passengers on a fourth flight (United Airlines Flight 93, which had departed from Newark, New Jersey) attempted to overpower the terrorists on their aircraft. The plane crashed about eighty miles from Pittsburgh. The worst, however, was yet to come.

In the stairwells of the towers, as occupants of the buildings fled downward, firemen climbed higher into the buildings. Their mission was to attempt to put out the fire and to find the living and bring them to safety. But the burning fuel from the airplanes generated

IMPORTANT EVENTS

1989 George H. W. Bush becomes president
Tiananmen Square massacre in China
Bush vetoes increase in minimum wage
World accord controls ozone-killing
   chemicals
Berlin Wall opens
U.S. troops invade Panama

1990 Communist regimes in eastern Europe
   collapse
Sandinistas lose Nicaragua election
Recession begins; personal incomes fall
Americans with Disabilities Act passed
Iraq invades Kuwait
Reunification of Germany
Bush-Congress budget agreement raises
   taxes; Bush reneges on "no new taxes"
Clean Air Act reauthorization requires
   reduction in emission of pollutants
South Africa begins to dismantle apartheid

1991 Persian Gulf War
START I treaty reduces nuclear warheads
Ethnic wars flare in former Yugoslavia
Hill testifies at Thomas confirmation
   hearings; Thomas confirmed
USSR dissolves into independent states

1992 Los Angeles riots erupt
Federal deficit hits $4 trillion
Planned Parenthood v. Casey upholds the
   right to an abortion
Clinton elected president
Twenty-seventh Amendment prohibits
   future midterm congressional pay raises
U.S. troops sent to Somalia
Canada, Mexico, and U.S. sign NAFTA

1993 Clinton becomes president
Clinton lifts restrictions on abortion
   counseling
START-II treaty reduces warheads and
   ICBMs
H. Clinton heads task force on healthcare
Clinton's proposal to lift ban on homo-
   sexuals in the military stirs controversy
Clinton appoints Ginsberg to Court
Congress approves NAFTA
Agreement for Palestinian self-rule
Motor-voter and family-leave acts passed
Gun control laws require waiting period for
   handguns and ban sale of assault weapons

1994 Republican candidates for Congress propose
   Contract with America
Clinton appoints Breyer to Court
Genocide in Rwanda
U.S. troops sent to Haiti
Clinton signs crime bill into law
Republicans win House and Senate

1995 Bombing in Oklahoma City kills 168 people
U.S. opens diplomatic relations with
   Vietnam
World Conference on Women
U.S. diplomats broker peace for Bosnia

1996 Telecommunications Act allows telephone
   and cable companies to compete
Helms-Burton Act tightens Cuba embargo
Freedom to Farm Act mandates phase-out
   of federal farm subsidies
Convictions in first Whitewater trials
Clinton signs welfare act eliminating Aid to
   Families with Dependent Children
Guatemalan civil war ends
Clinton reelected

1997 Albright is first woman secretary of state
U.S. ratifies Chemical Weapons Convention

1998 Independent counsel investigates Clinton's
   relationship with Lewinsky
India and Pakistan explode nuclear devices
U.S. signs Global Warming Convention
Republicans lose seats in House
House votes to impeach Clinton

1999 Senate votes to acquit Clinton
NATO bombs Serbia over Kosovo crisis
Senate rejects Comprehensive Test Ban
   Treaty

2000 Gore wins popular vote in presidential
   election of 2000
Supreme Court decision in *Bush v. Gore*

2001 George W. Bush becomes president
Jeffords leaves the GOP; Democrats gain
   control of the Senate
Economic downturn
Terrorist attacks against World Trade Center
   and Pentagon kill thousands
The war against terrorism
Anthrax outbreak

2002 War on terrorism continues
Escalation of Palestinian-Israeli violence

temperatures in excess of 2,000 degrees Fahrenheit. The inner steel cores of the towers could not withstand the heat. First the south tower and then the north tower collapsed.

Because of the total destruction at what became known as "ground zero," the placing of the names of missing people on multiple lists, and other factors, the exact death toll was extremely difficult to determine. Initial reports suggested that as many as 6,500 people perished in the attack. As city officials painstakingly verified the name of each casualty, however, the number of fatalities steadily decreased. By May 2002, city officials placed the number of confirmed dead or missing and presumed dead at 2,823. Among the dead were 343 firemen, including 95 of the 452 people serving in the elite units of the department's Special Operations Command. Nationals from 86 countries were also among the casualties. At the Pentagon 189 people were killed, and 44 died in the crash outside Pittsburgh.

Osama bin Laden and his organization al-Qaeda (the base) soon became the primary suspects. Bin Laden, a wealthy Saudi, had been implicated in the 1998 bombings of the American embassies in Kenya and Tanzania as well as a 2000 attack on the U.S.S. *Cole* at anchor in Yemen. A Muslim fundamentalist, bin Laden had become deeply offended and angered by the presence of U.S. military personnel in Saudi Arabia, the guardian of the Islamic holy places in Mecca and Medina. And bin Laden grew equally angered over what he perceived as the consistent pro-Israel and anti-Palestine stance of the United States.

The task of responding to the September 11 attacks fell to George W. Bush. Bush, the son of a former president, had been elected in the most controversial election since the Hayes-Tilden contest of 1876. After September 11, Bush and his advisers spoke of a new war: a war against terrorists and any political state that sponsored or protected them. By a vote of 420 to 1 in the House and 98 to 0 in the Senate, Congress soon passed a use-of-force resolution giving the president the power "to use all necessary and appropriate force against those nations, organizations, or persons he determines planned, authorized, committed, or aided the terrorist attacks that occurred on September 11, 2001, or harbored such organizations or persons, in order to prevent any future acts of international terrorism against the United States by such nations, organizations or persons." And NATO, for the first time in its history, invoked the collective security provision contained in Article 5 of its charter.

The Bush administration identified the extreme Islamic Taliban regime in Afghanistan as a government that had since 1996 harbored bin Laden. Bush ordered the Taliban to turn bin Laden over to the United States and to destroy al-Qaeda's training camps in Afghanistan. The Taliban refused, and on October 7, 2001, the United States initiated military action against Afghanistan. Most of the international community endorsed the U.S. war against terrorism. At home, meanwhile, an outbreak of anthrax bacteria poisoning raised alarms about the nation's security in the face of terrorism.

The American people rallied behind the president and patriotism soared, even as the economy suffered. The sense of unity, however, masked fundamental differences between Republicans and Democrats over the same issues that had divided the parties in the 1990s: taxes, Social Security, healthcare, education, and defense policy.

The 1990s was a decade of political volatility and cultural conflict. Many Americans abjured political participation, denouncing the government for being corrupt, arrogant, and downright stupid. They rejected the Democratic Party for having lost touch with their cultural and moral values, and they rejected the Republicans for failing to represent their economic and social needs. Some Americans wanted new political parties.

America's president from 1989 to 1993 was George H. W. Bush. Victory in the Persian Gulf War in 1991 seemed to guarantee his reelection in 1992. But the economy had stagnated, and the president seemed without a plan to spur recovery. The Cold War had ended, but the president seemed to lack vision for the new world order he had proclaimed. And Ross Perot, a multibillionaire who vowed he could fix the fiscal deficit, waged a popular third-party campaign. But the winner and president-elect was the Democratic candidate, Governor Bill Clinton of Arkansas.

Politics grew even more volatile during Clinton's two presidential terms. In 1994, just two years after Clinton defeated Bush, the "Republican Revolution" led by Representative Newt Gingrich routed the Democrats in congressional elections, winning control of both houses of Congress. In 1996, however, Clinton won reelection. Prosperity, low inflation, a booming stock market, and skill as a campaigner contributed to Clinton's victory.

But the president had a formidable enemy: himself, notably his history of philandering and lying. In 1998 Clinton was impeached by the House of Representatives, which alleged that he had committed perjury and obstructed justice. And while the Senate acquitted the president, Clinton had permanently tarnished his historical reputation.

For both Bush and Clinton, the 1990s was a decade of power and perils in world affairs. The Bush administration witnessed the dramatic end of the Cold War, symbolized by the collapse of Communist regimes in eastern Europe, the reunification of Germany, and the dissolution of the Soviet Union. Disorder, however—created by ethnic wars, natural disasters, economic crises, and religious conflict—soon followed, disappointing Americans who wanted less overseas activism. The Clinton administration struggled to articulate new doctrines and to clarify U.S. interests in the absence of a Soviet threat. Moreover, some threats, long overshadowed by the Cold War, became more pressing: nuclear proliferation, chemical warfare, population explosion, drug trafficking, the spread of diseases, terrorism, and pollution of the natural environment.

The decade of the 1990s concluded what some called the "American century." As Americans looked to the new century, the nation was at peace and in an extended period of prosperity. A presidential election was on the horizon, and many expected the Democratic nominee, Vice President Al Gore, to ride the good times to victory. Gore would carry the popular vote in November 2000, but disputed returns from Florida led to a 5-4 Supreme Court decision that stopped vote recounts in Florida and gave the state to Bush. More than a month after the election, the Supreme Court decision meant that George W. Bush won a majority of the electoral votes to become the forty-third president. ■

Economic and Social Anxieties: The Presidency of George H. W. Bush

As president from 1989 to 1993, George H. W. Bush had a rough ride. He and the Democratic Congress seemed unable to work together or agree on anything. Bush vetoed thirty-seven bills during his presidency, only one of which was overridden. Rarely in American history had the relationship between Congress and the president been so sour and the legislative results so meager.

Decisive presidential leadership might have broken the gridlock, but Bush was a political chameleon. Once a supporter of family planning and a woman's right to an abortion, he had switched his position and denounced abortion. In the 1980 Republican primaries, he had dismissed Ronald Reagan's supply-side economic ideas as "voodoo economics," but he quickly endorsed those policies when he became Reagan's running mate in 1980. He thus seemed to lack firm convictions of his own. Still, when he was inaugurated in 1989, the country had enjoyed six straight years of economic growth, and both unemployment and inflation were low.

Soon, however, the economy took a nosedive, and by mid-1990 signs of recession were everywhere. Workers were laid off or furloughed, but Bush took no action. The Bush administration, one columnist wrote, was "leading a retreat from social responsibility." The president had vetoed an increase in the minimum wage and defended tax breaks for the rich while opposing extended relief payments to the long-term unemployed.

Economic and Social Problems

However, the social ills that had plagued the United States in the 1980s—AIDS, homelessness, drug and alcohol addiction, racism and inequality, poverty among children, the day-to-day struggles of single-parent families—persisted unabated, and even the middle class experienced a decline in the standard of living. Scholars who tracked the "social health" of the nation diagnosed America's well-being as at its lowest level since 1970. Problems that reached their worst recorded levels in 1990 were child abuse, teen suicide, the gap between rich and poor, and lack of health insurance coverage.

Healthcare, in particular, caused increasing anxiety. With few incentives to control healthcare costs and the spread of expensive technologies, medical expenses were rising rapidly, and so were health insurance premiums. In fact, many people could not afford health insurance: some 33 million Americans, about 13 percent of the population, had no health insurance at all. Three-fourths of these people were employed but worked at minimum-wage jobs that did not provide health benefits. Additional tens of millions had such limited coverage that they constantly were at risk of financial devastation.

Also fueling Americans' anxieties were the growing numbers of job layoffs, some temporary but many permanent. In a practice called "outsourcing," companies stopped making their components and began ordering them from factories in other states or other countries, where wages were far lower and benefit packages nonexistent. Other businesses replaced workers with computers and other machines to cut costs and increase productivity. And still others were deciding whether to reduce labor costs by opting for technology, outsourcing, or moving their plants to Mexico, South Korea, and other low-wage countries.

One group, however, made real progress in 1990. That year, President Bush signed the Americans

Americans with Disabilities Act

with Disabilities Act, which banned job discrimination, in companies with twenty-five or more employees, against the blind, deaf, mentally retarded, and physically impaired, as well as against those who are HIV-positive or have cancer. The act, which covered 87 percent of all wage earners, also required that "reasonable accommodations," such as wheelchair ramps, be made available to people with disabilities.

Bush's domestic problems were complicated by a pledge he had made at the 1988 Republican convention: "Read my lips: No new taxes."

Failed Promises

But during the 1990 budget summit with Congress, to keep the budget deficit from rising even higher, he agreed to a tax increase.

Other campaign pledges were broken, too. As a candidate in 1988, Bush had promised that he would be the "education president" as well as the "environmental president"; he failed in both areas. Other than argue for government vouchers that parents could use to pay tuition at public or private schools of their choice, his administration did little to support educational reform. Bush got good marks from environmentalists for signing the 1990 reauthorization of the Clean Air Act, which limited emissions of sulfur dioxide and nitrogen oxides, but his Council on Competitiveness gutted enforcement. The council declared that environmental regulations should be eliminated because they slowed economic growth and cost jobs. In addition, the Justice Department overruled the Environmental Protection Agency's move to prosecute large corporate polluters.

As the criticism of President Bush's performance grew, his credibility fell, especially during the confirmation hearings on Clarence Thomas,

Clarence Thomas Nomination

whom Bush nominated to the Supreme Court. Few believed this inexperienced federal judge was, as Bush put it, the "best man for the job." But Thomas, an African American, was highly conservative. He opposed affirmative action in hiring, believed in returning prayer to the schools, and opposed abortion.

Bush's nomination of Thomas was clever but cynical. Eleanor Holmes Norton, the African American congressional delegate from Washington, D.C., denounced the choice as "calculated . . . to mute the expected reaction to yet another conservative nominee." Then, in October, the nation was electrified by the testimony of Anita Hill, an African American law professor at the University of Oklahoma, who charged that Thomas had sexually harassed her when she worked for him in the early 1980s. The Senate confirmed Thomas, but Hill's testimony—and the Senate's ultimate rejection of it—so angered many women that they vowed to oppose the Republican Party in 1992.

The End of the Cold War and Global Disorder

When Bush became president, the Cold War was waning. A cautious, reactive conservative, Bush seemed to set few long-range goals except to envision the United States as the supreme power in a unipolar world.

In the mid-1980s, Communist Party chief Mikhail S. Gorbachev had set loose cascading changes in the Soviet Union (see page 567). He also

Collapse of Communist Regimes

had encouraged the people of East Germany and eastern Europe to go their own ways. No longer would a financially hobbled Moscow prop up unpopular Communist regimes. In October 1989 East Germans startled the world by repudiating their Communist government, and in November Germans tore down the Berlin Wall. On October 2, 1990, the two Germanys reunited. Veteran

Communist oligarchs also fell in Poland, Hungary, Czechoslovakia, Romania, and Bulgaria.

The Union of Soviet Socialist Republics itself collapsed: in 1990 the Baltic states of Lithuania, Latvia, and Estonia declared independence; and in 1991 the Soviet Union disintegrated into independent successor states (see Map 33.1). The breakup of the Soviet empire, dismantling of the Warsaw Pact, repudiation of communism by its own leaders, German reunification, and a significantly reduced risk of nuclear war signaled the end of the Cold War.

The Cold War ended because of the relative decline of the United States and the Soviet Union in the international system. Between the 1950s and the 1980s, the contest had undermined the power of the

Why the Cold War Ended

two major protagonists. They moved gradually toward a cautious cooperation whose urgent goals were the restoration of their economic well-being and the preservation of their diminishing global positions.

Four influential trends explain this gradual decline and the resulting attractions of détente. The first was the burgeoning economic cost of the Cold War—trillions of dollars spent on weapons and interventions. Second, challenges from within their own spheres of influence help explain why the two major powers welcomed détente. Cuba's anti-American revolution and France's withdrawal from NATO in the 1960s are but two indications that the United States was losing

Map 33.1   The End of the Cold War in Europe   When Mikhail Gorbachev came to power in the Soviet Union in 1985, he initiated reforms that ultimately undermined the communist regimes in eastern Europe and East Germany and led to the breakup of the Soviet Union itself, ensuring an end to the Cold War.

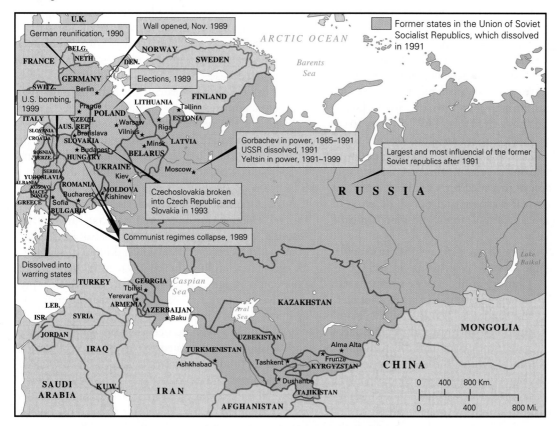

power. The uprisings in Hungary and Czechoslovakia and the Sino-Soviet rift undercut the Soviet Union's hegemony within its network of allies.

Third, the Cold War ended because of the emergence of the Third World, which introduced new players into the international game, further diffused power, and challenged bipolarism. Soviet-American détente represented a means to apply leverage to volatile Third World nations. Finally, the worldwide antinuclear movement of the 1980s pressed leaders, especially in western Europe, to seek détente in order to stop the arms race.

These four elements combined to weaken the standing of the two adversaries and ultimately to persuade them to halt their nations' declines by ending the Cold War. Because the Soviet Union fell much harder than the United States, American leaders crowed that they had won the Cold War. But doubters calculated a high price in dollars and deaths for the United States, too.

As the Cold War drew to a close, Bush struggled futilely to shape the agenda of a new world order. His

START Treaties

administration sustained a large defense budget and continued to use military force abroad, denying Americans the "peace dividend" they hoped would reduce taxes and free up funds to address domestic problems. Still, in mid-1991 the Soviet Union and the United States signed the START I treaty to reduce their long-range nuclear weapons by one-third. In 1993 Bush signed the START II agreement with Russia's president Boris Yeltsin, who had ousted Gorbachev. This accord provided for a further 50 percent reduction of nuclear weapons and the elimination of all multiple warhead (MIRV) intercontinental ballistic missiles (ICBMs).

Bush also struggled to define America's policy toward the People's Republic of China. In June 1989

Tiananmen Square

Chinese armed forces stormed into Beijing's Tiananmen Square, slaughtering hundreds—perhaps thousands—of unarmed students and other citizens who for weeks had been holding peaceful prodemocracy rallies. Bush officials initially expressed revulsion, but muted their response in the belief that America's global security and trade needs required friendly Sino-American ties. A symbol of improved relations and of changes within China was the opening in 1992, near Tiananmen Square, of the largest McDonald's restaurant in the world. Some Chinese citizens recoiled from the Golden Arches, charging cultural imperialism. But others embraced America's icon, not for its hamburgers, but for what McDonald's represented to them: modernization, good management, cleanliness, equality.

Within the Western Hemisphere, immigration often disturbed U.S.–Latin American relations. By

Peace and War in Latin America

1992 probably 2.5 to 4 million "illegal aliens" from around the world lived in the United States; most of them had come for economic reasons, and most of them had come from Mexico. When the Cold War ended, Latin America still staggered under external debt, poverty, and environmental calamities such as deforestation of the Amazon River basin in Brazil and carbon monoxide emissions that threatened the public health of Mexico City and Santiago de Chile. A positive note was the North American Free Trade Agreement (NAFTA) with Canada and Mexico. Approved by Congress in 1993, the pact created the world's largest tariff-free trade bloc. Critics, however, claimed that the agreement would cost many U.S. workers their jobs because corporations would move south to exploit less expensive Mexican labor and minimal environmental controls.

In Central America, the Bush administration cooled the zeal with which Reagan had meddled because the interventions had largely failed. The death-dealing, U.S.-financed contra war had not forced the Sandinistas from power in Nicaragua. Instead, in 1989 the Central American presidents devised a workable plan for free elections in Nicaragua (the Sandinista Front lost the 1990 elections) and the disbanding of the contras. In December 1991 U.N. diplomats mediated an agreement ending the civil war in El Salvador. In Guatemala in late 1996 Norwegian and U.N. representatives brokered a peace accord that terminated a civil war that had been raging since 1954.

As the Cold War receded, the drug war accelerated, and Washington attempted to use the U.S. military to quash drug producers and traffickers in Colombia, Bolivia, and Peru, sources of cocaine. While the U.S. concentrated on eradication programs and the interdiction of supplies, many Latin Americans stressed the need to halt consumer demand inside the United States.

Drugs became conspicuous in relations with Panama. Soon after General Manuel Antonio Noriega took power in 1983, he cut deals with Colombia's cocaine barons. Noriega also went on the CIA payroll and helped the United States aid the contras. Appreciative, Washington turned a blind eye to his drug trafficking. When exposés of Noriega's sordid record provoked protests in Panama, however, Bush decided to dump the dictator. On December 20, 1989, 22,500 U.S. troops invaded Panama. More than three hundred Panamanians died; twenty-three American soldiers perished. Noriega was captured and taken to Miami, where, in 1992, he was convicted of drug trafficking and imprisoned. Devastated Panama, meanwhile, became even more dependent on the United States, which offered little reconstruction aid.

Invasion of Panama

Seeking to end apartheid in South Africa, the United States maintained sanctions against the segregated nation, costing South Africa billions of dollars.

End of Apartheid in South Africa

Fearing economic disaster and an ultimately successful black revolt, South African president F. W. de Klerk in 1990 lifted restrictions on dissent and legalized the militantly anti-apartheid African National Congress (ANC). De Klerk also released from prison his nation's most celebrated critic, ANC leader Nelson Mandela. In 1994 Mandela became his nation's first black president. When apartheid ended, the U.S. Congress repealed sanctions, and American companies invested once again in South Africa.

The Middle East became the site of the Bush presidency's major foreign policy venture. When Iraq's dictator, Saddam Hussein, sent troops to invade his peaceful neighbor Kuwait in August 1990, oil-rich Saudi Arabia, long a U.S. ally, felt threatened. Bush dispatched more than 500,000 U.S. forces to the region. He also rallied a deeply divided

Persian Gulf War

In the Persian Gulf War of early 1991, Operation Desert Storm forced Iraqi troops out of Kuwait. Much of that nation's oil industry was destroyed by bombs and the retreating Iraqis, who torched oil facilities as they left. Oil wells burned for months, darkening the sky over these American forces and causing environmental damage.   (Bruno Barbey/Magnum Photos, Inc.)

Congress to authorize "all necessary means" to oust Iraq from Kuwait. The United Nations helped organize a coalition of forces. Although many Americans believed that economic sanctions imposed on Iraq should be given more time to work, Bush would not wait.

Operation Desert Storm began on January 16, 1991, with the greatest air armada in history pummeling Iraqi targets. American missiles reinforced round-the-clock bombing raids on Baghdad, Iraq's capital. In late February, coalition forces launched a ground war that quickly routed the Iraqis from Kuwait. The war's toll: at least 40,000 Iraqis dead; 240 coalition soldiers dead, including 148 Americans. But Saddam Hussein remained in power. A decade later, economic sanctions were still being applied against Iraq, and U.S. air attacks continued to punish Iraqi violations of the "no-fly zone."

When Somalia's repressive dictator was driven from power in 1991, public authority broke down as rival clans vied for power. While gun-toting bandits stole international relief supplies, hundreds of thousands of Somalis died of starvation. Appalled by television pictures of starving children, President Bush ordered 28,150 American troops to Somalia in December 1992 to ensure the delivery of relief aid. A U.N. peacekeeping force, including 9,000 Americans, took over in mid-1993. After changing the mission from feeding to reforming Somalia, the Clinton administration soon admitted defeat and in early 1994 withdrew U.S. troops; U.N. peacekeepers left about a year later. Somalia returned to violent politics and dire hunger.

Operation Restore Hope in Somalia

Economic Doldrums, American Voters, and the Election of 1992

Given the success in the Persian Gulf, Republicans were confident they would win the 1992 presidential election. The Republican coalition was intact, uniting economic conservatives, cultural conservatives (the fundamentalist and evangelical Christians who advocated "family values"), "Reagan Democrats" (blue-collar workers

and one-time Democrats who had supported Bush as Reagan's heir), white voters in the South, young Americans who had come of age politically during the Reagan years, and antitax and antigovernment conservatives in America's ever-growing suburbs. In the 1980s what had held the Republican coalition together were economic growth, anticommunism, and Ronald Reagan. In 1992, however, these three factors were absent.

As the 1992 presidential election neared, the stagnant economy pushed the Gulf War into the background. Between 1989 and 1992, the economy had grown slowly or not at all; the gross domestic product had averaged an increase of only 0.7 percent a year, the worst showing since the Great Depression of the 1930s. Even for Americans with jobs, personal income was stagnant. In fact, in 1991 median household incomes fell by 3.5 percent.

A Stagnant Economy

Some city and state governments faced bankruptcy. California, out of money in mid-1992, paid its workers and bills in IOUs. A series of "tax revolts," beginning with Proposition 13 in 1978, had cut property taxes just as California's population was booming. But California was not alone; some thirty states were in serious financial difficulty in the 1990s. Businesses, too, were deeply burdened with debt. And as companies tottered, the American people grew anxious about their jobs. Meanwhile, Bush's ratings waned. By January 1992 his approval rating had dropped to half of what it had been after the Persian Gulf War just ten months before.

The Democrats had problems of their own, particularly in the 102nd Congress, which they controlled. The most blatant scandal involved the House bank, where members of Congress wrote thousands of bad checks, all of which the bank covered at no fee. In the Senate, several members had done favors for Charles Keating, who had plundered a large California savings and loan association, causing many unsuspecting small investors to lose their savings. Many Americans also blamed Congress for the gridlock in Washington. Then, with few accomplishments to their credit, the members of Congress voted themselves a pay raise.

Scandals in Congress

In 1992 the Democrats nominated Governor Bill Clinton of Arkansas for president. Clinton was a baby

Bill Clinton

boomer whose message to the voters was mixed. Calling himself a "New Democrat," Clinton sought to inch his party to the right to make it more attractive to white suburbanites, Reagan Democrats, and members of the business community. He emphasized the need to move people off welfare, and he called for more police officers on the streets and for capital punishment. But he also advocated greater public investment in building roads, bridges, and communications infrastructure; universal access to apprenticeship programs and college educations; basic healthcare for all Americans; and a shift of funds from defense to civilian programs. Clinton's running mate, Tennessee senator Albert Gore, was also a baby boomer from the South. Gore appealed to environmentalists as the author of a bestselling book, *Earth in the Balance: Ecology and the Human Spirit* (1992).

Clinton was not Bush's only opponent in 1992. In April 1992, H. Ross Perot, who had amassed a fortune in the computer industry, announced

Ross Perot

on a television call-in show that he would run for president if voters in all fifty states put his name on the ballot. Many people responded to Perot's candidacy, convinced that he had the answers.

Still the chameleon, in 1992 Bush reverted to an earlier identity: "I care," he told the voters. Yet during race riots in Los Angeles, he revealed

Los Angeles Riots

his inability to respond to a domestic crisis. The violence erupted after a California jury had discounted videotaped evidence and acquitted four police officers charged with beating Rodney King, an African American motorist pulled over after a high-speed chase. Forty-four died in the rioting and a billion dollars in property losses was incurred.

President Bush paid a two-day trip to Los Angeles and advocated emergency aid, but he missed an opportunity to take a bold step in addressing the nation's urban and racial problems. He gave no civil rights talks, and he avoided meeting with the nation's mayors. It seemed to increasing numbers of voters that President Bush did not really care.

Clinton won the election with only 43 percent of the popular vote (Bush received 37 percent, Perot 19 percent). Clinton swept all of New England and the West

Clinton's Victory

Coast and much of the industrial heartland of the Midwest. He also made deep inroads into the South and ran well in the suburbs. The Republican coalition had not held. And Perot, by capturing almost one-fifth of the popular vote, demonstrated the public's dissatisfaction with both major parties.

Voters also changed Congress. Though party distribution remained about the same, with the Democrats in control of both houses, four more women were sent to the Senate and nineteen more to the House. Voters also elected more African American and Hispanic American representatives. Many of the first-term members of Congress were—like Clinton—in their forties with advanced degrees, no military service, and considerable experience in politics at the state level.

Bill Clinton, Newt Gingrich, and Political Stalemate

President Bill Clinton was one of the most paradoxical presidents in American history. In a 1996 story for the *New York Times*, the journalist Todd S. Purdum observed that Clinton was "one of the biggest, most talented, articulate, intelligent, open, colorful characters ever to inhabit the White House. [Clinton] can also be an undisciplined, fumbling, obtuse, defensive, self-justifying rogue. . . . He is breathtakingly bright while capable of doing really dumb things."

Clinton's immediate goal as president was to mobilize the nation to pull itself out of its economic, social, and political doldrums. In his inaugural address, he called on Americans to "take more responsibility, not only for ourselves and our families, but for our communities and our country." One of Clinton's first acts was to overturn Bush's "gag rule," which had prohibited abortion counseling in clinics that received federal funds. And he appointed his wife, Hillary Rodham Clinton, to draft a plan for healthcare reform. Seemingly off to a fast start, Clinton soon ran into trouble over a campaign pledge to lift the ban on homosexuals in the military. Finally accepting a "Don't ask, don't tell" compromise, he alienated both liberals and conservatives, both the gay community and the military.

In 1993 the president turned his attention to the economy. His economic plan called for higher taxes

**Economic
Proposals**

for the middle class, a 10 percent surtax on individuals with taxable incomes over $250,000, an energy tax, and a higher corporate tax. He also proposed to cut government spending through a smaller defense budget and a downsized bureaucracy, and he offered an immediate stimulus to the economy through public works projects.

With reduced spending and higher taxes, the federal deficit declined by some $83 billion during Clinton's first fiscal year in office. The president touted the accomplishment but could not take credit alone. The economy rebounded in 1993, outperforming estimates, increasing tax revenues, and cutting interest on the federal debt. Spending for healthcare and for Social Security fell below estimates. The decline in the fiscal deficit begun in 1993 continued, and by the time Clinton left office in January 2001, the nation boasted of budget surpluses.

Clinton's early successes included the so-called motor-voter act, which enabled people to register to

**Legislative
Successes**

vote when they applied for drivers' licenses, and the Family and Medical Leave Act, which required employers to grant workers unpaid family or medical leave of up to twelve weeks. He also signed into law measures dealing with the sale of firearms. The Brady Bill (1993) required a short waiting period (to allow for a background check) before the sale of a handgun; a second law banned the sale of assault weapons. And in 1994 Clinton secured the enactment of a $30.2 billion crime bill that provided funds for building prisons and increasing the size of urban police forces. Finally, with considerable opposition from his own party and from organized labor, Clinton secured congressional approval of NAFTA (see page 39).

When Byron R. White, a conservative justice, retired in 1993, Clinton altered the outlook of the

**Supreme Court
Appointments**

Supreme Court by appointing Ruth Bader Ginsburg, an experienced women's rights advocate and federal appeals court judge. The next year he named Stephen Breyer, a federal judge from Massachusetts, to succeed Justice Harry

Blackmun. The Court would be less conservative, but it was deeply divided over cases involving gay rights, free speech, and voting rights.

The 1994–1995 term produced conservative rulings that placed limits on affirmative action and school desegregation, but a year later the new justices began to speak up. In *U.S. v. Virginia*, the Court held that the Virginia Military Institute could not exclude women because to do so would violate the constitutional guarantee of "equal protection of the laws." Also in 1996, in a landmark gay rights case (*Romer v. Evans*), the Court ruled unconstitutional a Colorado amendment that nullified civil rights protections for homosexuals.

Almost everyone agreed that the nation's healthcare system was in crisis and that its welfare system

**Defeat of
Healthcare
Reform**

was a failure. Different constituencies, however, had vastly different "solutions" to offer. The result was continued gridlock between Democrats and Republicans, and between the White House and Congress, and eventual defeat for healthcare reforms. The failure to deliver on healthcare was Clinton's major defeat, and it was one he shared with his wife, who cochaired the president's task force on healthcare reform.

On the stump in 1992, Bill Clinton had praised his wife, Hillary Rodham Clinton, as a major asset. A Yale

**A Controversial
Couple**

law school graduate, Hillary Clinton had her own career as a lawyer, feminist, and social activist. Both she and her husband were controversial. Bill Clinton conceded that he had smoked marijuana in the 1960s but insisted that he had not inhaled. Few people believed him. As president, Clinton was the defendant in a civil lawsuit alleging sexual harassment. In addition, a scandal dating back to the mid-1980s began to embarrass both the Clintons. It involved the Whitewater Development Company, and in 1994 Kenneth Starr was appointed special prosecutor to investigate the matter.

Hillary Clinton was also a magnet for criticism, having been in the middle of several of the defining controversies of the Clinton administration, including the firing of the White House travel office staff in 1993 and the suicide later that year of her friend and former law partner, deputy White House counsel Vincent Foster.

Two years into the Clinton administration, disgusted and angry voters vowed again to "throw the rascals out." This time the target was

Newt Gingrich and the Contract with America

the Democratic-controlled Congress, and conservative Republicans stood ready to lead the assault. Meeting in 1989 and 1990, a group led by Newt Gingrich, a Republican representative from Georgia, had drafted a ten-point legislative agenda. Gingrich hoped the program would be endorsed by all Republican candidates and enacted in the first one hundred days of the new Congress. Bush rejected the plan in 1992 and went down to defeat. Gingrich resurrected the plan for the 1994 congressional elections.

This time more than three hundred Republican candidates for the House of Representatives stood on the steps of the U.S. Capitol and proclaimed their endorsement of the "Contract with America." The document called for a balanced-budget amendment to the Constitution; a presidential line-item veto; the prohibition of welfare payments to unmarried mothers under eighteen and a two-years-and-out limit on welfare benefits; more prisons and longer prison sentences; a $500-per-child tax credit; increased defense spending; a reduced capital gains tax; and congressional term limits.

In 1994 the Republican Party scored one of the most smashing victories in American political history, winning both houses of Congress for

The "Republican Revolution"

the first time since 1954. Not a single Republican incumbent lost, and many newcomers were elected, 73 in the House alone. Gingrich became Speaker of the House, and Bob Dole of Kansas became majority leader of the Senate. After the election Republicans set out to reverse sixty years of federal dominance and to dismantle the welfare state.

Anger, Apathy, and the Election of 1996

 On April 19, 1995, 168 children, women, and men were killed in a powerful bomb blast that destroyed the nine-story Alfred P. Murrah Federal Building in downtown Oklahoma City. Americans were dazed, saddened, and in-

censed. Many Americans initially thought the bomb had come from abroad, perhaps set off by Middle Eastern terrorists. That, however, was not the case. Timothy McVeigh, a native-born white American and a veteran of the Persian Gulf War, was responsible. McVeigh hated the federal government, which he condemned for betraying the American people and the Constitution. He was convicted of the crime in 1997 and executed in 2001.

After his arrest, McVeigh said he was agitated by a tragedy in Waco, Texas, in 1993, when the FBI led an

Hostility to Government and Political Alienation

assault on the compound of a religious sect known as the Branch Davidians; a fire had broken out, and some eighty people died. McVeigh called the attack a deliberate slaughter by the FBI. In the months that followed McVeigh's arrest, reporters and government investigators discovered various networks of Militiamen, Patriots, tax resisters, and Aryan-supremacist groups that thrived on the growing climate of fear and hatred.

While terrorism was relatively new to the American experience, hostility to the government was not. As the historian Michael Kazin has noted, "Throughout American history groups on the right and the left have seen the Federal Government as an alien force, inimical to their interests." Such groups, no matter what their form, believe that the government has betrayed the people; its leaders are corrupt; and the Constitution has been subverted. In the 1990s increasing numbers of Americans seemed to share this outlook.

For many Americans, the roots of hostility to government were planted during the Vietnam War. In the 1960s, student radicals had opposed the draft and demanded the right to smoke marijuana. At the same time, leftists saw government as an instrument of the ruling classes, and libertarians called for freedom from government restraints. In the 1990s, conservatives railed against taxes and proclaimed the unfettered right to own handguns and assault weapons. The scandals—Watergate, Iran-contra—of the decades in between had only deepened Americans' distrust of the federal government. And in Clinton's era, scandal undermined the presidency once again.

In quite a different way, President Ronald Reagan also fueled hostility to the government. In his inaugural address in 1981, he had asserted that "government is not the solution to our problem; government *is* the problem." Reagan's continuing antigovernment rhetoric drew many devoted listeners. And his compounding of the federal debt (aided by a fiscally irresponsible Congress) from $1 trillion to $3 trillion set severe financial constraints on what the government could afford to do in the future. When George H. W. Bush left office in 1993, the federal debt was $4.4 trillion. No wonder many Americans believed government was more a burden than a benefit.

Soon the Republicans in the 104th Congress, led by Newt Gingrich, proceeded to anger voters even

Failures and Successes of the "Republican Revolution"

more. Americans, it turned out, applauded economy in government, but were resistant to personal sacrifice. And under the Contract with America, most of those whose benefits would be cut were members of the middle class. People worried especially about Medicare and Medicaid, aid to education and college loans, Social Security, and veterans' benefits. When the Republicans attempted to turn over to the states responsibility for child nutrition programs, including school lunches, the Democrats resisted and the public rallied to their side. Republicans later repeated the mistake in pushing to cut spending for education and to repeal decades of environmental and occupational safety legislation.

The Republicans also erred when they used the threat of a federal government shutdown as a bargaining chip in their quest for a balanced budget by the year 2002. When the government temporarily closed its doors in 1995 and 1996, the public was inconvenienced and angry. Most Americans perceived Congress as ideologically inflexible but tended to see Clinton as moderate and reasonable.

Republicans in the 104th Congress were clearly frustrated. Their proposed constitutional amendments were defeated, and Clinton vetoed their tax cuts. Congress did, however, pass several significant acts, including the line-item veto, which allowed the president to cut specific spending items from the federal budget. Of far-reaching influence, the Telecommunications Act of 1996 made sweeping changes in federal law, allowing telephone companies and cable companies to compete, deregulating cable rates, and permitting media companies to own more television and radio sta-

tions. With the Freedom to Farm Act of 1996, Congress also made historic changes in farm policy, throwing out the 1938 law that established agricultural subsidies and mandating the seven-year phase-out of payments to farmers. Most important, it passed a welfare reform act (The Personal Responsibility and Work Opportunity Act) that eliminated the provision in the Social Security Act of 1935 that guaranteed cash assistance for poor children (Aid to Families with Dependent Children). Instead, under the new law each state received a lump sum of federal money to design and run its own "welfare-to-work" programs. In addition to reducing food stamps and restricting welfare eligibility for legal immigrants, the law mandated that the head of every family on welfare must find work within two years, or the family loses benefits. And it decreed that no one can get more than five years of welfare benefits over a lifetime.

While the Republican 104th Congress failed to secure most of its legislative goals, it did recast the American political debate. Many Democrats conceded that the government could not solve all problems and needed to be shrunk. Both Congress and the president urged returning power to the states.

As the 1996 election neared, some political observers predicted that voters would send Clinton back

The 1996 Election

to Arkansas and put a conservative Republican in the White House. But these pundits overlooked an essential segment of the electorate: women. For years, political scholars had identified a "gender gap" in voting behavior: women were more likely than men to vote Democratic. Now, women tended to view the 104th Congress as hostile to measures essential to family welfare.

"Women are still bigger believers in government," explained Andrew Kohut, a veteran pollster, in 1996. "Women are stronger environmentalists, more critical of business and less critical of government." Issues like health insurance, daycare for children, and education were also of keen importance to women, who feared for the future of safety-net programs and believed that the government should do more to help families. Looking to the 1996 elections, Democrats hoped that women could do for them what "angry white men" had done for the Republicans in 1994.

Among the Republican hopefuls in 1996 was Bob Dole of Kansas. Dole, the Senate majority leader, had

President Bill Clinton suffered political repudiation in the Republican sweep of Congress in 1994. But two years later his popularity was on the upswing. Here he and Hillary Clinton and Vice President Al Gore (with wife Tipper) celebrate their renomination at the 1996 Democratic National Convention in Chicago.   (Wide World Photos, Inc.)

served in Congress for thirty-five years, and many Republicans believed that he had earned his party's presidential nomination.

Clinton was reelected with only 49 percent of the popular vote. Still, he easily defeated Dole (41 percent) and Ross Perot (8 percent), who ran again, this time as the Reform Party candidate. Although the Republicans lost the contest for the White House, they retained control of both houses of Congress.

Clinton had won, in part, because he stole some of the conservatives' thunder. He called for a balanced budget, declared "the era of big government" was over, and invoked family values such as "fighting for the family-leave law or the assault-weapons ban or the Brady Bill or the V-chip for parents or trying to keep tobacco out of the hands of kids." Clinton's movement to the right reflected the strength of conservatism in the United States as the nation neared the new millennium.

The Prospects and Perils of Hegemonic Power: Military Interventions, Peace Diplomacy, Trade, and Culture

Clinton and his secretaries of state, the veteran diplomat Warren Christopher and Madeleine Albright, the first woman ever to hold that high post, championed domestic themes in their foreign policy agenda—especially the expansion of economic prosperity, democracy, and environmental controls. Clinton had difficulty with congressional Republicans, who derailed his ambassadorial appointments, cut foreign aid, refused to pay America's U.N. dues, and blocked major treaties. Clinton sustained a large military budget ($270 billion in 1999) and repeatedly deployed U.S. armed forces abroad.

One consequence of the end of the Cold War proved savage: ethnic wars in Yugoslavia, from which Slovenia, Croatia, and Macedonia seceded in 1991, followed the next year by Bosnia-Herzegovina. Yugoslavia (primarily Serbia but including Montenegro) fought these moves toward independence. Bosnian Muslims, Serbs, and Croats were soon killing one another by the hundreds of thousands. Clinton talked tough against Serbian aggression and atrocities in Bosnia-Herzegovina, especially the Serbs' cruel "ethnic cleansing" of Muslims through massacres and rape camps. On occasion he ordered U.S. airpower to strike Serb positions. In late 1995, after American diplomats, meeting with the belligerents in Dayton, Ohio, brokered an agreement for a new multiethnic state in Bosnia-Herzegovina, Clinton contributed thousands of U.S. troops to a NATO Implementation Force that continued to keep a fragile peace as the twentieth century closed.

Ethnic Wars in Former Yugoslavia

Still, troubles persisted in the Balkans, and in March 1999, U.S. and NATO forces began to bomb Yugoslavia (Serbia) to stop the ethnic cleansing of its province of Kosovo, whose majority were ethnic Albanians. Yugoslav president Slobodan Milošević finally relented in June, withdrawing his brutal military from Kosovo, where U.S. troops joined a U.N. peacekeeping force. The International War Crimes Tribunal indicted Milošević and his top aides for atrocities. In June 2001, a new government in Yugoslavia turned Milošević over to the international court to await trial.

Russia strongly protested the bombing of Yugoslavia. Economically hobbled, Russia found itself increasingly isolated. Just before the Kosovo crisis, Washington had expanded NATO to include Poland, Hungary, and the Czech Republic. Moscow read the expansion as an anti-Russian step. In 1997 Washington and Moscow had negotiated a START-III agreement, cutting strategic nuclear weapons once again, but the Russians bristled against the U.S. decision to move ahead on an antiballistic missile system. By 2000 a "Cold Peace" characterized U.S.-Russian relations over this issue as well as over Russia's inability to curb its rampant political and business corruption and refusal to launch effective reforms.

The Middle East also continued to draw intense U.S. interest. As Saudi Arabia punished the Palestine Liberation Organization (PLO) for its support of Iraq in the Persian Gulf War by trimming financial assistance, and as the *intifada* raised Israel's costs of maintaining control over occupied territories (see Map 31.2 on page 560), the PLO and Israel seemed more willing to settle their differences. U.S. diplomats encouraged Arab and Israeli leaders to attend a peace conference in Madrid in the fall of 1991. In September 1993 the PLO's Yasir Arafat and Israel's prime minister Yitzhak Rabin signed an agreement for Palestinian self-rule in the Gaza Strip and the West Bank's Jericho. In 1994 Israel signed a peace accord with Jordan. Radical Palestinians, however, continued to stage bloody terrorist attacks on Israelis, while extremist Israelis killed Palestinians. Only after American-conducted negotiations and renewed violence in the West Bank did Israel agree in early 1997 to withdraw its forces from the West Bank city of Hebron.

Arab-Israeli Agreements

Palestinian-Israeli tensions remained high, and a new *intifada* erupted in late 2000. During the uprising, Palestinian suicide bombers targeted Israeli civilians. Israel in turn targeted suspected terrorists. Then, during Passover 2002, a suicide bomber killed twenty-eight Israelis who were dining at a hotel. Israel responded by sending troops into the occupied territories with the intent of destroying the terrorist infrastructure. The operation led to the detention of four thousand Palestinians, the destruction of property, and the deaths of an undetermined number of civilians. Between the bombings and Israel's military response, peace seemed a distant dream.

Ethnic rivalry also created turmoil in Africa. In mid-1994, in Rwanda, the majority Hutus butchered eight hundred thousand of the minority Tutsis. The United States and the United Nations responded too late, with Clinton resisting appeals for intervention to stop the killing. In 1998, Clinton apologized for not "calling these crimes by their rightful name: genocide."

Genocide in Rwanda

Throughout Latin America, the Clinton administration continued to promote liberalized trade, private enterprise economies, orderly immigration, democratization, and the war against drugs. In the early 1990s in poverty-wracked and environmentally devastated Haiti, a military coup and political instability provoked U.S. economic sanctions. Tens of thousands of black Haitians

Pressures Against Haiti and Cuba

fled in boats for U.S. territory, spawning an immigration crisis. In September 1994, President Clinton sent Jimmy Carter as his emissary to the Caribbean island nation. The former president cut a deal granting amnesty to the generals, who stepped down. Clinton soon ordered U.S. troops to Haiti. In early 1996 American forces departed, their mission to revitalize Haiti unfulfilled.

As for Cuba, Clinton improved telecommunications and cultural linkages while maintaining the punishing economic embargo. Then in March 1996, after an airplane manned by a provocative anti-Castro group was shot down by Cuban fighter pilots near Cuba, Clinton, on the eve of the Florida primary, pandered to the politically influential Cuban-American community and signed the Helms-Burton Act, which among other things allowed American nationals and companies to sue in U.S. courts foreign companies that were using formerly American-owned properties in Cuba. The Castro government had seized these assets in the early days of the Cuban Revolution. After Canada and the European Union, both of which traded with and invested in Cuba, condemned the measure, Clin-

ton suspended the act's provision that permitted the suing of foreign companies, but Cuban-American relations remained at an impasse, influenced more by domestic U.S. politics than by calculations of national security.

Seeing flourishing foreign trade as essential to U.S. prosperity and to world economic and political stability, the Clinton administration strove to open foreign markets to American products and to close the U.S. trade gap (which in 1998 reached a record deficit of $233.4 billion). Besides guiding NAFTA through Congress, Clinton announced in 1994, when granting China most-favored-nation trading status, that the United States was decoupling trade and human-rights issues. Thus in 1999 the United States supported China's membership in the World Trade Organization (WTO) in return for increased U.S. access to the Chinese domestic market.

Trade Expansion and Globalization

The WTO became the main body regulating and settling disputes over international trade. As a symbol of globalization—the greater movement of goods,

Protesting that the World Trade Organization (WTO) possessed the dangerous power to challenge any nation's environmental laws if the WTO deemed them barriers to trade, chanting demonstrators marched in the streets of Seattle on November 30, 1999. Critics of the WTO have claimed that sea turtles and dolphins have already been victimized by the WTO. Demonstrators identified the WTO as an example of globalization gone wrong. The WTO meeting went on, but the results proved meager because nations could not agree on rules governing dumping, subsidies for farm goods, genetically altered foods, and lower tariffs on high-tech goods.   (Paul David Brown/Seattle Post-Intelligencer)

services, money, and people across national borders—the WTO became a target of environmental and labor groups, such as the Sierra Club and the AFL-CIO. They charged that the powerful organization of 135 nations served corporate interests and had the dangerous authority to overrule national laws protecting labor standards, human rights, and public health. When the WTO held a summit meeting in Seattle in late 1999, antiglobalization groups and individuals protested. Other meetings of the powerful also sparked protests. This was especially true in 2001 during the Summit of the Americas talks in Quebec City, Canada, and the gathering of the Group of 8 (leaders of the world's leading industrial democracies plus Russia) in Genoa, Italy. At Quebec the leaders of Western Hemisphere nations (minus Cuba) discussed plans to create the Free Trade Area of the Americas—a NAFTA arrangement that would extend from Canada to the tip of South America.

Trade issues lay at the center of tense U.S.-Japanese relations. Most nettlesome was the huge trade deficit in Japan's favor. American manufacturers protested that Japan's tariffs, cartels, and government subsidies blocked U.S. goods from Japanese markets. The Japanese countered that obsolete equipment, poor education, and inadequate spending on research and development undercut U.S. competitiveness. Trade talks with Japan proved divisive and produced small gains, but both nations knew that their economies were too interdependent for one to punish or isolate the other. By the late 1990s, as Japan's economy stagnated and America's galloped, "Japan bashing" declined and McDonald's became Japan's largest restaurant chain.

The question of trade also influenced U.S. policy toward Vietnam. Military veterans and families of missing-in-action (MIA) soldiers berated Clinton's 1994 decision to lift the trade embargo against Vietnam and his 1995 opening of full diplomatic relations. American businesses such as Otis, General Electric, and Pepsico welcomed the new economic opportunities there. "English is the language of money, the language of our future," remarked a Vietnamese diplomat.

Weapons proliferation alarmed people everywhere. Sales of arms, including surface-to-surface missiles, accelerated across the post–Cold War world, and the United States continued to be the world's largest arms merchant. Nuclear proliferation continued to

Weapons of Mass Destruction

worry leaders, especially after India and Pakistan exploded nuclear devices in 1998. The Comprehensive Nuclear-Test-Ban Treaty of 1996 had 151 signatories, including the United States. But the Clinton administration seemed lackluster in its advocacy of U.S. ratification. In October 1999 the Republican-dominated Senate rejected the treaty by a vote of 51 to 48 (67 votes were needed). Secretary Albright soon announced that the United States would honor the treaty anyway. Two years earlier the United States had finally ratified the Chemical Weapons Convention, which required the destruction of chemical weapons such as poison gas. The United States refused, however, to join a hundred other nations in endorsing a treaty banning antipersonnel land mines.

Environmental and Population Crises

Environmental woes also continued to disturb world order and political stability. Acid rain, toxic waste, deterioration of the protective ozone layer (which blocks the sun's carcinogenic ultraviolet rays), soil erosion, water pollution, and destruction of tropical forests spoiled the natural environment, killed wildlife, and poisoned land. Warming of the earth's climate due to the greenhouse effect—the buildup of carbon dioxide and other gases in the atmosphere—threatened a rise in ocean levels, potentially flooding occupied land and dislocating millions of people.

Unlike his predecessor, Clinton actively advanced environmental issues. In 1993 he signed the Biodiversity Treaty and sent it to the Senate, where it remains pending. The United States also signed the Global Warming Convention (1997) to reduce greenhouse gas emissions (not yet ratified). And in the fall of 1997 Clinton transmitted the 1982 Convention on the Law of the Sea to the Senate. It too has yet to be ratified.

Human Rights for Women

In the mid-1990s the State Department and the United Nations studied the treatment of women as a worldwide human rights issue. Their reports revealed that 70 percent of the world's poor people were women. Women faced not only job discrimination and political discrimination but also forced sterilization and abortion, coerced prostitution, and genital mutilation. The 1995 Fourth

World Conference on Women, held in Beijing, called for the "empowerment of women" through "human rights and fundamental freedoms." Gender issues and international relations became intertwined. The United States soon made genital mutilation and other gender-based abuses grounds for asylum.

The export of American popular culture became one of the 1990s' most prominent features. After the Cold War ended, American culture became particularly coveted in eastern Europe and the former Soviet republics. Many residents of former Communist countries strove to learn the English language like their counterparts in western Europe. Interest in American basketball soared everywhere. Images of the slam-dunking Chicago Bulls hero Michael Jordan adorned T-shirts worldwide, and players from foreign lands, including eastern Europe, increasingly enrolled in U.S. colleges to play hoops.

Globalization of American Culture

American movies, TV programs, music, books, computer software, and other "intellectual property" dominated world markets in the 1990s. The TV soap opera *The Young and the Restless* became popular in New Delhi; people in Warsaw watched *Dr. Quinn, Medicine Woman*. Time Warner, Inc., sold TV programs in 175 countries. On the Internet an estimated 90 percent of all global traffic was in English. The popularity of U.S. culture abroad stemmed in good part from the themes it presented: wealth, individuality, freedom, optimism, sex, violence, mobility, technological progress.

Some world affairs specialists predicted the growth of a single global culture, with the United States at its center. The globalization of American culture, however, did not unfold conflict-free: some peoples protested the emasculation of their native ways by U.S. imports that seemed tawdry, unhealthy, and violent. Yet, with power in the world "no longer defined solely by territory or industrial capacity, but increasingly by the development of intellectual capital," the scholar Barry Fulton has suggested, the United States was well positioned to lead the so-called Information Age of the twenty-first century.

At the start of the twenty-first century, the United States held immense power, measured in many ways. As "globocop" it intervened in other countries. As

banker and trader, it pressed other nations to open their markets to U.S. commerce. Accelerated by the World Wide Web and the Internet, American culture spread everywhere. Yet, throughout history, hegemonic powers have had difficulty sustaining their supremacy. Would America, too, falter? By 2000 many nations and peoples had grown wary and critical of the United States. French foreign minister Hubert Vedrine declared, "we cannot accept either a politically unipolar world, not a culturally uniform world, nor the unilateralism of a single hyper-power" like the United States.

Clinton's Second Term: Scandal, Impeachment, and Political Survival

 Misconduct and scandals had tainted the Clinton White House from the beginning. Bill Clinton's character was often the issue, and allegations of his marital infidelity abounded. But, as one reporter noted, "If Ronald Reagan was the Teflon President, then Bill Clinton is the Timex President. He takes his lickings, keeps on ticking."

The scandal involving the Whitewater Development Company continued to dog the White House. In the mid-1980s, the Clintons had been partners in the company with James McDougal, who was later indicted for conspiracy and mail fraud, along with his wife, Susan, and Jim Guy Tucker, Clinton's successor as governor of Arkansas. During the 1996 elections, Kenneth Starr, the independent counsel investigating Whitewater, began to produce indictments and even convictions: the McDougals and Tucker were found guilty. Hillary Clinton, testifying before a Senate committee, could not explain how long-lost law-firm billing records from Little Rock, which had been subpoenaed, had disappeared for two years before surfacing in the family quarters of the White House. At a later point, the Clinton administration said it was a mistake that in 1993 and 1994 the FBI had sent over to the White House the confidential records of some nine hundred Republicans. Others thought the manipulation of federal agencies smelled of an earlier scandal, Watergate.

Whitewater Indictments and Investigation

Meanwhile, Starr expanded his investigation of Bill Clinton to matters unrelated to Whitewater, including allegations of illegal campaign contri-

Monica Lewinsky

butions, sexual harassment, and, finally, lying to a grand jury about the nature of his relationship with a White House intern named Monica S. Lewinsky. In early 1998 Linda Tripp, a former White House employee, informed Starr's office that Clinton had had a sexual affair, and she had tapes of telephone conversations to prove it. A week later, in a sworn deposition to the grand jury investigating sexual harassment, Clinton denied the affair. But in late July, Starr granted Lewinsky and her mother full immunity in exchange for testimony, and the next day Clinton's lawyer announced that the president would also testify.

On the night of August 13, 1998, Bill Clinton confessed to his wife that he had had a sexual relationship with Monica Lewinsky. Four days later, Clinton testified, telling the grand jury that he recalled a half-dozen sexual encounters with Lewinsky, beginning in late 1995 and ending by 1997. That evening, he spoke from the Oval Office. "I have sinned," he told the American people, and he expressed "sorrow" for the "hurt" he had caused his family, his staff, Lewinsky and her family, and the American people. "I have asked all for their forgiveness." Meanwhile, Starr was preparing a 445-page impeachment report for consideration by Congress.

The Starr report described ten sexual encounters between Clinton and Lewinsky and mapped out eleven

Impeachment by the House

possible grounds for impeachment of the president. On December 19, the House passed two articles of impeachment against Clinton, one alleging that the president had committed perjury in his August 17 grand-jury testimony, the other that he had obstructed justice. With the House vote, Clinton became only the second president to face a trial in the Senate, where a two-thirds majority is needed to remove a president from office.

The 1998 congressional elections left the Republican majority in the Senate unchanged at 55 to 45, and

Acquittal by the Senate

everyone expected that the Senate vote would generally break along party lines. After a five-week trial, the Senate, by a 55-to-45 vote, found the president not guilty of perjury. And

voting 50 to 50, the Senate cleared him of obstructing justice.

Problems also beset the nation's schools. In the 1990s students in Paducah, Kentucky; Jonesboro, Arkansas; Springfield, Oregon; and

Columbine

elsewhere opened fire on their schoolmates. On Tuesday, April 20, 1999, Dylan Klebold and Eric Harris came to their high school in Littleton, Colorado, armed with two shotguns, two semiautomatic rifles, and thirty pipe bombs filled with gunpowder, nails, and broken glass. Walking toward the school, one of the boys pointed a rifle at a seventeen-year-old student and fatally shot her in the head. It was a little after 11 A.M. At the end of the day, fifteen people, including Klebold and Harris, lay dead. Why, asked society? Were guns too readily available? Was there too much violence on television? Was America a sick society?

The 2000 Elections, a New Bush, and Terrorism

As America entered a new century, its people yearned for a president with character and leadership. Some Americans embraced Senator John McCain, a Republican from Arizona who championed campaign finance reform. McCain was also a war hero who had survived five and a half years in North Vietnam as a prisoner of war. The Democratic presidential race also featured a genuine hero; Bill Bradley had been an All-American basketball player at Princeton, a Rhodes scholar at Oxford University, a Hall of Fame basketball player for the New York Knicks, and a U.S. senator from New Jersey. Bradley joined McCain in demanding campaign finance reform.

The race for the presidency accelerated in early 2000, with primary elections, party caucuses, and state

Super Tuesday

party conventions scheduled in thirty-two states during the first three months of the year, beginning in Iowa in January. The front runners were George W. Bush, the Republican governor of Texas, and Al Gore, Jr., Democratic vice president under Clinton. Loyalists in both parties supported Bush and Gore politically and financially. On Super Tuesday in March, Gore swept the Democratic primaries, including California and New York, and Bush won all but a handful of states in New England. McCain and Bradley ended their campaigns, and Gore and Bush squared off for the November election.

In 2000 the United States was riding a wave of great prosperity. Indeed, the economic expansion that had begun in 1991 became in early 2000 the longest-running expansion in American history. Moreover, inflation remained low and the stock market soared. In January 2000 the Dow Jones Industrial Average hit a record high closing of 11,722; two months later the technology stocks on the Nasdaq closed at an all-time high of 5,048. Virtually all economic data seemed to bode well for Al Gore as the nominee of the incumbent party.

Bush, however, had an immense war chest. Even before officially securing the Republican nomination,

The Polls—a Close Race

he had raised $67 million, some of which he used for ads against the Democrats. At the time of the Republican Convention, the Gallup Poll gave Bush an eleven-percentage-point edge over Gore. This margin increased to seventeen points by the end of the convention. Gore then closed the gap, and when the Democratic Convention ended, the two candidates were about even. By the eve of the election, the Gallup poll indicated the race was too close to call.

On November 8, the day after the election, a winner had not emerged. Gore had 267 electoral votes and Bush had 246 (see Map 33.2). Neither candidate had the 270 electoral votes needed to become president. Not included in the totals were the 25 electoral votes from Florida, a state where the popular vote was extremely close, where the governor, Jeb Bush, was George W. Bush's brother, and where the cochairperson of the Bush campaign was the secretary of state.

The initial vote count in Florida gave Bush a slim victory margin. A machine recount began, as did hand recounts in some counties. Bush's

Florida and the Supreme Court

lead sank to 930, and the Gore team hoped that hand recounts in Broward, Palm Beach, and Miami-Dade counties would swing the election to him. Legal action began first in the Florida courts and then in the United States Supreme

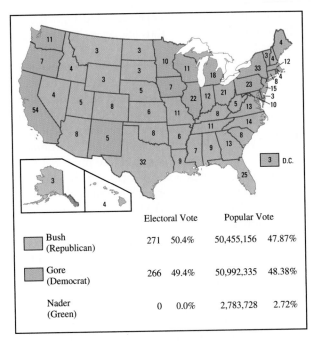

Map 33.2   Presidential Election, 2000   In the most disputed U.S. presidential election since 1876, George W. Bush received fewer popular votes but more electoral votes (271 to 266) than Al Gore. Although Florida became the focal point of the dispute, the popular vote was extremely close in several other states. Votes for Green Party candidate Ralph Nader hurt Gore, especially in Florida.

Court. Finally, on December 12, a divided Supreme Court rendered its decision in the case of *Bush v. Gore*. By a 5-4 vote along conservative versus liberal lines, the Court prevented further recounts in Florida and thus allowed to stand earlier recounts that gave Bush a 537-vote victory. The final electoral count was Bush 271, Gore 266, with 1 abstention. Gore, however, did defeat Bush in the nationwide popular vote by 539,947 votes.

The Senate races mirrored the presidential election's closeness. The new Senate had fifty Democrats and fifty Republicans. Thus the Bush administration began with the deciding vote in the Senate held by Vice President Dick Cheney. Within months of his inauguration Bush had taken positions of deep concern to moderate Republicans, one of whom, Jim Jeffords of Vermont, became an independent and aligned himself with the Democrats, thus allowing them to organize the Senate.

During the first several months of his presidency, Bush embraced positions that were pleasing to social

Early Bush Positions

conservatives, the energy industry, tax reduction advocates, and the insurance industry. Conversely, his policies concerned liberals and environmentalists. Because of the projected budget surpluses, he was able to secure enactment of a ten-year tax reduction program. The initial phase of the plan sent rebates of up to $300 to individual taxpayers. Those filing joint returns received a maximum of $600.

Shortly after taking office, Bush stated his belief that the drilling for oil in the Arctic National Wildlife Refuge should be authorized. He also rejected the Kyoto Treaty, which called for reductions in carbon dioxide emissions. Power plants burning fossil fuels are a major source of CO_2. Critics saw the Bush positions as paybacks to the oil, gas, coal, and electric power industries, which had backed his campaign.

Bush's reinstatement of the policy that prohibited the use of federal funds for abortion services or counseling abroad alarmed others. To many, this seemed a political payback to social conservatives. Liberals opposed his proposal to place a cap on the amount for which one could sue a health maintenance organization. These and other issues, such as the administration's education, Social Security, and defense proposals, deeply divided Democrats and Republicans.

The divisions between the two parties intensified in mid-2001 when the economy moved toward reces-

Economic Slowdown

sion. The stock market highs of early 2000 vanished. By March 2001 the Nasdaq had lost 64 percent of its March 2000 value; in subsequent months it would fall even more. The Dow Jones Industrial Average and the Standard & Poor's index also retreated. Unemployment began to rise, and the projected surplus began to vanish. Other problems also concerned Americans.

Violence in the schools, as well as hate crimes against African Americans, Jews, and gays, seemed to pale when Americans encountered escalating terrorism. The 2001 attacks on the World Trade Center and the Pentagon were the latest in a series of attacks dat-

President George W. Bush (b. 1946) proudly hails from Texas, where his career in the gas and oil business and his partnership in the Texas Rangers baseball franchise preceded his election as governor. Despite a bachelor's degree from Yale and a master's degree from Harvard, Bush at times struggled to express himself clearly, becoming the brunt of many jokes that doubted his intelligence. But adept management of Bush's presentations by political advisers, and his resolute response to terrorism, quieted criticism of the conservative forty-third president. (Sygma/Corbis)

Terrorism

ing back at least two decades. In 1983, 241 marines were killed when a truck loaded with explosives was driven into their barracks in Lebanon. The 1993 bombing of the World Trade Center by Islamic terrorists did comparatively little damage, but Tim McVeigh's bombing of the Murrah Federal Building in Oklahoma City took 168 lives, and the 1998 bombings of the U.S. embassies in Kenya and Tanzania claimed 224 lives, including those of 12 Americans. And 17 Americans died in the attack on the U.S.S. *Cole* in October 2000.

Osama bin Laden probably masterminded several of the attacks.

The terrorist attacks of September 11, 2001, had an immediate and broad-based impact. For some Americans, this was a defining moment comparable to December 7, 1941. An already ailing economy sustained a traumatic shock. The stock market suffered its worst percentage decline since the Great Depression. As people cancelled reservations, the airline industry began announcing layoffs, which eventually neared the 100,000 mark. Hotels, restaurants, and the tourist industry reported sharp declines. Americans wondered what would happen next. Fears of biological and chemical attacks abounded. In October, Americans learned of anthrax being spread through the mails. By late October anthrax had killed four people. It also led to the closing of congressional office buildings, other federal buildings in the nation's capital, and U.S. postal facilities in various cities. Moreover, the anthrax scare led to concern about the nation's vulnerability to a once dreaded disease—smallpox.

As for the government, it announced a war against terrorism. This war involved building a global antiterrorist coalition, conducting an extensive air campaign against the Taliban and al-Qaeda, supporting indigenous opposition forces in Afghanistan and using American troops there, freezing the assets of suspected terrorists and terrorist organizations, and detaining hundreds of suspect Middle Easterners living in the United States. Screening at airports was enhanced, and armed national guardsmen appeared in air terminals. President Bush created the Office of Homeland Security and named former governor Tom Ridge of Pennsylvania as the agency's director. And while the government encouraged Americans to be tolerant of people of Middle Eastern backgrounds, hate crimes increased. Government officials suggested that civil liberties might have to be restricted in order to deal with the new crisis.

In November 2001, the Taliban regime was toppled and, a few weeks later, forces in its last stronghold surrendered. And while pockets of resistance remained, al-Qaeda forces in Afghanistan were on the run (see Map 33.3). Still, neither Osama bin Laden nor the head of the Taliban, Mullah Muhammad Omar, had been captured or killed. As the quest for bin Laden and Omar continued, Americans pondered the next steps

September 11 and Its Impact

On September 11, 2001, rescue workers carry away from the World Trade Center the dead body of Father Mychal Judge. A chaplain for the New York City fire department, the Franciscan priest had gone to the site to help victims of the terrorist attacks. Rubble collapsed on him. Born in Brooklyn in 1933 to Irish immigrant parents, Judge earned respect as a man of compassion. Another priest said of him, "He just felt so bad for people who were not cared for." His rescuers took Father Judge to the sanctuary of a nearby church. (Reuters NewMedia Inc./Corbis)

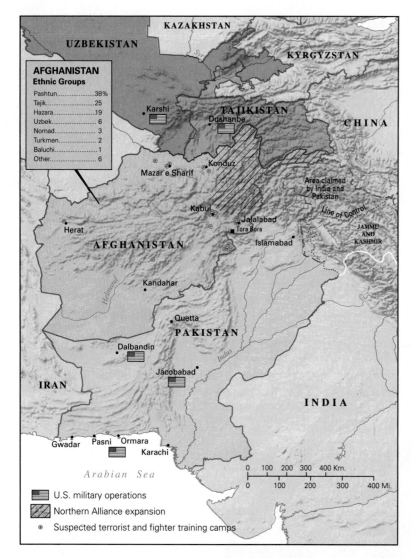

Map 33.3 Afghanistan and the War on Terrorism Prior to conducting military operations against the Taliban regime in Afghanistan and the al-Qaeda forces of Osama bin Laden, the United States secured permission to operate from bases in Pakistan, Uzbekistan, and Tajikistan. In the war the United States conducted extensive bombing raids in support of forces, especially the Northern Alliance, combating the Taliban. With military air support the opposition forces soon captured the Taliban/al-Qaeda strongholds of Mazar e Sharif, Kabul, and Kandahar.

to be taken in a war with no borders and no anticipated termination date. Would the next phase of the war involve Somalia, Yemen, Iraq, Sudan, the Philippines, or some other country in which or from which terrorists operated?

Summary

The 1990s began with challenges to the old world order. Like a retreating glacier, the Cold War left behind a scarred landscape and debris that complicated the shaping of a new world order. Localized conflicts and ethnic rivalries, such as those in the Balkans, the Middle East, and Africa, crowded the international agenda, as did human rights, the natural environment, and the proliferation of deadly weapons. In the 1990s Bush and Clinton officials spoke of America's "world responsibilities" to spread democracy and free-market economics abroad and to intervene for humanitarian purposes. Clinton himself reasserted traditional notions of U.S. world leadership. His military interventions in a host of countries—especially against what Washington officials called "rogue states"—and trade and cultural expansion demonstrated a traditional American desire to make the world more American and to sustain U.S. hegemony against all challengers.

The personal behavior of President Clinton led not only to his impeachment and trial but to a continued erosion of the respect Americans had for the central government. The 2000 presidential election was, at best, a muddied affair. The American people waited for thirty-six days before learning who was to be their next president. They then accepted a leader who had received a half million fewer votes than the loser and who had gained the office through a Supreme Court decision.

At the time George W. Bush assumed the presidency, many nations had grown envious of America's prosperity and power and were struggling to adopt American economic and political institutions, especially as American culture spread worldwide. But perils also confronted America and the world in the new century. Some foreign peoples hated America. The first targets of terrorism directed at the United States in the new century had symbolic value. The World Trade Center was a symbol of America's economic might, and the Pentagon of its military prowess. Attacks on those symbols led to the nation's first war of the twenty-first century.

LEGACY FOR A PEOPLE AND A NATION
The Internet

In the 1990s America—and the world—went online, forever changing the way people communicate (e-mail), do business (e-commerce), and experience life. Although a crude version of the Internet known as ARPANET went online in 1969, when two bulky computers were linked by a 15-foot cable, it was a series of developments in the late 1980s and 1990s that stimulated the Net revolution. First, Tim Berners-Lee, a British physicist, devised the three basic elements of the Web's operation: URL (uniform resource locator), HTML (hypertext markup language), and HTTP (hypertext transfer protocol). Then in 1993 the first commercial "browser" to aid navigation through the Web hit the market. Called Mosaic, it was soon followed by a much more successful product: Netscape. The prospect of millions of computers connected worldwide had become a reality.

By 2000 there were nearly 200 million Internet users worldwide, including 80 million Americans. By 2003 more than 500 million people will be surfing the World Wide Web. For their Christmas shopping in 1999, for example, millions of Americans avoided the malls and clicked through their gift lists. Some bought books from Amazon.com, while others bid on items being auctioned at eBay. Psychologists at Carnegie Mellon University, surveying the lives of Net users, found that people who spend even a few hours a week online suffer higher levels of loneliness and depression. Seemingly nothing, however, can slow down the digitized transformations in communications and the diffusion of information. Indeed, for the American people and nation in the new millennium, there could be no more fitting legacy than the Internet.

For Further Reading, see the Appendix. For Web resources, go to history.college.hmco.com/students.

APPENDIX

Suggestions for Further Reading

Chapter 16

National Policy, Politics, and Constitutional Law

Herman Belz, *Emancipation and Equal Rights* (1978); Michael Les Benedict, *A Compromise of Principle: Congressional Republicans and Reconstruction, 1863–1869* (1974); Michael Les Benedict, *The Impeachment and Trial of Andrew Johnson* (1973); Adrian Cook, *The Alabama Claims* (1975); David Donald, *Charles Sumner and the Rights of Man* (1970); Harold M. Hyman, *A More Perfect Union* (1973); William S. McFeely, *Grant* (1981); William S. McFeely, *Yankee Stepfather: General O. O. Howard and the Freedmen* (1968); Eric L. McKitrick, *Andrew Johnson and Reconstruction* (1966); Joel Silbey, *A Respectable Minority: The Democratic Party in the Civil War Era* (1977); Brooks D. Simpson, *The Reconstruction Presidents* (1998); Kenneth M. Stampp, *The Era of Reconstruction* (1965); Hans L. Trefousse, *Andrew Johnson* (1989).

The Freed Slaves

Ira Berlin, ed., *Freedom: A Documentary History of Emancipation, 1861–1867* (1984); Orville Vernon Burton, *In My Father's House Are Many Mansions* (1985); Edmund L. Drago, *Black Politicians and Reconstruction in Georgia* (1982); Eric Foner, *One Kind of Freedom* (1983); Gerald Jaynes, *Branches Without Roots: The Genesis of the Black Working Class in the American South, 1862–1882* (1986); Leon Litwack, *Been in the Storm So Long* (1979); Edward Magdol, *A Right to the Land* (1977); Robert Morris, *Reading, 'Riting and Reconstruction* (1981); Howard Rabinowitz, ed., *Southern Black Leaders in Reconstruction* (1982); Emma Lou Thornbrough, ed., *Black Reconstructionists* (1972).

Politics and Reconstruction in the South

Robert W. Coakley, *The Role of Federal Military Forces in Domestic Disorders, 1789–1878* (1988); Richard N. Current, *Those Terrible Carpetbaggers* (1988); W. E. B. Du Bois, *Black Reconstruction* (1935); Paul D. Escott, *Many Excellent People: Power and Privilege in North Carolina, 1850–1900* (1985);

Michael W. Fitzgerald, *The Union League Movement in the Deep South* (1989); Eric Foner, *Reconstruction: America's Unfinished Revolution, 1863–1877* (1988); William C. Harris, *The Day of the Carpetbagger* (1979); Thomas Holt, *Black over White: Negro Political Leadership in South Carolina During Reconstruction* (1977); J. Morgan Kousser and James M. McPherson, eds., *Region, Race and Reconstruction* (1982); Michael Perman, *The Road to Redemption* (1984); George C. Rable, *But There Was No Peace* (1984); James Roark, *Masters Without Slaves* (1977); Mark W. Summers, *Railroads, Reconstruction, and the Gospel of Prosperity* (1984); Allen Trelease, *White Terror* (1967); Ted Tunnell, *Crucible of Reconstruction* (1984); Michael Wayne, *The Reshaping of Plantation Society* (1983).

Women, Family, and Social History

Virginia I. Burr, ed., *The Secret Eye* (1990); Ellen Carol Dubois, *Feminism and Suffrage* (1978); Elizabeth Jacoway, *Yankee Missionaries in the South* (1979); Jacqueline Jones, *Soldiers of Light and Love* (1980); Robert C. Kenzer, *Kinship and Neighborhood in a Southern Community* (1987); Mary P. Ryan, *Women in Public* (1990); Rebecca Scott, "The Battle over the Child," *Prologue* 10 (Summer 1978): 101–113.

The End of Reconstruction

Michael Les Benedict, "Southern Democrats in the Crisis of 1876–1877," *Journal of Southern History* 66 (November 1980): 489–524; William Gillette, *Retreat from Reconstruction, 1869–1879* (1980); John G. Sproat, *"The Best Men": Liberal Reformers in the Gilded Age* (1968); C. Vann Woodward, *Reunion and Reaction* (1951).

Reconstruction's Legacy for the South and the Nation

Edward L. Ayers, *The Promise of the New South* (1992); David W. Blight, *Race and Reunion: The Civil War in American Memory, 1863–1915* (2001); Norman L. Crockett, *The Black Towns* (1979); Steven Hahn, *The Roots of Southern Populism* (1983); Jay R. Mandle, *The Roots of Black Poverty* (1978); Nell Irvin Painter, *Exodusters* (1976); Howard Rabinowitz, *Race*

Relations in the Urban South, 1865–1890 (1978); Roger L. Ransom and Richard Sutch, *One Kind of Freedom* (1977); Jonathan M. Wiener, *Social Origins of the New South* (1978).

Chapter 17

Native Americans

Leonard A. Carlson, *Indians, Bureaucrats, and Land: The Dawes Act and the Decline of Indian Farming* (1981); David Courtwright, *Violent Land* (1996); Frederick E. Hoxie, *A Final Promise: The Campaign to Assimilate the Indians, 1880–1920* (1984); Janet A. McDonnell, *The Dispossession of the American Indian* (1991); Francis Paul Prucha, *The Great Father: The United States Government and the American Indians* (1984); Robert M. Utley, *The Indian Frontier of the American West, 1846–1890* (1984); Richard White, *The Roots of Dependency* (1983).

The Western Frontier

Ray A. Billington and Martin Ridge, *Westward Expansion*, 5th ed. (1982); Sara Deutsch, *No Separate Refuge: Culture, Class, and Gender on an Anglo-Hispanic Frontier in the American Southwest* (1987); James R. Grossman, ed., *The Frontier in American Culture* (1994); Julie Roy Jeffrey, *Frontier Women* (1979); Patricia Limerick, *The Legacy of Conquest: The Unbroken Past of the American West* (1987); Peggy Pascoe, *Relations of Rescue: The Search for Female Moral Authority in the American West* (1990); Robert J. Rosenbaum, *Mexican Resistance in the Southwest* (1981); Richard White, *"It's Your Misfortune and None of My Own": A New History of the American West* (1991).

Water and the Environment

Roderick Nash, *American Environmentalism*, 3d ed. (1990); Thurman Wilkins, *John Muir: Apostle of Nature* (1995); Donald Worster, *Rivers of Empire: Water, Aridity, and the Growth of the American West* (1985); Donald Worster, *An Unsettled Country: Changing Landscapes of the American West* (1994).

Railroads

Alfred D. Chandler, ed., *Railroads* (1965); Edward C. Kirkland, *Men, Cities, and Transportation* (1948); Alan Trachtenberg, *The Incorporation of America* (1982).

Ranching and Settlement of the Plains

William Cronon, *Nature's Metropolis: Chicago and the Great West* (1991); Gilbert C. Fite, *The Farmer's Frontier* (1963); Robert V. Hine, *Community on the American Frontier* (1980); Richard W. Slatta, *Cowboys of the Americas* (1990).

Chapter 18

General

Daniel J. Boorstin, *The Americans: The Democratic Experience* (1973); Stephen Diner, *A Very Different Age* (1998); Samuel P. Hays, *The Response to Industrialism* (1975); Thomas J. Schlereth, *Victorian America: Transformations in Everyday Life* (1991).

Technology and Invention

Gary Cross and Rich Szostak, *Technology and American Society* (1995); David Hounshell, *From the American System to Mass Production* (1984); Thomas Parke Hughes, *American Genesis: A Century of Technological Enthusiasm* (1989); John P. Kasson, *Civilizing the Machine: Technology and Republican Values in America* (1976); Leo Marx, *The Machine in the Garden: Technology and the Pastoral Ideal* (1964); Andre Millard, *Edison and the Business of Innovation* (1990).

Industrialism, Industrialists, and Corporate Growth

W. Eliot Brownlee, *Dynamics of Ascent: A History of the American Economy*, 2d ed. (1979); Vincent P. Carosso, *The Morgans* (1987); Alfred D. Chandler, *The Visible Hand: The Managerial Revolution in American Business* (1977); David F. Hawkes, *John D.: The Founding Father of the Rockefellers* (1980); Robert Higgs, *The Transformation of the American Economy, 1865–1914* (1971); Glen Porter, *The Rise of Big Business* (1973); Martin J. Sklar, *The Corporate Reconstruction of American Capitalism* (1988); Richard Tedlow, *The Rise of the American Business Corporation* (1991); Joseph Wall, *Alfred I. du Pont: The Man and His Family* (1990).

Work and Labor Organization

Alan Derickson, *Workers' Health, Workers' Democracy: The Western Miners' Struggle, 1891–1925* (1988); Sarah Eisenstein, *Give Us Bread, Give Us Roses: Working Women's Consciousness in the United States* (1983); Leon Fink, *Workingmen's Democracy: The Knights of Labor and American Politics* (1982); Philip S. Foner, *The Great Labor Uprising of 1877* (1977); Herbert G. Gutman, *Work, Culture and Society in Industrializing America* (1976); Alice Kessler-Harris, *Out to Work: A History of Wage Earning Women in the United States* (1982); Harold Livesay, *Samuel Gompers and Organized Labor in America* (1978); Ruth Milkman, ed., *Women, Work, and Protest* (1985); David Montgomery, *The Fall of the House of Labor: The Workplace, the State, and American Labor Activism, 1865–1925* (1987); Stephen H. Norwood, *Labor's Flaming Youth: Telephone Operators and Worker Militancy* (1990); Elizabeth Ann Payne, *Reform, Labor, and Feminism: Margaret Dreier Robins and the Women's Trade Union League* (1988).

Living Standards and New Conveniences

Susan Porter Benson, *Counter Cultures: Saleswomen, Managers, and Customers in American Department Stores, 1890–1940* (1986); T. J. Jackson Lears and Richard W. Fox, eds., *The Culture of Consumption* (1983); Harvey A. Levenstein, *Revolution at the Table: The Transformation of the American Diet* (1988); Daniel Pope, *The Making of Modern Advertising* (1983); Susan Strasser, *Satisfaction Guaranteed: The Making of the American Mass Market* (1989); Gwendolyn Wright, *Building the Dream: A Social History of Housing in America* (1983).

Attitudes Toward Industrialism

Louis Galambos and Barbara Barron Spence, *The Public Image of Big Business in America* (1975); Richard Hofstadter, *Social Darwinism in American Thought*, rev. ed. (1955); T. J. Jackson Lears, *No Place of Grace: Antimodernism and the Transformation of American Culture* (1981); John L. Thomas, *Alternative America: Henry George, Edward Bellamy, Henry Demarest Lloyd, and the Adversary Tradition* (1983).

Southern Industrialism

Edward Ayers, *The Promise of the New South* (1992); James C. Cobb, *Industrialization and Southern Society, 1877–1984* (1984); C. Vann Woodward, *Origins of the New South* (1951); Gavin Wright, *Old South, New South* (1986).

Chapter 19

Urban Growth

Howard P. Chudacoff and Judith E. Smith, *The Evolution of American Urban Society*, 5th ed. (1999); David Goldfield, *Cotton Fields and Skyscrapers: Southern City and Region* (1982); Kenneth T. Jackson, *The Crabgrass Frontier: The Suburbanization of the United States* (1985); Jon Teaford, *The Unheralded Triumph: City Government in America, 1870–1900* (1984).

Immigration, Ethnicity, and Religion

Aaron I. Abell, *American Catholicism and Social Action* (1960); John Bodnar, *The Transplanted* (1985); Sucheng Chan, ed., *Entry Denied: Exclusion and the Chinese Community in America, 1882–1943* (1990); Donna R. Gabaccia, *From the Other Side: Women, Gender, and Immigrant Life in the United States* (1994); John Higham, *Strangers in the Land: Patterns of American Nativism* (1955); Matthew Frye Jacobson, *Whiteness of a Different Color: European Immigrants and the Alchemy of Race* (1998); Matt S. Maier and Felciano Rivera, *The Chicanos* (1972); Henry F. May, *Protestant Churches and Industrial America* (1949); Werner Sollors, *Beyond Ethnicity* (1986); Ron

Takaki, *Iron Cages: Race and Culture in Nineteenth-Century America* (1979); Stephan Thernstrom, ed., *Harvard Encyclopedia of American Ethnic Groups* (1980).

Urban Services

Christine Boyer, *Dreaming the Rational City: The Myth of American City Planning* (1983); Lawrence A. Cremin, *American Education: The Metropolitan Experience* (1988); David R. Johnson, *American Law Enforcement* (1981); Martin V. Melosi, *Garbage in the Cities* (1981); Mark Rose, *Cities of Light and Heat* (1995); Stanley K. Schultz, *Constructing Urban Culture: American Cities and City Planning* (1989).

Family and Individual Life Cycles

George Chauncey, *Gay New York* (1995); Howard P. Chudacoff, *The Age of the Bachelor* (1999); Howard P. Chudacoff, *How Old Are You? Age in American Culture* (1989); Carl N. Degler, *At Odds: Women and the Family in America* (1980); Carole Haber, *Beyond Sixty-five: Dilemmas of Old Age in America's Past* (1983); E. Anthony Rotundo, *American Manhood* (1994).

Mass Entertainment and Leisure

Jessica H. Foy and Thomas J. Schlereth, eds., *American Home Life, 1880–1930* (1992); Donna R. Gabaccia, *We Are What We Eat: Ethnic Food and the Making of Americans* (1998); Katrina Hazzard-Gordon, *Lookin': The Rise of Social Dance Formulations in African-American Culture* (1990); John F. Kasson, *Amusing the Million: Coney Island at the Turn of the Century* (1978); David Nasaw, *Going Out: The Rise and Fall of Popular Amusements* (1993); Kathy Peiss, *Cheap Amusements: Working Women and Leisure in Turn-of-the-Century New York* (1986); Benjamin G. Rader, *American Sports*, 4th ed. (1999); Roy Rosenzweig, *Eight Hours for What We Will! Workers and Leisure in an Industrial City, 1870–1920* (1983); Robert Sklar, *Movie-Made America* (1976); Ronald A. Smith, *Sports and Freedom: The Rise of Big-Time College Athletics* (1988); Robert V. Snyder, *The Voice of the City: Vaudeville and Popular Culture in New York City, 1880–1920* (1990).

Mobility and Race Relations

James Borchert, *Alley Life in Washington* (1980); Jacqueline Jones, *Labor of Love, Labor of Sorrow: Black Women, Work and the Family from Slavery to the Present* (1985); David M. Katzman, *Before the Ghetto* (1973); Kenneth L. Gilbert Osofsky, *Harlem: The Making of a Ghetto* (1966); Howard N. Rabinowitz, *Race Relations in the Urban South* (1978); Allan H. Spear, *Black Chicago* (1967); Stephan Thernstrom, *The Other Bostonians: Poverty and Progress in the American Metropolis* (1973); Olivier Zunz, *The Changing Face of Inequality* (1982).

Boss Politics

Alexander B. Callow, Jr., ed., *The City Boss in America* (1976); Leo Hershkowitz, *Tweed's New York: Another Look* (1977); Terrence J. McDonald, *The Parameters of Urban Fiscal Policy* (1986); Zane L. Miller, *Boss Cox's Cincinnati* (1968).

Urban Reform

John D. Buenker, *Urban Liberalism and Progressive Reform* (1973); Allen F. Davis, *Spearheads for Reform* (1967); Rivka Shpak Lissack, *Pluralism and Progressives: Hull House and the New Immigrants, 1890–1919* (1989); Roy M. Lubove, *The Progressives and the Slums* (1962); Robyn Muncy, *Creating a Female Dominion in American Reform* (1991); Martin J. Schiesl, *The Politics of Efficiency* (1977); Kathryn Kish Sklar, *Florence Kelley and the Nation's Work* (1995).

Chapter 20

General

Charles W. Calhoun, ed., *The Gilded Age: Essays on the Origins of Modern America* (1995); Sean Denis Cashman, *America in the Gilded Age* (1984); Steven J. Diner, *A Very Different Age* (1998); H. Wayne Morgan, ed., *The Gilded Age* (1970).

Parties and Political Issues

John M. Dobson, *Politics in the Gilded Age* (1972); Ari A. Hoogenboom, *Outlawing the Spoils: The Civil Service Movement* (1961); Morton Keller, *Affairs of State* (1977); Paul Kleppner, *The Third Electoral System, 1853–1892* (1979); Michael E. McGerr, *The Decline of Popular Politics* (1986); A. M. Paul, *Conservative Crisis and the Rule of Law: Attitudes of Bar and Bench, 1887–1895* (1969).

The Presidency

Kenneth E. Davison, *The Presidency of Rutherford B. Hayes* (1972); Lewis L. Gould, *The Presidency of William McKinley* (1981); Homer E. Socolotsky and Allen B. Spetter, *The Presidency of Benjamin Harrison* (1987); Richard G. Welch, *The Presidency of Grover Cleveland* (1988).

Women's Rights and Disfranchisement of African Americans

Edward L. Ayers, *The Promise of the New South* (1992); Paula Baker, *The Moral Framework of Public Life* (1991); Beverly Beeton, *Women Vote in the West: The Suffrage Movement, 1869–1896* (1986); Glenda Elizabeth Gilmore, *Gender & Jim Crow* (1996); C. Vann Woodward, *The Strange Career of Jim Crow*, 3d rev. ed. (1974).

Protest and Socialism

William M. Dick, *Labor and Socialism in America* (1972); Nick Salvatore, *Eugene V. Debs: Citizen and Socialist* (1982); Carlos A. Schwantes, *Coxey's Army* (1985); David Shannon, *The Socialist Party of America* (1955).

Populism and the Election of 1896

Donna A. Barnes, *Farmers in Rebellion: The Rise and Fall of the Southern Farmers Alliance and People's Party in Texas* (1984); Paul W. Glad, *McKinley, Bryan, and the People* (1964); Lawrence Goodwyn, *Democratic Promise: The Populist Movement in America* (1976); Steven Hahn, *The Roots of Southern Populism* (1983); Robert C. McMath, Jr., *American Populism* (1993); Walter T. K. Nugent, *The Tolerant Populists* (1963); Jeffrey Ostler, *Prairie Populism* (1993); Allan Weinstein, *Prelude to Populism: Origins of the Silver Issue* (1970).

Chapter 21

General

Paul M. Boyer, *Urban Masses and Moral Order in America, 1820-1920* (1978); Walter M. Brasch, *Forerunners of Revolution: Muckrakers and the American Social Conscience* (1990); John M. Cooper, Jr., *The Pivotal Decades* (1990); Richard Hofstadter, *The Age of Reform* (1955); Gabriel Kolko, *The Triumph of Conservatism* (1963); Arthur Link and Richard L. McCormick, *Progressivism* (1983); Daniel T. Rodgers, *Atlantic Crossings: Social Politics in a Progressive Age* (1998); Robert Wiebe, *The Search for Order* (1968).

Regional Studies

William A. Link, *The Paradox of Southern Progressivism* (1992); Richard White, *"It's Your Misfortune and None of My Own": A History of the American West* (1991); C. Vann Woodward, *Origins of the New South* (1951).

Legislative Issues and Reform Groups

Ruth H. Crocker, *Social Work and Social Order* (1992); Robert M. Crunden, *Ministers of Reform: The Progressives' Achievement in American Civilization* (1982); Ruth Rosen, *The Lost Sisterhood: Prostitution in America, 1900–1918* (1982); W. J. Rorabaugh, *The Alcoholic Republic* (1979); Kathryn Kish Sklar, *Florence Kelley and the Nation's Work* (1995); Walter I. Trattner, *Crusade for the Children* (1970); James Harvey Young, *Pure Food* (1989). (For works that cover socialism, see the listings under "Protest and Socialism," Chapter 20.)

Education, Law, and the Social Sciences

Jerold S. Auerback, *Unequal Justice: Lawyers and Social Change in Modern America* (1976); Lawrence Cremin, *The Transformation of the School: Progressivism in American Education* (1961); Ellen Fitzpatrick, *Endless Crusade: Women Social Scientists and Progressive Reform* (1990); Thomas L. Haskell, *The Emergence of Professional Social Science* (1977); Helen Horowitz, *Alma Mater: Design and Experience in Women's Colleges* (1984); Lawrence Veysey, *The Emergence of the American University* (1970).

Women

Ellen Chesler, *Woman of Valor: The Life of Margaret Sanger* (1992); Nancy F. Cott, *The Grounding of American Feminism* (1987); Linda Gordon, *Woman's Body, Woman's Right: A Social History of Birth Control in America* (1976); Evelyn Higginbotham, *Righteous Discontent: The Women's Movement in the Black Baptist Church, 1880–1920* (1993); Rosalind Rosenberg, *Beyond Separate Spheres: Intellectual Roots of Modern Feminism* (1982); Sheila M. Rothman, *Woman's Proper Place* (1978).

African Americans

John Dittmer, *Black Georgia in the Progressive Era* (1977); George Frederickson, *The Black Image in the White Mind* (1971); Louis R. Harlan, *Booker T. Washington*, 2 vols. (1972 and 1983); David Levering Lewis, *W. E. B. Du Bois* (1993); August Meier, *Negro Thought in America, 1880–1915* (1963).

Roosevelt, Taft, and Wilson

Francis L. Broderick, *Progressivism at Risk: Electing a President in 1912* (1989); John M. Cooper, Jr., *The Warrior and the Priest: Woodrow Wilson and Theodore Roosevelt* (1983); August Hecksher, *Woodrow Wilson* (1991); Edmund Morris, *The Rise of Theodore Roosevelt* (1979).

Chapter 22

General

Robert L. Beisner, *From the Old Diplomacy to the New, 1865–1900*, 2d ed. (1986); Daniel R. Headrick, *The Invisible Weapon: Telecommunications and International Politics, 1851–1945* (1991); Ronald J. Jensen, *The Alaska Purchase and Russian-American Relations* (1975); Paul Kennedy, *The Rise and Fall of the Great Powers* (1987); Paul A. C. Koistinen, *Mobilizing for Modern War: The Political Economy of American Warfare, 1865–1919* (1997); Walter LaFeber, *The American Search for Opportunity, 1865–1913* (1993); Walter LaFeber, *The New Empire*, anniv. ed. (1998); Emily Rosenberg, *Spreading the*

American Dream (1982); William Appleman Williams, *The Tragedy of American Diplomacy*, new ed. (1988).

Imperial Promoters

Howard K. Beale, *Theodore Roosevelt and the Rise of America to World Power* (1956); H. W. Brands, *T.R.* (1997); John M. Cooper, Jr., *The Warrior and the Priest* (1983) (on Roosevelt and Wilson); Edward P. Crapol, *James G. Blaine* (1999); Lewis L. Gould, *The Presidency of William McKinley* (1981); William C. Widenor, *Henry Cabot Lodge and the Search for an American Foreign Policy* (1980).

Economic and Financial Expansion

Robert B. Davies, *Peacefully Working to Conquer the World: Singer Sewing Machines in Foreign Markets, 1854–1920* (1976); David Pletcher, *The Diplomacy of Trade and Investment* (1998); Emily Rosenberg, *Financial Missionaries to the World: The Politics and Culture of Dollar Diplomacy, 1900–1930* (1999); Mira Wilkins, *The Emergence of the Multinational Enterprise* (1970); William Appleman Williams, *The Roots of the Modern American Empire* (1969).

Ideology and Culture

Gail Bederman, *Manliness & Civilization* (1995); Alexander DeConde, *Ethnicity, Race, and American Foreign Policy* (1992); Thomas G. Dyer, *Theodore Roosevelt and the Idea of Race* (1980); Michael H. Hunt, *Ideology and U.S. Foreign Policy* (1987); Robert D. Johnson, ed., *On Cultural Ground* (1994); Amy Kaplan and Donald E. Pease, eds., *Cultures of United States Imperialism* (1993); Catherine A. Lutz and Jane L. Collins, *Reading National Geographic* (1993); Robert Rydell, *World of Fairs* (1993); Robert Rydell, *All the World's a Fair* (1985); David Spurr, *The Rhetoric of Empire* (1993).

Religious Missionaries

Wayne Flynt and Gerald W. Berkley, *Taking Christianity to China* (1997); John K. Fairbank, ed., *The Missionary Enterprise in China and America* (1974); Gael Graham, *Gender, Culture, and Christianity: American Protestant Mission Schools in China, 1880–1930* (1995); Patricia R. Hill, *The World Their Household* (1985); Jane Hunter, *The Gospel of Gentility: American Missionaries in Turn-of-the-Century China* (1984); Irwin T. Hyatt, Jr., *Our Ordered Lives Confess* (1976).

Navalism and the Navy

Benjamin F. Cooling, *Gray Steel and Blue Water Navy* (1979); Frederick C. Drake, *The Empire of the Seas: A Biography of Rear Admiral Robert W. Shufelt* (1984); Kenneth J. Hagan, *This People's Navy* (1991); Mark R. Shulman, *Navalism and the*

Emergence of American Sea Power (1995); Robert Seager II, *Alfred Thayer Mahan* (1977); Ronald Spector, *Admiral of the New Empire: The Life and Career of George Dewey* (1974).

The Spanish-American-Cuban-Filipino War

Graham A. Cosmas, *An Army for Empire* (1971); Kristin L. Hoganson, *Fighting for American Manhood* (1998); Gerald F. Linderman, *The Mirror of War* (1974); John Offner, *An Unwanted War* (1992); Louis A. Pérez, Jr., *The War of 1898* (1998); David F. Trask, *The War with Spain in 1898* (1981).

Anti-Imperialism and the Peace Movement

Robert L. Beisner, *Twelve Against Empire* (1968); Charles DeBenedetti, *Peace Reform in American History* (1980); C. Roland Marchand, *The American Peace Movement and Social Reform, 1898–1918* (1973); David S. Patterson, *Toward a Warless World* (1976).

Cuba, Mexico, Panama, and Latin America

Arturo M. Carrión, *Puerto Rico* (1983); Judith Ewell, *Venezuela and the United States* (1996); David Healy, *Drive to Hegemony: The United States in the Caribbean, 1898–1917* (1989); Walter LaFeber, *Inevitable Revolutions: The United States in Central America*, 2d rev. ed. (1993); Walter LaFeber, *The Panama Canal*, updated ed. (1990); Lester D. Langley, *The Banana Wars* (2002); Thomas M. Leonard, *United States-Latin American Relations, 1850–1903* (1999); John Major, *Prize Possession: The United States and the Panama Canal, 1903–1979* (1993); David McCullough, *The Path Between the Seas: The Creation of the Panama Canal, 1870–1914* (1977); Louis A. Pérez, Jr., *Cuba and the United States*, 2d ed. (1997); Louis A. Pérez, Jr., *Cuba Under the Platt Amendment, 1902–1934* (1986); Fredrick B. Pike, *The United States and Latin America* (1992); Brenda G. Plummer, *Haiti and the Great Powers, 1902–1915* (1988); Stephen J. Randall, *Colombia and the United States* (1992); Lars Schoultz, *Beneath the United States* (1998); Josefina Vázquez and Lorenzo Meyer, *The United States and Mexico* (1985).

Hawai'i, China, Japan, and the Pacific

Warren I. Cohen, *America's Response to China*, 3d ed. (1989); Michael H. Hunt, *The Making of a Special Relationship* (1983) (on China); Walter LaFeber, *The Clash: A History of U.S. Japanese Relations* (1997); Brian M. Linn, *Guardians of Empire* (1997); Charles J. McClain, *In Search of Equality: The Chinese Struggle Against Discrimination in Nineteenth-Century America* (1994); Thomas J. McCormick, *China Market* (1967); Craig Storti, *Incident at Bitter Creek: The Story of the Rock Springs Chinese Massacre* (1991); Merze Tate, *Hawaii: Reciprocity or Annexation* (1968).

The Philippines and the Insurrection

John M. Gates, *Schoolbooks and Krags* (1973) (on the U.S. Army); Stanley Karnow, *In Our Image* (1989); Brian M. Linn, *The Philippine War* (2000); Glenn A. May, *Battle for Batangas* (1991); Stuart C. Miller, *"Benevolent Assimilation"* (1982); Richard E. Welch, *Response to Imperialism: American Resistance to the Philippine War* (1972).

Great Britain and Canada

Robert Bothwell, *Canada and the United States* (1992); Kenneth Bourne, *Britain and the Balance of Power in North America, 1815–1908* (1967); David Dimbleby and David Reynolds, *An Ocean Apart* (1988); Kurkpatrick Dorsey, *The Dawn of Conservation Diplomacy* (1999); Bradford Perkins, *The Great Rapprochement* (1968); William N. Tilchin, *Theodore Roosevelt and the British Empire* (1997).

Chapter 23

General

John W. Chambers, *The Tyranny of Change* (1992); Paul Fussell, *The Great War and Modern Memory* (1975); Ellis W. Hawley, *The Great War and the Search for a Modern Order*, 2d ed. (1999); Clayton D. James and Anne S. Wells, *America and the Great War* (1998); Daniel T. Rodgers, *Atlantic Crossings: Social Politics in a Progressive Age* (1998); John A. Thompson, *Reformers and War* (1987).

Wilson, Wilsonianism, and World War I

Lloyd E. Ambrosius, *Wilsonian Statecraft* (1991); Frederick S. Calhoun, *Power and Principle* (1986); Kendrick A. Clements, *The Presidency of Woodrow Wilson* (1992); John W. Coogan, *The End of Neutrality* (1981); Robert H. Ferrell, *Woodrow Wilson and World War I* (1985); Manfred Jonas, *The United States and Germany* (1984); Thomas J. Knock, *To End All Wars* (1992); N. Gordon Levin, Jr., *Woodrow Wilson and World Politics* (1968); Arthur S. Link, *Woodrow Wilson: Revolution, War and Peace* (1979); Arthur S. Link, *Wilson* (1947–1965); Bert E. Park, *Ailing, Aging, Addicted* (1993) (on Wilson's health); Frank Ninkovich, *Wilsonian Century* (1999); J. W. Schulte Nordholt, *Woodrow Wilson* (1991); Tony Smith, *America's Mission: The United States and the Worldwide Struggle for Democracy in the Twentieth Century* (1994); Edwin A. Weinstein, *Woodrow Wilson: A Medical and Psychological Biography* (1981).

Fighting and Remembering the Great War in Europe

Allan M. Brandt, *No Magic Bullet: A Social History of Venereal Disease in the United States Since 1880* (1985); John W. Chambers, *To Raise an Army* (1987); J. Garry Clifford, *The Citizen Soldiers* (1972); Edward M. Coffman, *The War to End All Wars* (1968); James J. Cooke, *The U.S. Air Service in the Great War: 1917–1919* (1996); Byron Farwell, *Over There* (1999); Martin Gilbert, *The First World War* (1994); Paul G. Halpern, *A Naval History of World War I* (1994); Jennifer D. Kenne, *Doughboys, the Great War, and the Remaking of America* (2001); G. Kurt Piehler, *Remembering War the American Way* (1995); Donald Smythe, *Pershing* (1986); Russell F. Weigley, *The American Way of War* (1973).

The Home Front

William J. Breen, *Labor Market Politics and the Great War* (1997); Thomas A. Britten, *American Indians in World War I* (1997); Craig W. Campbell, *Reel America and World War I* (1985); Valerie Jean Conner, *The National War Labor Board* (1983); Alfred W. Crosby, *America's Forgotten Pandemic: The Influenza of 1918* (1989); Robert D. Cuff, *The War Industries Board* (1973); Leslie M. DeBauche, *Reel Patriotism* (1997); David M. Kennedy, *Over Here* (1980); Paul A. C. Koistinen, *Mobilizing for Modern War* (1997); Joseph A. McCartin, *Labor's Great War* (1997); Ronald Schaffer, *America in the Great War: The Rise of the War Welfare State* (1991); Stephen L. Vaughn, *Holding Fast the Inner Lines: Democracy, Nationalism, and the Committee on Public Information* (1979); Neil A. Wynn, *From Progressivism to Prosperity* (1986).

Women and the War

Frances H. Early, *A World Without War: How U.S. Feminists and Pacifists Resisted World War I* (1997); Lettie Gavin, *American Women in World War I* (1997); Maurine W. Greenwald, *Women, War, and Work* (1980); Kathleen Kennedy, *Disloyal Mothers and Scurrilous Citizens: Women and Subversion During World War I* (1999); Erika A. Kuhlman, *Petticoats and White Feathers* (1997); Dorothy Schneider and Carl J. Schneider, *Into the Breach: American Women Overseas in World War I* (1991); Barbara J. Steinson, *American Women's Activism in World War I* (1982).

African Americans and Migration

Arthur E. Barbeau and Florette Henri, *The Unknown Soldiers* (1974); Marvin E. Fletcher, *The Black Soldier and Officer in the United States Army, 1891–1917* (1974); James B. Grossman, *Land of Hope: Chicago, Black Southerners, and the Great Migration* (1989); Robert V. Haynes, *A Night of Violence: The Houston Riot of 1917* (1976); Carole Marks, *Farewell—We're Good and Gone: The Great Black Migration* (1989); Elliot M. Rudwick, *Race Riot at East St. Louis, July 2, 1917* (1964); Joe

William Trotter, Jr., ed., *The Great Migration in Historical Perspective* (1991); William M. Tuttle, Jr., *Race Riot: Chicago in the Red Summer of 1919*, rev. ed. (1996).

Dissenters, Wartime Civil Liberties, and the Red Scare

Charles Chatfield, *The American Peace Movement* (1992); Stanley Coben, *A. Mitchell Palmer* (1963); Charles DeBenedetti, *Origins of the Modern Peace Movement* (1978); Sondra Herman, *Eleven Against War* (1969); C. Roland Marchand, *The American Peace Movement and Social Reform* (1973); Elizabeth McKillen, *Chicago Labor and the Quest for a Democratic Diplomacy* (1995); Paul L. Murphy, *World War I and the Origin of Civil Liberties* (1979); Robert K. Murray, *Red Scare* (1955); William Pencak, *For God and Country: The American Legion, 1919–1941* (1989); H. C. Peterson and Gilbert C. Fite, *Opponents of War, 1917–1918* (1968); Richard Polenberg, *Fighting Faiths: The Abrams Case, the Supreme Court, and Free Speech* (1987); William Preston, *Aliens and Dissenters* (1995).

The United States and the Bolshevik Revolution

Peter G. Filene, *Americans and the Soviet Experiment, 1917–1933* (1967); David S. Foglesong, *America's Secret War Against Bolshevism* (1995); Christopher Lasch, *The American Liberals and the Russian Revolution* (1962); David McFadden, *Alternative Paths* (1993); Norman E. Saul, *War and Revolution* (2001); Betty M. Unterberger, *The United States, Revolutionary Russia, and the Rise of Czechoslovakia* (1989).

Paris Peace Conference, Treaty of Versailles, and League Fight

Manfred F. Boemeke et al., eds., *The Treaty of Versailles* (1998); Lloyd Ambrosius, *Woodrow Wilson and the American Diplomatic Tradition* (1987); John M. Cooper, Jr., *Breaking the Heart of the World* (2001); Warren F. Kuehl, *Seeking World Order* (1969); Ralph A. Stone, *The Irreconcilables* (1970); Arthur Walworth, *Wilson and the Peacemakers* (1986); William C. Widenor, *Henry Cabot Lodge and the Search for an American Foreign Policy* (1980).

Chapter 24

Overviews of the 1920s

Paul A. Carter, *Another Part of the Twenties* (1977); Lynn Dumenil, *Modern Temper* (1995); David J. Goldberg, *Discontented America: The United States in the 1920s* (1999); William E. Leuchtenburg, *The Perils of Prosperity* (1958); Geoffrey Perrett, *America in the Twenties* (1982).

Business and the Economy

William W. Barber, *Herbert Hoover, the Economists, and American Economic Policy, 1921–1933* (1986); David Montgomery, *The Fall of the House of Labor* (1987); Allan Nevins, *Ford*, 2 vols. (1954–1957); Emily Rosenberg, *Spreading the American Dream* (1982).

Politics and Law

Christine Bolt, *American Indian Policy and American Reform* (1987); Allan J. Lichtman, *Prejudice and the Old Politics: The Presidential Election of 1928* (1979); Alpheus Mason, *The Supreme Court from Taft to Warren* (1958); Robert K. Murray, *The Politics of Normalcy* (1973); George Tindall, *The Emergence of the New South* (1967); Joan Hoff Wilson, *Herbert Hoover: The Forgotten Progressive* (1975).

African Americans, Asians, and Hispanics

Roger Daniels, *Asian America* (1988); James R. Grossman, *Land of Hope* (1989); Gilbert Osofsky, *Harlem: The Making of a Ghetto* (1965); George Sanchez, *Becoming Mexican American* (1993); Judith Stein, *The World of Marcus Garvey* (1986); Ronald Takaki, *Strangers from a Different Shore* (1989).

Women, Family, and Lifestyles

W. Andrew Achenbaum, *Shades of Gray: Old Age, American Values, and Federal Policies Since 1920* (1983); Beth Bailey, *From Front Porch to Back Seat: Courtship in Twentieth Century America* (1988); Dorothy M. Brown, *Setting a Course: American Women in the 1920s* (1987); George Chauncey, *Gay New York* (1995); Howard P. Chudacoff, *How Old Are You? Age in American Culture* (1989); Nancy F. Cott, *The Grounding of Modern Feminism* (1987); Elizabeth Lillian Faderman, *Odd Girls and Twilight Lovers* (1991); Lois Scharf, *To Work and to Wed* (1980); Susan Strasser, *Never Done: A History of American Housework* (1982); Winifred D. Wandersee, *Women's Work and Family Values, 1920–1940* (1981).

Lines of Defense

Paul Avrich, *Sacco and Vanzetti* (1991); Norman H. Clark, *Deliver Us From Evil: An Interpretation of American Prohibition* (1976); John Higham, *Strangers in the Land: Patterns of American Nativism* (1955); Edward J. Larson, *Summer for the Gods* (1997); Nancy Maclean, *Behind the Mask of Chivalry: The Making of the Second Ku Klux Klan* (1994); George M. Marsden, *Fundamentalism and American Culture* (1980).

Mass Culture

Stanley Coben, *Rebellion Against Victorianism* (1991); Susan J. Douglas, *Inventing American Broadcasting* (1987); Paula Fass, *The Damned and the Beautiful: American Youth in the 1920s* (1977); James J. Flink, *The Car Culture* (1975); Richard Wightman Fox and T. Jackson Lears, eds., *The Culture of Consumption* (1983); William R. Leach, *Land of Desire* (1993); Harvey J. Levenstein, *Revolution at the Table: The Transformation of the American Diet* (1988); Roland Marchand, *Advertising the American Dream* (1985); Virginia Scharff, *Taking the Wheel: Women and the Coming of the Motor Age* (1991); Ronald A. Smith, *Sports and Freedom: The Rise of Big-Time College Athletics* (1988).

Literature and Thought

Mary Campbell, *Harlem Renaissance: Art of Black America* (1987); Robert Crunden, *From Self to Society: Transition in American Thought, 1919–1941* (1972); Cary D. Mintz, *Black Culture and the Harlem Renaissance* (1988); Kenneth M. Wheller and Virginia L. Lussier, eds., *Women and the Arts and the 1920s in Paris and New York* (1982).

Boom and Bust: The Crash

Peter Fearon, *War, Prosperity, and Depression* (1987); John Kenneth Galbraith, *The Great Crash: 1929* (1989).

Chapter 25

Hoover and the Worsening Depression

Michael A. Bernstein, *The Great Depression: Delayed Recovery and Economic Change in America, 1929–1939* (1988); Martin L. Fausold, *The Presidency of Herbert C. Hoover* (1985); John A. Garraty, *The Great Depression* (1986); James S. Olson, *Herbert Hoover and the Reconstruction Finance Corporation, 1931–1933* (1977); Jordan A. Schwarz, *Interregnum of Despair* (1970).

The New Deal

Anthony J. Badger, *The New Deal: The Depression Years, 1933–1940* (1989); Alan Brinkley, *Liberalism and Its Discontents* (1998); Alan Brinkley, *The End of Reform: New Deal Liberalism in Recession and War* (1995); Steve Fraser and Gary Gerstle, eds., *The Rise and Fall of the New Deal Order, 1930–1980* (1989); David M. Kennedy, *Freedom from Fear: The American People in Depression and War, 1929–1945* (1999); William E. Leuchtenburg, *Franklin D. Roosevelt and the New Deal* (1963); Albert U. Romasco, *The Politics of Recovery: Roosevelt's New Deal* (1983).

Franklin and Eleanor Roosevelt

James MacGregor Burns, *Roosevelt: The Lion and the Fox* (1956); Blanche Wiesen Cook, *Eleanor Roosevelt: Volume One, 1884–1933* (1992), and *Volume Two, 1933–1938* (1999); Frank Freidel, *Franklin D. Roosevelt: A Rendezvous with Destiny*

(1990); Joseph P. Lash, *Eleanor and Franklin* (1971); Arthur M. Schlesinger, Jr., *The Age of Roosevelt*, 3 vols. (1957–1960).

Voices from the Depression

James Agee, *Let Us Now Praise Famous Men* (1941); Federal Writers' Project, *These Are Our Lives* (1939); Robert S. McElvaine, ed., *Down and Out in the Great Depression* (1983); Studs Terkel, *Hard Times: An Oral History of the Great Depression* (1970).

Alternatives to the New Deal

Alan Brinkley, *Voices of Protest: Huey Long, Father Coughlin, and the Great Depression* (1982); William Ivy Hair, *The Kingfish and His Realm: The Life and Times of Huey P. Long* (1992); Robin D. G. Kelley, *Hammer and Hoe: Alabama Communists During the Great Depression* (1991); Fraser M. Ottanelli, *The Communist Party of the United States from the Depression to World War II* (1991); Leo Ribuffo, *The Old Christian Right: The Protestant Far Right from the Great Depression to the Cold War* (1983); Donald Warren, *Radio Priest: Charles Coughlin, the Father of Hate Radio* (1996).

Workers and Organized Labor

Irving Bernstein, *Turbulent Years: A History of the American Worker, 1933–1941* (1969); Lizabeth Cohen, *Making a New Deal: Industrial Workers in Chicago, 1919–1939* (1991); Melvin Dubofsky and Warren Van Tine, *John L. Lewis* (1977); Gary Gerstle, *Working-Class Americanism: The Politics of Labor in a Textile City, 1914–1960* (1989); Nelson Lichtenstein, *The Most Dangerous Man in Detroit: Walter Reuther and the Fate of American Labor* (1995); Robert H. Zieger, *The CIO, 1935–1955* (1995).

People of Color

Dan T. Carter, *Scottsboro*, rev. ed. (1979); James Goodman, *Stories of Scottsboro* (1994); Camille Guerin-Gonzales, *Mexican Workers and American Dreams: Immigration, Repatriation, and California Farm Labor, 1900–1939* (1994); Laurence C. Kelly, *The Assault on Assimilation: John Collier and the Origins of Indian Policy Reform* (1983); George Lipsitz, *The Possessive Investment in Whiteness: How White People Profit from Identity Politics* (1998); Kenneth R. Philp, *Termination Revisited: American Indians on the Trail to Self-Determination, 1933-1953* (1999); George J. Sanchez, *Becoming Mexican American: Ethnicity, Culture and Identity in Chicano Los Angeles, 1900–1945* (1993); Harvard Sitkoff, *A New Deal for Blacks* (1978); Patricia Sullivan, *Days of Hope: Race and Democracy in the New Deal Era* (1996); Mark V. Tushnet, *The NAACP's Legal Strategy Against Segregated Education, 1925–1950* (1987); Nancy J. Weiss, *Farewell to the Party of Lincoln: Black Politics in the Age of FDR* (1983).

Women

Glen H. Elder, Jr., *Children of the Great Depression* (1974); Linda Gordon, *Pitied but Not Entitled: Single Mothers and the History of Welfare, 1890–1935* (1994); Lois Scharf, *To Work and to Wed: Female Employment, Feminism, and the Great Depression* (1980); Winifred Wandersee, *Women's Work and Family Values, 1920–1940* (1981); Susan Ware, *Holding Their Own: American Women in the 1930s* (1982); Susan Ware, *Beyond Suffrage: Women in the New Deal* (1981).

Cultural and Intellectual History

Michael Denning, *The Cultural Front: The Laboring of American Culture in the Twentieth Century* (1997); Barbara Melosh, *Engendering Culture: Manhood and Womanhood in New Deal Public Art and Theater* (1991); Richard H. Pells, *Radical Visions and American Dreams: Culture and Social Thought in the Depression Years* (1973).

Chapter 26

General

Warren I. Cohen, *Empire Without Tears* (1987); Justus D. Doenecke and John E. Wilz, *From Isolation to War*, 2d ed. (1991); Elting E. Morison, *Turmoil and Tradition* (1964) (on Stimson); Brenda G. Plummer, *Rising Wind: Black Americans and U.S. Foreign Affairs, 1935–1960* (1996); Emily S. Rosenberg, *Spreading the American Dream* (1982); Joan Hoff Wilson, *Herbert Hoover* (1975).

Arms Control and the Military

Thomas H. Buckley, *The United States and the Washington Conference, 1921–1922* (1970); Emily O. Goldman, *Sunken Treaties* (1994); Paul A. C. Koistinen, *Planning War, Pursuing Peace: The Political Economy of American Warfare, 1920–1939* (1998); Brian M. Linn, *Guardians of Empire: The U.S. Army and the Pacific, 1902–1940* (1997); Michael S. Sherry, *The Rise of American Airpower* (1987).

Peace Groups and Leaders

Harriet H. Alonso, *The Women's Peace Union and the Outlawry of War* (1989); Charles Chatfield, *For Peace and Justice* (1971); Charles DeBenedetti, *The Peace Reform in American History* (1980); Carrie A. Foster, *The Women and the Warriors* (1995); Robert D. Johnson, *The Peace Progressives and American Foreign Relations* (1995); Warren F. Kuehl and Lynne K. Dunn, *Keeping the Covenant* (1997); Linda A. Schott, *Reconstructing Women's Thoughts: The Women's International League for Peace and Freedom Before World War II* (1997); Lawrence Wittner, *Rebels Against War* (1984).

Economic and Financial Relations

Michael Butler, *Cautious Visionary: Cordell Hull and Trade Reform, 1933-1937* (1998); Michael J. Hogan, *Informal Entente: The Private Structure of Cooperation in Anglo-American Economic Diplomacy* (1977); Charles Kindleberger, *The World in Depression* (1973); Stephen J. Randall, *United States Foreign Oil Policy, 1919–1948* (1986); Emily S. Rosenberg, *Financial Missionaries: The Politics and Culture of Dollar Diplomacy, 1900–1930* (1999); Mira Wilkins, *The Maturing of Multinational Enterprise* (1974); Joan Hoff Wilson, *American Business and Foreign Policy, 1920–1933* (1971).

Cultural Expansion and Philanthropy

Frank Costigliola, *Awkward Dominion* (1984); Marcos Cueto, ed., *Missionaries of Science: The Rockefeller Foundation and Latin America* (1994); Mary Nolan, *Visions of Modernity: American Business and the Modernization of Germany* (1994); Thomas J. Saunders, *Hollywood in Berlin* (1994).

Latin America and the Good Neighbor Policy

G. Pope Atkins and Larman C. Wilson, *The Dominican Republic and the United States* (1998); Bruce J. Calder, *The Impact of Intervention: The Dominican Republic During the U.S. Occupation of 1916–1924* (1984); Arturo Morales Carrión, *Puerto Rico* (1983); Paul J. Dosal, *Doing Business with the Dictators* (1993); Paul W. Drake, *The Money Doctors in the Andes* (1989); Linda B. Hall, *Oil, Banks, and Politics: The United States and Postrevolutionary Mexico, 1917–1924* (1995); Walter LaFeber, *Inevitable Revolutions: The United States in Central America*, 2d and extended ed. (1993); Lester D. Langley, *The United States and the Caribbean, 1900–1970* (1980); Abraham F. Lowenthal, ed., *Exporting Democracy* (1991); John Major, *Prize Possession: The United States and the Panama Canal, 1903–1979* (1993); Louis A. Pérez, *Cuba and the United States*, 2d ed. (1997); Louis A. Pérez, Jr., *On Becoming Cuban* (1999); Fredrick B. Pike, *FDR's Good Neighbor Policy* (1995); Brenda G. Plummer, *Haiti and the United States* (1992); W. Dirk Raat, *Mexico and the United States* (1997); Mary A. Renta, *Taking Haiti* (2001).

Isolationists and Isolationism

Wayne S. Cole, *Roosevelt and the Isolationists, 1932–1945* (1983); Manfred Jonas, *Isolationism in America, 1935–1941* (1966); Thomas C. Kennedy, *Charles A. Beard and American Foreign Policy* (1975); Richard C. Lower, *A Bloc of One: The Political Career of Hiram W. Johnson* (1993); Richard Lowitt, *George W. Norris* (1963–1978); John Wiltz, *In Search of Peace: The Senate Munitions Inquiry* (1963).

Europe, Roosevelt's Policies, and the Coming of World War II

J. Garry Clifford and Samuel R. Spencer, Jr., *The First Peacetime Draft* (1986); David H. Culbert, *News for Everyman* (1976) (on radio); Robert Dallek, *Franklin D. Roosevelt and American Foreign Policy* (1995); Robert A. Divine, *Roosevelt and World War II* (1969); Justus D. Doenecke, *Storm on the Horizon* (2001); Manfred Jonas, *The United States and Germany* (1984); Warren F. Kimball, *The Juggler* (1991); Warren F. Kimball, *The Most Unsordid Act: Lend-Lease, 1939-1941* (1969); Melvyn P. Leffler, *The Elusive Quest: America's Pursuit of European Stability and French Security, 1919–1933* (1979); Thomas R. Maddux, *Years of Estrangement: American Relations with the Soviet Union, 1933–1941* (1980); David Reynolds, *The Creation of the Anglo-American Alliance* (1982); David Reynolds, *From Munich to Pearl Harbor* (2001); David F. Schmitz, *The United States and Fascist Italy* (1988); James C. Schneider, *Should America Go to War?* (1989); Richard Steele, *Propaganda in an Open Society* (1985); Donald C. Watt, *How War Came* (1989); Theodore A. Wilson, *The First Summit* (1991).

China, Japan, and the Coming of War in Asia

Dorothy Borg and Shumpei Okomoto, eds., *Pearl Harbor as History* (1973); R. J. C. Butow, *Tojo and the Coming of War* (1961); Warren I. Cohen, *America's Response to China*, 3d ed. (1990); Hilary Conroy and Harry Wray, eds., *Pearl Harbor Reexamined* (1990); Waldo H. Heinrichs, Jr., *Threshold of War* (1988); Akira Iriye, *The Origins of the Second World War in Asia and the Pacific* (1987); Akira Iriye, *Across the Pacific* (1967); Akira Iriye, *After Imperialism* (1965); T. Christopher Jespersen, *American Images of China* (1996); Walter LaFeber, *The Clash: A History of U.S.-Japan Relations* (1997); James Morley, ed., *The Final Confrontation* (1994); Jonathan Utley, *Going to War with Japan* (1985).

Attack on Pearl Harbor

David Kahn, *The Codebreakers* (1967); Robert W. Love, Jr., ed., *Pearl Harbor Revisited* (1995); Martin V. Melosi, *The Shadow of Pearl Harbor* (1977); Gordon W. Prange, *Pearl Harbor* (1986); Gordon W. Prange, *At Dawn We Slept* (1981); John Toland, *Infamy* (1982); Roberta Wohlstetter, *Pearl Harbor* (1962).

Chapter 27

The Second World War

John W. Dower, *War Without Mercy: Race and Power in the Pacific War* (1986); John Keegan, *The Second World War* (1989); David M. Kennedy, *Freedom from Fear: The American People in Depression and War, 1929–1945* (1999); Gordon W.

Prange et al., *At Dawn We Slept: The Untold Story of Pearl Harbor* (1981); Ronald H. Spector, *Eagle Against the Sun: The American War with Japan* (1984); Gerhard L. Weinberg, *A World at Arms: A Global History of World War II* (1994).

Fighting the War: Americans in Combat

Stephen E. Ambrose, *The Victors* (1998); Stephen E. Ambrose, *Citizen Soldiers* (1997); Stephen E. Ambrose, *D-Day, June 6, 1944* (1994); Allan Berube, *Coming Out Under Fire: The History of Gay Men and Women in World War II* (1990); Paul Fussell, *Wartime* (1989); Gerald F. Linderman, *The World Within the War: America's Combat Experience in World War II* (1997); David Reynolds, *Rich Relations: The American Occupation of Britain, 1942–1945* (1995).

Wartime Diplomacy

Russell Buhite, *Decisions at Yalta* (1986); Robert Dallek, *Franklin D. Roosevelt and American Foreign Policy, 1932–1945* (1979); Henry L. Feingold, *Bearing Witness: How America and Its Jews Responded to the Holocaust* (1995); George C. Herring, *Aid to Russia, 1941–1946* (1973); Akira Iriye, *Power and Culture: The Japanese-American War, 1941–1945* (1981); Warren Kimball, *Forged in War: Roosevelt, Churchill, and the Second World War* (1997); Walter LaFeber, *The Clash: A History of U.S.-Japan Relations* (1997); Keith Sainsbury, *Churchill and Roosevelt at War* (1994); Mark Stoler, *The Politics of the Second Front* (1977); David S. Wyman, *The Abandonment of the Jews* (1984).

Mobilizing for War

Amy Bentley, *Eating for Victory: Food Rationing and the Politics of Domesticity* (1998); George Q. Flynn, *The Draft, 1940–1973* (1993); Clayton R. Koppes and Gregory D. Black, *Hollywood Goes to War* (1987); Nelson Lichtenstein, *Labor's War at Home: The CIO in World War II* (1983); George H. Roeder, Jr., *The Censored War: American Visual Experience During World War II* (1993); Lawrence R. Samuel, *Pledging Allegiance: American Identity and the Bond Drive of World War II* (1997); Bartholomew H. Sparrow, *From the Outside In: World War II and the American State* (1996); Allen M. Winkler, *The Politics of Propaganda: The Office of War Information, 1942–1945* (1978).

The Home Front

John Morton Blum, *V Was for Victory: Politics and American Culture During World War II* (1976); John D'Emilio, *Sexual Politics, Sexual Communities: The Making of a Homosexual Minority in the United States, 1940–1970* (1983); William L. O'Neill, *A Democracy at War: America's Fight at Home and Abroad in World War II* (1993); Studs Terkel, ed., *"The Good War": An Oral History of World War Two* (1984); William M.

Tuttle, Jr., *"Daddy's Gone to War": The Second World War in the Lives of America's Children* (1993).

The Internment of Japanese-Americans and Enemy Aliens

Roger Daniels, *Prisoners Without Trial* (1993); Stephen Fox, *The Unknown Internment: An Oral History of the Relocation of Italian Americans During World War II* (1990); Peter Irons, *Justice at War* (1983); Arnold Krammer, *Undue Process: The Untold Story of America's German Alien Internees* (1997).

African Americans and Wartime Violence

Dominic J. Capeci, Jr., *The Harlem Riot of 1943* (1977); Dominic J. Capeci, Jr., and Martha Wilkerson, *Layered Violence: The Detroit Rioters of 1943* (1991); Mauricio Mazon, *The Zoot-Suit Riots* (1984); Neil A. Wynn, *The Afro-American and the Second World War*, rev. ed. (1993).

Women at War

Karen T. Anderson, *Wartime Women* (1981); D'Ann Campbell, *Women at War with America* (1984); Susan M. Hartmann, *The Home Front and Beyond* (1982); Judy Barrett Litoff and David C. Smith, eds., *We're in This War, Too: World War II Letters from American Women in Uniform* (1994); Leisa D. Meyer, *Creating GI Jane: Sexuality and Power in the Women's Army Corps During World War II* (1996); Ruth Milkman, *Gender at Work: The Dynamics of Job Discrimination by Sex During World War II* (1987); Leila J. Rupp, *Mobilizing Women for War: German and American Propaganda, 1939–1945* (1978).

The Atomic Bomb and Japan's Surrender

Gar Alperovitz, *The Decision to Use the Atomic Bomb and the Architecture of an American Myth*, 2d ed. (1995); Michael Hogan, ed., *Hiroshima in History and Memory* (1995); Robert Jay Lifton and Greg Mitchell, *Hiroshima in America: Fifty Years of Denial* (1995); Martin J. Sherwin, *A World Destroyed: The Atomic Bomb and the Grand Alliance* (1975); Ronald Takaki, *Hiroshima: Why America Dropped the Atomic Bomb* (1995); J. Samuel Walker, *Prompt and Utter Destruction: Truman and the Use of the Atomic Bombs Against Japan* (1997).

Chapter 28

An Age of Consensus

John Patrick Diggins, *The Proud Decades: America in War and Peace, 1941–1960* (1988); David Halberstam, *The Fifties* (1993); Marty Jezer, *The Dark Ages: Life in the United States, 1945–1960* (1982); William L. O'Neill, *American High: The Years of Confidence, 1945–1960* (1986); James T. Patterson, *Grand Expectations: The United States, 1945–1974* (1996).

Cold War Culture

Paul Boyer, *By the Bomb's Early Light: American Thought and Culture at the Dawn of the Atomic Age* (1985); Tom Engelhardt, *The End of Victory Culture* (1995); William S. Graebner, *The Age of Doubt: American Thought and Culture in the 1940s* (1991); Lary May, ed., *Recasting America: Culture and Politics in the Age of Cold War* (1989); Richard H. Pells, *The Liberal Mind in a Conservative Age* (1985); Stephen J. Whitfield, *The Culture of the Cold War*, rev. ed. (1996).

The Truman Presidency

Alonzo L. Hamby, *Man of the People: The Life of Harry S. Truman* (1995); Michael J. Hogan, *A Cross of Iron: Harry S. Truman and the Origins of the National Security State* (1998); David McCullough, *Truman* (1992); Paul G. Pierpaoli, Jr., *Truman and Korea: The Political Culture of the Cold War* (1999).

Eisenhower and the Politics of the 1950s

Stephen E. Ambrose, *Eisenhower: The President* (1984); Fred I. Greenstein, *The Hidden-Hand Presidency* (1982); Chester J. Pach, Jr., and Elmo Richardson, *The Presidency of Dwight D. Eisenhower*, rev. ed. (1991); Geoffrey Perret, *Eisenhower* (1999).

McCarthyism

Richard M. Fried, *Nightmare in Red* (1990); Robert Griffith, *The Politics of Fear: Joseph R. McCarthy and the Senate*, rev. ed. (1987); John Earl Haynes and Harvey Klehr, *Venona: Decoding Soviet Espionage in America* (1999); David M. Oshinsky, *A Conspiracy So Immense: The World of Joe McCarthy* (1983); Ellen W. Schrecker, *Many Are the Crimes: McCarthyism in America* (1998); Ellen W. Schrecker, *No Ivory Tower: McCarthyism in the Universities* (1986).

Race Relations and the Civil Rights Movement

Taylor Branch, *Parting the Waters: America in the King Years, 1954–1963* (1988); William H. Chafe, *Civilities and Civil Rights: Greensboro, North Carolina, and the Black Struggle for Freedom* (1980); David J. Garrow, *Bearing the Cross: Martin Luther King, Jr., and the Southern Christian Leadership Conference* (1986); Richard Kluger, *Simple Justice: The History of Brown v. Board of Education and Black America's Struggle for Equality* (1975); Thomas J. Sugrue, *The Origins of the Urban Crisis: Race and Inequality in Postwar Detroit* (1996); Jules Tygiel, *Baseball's Great Experiment: Jackie Robinson and His Legacy*, rev. ed. (1997); Juan Williams, *Thurgood Marshall: American Revolutionary* (1998).

The Baby Boom, Youth Culture, and Cold War Families

James Gilbert, *A Cycle of Outrage: America's Reaction to the Juvenile Delinquent* (1986); Landon Y. Jones, *Great Expectations: America and the Baby Boom Generation* (1980); Elaine Tyler May, *Homeward Bound: American Families in the Cold War Era* (1988); Grace Palladino, *Teenagers* (1996).

Suburbia and the Spread of Education

Dolores Hayden, *Redesigning the American Dream* (1984); Kenneth T. Jackson, *Crabgrass Frontier: The Suburbanization of the United States* (1985); Diane Ravitch, *The Troubled Crusade: American Education, 1945–1980* (1983); Joel Spring, *The Sorting Machine: National Educational Policy Since 1945* (1976).

Women's Lives and Women's Rights

Wini Breines, *Young, White, and Miserable: Growing Up Female in the Fifties* (1992); Barbara Ehrenreich, *The Hearts of Men: American Dreams and the Flight from Commitment* (1983); Cynthia Harrison, *On Account of Sex: The Politics of Women's Issues, 1945–1968* (1988); Susan Lynn, *Progressive Women in Conservative Times* (1992); Glenna Matthews, *"Just a Housewife"* (1987); Joanne J. Meyerowitz, ed., *Not June Cleaver: Women and Gender in Postwar America, 1945–1960* (1994); Leila J. Rupp and Verta Taylor, *Survival in the Doldrums: The American Women's Rights Movement, 1945 to the 1960s* (1987).

The Affluent Society

Loren Baritz, *The Good Life: The Meaning of Success for the American Middle Class* (1982); John Kenneth Galbraith, *The Affluent Society* (1958); Ann Markusen et al., *Rise of the Gunbelt: The Military Remapping of Industrial America* (1991); Kirkpatrick Sale, *Power Shift: The Rise of the Southern Rim and Its Challenge to the Eastern Establishment* (1975).

The Other America

J. Wayne Flint, *Dixie's Forgotten People: The South's Poor Whites* (1979); Mario T. Garcia, *Mexican Americans: Leadership, Ideology, and Identity, 1930–1960* (1990); Michael Harrington, *The Other America*, rev. ed. (1981); Dorothy K. Newman et al., *Politics and Prosperity: Black Americans and White Institutions, 1940–75* (1978); James T. Patterson, *America's Struggle Against Poverty, 1900–1994*, rev. ed. (1994).

Chapter 29

The Cold War: Overviews

Warren Cohen, *America in the Age of Soviet Power, 1945–1991* (1993); John Lewis Gaddis, *We Now Know* (1997); John Lewis Gaddis, *The Long Peace* (1987); John Lewis Gaddis, *Strategies of Containment* (1982); Walter Isaacson and Evan Thomas, *The Wise Men* (1986); Robert H. Johnson, *Improbable Dangers: U.S. Perceptions of Threat in the Cold War and After* (1994); Walter LaFeber, *America, Russia, and the Cold War* (2001); Deborah Larson, *Anatomy of Dis-*

trust (1997); Ralph Levering, *The Cold War*, 2d ed. (1994); Thomas McCormick, *America's Half-Century*, 2d ed. (1994); Thomas G. Paterson, *On Every Front: The Making and Unmaking of the Cold War*, rev. ed. (1992); Thomas G. Paterson, *Meeting the Communist Threat* (1988); Michael S. Sherry, *In the Shadow of War* (1995).

Relations with the Third World: Overviews

Richard J. Barnet, *Intervention and Revolution* (1972); Edward H. Berman, *The Influence of the Carnegie, Ford, and Rockefeller Foundations on American Foreign Policy* (1983); Scott L. Bills, *Empire and Cold War* (1990); Thomas Borstelmann, *The Cold War and the Color Line* (2001); H. W. Brands, *The Specter of Neutralism* (1989); Peter L. Hahn and Mary Ann Heiss, eds., *Empire and Revolution* (2001); Mary L. Dudziak, *Cold War Civil Rights* (2000); Gabriel Kolko, *Confronting the Third World* (1988); Michael L. Krenn, *Black Diplomacy: African Americans and the State Department, 1945–1969* (1998); Brenda G. Plummer, *Rising Wind: Black Americans and U.S. Foreign Affairs, 1935–1960* (1996); David F. Schmitz, *Thank God They're on Our Side: The U.S. and Right-Wing Dictatorships, 1921–1965* (1999); Penny M. von Eschen, *Race Against Empire: Black Americans and Anticolonialism, 1937–1957* (1996).

Truman, Cold War Origins, Containment, and the National Security State

James Chace, *Acheson* (1998); Carolyn W. Eisenberg, *Drawing the Line: The American Decision to Divide Germany, 1944–1949* (1996); Richard M. Fried, *The Russians Are Coming! The Russians Are Coming!* (1998); Frazer Harbutt, *The Iron Curtain* (1986); Walter Hixson, *George F. Kennan* (1990); Michael J. Hogan, *A Cross of Iron: Harry S. Truman and the Origins of the National Security State* (1998); Michael J. Hogan, *The Marshall Plan* (1987); Lawrence S. Kaplan, *The United States and NATO* (1984); Gabriel Kolko and Joyce Kolko, *The Limits of Power* (1972); Melvyn Leffler, *The Specter of Communism* (1994); Melvyn Leffler, *A Preponderance of Power: National Security, the Truman Administration, and the Cold War* (1992); Alan Milward, *The Reconstruction of Western Europe* (1984); Wilson D. Miscamble, *George F. Kennan and the Making of American Foreign Policy, 1947–1950* (1992); Ann Markusen et al., *The Rise of the Gunbelt* (1991); Arnold A. Offner, *Another Such Victory* (2002); Thomas A. Schwartz, *America's Germany* (1991); Mark A. Stoler, *George C. Marshall* (1989); Lawrence S. Wittner, *American Intervention in Greece, 1943–1949* (1982); Vladislav Zubok and Constantine Pleshakov, *Inside the Kremlin's Cold War* (1996).

Eisenhower-Dulles Foreign Policy

Stephen E. Ambrose, *Eisenhower*, 2 vols. (1982, 1984); Jeff Broadwater, *Eisenhower and the Anti-Communist Crusade* (1992); Robert A. Divine, *Eisenhower and the Cold War* (1981); Fred Greenstein, *The Hidden-Hand Presidency* (1982); Townsend Hoopes, *The Devil and John Foster Dulles* (1973); Richard Immerman, *John Foster Dulles* (1998).

The CIA and Counterinsurgency

Douglas S. Blaufarb, *The Counterinsurgency Era* (1977); Peter Grose, *Gentleman Spy: The Life of Allen Dulles* (1994); Rhodi Jeffreys-Jones, *The CIA and American Democracy* (1989); Loch K. Johnson, *America's Secret Power* (1989); Mark Lowenthal, *U.S. Intelligence* (1984); John Ranelagh, *The Agency* (1986); Jeffrey T. Richelson, *A Century of Spies* (1995); Jeffrey T. Richelson, *The U.S. Intelligence Community* (1999); Evan Thomas, *The Very Best Men* (1995).

Atomic Diplomacy, Nuclear Arms Race, and Public Attitudes

Howard Ball, *Justice Downwind: America's Atomic Testing Program in the 1950s* (1986); Paul Boyer, *Fallout* (1998); Paul Boyer, *By the Bomb's Early Light* (1986); McGeorge Bundy, *Danger and Survival* (1988); Campbell Craig, *Destroying the Village: Eisenhower and Thermonuclear War* (1998); Robert A. Divine, *The Sputnik Challenge* (1993); Robert A. Divine, *Blowing on the Wind: The Nuclear Test Ban Debate, 1954–1960* (1978); Margot Henriksen, *Dr. Strangelove's America* (1997); Gregg Herken, *The Winning Weapon* (1981); Richard G. Hewlett and Jack M. Hall, *Atoms for Peace and War, 1953–1961* (1989); David Holloway, *Stalin and the Bomb* (1994); Robert Jervis, *The Meaning of the Nuclear Revolution* (1989); Milton Katz, *Ban the Bomb* (1986); Stuart W. Leslie, *The Cold War and American Science* (1994); Richard Rhodes, *Dark Sun: The Making of the Hydrogen Bomb* (1995); David N. Schwartz, *NATO's Nuclear Dilemmas* (1983); Martin Sherwin, *A World Destroyed* (1975); Spencer Weart, *Nuclear Fear* (1988); Allan M. Winkler, *Life Under a Cloud* (1993); Lawrence S. Wittner, *The Struggle Against the Bomb* (1993, 1998).

Cultural Relations and Expansion

Robert H. Haddow, *Pavilions of Plenty* (1997); Walter L. Hixson, *Parting the Curtain: Propaganda, Culture, and the Cold War* (1997); Frank A. Ninkovich, *The Diplomacy of Ideas* (1981); Richard Pells, *Not Like Us: How Europeans Have Loved, Hated, and Transformed American Culture Since World War II* (1997); Reinhold Wagnleitner, *Coca-Colonization and the Cold War* (1994).

Japan, China, and Asian Issues

Gordon Chang, *Friends and Enemies* (1990); Thomas J. Christensen, *Useful Adversaries* (1996); Warren I. Cohen, *America's Response to China*, 3d ed. (1990); Nick Cullather, *Illusions of In-*

fluence: The Political Economy of United States–Philippines Relations, 1942–1960 (1994); Kyoko Hirano, Mr. Smith Goes to Tokyo: Japanese Cinema Under the American Occupation, 1945–1952 (1992); Walter LaFeber, The Clash: A History of U.S.-Japan Relations (1997); Paul G. Lauren, ed., The "China Hands" Legacy (1987); Robert J. McMahon, The Limits of Empire: The United States and Southeast Asia Since World War II (1999); Dennis Merrill, Bread and the Ballot: The United States and India's Economic Development, 1947–1963 (1990); Andrew J. Rotter, Comrades at Odds (2000) (on India); Michael Schaller, Douglas MacArthur (1989); Michael Schaller, The American Occupation of Japan (1985); Nancy B. Tucker, Taiwan, Hong Kong, and the United States (1994); Nancy B. Tucker, Patterns in the Dust: Chinese-American Relations and the Recognition Controversy, 1945–1950 (1983); Philip West et al., eds., America's Wars in Asia (1998).

The Korean War

Roy E. Appleman, Disaster in Korea (1992); Roy E. Appleman, Escaping the Trap (1990); Roy E. Appleman, Ridgeway Duels for Korea (1990); Conrad C. Crane, American Airpower Strategy in Korea (2000); Bruce Cumings, Korea's Place in the Sun (1997); Bruce Cumings, The Origins of the Korean War (1980, 1991); Rosemary Foot, A Substitute for Victory (1990); Rosemary Foot, The Wrong War (1985); Sergei Goncharov et al., Uncertain Partners: Stalin, Mao, and the Korean War (1993); Chen Jian, China's Road to the Korean War (1995); Burton I. Kaufman, The Korean War, 2d ed. (1997); William Stueck, The Korean War (1995); Shu Guang Zhang, Mao's Military Romanticism (1996).

Vietnam

David L. Anderson, ed., Shadow on the White House (1993); David L. Anderson, Trapped by Success (1991); Lloyd C. Gardner, Approaching Vietnam (1988); George C. Herring, America's Longest War, 3d ed. (1996); Gary R. Hess, Vietnam and the United States, rev. ed. (1998); Gabriel Kolko, Anatomy of a War (1986); David G. Marr, Vietnam 1945 (1995); Andrew Rotter, The Path to Vietnam (1987); Robert D. Schulzinger, A Time for War (1997); Robert R. Tomes, Apocalypse Then: American Intellectuals and the Vietnam War, 1954–1975 (1998); Marilyn B. Young, The Vietnam Wars (1991).

Latin America

John Coatsworth, Central America and the United States (1994); Michael Conniff, Panama and the United States (1992); Nick Cullather, Secret History: The CIA's Classified Account of Its Operations in Guatemala, 1952–1954 (1999); Mark T. Gilderhus, The Second Century (2000); Piero Gleijeses,

Shattered Hope: The Guatemalan Revolution and the United States, 1944–1954 (1991); Richard Immerman, The CIA in Guatemala (1982); Walter LaFeber, Inevitable Revolutions: The United States in Central America (1993); Walter LaFeber, The Panama Canal (1990); Lester Langley, America and the Americas (1989); A. W. Maldonado, Teodoro Moscoso and Puerto Rico's Operation Bootstrap (1997); Thomas G. Paterson, Contesting Castro (1994); Louis A. Pérez, Jr., Cuba and the United States, 2d ed. (1997); W. Dirk Raat, Mexico and the United States, 2d ed. (1997); Stephen G. Rabe, Eisenhower and Latin America (1988); Lars Schoultz, Beneath the United States (1998); Peter H. Smith, Talons of the Eagle (1996).

Middle East and Africa

Nigel J. Ashton, Eisenhower, Macmillan, and the Problem of Nasser (1996); James A. Bill, The Eagle and the Lion: The Tragedy of American-Iranian Relations (1988); Thomas Borstelmann, Apartheid's Reluctant Uncle: The United States and Southern Africa in the Early Cold War (1993); Michael J. Cohen, Truman and Israel (1990); Michael J. Cohen, Palestine and the Great Powers, 1945–1948 (1983); Mark Gasiorowski, U.S. Foreign Policy and the Shah (1991); Peter L. Hahn, The United States, Great Britain, and Egypt, 1945–1956 (1991); Mary Ann Heiss, Empire and Nationhood: The United States, Great Britain, and Iranian Oil, 1950–1954 (1997); Burton I. Kaufman, The Arab Middle East and the United States (1996); Diane Kunz, The Economic Diplomacy of the Suez Crisis (1991); Aaron D. Miller, Search for Security (1980); Thomas J. Noer, Cold War and Black Liberation (1985); David Schoenbaum, The United States and the State of Israel (1993); Daniel Yergin, The Prize: The Epic Quest for Oil, Money, and Power (1991).

Chapter 30

The 1960s

David Burner, Making Peace with the 60s (1996); David Chalmers, And the Crooked Places Made Straight: The Struggle for Social Change in the 1960s (1991); David Farber, The Age of Great Dreams (1994); David Farber, ed., The Sixties (1994); James J. Farrell, The Spirit of the Sixties (1997); Godfrey Hodgson, America in Our Time (1976); Michael Kazin and Maurice Isserman, America Divided: The Civil War of the 1960s (2000); Allen J. Matusow, The Unraveling of America: A History of Liberalism in the 1960s (1984); James T. Patterson, Grand Expectations: The United States, 1945–1974 (1996).

The Kennedy Presidency

Irving Bernstein, Promises Kept: John F. Kennedy's New Frontier (1991); James Giglio, The Presidency of John F. Kennedy

(1991); David Halberstam, *The Best and the Brightest* (1972); Thomas C. Reeves, *A Question of Character* (1991); Arthur M. Schlesinger, Jr., *Robert Kennedy and His Times* (1978); Arthur M. Schlesinger, Jr., *A Thousand Days: John F. Kennedy in the White House* (1965); Ronald Steel, *In Love with Night: The American Romance with Robert Kennedy* (1999).

The Kennedy Assassination

Edward Jay Epstein, *Legend: The Secret World of Lee Harvey Oswald* (1978); Henry Hurt, *Reasonable Doubt* (1985); Gerald Posner, *Case Closed* (1993); Anthony Summers, *Conspiracy* (1980).

Lyndon B. Johnson and the Great Society

Irving Bernstein, *Guns or Butter: The Presidency of Lyndon Johnson* (1996); Robert Dallek, *Flawed Giant: Lyndon Johnson and His Times, 1961–1973* (1998); Doris Kearns, *Lyndon Johnson and the American Dream* (1976); James T. Patterson, *America's Struggle Against Poverty, 1900–1994*, rev. ed. (1994); John E. Schwarz, *America's Hidden Success: A Reassessment of Twenty Years of Public Policy* (1983).

Civil Rights, Black Power, and Urban Riots

Taylor Branch, *Pillar of Fire: America in the King Years, 1963–1965* (1998); Taylor Branch, *Parting the Waters: America in the King Years, 1954–1963* (1988); Clayborne Carson, *In Struggle: SNCC and the Black Awakening of the 1960s* (1981); John Dittmer, *Local People: The Struggle for Civil Rights in Mississippi* (1994); David J. Garrow, *Bearing the Cross: Martin Luther King, Jr., and the Southern Christian Leadership Conference* (1986); Malcolm X and Alex Haley, *The Autobiography of Malcolm X* (1965); August Meier and Elliott Rudwick, *CORE* (1973); Belinda Robnett, *How Long? How Long? African-American Women in the Struggle for Civil Rights* (1997).

The New Left and Protest for Peace and Justice

Terry H. Anderson, *The Movement and the Sixties* (1995); Wini Breines, *Community and Organization in the New Left, 1962–1968*, rev. ed. (1989); Charles DeBenedetti, *An American Ordeal: The Antiwar Movement of the Vietnam Era* (1990); John D'Emilio, *Sexual Politics, Sexual Communities: The Making of a Homosexual Minority in the United States, 1940–1970* (1983); Todd Gitlin, *The Sixties* (1987); James Miller, *"Democracy Is in the Streets": From Port Huron to the Siege of Chicago* (1987).

The Counterculture

James Miller, *Flowers in the Dustbin: The Rise of Rock and Roll, 1947–1977* (1999); Tim Miller, *The Hippies and American Values* (1991); Jay Stevens, *Storming Heaven: LSD and the American Dream* (1987); Jon Weiner, *Come Together: John Lennon in His Time* (1984); Tom Wolfe, *The Electric Kool-Aid Acid Test* (1968).

The Rebirth of Feminism

Alice Echols, *Daring to Be Bad: Radical Feminism in America, 1965–1975* (1989); Sara Evans, *Personal Politics* (1978); Jo Freeman, *The Politics of Women's Liberation* (1975); David J. Garrow, *Liberty and Sexuality: The Right to Privacy and the Making of* Roe v. Wade (1994); Cynthia Harrison, *On Account of Sex: The Politics of Women's Issues, 1945–1968* (1988); Ruth Rosen, *The World Split Open: How the Modern Women's Movement Changed America* (2000).

Year of Shocks: 1968

David Farber, *Chicago '68* (1988); Ronald Fraser et al., *1968: A Student Generation in Revolt* (1988); Charles Kaiser, *1968 in America* (1988); Jules Witcover, *The Year the Dream Died: Revisiting 1968 in America* (1997) .

Richard M. Nixon and the Resurgence of Conservatism

Stephen E. Ambrose, *Nixon*, 3 vols. (1987–1991); Mary C. Brennan, *Turning Right in the Sixties: The Conservative Capture of the GOP* (1995); Dan T. Carter, *The Politics of Rage: George Wallace, the Origins of the New Conservatism, and the Transformation of American Politics* (1995); Robert Alan Goldberg, *Barry Goldwater* (1995); Herbert S. Parmet, *Richard Nixon and His America* (1990); Melvin Small, *The Presidency of Richard Nixon* (1999); Garry Wills, *Nixon Agonistes* (1970).

Watergate

Stanley I. Kutler, ed., *Abuse of Power: The New Nixon Tapes* (1997); Stanley I. Kutler, *The Wars of Watergate* (1990); J. Anthony Lukas, *Nightmare: The Underside of the Nixon Years* (1976); Kim McQuaid, *The Anxious Years: America in the Vietnam-Watergate Era* (1989); Theodore H. White, *Breach of Faith* (1975); Bob Woodward, *Shadow: Five Presidents and the Legacy of Watergate* (1999); Bob Woodward and Carl Bernstein, *All the President's Men* (1974).

Chapter 31

General

See works listed under Chapter 29 and Richard J. Barnet, *Intervention and Revolution* (1972); Edward H. Berman, *The Influence of the Carnegie, Ford, and Rockefeller Foundations on*

American Foreign Policy (1983); Alvin Z. Rubenstein and Donald E. Smith, eds., Anti-Americanism in the Third World (1985).

Foreign Policy in the 1960s: Kennedy and Johnson

Michael Beschloss, The Crisis Years (1991); James A. Bill, George Ball (1997); Kai Bird, The Color of Truth: McGeorge Bundy and William Bundy (1998); H. W. Brands, The Wages of Globalism (1995); Warren I. Cohen, Dean Rusk (1980); Warren I. Cohen and Nancy B. Tucker, eds., Lyndon Johnson Confronts the World (1995); Robert Dallek, Flawed Giant: Lyndon Johnson and His Times, 1961–1973 (1998); Fritz Fisher, Making Them Like Us: Peace Corps Volunteers in the 1960s (1998); James N. Giglio, The Presidency of John F. Kennedy (1991); David Halberstam, The Best and the Brightest (1972); Seymour Hersh, The Other Side of Camelot (1997); Elizabeth Cobbs Hoffman, All You Need Is Love: The Peace Corps and the Spirit of the 1960s (1998); Doris Kearns, Lyndon Johnson and the American Dream (1976); Diane Kunz, ed., The Diplomacy of the Crucial Decade (1994); Herbert S. Parmet, JFK (1983); Thomas G. Paterson, ed., Kennedy's Quest for Victory (1989); Gerald T. Rice, The Bold Experiment: JFK's Peace Corps (1985); Arthur M. Schlesinger, Jr., Robert Kennedy and His Times (1978); Deborah Shapley, Promise and Power: The Life and Times of Robert McNamara (1993); Mark J. White, Kennedy (1998); Randall Woods, Fulbright (1995); Thomas W. Zeiler, Dean Rusk (1999).

Cuba and the Missile Crisis

Graham Allison and Philip Zelikow, Essence of Decision: Explaining the Cuban Missile Crisis, 2d ed. (1999); James G. Blight, The Shattered Crystal Ball (1990); James G. Blight et al., Cuba on the Brink (1993); James G. Blight and Peter Kornbluh, eds., Politics of Illusion: The Bay of Pigs Invasion Reexamined (1998); James G. Blight and David A. Welch, On the Brink (1989); Raymond Garthoff, Reflections on the Cuban Missile Crisis, rev. ed. (1989); Trumbull Higgins, The Perfect Failure: Kennedy, Eisenhower, and the CIA at the Bay of Pigs (1987); Donna R. Kaplowitz, Anatomy of a Failed Embargo: U.S. Sanctions Against Cuba (1998); Ernest R. May and Philip Zelikow, eds., The Kennedy Tapes (1997); James Nathan, ed., The Cuban Missile Crisis Revisited (1992); Thomas G. Paterson, Contesting Castro (1994); Louis A. Pérez, Jr., Cuba and the United States, 2d ed. (1997); Scott D. Sagan, The Limits of Safety (1993); Mark J. White, The Cuban Missile Crisis (1996).

The Vietnam War

See Herring, Hess, Kolko, Morgan, Schulzinger, Tomes, and Young listed under Chapter 29 and David L. Anderson, Facing My Lai (1998); Loren Baritz, Backfire (1985); David M. Barrett, Uncertain Warriors (1993); Eric M. Bergerud, The Dynamics of Defeat (1991); Larry Berman, Lyndon Johnson's War (1989); Larry Berman, Planning a Tragedy (1982); Robert K. Brigham, Guerilla Diplomacy: The NFL's Foreign Relations and the Viet Nam War (1999); Robert Buzzanco, Vietnam and the Transformation of American Life (1999); Robert Buzzanco, Masters of War: Military Dissent and Politics in the Vietnam Era (1996); Larry Cable, Unholy Grail (1991); Mark Clodfelter, The Limits of Power: The American Bombing of North Vietnam (1989); Charles DeBenedetti and Charles Chatfield, An American Ordeal: The Antiwar Movement of the Vietnam War (1990); David L. DiLeo, George Ball, Vietnam, and the Rethinking of Containment (1991); Frances FitzGerald, Fire in the Lake (1972); Lloyd C. Gardner, Pay Any Price (1995); William C. Gibbons, The U.S. Government and the Vietnam War (1986–1994); George C. Herring, LBJ and Vietnam (1994); Michael H. Hunt, Lyndon Johnson's War (1996); Jeffrey Kimball, Nixon's Vietnam War (1998); Fredrick Logevall, Choosing War (1999); Robert S. McNamara, James G. Blight, and Robert K. Brigham, Argument Without End: In Search of Answers to the Vietnam Tragedy (1999); Edwin E. Moïse, Tonkin Gulf and the Escalation of the Vietnam War (1996); William Prochnau, Once upon a Distant War (1995) (on journalists); William Shawcross, Sideshow: Kissinger, Nixon, and the Destruction of Cambodia (1979); Kevin Sim and Michael Bilton, Four Hours in My Lai (1992); Melvin Small, Johnson, Nixon and the Doves (1988); Ronald H. Spector, After Tet: The Bloodiest Year in Vietnam (1992); Ronald H. Spector, United States Army in Vietnam (1983); Brian VanDerMark, Into the Quagmire (1991).

Legacy and Lessons of the Vietnam War

Eric T. Dean, Jr., Shook Over Hell: Post-Traumatic Stress, Vietnam, and the Civil War (1998); John Hellman, American Myth and the Legacy of Vietnam (1986); Herbert Hendin and Ann P. Haas, Wounds of War: The Psychological Aftermath of Combat in Vietnam (1984); Ole R. Holsti and James Rosenau, American Leadership in World Affairs: Vietnam and the Breakdown of Consensus (1984); Myra MacPherson, Long Time Passing (1984); Charles E. Neu, ed., After Vietnam (2000); Norman Podhoretz, Why We Were in Vietnam (1982); Earl C. Ravenal, Never Again (1978); Harry G. Summers, Jr., On Strategy (1982); Fred Turner, Echoes of Combat: The Vietnam War in American Memory (1996).

Nixon, Kissinger, and Détente

Stephen Ambrose, Nixon, 3 vols. (1987–1991); Michael B. Froman, The Development of the Idea of Détente (1992); Raymond L. Garthoff, Détente and Confrontation (1985); John R. Greene, The Limits of Power (1992); Seymour Hersh, The Price of Power (1983); Joan Hoff, Nixon Reconsidered (1994);

Walter Isaacson, *Kissinger* (1992); Herbert S. Parmet, *Richard Nixon and His America* (1990); Andrew J. Pierre, *The Global Politics of Arms Sales* (1982); Robert D. Schulzinger, *Henry Kissinger* (1989); Melvin Small, *The Presidency of Richard Nixon* (1999).

Carter Foreign Policy and Human Rights

Anne H. Cahn, *Killing Détente: The Right Attacks the CIA* (1998); Gary M. Fink and Hugh Davis Graham, eds., *The Carter Presidency* (1998); Burton I. Kaufman, *The Presidency of James Earl Carter, Jr.* (1993); David S. McLellan, *Cyrus Vance* (1985); Richard A. Melanson, *Reconstructing Consensus* (1990); A. Glenn Mower, Jr., *Human Rights and American Foreign Policy* (1987); John Newhouse, *Cold Dawn* (1973) (on SALT); Kenneth A. Oye et al., *Eagle Entangled* (1979); Gaddis Smith, *Morality, Reason, and Power* (1986); Robert A. Strong, *Working in the World* (2000); Strobe Talbott, *Endgame: The Inside Story of SALT II* (1979); Sandy Vogelsang, *American Dream, Global Nightmare* (1980).

Reagan's Foreign Policy and Military Buildup

Dana H. Allin, *Cold War Illusions* (1995); Michael R. Beschloss and Strobe Talbott, *At the Highest Levels* (1993); Archie Brown, *The Gorbachev Factor* (1996); Lou Cannon, *President Reagan* (1991); Theodore Draper, *A Very Thin Line: The Iran-Contra Affairs* (1991); Raymond L. Garthoff, *The Great Transition* (1994); Haynes Johnson, *Sleepwalking Through History* (1991); Robert G. Kaiser, *Why Gorbachev Happened* (1991); Peter Kornbluh and Malcolm Byrne, eds., *The Iran-Contra Scandal* (1993); Michael McGwire, *Perestroika and Soviet National Security* (1991); Don Oberdorfer, *From the Cold War to a New Era* (1998); Kenneth A. Oye et al., eds., *Eagle Resurgent?* (1987); William E. Pemberton, *Exit with Honor* (1997); Michael Schaller, *Reckoning with Reagan* (1992); Strobe Talbott, *The Master of the Game: Paul Nitze and the Nuclear Peace* (1988); Strobe Talbott, *Deadly Gambit* (1984); Daniel Wirls, *Buildup* (1992).

Latin America: General

David W. Dent, ed., *U.S.–Latin American Policymaking* (1995); Guy Gugliotta and Jeff Leen, *Kings of Cocaine* (1989); Lester Langley, *America and the Americas* (1989); Abraham F. Lowenthal, ed., *Exporting Democracy* (1991); Abraham F. Lowenthal, *Partners in Conflict*, rev. ed. (1990); Donald J. Mabry, ed., *The Latin American Narcotics Trade and U.S. National Security* (1989); W. Dirk Raat, *Mexico and the United States*, 2d ed. (1997); Stephen G. Rabe, *The Most Dangerous Area in the World: John F. Kennedy Confronts Communist Revolution in Latin America* (1999); Lars Schoultz, *Beneath the United States* (1998); Peter H. Smith, *Talons of the Eagle* (1996).

Central America and Panama

Cynthia J. Arnson, *Crossroads* (1989); Morris J. Blachman et al., eds., *Confronting Revolution* (1986); E. Bradford Burns, *At War in Nicaragua* (1987); John Coatsworth, *Central America and the United States* (1994); Michael L. Conniff, *Panama and the United States* (1992); Walter LaFeber, *Inevitable Revolutions*, 2d ed. (1993); Walter LaFeber, *The Panama Canal*, updated ed. (1989); William M. LeoGrande, *Our Own Backyard* (1998); Robert A. Pastor, *Whirlpool: U.S. Foreign Policy Toward Latin America and the Caribbean* (1992); Robert A. Pastor, *Condemned to Repetition: The United States and Nicaragua* (1987); Peter Dale Scott and Jonathan Marshall, *Cocaine Politics* (1991); Christian Smith, *Resisting Reagan: The U.S.–Central America Peace Movement* (1996).

The Middle East and Iranian Hostage Crisis

James A. Bill, *The Eagle and the Lion: The Tragedy of American-Iranian Relations* (1988); William J. Burns and Richard W. Cottam, *Iran and the United States* (1988); Mark Gasiorowski, *U.S. Foreign Policy and the Shah* (1991); Burton I. Kaufman, *The Arab Middle East and the United States* (1996); William B. Quandt, *Peace Process* (1993); Cheryl A. Rubenberg, *Israel and the American National Interest* (1986); David Schoenbaum, *The United States and the State of Israel* (1993); Daniel Yergin, *The Prize: The Epic Quest for Oil, Money, and Power* (1991).

Africa

Pauline H. Baker, *The United States and South Africa: The Reagan Years* (1989); Christopher Coker, *The United States and South Africa, 1968–1985* (1986); David N. Gibbs, *The Political Economy of Third World Intervention : Mines, Money, and U.S. Policy in the Congo Crises* (1991); Richard D. Mahoney, *JFK: Ordeal in Africa* (1983); Robert K. Massie, *Loosing the Bonds: The United States and South Africa in the Apartheid Years* (1997); Thomas J. Noer, *Cold War and Black Liberation* (1985); Peter J. Schraeder, *United States Policy Toward Africa* (1994).

Asia

Walter LaFeber, *The Clash: A History of U.S.-Japan Relations* (1997); James Mann, *About Face: A History of America's Curious Relationship with China, From Nixon to Clinton* (1999); Robert McMahon, *The Limits of Empire: The United States and Southeast Asia Since World War II* (1999); Robert S. Ross, *Negotiating Cooperation: The United States and China, 1969–1989* (1995); Michael Schaller, *Altered States: The United States and Japan Since the Occupation* (1997); Nancy B. Tucker, *Taiwan, Hong Kong, and the United States* (1994). See above for Vietnam.

The World Economy and the Natural Environment

Richard J. Barnet, *The Lean Years* (1980); Richard J. Barnet and John Cavanaugh, *Global Dreams* (1994); Richard J. Barnet and Ronald Müller, *Global Reach* (1974); Richard E. Benedick, *Ozone Diplomacy* (1991); David P. Calleo, *The Imperious Economy* (1982); Alfred E. Eckes, *The United States and the Global Struggle for Minerals* (1979); David E. Fisher, *Fire & Ice: The Greenhouse Effect, Ozone Depletion, and Nuclear Winter* (1990); Edward M. Graham and Paul R. Krugman, *Foreign Direct Investment in the United States* (1989); Stephen D. Krasner, *Defending the National Interest* (1978); Diane B. Kunz, *Butter and Guns* (1997); John McCormick, *Reclaiming Paradise: The Global Environmental Movement* (1989); Joan E. Spero and Jeffrey A. Hart, *The Politics of International Economic Relations*, 5th ed. (1997); Richard P. Tucker, *Insatiable Appetite* (2000); Herman Van Der Wee, *The Search for Prosperity: The World Economy, 1945–1980* (1986).

Chapter 32

The Ford and Carter Administrations

Gary M. Fink and Hugh Davis Graham, eds., *The Carter Presidency* (1998); John Robert Greene, *The Presidency of Gerald R. Ford* (1995); Erwin C. Hargrove, *Jimmy Carter as President* (1989); Charles O. Jones, *The Trusteeship Presidency: Jimmy Carter and the United States Congress* (1988); Burton I. Kaufman, *The Presidency of James Earl Carter, Jr.* (1993).

Women and Children's Struggles

Marian Wright Edelman, *Families in Peril* (1987); Barbara Ehrenreich, *The Hearts of Men: American Dreams and the Flight from Commitment* (1983); David T. Ellwood, *Poor Support: Poverty in the American Family* (1988); Susan Faludi, *Backlash: The Undeclared War Against American Women* (1991); Sylvia Ann Hewlett, *When the Bough Breaks: The Cost of Neglecting Our Children* (1991); Arlie Russell Hochschild, *The Second Shift: Working Parents and the Revolution at Home* (1989); Kristin Luker, *Abortion and the Politics of Motherhood* (1984).

People of Color and New Immigrants

Leslie W. Dunbar, ed., *Minority Report: What Has Happened to Blacks, Hispanics, American Indians, and Other Minorities in the Eighties* (1984); Reynolds Farley and Walter R. Allen, *The Color Line and the Quality of Life in America* (1987); Ronald P. Formisano, *Boston Against Busing* (1991); Joane Nagel, *American Indian Ethnic Revival: Red Power and the Resurgence of Identity and Culture* (1996); Paul Chaat Smith and Robert Allen Warrior, *Like a Hurricane: The Indian Movement from Alcatraz to Wounded Knee* (1996); Sanford J. Ungar, *Fresh Blood: The New Immigrants* (1995); William Julius Wilson, *The Truly Disadvantaged: The Inner City, the Underclass, and Public Policy* (1987).

The New Conservatism and the Election of 1980

William C. Berman, *America's Right Turn* (1994); Sara Diamond, *Not by Politics Alone: The Enduring Influence of the Christian Right* (1998); Lee Edwards, *The Conservative Revolution* (1999); Jack W. Germond and Jules Witcover, *Blue Smoke and Mirrors: How Reagan Won and Why Carter Lost the Election of 1980* (1981); Godfrey Hodgson, *The World Turned Right Side Up: A History of the Conservative Ascendancy in America* (1996).

Ronald Reagan and His Presidency

Lou Cannon, *President Reagan* (1991); Paul D. Erickson, *Reagan Speaks: The Making of an American Myth* (1985); Mark Hertsgaard, *On Bended Knee: The Press and the Reagan Presidency* (1988); Haynes Johnson, *Sleepwalking Through History: America in the Reagan Years* (1991); Jane Mayer and Doyle McManus, *Landslide: The Unmaking of the President, 1984–1988* (1988); Garry Wills, *Reagan's America* (1987).

"Reaganomics"

Joan Claybrook, *Retreat from Safety: Reagan's Attack on America's Health* (1984); Jonathan Lash, *A Season of Spoils: The Story of the Reagan Administration's Attack on the Environment* (1984); Robert Lekachman, *Greed Is Not Enough: Reaganomics* (1982); William A. Niskanen, *Reaganomics* (1988).

A Polarized Society in the 1980s

Chandler Davidson, *Race and Class in Texas Politics* (1990); Thomas Byrne Edsall and Mary D. Edsall, *Chain Reaction: The Impact of Race, Rights, and Taxes on American Politics* (1991); Michael Harrington, *The New American Poverty* (1984); Katherine S. Newman, *Declining Fortunes: The Withering of the American Dream* (1993); Randy Shilts, *And the Band Played On: Politics, People and the AIDS Epidemic* (1987); Studs Terkel, *The Great Divide* (1988); Edward N. Wolff, *Top Heavy: A Study of Increasing Inequality in America* (1995).

Presidential Politics: The Elections of 1984 and 1988

Richard Ben Cramer, *What It Takes* (1992); Thomas Ferguson and Joel Rogers, *Right Turn: The Decline of the Democrats and the Future of American Politics* (1986); Jack W. Germond and Jules Witcover, *Wake Us When It's Over: Presidential Politics of 1984* (1985); Peter Goldman and Tom Mathews, *The Quest for the Presidency: The 1988 Campaign* (1989).

Chapter 33

The Bush Administration

Donald L. Bartlett and James B. Steele, *America: What Went Wrong?* (1992); Michael Duffy and Don Goodgame, *Marching in Place: The Status Quo Presidency of George Bush* (1992); John Robert Greene, *The Presidency of George Bush* (2000); Herbert S. Parmet, *George Bush: The Life of a Lone Star Yankee* (1998).

Politics and the Election of 1992

Alan Ehrenhalt, *The United States of Ambition: Politicians, Power, and the Pursuit of Office* (1991); William Greider, *Who Will Tell the People: The Betrayal of American Democracy* (1992); Kathleen Hall Jamieson, *Dirty Politics* (1992); Kevin Phillips, *The Politics of Rich and Poor* (1990); Gerald Posner, *Citizen Perot* (1996); Ruy A. Teixeira, *The Disappearing American Voter* (1992).

American Society in the 1990s

Robert H. Frank and Philip J. Cook, *The Winner-Take-All Society* (1995); Herbert J. Gans, *The War Against the Poor* (1995); David M. Gordon, *Fat and Mean: The Corporate Squeeze of Working Americans and the Myth of Managerial "Downsizing"* (1996); Jennifer L. Hochschild, *Facing Up to the American Dream: Race, Class, and the Soul of the Nation* (1995); Katherine S. Newman, *Declining Fortunes: The Withering of the American Dream* (1993); Robert J. Samuelson, *The Good Life and Its Discontents: The American Dream in an Age of Entitlements* (1995).

Disgruntled Americans: Political Apathy, Antigovernment Movements, and Culture Wars

Stephen Ansolabehere and Shanto Iyengar, *Going Negative: How Attack Ads Shrink and Polarize the Electorate* (1995); E. J. Dionne, Jr., *Why Americans Hate Politics* (1991); James Fallows, *Breaking the News: How the Media Undermine American Democracy* (1996); Thomas Ferguson, *Golden Rule: The Investment Theory of Party Competition and the Logic of Money-Driven Political Systems* (1995); William Martin, *With God on Our Side: The Rise of the Religious Right in America* (1996); Larry J. Sabato and Glenn R. Simpson, *Dirty Little Secrets: The Persistence of Corruption in American Politics* (1996); Kenneth S. Stern, *A Force upon the Plain: The American Militia Movement and the Politics of Hate* (1996).

The 1996 Election and the Future of American Politics

E. J. Dionne, Jr., *They Only Look Dead: Why Progressives Will Dominate the Next Political Era* (1996); Martin Plissner, *The Control Room: How Television Calls the Shots in Presidential Elections* (1999); Jake H. Thompson, *Bob Dole* (1994); Jacob Weisberg, *In Defense of Government: The Fall and Rise of Public Trust* (1996); Bob Woodward, *The Choice* (1996).

Clinton's Presidency, Impeachment, and Survival

Alan M. Dershowitz, *Sexual McCarthyism: Clinton, Starr and the Emerging Constitutional Crisis* (1998); Michael Isikoff, *Uncovering Clinton: A Reporter's Story* (1999); David Maraniss, *First in His Class: A Biography of Bill Clinton* (1995); Roger Morris, *Partners in Power: The Clintons and Their America* (1996); Richard A. Posner, *Affair of State: The Investigation, Impeachment, and Trial of President Clinton* (1999); Richard Reeves, *Running in Place: How Bill Clinton Disappointed America* (1996); James B. Stewart, *Blood Sport: The President and His Adversaries* (1996); Jeffrey Toobin, *A Vast Conspiracy: The Real Story of the Sex Scandal That Nearly Brought Down a President* (2000); Bob Woodward, *The Agenda: Inside the Clinton White House* (1994).

The Foreign Policies and Wars of Bush and Clinton

See some works listed under Chapter 31 and Deborah Amos, *Lines in the Sand: Desert Storm and the Remaking of the Arab World* (1992); Michael R. Beschloss and Strobe Talbott, *At the Highest Levels: The Inside Story of the End of the Cold War* (1993); John Coatsworth, *Central America and the United States* (1994); Michael Conniff, *Panama and the United States* (1992); Timothy J. Dunn, *The Militarization of the U.S.-Mexico Border* (1996); Lawrence Freedman and Efraim Karsh, *The Gulf Conflict, 1990–1991* (1993); Stephen Graubard, *Mr. Bush's War* (1992); David Halberstam, *War in a Time of Peace* (2001); Avigdor Haselkorn, *The Continuing Storm: Iraq, Poisonous Weapons, and Deterrence* (1999); John L. Hirsch and Robert B. Oakley, *Somalia and Operation Restore Hope* (1995); Michael Hogan, ed., *The End of the Cold War* (1992); William G. Hyland, *Clinton's World* (1999); Burton I. Kaufman, *The Arab Middle East and the United States* (1996); Robert K. Massie, *Loosing the Bonds: The United States and South Africa in the Apartheid Years* (1998); James Mayall, ed., *The New Interventionism* (1996); Kenneth A. Oye et al., eds., *Eagle in a New World* (1992); Jean Edward Smith, *George Bush's War* (1992); Peter H. Smith, *Talons of the Eagle* (1996) (on U.S.-Latin America); Stephen R. Weissman, *A Culture of Deference: Congress's Failure of Leadership in Foreign Policy* (1995); Susan Woodward, *Balkan Tragedy* (1995).

Global Economic and Cultural Issues

Richard J. Barnet and John Cavangh, *Global Dreams: Imperial Corporations and the New World Order* (1994); Thomas L. Friedman, *The Lexus and the Olive Tree* (1999) (on globalization); Laurie Garrett, *Microbes Versus Mankind: The Coming Plague* (1997); George W. Grayson, *The North American Free Trade Agreement* (1995); Frank Ninkovich, *Information Policy and Cultural Diplomacy* (1996); Richard Pells, *Not Like Us: How Europeans Have Loved, Hated, and Transformed American Culture Since World War II* (1997); Robert Soloman, *Money on the Move: The Revolution in International Finance Since 1980* (1999); Paul B. Stares, *Global Habit: The Drug Problem in a Borderless World* (1996); Jessica Stern, *The Ultimate Terrorists* (1999).

Historical Reference Books by Subject:
Encyclopedias, Dictionaries, Atlases, Chronologies, and Statistics

American History: General

Gorton Carruth, ed., *The Encyclopedia of American Facts and Dates* (1997); *Dictionary of American History* (1976) and Joan Hoff and Robert H. Ferrell, eds., *Supplement* (1996); John M. Farragher, ed., *The American Heritage Encyclopedia of American History* (1998); Eric Foner and John A. Garraty, eds., *The Reader's Companion to American History* (1991); Bernard Grun, *The Timetables of History* (1991); *International Encyclopedia of the Social Sciences* (1968–); Richard B. Morris and Jeffrey B. Morris, eds., *Encyclopedia of American History* (1996); Harry Ritter, *Dictionary of Concepts in History* (1986); Lawrence Urdang, ed., *The Timetables of American History* (1996); U.S. Bureau of the Census, *Historical Statistics of the United States* (1975).

American History: General, Twentieth Century

John D. Buenker and Edward R. Kantowicz, eds., *Historical Dictionary of the Progressive Era, 1890–1920* (1988); David Farber and Beth Bailey, *The Columbia Guide to America in the 1960s* (2001); Robert H. Ferrell and John S. Bowman, eds., *The Twentieth Century: An Almanac* (1984); George H. Gallup, *The Gallup Poll: Public Opinion, 1935–1971* (1972), *1972–1977* (1978), and annual reports (1979–); Lois Gordon and Alan Gordon, *American Chronicles: Year by Year Through the Twentieth Century* (1999): Stanley Hochman, *The Penguin Dictionary of Contemporary American History* (1997); Stanley I. Kutler, ed., *Encyclopedia of the United States in the Twentieth Century* (1995); Peter B. Levy, *Encyclopedia of the Reagan-Bush Years* (1996); James S. Olson, *Historical Dictionary of the 1920s* (1988), and *Historical Dictionary of the 1950s* (2000); Thomas Parker and Douglas Nelson, *Day by Day: The Sixties* (1983).

American History: General Atlases and Gazetteers

Geoffrey Barraclough, ed., *The Times Atlas of World History* (1994); Rodger Doyle, *Atlas of Contemporary America* (1994); Robert H. Ferrell and Richard Natkiel, *Atlas of American History* (1997); Edward W. Fox, *Atlas of American History* (1964); Archie Hobson, *The Cambridge Gazetteer of the United States and Canada* (1996); Eric Homberger, *The Penguin Historical Atlas of North America* (1995); National Geographic Society, *Historical Atlas of the United States* (1994); U.S. Department of the Interior, *National Atlas of the United States* (1970). Other atlases are listed under specific categories.

American History: General Biographies

Lucian Boia, ed., *Great Historians of the Modern Age* (1991); John S. Bowman, *The Cambridge Dictionary of American Biography* (1995); *Current Biography* (1940–); *Dictionary of American Biography* (1928–); John A. Garraty and Mark C. Carnes, eds., *American National Biography* (1999); John Garraty and Jerome L. Sternstein, eds., *The Encyclopedia of American Biography* (1996); *National Cyclopedia of American Biography* (1898–). Other biographical works appear under specific categories.

African Americans

Molefi Asante and Mark T. Mattson, *Historical and Cultural Atlas of African-Americans* (1991); James Ciment, *Atlas of African-American History* (2001); Jonathan Earle, *The Routledge Atlas of African American History* (2000); John N. Ingham, *African-American Business Leaders* (1993); Rayford W. Logan and Michael R. Winston, eds., *The Dictionary of American Negro Biography* (1983); Sharon Harley, *The Timetables of African-American History* (1995); Darlene C. Hine et al., eds., *Black Women in White America* (1994); Charles D. Lowery and John F. Marszalek, eds., *Encyclopedia of African-American Civil Rights* (1992); Larry G. Murphy et al., eds., *Encyclopedia of African American Religions* (1993); Jack Salzman et al., eds., *Encyclopedia of African-American Culture and History* (1996); Jessie Carney Smith, ed., *Notable Black American Women* (1992). See also "Slavery."

American Revolution and Colonies

Ian Barnes, *The Historical Atlas of the American Revolution* (2000); Richard Blanco and Paul Sanborn, eds., *The American Revolution* (1993); Lester J. Cappon, ed., *Atlas of Early American History: The Revolutionary Era, 1760–1790* (1976); Jacob E. Cooke, ed., *Encyclopedia of the American Colonies* (1993); John M. Faragher, ed., *The Encyclopedia of Colonial and Revolutionary America* (1990); Jack P. Greene and J. R. Pole, eds., *The Blackwell Encyclopedia of the American Revolution* (1991); Gregory Palmer, ed., *Biographical Sketches of Loyalists of the American Revolution* (1984); John W. Raimo, ed., *Biographical Directory of American Colonial and Revolutionary Governors, 1607–1789* (1980); *Rand-McNally Atlas of the American Revolution* (1974); Seymour I. Schwartz, *The French and Indian War, 1754–1763* (1995).

Architecture

William D. Hunt, Jr., ed., *Encyclopedia of American Architecture* (1980).

Asian Americans

Monique Avakian, *Atlas of Asian-American History* (2001); Hyung-Chan Kim, ed., *Dictionary of Asian American History* (1986); Brian Niiya, ed., *Japanese American History* (1993); Lynn Pan, ed., *The Encyclopedia of the Chinese Overseas* (1999). See also "Immigration and Ethnic Groups."

Business and the Economy

Christine Ammer and Dean S. Ammer, *Dictionary of Business and Economics* (1983); Douglas Auld and Graham Bannock, *The American Dictionary of Economics* (1983); Michael J. Freeman, *Atlas of World Economy* (1991); John N. Ingham, *Biographical Dictionary of American Business Leaders* (1983); John N. Ingham and Lynne B. Feldman, *Contemporary American Business Leaders* (1990); Neil A. Hamilton, *American Business Leaders* (1999); William H. Mulligan, Jr., ed., *A Historical Dictionary of American Industrial Language* (1988); Paul Paskoff, ed., *Encyclopedia of American Business History and Biography* (1989); Glenn Porter, *Encyclopedia of American Economic History* (1980); Richard Robinson, *United States Business History, 1602–1988* (1990); Malcolm Warner, ed., *International Encyclopedia of Business and Management* (1996). See also "African Americans," "Native Americans and Indian Affairs," and "Transportation."

Cities and Towns

John L. Androit, ed., *Township Atlas of the United States* (1979); David J. Bodenhamer and Robert J. Barrows, eds., *The Encyclopedia of Indianapolis* (1994); *The Comparative Guide to American Suburbs* (2001); Gary A. Goreham, ed., *Encyclopedia of Rural America* (1997); Melvin G. Holli and Peter d'A. Jones, eds., *Biographical Dictionary of American Mayors, 1820–1980: Big City Mayors* (1981); Eric Homberger and Alice Hudson, *The Historical Atlas of New York City* (1998); Kenneth T. Jackson, ed., *Encyclopedia of New York City* (1995); John E. Kleber et al., eds., *The Encyclopedia of Louisville* (2000); George T. Kurian, *World Encyclopedia of Cities* (1994); Ory M. Nergal, ed., *The Encyclopedia of American Cities* (1980); Neil Larry Shumsky, ed., *Encyclopedia of Urban America* (1998); David D. Van Tassel and John J. Grabowski, eds., *The Dictionary of Cleveland Biography* (1996); David D. Van Tassel and John J. Grabowski, eds., *The Encyclopedia of Cleveland History* (1987). See also "Politics and Government."

Civil War and Reconstruction

Mark M. Boatner III, *The Civil War Dictionary* (1988); Richard N. Current, ed., *Encyclopedia of the Confederacy* (1993); John T. Hubbell and James W. Geary, eds., *Biographical Dictionary of the Union* (1995); Kenneth C. Martis, *The Historical Atlas of the Congresses of the Confederate States of America: 1861–1865* (1994); James M. McPherson, ed., *The Atlas of the Civil War* (1994); Mark E. Neely, Jr., *The Abraham Lincoln Encyclopedia* (1982); Craig L. Symonds, *A Battlefield Atlas of the Civil War* (1983); Hans L. Trefousse, *Historical Dictionary of Reconstruction* (1991); U.S. War Department, *The Official Atlas of the Civil War* (1958); Jon L. Wakelyn, ed., *Biographical Dictionary of the Confederacy* (1977); Ezra J. Warner and W. Buck Yearns, *Biographical Register of the Confederate Congress* (1975); Steven E. Woodworth, ed., *The American Civil War* (1996). See also "South" and "Politics and Government."

The Cold War

Thomas S. Arms, *Encyclopedia of the Cold War* (1994); Michael Kort, *The Columbia Guide to the Cold War* (1998); Thomas Parrish, *The Cold War Encyclopedia* (1996); Richard A. Schwartz, *Cold War Culture: The Media and the Arts* (1998); Joseph Smith and Simon Davis, *Historical Dictionary of the Cold War* (2000); Brandon Toropov, *Encyclopedia of Cold War Politics* (2000). See also "Foreign Relations" and "Military and Wars."

Constitution, Supreme Court, and Judiciary

David Bradley and Shelly F. Fishkin, eds., *The Encyclopedia of Civil Rights* (1997); Congressional Quarterly, *The Supreme Court A to Z* (1994); Kermit L. Hall, ed., *The Oxford Companion to the Supreme Court of the United States* (1992); Kermit L. Hall, ed., *The Oxford Guide to United States Supreme Court Decisions* (1999); Richard F. Hixson, *Mass Media and the Con-*

stitution (1989); Robert J. Janosik, ed., *Encyclopedia of the American Judicial System* (1987); John W. Johnson, ed., *Historic U.S. Court Cases* (2001); Leonard W. Levy et al., eds., *Encyclopedia of the American Constitution* (1986); Fred R. Shapiro, *The Oxford Dictionary of American Legal Quotations* (1993); Melvin I. Urofsky, ed., *The Supreme Court Justices* (1994). See also "Politics and Government" and "Sexuality."

Crime, Violence, Police, and Prisons

William G. Bailey, *Encyclopedia of Police Science* (1994); Marilyn D. McShane and Frank P. Williams III, eds., *Encyclopedia of American Prisons* (1995); Michael Newton and Judy Ann Newton, *Racial and Religious Violence in America* (1991); Michael Newton and Judy Newton, *The Ku Klux Klan* (1990); Carl Sifakis, *Encyclopedia of Assassinations* (2001); Carl Sifakis, *The Encyclopedia of American Crime* (2000); Carl Sifakis, *The Mafia Encyclopedia* (1999).

Culture and Folklore

Jan Harold Brunvald, *American Folklore* (1996); Mary K. Cayton and Peter W. Williams, eds., *Encyclopedia of American Cultural and Intellectual History* (2001); Hennig Cohen and Tristam Potter Coffin, eds., *The Folklore of American Holidays* (1987); Richard M. Dorson, ed., *Handbook of American Folklore* (1983); Robert L. Gale, *A Cultural Encyclopedia of the 1850s in America* (1993); Robert L. Gale, *The Gay Nineties in America* (1992); M. Thomas Inge, ed., *Handbook of American Popular Culture* (1979–1981); Wolfgang Mieder et al., eds., *A Dictionary of American Proverbs* (1992); J. F. Rooney, Jr., et al., eds., *This Remarkable Continent: An Atlas of United States and Canadian Society and Cultures* (1982); Jane Stern and Michael Stern, *Encyclopedia of Pop Culture* (1992); Justin Wintle, ed., *Makers of Nineteenth Century Culture, 1800–1914* (1982). See also "The Cold War," "Entertainment and the Arts," "Mass Media and Journalism," "Music," and "Sports."

Education and Libraries

Lee C. Deighton, ed., *The Encyclopedia of Education* (1971); Joseph C. Kiger, ed., *Research Institutions and Learned Societies* (1982); John F. Ohles, ed., *Biographical Dictionary of American Educators* (1978); Wayne A. Wiegard and Donald E. Davis, Jr., eds., *Encyclopedia of Library History* (1994).

Entertainment and the Arts

Tim Brooks and Earle Marsh, *The Complete Directory to Prime Time Network and Cable TV Shows, 1946–Present* (1999); Barbara N. Cohen-Stratyner, *Biographical Dictionary of Dance* (1982); John Dunning, *Tune in Yesterday* (radio)

(1967); Larry Langman and Edgar Borg, *Encyclopedia of American War Films* (1989); Larry Langman and David Ebner, *Encyclopedia of American Spy Films* (1990); Don Rubin, *World Encyclopedia of Contemporary Theatre: The Americas* (2000); Andrew Sarris, *The American Cinema: Directors and Directions, 1929–1968* (1968); Anthony Slide, *The American Film Industry* (1986); Anthony Slide, *The Encyclopedia of Vaudeville* (1994); Evelyn M. Truitt, *Who Was Who on Screen* (1984); Don B. Wilmeth and Tice L. Miller, eds., *The Cambridge Guide to American Theatre* (1993). See also "The Cold War," "Culture and Folklore," "Mass Media and Journalism," "Music," and "Sports."

Environment and Conservation

André R. Cooper, ed., *Cooper's Comprehensive Environmental Desk Reference* (1996); Forest History Society, *Encyclopedia of American Forest and Conservation History* (1983); Irene Franck and David Brownstone, *The Green Encyclopedia* (1992); Robert J. Mason and Mark T. Mattson, *Atlas of United States Environmental Issues* (1990); Robert Paehlke, ed., *Conservation and Environmentalism* (1995); World Resources Institute, *Environmental Almanac* (1992).

Exploration: From Columbus to Space

Silvio A. Bedini, ed., *The Christopher Columbus Encyclopedia* (1992); Michael Cassutt, *Who's Who in Space* (1987); W. P. Cumming et al., *The Discovery of North America* (1972); William Goetzmann and Glyndwr Williams, *The Atlas of North American Exploration* (1992); Clive Holland, *Arctic Exploration and Development* (1993); Adrian Johnson, *America Explored* (1974); Kenneth Nebenzahl, *Atlas of Columbus and the Great Discoveries* (1990). See also "Science and Technology."

Foreign Relations

Gérard Chaliand and Jean-Pierre Rageau, *Strategic Atlas* (1990); Alexander DeConde, ed., *Encyclopedia of American Foreign Policy* (1978); Margaret B. Denning and J. K. Sweeney, *Handbook of American Diplomacy* (1992); Graham Evans and Jeffrey Newnham, *The Penguin Dictionary of International Relations* (1999); John E. Findling, *Dictionary of American Diplomatic History* (1989); Chas. W. Freeman, Jr., *The Diplomat's Dictionary* (1999); Don Smith and Michael Kidron, *The State of the World Atlas* (1995); Bruce W. Jentleson and Thomas G. Paterson, eds., *Encyclopedia of U.S. Foreign Relations* (1997); Warren F. Kuehl, ed., *Biographical Dictionary of Internationalists* (1983); Edward Lawson, *Encyclopedia of Human Rights* (1991); Jack C. Plano and Roy Olton, eds., *The International Relations Dictionary* (1988). See also "The Cold War," "Peace Movements and Pacifism,"

"Politics and Government," "Military and Wars," and specific wars.

Hispanics

Nicolás Kanellos, ed., *The Hispanic-American Almanac* (1993); Nicolás Kanellos, ed., *Reference Library of Hispanic America* (1993); Francisco Lomelí, ed., *Handbook of Hispanic Cultures in the United States* (1993); Matt S. Meier, *Mexican-American Biographies* (1988); Matt S. Meier, *Notable Latino Americans* (1997); Matt S. Meier and Feliciano Rivera, *Dictionary of Mexican American History* (1981); Joseph C. Tardiff and L. Mpho Mabunda, eds., *Dictionary of Hispanic Biography* (1996). See also "Immigration and Ethnic Groups."

Immigration and Ethnic Groups

James P. Allen and Eugene J. Turner, *We the People: Atlas of America's Ethnic Diversity* (1988); Gerald Chaliand and Jean-Pierre Rageau, *The Penguin Atlas of Diasporas* (1995); Francesco Cordasco, ed., *Dictionary of American Immigration History* (1990); Salvatore J. LaGumina et al., eds., *The Italian American Experience* (2000); David Levinson and Melvin Ember, eds., *American Immigrant Cultures* (1997); Judy B. Litoff and Judith McDonnell, eds., *European Immigrant Women in the United States* (1994); Sally M. Miller, ed., *The Ethnic Press in the United States* (1987); Stephan Thernstrom, ed., *Harvard Encyclopedia of American Ethnic Groups* (1980); Rudolph J. Vecoli et al., eds., *Gale Encyclopedia of Multicultural America* (1995). See also "Asian Americans," "Jewish Americans," and "Hispanics."

Jewish Americans

American Jewish Yearbook (1899–); Jack Fischel and Sanford Pinsker, eds., *Jewish-American History and Culture* (1992); E. Paula Hyman and Deborah Dash Moore, eds., *Jewish Women in America* (1998); Geoffrey Wigoder, *Dictionary of Jewish Biography* (1991). See also "Immigration and Ethnic Groups."

Labor

Ronald L. Filippelli, *Labor Conflict in the United States* (1990); Gary M. Fink, ed., *Biographical Dictionary of American Labor* (1984); Gary M. Fink, ed., *Labor Unions* (1977); Philip S. Foner, *First Facts of American Labor* (1984).

Literature

James T. Callow and Robert J. Reilly, *Guide to American Literature* (1976–1977); *Dictionary of Literary Biography* (1978–); Eugene Ehrlich and Gorton Carruth, *The Oxford Illustrated Literary Guide to the United States* (1992); Jon Tuska and Vicki Piekarski, *Encyclopedia of Frontier and Western Fiction* (1983). See also "Culture and Folklore," "The South," and "Women."

Mass Media and Journalism

Robert V. Hudson, *Mass Media* (1987); Joseph P. McKerns, ed., *Biographical Dictionary of American Journalism* (1989); Michael D. Murray, ed., *Encyclopedia of Television News* (1998); William H. Taft, ed., *Encyclopedia of Twentieth-Century Journalists* (1986). See also "The Cold War," "Constitution, Supreme Court, and Judiciary," "Entertainment and the Arts," and "Immigration and Ethnic Groups."

Medicine and Nursing

Rima D. Apple, ed., *Women, Health, and Medicine in America* (1990); Vern L. Bullough et al., eds., *American Nursing: A Biographical Dictionary* (1988); Martin Kaufman et al., eds., *Dictionary of American Nursing Biography* (1988); Martin Kaufman et al., eds., *Dictionary of American Medical Biography* (1984); George L. Maddox, ed., *The Encyclopedia of Aging* (1995).

Military and Wars

William M. Arkin et al., *Encyclopedia of the U.S. Military* (1990); Charles D. Bright, ed., *Historical Dictionary of the U.S. Air Force* (1992); John W. Chambers, ed., *Oxford Companion to United States Military History* (2000); Andre Corvisier, ed., *A Dictionary of Military History* (1994); R. Ernest Dupuy and Trevor N. Dupuy, *The Harper Encyclopedia of Military History* (1993); David S. Frazier, ed., *The United States and Mexico at War* (1998); John E. Jessup, ed., *Encyclopedia of the American Military* (1994); Kenneth Macksey and William Woodhouse, *The Penguin Encyclopedia of Modern Warfare* (1992); Franklin D. Margiotta, ed., *Brassey's Encyclopedia of Naval Forces and Warfare* (1996); David F. Marley, *Pirates and Privateers of the Americas* (1994); James I. Matray, ed., *Historical Dictionary of the Korean War* (1991); Stanley Sandler, ed., *The Korean War* (1995); Roger J. Spiller and Joseph G. Dawson III, eds., *Dictionary of American Military Biography* (1984); Jerry K. Sweeney, ed., *A Handbook of American Military History* (1996); Peter G. Tsouras et al., *The United States Army* (1991); U.S. Military Academy, *The West Point Atlas of American Wars, 1689–1953* (1959); Bruce W. Watson et al., eds., *United States Intelligence* (1990); Bruce W. Watson and Susan M. Watson, *The United States Air Force* (1992); Bruce W. Watson and Susan M. Watson, *The United States Navy* (1991). See also "American Revolution and Colonies," "Civil War and Reconstruction," "The Cold War," "Vietnam War," and "World War II."

Music

John Chilton, *Who's Who of Jazz* (1985); Donald Clarke et al., eds., *The Penguin Encyclopedia of Popular Music* (1999); Edward Jablonski, *The Encyclopedia of American Music* (1981); Ellen Koskoff, *Garland Encyclopedia of World Music: The United States and Canada* (2000); Roger Lax and Frederick Smith, *The Great Song Thesaurus* (1989); Philip D. Morehead, *The New International Dictionary of Music* (1993); Austin Sonnier, Jr., *A Guide to the Blues* (1994). See also "Culture and Folklore" and "Entertainment and the Arts."

Native Americans and Indian Affairs

Gretchen M. Bataille, ed., *Native American Women* (1992); Michael Coe et al., *Atlas of Ancient America* (1986); Mary B. Davis, ed., *Native America in the Twentieth Century* (1994); Rayna Green, *The British Museum Encyclopedia of Native North America* (1999); *Handbook of North American Indians* (1978–); Sam D. Gill and Irene F. Sullivan, *Dictionary of Native American Mythology* (1992); J. Norman Heard et al., *Handbook of the American Frontier: Four Centuries of Indian–White Relationships* (1987–); Bruce E. Johansen, ed., *The Encyclopedia of Native American Economic History* (1999); Bruce E. Johansen, ed., *The Encyclopedia of Native American Legal Tradition* (1998); Bruce E. Johansen et al., eds., *The Encyclopedia of Native American Biography* (1997); Barry Klein, ed., *Reference Encyclopedia of the American Indian* (1993); Richard B. Lee and Richard Daly, eds., *The Cambridge Encyclopedia of Hunters and Gatherers* (2000); Barry M. Plitzker, ed., *A Native American Encyclopedia* (2000); Francis P. Prucha, *Atlas of American Indian Affairs* (1990); Carl Waldman, *Encyclopedia of Native American Tribes* (1988); Carl Waldman, *Atlas of the North American Indian* (2000).

The New Deal and Franklin D. Roosevelt

Otis L. Graham, Jr., and Meghan R. Wander, eds., *Franklin D. Roosevelt: His Life and Times* (1985); James S. Olson, ed., *Historical Dictionary of the New Deal* (1985). See also "Politics and Government."

Peace Movements and Pacifism

Harold Josephson et al., eds., *Biographical Dictionary of Modern Peace Leaders* (1985); Ervin Laszlo and Jong Y. Yoo, eds., *World Encyclopedia of Peace* (1986); Robert S. Meyer, *Peace Organizations Past and Present* (1988); Nancy L. Roberts, *American Peace Writers, Editors, and Periodicals* (1991). See also "Foreign Relations," "Military and Wars," and specific wars.

Politics and Government: General

J. Clark Archer et al., *Atlas of American Politics, 1960–2000* (2001); Erik W. Austin and Jerome M. Clubb, *Political Facts of the United States Since 1789* (1986); *The Columbia Dictionary of Political Biography* (1991); Jack P. Greene, ed., *Encyclopedia of American Political History* (1984); Leon Hurwitz, *Historical Dictionary of Censorship in the United States* (1985); George T. Kurian, ed., *A Historical Guide to the U.S. Government* (1998); John J. Patrick et al., *The Oxford Guide to the United States Government* (2001); Jack Plano, *The American Political Dictionary* (2001); Philip Rees, *Biographical Dictionary of the Extreme Right Since 1890* (1991); Charles R. Ritter et al., *American Legislative Leaders, 1850–1910* (1989); William Safire, *Safire's Political Dictionary* (1993); Robert Scruton, *A Dictionary of Political Thought* (1982); Jay M. Shafritz, *The HarperCollins Dictionary of American Government and Politics* (1992). See also "Cities and Towns," "Constitution, Supreme Court, and Judiciary," "States," and the following sections.

Politics and Government: Congress

American Enterprise Institute, *Vital Statistics on Congress* (1980–); Donald C. Brown et al., eds., *The Encyclopedia of the United States Congress* (1995); Stephen G. Christianson, *Facts About the Congress* (1996); Congressional Quarterly, *Biographical Directory of the American Congress, 1774–1996* (1997); Congressional Quarterly, *Congress and the Nation* (1965–); Kenneth C. Martis, *Historical Atlas of Political Parties in the United States Congress, 1789–1989* (1989); Kenneth C. Martis, *Historical Atlas of United States Congressional Districts, 1789–1983* (1982); Joel H. Silbey, ed., *Encyclopedia of the American Legislative System* (1994).

Politics and Government: Election Statistics

Congressional Quarterly, *Guide to U.S. Elections* (1994); Congressional Quarterly, *Presidential Elections, 1789–1996* (1997); L. Sandy Maisel, ed., *Political Parties and Elections in the United States* (1991); Yanek Mieczkowski, *The Routledge Historical Atlas of Presidential Elections* (2001); Svend Petersen and Louis Filler, *A Statistical History of the American Presidential Elections* (1981); Richard M. Scammon et al., eds., *America Votes* (1956–); Harold W. Stanley and Richard G. Niemi, *Vital Statistics on American Politics* (1988–); Lyn Ragsdale, *Vital Statistics on the Presidency* (1998); G. Scott Thomas, *The Pursuit of the White House* (1987).

Politics and Government: Parties

Earl R. Kruschke, *Encyclopedia of Third Parties in the United States* (1991); George T. Kurian, ed., *The Encyclopedia of the Republican Party* and *The Encyclopedia of the Democratic Party* (1996); Edward L. Schapsmeier and Frederick H. Schapsmeier, eds., *Political Parties and Civic Action Groups* (1981). See also other listings for "Politics and Government."

Politics and Government: Presidency and Executive Branch

Alan Brinkley and Davis Dyer, eds., *The Reader's Companion to the American Presidency* (2000); Henry F. Graff, *The Presidents* (1996); Mark Grossman, *Encyclopedia of the United States Cabinet* (2000); Bernard S. Katz and C. Daniel Vencill, eds., *Biographical Dictionary of the United States Secretaries of the Treasury, 1789–1995* (1996); Richard S. Kirkendall, ed., *The Harry S Truman Encyclopedia* (1989); Leonard W. Levy and Louis Fisher, eds., *Encyclopedia of the American Presidency* (1993); Merrill D. Peterson, ed., *Thomas Jefferson* (1986); Lyn Ragsdale, *Vital Statistics on the Presidency* (1998); Robert A. Rutland, ed., *James Madison and the American Nation* (1995); Robert Sobel, ed., *Biographical Directory of the United States Executive Branch, 1774–1977* (1977). See other categories for various presidents.

Politics and Government: Radicalism and the Left

Mari Jo Buhle et al., eds., *The American Radical* (1994); Mari Jo Buhle et al., eds., *Encyclopedia of the American Left* (1998); David DeLeon, ed., *Leaders of the 1960s* (1994); Bernard K. Johnpoll and Harvey Klehr, eds., *Biographical Dictionary of the American Left* (1986).

Religion and Cults

Henry Bowden, *Dictionary of American Religious Biography* (1993); S. Kent Brown et al., eds., *Historical Atlas of Mormonism* (1995); Bret Carroll, *The Routledge Historical Atlas of Religion in America* (2001); Edwin Gaustad and Philip L. Barlow, *New Historical Atlas of Religion in America* (1998); Michael Glazier and Thomas J. Shelley, eds., *The Encyclopedia of American Catholic History* (1997); Bill J. Leonard, *Dictionary of Baptists in America* (1994); Donald Lewis, ed., *A Dictionary of Evangelical Biography* (1995); Charles H. Lippy and Peter W. Williams, eds., *Encyclopedia of the American Religious Experience* (1988); J. Gordon Melton, *The Encyclopedia of American Religions* (1992); J. Gordon Melton, *The Encyclopedic Handbook of Cults in America* (1992); Mark A. Noll and Nathan O. Hatch, eds., *Eerdman's Handbook to Christianity in America* (1983); Stephen R. Prothero et al., *The Encyclopedia of American Religious History* (1996); Wade C. Roof, ed., *Contemporary American Religion* (2000); Paul J. Weber and W. Landis Jones, *U.S. Religious Interest Groups* (1994). See also "African Americans" and "South."

Science and Technology

James W. Cortada, *Historical Dictionary of Data Processing* (1987); Clark A. Elliott, *Biographical Index to American Science: The Seventeenth Century to 1920* (1990); Charles C. Gillespie et al., eds., *Dictionary of Scientific Biography* (1970–); Na-

tional Academy of Sciences, *Biographical Memoirs* (1877–); Roy Porter, ed., *The Biographical Dictionary of Scientists* (1994). See also "Exploration."

Sexuality

Robert T. Francoeur, ed., *The International Encyclopedia of Sexuality* (1998); Wayne R. Dynes, ed., *Encyclopedia of Homosexuality* (1990); Steve Hogan and Lee Hudson, *Completely Queer: The Gay and Lesbian Encyclopedia* (1998); Arthur S. Leonard, ed., *Sexuality and the Law* (1993); Neil Schlager, ed., *Gay & Lesbian Almanac* (1998); Michael J. Tyrkus, ed., *Gay & Lesbian Biography* (1997); Bonnie Zimmerman and George Haggerty, eds., *Encyclopedia of Lesbian and Gay Histories and Cultures* (1999). See also "Social History and Reform."

Slavery

Seymour Drescher and Stanley L. Engerman, eds., *A Historical Guide to World Slavery* (1998); Paul Finkelman and Joseph C. Miller, eds., *Macmillan Encyclopedia of World Slavery* (1998); Randall M. Miller and John D. Smith, eds., *Dictionary of Afro-American Slavery* (1997); Junius P. Rodriguez, ed., *The Historical Encyclopedia of World Slavery* (1997). See also "African Americans."

Social History and Reform

Mary K. Cayton et al., eds., *Encyclopedia of American Social History* (1993); Louis Filler, *Dictionary of American Social Change* (1982); Robert S. Fogarty, *Dictionary of American Communal and Utopian History* (1980); Joseph M. Hawes and Elizabeth I. Nybakken, eds., *American Families* (1991); David Hey, ed., *The Oxford Companion to Local and Family History* (1996); Harold M. Keele and Joseph C. Kiger, eds., *Foundations* (1984); Mark E. Lender, *Dictionary of American Temperance Biography* (1984); Patricia M. Melvin, ed., *American Community Organizations* (1986); Randall M. Miller and Paul A. Cimbala, eds., *American Reform and Reformers* (1996); Roger S. Powers and William B. Vogele, eds., *Protest, Power, and Change* (1996); Alvin J. Schmidt, *Fraternal Organizations* (1980); Peter N. Stearns, ed., *Encyclopedia of Social History* (1993); Walter I. Trattner, *Biographical Dictionary of Social Welfare in America* (1986). See also "Crime, Violence, Police, and Prisons" and "Sexuality."

South

Edward L. Ayers and Brad Mittendorf, eds., *The Oxford Book of the American South* (1997); Robert Bain et al., eds., *Southern Writers* (1979); Kenneth Coleman and Charles S. Gurr, eds., *Dictionary of Georgia Biography* (1983); Andrew Frank, *The Routledge Historical Atlas of the American South* (1999);

Samuel S. Hill, ed., *Encyclopedia of Religion in the South* (1998); William S. Powell, ed., *Dictionary of North Carolina Biography* (1979–1996); David C. Roller and Robert W. Twyman, eds., *The Encyclopedia of Southern History* (1979); A. Ray Stephens and William M. Holmes, *Historical Atlas of Texas* (1990); James M. Volo and Dorothy D. Volo, *Encyclopedia of the Antebellum South* (2000); Walter P. Webb et al., eds., *The Handbook of Texas* (1952, 1976); Charles R. Wilson et al., eds., *Encyclopedia of Southern Culture* (1989). See also "Civil War and Reconstruction," "Politics and Government," and "States."

Sports

Peter C. Bjarkman, ed., *Encyclopedia of Major League Baseball Team Histories* (1991); Ralph Hickok, *A Who's Who of Sports Champions* (1995); Ralph Hickok, *The Encyclopedia of North American Sports History* (1991); David Levinson and Karen Christensen, eds., *Encyclopedia of World Sport* (1996); Jonathan F. Light, *The Cultural Encyclopedia of Baseball* (1997); David L. Porter, *Biographical Dictionary of American Sports: Baseball* (2000), *Basketball and Other Indoor Sports* (1989), *Football* (1987), and *Outdoor Sports* (1988); Victoria Sherrow, *Encyclopedia of Women and Sports* (1996); David Wallechinsky, *The Complete Book of the Summer Olympics* (1996); David Wallechinsky, *The Complete Book of the Winter Olympics* (1993). See also "Culture and Folklore."

States

Gary Alampi, ed., *Gale State Rankings Reporter* (1994); Roy R. Glashan, comp., *American Governors and Gubernatorial Elections, 1775–1978* (1979); John Hoffmann, ed., *A Guide to the History of Illinois* (1991); Edith R. Hornor, *Almanac of the Fifty States* (1997); Joseph E. Kallenback and Jessamine S. Kallenback, *American State Governors, 1776–1976* (1977); Joseph N. Kane et al., eds., *Facts About the States* (1994); John E. Kleber et al., eds., *The Kentucky Encyclopedia* (1992); Thomas A. McMullin and Marie Mullaney, *Biographical Directory of the Governors of the United States, 1983–1987* (1988) and *1988–1993* (1994); Marie Mullaney, *Biographical Directory of the Governors of the United States, 1988–1994* (1994); Thomas J. Noel, *Historical Atlas of Colorado* (1994); John W. Raimo, ed., *Biographical Directory of the Governors of the United States, 1978–1983* (1985); James W. Scott and Ronald L. De Lorme, *Historical Atlas of Washington* (1988); Benjamin F. Shearer and Barbara S. Shearer, *State Names, Seals, Flags, and Symbols* (1994); Robert Sobel and John W. Raimo, eds., *Biographical Directory of the Governors of the United States, 1789–1978* (1978); Richard W. Wilkie and Jack Tager, eds., *Historical Atlas of Massachusetts* (1991). See also "Politics and Government," "South," and "West and Frontier."

Transportation

Keith L. Bryant, ed., *Railroads in the Age of Regulation, 1900–1980* (1988); Rene De La Pedraja, *A Historical Dictionary of the U.S. Merchant Marine and Shipping Industry* (1994); Robert L. Frey, ed., *Railroads in the Nineteenth Century* (1988); John Stover, *The Routledge Historical Atlas of the American Railroads* (1999). See also "Business and the Economy."

Vietnam War

John S. Bowman, ed., *The Vietnam War: An Almanac* (1986); Stanley I. Kutler, ed., *Encyclopedia of the Vietnam War* (1996); James S. Olson, ed., *Dictionary of the Vietnam War* (1988); Harry G. Summers, Jr., *Vietnam War Almanac* (1985); Spencer C. Tucker, ed., *Encyclopedia of the Vietnam War* (2000). Also see "Peace Movements and Pacifism" and "Military and Wars."

West and Frontier

William A. Beck and Ynez D. Haase, *Historical Atlas of the American West* (1989); Doris O. Dawdy, *Artists of the American West* (1974–1984); J. Norman Heard, *Handbook of the American Frontier* (1987); Howard R. Lamar, ed., *The New Encyclopedia of the American West* (1998); Clyde A. Milner III et al., eds., *The Oxford History of the American West* (1994); Jay Robert Nash, *Encyclopedia of Western Lawmen and Outlaws* (1992); Doyce B. Nunis, Jr., and Gloria R. Lothrop, eds., *A Guide to the History of California* (1989); Charles Phillips and Alan Axelrod, eds., *Encyclopedia of the American West* (1996); Dan L. Thrapp, *The Encyclopedia of Frontier Biography* (1988–1994); David Walker, *Biographical Directory of American Territorial Governors* (1984). See also "Cities and Towns," "Literature," and "Native Americans and Indian Affairs."

Women

Anne Gibson and Timothy Fast, *The Women's Atlas of the United States* (1986); Karen Greenspan, *The Timetables of Women's History* (1996); Maggie Humm, *The Dictionary of Feminist Theory* (1990); Edward T. James et al., *Notable American Women, 1607–1950* (1971); Lina Mainiero, ed., *American Women Writers* (1979–1982); Wilma Mankiller et al., *The Reader's Companion to U.S. Women's History* (1998); Kirstin Olsen, *Chronology of Women's History* (1994); Sandra Opdycke, *The Routledge Historical Atlas of Women in America* (2000); Barbara G. Shortridge, *Atlas of American Women* (1987); Barbara Sicherman and Carol H. Green, eds., *Notable American Women, The Modern Period* (1980); Helen Tierney, ed., *Women's Studies Encyclopedia* (1991); James Trager, *The Women's Chronology* (1994); Angela H. Zophy and Frances M. Kavenik, eds., *Handbook of American*

Women's History (1990). See also "African Americans," "Immigration and Ethnic Groups," "Medicine and Nursing," "Native Americans and Indian Affairs," and "Sports."

World War I

David F. Burg and L. Edward Purcell, *Almanac of World War I* (1998); Martin Gilbert, *Atlas of World War I* (1994); Holger H. Herwig and Neil M. Heyman, *Biographical Dictionary of World War I* (1982); George T. Kurian, *Encyclopedia of the First World War* (1990); Stephen Pope and Elizabeth-Anne Wheal, *The Dictionary of the First World War* (1995); U.S. Military Academy, *The West Point Atlas of American Wars: 1900–1918* (1997); Anne C. Venzon, *The United States in the First World War* (1995). See also "Military and Wars."

World War II

David G. Chandler and James Lawton Collins, Jr., eds., *The D-Day Encyclopedia* (1993); I. C. B. Dear and M. R. D. Foot, eds., *The Oxford Companion to World War II* (1995); Simon Goodenough, *War Maps: Great Land Battles of World War II* (1988); Robert Goralski, *World War II Almanac* (1981); John Keegan, ed., *The Times Atlas of the Second World War* (1989); George T. Kurian, *Encyclopedia of the Second World War* (1991); Norman Polmer and Thomas B. Allen, *World War II: America at War* (1991); U.S. Military Academy, *Campaign Atlas to the Second World War: Europe and the Mediterranean* (1980); Peter Young, ed., *The World Almanac Book of World War II* (1981). See also "Military and Wars."

Documents

DECLARATION OF INDEPENDENCE IN CONGRESS, JULY 4, 1776

When, in the course of human events, it becomes necessary for one people to dissolve the political bonds which have connected them with another, and to assume, among the powers of the earth, the separate and equal station to which the laws of nature and of nature's God entitle them, a decent respect to the opinions of mankind requires that they should declare the causes which impel them to the separation.

We hold these truths to be self-evident: That all men are created equal; that they are endowed by their Creator with certain unalienable rights; that among these are life, liberty, and the pursuit of happiness; that, to secure these rights, governments are instituted among men, deriving their just powers from the consent of the governed; that whenever any form of government becomes destructive of these ends, it is the right of the people to alter or to abolish it, and to institute new government, laying its foundation on such principles, and organizing its powers in such form, as to them shall seem most likely to effect their safety and happiness. Prudence, indeed, will dictate that governments long established should not be changed for light and transient causes; and accordingly all experience hath shown that mankind are more disposed to suffer, while evils are sufferable, than to right themselves by abolishing the forms to which they are accustomed. But when a long train of abuses and usurpations, pursuing invariably the same object, evinces a design to reduce them under absolute despotism, it is their right, it is their duty, to throw off such government, and to provide new guards for their future security. Such has been the patient sufferance of these colonies; and such is now the necessity which constrains them to alter their former systems of government. The history of the present King of Great Britain is a history of repeated injuries and usurpations, all having in direct object the establishment of an absolute tyranny over these states. To prove this, let facts be submitted to a candid world.

He has refused his assent to laws, the most wholesome and necessary for the public good.

He has forbidden his governors to pass laws of immediate and pressing importance, unless suspended in their operation till his assent should be obtained; and, when so suspended, he has utterly neglected to attend to them.

He has refused to pass other laws for the accommodation of large districts of people, unless those people would relinquish the right of representation in the legislature, a right inestimable to them, and formidable to tyrants only.

He has called together legislative bodies at places unusual, uncomfortable, and distant from the depository of their public records, for the sole purpose of fatiguing them into compliance with his measures.

He has dissolved representative houses repeatedly, for opposing, with manly firmness, his invasions on the rights of the people.

He has refused for a long time, after such dissolutions, to cause others to be elected; whereby the legislative powers, incapable of annihilation, have returned to the people at large for their exercise; the state remaining, in the mean time, exposed to all the dangers of invasions from without and convulsions within.

He has endeavored to prevent the population of these states; for that purpose obstructing the laws for naturalization of foreigners; refusing to pass others to encourage their migration hither, and raising the conditions of new appropriations of lands.

He has obstructed the administration of justice, by refusing his assent to laws for establishing judiciary powers.

He has made judges dependent on his will alone, for the tenure of their offices, and the amount and payment of their salaries.

He has erected a multitude of new offices, and sent hither swarms of officers to harass our people and eat out their substance.

He has kept among us, in times of peace, standing armies, without the consent of our legislatures.

He has affected to render the military independent of, and superior to, the civil power.

He has combined with others to subject us to a jurisdiction foreign to our constitution, and unacknowledged by our laws, giving his assent to their acts of pretended legislation:

For quartering large bodies of armed troops among us;

For protecting them, by a mock trial, from punishment for any murders which they should commit on the inhabitants of these states;

For cutting off our trade with all parts of the world;

For imposing taxes on us without our consent;

For depriving us, in many cases, of the benefits of trial by jury;

For transporting us beyond seas, to be tried for pretended offenses;

For abolishing the free system of English laws in a neighboring province, establishing therein an arbitrary government, and enlarging its boundaries, so as to render it at once an example and fit instrument for introducing the same absolute rule into these colonies;

For taking away our charters, abolishing our most valuable laws, and altering fundamentally the forms of our governments;

For suspending our own legislatures, and declaring themselves invested with power to legislate for us in all cases whatsoever.

He has abdicated government here, by declaring us out of his protection and waging war against us.

He has plundered our seas, ravaged our coasts, burned our towns, and destroyed the lives of our people.

He is at this time transporting large armies of foreign mercenaries to complete the works of death, desolation, and tyranny already begun with circumstances of cruelty and perfidy scarcely paralleled in the most barbarous ages, and totally unworthy the head of a civilized nation.

He has constrained our fellow-citizens, taken captive on the high seas, to bear arms against their country, to become the executioners of their friends and brethren, or to fall themselves by their hands.

He has excited domestic insurrection among us, and has endeavored to bring on the inhabitants of our frontiers the merciless Indian savages, whose known rule of warfare is an undistinguished destruction of all ages, sexes, and conditions.

In every stage of these oppressions we have petitioned for redress in the most humble terms; our repeated petitions have been answered only by repeated injury. A prince, whose character is thus marked by every act which may define a tyrant, is unfit to be the ruler of a free people.

Nor have we been wanting in our attentions to our British brethren. We have warned them, from time to time, of attempts by their legislature to extend an unwarrantable jurisdiction over us. We have reminded them of the circumstances of our emigration and settlement here. We have appealed to their native justice and magnanimity; and we have conjured them, by the ties of our common kindred, to disavow these usurpations, which would inevitably interrupt our connections and correspondence. They, too, have been deaf to the voice of justice and of consanguinity. We must, therefore, acquiesce in the necessity which denounces our separation, and hold them, as we hold the rest of mankind, enemies in war, in peace friends.

We, therefore, the representatives of the United States of America, in General Congress assembled, appealing to the Supreme Judge of the world for the rectitude of our intentions, do, in the name and by the authority of the good people of these colonies, solemnly publish and declare, that these United Colonies are, and of right ought to be, FREE AND INDEPENDENT STATES; that they are absolved from all allegiance to the British crown, and that all political connection between them and the state of Great Britain is, and ought to be, totally dissolved; and that, as free and independent states, they have full power to levy war, conclude peace, contract alliances, establish commerce, and do all other acts and things which independent states may of right do. And for the support of this declaration, with a firm reliance on the protection of Divine Providence, we mutually pledge to each other our lives, our fortunes, and our sacred honor.

ARTICLES OF CONFEDERATION

(The text of the Articles of Confederation can be found at college.hmco.com.)

CONSTITUTION OF THE UNITED STATES OF AMERICA AND AMENDMENTS*

Preamble

We the people of the United States, in order to form a more perfect union, establish justice, insure domestic tranquillity, provide for the common defense, promote the general welfare, and secure the blessings of liberty to ourselves and our posterity, do ordain and establish this Constitution for the United States of America.

Article I

Section 1 All legislative powers herein granted shall be vested in a Congress of the United States, which shall consist of a Senate and a House of Representatives.

Section 2 The House of Representatives shall be composed of members chosen every second year by the people of the several States, and the electors in each State shall have the qualifications requisite for electors of the most numerous branch of the State Legislature.

---

*Passages no longer in effect are printed in italic type.

No person shall be a Representative who shall not have attained to the age of twenty-five years, and been seven years a citizen of the United States, and who shall not, when elected, be an inhabitant of that State in which he shall be chosen.

Representatives and direct taxes shall be apportioned among the several States which may be included within this Union, according to their respective numbers, *which shall be determined by adding to the whole number of free persons, including those bound to service for a term of years and excluding Indians not taxed, three-fifths of all other persons.* The actual enumeration shall be made within three years after the first meeting of the Congress of the United States, and within every subsequent term of ten years, in such manner as they shall by law direct. The number of Representatives shall not exceed one for every thirty thousand, but each State shall have at least one Representative; *and until such enumeration shall be made, the State of New Hampshire shall be entitled to choose three, Massachusetts eight, Rhode Island and Providence Plantations one, Connecticut five, New York six, New Jersey four, Pennsylvania eight, Delaware one, Maryland six, Virginia ten, North Carolina five, South Carolina five, and Georgia three.*

When vacancies happen in the representation from any State, the Executive authority thereof shall issue writs of election to fill such vacancies.

The House of Representatives shall choose their Speaker and other officers; and shall have the sole power of impeachment.

Section 3 The Senate of the United States shall be composed of two Senators from each State, *chosen by the legislature thereof,* for six years; and each Senator shall have one vote.

Immediately after they shall be assembled in consequence of the first election, they shall be divided as equally as may be into three classes. The seats of the Senators of the first class shall be vacated at the expiration of the second year, of the second class at the expiration of the fourth year, and of the third class at the expiration of the sixth year, so that one-third may be chosen every second year; *and if vacancies happen by resignation or otherwise, during the recess of the legislature of any State, the Executive thereof may make temporary appointments until the next meeting of the legislature, which shall then fill such vacancies.*

No person shall be a Senator who shall not have attained to the age of thirty years, and been nine years a citizen of the United States, and who shall not, when elected, be an inhabitant of that State for which he shall be chosen.

The Vice-President of the United States shall be President of the Senate, but shall have no vote, unless they be equally divided.

The Senate shall choose their other officers, and also a President *pro tempore,* in the absence of the Vice-President,

or when he shall exercise the office of President of the United States.

The Senate shall have the sole power to try all impeachments. When sitting for that purpose, they shall be on oath or affirmation. When the President of the United States is tried, the Chief Justice shall preside: and no person shall be convicted without the concurrence of two-thirds of the members present.

Judgment in cases of impeachment shall not extend further than to removal from the office, and disqualification to hold and enjoy any office of honor, trust or profit under the United States: but the party convicted shall nevertheless be liable and subject to indictment, trial, judgment and punishment, according to law.

Section 4 The times, places and manner of holding elections for Senators and Representatives shall be prescribed in each State by the legislature thereof; but the Congress may at any time by law make or alter such regulations, except as to the places of choosing Senators.

The Congress shall assemble at least once in every year, and such meeting *shall be on the first Monday in December, unless they shall by law appoint a different day.*

Section 5 Each house shall be the judge of the elections, returns and qualifications of its own members, and a majority of each shall constitute a quorum to do business; but a smaller number may adjourn from day to day, and may be authorized to compel the attendance of absent members, in such manner, and under such penalties, as each house may provide.

Each house may determine the rules of its proceedings, punish its members for disorderly behavior, and with the concurrence of two-thirds, expel a member.

Each house shall keep a journal of its proceedings, and from time to time publish the same, excepting such parts as may in their judgment require secrecy; and the yeas and nays of the members of either house on any question shall, at the desire of one-fifth of those present, be entered on the journal.

Neither house, during the session of Congress, shall, without the consent of the other, adjourn for more than three days, nor to any other place than that in which the two houses shall be sitting.

Section 6 The Senators and Representatives shall receive a compensation for their services, to be ascertained by law and paid out of the treasury of the United States. They shall in all cases except treason, felony and breach of the peace, be privileged from arrest during their attendance at the session of their respective houses, and in going to and returning from the same; and for any speech or debate in either house, they shall not be questioned in any other place.

No Senator or Representative shall, during the time for which he was elected, be appointed to any civil office under the authority of the United States, which shall have been created, or the emoluments whereof shall have been increased, during such time; and no person holding any office under the United States shall be a member of either house during his continuance in office.

Section 7   All bills for raising revenue shall originate in the House of Representatives; but the Senate may propose or concur with amendments as on other bills.

Every bill which shall have passed the House of Representatives and the Senate, shall, before it become a law, be presented to the President of the United States; if he approve he shall sign it, but if not he shall return it with objections to that house in which it originated, who shall enter the objections at large on their journal, and proceed to reconsider it. If after such reconsideration two-thirds of that house shall agree to pass the bill, it shall be sent, together with the objections, to the other house, by which it shall likewise be reconsidered, and, if approved by two-thirds of that house, it shall become a law. But in all such cases the votes of both houses shall be determined by yeas and nays, and the names of the persons voting for and against the bill shall be entered on the journal of each house respectively. If any bill shall not be returned by the President within ten days (Sundays excepted) after it shall have been presented to him, the same shall be a law, in like manner as if he had signed it, unless the Congress by their adjournment prevent its return, in which case it shall not be a law.

Every order, resolution, or vote to which the concurrence of the Senate and House of Representatives may be necessary (except on a question of adjournment) shall be presented to the President of the United States; and before the same shall take effect, shall be approved by him, or being disapproved by him, shall be repassed by two-thirds of the Senate and House of Representatives, according to the rules and limitations prescribed in the case of a bill.

Section 8   The Congress shall have power

To lay and collect taxes, duties, imposts, and excises, to pay the debts and provide for the common defense and general welfare of the United States; but all duties, imposts and excises shall be uniform throughout the United States;

To borrow money on the credit of the United States;

To regulate commerce with foreign nations, and among the several States, and with the Indian tribes;

To establish an uniform rule of naturalization, and uniform laws on the subject of bankruptcies throughout the United States;

To coin money, regulate the value thereof, and of foreign coin, and fix the standard of weights and measures;

To provide for the punishment of counterfeiting the securities and current coin of the United States;

To establish post offices and post roads;

To promote the progress of science and useful arts by securing for limited times to authors and inventors the exclusive right to their respective writings and discoveries;

To constitute tribunals inferior to the Supreme Court;

To define and punish piracies and felonies committed on the high seas and offenses against the law of nations;

To declare war, grant letters of marque and reprisal, and make rules concerning captures on land and water;

To raise and support armies, but no appropriation of money to that use shall be for a longer term than two years;

To provide and maintain a navy;

To make rules for the government and regulation of the land and naval forces;

To provide for calling forth the militia to execute the laws of the Union, suppress insurrections, and repel invasions;

To provide for organizing, arming, and disciplining the militia, and for governing such part of them as may be employed in the service of the United States, reserving to the States respectively the appointment of the officers, and the authority of training the militia according to the discipline prescribed by Congress;

To exercise exclusive legislation in all cases whatsoever, over such district (not exceeding ten miles square) as may, by cession of particular States, and the acceptance of Congress, become the seat of government of the United States, and to exercise like authority over all places purchased by the consent of the legislature of the State, in which the same shall be, for erection of forts, magazines, arsenals, dockyards, and other needful buildings; —and

To make all laws which shall be necessary and proper for carrying into execution the foregoing powers, and all other powers vested by this Constitution in the government of the United States, or in any department or officer thereof.

Section 9   The migration or importation of such persons as any of the States now existing shall think proper to admit shall not be prohibited by the Congress prior to the year 1808; but a tax or duty may be imposed on such importation, not exceeding $10 for each person.

The privilege of the writ of habeas corpus shall not be suspended, unless when in cases of rebellion or invasion the public safety may require it.

No bill of attainder or ex post facto law shall be passed.

No capitation, or other direct, tax shall be laid, unless in proportion to the census or enumeration herein before directed to be taken.

No tax or duty shall be laid on articles exported from any State.

No preference shall be given by any regulation of commerce or revenue to the ports of one State over those of another; nor shall vessels bound to, or from, one State, be obliged to enter, clear, or pay duties in another.

No money shall be drawn from the treasury, but in consequence of appropriations made by law; and a regular statement and account of the receipts and expenditures of all public money shall be published from time to time.

No title of nobility shall be granted by the United States: and no person holding any office of profit or trust under them, shall, without the consent of the Congress, accept of any present, emolument, office, or title, of any kind whatever, from any king, prince, or foreign state.

Section 10   No State shall enter into any treaty, alliance, or confederation; grant letters of marque and reprisal; coin money; emit bills of credit; make anything but gold and silver coin a tender in payment of debts; pass any bill of attainder, ex post facto law, or law impairing the obligation of contracts, or grant any title of nobility.

No State shall, without the consent of Congress, lay any imposts or duties on imports or exports, except what may be absolutely necessary for executing its inspection laws: and the net produce of all duties and imposts, laid by any State on imports or exports, shall be for the use of the treasury of the United States; and all such laws shall be subject to the revision and control of the Congress.

No State shall, without the consent of Congress, lay any duty of tonnage, keep troops or ships of war in time of peace, enter into any agreement or compact with another State, or with a foreign power, or engage in war, unless actually invaded, or in such imminent danger as will not admit of delay.

Article II

Section 1   The executive power shall be vested in a President of the United States of America. He shall hold his office during the term of four years, and, together with the Vice-President, chosen for the same term, be elected as follows:

Each State shall appoint, in such manner as the legislature thereof may direct, a number of electors, equal to the whole number of Senators and Representatives to which the State may be entitled in the Congress; but no Senator or Representative, or person holding an office of trust or profit under the United States, shall be appointed an elector.

The electors shall meet in their respective States, and vote by ballot for two persons, of whom one at least shall not be an inhabitant of the same State with themselves. And they shall make a list of all the persons voted for, and of the number of votes for each; which list they shall sign and certify, and transmit sealed to the seat of government of the United States, directed to the President of the Senate. The President of the Senate shall, in the presence of the Senate and House of Representatives, open all the certificates, and the votes shall then be counted. The person having the greatest number of votes shall be the President, if such number be a majority of the whole number of electors appointed; and if there be more than one who have such majority, and have an equal number of votes, then the House of Representatives shall immediately choose by ballot one of them for President; and if no person have a majority, then from the five highest on the list said house shall in like manner choose the President. But in choosing the President the votes shall be taken by States, the representation from each State having one vote; a quorum for this purpose shall consist of a member or members from two-thirds of the States, and a majority of all the States shall be necessary to a choice. In every case, after the choice of the President, the person having the greatest number of votes of the electors shall be the Vice-President. But if there should remain two or more who have equal votes, the Senate shall choose from them by ballot the Vice-President.

The Congress may determine the time of choosing the electors and the day on which they shall give their votes; which day shall be the same throughout the United States.

No person except a natural-born citizen, *or a citizen of the United States at the time of the adoption of this Constitution,* shall be eligible to the office of President; neither shall any person be eligible to that office who shall not have attained to the age of thirty-five years, and been fourteen years a resident within the United States.

In cases of the removal of the President from office or of his death, resignation, or inability to discharge the powers and duties of the said office, the same shall devolve on the Vice-President, and the Congress may by law provide for the case of removal, death, resignation, or inability, both of the President and Vice-President, declaring what officer shall then act as President, and such officer shall act accordingly, until the disability be removed, or a President shall be elected.

The President shall, at stated times, receive for his services a compensation, which shall neither be increased nor diminished during the period for which he shall have been elected, and he shall not receive within that period any other emolument from the United States, or any of them.

Before he enter on the execution of his office, he shall take the following oath or affirmation:—"I do solemnly swear (or affirm) that I will faithfully execute the office of the President of the United States, and will to the best of my ability preserve, protect and defend the Constitution of the United States."

Section 2   The President shall be commander in chief of the army and navy of the United States, and of the militia of the several States, when called into the actual service of the United States; he may require the opinion, in writing, of the principal officer in each of the executive departments, upon any subject relating to the duties of their respective offices, and he shall have power to grant reprieves and pardons for offenses against the United States, except in cases of impeachment.

He shall have power, by and with the advice and consent of the Senate, to make treaties, provided two-thirds of the Senators present concur; and he shall nominate, and by and with the advice and consent of the Senate, shall appoint ambassadors, other public ministers and consuls, judges of the Supreme Court, and all other officers of the United States, whose appointments are not herein otherwise provided for, and which shall be established by law: but Congress may by law vest the appointment of such inferior officers, as they think proper, in the President alone, in the courts of law, or in the heads of departments.

The President shall have power to fill up all vacancies that may happen during the recess of the Senate, by granting commissions which shall expire at the end of their next session.

Section 3 He shall from time to time give to the Congress information of the state of the Union, and recommend to their consideration such measures as he shall judge necessary and expedient; he may, on extraordinary occasions, convene both houses, or either of them, and in case of disagreement between them, with respect to the time of adjournment, he may adjourn them to such time as he shall think proper; he shall receive ambassadors and other public ministers; he shall take care that the laws be faithfully executed, and shall commission all the officers of the United States.

Section 4 The President, Vice-President and all civil officers of the United States shall be removed from office on impeachment for, and on conviction of, treason, bribery, or other high crimes and misdemeanors.

Article III

Section 1 The judicial power of the United States shall be vested in one Supreme Court, and in such inferior courts as the Congress may from time to time ordain and establish. The judges, both of the Supreme and inferior courts, shall hold their offices during good behavior, and shall, at stated times, receive for their services a compensation which shall not be diminished during their continuance in office.

Section 2 The judicial power shall extend to all cases, in law and equity, arising under this Constitution, the laws of the United States, and treaties made, or which shall be made, under their authority;—to all cases affecting ambassadors, other public ministers and consuls;—to all cases of admiralty and maritime jurisdiction;—to controversies to which the United States shall be a party;—to controversies between two or more States;—*between a State and citizens of another State;*—between citizens of different States;—between citizens of the same State claiming lands under grants of different States, and between a State, or the citizens thereof, and foreign states, citizens or subjects.

In all cases affecting ambassadors, other public ministers and consuls, and those in which a State shall be party, the Supreme Court shall have original jurisdiction. In all the other cases before mentioned, the Supreme Court shall have appellate jurisdiction, both as to law and fact, with such exceptions, and under such regulations, as the Congress shall make.

The trial of all crimes, except in cases of impeachment, shall be by jury; and such trial shall be held in the State where said crimes shall have been committed; but when not committed within any State, the trial shall be at such place or places as the Congress may by law have directed.

Section 3 Treason against the United States shall consist only in levying war against them, or in adhering to their enemies, giving them aid and comfort. No person shall be convicted of treason unless on the testimony of two witnesses to the same overt act, or on confession in open court.

The Congress shall have power to declare the punishment of treason, but no attainder of treason shall work corruption of blood, or forfeiture except during the life of the person attainted.

Article IV

Section 1 Full faith and credit shall be given in each State to the public acts, records, and judicial proceedings of every other State. And the Congress may by general laws prescribe the manner in which such acts, records, and proceedings shall be proved, and the effect thereof.

Section 2 The citizens of each State shall be entitled to all privileges and immunities of citizens in the several States.

A person charged in any State with treason, felony, or other crime, who shall flee from justice, and be found in another State, shall on demand of the executive authority of the State from which he fled, be delivered up, to be removed to the State having jurisdiction of the crime.

No person held to service or labor in one State, under the laws thereof, escaping into another, shall, in consequence of any law or regulation therein, be discharged from such service or labor, but shall be delivered up on claim of the party to whom such service or labor may be due.

Section 3 New States may be admitted by the Congress into this Union; but no new State shall be formed or erected within the jurisdiction of any other State; nor any State be formed by the junction of two or more States, or parts of States, without the consent of the legislatures of the States concerned as well as of the Congress.

The Congress shall have power to dispose of and make all needful rules and regulations respecting the territory or other property belonging to the United States; and nothing in this Constitution shall be so construed as to prejudice any claims of the United States, or of any particular State.

Section 4   The United States shall guarantee to every State in this Union a republican form of government, and shall protect each of them against invasion; and on application of the legislature, or of the executive (when the legislature cannot be convened), against domestic violence.

Article V

The Congress, whenever two-thirds of both houses shall deem it necessary, shall propose amendments to this Constitution, or, on the application of the legislatures of two-thirds of the several States, shall call a convention for proposing amendments, which, in either case, shall be valid to all intents and purposes, as part of this Constitution, when ratified by the legislatures of three-fourths of the several States, or by conventions in three-fourths thereof, as the one or the other mode of ratification may be proposed by the Congress; provided *that no amendments which may be made prior to the year one thousand eight hundred and eight shall in any manner affect the first and fourth clauses in the ninth section of the first article;* and that no State, without its consent, shall be deprived of its equal suffrage in the Senate.

Article VI

All debts contracted and engagements entered into, before the adoption of this Constitution, shall be as valid against the United States under this Constitution, as under the Confederation.

This Constitution, and the laws of the United States which shall be made in pursuance thereof; and all treaties made, or which shall be made, under the authority of the United States, shall be the supreme law of the land; and the judges in every State shall be bound thereby, anything in the Constitution or laws of any State to the contrary notwithstanding.

The Senators and Representatives before mentioned, and the members of the several State legislatures, and all executive and judicial officers, both of the United States and of the several States, shall be bound by oath or affirmation to support this Constitution; but no religious test shall ever be required as a qualification to any office or public trust under the United States.

Article VII

The ratification of the conventions of nine States shall be sufficient for the establishment of this Constitution between the States so ratifying the same.

Done in Convention by the unanimous consent of the States present, the seventeenth day of September in the year of our Lord one thousand seven hundred and eighty-seven and of the Independence of the United States of America the twelfth. In witness whereof we have hereunto subscribed our names.

AMENDMENTS TO THE CONSTITUTION*

Amendment I

Congress shall make no law respecting an establishment of religion, or prohibiting the free exercise thereof; or abridging the freedom of speech, or of the press; or the right of the people peaceably to assemble, and to petition the government for a redress of grievances.

Amendment II

A well-regulated militia being necessary to the security of a free State, the right of the people to keep and bear arms shall not be infringed.

Amendment III

No soldier shall, in time of peace, be quartered in any house without the consent of the owner, nor in time of war, but in a manner to be prescribed by law.

Amendment IV

The right of the people to be secure in their persons, houses, papers, and effects, against unreasonable searches and seizures, shall not be violated, and no warrants shall issue but upon probable cause, supported by oath or affirmation, and particularly describing the place to be searched, and the persons or things to be seized.

Amendment V

No person shall be held to answer for a capital, or otherwise infamous crime, unless on a presentment or indictment of a grand jury, except in cases arising in the land or naval forces, or in the militia, when in actual service in time of war or public danger; nor shall any person be subject for the same of-

---

*The first ten Amendments (the Bill of Rights) were adopted in 1791.

fense to be twice put in jeopardy of life or limb; nor shall be compelled in any criminal case to be a witness against himself, nor be deprived of life, liberty, or property, without due process of law; nor shall private property be taken for public use without just compensation.

Amendment VI

In all criminal prosecutions, the accused shall enjoy the right to a speedy and public trial, by an impartial jury of the State and district wherein the crime shall have been committed, which district shall have been previously ascertained by law, and to be informed of the nature and cause of the accusation; to be confronted with the witnesses against him; to have compulsory process for obtaining witnesses in his favor, and to have the assistance of counsel for his defense.

Amendment VII

In suits at common law, where the value in controversy shall exceed twenty dollars, the right of trial by jury shall be preserved, and no fact tried by a jury shall be otherwise reexamined in any court of the United States, than according to the rules of the common law.

Amendment VIII

Excessive bail shall not be required, nor excessive fines imposed, nor cruel and unusual punishments inflicted.

Amendment IX

The enumeration in the Constitution, of certain rights, shall not be construed to deny or disparage others retained by the people.

Amendment X

The powers not delegated to the United States by the Constitution, nor prohibited by it to the States, are reserved to the States respectively, or to the people.

Amendment XI

[Adopted 1798]
The judicial power of the United States shall not be construed to extend to any suit in law or equity, commenced or prosecuted against one of the United States by citizens of another State, or by citizens or subjects of any foreign state.

Amendment XII

[Adopted 1804]

The electors shall meet in their respective States, and vote by ballot for President and Vice-President, one of whom, at least, shall not be an inhabitant of the same State with themselves; they shall name in their ballots the person voted for as President, and in distinct ballots the person voted for as Vice-President, and they shall make distinct lists of all persons voted for as President, and of all persons voted for as Vice-President, and of the number of votes for each, which lists they shall sign and certify, and transmit sealed to the seat of government of the United States, directed to the President of the Senate;—the President of the Senate shall, in the presence of the Senate and House of Representatives, open all the certificates and the votes shall then be counted;—the person having the greatest number of votes for President shall be the President, if such number be a majority of the whole number of electors appointed; and if no person have such majority, then from the persons having the highest numbers not exceeding three on the list of those voted for as President, the House of Representatives shall choose immediately, by ballot, the President. But in choosing the President, the votes shall be taken by States, the representation from each State having one vote; a quorum for this purpose shall consist of a member or members from two-thirds of the States, and a majority of all the States shall be necessary to a choice. And if the House of Representatives shall not choose a President whenever the right of choice shall devolve upon them, before *the fourth day of March* next following, then the Vice-President shall act as President, as in the case of the death or other constitutional disability of the President.

The person having the greatest number of votes as Vice-President shall be the Vice-President, if such number be a majority of the whole number of electors appointed; and if no person have a majority, then from the two highest numbers on the list the Senate shall choose the Vice-President; a quorum for the purpose shall consist of two-thirds of the whole number of Senators, and a majority of the whole number shall be necessary to a choice. But no person constitutionally ineligible to the office of President shall be eligible to that of Vice-President of the United States.

Amendment XIII

[Adopted 1865]

Section 1   Neither slavery nor involuntary servitude, except as a punishment for crime whereof the party shall have been duly convicted, shall exist within the United States, or any place subject to their jurisdiction.

Section 2   Congress shall have power to enforce this article by appropriate legislation.

Amendment XIV

[Adopted 1868]

Section 1 All persons born or naturalized in the United States, and subject to the jurisdiction thereof, are citizens of the United States and of the State wherein they reside. No State shall make or enforce any law which shall abridge the privileges or immunities of citizens of the United States; nor shall any State deprive any person of life, liberty, or property, without due process of law; nor deny to any person within its jurisdiction the equal protection of the laws.

Section 2 Representatives shall be apportioned among the several States according to their respective numbers, counting the whole number of persons in each State, excluding Indians not taxed. But when the right to vote at any election for the choice of Electors for President and Vice-President of the United States, Representatives in Congress, the executive and judicial officers of a State, or the members of the legislature thereof, is denied to any of the male inhabitants of such State, being twenty-one years of age and citizens of the United States, or in any way abridged, except for participation in rebellion, or other crime, the basis of representation therein shall be reduced in the proportion which the number of such male citizens shall bear to the whole number of male citizens twenty-one years of age in such State.

Section 3 No person shall be a Senator or Representative in Congress, or Elector of President and Vice-President, or hold any office, civil or military, under the United States, or under any State, who, having previously taken an oath, as a member of Congress, or as an officer of the United States, or as a member of any State legislature, or as an executive or judicial officer of any State, to support the Constitution of the United States, shall have engaged in insurrection or rebellion against the same, or given aid or comfort to the enemies thereof. Congress may, by a vote of two-thirds of each house, remove such disability.

Section 4 The validity of the public debt of the United States, authorized by law, including debts incurred for payment of pensions and bounties for services in suppressing insurrection or rebellion, shall not be questioned. But neither the United States nor any State shall assume or pay any debt or obligation incurred in aid of insurrection or rebellion against the United States, or any claim for the loss of emancipation of any slave; but all such debts, obligations, and claims shall be held illegal and void.

Section 5 The Congress shall have power to enforce, by appropriate legislation, the provisions of this article.

Amendment XV

[Adopted 1870]

Section 1 The right of citizens of the United States to vote shall not be denied or abridged by the United States or by any State on account of race, color, or previous condition of servitude.

Section 2 The Congress shall have power to enforce this article by appropriate legislation.

Amendment XVI

[Adopted 1913]

The Congress shall have power to lay and collect taxes on incomes, from whatever source derived, without apportionment among the several States, and without regard to any census or enumeration.

Amendment XVII

[Adopted 1913]

Section 1 The Senate of the United States shall be composed of two Senators from each State, elected by the people thereof, for six years; and each Senator shall have one vote. The electors in each State shall have the qualifications requisite for electors of [voters for] the most numerous branch of the State legislatures.

Section 2 When vacancies happen in the representation of any State in the Senate, the executive authority of such State shall issue writs of election to fill such vacancies: Provided, that the Legislature of any State may empower the executive thereof to make temporary appointments until the people fill the vacancies by election as the Legislature may direct.

Section 3 This amendment shall not be so construed as to affect the election or term of any Senator chosen before it becomes valid as part of the Constitution.

Amendment XVIII

[Adopted 1919; Repealed 1933]

Section 1 After one year from the ratification of this article the manufacture, sale, or transportation of intoxicating liquors within, the importation thereof into, or the exportation thereof from the United States and all territory subject to the jurisdiction thereof, for beverage purposes, is hereby prohibited.

Section 2 The Congress and the several States shall have concurrent power to enforce this article by appropriate legislation.

Section 3 This article shall be inoperative unless it shall have been ratified as an amendment to the Constitution by the legislatures of the several States, as provided by the Constitution, within seven years from the date of the submission thereof to the States by the Congress.

Amendment XIX

[Adopted 1920]

Section 1 The right of citizens of the United States to vote shall not be denied or abridged by the United States or by any State on account of sex.

Section 2 The Congress shall have power to enforce this article by appropriate legislation.

Amendment XX

[Adopted 1933]

Section 1 The terms of the President and Vice-President shall end at noon on the 20th day of January, and the terms of Senators and Representatives at noon on the 3rd day of January, of the years in which such terms would have ended if this article had not been ratified; and the terms of their successors shall then begin.

Section 2 The Congress shall assemble at least once in every year, and such meeting shall begin at noon on the 3d day of January, unless they shall by law appoint a different day.

Section 3 If, at the time fixed for the beginning of the term of the President, the President-elect shall have died, the Vice-President–elect shall become President. If a President shall not have been chosen before the time fixed for the beginning of his term, or if the President-elect shall have failed to qualify, then the Vice-President–elect shall act as President until a President shall have qualified; and the Congress may by law provide for the case wherein neither a President-elect nor a Vice-President–elect shall have qualified, declaring who shall then act as President, or the manner in which one who is to act shall be selected, and such persons shall act accordingly until a President or Vice-President shall have qualified.

Section 4 The Congress may by law provide for the case of the death of any of the persons from whom the House of Representatives may choose a President whenever the right of choice shall have devolved upon them, and for the case of the death of any of the persons from whom the Senate may choose a Vice-President whenever the right of choice shall have devolved upon them.

Section 5 Sections 1 and 2 shall take effect on the 15th day of October following the ratification of this article.

Section 6 This article shall be inoperative unless it shall have been ratified as an amendment to the Constitution by the Legislatures of three-fourths of the several States within seven years from the date of its submission.

Amendment XXI

[Adopted 1933]

Section 1 The eighteenth article of amendment to the Constitution of the United States is hereby repealed.

Section 2 The transportation or importation into any State, Territory, or Possession of the United States for delivery or use therein of intoxicating liquors, in violation of the laws thereof, is hereby prohibited.

Section 3 This article shall be inoperative unless it shall have been ratified as an amendment to the Constitution by conventions in the several States, as provided in the Constitution, within seven years from the date of submission thereof to the States by the Congress.

Amendment XXII

[Adopted 1951]

Section 1 No person shall be elected to the office of President more than twice, and no person who has held the office of President, or acted as President, for more than two years of a term to which some other person was elected President shall be elected to the office of President more than once. But this article shall not apply to any person holding the office of President when this article was proposed by the Congress, and shall not prevent any person who may be holding the office of President, or acting as President, during the term within which this article becomes operative from holding the office of President or acting as President during the remainder of such term.

Section 2 This article shall be inoperative unless it shall have been ratified as an amendment to the Constitution by the legislatures of three-fourths of the several States within seven years from the date of its submission to the States by the Congress.

Amendment XXIII

[Adopted 1961]

Section 1 The District constituting the seat of Government of the United States shall appoint in such manner as the Congress may direct:

A number of electors of President and Vice-President equal to the whole number of Senators and Representatives in Congress to which the District would be entitled if it were a State, but in no event more than the least populous State; they shall be in addition to those appointed by the States, but they shall be considered for the purposes of the election of President and Vice-President, to be electors appointed by a State; and they shall meet in the District and perform such duties as provided by the twelfth article of amendment.

Section 2 The Congress shall have the power to enforce this article by appropriate legislation.

Amendment XXIV

[Adopted 1964]

Section 1 The right of citizens of the United States to vote in any primary or other election for President or Vice-President, for electors for President or Vice-President, or for Senator or Representative in Congress, shall not be denied or abridged by the United States or any State by reason of failure to pay any poll tax or other tax.

Section 2 The Congress shall have the power to enforce this article by appropriate legislation.

Amendment XXV

[Adopted 1967]

Section 1 In case of the removal of the President from office or of his death or resignation, the Vice-President shall become President.

Section 2 Whenever there is a vacancy in the office of the Vice-President, the President shall nominate a Vice-President who shall take office upon confirmation by a majority vote of both Houses of Congress.

Section 3 Whenever the President transmits to the President pro tempore of the Senate and the Speaker of the House of Representatives his written declaration that he is unable to discharge the powers and duties of his office, and until he transmits to them a written declaration to the contrary, such powers and duties shall be discharged by the Vice-President as Acting President.

Section 4 Whenever the Vice-President and a majority of either the principal officers of the executive departments or of such other body as Congress may by law provide, transmit to the President pro tempore of the Senate and the Speaker of the House of Representatives their written declaration that the President is unable to discharge the powers and duties of his office, the Vice-President shall immediately assume the powers and duties of the office as Acting President.

Thereafter, when the President transmits to the President pro tempore of the Senate and the Speaker of the House of Representatives his written declaration that no inability exists, he shall resume the powers and duties of his office unless the Vice-President and a majority of either the principal officers of the executive department[s] or of such other body as Congress may by law provide, transmit within four days to the President pro tempore of the Senate and the Speaker of the House of Representatives their written declaration that the President is unable to discharge the powers and duties of his office. Thereupon Congress shall decide the issue, assembling within forty-eight hours for that purpose if not in session. If the Congress, within twenty-one days after receipt of the latter written declaration, or, if Congress is not in session, within twenty-one days after Congress is required to assemble, determines by two-thirds vote of both Houses that the President is unable to discharge the powers and duties of his office, the Vice-President shall continue to discharge the same as Acting President; otherwise, the President shall resume the powers and duties of his office.

Amendment XXVI

[Adopted 1971]

Section 1 The right of citizens of the United States, who are eighteen years of age or older, to vote shall not be denied or abridged by the United States or by any State on account of age.

Section 2 The Congress shall have power to enforce this article by appropriate legislation.

Amendment XXVII

[Adopted 1992]

No law, varying the compensation for the services of the Senators and Representatives, shall take effect, until an election of Representatives shall have intervened.

The American People and Nation: A Statistical Profile

Population of the United States

Year	Number of States	Population	Percent Increase	Population Per Square Mile	Percent Urban/ Rural	Percent Male/ Female	Percent White/ Non- white	Persons Per House- hold	Median Age
1790	13	3,929,214		4.5	5.1/94.9	NA/NA	80.7/19.3	5.79	NA
1800	16	5,308,483	35.1	6.1	6.1/93.9	NA/NA	81.1/18.9	NA	NA
1810	17	7,239,881	36.4	4.3	7.3/92.7	NA/NA	81.0/19.0	NA	NA
1820	23	9,638,453	33.1	5.5	7.2/92.8	50.8/49.2	81.6/18.4	NA	16.7
1830	24	12,866,020	33.5	7.4	8.8/91.2	50.8/49.2	81.9/18.1	NA	17.2
1840	26	17,069,453	32.7	9.8	10.8/89.2	50.9/49.1	83.2/16.8	NA	17.8
1850	31	23,191,876	35.9	7.9	15.3/84.7	51.0/49.0	84.3/15.7	5.55	18.9
1860	33	31,443,321	35.6	10.6	19.8/80.2	51.2/48.8	85.6/14.4	5.28	19.4
1870	37	39,818,449	26.6	13.4	25.7/74.3	50.6/49.4	86.2/13.8	5.09	20.2
1880	38	50,155,783	26.0	16.9	28.2/71.8	50.9/49.1	86.5/13.5	5.04	20.9
1890	44	62,947,714	25.5	21.2	35.1/64.9	51.2/48.8	87.5/12.5	4.93	22.0
1900	45	75,994,575	20.7	25.6	39.6/60.4	51.1/48.9	87.9/12.1	4.76	22.9
1910	46	91,972,266	21.0	31.0	45.6/54.4	51.5/48.5	88.9/11.1	4.54	24.1
1920	48	105,710,620	14.9	35.6	51.2/48.8	51.0/49.0	89.7/10.3	4.34	25.3
1930	48	122,775,046	16.1	41.2	56.1/43.9	50.6/49.4	89.8/10.2	4.11	26.4
1940	48	131,669,275	7.2	44.2	56.5/43.5	50.2/49.8	89.8/10.2	3.67	29.0
1950	48	150,697,361	14.5	50.7	64.0/36.0	49.7/50.3	89.5/10.5	3.37	30.2
1960	50	179,323,175	18.5	50.6	69.9/30.1	49.3/50.7	88.6/11.4	3.33	29.5
1970	50	203,302,031	13.4	57.4	73.6/26.4	48.7/51.3	87.6/12.4	3.14	28.0
1980	50	226,542,199	11.4	64.1	73.7/26.3	48.6/51.4	85.9/14.1	2.75	30.0
1990	50	248,718,301	9.8	70.3	75.2/24.8	48.7/51.3	83.9/16.1	2.63	32.8
2000	50	281,421,906	13.2	75.7	NA	49.1/50.9	75.1/24.9	2.59	35.3

NA = Not available.

Vital Statistics

Year	Birth Rate*	Death Rate*	Life Expectancy in Years					Marriage Rate	Divorce Rate
			Total Population	White Females	Nonwhite Females	White Males	Nonwhite Males		
1790	NA	NA	NA	NA	NA	NA	NA	NA	NA
1800	55.0	NA	NA	NA	NA	NA	NA	NA	NA
1810	54.3	NA	NA	NA	NA	NA	NA	NA	NA
1820	55.2	NA	NA	NA	NA	NA	NA	NA	NA
1830	51.4	NA	NA	NA	NA	NA	NA	NA	NA
1840	51.8	NA	NA	NA	NA	NA	NA	NA	NA
1850	43.3	NA	NA	NA	NA	NA	NA	NA	NA
1860	44.3	NA	NA	NA	NA	NA	NA	NA	NA
1870	38.3	NA	NA	NA	NA	NA	NA	NA	NA
1880	39.8	NA	NA	NA	NA	NA	NA	NA	NA
1890	31.5	NA	NA	NA	NA	NA	NA	NA	NA
1900	32.3	17.2	47.3	48.7	33.5	46.6	32.5	NA	NA
1910	30.1	14.7	50.0	52.0	37.5	48.6	33.8	NA	NA
1920	27.7	13.0	54.1	55.6	45.2	54.4	45.5	12.0	1.6
1930	21.3	11.3	59.7	63.5	49.2	59.7	47.3	9.2	1.6
1940	19.4	10.8	62.9	66.6	54.9	62.1	51.5	12.1	2.0
1950	24.1	9.6	68.2	72.2	62.9	66.5	59.1	11.1	2.6
1960	23.7	9.5	69.7	74.1	66.3	67.4	61.1	8.5	2.2
1970	18.4	9.5	70.8	75.6	69.4	68.0	61.3	10.6	3.5
1980	15.9	8.8	73.7	78.1	73.6	70.7	65.3	10.6	5.2
1990	16.6	8.6	75.4	79.4	75.2	72.7	67.0	9.8	4.7
1998	14.5†	8.8†	76.7	79.9	76.1°	74.6	68.9°	8.3	4.2

Note: Data per one thousand for Birth, Death, Marriage, and Divorce Rates.

NA = Not available. *Data for 1800, 1810, 1830, 1850, 1870, and 1890 for whites only. †Data for 1999. °Data for 1996.

Immigrants to the United States

Immigration Totals by Decade			
Years	Number	Years	Number
1820–1830	151,824	1911–1920	5,735,811
1831–1840	599,125	1921–1930	4,107,209
1841–1850	1,713,251	1931–1940	528,431
1851–1860	2,598,214	1941–1950	1,035,039
1861–1870	2,314,824	1951–1960	2,515,479
1871–1880	2,812,191	1961–1970	3,321,677
1881–1890	5,246,613	1971–1980	4,493,314
1891–1900	3,687,546	1981–1990	7,338,062
1901–1910	8,795,386	1991–1998	7,605,068
		Total	64,599,082

Major Sources of Immigrants by Country or Region (in thousands)

Period	Asia[a]	Germany	Mexico	Italy	Great Britain (UK)[b]	Ireland	Canada	Austria and Hungary	Soviet Union (Russia)	Caribbean	Central America and South America	Norway and Sweden
1820–1830	—	8	5	—	27	54	2	—	—	4	—	—
1831–1840	—	152	7	2	76	207	14	—	—	12	—	1
1841–1850	—	435	3	2	267	781	42	—	—	14	4	14
1851–1860	42	952	3	9	424	914	59	—	—	11	2	21
1861–1870	65	787	2	12	607	436	154	8	3	9	1	109
1871–1880	124	718	5	56	548	437	384	73	39	14	1	211
1881–1890	70	1,453	2[c]	307	807	655	393	354	213	29	3	568
1891–1900	75	505	1[c]	652	272	388	3	593	505	33	2	321
1901–1910	324	341	50	2,046	526	339	179	2,145	1,597	108	25	440
1911–1920	247	144	219	1,110	341	146	742	896	921	123	59	161
1921–1930	112	412	459	455	340	211	925	64	62	75	58	166
1931–1940	17	114	22	68	32	11	109	11	1	16	14	9
1941–1950	37	227	61	58	139	20	172	28	—	50	43	21
1951–1960	153	478	300	185	203	48	378	104	—	123	136	45
1961–1970	428	191	454	214	214	33	413	26	2	470	359	33
1971–1980	1,588	74	640	129	137	11	170	16	39	741	430	10
1981–1990	2,738	92	2,336	67	160	32	157	25	58	872	930	15
1991–1998	2,347	73	1,932	58	129	55	158	21	386	823	866	15
Total	8,366	7,156	5,820	5,431	5,249	4,780	4,454	4,364	3,830	3,526	2,936	2,161

Notes: Numbers for periods are rounded. Dash indicates less than 1,000. [a]Includes Middle East. [b]Since 1925, includes England, Scotland, Wales, and Northern Ireland data. [c]No data available for 1886–1894.

The American Worker

Year	Total Number of Workers	Males as Percent of Total Workers	Females as Percent of Total Workers	Married Women as Percent of Female Workers	Female Workers as Percent of Female Population	Percent of Labor Force Unemployed	Percent of Workers in Labor Unions
1870	12,506,000	85	15	NA	NA	NA	NA
1880	17,392,000	85	15	NA	NA	NA	NA
1890	23,318,000	83	17	14	19	4 (1894 = 18)	NA
1900	29,073,000	82	18	15	21	5	3
1910	38,167,000	79	21	25	25	6	6
1920	41,614,000	79	21	23	24	5 (1921 = 12)	12
1930	48,830,000	78	22	29	25	9 (1933 = 25)	11.6
1940	53,011,000	76	24	36	27	15 (1944 = 1)	26.9
1950	62,208,000	72	28	52	31	5.3	31.5
1960	69,628,000	67	33	55	38	5.5	31.4
1970	82,771,000	62	38	59	43	4.9	27.3
1980	106,940,000	58	42	55	52	7.1	21.9
1990	125,840,000	55	45	54	58	5.6	16.1
1999	140,900,000[a]	54[b]	46[b]	53	60	4.2	13.9

[a] Data for 2000.

[b] Data for 1998.

NA = Not available.

The American Economy

Year	Gross National Product (GNP) and Gross Domestic Product (GDP)[a] (in $ billions)	Steel Production (in tons)	Corn Production (millions of bushels)	Automobiles Registered	New Housing Starts	Foreign Trade (in $ millions)	
						Exports	Imports
1790	NA	NA	NA	NA	NA	20	23
1800	NA	NA	NA	NA	NA	71	91
1810	NA	NA	NA	NA	NA	67	85
1820	NA	NA	NA	NA	NA	70	74
1830	NA	NA	NA	NA	NA	74	71
1840	NA	NA	NA	NA	NA	132	107
1850	NA	NA	592[d]	NA	NA	152	178
1860	NA	13,000	839[e]	NA	NA	400	362
1870	7.4[b]	77,000	1,125	NA	NA	451	462
1880	11.2[c]	1,397,000	1,707	NA	NA	853	761
1890	13.1	4,779,000	1,650	NA	328,000	910	823
1900	18.7	11,227,000	2,662	8,000	189,000	1,499	930
1910	35.3	28,330,000	2,853	458,300	387,000 (1918 = 118,000)	1,919	1,646
1920	91.5	46,183,000	3,071	8,131,500	247,000 (1925 = 937,000)	8,664	5,784
1930	90.7	44,591,000	2,080	23,034,700	330,000 (1933 = 93,000)	4,013	3,500
1940	100.0	66,983,000	2,457	27,465,800	603,000 (1944 = 142,000)	4,030	7,433
1950	286.5	96,836,000	3,075	40,339,000	1,952,000	9,997	8,954
1960	506.5	99,282,000	4,314	61,682,300	1,365,000	19,659	15,093
1970	1,016.0	131,514,000	4,200	89,279,800	1,434,000	42,681	40,356
1980	2,819.5	111,835,000	6,600	121,601,000	1,292,000	220,626	244,871
1990	5,764.9	98,906,000	7,933	143,550,000	1,193,000	394,030	485,453
2000	9,256.1[f]	107,395,010[g]	9,970	131,839,000	1,593,000	782,000	1,217,000

[a]In December 1991 the Bureau of Economic Analysis of the U.S. government began featuring Gross Domestic Product rather than Gross National Product as the primary measure of U.S. production.

[b]Figure is average for 1869–1878.

[c]Figure is average for 1879–1888.

[d]Figure for 1849.

[e]Figure for 1859.

[f]Figure for 1999.

[g]Figure for 1998.

NA = Not available.

Federal Budget Outlays and Debt

Year	Defense[a]	Veterans Benefits[a]	Income Security[a]	Social Security[a]	Health and Medicare[a]	Education[a,d]	Net Interest Payments[a]	Federal Debt (dollars)
1790	14.9	4.1[b]	NA	NA	NA	NA	55.0	75,463,000[c]
1800	55.7	.6	NA	NA	NA	NA	31.3	82,976,000
1810	48.4 (1814: 79.7)	1.0	NA	NA	NA	NA	34.9	53,173,000
1820	38.4	17.6	NA	NA	NA	NA	28.1	91,016,000
1830	52.9	9.0	NA	NA	NA	NA	12.6	48,565,000
1840	54.3 (1847: 80.7)	10.7	NA	NA	NA	NA	.7	3,573,000
1850	43.8	4.7	NA	NA	NA	NA	1.0	63,453,000
1860	44.2 (1865: 88.9)	1.7	NA	NA	NA	NA	5.0	64,844,000
1870	25.7	9.2	NA	NA	NA	NA	41.7	2,436,453,000
1880	19.3	21.2	NA	NA	NA	NA	35.8	2,090,909,000
1890	20.9 (1899: 48.6)	33.6	NA	NA	NA	NA	11.4	1,222,397,000
1900	36.6	27.0	NA	NA	NA	NA	7.7	1,263,417,000
1910	45.1 (1919: 59.5)	23.2	NA	NA	NA	NA	3.1	1,146,940,000
1920	37.1	3.4	NA	NA	NA	NA	16.0	24,299,321,000
1930	25.3	6.6	NA	NA	NA	NA	19.9	16,185,310,000
1940	17.5 (1945: 89.4)	6.0	16.0	.3	.5	20.8	9.4	42,967,531,000
1950	32.2	20.3	9.6	1.8	.6	.6	11.3	256,853,000,000
1960	52.2	5.9	8.0	12.6	.9	1.0	7.5	290,525,000,000
1970	41.8	4.4	8.0	15.5	6.2	4.4	7.3	308,921,000,000
1980	22.7	3.6	14.6	20.1	9.4	5.4	8.9	909,050,000,000
1990	23.9	2.3	11.7	19.8	12.4	3.1	14.7	3,266,073,000,000
2000	16.2	2.6	14.0	22.7	19.9	3.5	12.3	5,686,338,000,000

[a]Figures represent percentage of total federal spending for each category. Not included are transportation, commerce, housing, and various other categories.

[b]1789–1791 figure.

[c]1791 figure.

[d]Includes training, employment, and social services.

NA = Not available.

The Fifty States, District of Columbia, and Puerto Rico

State	Date of Admission (with Rank)	Capital City	Population (2000) (with Rank)	Racial/Ethnic Distribution (1998)	Per Capita Personal Income (1998) (with Rank)	Total Area in Square Miles (with Rank)
Alabama (AL)	Dec. 14, 1819 (22)	Montgomery	4,447,100 (23)	White: 3,141,000; Black: 1,132,000; Hispanic: 36,000; Asian: 28,000; Native American: 15,000	$21,442 (40)	52,423 (30)
Alaska (AK)	Jan. 3, 1959 (49)	Juneau	626,932 (48)	White: 444,000; Black: 24,000; Hispanic: 19,000; Asian: 28,000; Native American: 100,000	$25,675 (20)	656,424 (1)
Arizona (AZ)	Feb. 14, 1912 (48)	Phoenix	5,130,632 (20)	White: 3,182,000; Black: 169,000; Hispanic: 963,000; Asian: 98,000; Native American: 256,000	$23,060 (35)	114,006 (6)
Arkansas (AR)	June 15, 1836 (25)	Little Rock	2,673,400 (33)	White: 2,055,000; Black: 408,000; Hispanic: 44,000; Asian: 19,000; Native American: 14,000	$20,346 (46)	53,182 (29)
California (CA)	Sept. 9, 1850 (31)	Sacramento	33,871,648 (1)	White: 16,511,000; Black: 2,456,000; Hispanic: 9,454,000; Asian: 3,938,000; Native American: 309,000	$27,503 (1)	163,707 (3)
Colorado (CO)	Aug. 1, 1876 (38)	Denver	4,301,261 (24)	White: 3,125,000; Black: 172,000; Hispanic: 541,000; Asian: 96,000; Native American: 37,000	$28,657 (18)	104,100 (8)
Connecticut (CT)	Jan. 9, 1788 (5)	Hartford	3,405,565 (29)	White: 3,125,000; Black: 172,000; Hispanic: 238,000; Asian: 96,000; Native American: 37,000	$37,598 (1)	5,544 (48)
Delaware (DE)	Dec. 7, 1787 (1)	Dover	783,600 (45)	White: 560,000; Black: 144,000; Hispanic: 22,000; Asian: 15,000; Native American: 2,000	$29,814 (6)	2,489 (49)
District of Columbia (DC)	U.S. Capital, Dec. 1, 1800	Washington (coextensive with DC)	572,059 (not ranked)	White: 149,000; Black: 326,000; Hispanic: 30,000; Asian: 16,000; Native American: 2,000	$33,433 (not ranked)	68 (not ranked)
Florida (FL)	Mar. 3, 1845 (27)	Tallahassee	15,982,378 (4)	White: 10,239,000; Black: 2,268,000; Hispanic: 2,080,000; Asian: 271,000; Native American: 58,000	$25,852 (19)	65,756 (22)
Georgia (GA)	Jan. 2, 1788 (4)	Atlanta	8,186,453 (10)	White: 5,100,000; Black: 2,181,000; Hispanic: 193,000; Asian: 149,000; Native American: 18,000	$25,020 (23)	59,441 (24)
Hawai'i (HI)	Aug. 21, 1959 (50)	Honolulu	1,211,537 (42)	White: 344,000; Black: 35,000; Hispanic: 51,000; Asian: 757,000; Native American: 7,000	$26,137 (17)	10,932 (43)
Idaho (ID)	July 3, 1890 (43)	Boise	1,293,953 (39)	White: 1,109,000; Black: 7,000; Hispanic: 82,000; Asian: 14,000; Native American: 17,000	$21,081 (43)	83,574 (14)
Illinois (IL)	Dec. 3, 1818 (21)	Springfield	12,419,293 (5)	White: 8,630,000; Black: 1,840,000; Hispanic: 1,145,000; Asian: 403,000; Native American: 27,000	$28,873 (8)	57,918 (25)

The Fifty States, District of Columbia, and Puerto Rico (continued)

State	Date of Admission (with Rank)	Capital City	Population (2000) (with Rank)	Racial/Ethnic Distribution (1998)	Per Capita Personal Income (1998) (with Rank)	Total Area in Square Miles (with Rank)
Indiana (IN)	Dec. 11, 1816 (19)	Indianapolis	6,080,485 (14)	White: 5,206,000; Black: 491,000; Hispanic: 132,000; Asian: 56,000; Native American: 15,000	$24,219 (29)	36,420 (38)
Iowa (IA)	Dec. 28, 1846 (29)	Des Moines	2,926,324 (30)	White: 2,709,000; Black: 57,000; Hispanic: 52,000; Asian: 36,000; Native American: 8,000	$23,925 (32)	56,276 (26)
Kansas (KS)	Jan. 29, 1861 (34)	Topeka	2,688,418 (32)	White: 2,278,000; Black: 155,000; Hispanic: 137,000; Asian: 46,000; Native American: 23,000	$24,981 (24)	82,282 (15)
Kentucky (KY)	June 1, 1792 (15)	Frankfort	4,041,769 (25)	White: 3,591,000; Black: 285,000; Hispanic: 28,000; Asian: 27,000; Native American: 6,000	$21,506 (39)	40,411 (37)
Louisiana (LA)	Apr. 30, 1812 (18)	Baton Rouge	4,408,976 (22)	White: 2,787,000; Black: 1,407,000; Hispanic: 100,000; Asian: 55,000; Native American: 19,000	$21,346 (41)	51,843 (31)
Maine (ME)	Mar. 15, 1820 (23)	Augusta	1,274,923 (40)	White: 1,215,000; Black: 6,000; Hispanic: 8,000; Asian: 9,000; Native American: 6,000	$22,952 (36)	35,387 (39)
Maryland (MD)	Apr. 28, 1788 (7)	Annapolis	5,296,486 (19)	White: 3,329,000; Black: 1,428,000; Hispanic: 158,000; Asian: 204,000; Native American: 16,000	$29,943 (5)	12,407 (42)
Massachusetts (MA)	Feb. 6, 1788 (6)	Boston	6,349,097 (13)	White: 5,217,000; Black: 395,000; Hispanic: 298,000; Asian: 223,000; Native American: 15,000	$32,797 (3)	10,555 (44)
Michigan (MI)	Jan. 26, 1837 (26)	Lansing	9,938,444 (8)	White: 7,961,000; Black: 1,405,000; Hispanic: 234,000; Asian: 158,000; Native American: 60,000	$25,857 (18)	96,705 (11)
Minnesota (MN)	May 11, 1858 (32)	Saint Paul	4,919,479 (21)	White: 4,328,000; Black: 141,000; Hispanic: 76,000; Asian: 124,000; Native American: 58,000	$27,510 (11)	86,943 (12)
Mississippi (MS)	Dec. 10, 1817 (20)	Jackson	2,844,658 (31)	White: 1,701,000; Black: 1,003,000; Hispanic: 18,000; Asian: 19,000; Native American: 10,000	$18,958 (50)	48,434 (32)
Missouri (MO)	Aug. 10, 1821 (24)	Jefferson City	5,595,211 (17)	White: 4,668,000; Black: 613,000; Hispanic: 77,000; Asian: 60,000; Native American: 21,000	$24,427 (28)	69,709 (21)
Montana (MT)	Nov. 8, 1889 (41)	Helena	902,195 (44)	White: 803,000; Black: 3,000; Hispanic: 13,000; Asian: 5,000; Native American: 56,000	$20,172 (47)	147,046 (4)
Nebraska (NE)	Mar. 1, 1867 (37)	Lincoln	1,711,263 (38)	White: 1,493,000; Black: 67,000; Hispanic: 66,000; Asian: 22,000; Native American: 15,000	$24,754 (27)	77,358 (16)
Nevada (NV)	Oct. 3, 1864 (36)	Carson City	1,998,257 (35)	White: 1,248,000; Black: 133,000; Hispanic: 253,000; Asian: 81,000; Native American: 31,000	$27,200 (14)	110,567 (7)

The Fifty States, District of Columbia, and Puerto Rico (continued)

State	Date of Admission (with Rank)	Capital City	Population (2000) (with Rank)	Racial/Ethnic Distribution (1998)	Per Capita Personal Income (1998) (with Rank)	Total Area in Square Miles (with Rank)
New Hampshire (NH)	June 21, 1788 (9)	Concord	1,235,786 (41)	White: 1,109,000; Black: 9,000; Hispanic: 16,000; Asian: 14,000; Native American: 2,000	$29,022 (7)	9,351 (46)
New Jersey (NJ)	Dec. 18, 1787 (3)	Trenton	8,414,350 (9)	White: 5,586,000; Black: 1,188,000; Hispanic: 866,000; Asian: 453,000; Native American: 22,000	$33,937 (2)	8,722 (47)
New Mexico (NM)	Jan. 6, 1912 (47)	Santa Fe	1,819,046 (36)	White: 834,000; Black: 45,000; Hispanic: 669,000; Asian: 26,000; Native American: 163,000	$19,936 (48)	121,598 (5)
New York (NY)	July 26, 1788 (11)	Albany	18,976,457 (3)	White: 11,895,000; Black: 3,220,000; Hispanic: 1,990,000; Asian: 995,000; Native American: 76,000	$31,734 (4)	54,471 (27)
North Carolina (NC)	Nov. 21, 1789 (12)	Raleigh	8,049,313 (11)	White: 5,545,000; Black: 1,665,000 Hispanic: 139,000; Asian: 100,000; Native American: 98,000	$24,036 (31)	53,821 (28)
North Dakota (ND)	Nov. 2, 1889 (39)	Bismarck	642,200 (47)	White: 593,000; Black: 4,000; Hispanic: 6,000; Asian: 5,000; Native American: 30,000	$21,675 (38)	70,704 (19)
Ohio (OH)	Mar. 1, 1803 (17)	Columbus	11,353,140 (7)	White: 9,610,000; Black: 1,290,000; Hispanic: 158,000; Asian: 129,000; Native American: 23,000	$25,134 (21)	44,828 (34)
Oklahoma (OK)	Nov. 16, 1907 (46)	Oklahoma City	3,450,654 (27)	White: 2,668,000; Black: 262,000; Hispanic: 109,000; Asian: 45,000; Native American: 263,000	$21,072 (44)	69,903 (20)
Oregon (OR)	Feb. 14, 1859 (33)	Salem	3,421,399 (28)	White: 2,888,000; Black: 61,000; Hispanic: 182,000; Asian: 106,000; Native American: 45,000	$24,766 (26)	98,386 (9)
Pennsylvania (PA)	Dec. 12, 1787 (2)	Harrisburg	12,281,054 (6)	White: 10,354,000; Black: 1,166,000; Hispanic: 265,000; Asian: 198,000; Native American: 18,000	$26,792 (16)	46,058 (33)
Puerto Rico (PR)	Ascession 1898; Commonwealth Status 1952	San Juan	3,808,610 (not ranked)	White: <1,000; Black: <1,000; Hispanic: 3,856,000; Asian: <1,000	$7,882* (not ranked)	3,427* (not ranked)
Rhode Island (RI)	May 29, 1790 (13)	Providence	1,048,319 (43)	White: 859,000; Black: 49,000; Hispanic: 52,000; Asian: 23,000; Native American: 5,000	$26,797 (15)	1,545 (50)
South Carolina (SC)	May 23, 1788 (8)	Columbia	4,012,012 (26)	White: 2,603,000; Black: 1,147,000; Hispanic: 42,000; Asian: 34,000; Native American: 9,000	$21,309 (42)	32,008 (40)
South Dakota (SD)	Nov. 2, 1889 (40)	Pierre	754,844 (46)	White: 662,000; Black: 5,000; Hispanic: 7,000; Asian: 5,000; Native American: 59,000	$22,114 (37)	77,121 (17)
Tennessee (TN)	June 1, 1796 (16)	Nashville	5,689,283 (16)	White: 4,413,000; Black: 900,000; Hispanic: 54,000; Asian: 53,000; Native American: 12,000	$23,559 (33)	42,149 (36)

The Fifty States, District of Columbia, and Puerto Rico (continued)

State	Date of Admission (with Rank)	Capital City	Population (2000) (with Rank)	Racial/Ethnic Distribution (1998)	Per Capita Personal Income (1998) (with Rank)	Total Area in Square Miles (with Rank)
Texas (TX)	Dec. 29, 1845 (28)	Austin	20,851,820 (2)	White: 11,038,000; Black: 2,430,000; Hispanic: 5,640,000; Asian: 556,000; Native American: 96,000	$24,957 (25)	268,601 (2)
Utah (UT)	Jan. 4, 1896 (45)	Salt Lake City	2,233,169 (32)	White: 1,866,000; Black: 19,000; Hispanic: 132,000; Asian: 53,000; Native American: 30,000	$21,019 (45)	84,904 (13)
Vermont (VT)	Mar. 4, 1791 (14)	Montpelier	608,827 (49)	White: 577,000; Black: 3,000; Hispanic: 5,000; Asian: 5,000; Native American: 2,000	$24,175 (30)	9,615 (45)
Virginia (VA)	June 25, 1788 (10)	Richmond	7,078,515 (12)	White: 4,943,000; Black: 1,363,000 Hispanic: 220,000; Asian: 247,000; Native American: 19,000	$27,385 (13)	42,777 (35)
Washington (WA)	Nov. 11, 1889 (42)	Olympia	5,894,121 (15)	White: 4,743,000; Black: 198,000; Hispanic: 315,000; Asian: 330,000; Native American: 103,000	$27,961 (11)	71,302 (18)
West Virginia (WV)	June 20, 1863 (35)	Charleston	1,808,344 (37)	White: 1,732,000; Black: 58,000; Hispanic: 9,000; Asian: 9,000; Native American: 3,000	$19,362 (49)	24,231 (41)
Wisconsin (WI)	May 29, 1848 (30)	Madison	5,363,675 (18)	White: 4,687,000; Black: 291,000; Hispanic: 120,000; Asian: 80,000; Native American: 56,000	$25,079 (22)	65,499 (23)
Wyoming (WY)	July 10, 1890 (44)	Cheyenne	493,782 (50)	White: 435,000; Black: 4,000; Hispanic: 27,000; Asian: 4,000; Native American: 11,000	$23,167 (34)	97,818 (10)

*1996 figure.

Presidential Elections

Year	Number of States	Candidates	Parties	Popular Vote	% of Popular Vote	Electoral Vote	% Voter Participation[a]
1789	10	**George Washington**	No party			69	
		John Adams	designations			34	
		Other candidates				35	
1792	15	**George Washington**	No party			132	
		John Adams	designations			77	
		George Clinton				50	
		Other candidates				5	
1796	16	**John Adams**	Federalist			71	
		Thomas Jefferson	Democratic-Republican			68	
		Thomas Pinckney	Federalist			59	
		Aaron Burr	Democratic-Republican			30	
		Other candidates				48	
1800	16	**Thomas Jefferson**	Democratic-Republican			73	
		Aaron Burr	Democratic-Republican			73	
		John Adams	Federalist			65	
		Charles C. Pinckney	Federalist			64	
		John Jay	Federalist			1	
1804	17	**Thomas Jefferson**	Democratic-Republican			162	
		Charles C. Pinckney	Federalist			14	
1808	17	**James Madison**	Democratic-Republican			122	
		Charles C. Pinckney	Federalist			47	
		George Clinton	Democratic-Republican			6	
1812	18	**James Madison**	Democratic-Republican			128	
		DeWitt Clinton	Federalist			89	
1816	19	**James Monroe**	Democratic-Republican			183	
		Rufus King	Federalist			34	
1820	24	**James Monroe**	Democratic-Republican			231	

Presidential Elections (continued)

Year	Number of States	Candidates	Parties	Popular Vote	% of Popular Vote	Electoral Vote	% Voter Participation[a]
		John Quincy Adams	Independent Republican			1	
1824	24	**John Quincy Adams**	Democratic-Republican	108,740	30.5	84	26.9
		Andrew Jackson	Democratic-Republican	153,544	43.1	99	
		Henry Clay	Democratic-Republican	47,136	13.2	37	
		William H. Crawford	Democratic-Republican	46,618	13.1	41	
1828	24	**Andrew Jackson**	Democratic	647,286	56.0	178	57.6
		John Quincy Adams	National Republican	508,064	44.0	83	
1832	24	**Andrew Jackson**	Democratic	701,780	54.2	219	55.4
		Henry Clay	National Republican	484,205	37.4	49	
		Other candidates		107,988	8.0	18	
1836	26	**Martin Van Buren**	Democratic	764,176	50.8	170	57.8
		William H. Harrison	Whig	550,816	36.6	73	
		Hugh L. White	Whig	146,107	9.7	26	
1840	26	**William H. Harrison**	Whig	1,274,624	53.1	234	80.2
		Martin Van Buren	Democratic	1,127,781	46.9	60	
1844	26	**James K. Polk**	Democratic	1,338,464	49.6	170	78.9
		Henry Clay	Whig	1,300,097	48.1	105	
		James G. Birney	Liberty	62,300	2.3		
1848	30	**Zachary Taylor**	Whig	1,360,967	47.4	163	72.7
		Lewis Cass	Democratic	1,222,342	42.5	127	
		Martin Van Buren	Free Soil	291,263	10.1		
1852	31	**Franklin Pierce**	Democratic	1,601,117	50.9	254	69.6
		Winfield Scott	Whig	1,385,453	44.1	42	
		John P. Hale	Free Soil	155,825	5.0		
1856	31	**James Buchanan**	Democratic	1,832,955	45.3	174	78.9
		John C. Frémont	Republican	1,339,932	33.1	114	
		Millard Fillmore	American	871,731	21.6	8	
1860	33	**Abraham Lincoln**	Republican	1,865,593	39.8	180	81.2
		Stephen A. Douglas	Democratic	1,382,713	29.5	12	
		John C. Breckinridge	Democratic	848,356	18.1	72	
		John Bell	Constitutional Union	592,906	12.6	39	
1864	36	**Abraham Lincoln**	Republican	2,206,938	55.0	212	73.8
		George B. McClellan	Democratic	1,803,787	45.0	21	

Presidential Elections (continued)

Year	Number of States	Candidates	Parties	Popular Vote	% of Popular Vote	Electoral Vote	% Voter Participation[a]
1868	37	**Ulysses S. Grant**	Republican	3,013,421	52.7	214	78.1
		Horatio Seymour	Democratic	2,706,829	47.3	80	
1872	37	**Ulysses S. Grant**	Republican	3,596,745	55.6	286	71.3
		Horace Greeley	Democratic	2,843,446	43.9	[b]	
1876	38	**Rutherford B. Hayes**	Republican	4,036,572	48.0	185	81.8
		Samuel J. Tilden	Democratic	4,284,020	51.0	184	
1880	38	**James A. Garfield**	Republican	4,453,295	48.5	214	79.4
		Winfield S. Hancock	Democratic	4,414,082	48.1	155	
		James B. Weaver	Greenback-Labor	308,578	3.4		
1884	38	**Grover Cleveland**	Democratic	4,879,507	48.5	219	77.5
		James G. Blaine	Republican	4,850,293	48.2	182	
		Benjamin F. Butler	Greenback-Labor	175,370	1.8		
		John P. St. John	Prohibition	150,369	1.5		
1888	38	**Benjamin Harrison**	Republican	5,447,129	47.9	233	79.3
		Grover Cleveland	Democratic	5,537,857	48.6	168	
		Clinton B. Fisk	Prohibition	249,506	2.2		
		Anson J. Streeter	Union Labor	146,935	1.3		
1892	44	**Grover Cleveland**	Democratic	5,555,426	46.1	277	74.7
		Benjamin Harrison	Republican	5,182,690	43.0	145	
		James B. Weaver	People's	1,029,846	8.5	22	
		John Bidwell	Prohibition	264,133	2.2		
1896	45	**William McKinley**	Republican	7,102,246	51.1	271	79.3
		William J. Bryan	Democratic	6,492,559	47.7	176	
1900	45	**William McKinley**	Republican	7,218,491	51.7	292	73.2
		William J. Bryan	Democratic; Populist	6,356,734	45.5	155	
		John C. Wooley	Prohibition	208,914	1.5		
1904	45	**Theodore Roosevelt**	Republican	7,628,461	57.4	336	65.2
		Alton B. Parker	Democratic	5,084,223	37.6	140	
		Eugene V. Debs	Socialist	402,283	3.0		
		Silas C. Swallow	Prohibition	258,536	1.9		
1908	46	**William H. Taft**	Republican	7,675,320	51.6	321	65.4
		William J. Bryan	Democratic	6,412,294	43.1	162	
		Eugene V. Debs	Socialist	420,793	2.8		
		Eugene W. Chafin	Prohibition	253,840	1.7		
1912	48	**Woodrow Wilson**	Democratic	6,296,547	41.9	435	58.8
		Theodore Roosevelt	Progressive	4,118,571	27.4	88	
		William H. Taft	Republican	3,486,720	23.2	8	
		Eugene V. Debs	Socialist	900,672	6.0		

Presidential Elections (continued)

Year	Number of States	Candidates	Parties	Popular Vote	% of Popular Vote	Electoral Vote	% Voter Partici-pation[a]
		Eugene W. Chafin	Prohibition	206,275	1.4		
1916	48	**Woodrow Wilson**	Democratic	9,127,695	49.4	277	61.6
		Charles E. Hughes	Republican	8,533,507	46.2	254	
		A. L. Benson	Socialist	585,113	3.2		
		J. Frank Hanly	Prohibition	220,506	1.2		
1920	48	**Warren G. Harding**	Republican	16,143,407	60.4	404	49.2
		James M. Cox	Democratic	9,130,328	34.2	127	
		Eugene V. Debs	Socialist	919,799	3.4		
		P. P. Christensen	Farmer-Labor	265,411	1.0		
1924	48	**Calvin Coolidge**	Republican	15,718,211	54.0	382	48.9
		John W. Davis	Democratic	8,385,283	28.8	136	
		Robert M. La Follette	Progressive	4,831,289	16.6	13	
1928	48	**Herbert C. Hoover**	Republican	21,391,993	58.2	444	56.9
		Alfred E. Smith	Democratic	15,016,169	40.9	87	
1932	48	**Franklin D. Roosevelt**	Democratic	22,809,638	57.4	472	56.9
		Herbert C. Hoover	Republican	15,758,901	39.7	59	
		Norman Thomas	Socialist	881,951	2.2		
1936	48	**Franklin D. Roosevelt**	Democratic	27,752,869	60.8	523	61.0
		Alfred M. Landon	Republican	16,674,665	36.5	8	
		William Lemke	Union	882,479	1.9		
1940	48	**Franklin D. Roosevelt**	Democratic	27,307,819	54.8	449	62.5
		Wendell L. Wilkie	Republican	22,321,018	44.8	82	
1944	48	**Franklin D. Roosevelt**	Democratic	25,606,585	53.5	432	55.9
		Thomas E. Dewey	Republican	22,014,745	46.0	99	
1948	48	**Harry S Truman**	Democratic	24,179,345	49.6	303	53.0
		Thomas E. Dewey	Republican	21,991,291	45.1	189	
		J. Strom Thurmond	States' Rights	1,176,125	2.4	39	
		Henry A. Wallace	Progressive	1,157,326	2.4		
1952	48	**Dwight D. Eisenhower**	Republican	33,936,234	55.1	442	63.3
		Adlai E. Stevenson	Democratic	27,314,992	44.4	89	
1956	48	**Dwight D. Eisenhower**	Republican	35,590,472	57.6	457	60.6
		Adlai E. Stevenson	Democratic	26,022,752	42.1	73	
1960	50	**John F. Kennedy**	Democratic	34,226,731	49.7	303	62.8
		Richard M. Nixon	Republican	34,108,157	49.5	219	
1964	50	**Lyndon B. Johnson**	Democratic	43,129,566	61.1	486	61.7
		Barry M. Goldwater	Republican	27,178,188	38.5	52	
1968	50	**Richard M. Nixon**	Republican	31,785,480	43.4	301	60.6
		Hubert H. Humphrey	Democratic	31,275,166	42.7	191	

Presidential Elections (continued)

Year	Number of States	Candidates	Parties	Popular Vote	% of Popular Vote	Electoral Vote	% Voter Participation[a]
		George C. Wallace	American Independent	9,906,473	13.5	46	
1972	50	**Richard M. Nixon**	Republican	47,169,911	60.7	520	55.2
		George S. McGovern	Democratic	29,170,383	37.5	17	
		John G. Schmitz	American	1,099,482	1.4		
1976	50	**James E. Carter**	Democratic	40,830,763	50.1	297	53.5
		Gerald R. Ford	Republican	39,147,793	48.0	240	
1980	50	**Ronald W. Reagan**	Republican	43,904,153	50.7	489	52.6
		James E. Carter	Democratic	35,483,883	41.0	49	
		John B. Anderson	Independent	5,720,060	6.6	0	
		Ed Clark	Libertarian	921,299	1.1	0	
1984	50	**Ronald W. Reagan**	Republican	54,455,075	58.8	525	53.3
		Walter F. Mondale	Democratic	37,577,185	40.6	13	
1988	50	**George H. W. Bush**	Republican	48,886,097	53.4	426	50.1
		Michael S. Dukakis	Democratic	41,809,074	45.6	111[c]	
1992	50	**William J. Clinton**	Democratic	44,909,326	43.0	370	55.2
		George H. W. Bush	Republican	39,103,882	37.4	168	
		H. Ross Perot	Independent	19,741,048	18.9	0	
1996	50	**William J. Clinton**	Democratic	47,402,357	49.2	379	49.1
		Robert J. Dole	Republican	39,196,755	40.7	159	
		H. Ross Perot	Reform	8,085,402	8.4	0	
		Ralph Nader	Green	684,902	0.7	0	
2000	50	**George W. Bush**	Republican	50,455,156	47.87	271	51.2
		Albert Gore	Democratic	50,992,335	48.38	266	

Candidates receiving less than 1 percent of the popular vote have been omitted. Thus the percentage of popular vote given for any election year may not total 100 percent.

Before the passage of the Twelfth Amendment in 1804, the Electoral College voted for two presidential candidates; the runner-up became vice president.

Before 1824, most presidential electors were chosen by state legislatures, not by popular vote.

[a]Percent of voting-age population casting ballots.

[b]Greeley died shortly after the election; the electors supporting him then divided their votes among minor candidates.

[c]One elector from West Virginia cast her Electoral College presidential ballot for Lloyd Bentsen, the Democratic Party's vice-presidential candidate.

Presidents and Vice Presidents

1. President	**George Washington**	1789–1797
Vice President	John Adams	1789–1797
2. President	**John Adams**	1797–1801
Vice President	Thomas Jefferson	1797–1801
3. President	**Thomas Jefferson**	1801–1809
Vice President	Aaron Burr	1801–1805
Vice President	George Clinton	1805–1809
4. President	**James Madison**	1809–1817
Vice President	George Clinton	1809–1813
Vice President	Elbridge Gerry	1813–1817
5. President	**James Monroe**	1817–1825
Vice President	Daniel Tompkins	1817–1825
6. President	**John Quincy Adams**	1825–1829
Vice President	John C. Calhoun	1825–1829
7. President	**Andrew Jackson**	1829–1837
Vice President	John C. Calhoun	1829–1833
Vice President	Martin Van Buren	1833–1837
8. President	**Martin Van Buren**	1837–1841
Vice President	Richard M. Johnson	1837–1841
9. President	**William H. Harrison**	1841
Vice President	John Tyler	1841
10. President	**John Tyler**	1841–1845
Vice President	None	
11. President	**James K. Polk**	1845–1849
Vice President	George M. Dallas	1845–1849
12. President	**Zachary Taylor**	1849–1850
Vice President	Millard Fillmore	1849–1850
13. President	**Millard Fillmore**	1850–1853
Vice President	None	
14. President	**Franklin Pierce**	1853–1857
Vice President	William R. King	1853–1857
15. President	**James Buchanan**	1857–1861
Vice President	John C. Breckinridge	1857–1861
16. President	**Abraham Lincoln**	1861–1865
Vice President	Hannibal Hamlin	1861–1865
Vice President	Andrew Johnson	1865
17. President	**Andrew Johnson**	1865–1869
Vice President	None	
18. President	**Ulysses S. Grant**	1869–1877
Vice President	Schuyler Colfax	1869–1873
Vice President	Henry Wilson	1873–1877
19. President	**Rutherford B. Hayes**	1877–1881
Vice President	William A. Wheeler	1877–1881
20. President	**James A. Garfield**	1881
Vice President	Chester A. Arthur	1881
21. President	**Chester A. Arthur**	1881–1885
Vice President	None	
22. President	**Grover Cleveland**	1885–1889
Vice President	Thomas A. Hendricks	1885–1889
23. President	**Benjamin Harrison**	1889–1893
Vice President	Levi P. Morton	1889–1893
24. President	**Grover Cleveland**	1893–1897
Vice President	Adlai E. Stevenson	1893–1897
25. President	**William McKinley**	1897–1901
Vice President	Garret A. Hobart	1897–1901
Vice President	Theodore Roosevelt	1901
26. President	**Theodore Roosevelt**	1901–1909
Vice President	Charles Fairbanks	1905–1909
27. President	**William H. Taft**	1909–1913
Vice President	James S. Sherman	1909–1913
28. President	**Woodrow Wilson**	1913–1921
Vice President	Thomas R. Marshall	1913–1921
29. President	**Warren G. Harding**	1921–1923
Vice President	Calvin Coolidge	1921–1923
30. President	**Calvin Coolidge**	1923–1929
Vice President	Charles G. Dawes	1925–1929
31. President	**Herbert C. Hoover**	1929–1933
Vice President	Charles Curtis	1929–1933
32. President	**Franklin D. Roosevelt**	1933–1945
Vice President	John N. Garner	1933–1941
Vice President	Henry A. Wallace	1941–1945
Vice President	Harry S Truman	1945
33. President	**Harry S Truman**	1945–1953
Vice President	Alben W. Barkley	1949–1953
34. President	**Dwight D. Eisenhower**	1953–1961
Vice President	Richard M. Nixon	1953–1961

Presidents and Vice Presidents (continued)

35. President	**John F. Kennedy**	1961–1963		40. President	**Ronald W. Reagan**	1981–1989
Vice President	Lyndon B. Johnson	1961–1963		Vice President	George H. W. Bush	1981–1989
36. President	**Lyndon B. Johnson**	1963–1969		41. President	**George H. W. Bush**	1989–1993
Vice President	Hubert H. Humphrey	1965–1969		Vice President	J. Danforth Quayle	1989–1993
37. President	**Richard M. Nixon**	1969–1974		42. President	**William J. Clinton**	1993–2001
Vice President	Spiro T. Agnew	1969–1973		Vice President	Albert Gore	1993–2001
Vice President	Gerald R. Ford	1973–1974		43. President	**George W. Bush**	2001–
38. President	**Gerald R. Ford**	1974–1977		Vice President	Richard Cheney	2001–
Vice President	Nelson A. Rockefeller	1974–1977				
39. President	**James E. Carter**	1977–1981				
Vice President	Walter F. Mondale	1977–1981				

For a complete list of Presidents, Vice Presidents, and Cabinet Members, go to college.hmco.com.

Party Strength in Congress

Period	Congress	House Majority Party		House Minority Party		House Others	Senate Majority Party		Senate Minority Party		Senate Others	Party of President	
1789–91	1st	Ad	38	Op	26		Ad	17	Op	9		F	Washington
1791–93	2nd	F	37	DR	33		F	16	DR	13		F	Washington
1793–95	3rd	DR	57	F	48		F	17	DR	13		F	Washington
1795–97	4th	F	54	DR	52		F	19	DR	13		F	Washington
1797–99	5th	F	58	DR	48		F	20	DR	12		F	J. Adams
1799–1801	6th	F	64	DR	42		F	19	DR	13		F	J. Adams
1801–03	7th	DR	69	F	36		DR	18	F	13		DR	Jefferson
1803–05	8th	DR	102	F	39		DR	25	F	9		DR	Jefferson
1805–07	9th	DR	116	F	25		DR	27	F	7		DR	Jefferson
1807–09	10th	DR	118	F	24		DR	28	F	6		DR	Jefferson
1809–11	11th	DR	94	F	48		DR	28	F	6		DR	Madison
1811–13	12th	DR	108	F	36		DR	30	F	6		DR	Madison
1813–15	13th	DR	112	F	68		DR	27	F	9		DR	Madison
1815–17	14th	DR	117	F	65		DR	25	F	11		DR	Madison
1817–19	15th	DR	141	F	42		DR	34	F	10		DR	Monroe
1819–21	16th	DR	156	F	27		DR	35	F	7		DR	Monroe
1821–23	17th	DR	158	F	25		DR	44	F	4		DR	Monroe
1823–25	18th	DR	187	F	26		DR	44	F	4		DR	Monroe
1825–27	19th	Ad	105	J	97		Ad	26	J	20		C	J. Q. Adams
1827–29	20th	J	119	Ad	94		J	28	Ad	20		C	J. Q. Adams
1829–31	21st	D	139	NR	74		D	26	NR	22		D	Jackson
1831–33	22nd	D	141	NR	58	14	D	25	NR	21	2	D	Jackson
1833–35	23rd	D	147	AM	53	60	D	20	NR	20	8	D	Jackson
1835–37	24th	D	145	W	98		D	27	W	25		D	Jackson
1837–39	25th	D	108	W	107	24	D	30	W	18	4	D	Van Buren
1839–41	26th	D	124	W	118		D	28	W	22		D	Van Buren
1841–43	27th	W	133	D	102	6	W	28	D	22	2	W	W. Harrison
												W	Tyler
1843–45	28th	D	142	W	79	1	W	28	D	25	1	W	Tyler
												D	Polk
1845–47	29th	D	143	W	77	6	D	31	W	25		D	Polk
1847–49	30th	W	115	D	108	4	D	36	W	21	1	W	Taylor
1849–51	31st	D	112	W	109	9	D	35	W	25	2	W	Fillmore
												W	Fillmore
1851–53	32nd	D	140	W	88	5	D	35	W	24	3	W	Fillmore
												D	Pierce
1853–55	33rd	D	159	W	71	4	D	38	W	22	2	D	Pierce
1855–57	34th	R	108	D	83	43	D	40	R	15	5	D	Buchanan
1857–59	35th	D	118	R	92	26	D	36	R	20	8	D	Buchanan
1859–61	36th	R	114	D	92	31	D	36	R	26	4	D	Buchanan

Party Strength in Congress (continued)

Period	Congress	House Majority Party		House Minority Party		Others	Senate Majority Party		Senate Minority Party		Others	Party of President	
1861–63	37th	R	105	D	43	30	R	31	D	10	8	R	Lincoln
1863–65	38th	R	102	D	75	9	R	36	D	9	5	R	Lincoln
1865–67	39th	U	149	D	42		U	42	D	10		R	Lincoln
												R	A. Johnson
1867–69	40th	R	143	D	49		R	42	D	11		R	A. Johnson
1869–71	41st	R	149	D	63		R	56	D	11		R	Grant
1871–73	42nd	R	134	D	104	5	R	52	D	17	5	R	Grant
1873–75	43rd	R	194	D	92	14	R	49	D	19	5	R	Grant
1875–77	44th	D	169	R	109	14	R	45	D	29	2	R	Grant
1877–79	45th	D	153	R	140		R	39	D	36	1	R	Hayes
1879–81	46th	D	149	R	130	14	D	42	R	33	1	R	Hayes
1881–83	47th	D	147	R	135	11	R	37	D	37	1	R	Garfield
												R	Arthur
1883–85	48th	D	197	R	118	10	R	38	D	36	2	R	Arthur
1885–87	49th	D	183	R	140	2	R	43	D	34		D	Cleveland
1887–89	50th	D	169	R	152	4	R	39	D	37		D	Cleveland
1889–91	51st	R	166	D	159		R	39	D	37		R	B. Harrison
1891–93	52nd	D	235	R	88	9	R	47	D	39	2	R	B. Harrison
1893–95	53rd	D	218	R	127	11	D	44	R	38	3	D	Cleveland
1895–97	54th	R	244	D	105	7	R	43	D	39	6	D	Cleveland
1897–99	55th	R	204	D	113	40	R	47	D	34	7	R	McKinley
1899–1901	56th	R	185	D	163	9	R	53	D	26	8	R	McKinley
1901–03	57th	R	197	D	151	9	R	55	D	31	4	R	McKinley
												R	T. Roosevelt
1903–05	58th	R	208	D	178		R	57	D	33		R	T. Roosevelt
1905–07	59th	R	250	D	136		R	57	D	33		R	T. Roosevelt
1907–09	60th	R	222	D	164		R	61	D	31		R	T. Roosevelt
1909–11	61st	R	219	D	172		R	61	D	32		R	Taft
1911–13	62nd	D	228	R	161	1	R	51	D	41		R	Taft
1913–15	63rd	D	291	R	127	17	D	51	R	44	1	D	Wilson
1915–17	64th	D	230	R	196	9	D	56	R	40		D	Wilson
1917–19	65th	D	216	R	210	6	D	53	R	42		D	Wilson
1919–21	66th	R	240	D	190	3	R	49	D	47		D	Wilson
1921–23	67th	R	301	D	131	1	R	59	D	37		R	Harding
1923–25	68th	R	225	D	205	5	R	51	D	43	2	R	Coolidge
1925–27	69th	R	247	D	183	4	R	56	D	39	1	R	Coolidge
1927–29	70th	R	237	D	195	3	R	49	D	46	1	R	Coolidge
1929–31	71st	R	267	D	167	1	R	56	D	39	1	R	Hoover
1931–33	72nd	D	220	R	214	1	R	48	D	47	1	R	Hoover
1933–35	73rd	D	310	R	117	5	D	60	R	35	1	D	F. Roosevelt
1935–37	74th	D	319	R	103	10	D	69	R	25	2	D	F. Roosevelt
1937–39	75th	D	331	R	89	13	D	76	R	16	4	D	F. Roosevelt

Party Strength in Congress *(continued)*

Period	Congress	House Majority Party		House Minority Party		Others	Senate Majority Party		Senate Minority Party		Others	Party of President	
1939–41	76th	D	261	R	164	4	D	69	R	23	4	D	F. Roosevelt
1941–43	77th	D	268	R	162	5	D	66	R	28	2	D	F. Roosevelt
1943–45	78th	D	218	R	208	4	D	58	R	37	1	D	F. Roosevelt
1945–47	79th	D	242	R	190	2	D	56	R	38	1	D	Truman
1947–49	80th	R	245	D	188	1	R	51	D	45		D	Truman
1949–51	81st	D	263	R	171	1	D	54	R	42		D	Truman
1951–53	82nd	D	234	R	199	1	D	49	R	47		D	Truman
1953–55	83rd	R	221	D	211	1	R	48	D	47	1	R	Eisenhower
1955–57	84th	D	232	R	203		D	48	R	47	1	R	Eisenhower
1957–59	85th	D	233	R	200		D	49	R	47		R	Eisenhower
1959–61	86th	D	284	R	153		D	65	R	35		R	Eisenhower
1961–63	87th	D	263	R	174		D	65	R	35		D	Kennedy
1963–65	88th	D	258	R	117		D	67	R	33		D	Kennedy
												D	L. Johnson
1965–67	89th	D	295	R	140		D	68	R	32		D	L. Johnson
1967–69	90th	D	246	R	187		D	64	R	36		D	L. Johnson
1969–71	91st	D	245	R	189		D	57	R	43		R	Nixon
1971–73	92nd	D	254	R	180		D	54	R	44	2	R	Nixon
1973–75	93rd	D	239	R	192	1	D	56	R	42	2	R	Nixon
1975–77	94th	D	291	R	144		D	60	R	37	3	R	Ford
1977–79	95th	D	292	R	143		D	61	R	38	1	D	Carter
1979–81	96th	D	276	R	157		D	58	R	41	1	D	Carter
1981–83	97th	D	243	R	192		R	53	D	46	1	R	Reagan
1983–85	98th	D	269	R	166		R	54	D	46		R	Reagan
1985–87	99th	D	253	R	182		R	53	D	47		R	Reagan
1987–89	100th	D	258	R	177		D	55	R	45		R	Reagan
1989–91	101st	D	259	R	174		D	55	R	45		R	Bush
1991–93	102nd	D	267	R	167	1	D	56	R	44		R	Bush
1993–95	103rd	D	258	R	176	1	D	57	R	43		D	Clinton
1995–97	104th	R	230	D	204	1	R	52	D	48		D	Clinton
1997–99	105th	R	227	D	207	1	R	55	D	45		D	Clinton
1999–2001	106th	R	223	D	211	1	R	55	D	45		D	Clinton
2001–2003	107th	R	221	D	212	2	D	50	R	49	1	R	Bush

AD = Administration; AM = Anti-Masonic; C = Coalition; D = Democratic; DR = Democratic-Republican; F = Federalist; J = Jacksonian; NR = National Republican; Op = Opposition; R = Republican; U = Unionist; W = Whig. Figures are for the beginning of the first session of each Congress, except the 93rd, which are for the beginning of the second session.

Justices of the Supreme Court

	Term of Service	Years of Service	Life Span		Term of Service	Years of Service	Life Span
John Jay	1789–1795	5	1745–1829	Joseph P. Bradley	1870–1892	22	1813–1892
John Rutledge	1789–1791	1	1739–1800	Ward Hunt	1873–1882	9	1810–1886
William Cushing	1789–1810	20	1732–1810	*Morrison R. Waite*	1874–1888	14	1816–1888
James Wilson	1789–1798	8	1742–1798	John M. Harlan	1877–1911	34	1833–1911
John Blair	1789–1796	6	1732–1800	William B. Woods	1880–1887	7	1824–1887
Robert H. Harrison	1789–1790	—	1745–1790	Stanley Mathews	1881–1889	7	1824–1889
James Iredell	1790–1799	9	1951–1799	Horace Gray	1882–1902	20	1828–1902
Thomas Johnson	1791–1793	1	1732–1819	Samuel Blatchford	1882–1893	11	1820–1893
William Paterson	1793–1806	13	1745–1806	Lucius Q. C. Lamar	1888–1893	5	1825–1893
*John Rutledge**	1795	—	1739–1800	*Melville W. Fuller*	1888–1910	21	1833–1910
Samuel Chase	1796–1811	15	1741–1811	David J. Brewer	1890–1910	20	1837–1910
Oliver Ellsworth	1796–1800	4	1745–1807	Henry B. Brown	1890–1906	16	1836–1913
Bushrod Washington	1798–1829	31	1762–1829	George Shiras, Jr.	1892–1903	10	1832–1924
Alfred Moore	1799–1804	4	1755–1810	Howell E. Jackson	1893–1895	2	1832–1895
John Marshall	1801–1835	34	1755–1835	Edward D. White	1894–1910	16	1845–1921
William Johnson	1804–1834	30	1771–1834	Rufus W. Peckham	1895–1909	14	1838–1909
H. Brockholst Livingston	1806–1823	16	1757–1823	Joseph McKenna	1898–1925	26	1843–1926
Thomas Todd	1807–1826	18	1765–1826	Oliver W. Holmes	1902–1932	30	1841–1935
Joseph Story	1811–1845	33	1779–1845	William D. Day	1903–1922	19	1849–1923
Gabriel Duval	1811–1835	24	1752–1844	William H. Moody	1906–1910	3	1853–1917
Smith Thompson	1823–1843	20	1768–1843	Horace H. Lurton	1910–1914	4	1844–1914
Robert Trimble	1826–1828	2	1777–1828	Charles E. Hughes	1910–1916	5	1862–1948
John McLean	1829–1861	32	1785–1861	Willis Van Devanter	1911–1937	26	1859–1941
Henry Baldwin	1830–1844	14	1780–1844	Joseph R. Lamar	1911–1916	5	1857–1916
James M. Wayne	1835–1867	32	1790–1867	*Edward D. White*	1910–1921	11	1845–1921
Roger B. Taney	1836–1864	28	1777–1864	Mahlon Pitney	1912–1922	10	1858–1924
Philip P. Barbour	1836–1841	4	1783–1841	James C. McReynolds	1914–1941	26	1862–1946
John Catron	1837–1865	28	1786–1865	Louis D. Brandeis	1916–1939	22	1856–1941
John McKinley	1837–1852	15	1780–1852	John H. Clarke	1916–1922	6	1857–1945
Peter V. Daniel	1841–1860	19	1784–1860	*William H. Taft*	1921–1930	8	1857–1930
Samuel Nelson	1845–1872	27	1792–1873	George Sutherland	1922–1938	15	1862–1942
Levi Woodbury	1845–1851	5	1789–1851	Pierce Butler	1922–1939	16	1866–1939
Robert C. Grier	1846–1870	23	1794–1870	Edward T. Sanford	1923–1930	7	1865–1930
Benjamin R. Curtis	1851–1857	6	1809–1874	Harlan F. Stone	1925–1941	16	1872–1946
John A. Campbell	1853–1861	8	1811–1889	*Charles E. Hughes*	1930–1941	11	1862–1948
Nathan Clifford	1858–1881	23	1803–1881	Owen J. Roberts	1930–1945	15	1875–1955
Noah H. Swayne	1862–1881	18	1804–1884	Benjamin N. Cardozo	1932–1938	6	1870–1938
Samuel F. Miller	1862–1890	28	1816–1890	Hugo L. Black	1937–1971	34	1886–1971
David Davis	1862–1877	14	1815–1886	Stanley F. Reed	1938–1957	19	1884–1980
Stephen J. Field	1863–1897	34	1816–1899	Felix Frankfurter	1939–1962	23	1882–1965
Salmon P. Chase	1864–1873	8	1808–1873	William O. Douglas	1939–1975	36	1898–1980
William Strong	1870–1880	10	1808–1895	Frank Murphy	1940–1949	9	1890–1949

Justices of the Supreme Court (continued)

	Term of Service	Years of Service	Life Span		Term of Service	Years of Service	Life Span
Harlan F. Stone	1941–1946	5	1872–1946	Abe Fortas	1965–1969	4	1910–1982
James F. Byrnes	1941–1942	1	1879–1972	Thurgood Marshall	1967–1991	24	1908–1993
Robert H. Jackson	1941–1954	13	1892–1954	*Warren C. Burger*	1969–1986	17	1907–1995
Wiley B. Rutledge	1943–1949	6	1894–1949	Harry A. Blackmun	1970–1994	24	1908–1998
Harold H. Burton	1945–1958	13	1888–1964	Lewis F. Powell, Jr.	1972–1987	15	1907–1998
Fred M. Vinson	1946–1953	7	1890–1953	*William H. Rehnquist*	1972–	—	1924–
Tom C. Clark	1949–1967	18	1899–1977	John P. Stevens III	1975–	—	1920–
Sherman Minton	1949–1956	7	1890–1965	Sandra Day O'Connor	1981–	—	1930–
Earl Warren	1953–1969	16	1891–1974	Antonin Scalia	1986–	—	1936–
John Marshall Harlan	1955–1971	16	1899–1971	Anthony M. Kennedy	1988–	—	1936–
William J. Brennan, Jr.	1956–1990	34	1906–1977	David H. Souter	1990–	—	1939–
Charles E. Whittaker	1957–1962	5	1901–1973	Clarence Thomas	1991–	—	1948–
Potter Stewart	1958–1981	23	1915–1985	Ruth Bader Ginsburg	1993–	—	1933–
Byron R. White	1962–1993	31	1917–	Stephen Breyer	1994–	—	1938–
Arthur J. Goldberg	1962–1965	3	1908–1990				

Note: Chief justices are in italics.

*Appointed and served one term, but not confirmed by the Senate.